D1484150

2 SAINT☆YOUNG MEN

C O N T E N T S

SAINT YOUNG MEN AND THE DEPICTION OF RELIGION IN CONTEMPORARY JAPAN

By Dr. Jolyon Baraka Thomas, Assistant Professor of Religious Studies, University of Pennsylvania

Contemporary Japanese society has an ambivalent relationship with religion.

According to the latest numbers compiled by the Japanese government, there are 180,853 discrete religious organizations in Japan, collectively boasting 181,164,731 adherents. This means that there is approximately one religious organization for every 1,000 people in Japan, and the total number of religious adherents amount to about 1.4 times the national population. When I share these numbers with students in my university classes, they reasonably assume that Japanese individuals must have dual affiliations, declaring themselves devotees of both Buddhism and Christianity, for example. Japan thus seems like one of the most religious places on earth.

But numbers can be misleading. The government's data come not from individuals, but rather statistics generated by religious institutions themselves. Independent research surveys about individuals' religious beliefs reveal a different picture. According to these reports, only about 20 percent of Japanese people describe themselves as religious, and very few describe religion as being particularly important. While a slight majority regularly participate in the cycle of ritual events that punctuate the calendar year, visiting Shintō shrines on New Year's Day (*hatsumōde*) or cleaning ancestral graves at Buddhist temples on the equinoxes (*ohigan*), most people prefer to use words like "custom" or "tradition," not religion, to explain these behaviors. If governmental statistics about religious affiliation suggest a country that is overwhelmingly religious, the survey data on religious belief suggest that Japan is one of the least religious countries in the world.

Against this backdrop, Hikaru Nakamura's rollicking slice-of-life comedy *Saint Young Men* skillfully inverts the position of religion in contemporary Japanese society. Rather than depicting contemporary urbanites wandering dispassionately past atmospheric shrines and temples, she depicts two among the most influential religious founders in world history living as roommates in a Tokyo suburb and reveling in the exotic aspects of everyday life in Japan. If statistics frame Japan's ambivalence about religion as excessively and minimally religious, *Saint Young Men* makes religion seem foreign and fun.

Nakamura weaves visual gags with cross-linguistic puns and dense allusions to a wide range of religious texts, local legends, and folk beliefs. Happily, this translation captures the irreverent double entendres and cultural nuances of the original—skillfully guiding readers through the text with notes that unobtrusively explain the religious connotations of everyday words, including slang.

Nakamura is also an excellent guide, leading her audience through the life stories of two of humanity's most inspiring religious teachers. The series rewards those already familiar with the Christian Gospels and Ashvaghosa's *Buddhacarita* (*The Acts of the Buddha*) with a steady stream of inside jokes, but it also introduces new audiences to the hagiographies of Jesus Christ and the Buddha Shakyamuni.

But just as official statistics about denominational affiliation only give us a partial picture of the position of religion in contemporary Japanese society, we would be wrong to assume that *Saint Young Men* is only about the formal doctrines of Buddhism and Christianity. In this second omnibus volume, for example, our heroes engage in the classic pastime of telling ghost stories to beat the oppressive summer heat. When that doesn't work, they escape to the air conditioning of a local diner, where a casual comment that "the customer is a god" (i.e., "always right") makes them fear that their cover has been blown. When they consider moving apartments, they get the "foreigner treatment" of being shown the most undesirable properties in a scene that indirectly reveals a longstanding Japanese taboo against occupying homes associated with inauspicious deaths.

These short vignettes capture the complicated place of religion in contemporary Japan, where formal doctrines have to "pass" in other guises, while tacit taboos reflect the continued vitality of old ideas about how to ritually care for the unruly dead. The experiences of Jesus and Buddha in *Saint Young Men* show that religion in contemporary Japan lives not just in the institutions that birthed Japan's famed UNESCO World Heritage Sites, but also in everyday acts of entertainment. Indeed, the same surveys that show that Japanese people have minimal religious belief also reveal that Japanese people hardly occupy a disenchanted world: A majority affirm the existence of ghosts, deities, "power spots," or other supernatural phenomena. Formal adherence to religion may be on the wane in Japan, but its people still prefer to inhabit a world characterized by miracles and spirits over a fully rationalized, demythologized universe. *Saint Young Men* embraces this ambivalence and brings that magic to life.

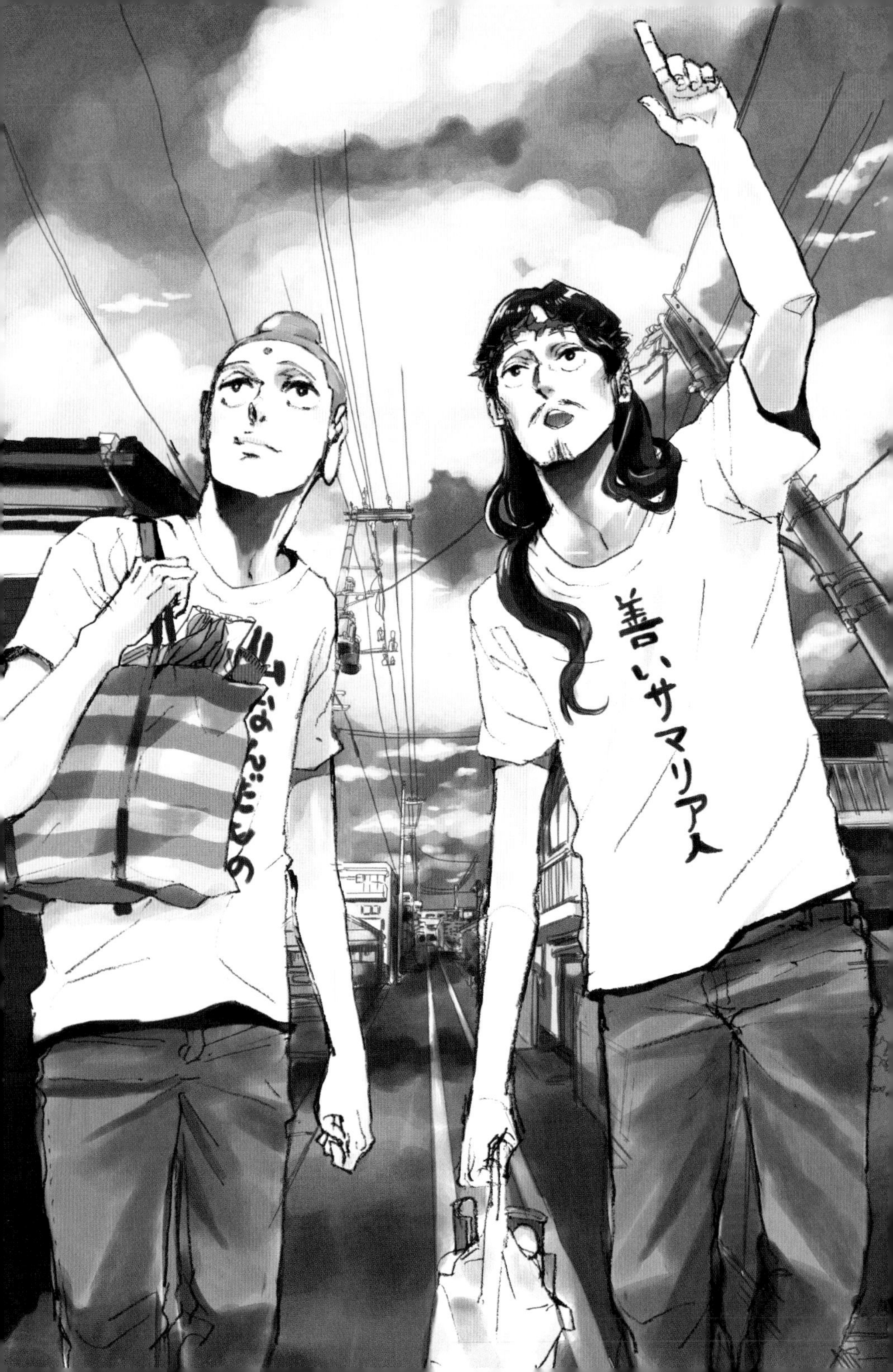
なんだもの
善いサマリア人

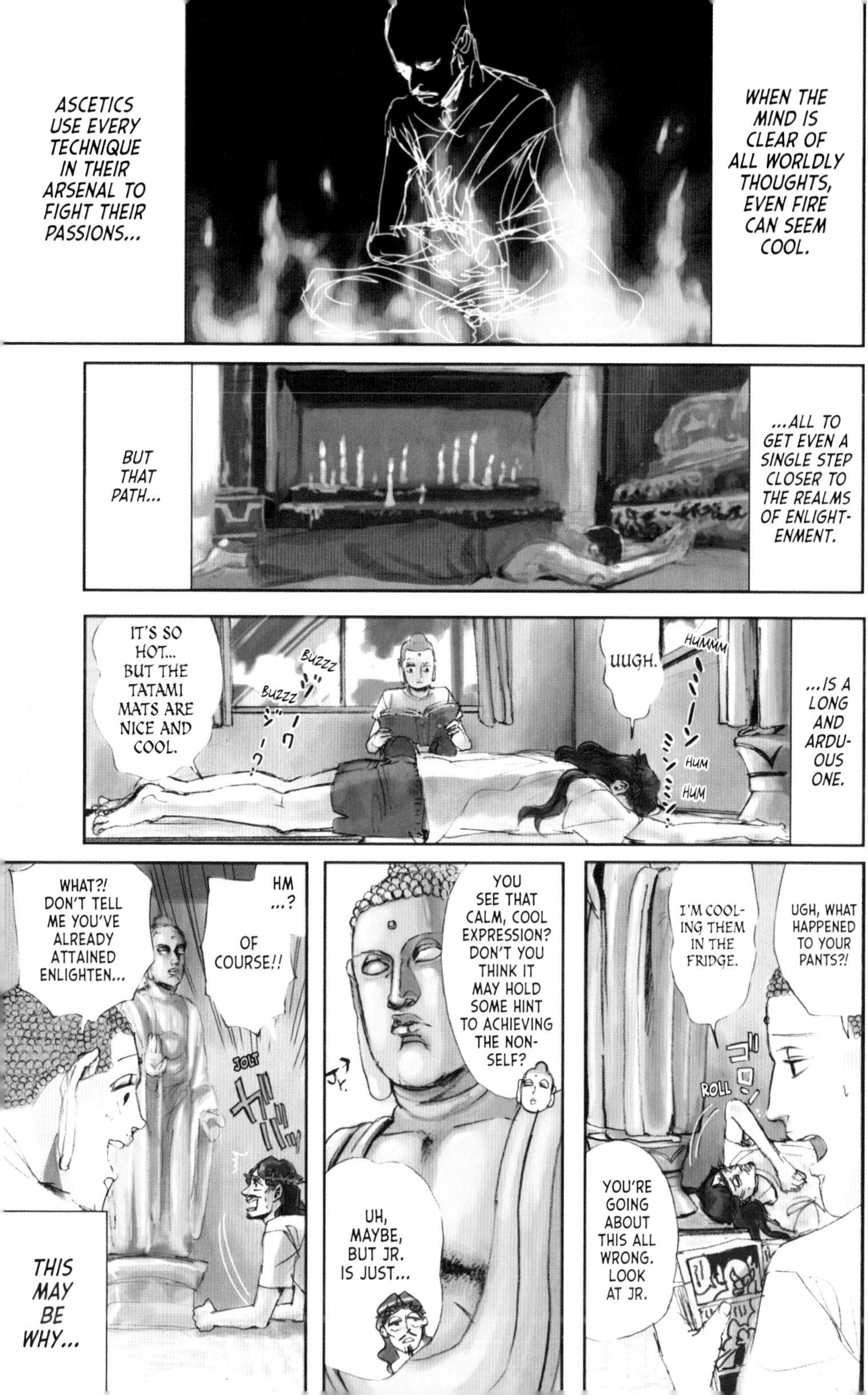
WHEN THE MIND IS CLEAR OF ALL WORLDLY THOUGHTS, EVEN FIRE CAN SEEM COOL.
ASCETICS USE EVERY TECHNIQUE IN THEIR ARSENAL TO FIGHT THEIR PASSIONS...
...ALL TO GET EVEN A SINGLE STEP CLOSER TO THE REALMS OF ENLIGHT-ENMENT.
BUT THAT PATH...
...IS A LONG AND ARDUOUS ONE.
HUMMM
HUM
HUM
UUGH.
IT'S SO HOT... BUT THE TATAMI MATS ARE NICE AND COOL.
BUZZZ
BUZZZ
UGH, WHAT HAPPENED TO YOUR PANTS?!
I'M COOL-ING THEM IN THE FRIDGE.
ROLL
YOU'RE GOING ABOUT THIS ALL WRONG. LOOK AT JR.
YOU SEE THAT CALM, COOL EXPRESSION? DON'T YOU THINK IT MAY HOLD SOME HINT TO ACHIEVING THE NON-SELF?
UH, MAYBE, BUT JR. IS JUST...
HM ...?
OF COURSE!!
WHAT?! DON'T TELL ME YOU'VE ALREADY ATTAINED ENLIGHTEN...
JOLT
THIS MAY BE WHY...

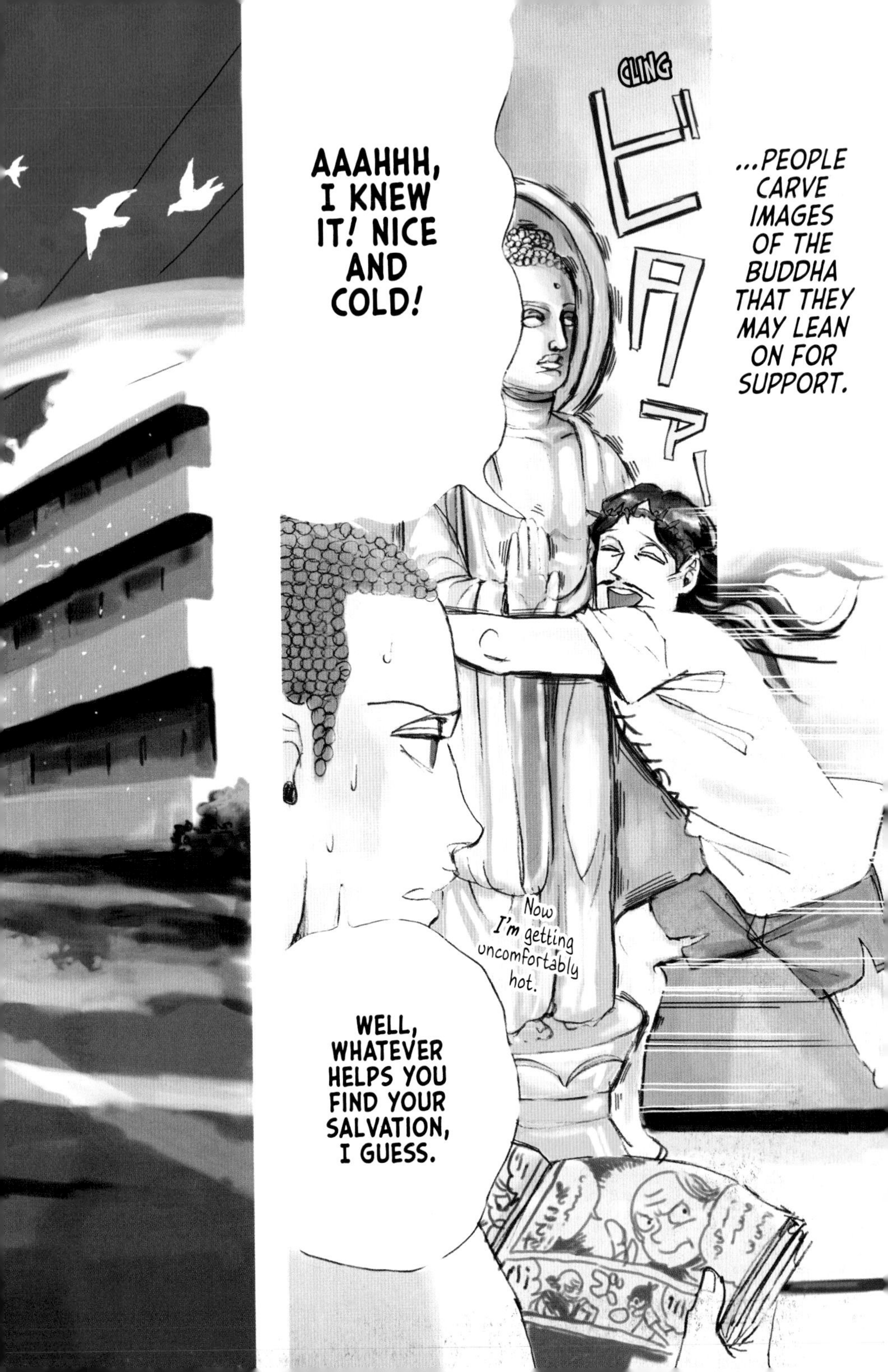
CLING
...PEOPLE CARVE IMAGES OF THE BUDDHA THAT THEY MAY LEAN ON FOR SUPPORT.
AAAHHH, I KNEW IT! NICE AND COLD!
Now I'm getting uncomfortably hot.
WELL, WHATEVER HELPS YOU FIND YOUR SALVATION, I GUESS.

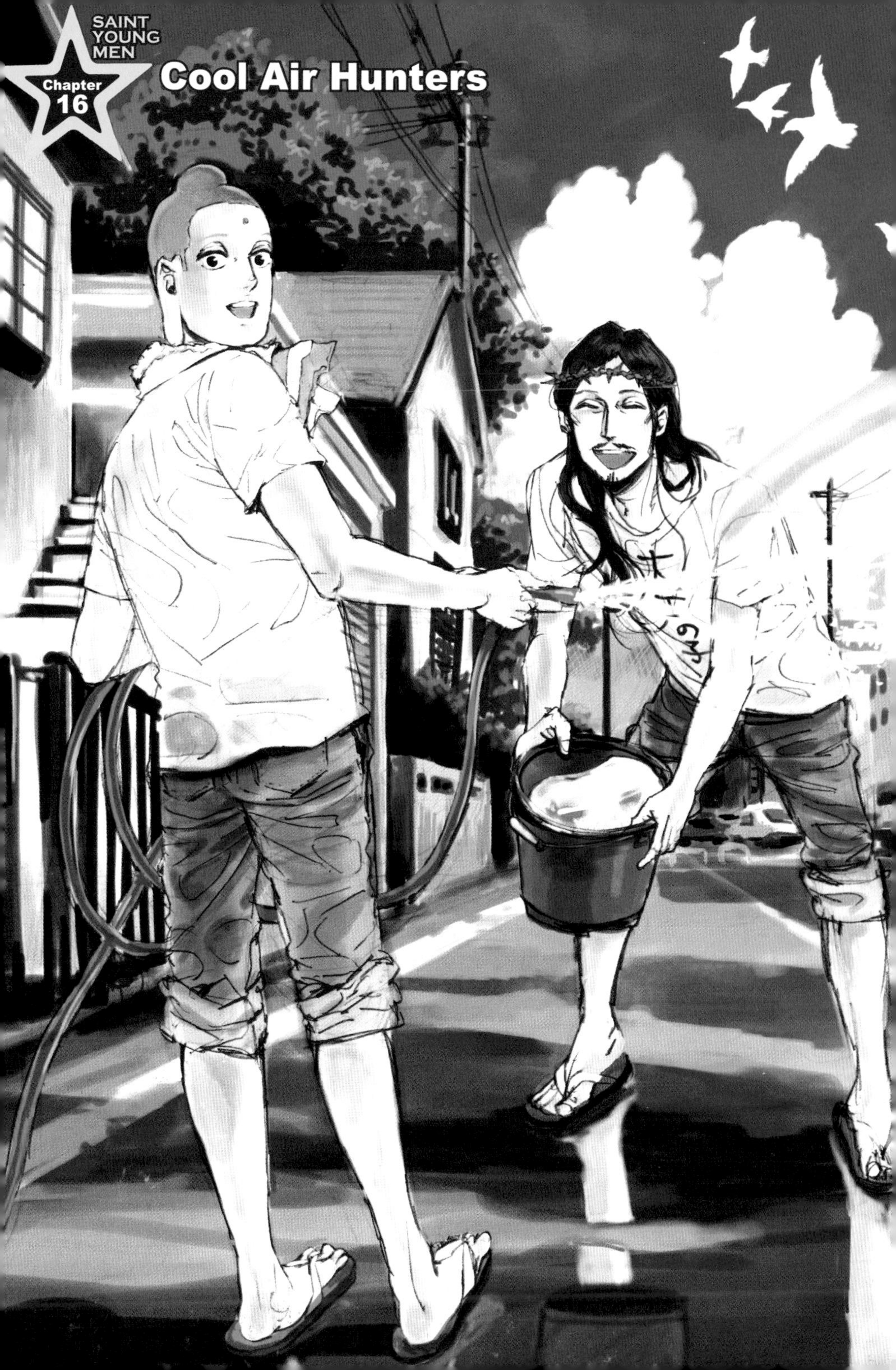
SAINT YOUNG MEN
Chapter 16
Cool Air Hunters

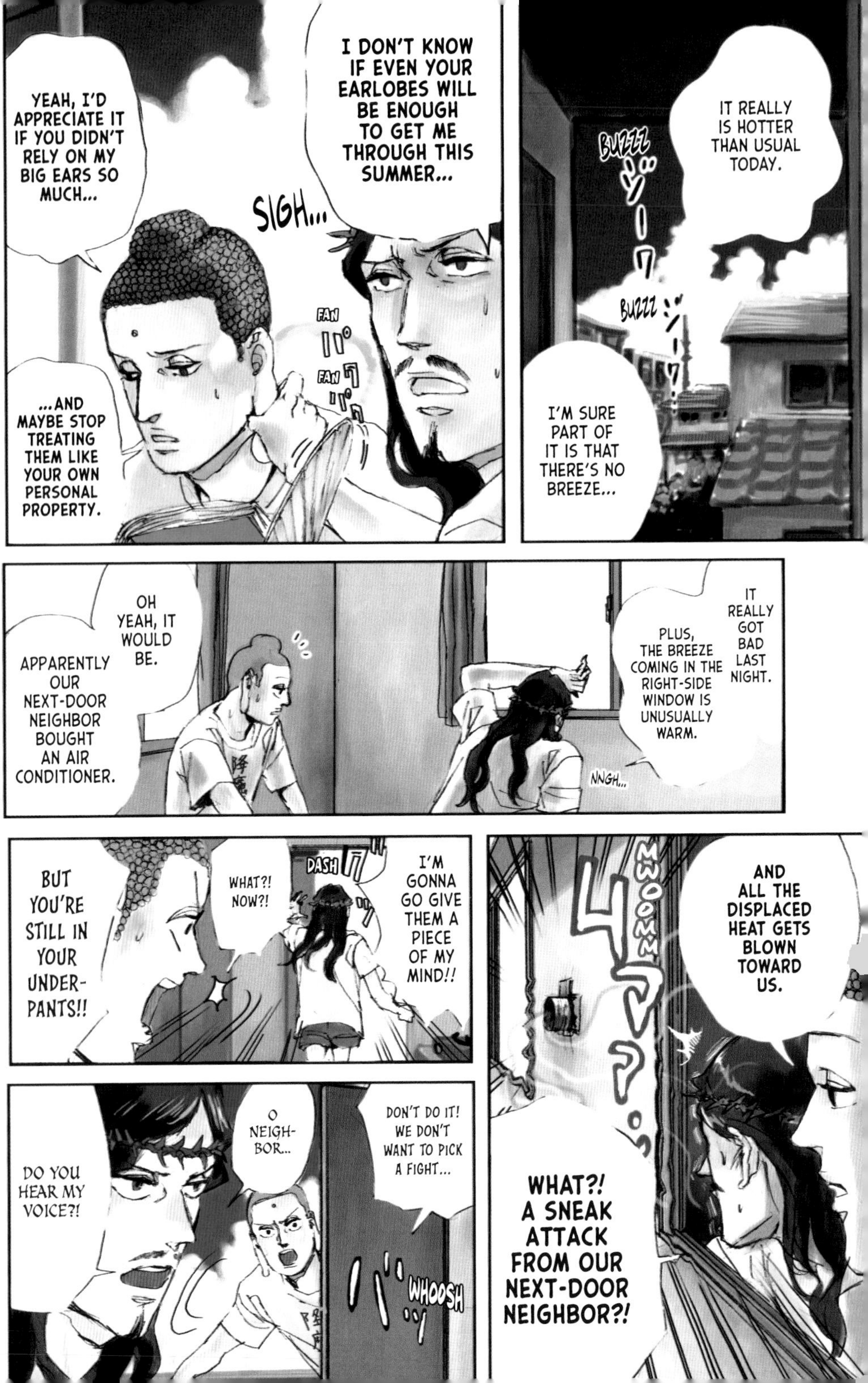
IT REALLY IS HOTTER THAN USUAL TODAY.
BUZZZ
BUZZZ
I'M SURE PART OF IT IS THAT THERE'S NO BREEZE...
I DON'T KNOW IF EVEN YOUR EARLOBES WILL BE ENOUGH TO GET ME THROUGH THIS SUMMER...
SIGH...
YEAH, I'D APPRECIATE IT IF YOU DIDN'T RELY ON MY BIG EARS SO MUCH...
FAN
FAN
...AND MAYBE STOP TREATING THEM LIKE YOUR OWN PERSONAL PROPERTY.
IT REALLY GOT BAD LAST NIGHT.
PLUS, THE BREEZE COMING IN THE RIGHT-SIDE WINDOW IS UNUSUALLY WARM.
NNGH...
OH YEAH, IT WOULD BE.
APPARENTLY OUR NEXT-DOOR NEIGHBOR BOUGHT AN AIR CONDITIONER.
AND ALL THE DISPLACED HEAT GETS BLOWN TOWARD US.
MWOOMM
WHAT?! A SNEAK ATTACK FROM OUR NEXT-DOOR NEIGHBOR?!
I'M GONNA GO GIVE THEM A PIECE OF MY MIND!!
DASH
WHAT?! NOW?!
BUT YOU'RE STILL IN YOUR UNDER-PANTS!!
DON'T DO IT! WE DON'T WANT TO PICK A FIGHT...
O NEIGH-BOR...
DO YOU HEAR MY VOICE?!
WHOOSH

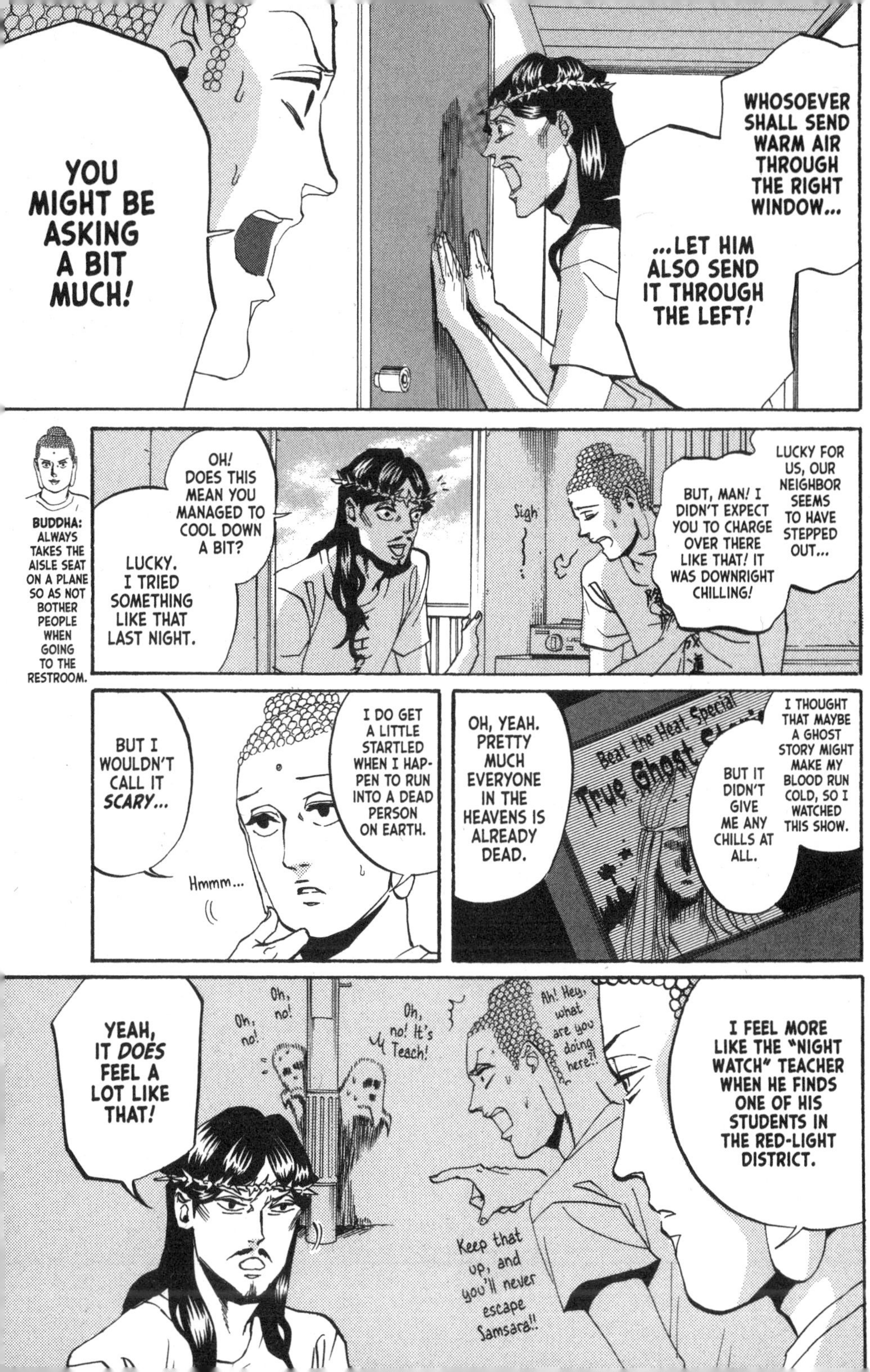

WHOSOEVER SHALL SEND WARM AIR THROUGH THE RIGHT WINDOW...
...LET HIM ALSO SEND IT THROUGH THE LEFT!
YOU MIGHT BE ASKING A BIT MUCH!
LUCKY FOR US, OUR NEIGHBOR SEEMS TO HAVE STEPPED OUT...
BUT, MAN! I DIDN'T EXPECT YOU TO CHARGE OVER THERE LIKE THAT! IT WAS DOWNRIGHT CHILLING!
Sigh
OH! DOES THIS MEAN YOU MANAGED TO COOL DOWN A BIT?
LUCKY. I TRIED SOMETHING LIKE THAT LAST NIGHT.
BUDDHA: ALWAYS TAKES THE AISLE SEAT ON A PLANE SO AS NOT BOTHER PEOPLE WHEN GOING TO THE RESTROOM.
I THOUGHT THAT MAYBE A GHOST STORY MIGHT MAKE MY BLOOD RUN COLD, SO I WATCHED THIS SHOW.
Beat the Heat Special
BUT IT DIDN'T GIVE ME ANY CHILLS AT ALL.
OH, YEAH. PRETTY MUCH EVERYONE IN THE HEAVENS IS ALREADY DEAD.
I DO GET A LITTLE STARTLED WHEN I HAPPEN TO RUN INTO A DEAD PERSON ON EARTH.
BUT I WOULDN'T CALL IT *SCARY*...
Hmmm...
I FEEL MORE LIKE THE "NIGHT WATCH" TEACHER WHEN HE FINDS ONE OF HIS STUDENTS IN THE RED-LIGHT DISTRICT.
Ah! Hey, what are you doing here?!
Keep that up, and you'll never escape Samsara!!
Oh, no! It's Teach!
Oh, no!
Oh, no!
YEAH, IT *DOES* FEEL A LOT LIKE THAT!

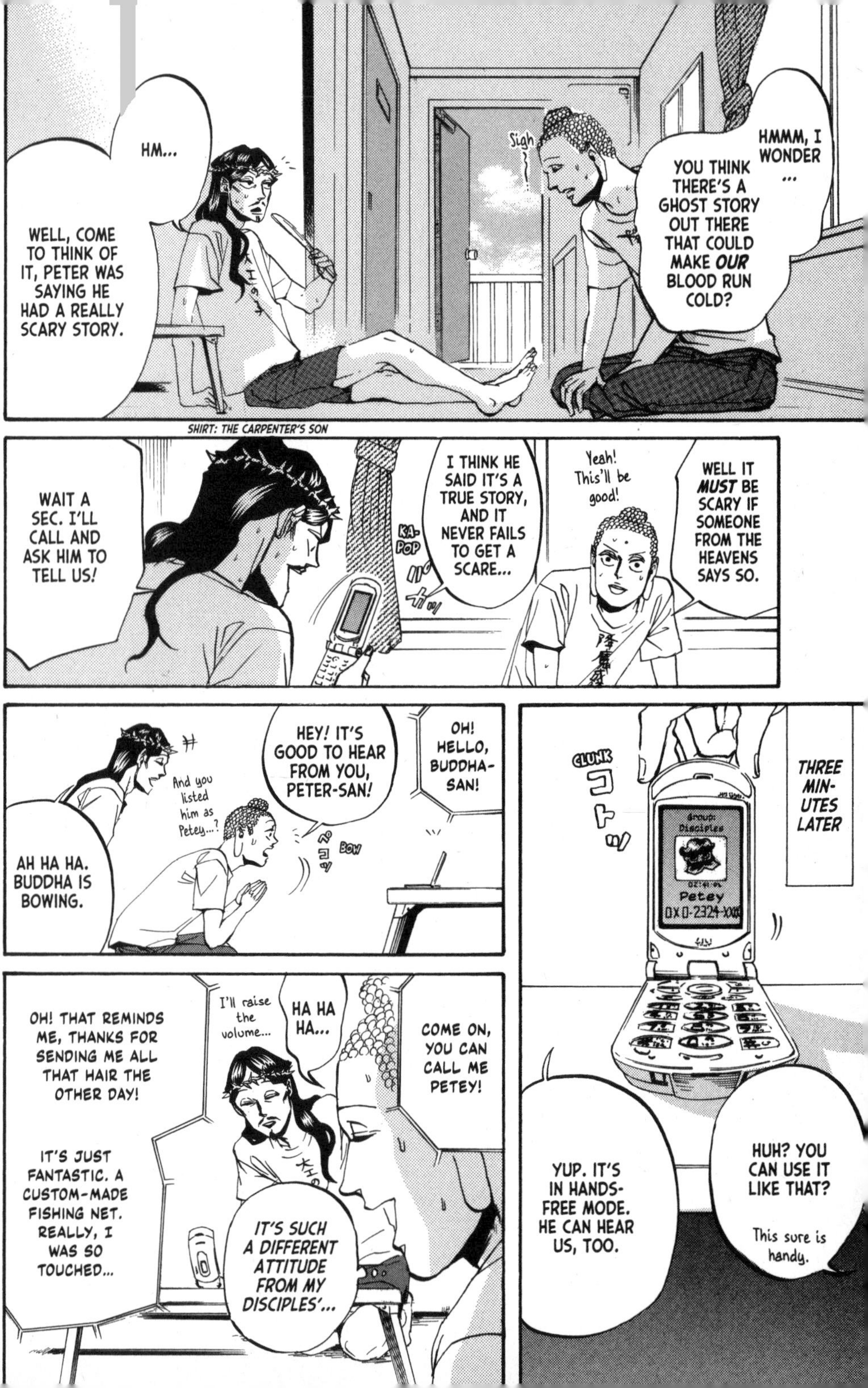
HMMM, I WONDER ...
YOU THINK THERE'S A GHOST STORY OUT THERE THAT COULD MAKE OUR BLOOD RUN COLD?
Sigh~
HM...
WELL, COME TO THINK OF IT, PETER WAS SAYING HE HAD A REALLY SCARY STORY.
SHIRT: THE CARPENTER'S SON
WELL IT MUST BE SCARY IF SOMEONE FROM THE HEAVENS SAYS SO.
Yeah! This'll be good!
I THINK HE SAID IT'S A TRUE STORY, AND IT NEVER FAILS TO GET A SCARE...
KA-POP
WAIT A SEC. I'LL CALL AND ASK HIM TO TELL US!
THREE MINUTES LATER
CLUNK
Group: Disciples
Petey
HUH? YOU CAN USE IT LIKE THAT?
This sure is handy.
YUP. IT'S IN HANDS-FREE MODE. HE CAN HEAR US, TOO.
OH! HELLO, BUDDHA-SAN!
HEY! IT'S GOOD TO HEAR FROM YOU, PETER-SAN!
BOW
And you listed him as Petey...?
AH HA HA. BUDDHA IS BOWING.
COME ON, YOU CAN CALL ME PETEY!
HA HA HA...
I'll raise the volume...
OH! THAT REMINDS ME, THANKS FOR SENDING ME ALL THAT HAIR THE OTHER DAY!
IT'S JUST FANTASTIC. A CUSTOM-MADE FISHING NET. REALLY, I WAS SO TOUCHED...
IT'S SUCH A DIFFERENT ATTITUDE FROM MY DISCIPLES'...

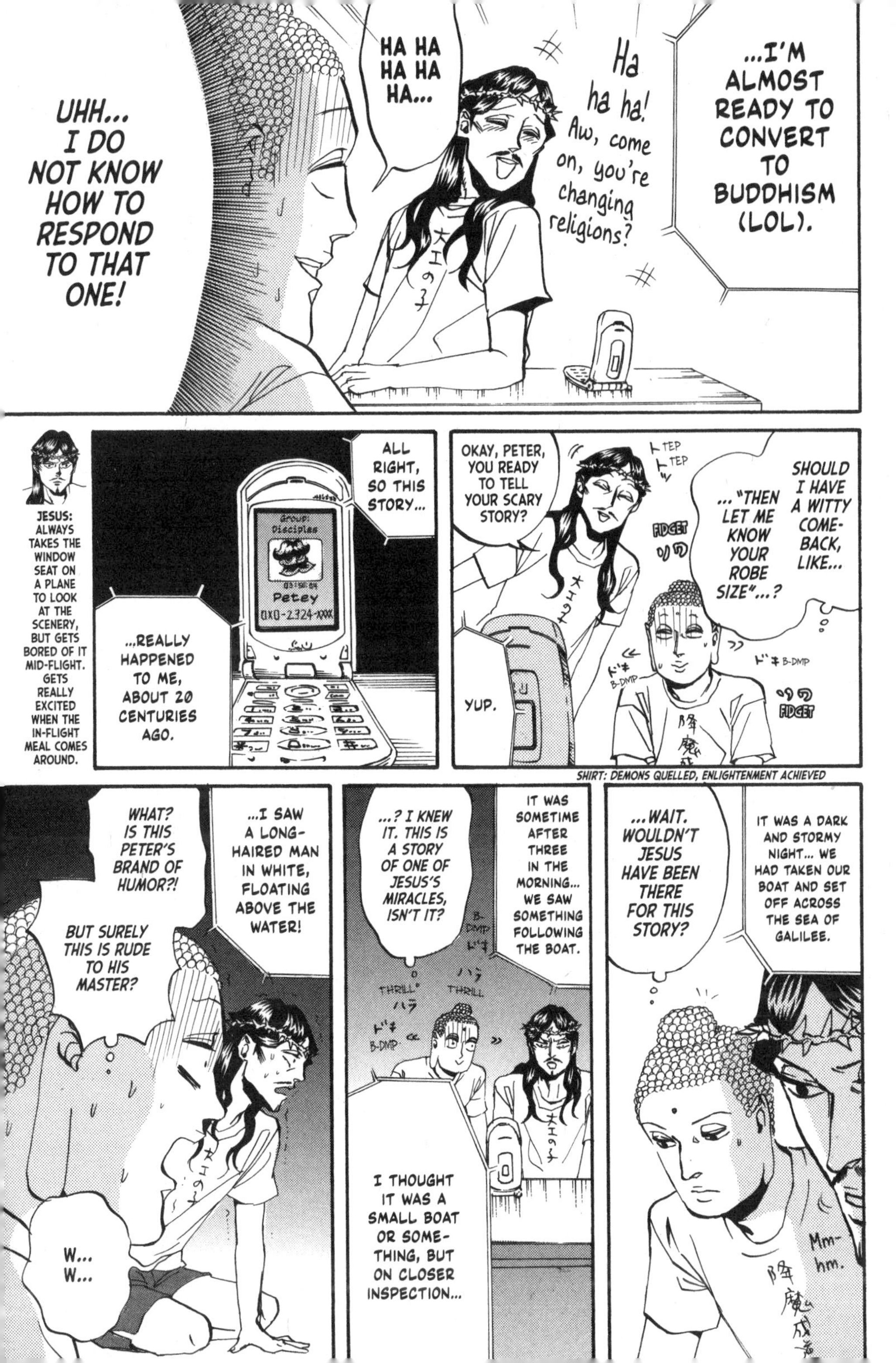

...I'M ALMOST READY TO CONVERT TO BUDDHISM (LOL).
Ha ha ha! Aw, come on, you're changing religions?
HA HA HA HA HA...
UHH... I DO NOT KNOW HOW TO RESPOND TO THAT ONE!
SHOULD I HAVE A WITTY COME-BACK, LIKE...
..."THEN LET ME KNOW YOUR ROBE SIZE"...?
TEP TEP
OKAY, PETER, YOU READY TO TELL YOUR SCARY STORY?
FIDGET
B-DMP
B-DMP
FIDGET
YUP.
ALL RIGHT, SO THIS STORY...
Group: Disciples
Petey
0X0-2324-XXXX
...REALLY HAPPENED TO ME, ABOUT 20 CENTURIES AGO.
JESUS: ALWAYS TAKES THE WINDOW SEAT ON A PLANE TO LOOK AT THE SCENERY, BUT GETS BORED OF IT MID-FLIGHT. GETS REALLY EXCITED WHEN THE IN-FLIGHT MEAL COMES AROUND.
SHIRT: DEMONS QUELLED, ENLIGHTENMENT ACHIEVED
IT WAS A DARK AND STORMY NIGHT... WE HAD TAKEN OUR BOAT AND SET OFF ACROSS THE SEA OF GALILEE.
...WAIT. WOULDN'T JESUS HAVE BEEN THERE FOR THIS STORY?
Mm-hm.
IT WAS SOMETIME AFTER THREE IN THE MORNING... WE SAW SOMETHING FOLLOWING THE BOAT.
...? I KNEW IT. THIS IS A STORY OF ONE OF JESUS'S MIRACLES, ISN'T IT?
B-DMP
THRILL
THRILL
B-DMP
I THOUGHT IT WAS A SMALL BOAT OR SOME-THING, BUT ON CLOSER INSPECTION...
...I SAW A LONG-HAIRED MAN IN WHITE, FLOATING ABOVE THE WATER!
WHAT? IS THIS PETER'S BRAND OF HUMOR?!
BUT SURELY THIS IS RUDE TO HIS MASTER?
W... W...

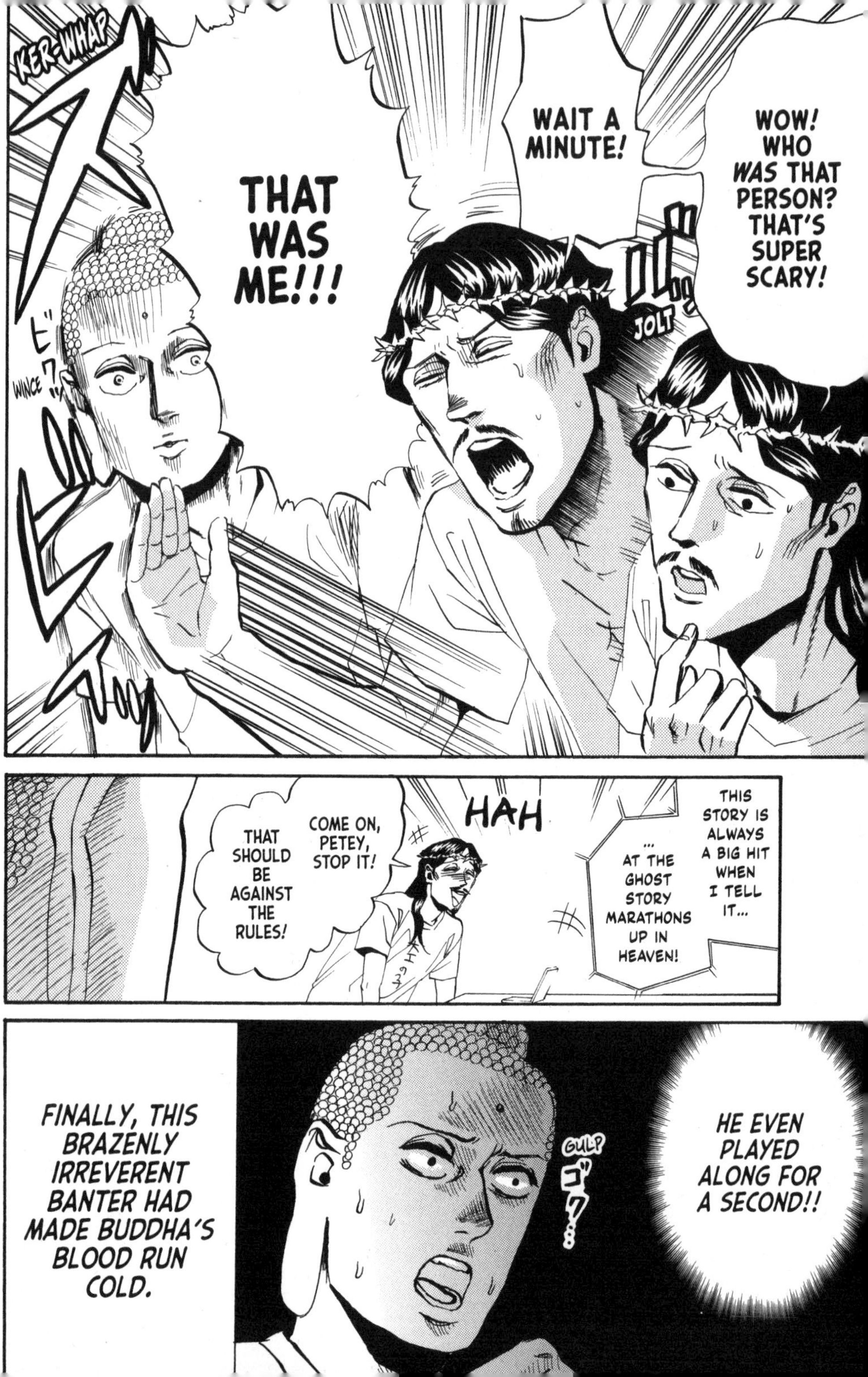
WOW! WHO WAS THAT PERSON? THAT'S SUPER SCARY!
JOLT
WAIT A MINUTE!
THAT WAS ME!!!
KER-WHAP
WINCE
THIS STORY IS ALWAYS A BIG HIT WHEN I TELL IT...
... AT THE GHOST STORY MARATHONS UP IN HEAVEN!
HAH
COME ON, PETEY, STOP IT!
THAT SHOULD BE AGAINST THE RULES!
HE EVEN PLAYED ALONG FOR A SECOND!!
GULP
FINALLY, THIS BRAZENLY IRREVERENT BANTER HAD MADE BUDDHA'S BLOOD RUN COLD.

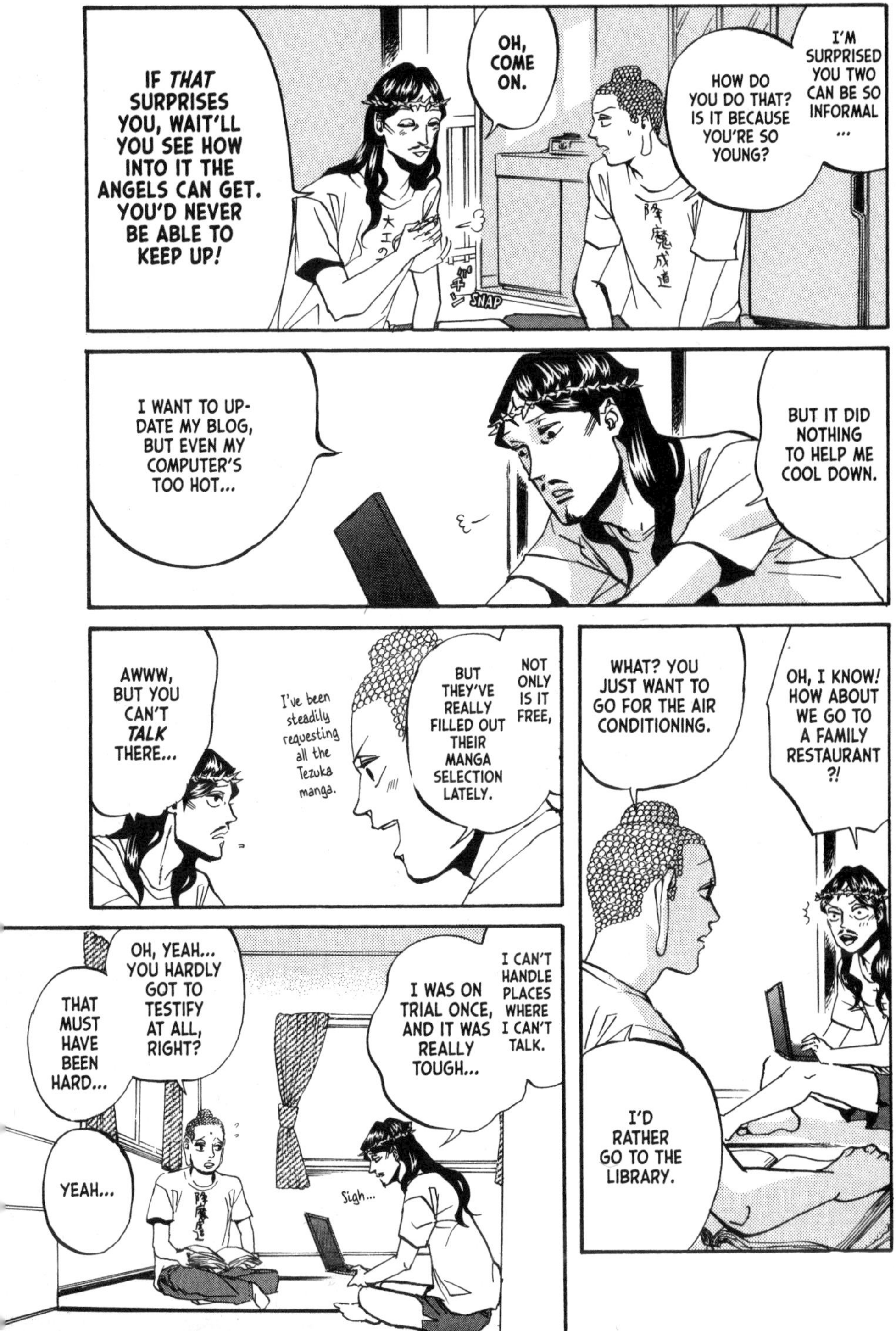
I'M SURPRISED YOU TWO CAN BE SO INFORMAL ...
HOW DO YOU DO THAT? IS IT BECAUSE YOU'RE SO YOUNG?
OH, COME ON.
IF *THAT* SURPRISES YOU, WAIT'LL YOU SEE HOW INTO IT THE ANGELS CAN GET. YOU'D NEVER BE ABLE TO KEEP UP!
SNAP
BUT IT DID NOTHING TO HELP ME COOL DOWN.
I WANT TO UP-DATE MY BLOG, BUT EVEN MY COMPUTER'S TOO HOT...
OH, I KNOW! HOW ABOUT WE GO TO A FAMILY RESTAURANT?!
WHAT? YOU JUST WANT TO GO FOR THE AIR CONDITIONING.
I'D RATHER GO TO THE LIBRARY.
NOT ONLY IS IT FREE,
BUT THEY'VE REALLY FILLED OUT THEIR MANGA SELECTION LATELY.
I've been steadily requesting all the Tezuka manga.
AWWW, BUT YOU CAN'T *TALK* THERE...
I CAN'T HANDLE PLACES WHERE I CAN'T TALK.
I WAS ON TRIAL ONCE, AND IT WAS REALLY TOUGH...
Sigh...
OH, YEAH... YOU HARDLY GOT TO TESTIFY AT ALL, RIGHT?
THAT MUST HAVE BEEN HARD...
YEAH...

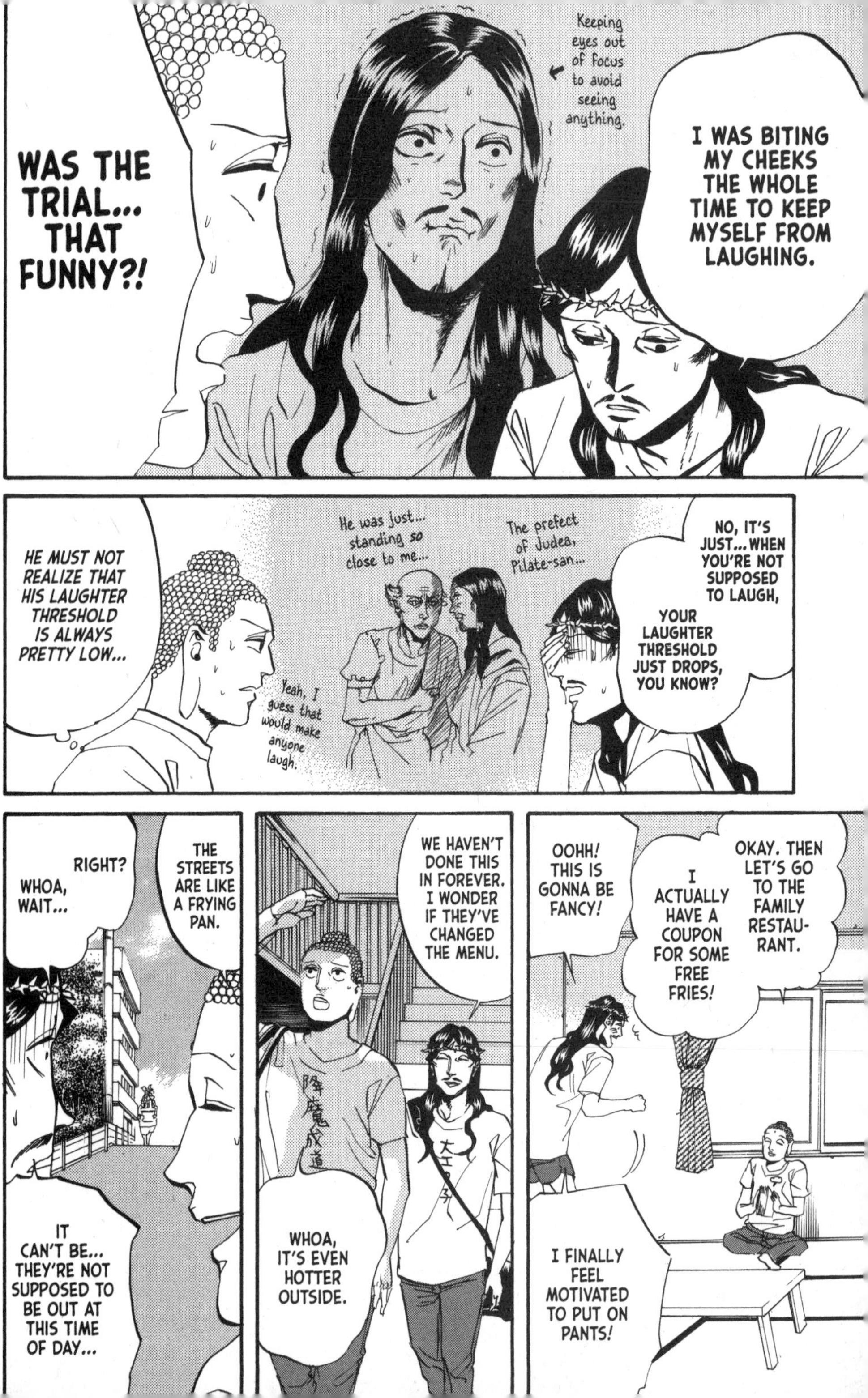
I WAS BITING MY CHEEKS THE WHOLE TIME TO KEEP MYSELF FROM LAUGHING.
Keeping eyes out of focus to avoid seeing anything.
WAS THE TRIAL... THAT FUNNY?!
NO, IT'S JUST... WHEN YOU'RE NOT SUPPOSED TO LAUGH,
YOUR LAUGHTER THRESHOLD JUST DROPS, YOU KNOW?
The prefect of Judea, Pilate-san...
He was just... standing so close to me...
Yeah, I guess that would make anyone laugh.
HE MUST NOT REALIZE THAT HIS LAUGHTER THRESHOLD IS ALWAYS PRETTY LOW...
OKAY. THEN LET'S GO TO THE FAMILY RESTAURANT.
I ACTUALLY HAVE A COUPON FOR SOME FREE FRIES!
OOHH! THIS IS GONNA BE FANCY!
I FINALLY FEEL MOTIVATED TO PUT ON PANTS!
WE HAVEN'T DONE THIS IN FOREVER. I WONDER IF THEY'VE CHANGED THE MENU.
WHOA, IT'S EVEN HOTTER OUTSIDE.
THE STREETS ARE LIKE A FRYING PAN.
RIGHT? WHOA, WAIT...
IT CAN'T BE... THEY'RE NOT SUPPOSED TO BE OUT AT THIS TIME OF DAY...

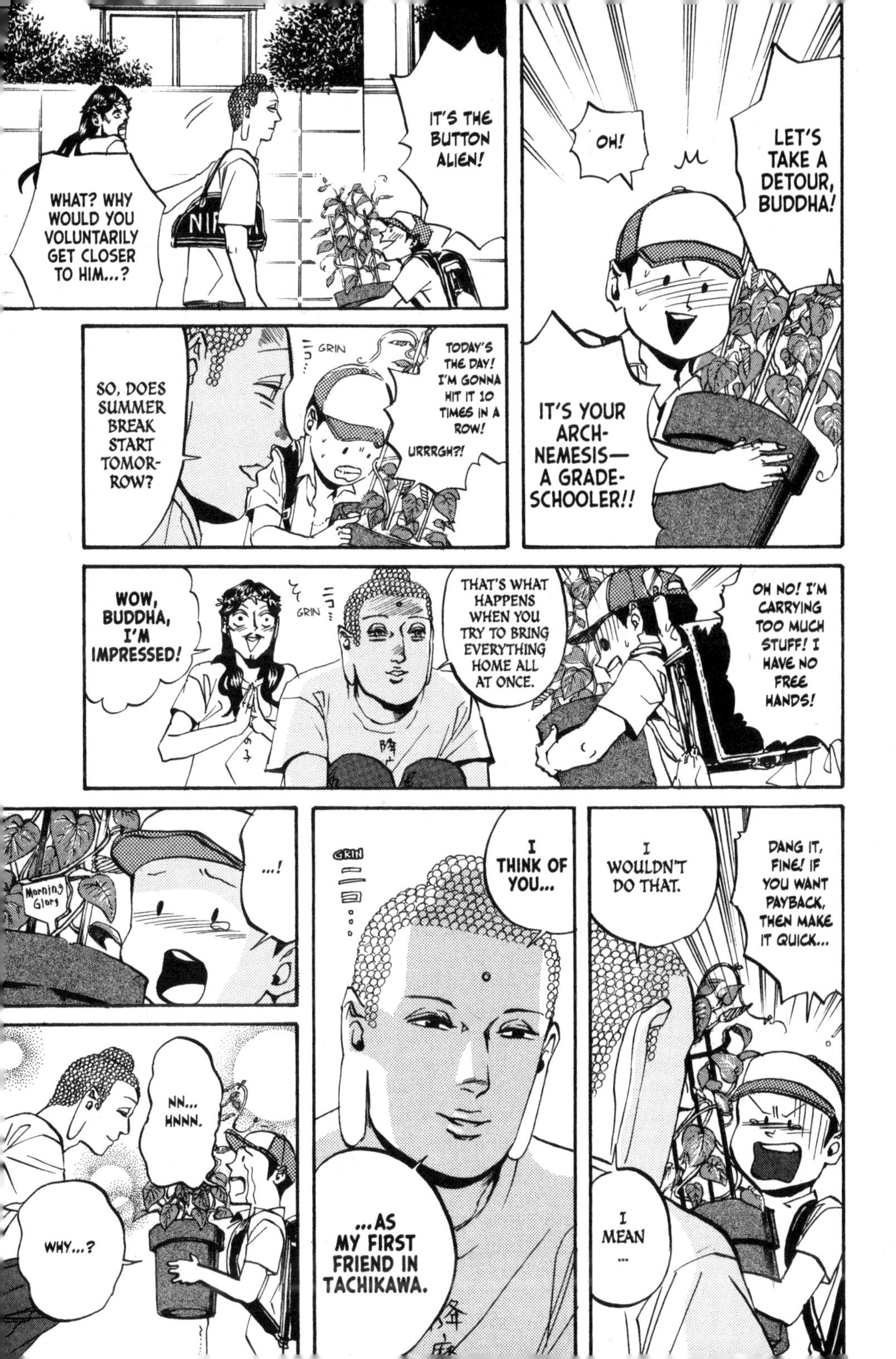
LET'S TAKE A DETOUR, BUDDHA!
OH!
IT'S YOUR ARCH-NEMESIS—A GRADE-SCHOOLER!!
IT'S THE BUTTON ALIEN!
WHAT? WHY WOULD YOU VOLUNTARILY GET CLOSER TO HIM...?
TODAY'S THE DAY! I'M GONNA HIT IT 10 TIMES IN A ROW!
GRIN
URRRGH?!
SO, DOES SUMMER BREAK START TOMORROW?
OH NO! I'M CARRYING TOO MUCH STUFF! I HAVE NO FREE HANDS!
THAT'S WHAT HAPPENS WHEN YOU TRY TO BRING EVERYTHING HOME ALL AT ONCE.
GRIN
WOW, BUDDHA, I'M IMPRESSED!
DANG IT, FINE! IF YOU WANT PAYBACK, THEN MAKE IT QUICK...
I WOULDN'T DO THAT.
I MEAN...
I THINK OF YOU...
GRIN
...AS MY FIRST FRIEND IN TACHIKAWA.
...!
Morning Glory
NN... HNNN.
WHY...?

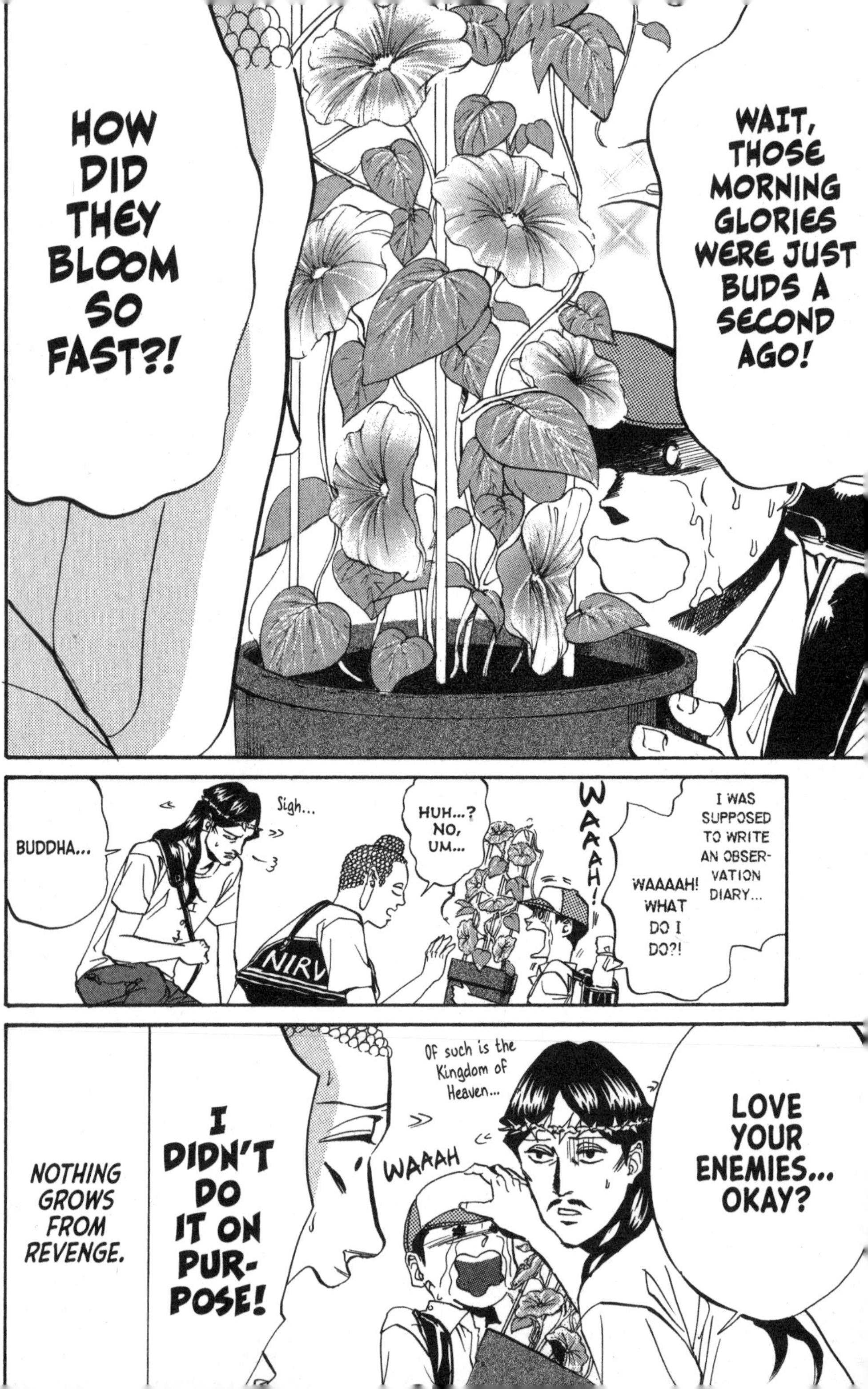
WAIT, THOSE MORNING GLORIES WERE JUST BUDS A SECOND AGO!
HOW DID THEY BLOOM SO FAST?!
I WAS SUPPOSED TO WRITE AN OBSERVATION DIARY...
WAAAH!
WAAAAH! WHAT DO I DO?!
HUH...? NO, UM...
Sigh...
BUDDHA...
LOVE YOUR ENEMIES... OKAY?
Of such is the Kingdom of Heaven...
WAAAH
I DIDN'T DO IT ON PURPOSE!
NOTHING GROWS FROM REVENGE.

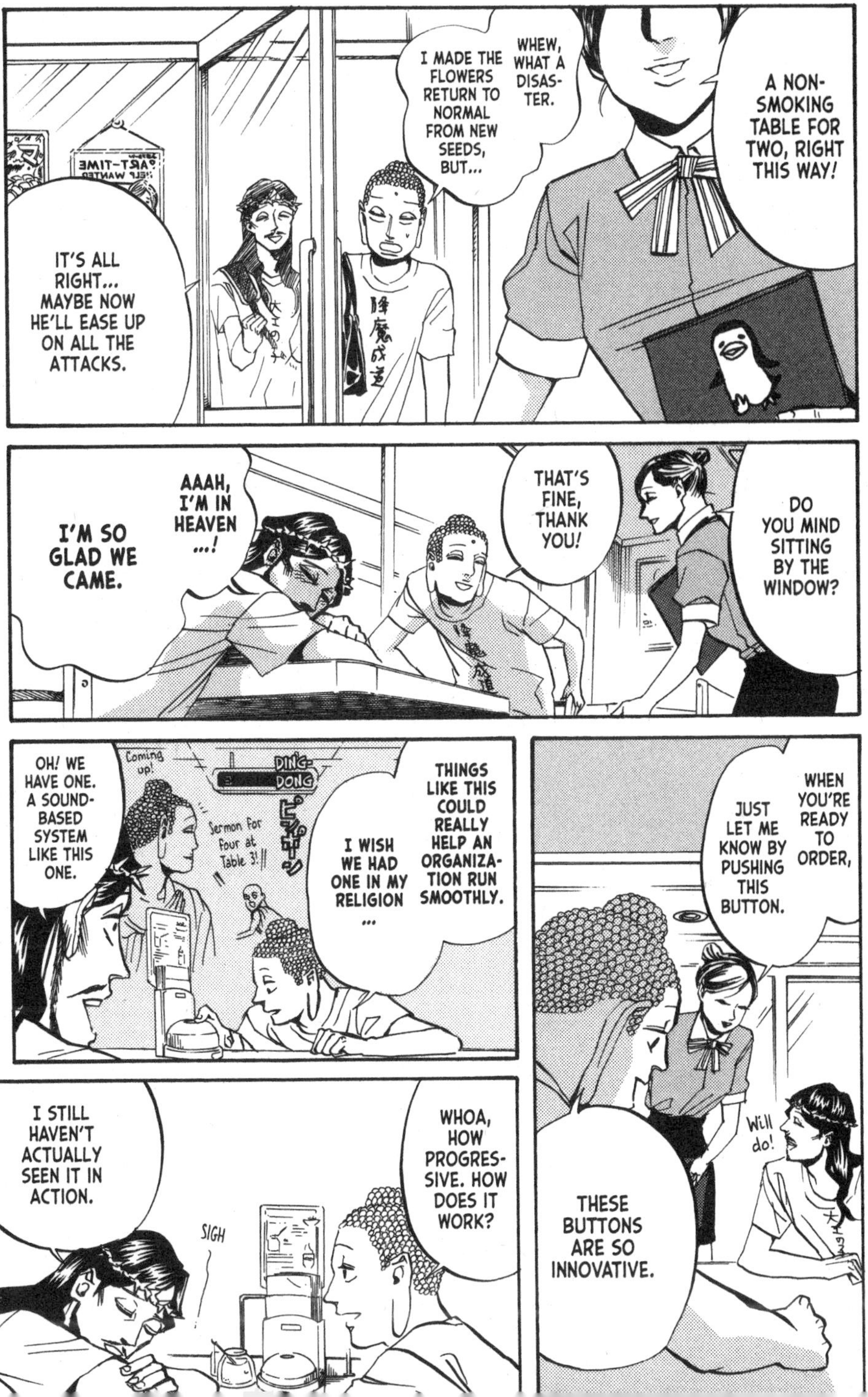
A NON-SMOKING TABLE FOR TWO, RIGHT THIS WAY!
WHEW, WHAT A DISASTER.
I MADE THE FLOWERS RETURN TO NORMAL FROM NEW SEEDS, BUT...
IT'S ALL RIGHT... MAYBE NOW HE'LL EASE UP ON ALL THE ATTACKS.
DO YOU MIND SITTING BY THE WINDOW?
THAT'S FINE, THANK YOU!
AAAH, I'M IN HEAVEN ...!
I'M SO GLAD WE CAME.
WHEN YOU'RE READY TO ORDER,
JUST LET ME KNOW BY PUSHING THIS BUTTON.
Will do!
THESE BUTTONS ARE SO INNOVATIVE.
THINGS LIKE THIS COULD REALLY HELP AN ORGANIZATION RUN SMOOTHLY.
I WISH WE HAD ONE IN MY RELIGION ...
DING-DONG
Coming up!
Sermon For Four at Table 3!!
OH! WE HAVE ONE. A SOUND-BASED SYSTEM LIKE THIS ONE.
WHOA, HOW PROGRESSIVE. HOW DOES IT WORK?
SIGH
I STILL HAVEN'T ACTUALLY SEEN IT IN ACTION.

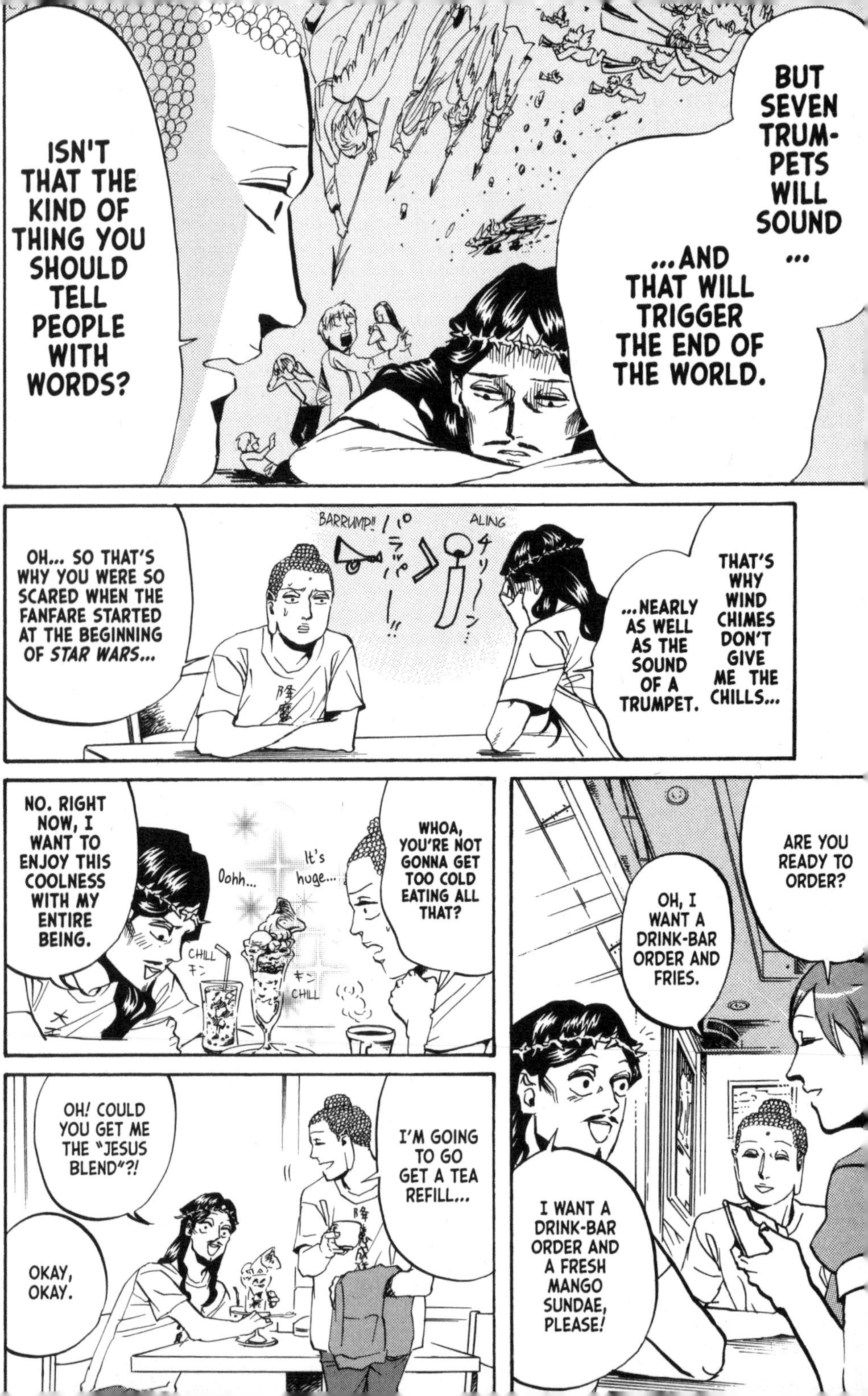
BUT SEVEN TRUMPETS WILL SOUND...
...AND THAT WILL TRIGGER THE END OF THE WORLD.
ISN'T THAT THE KIND OF THING YOU SHOULD TELL PEOPLE WITH WORDS?
THAT'S WHY WIND CHIMES DON'T GIVE ME THE CHILLS...
...NEARLY AS WELL AS THE SOUND OF A TRUMPET.
ALING
BARRUMP!!
OH... SO THAT'S WHY YOU WERE SO SCARED WHEN THE FANFARE STARTED AT THE BEGINNING OF *STAR WARS*...
ARE YOU READY TO ORDER?
OH, I WANT A DRINK-BAR ORDER AND FRIES.
I WANT A DRINK-BAR ORDER AND A FRESH MANGO SUNDAE, PLEASE!
WHOA, YOU'RE NOT GONNA GET TOO COLD EATING ALL THAT?
It's huge...
Oohh...
CHILL
CHILL
NO. RIGHT NOW, I WANT TO ENJOY THIS COOLNESS WITH MY ENTIRE BEING.
I'M GOING TO GO GET A TEA REFILL...
OH! COULD YOU GET ME THE "JESUS BLEND"?!
OKAY, OKAY.

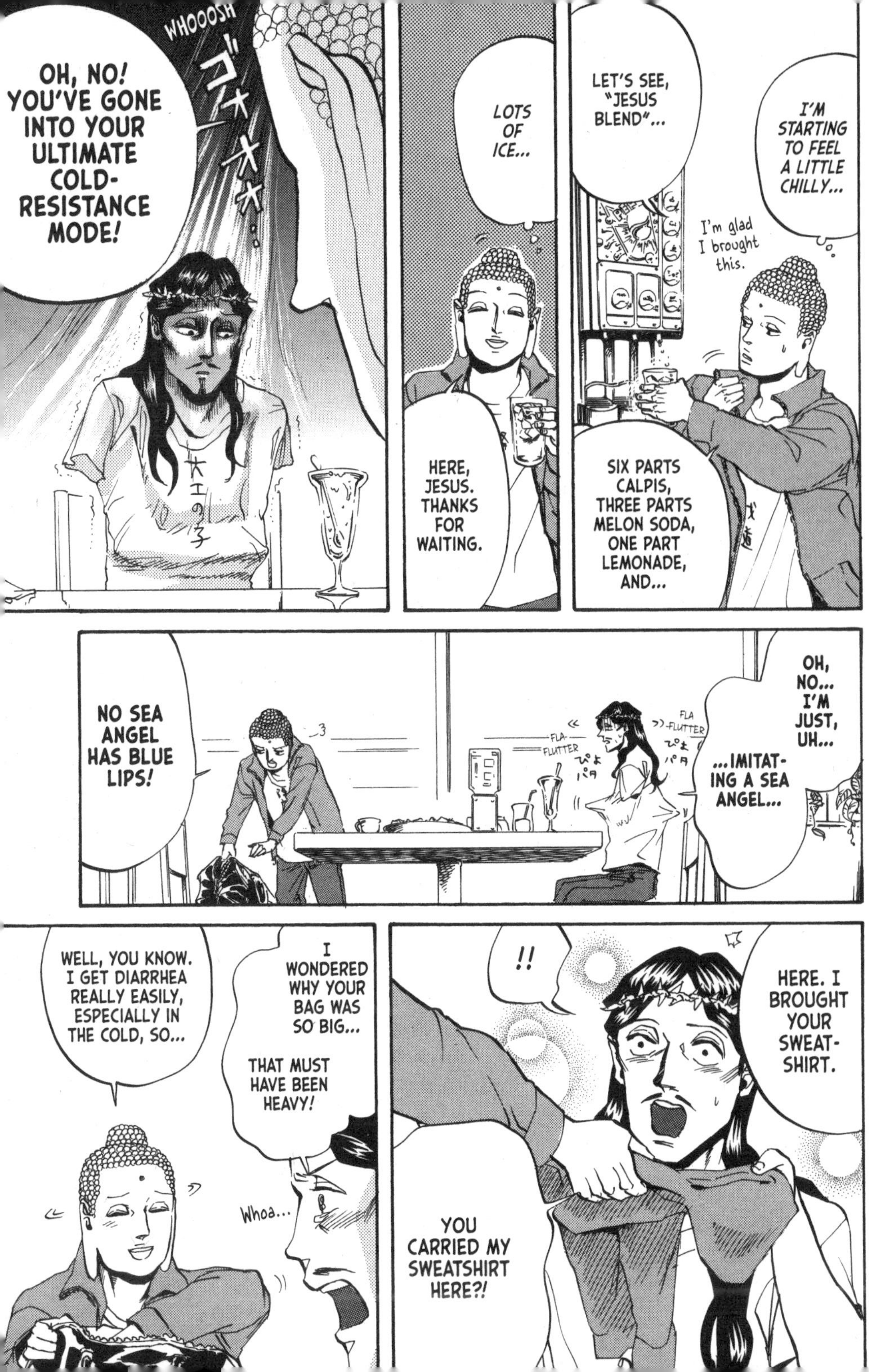
I'M STARTING TO FEEL A LITTLE CHILLY...
I'm glad I brought this.
LET'S SEE, "JESUS BLEND"...
SIX PARTS CALPIS, THREE PARTS MELON SODA, ONE PART LEMONADE, AND...
LOTS OF ICE...
HERE, JESUS. THANKS FOR WAITING.
WHOOOSH
OH, NO! YOU'VE GONE INTO YOUR ULTIMATE COLD-RESISTANCE MODE!
OH, NO... I'M JUST, UH...
...IMITATING A SEA ANGEL...
FLA-FLUTTER
FLA-FLUTTER
NO SEA ANGEL HAS BLUE LIPS!
HERE. I BROUGHT YOUR SWEATSHIRT.
!!
YOU CARRIED MY SWEATSHIRT HERE?!
I WONDERED WHY YOUR BAG WAS SO BIG...
WELL, YOU KNOW. I GET DIARRHEA REALLY EASILY, ESPECIALLY IN THE COLD, SO...
THAT MUST HAVE BEEN HEAVY!
Whoa...

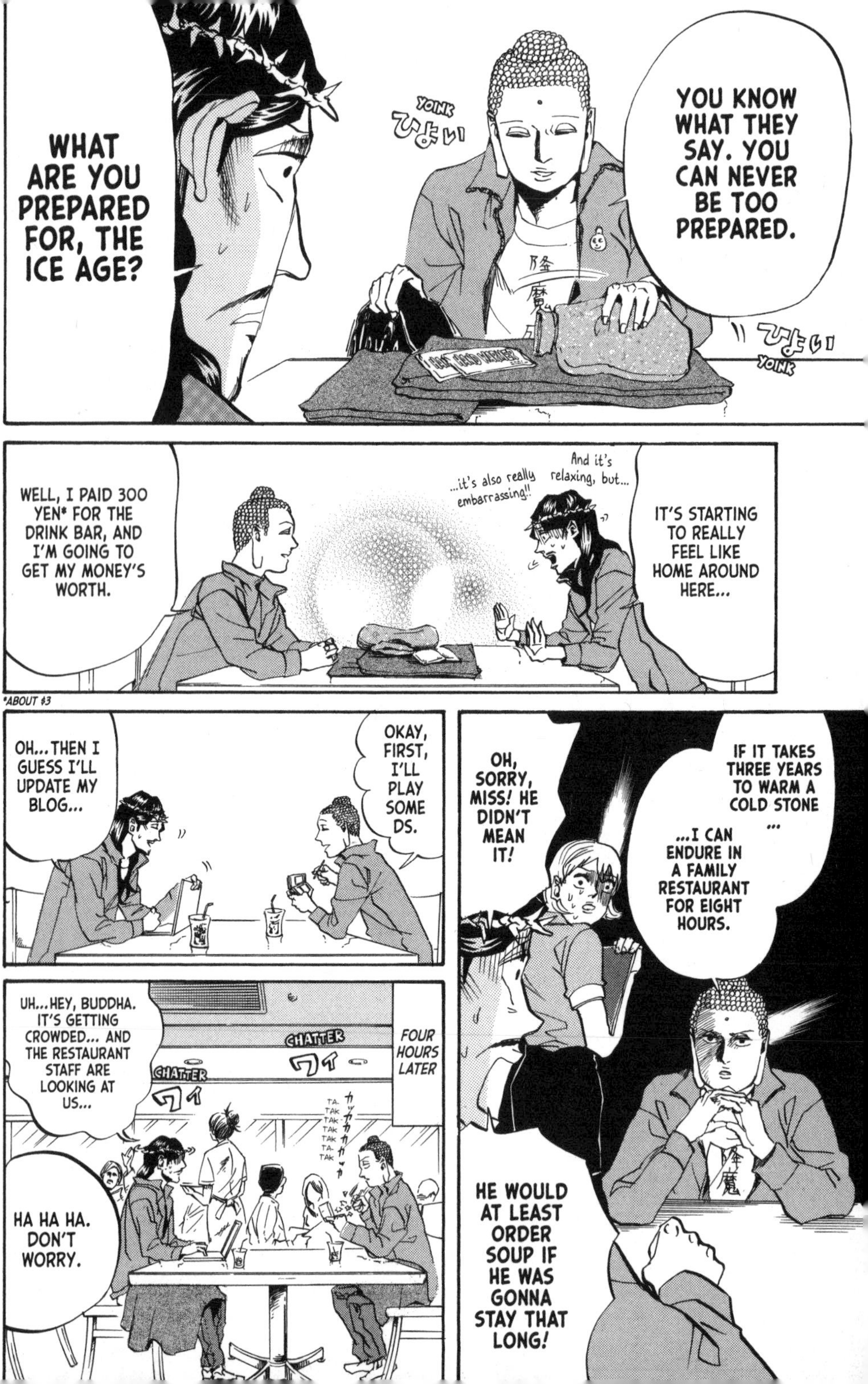
YOINK
ひょい
YOU KNOW WHAT THEY SAY. YOU CAN NEVER BE TOO PREPARED.
ひょい
YOINK
WHAT ARE YOU PREPARED FOR, THE ICE AGE?
IT'S STARTING TO REALLY FEEL LIKE HOME AROUND HERE...
And it's relaxing, but...
...it's also really embarrassing!!
WELL, I PAID 300 YEN* FOR THE DRINK BAR, AND I'M GOING TO GET MY MONEY'S WORTH.
IF IT TAKES THREE YEARS TO WARM A COLD STONE ...
...I CAN ENDURE IN A FAMILY RESTAURANT FOR EIGHT HOURS.
OH, SORRY, MISS! HE DIDN'T MEAN IT!
HE WOULD AT LEAST ORDER SOUP IF HE WAS GONNA STAY THAT LONG!
OKAY, FIRST, I'LL PLAY SOME DS.
OH...THEN I GUESS I'LL UPDATE MY BLOG...
FOUR HOURS LATER
CHATTER
ワイ
CHATTER
ワイ
UH...HEY, BUDDHA. IT'S GETTING CROWDED... AND THE RESTAURANT STAFF ARE LOOKING AT US...
TA-TAK-TAK-TAK-TAK-TA-TAK
カッカカカッカ
HA HA HA. DON'T WORRY.

*ABOUT $3

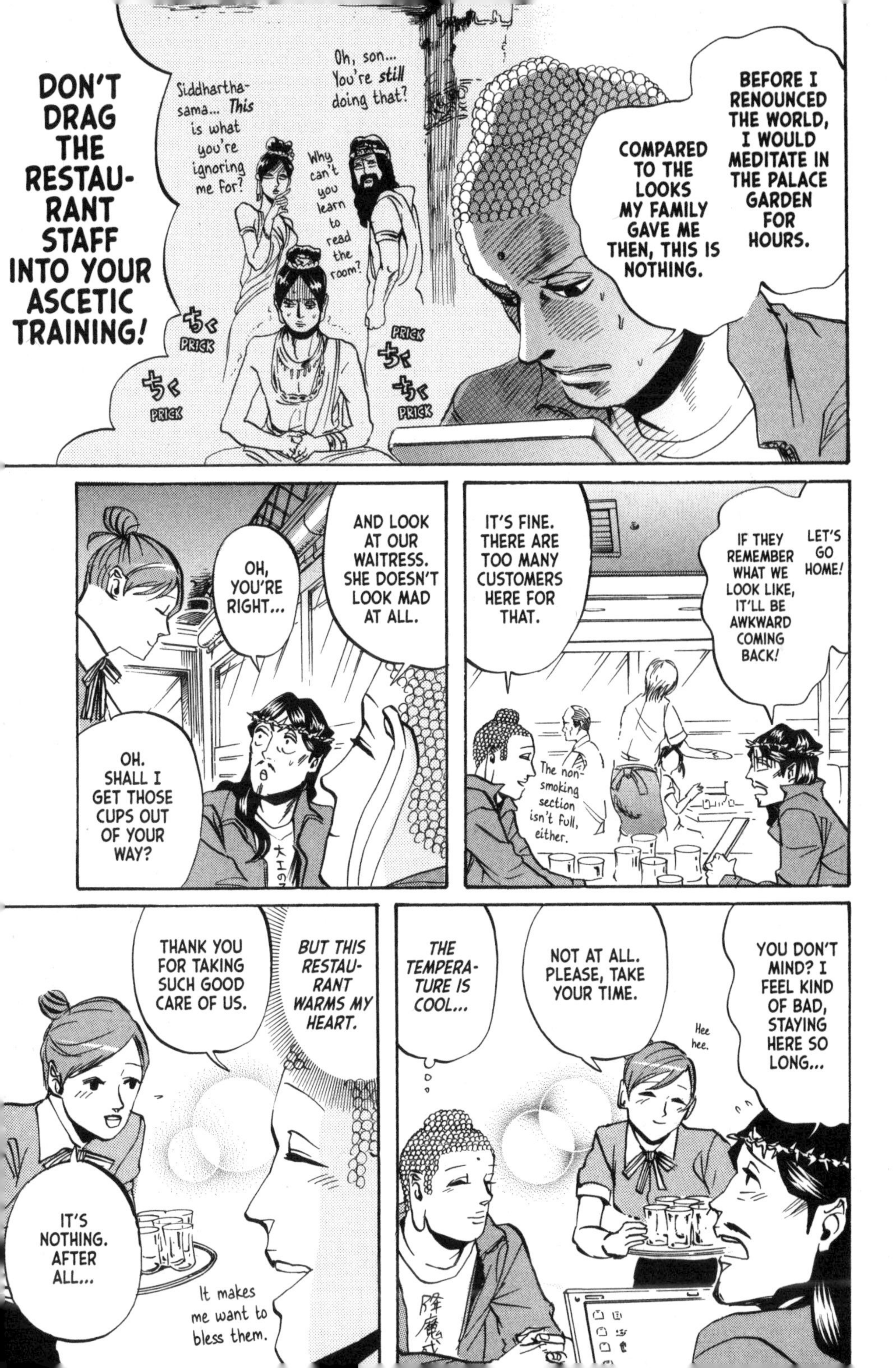
BEFORE I RENOUNCED THE WORLD, I WOULD MEDITATE IN THE PALACE GARDEN FOR HOURS.
COMPARED TO THE LOOKS MY FAMILY GAVE ME THEN, THIS IS NOTHING.
Oh, son... You're *still* doing that?
Why can't you learn to read the room?
Siddhartha-sama... *This* is what you're ignoring me for?
ちく PRICK
ちく PRICK
ちく PRICK
ちく PRICK
DON'T DRAG THE RESTAURANT STAFF INTO YOUR ASCETIC TRAINING!
LET'S GO HOME!
IF THEY REMEMBER WHAT WE LOOK LIKE, IT'LL BE AWKWARD COMING BACK!
IT'S FINE. THERE ARE TOO MANY CUSTOMERS HERE FOR THAT.
The non-smoking section isn't full, either.
AND LOOK AT OUR WAITRESS. SHE DOESN'T LOOK MAD AT ALL.
OH, YOU'RE RIGHT...
OH. SHALL I GET THOSE CUPS OUT OF YOUR WAY?
YOU DON'T MIND? I FEEL KIND OF BAD, STAYING HERE SO LONG...
NOT AT ALL. PLEASE, TAKE YOUR TIME.
Hee hee.
THE TEMPERATURE IS COOL...
BUT THIS RESTAURANT WARMS MY HEART.
THANK YOU FOR TAKING SUCH GOOD CARE OF US.
IT'S NOTHING. AFTER ALL...
It makes me want to bless them.

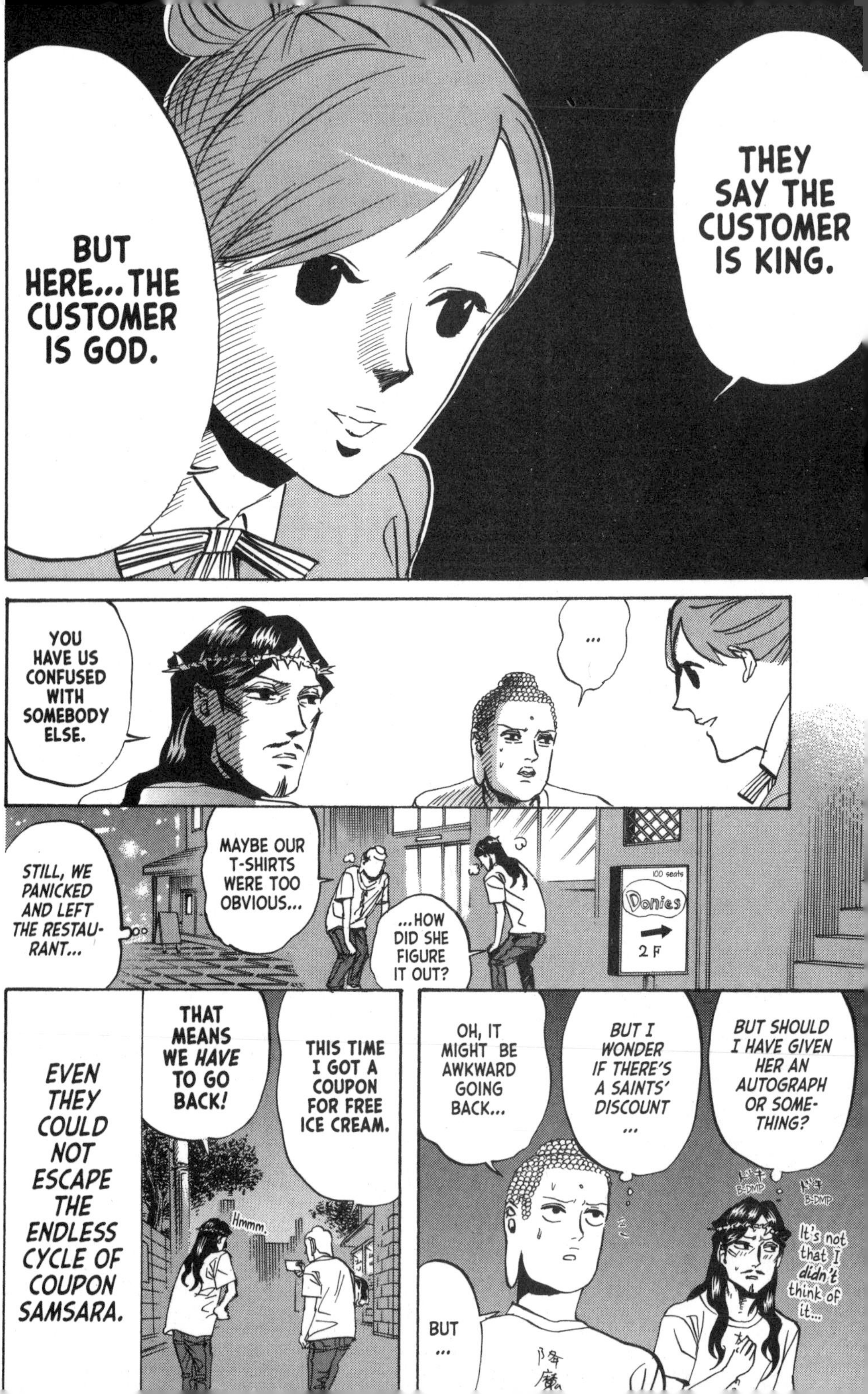
THEY SAY THE CUSTOMER IS KING.
BUT HERE... THE CUSTOMER IS GOD.
...
YOU HAVE US CONFUSED WITH SOMEBODY ELSE.
100 seats
Donies
2 F
...HOW DID SHE FIGURE IT OUT?
MAYBE OUR T-SHIRTS WERE TOO OBVIOUS...
STILL, WE PANICKED AND LEFT THE RESTAU-RANT...
BUT SHOULD I HAVE GIVEN HER AN AUTOGRAPH OR SOME-THING?
B-DMP
B-DMP
It's not that I didn't think of it...
BUT I WONDER IF THERE'S A SAINTS' DISCOUNT ...
OH, IT MIGHT BE AWKWARD GOING BACK...
BUT ...
THIS TIME I GOT A COUPON FOR FREE ICE CREAM.
THAT MEANS WE HAVE TO GO BACK!
Hmmm.
EVEN THEY COULD NOT ESCAPE THE ENDLESS CYCLE OF COUPON SAMSARA.

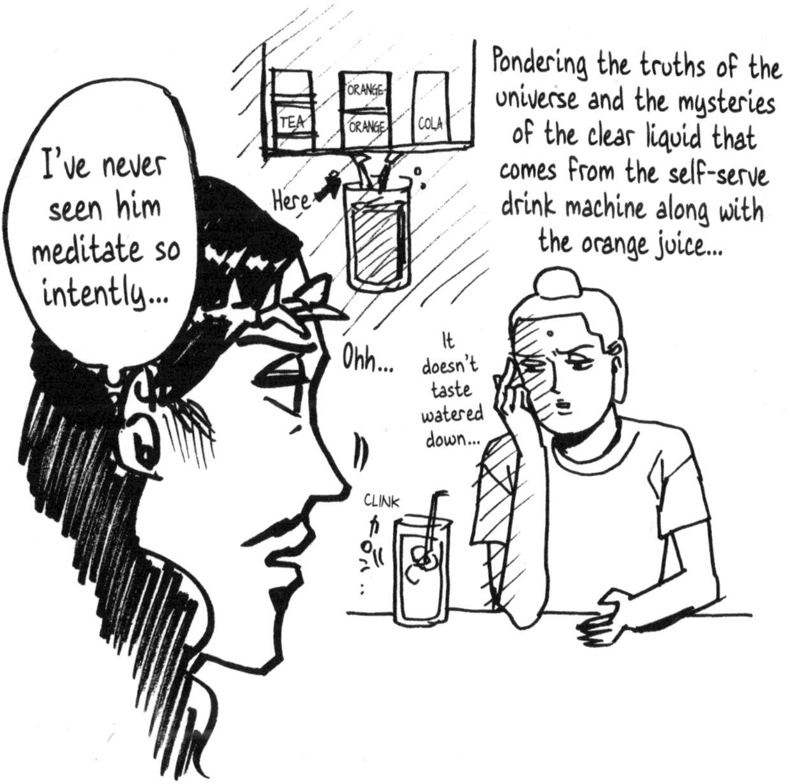
Pondering the truths of the universe and the mysteries of the clear liquid that comes from the self-serve drink machine along with the orange juice...
COLA
ORANGE-
ORANGE
TEA
Here
It doesn't taste watered down...
I've never seen him meditate so intently...
Ohh...
CLINK

CHAPTER 16 TRANSLATION NOTES

Achieving the non-self, page 5

The concept of non-self, or *anatman*, is an important concept in Buddhism stating that there is no permanent, underlying soul in living beings, including human beings. The ability to accept that there is no "self" is a step on the way to enlightenment.

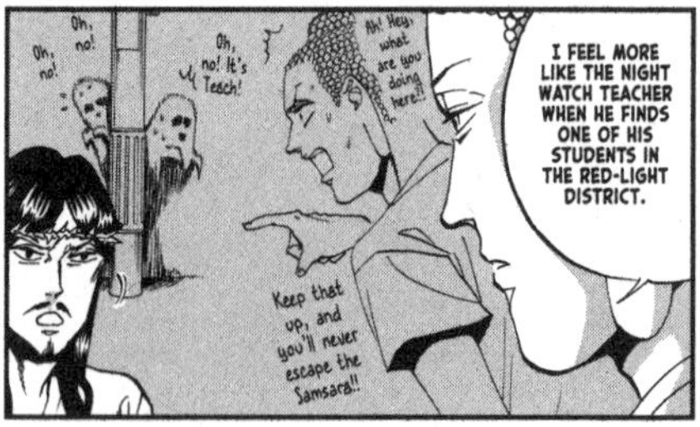
I FEEL MORE LIKE THE NIGHT WATCH TEACHER WHEN HE FINDS ONE OF HIS STUDENTS IN THE RED-LIGHT DISTRICT.
Ah! Hey, what are you doing here!?
Keep that up, and you'll never escape the Samsara!!
Oh, no! It's Teach!
Oh, no!
Oh, no!

Night Watch Teacher, page 9

Night Watch Teacher is a nickname given by the media to Osamu Mizutani, who was a teacher in Yokohama. He began patrolling the seedier side of town to find delinquent youths, help sort out their problems, and rehabilitate them.

Samsara, page 9

In Buddhism, the Wheel of Existence, or *Samsara*, is the cycle of life, death, and rebirth. This cycle is full of pain and suffering, and the goal of Buddhism is to find a way outside of the cycle in order to escape this pain and suffering.

The Carpenter's Son, page 10

Jesus Christ was raised by Mary and her husband Joseph, who was a carpenter by trade.

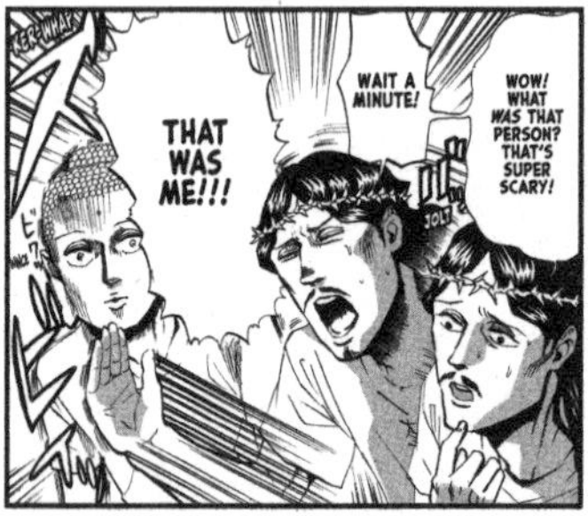
WOW! WHAT WAS THAT PERSON? THAT'S SUPER SCARY!
WAIT A MINUTE!
JOLT
THAT WAS ME!!!
KER-WHAP

Jesus walks on water, page 12

The Bible tells of a time when Jesus retired to the mountains to pray, while his disciples went on ahead in a boat to their next destination. A storm arose on the Sea of Galilee and as the sailors struggled to keep the boat from sinking, Jesus walked to their boat on water, and when he arrived, the wind ceased and they safely made it to their destination.

You're so young, page 13

Siddhartha Gautama was born sometime between the sixth and fourth centuries BCE (Before Common Era), and died at the age of 80. Jesus Christ was born around 1 CE (Common Era) and was crucified at age 33. In regards to earthly life, this would make the Buddha older both in terms of when he was born and how long he lived.

Jesus's trial, page 14

Before being crucified, Jesus was put on trial before a council of Jewish elders, and was then brought to the Roman prefect Pontius Pilate, as the Jewish community was not allowed to sentence anyone to death without Roman approval. At this trial before Pilate, Jesus remained silent in the face of his accusers, and spoke only when questioned by Pilate himself. Jesus further remained silent when sent to be judged by Herod, the governor of Galilee.

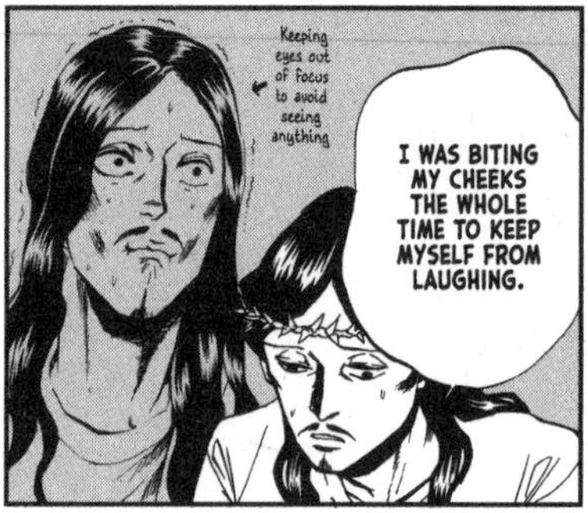
I WAS BITING MY CHEEKS THE WHOLE TIME TO KEEP MYSELF FROM LAUGHING.
Keeping eyes out of focus to avoid seeing anything

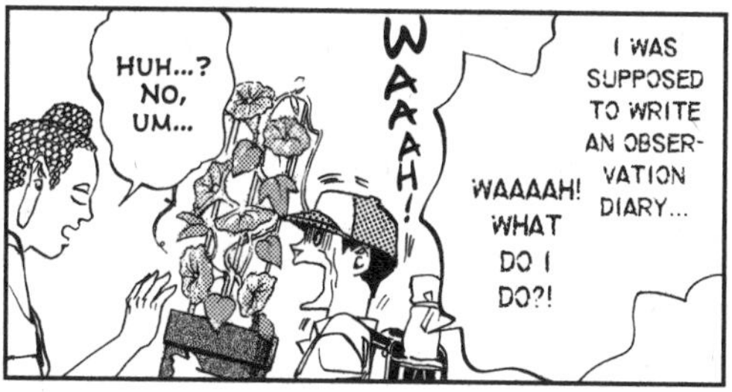
I WAS SUPPOSED TO WRITE AN OBSER-VATION DIARY...
WAAAAH! WHAT DO I DO?!
WAAAH!
HUH...? NO, UM...

Observation diary, page 16
Because the school year starts in April in Japan, summer vacation falls in the middle of the year, and is one month long. Students are usually given big projects to complete with all their free time, including long-term assignments such as observing plants over four weeks.

Of such is the kingdom of heaven, page 16
In the Sermon on the Mount (Matthew 5 - 7), Jesus teaches his disciples that instead of being kind only to their friends, they should love their enemies, as well. The next reference, "Of such is the Kingdom of Heaven," is from a different passage (Matthew 19:4). This is something Jesus said when people brought their children to be blessed, and the disciples told them not to bother Jesus. When he saw this, he told them not to forbid the children, because "of such is the Kingdom of Heaven."

Seven trumpets, page 18
This is a reference to the Book of Revelation, found at the end of the New Testament, which contains prophecies about the end of the world. Each of the trumpets will be sounded in turn, to signal the beginning of a different stage of the Apocalypse. The word "trumpet" is a translation from Greek, where the word specifically refers to a salpinx—a long, straight trumpet which was often used in ancient times as a signal.

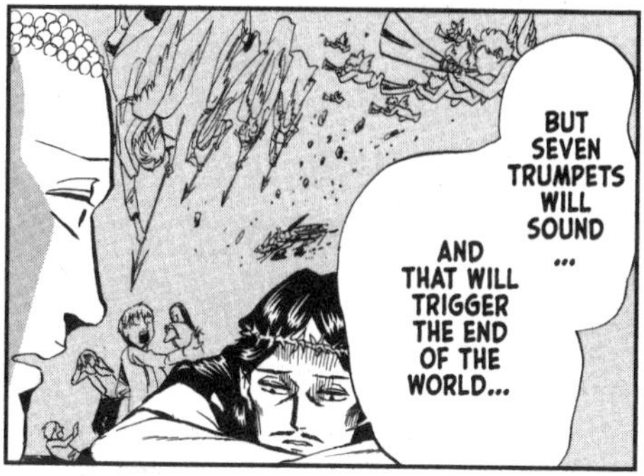
BUT SEVEN TRUMPETS WILL SOUND...
AND THAT WILL TRIGGER THE END OF THE WORLD...

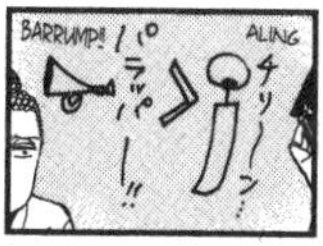
BARRUMP!
ALING

Wind chimes, page 18
The most common wind chime in Japan consists of a glass bell with a cylindrical clapper that has a piece of paper hanging from it to catch the wind and make it move. The sound of these chimes is believed to be refreshing enough to alleviate the agony of a hot, humid summer.

Calpis, page 19
Calpis is a cultured milk drink designed to improve digestion. It is usually sold as a concentrate, and diluted with water or milk before consumption.

Three years to warm a cold stone, page 20
This is a Japanese proverb to encourage perseverance.

SAINT☆YOUNG MEN

WHAT IS WITH THIS APART- MENT?!

~3DK ¥83,000

10 min. walking

5 0 1	¥66,000
3 0 2	¥48,000
4 0 2	¥80,000
1 0 5	¥83,000

Northwest Homes, Inc.

Studio with bath

¥30,000!!

Super Affordable

162㎡

DK   CLOSET

SAFES AND STORAGE

UB

Recom-mended

Apartment for Rent 3

Enjoy a quiet environment close to the station. For sale and rent.

4 AC units Furnished kitchen Shoe cabinet On-site parking, 1 space free.

WHOA ...!

OOHH! IT LOOKS LIKE IT'S GOT PLENTY OF STORAGE SPACE, TOO!

IT'S BIGGER THAN OUR PLACE, AND IT HAS A BATH...

...BUT IT'S CHEAPER!

Perfect House Rentals Sales

SHIRT: 30 PIECES OF SILVER

OH! JESUS!!

BUDDHA!! I FOUND AN INCREDIBLY INNOVATIVE WAY TO SOLVE OUR STORAGE PROBLEM!

KA-CHAK

BECAUSE BUDDHA SAID IF WE GOT ANY MORE STUFF WE WOULDN'T HAVE ROOM FOR IT ALL, BUT...

I WAS OUT GETTING BOXES TO SHIP STUFF BACK TO HEAVEN,

WHAT? BUT THERE'S STUFF ALL OVER THE FLOOR...

I FOUND A WAY TO UTILIZE SPACE MORE EFFECTIVELY!

ACTU-ALLY, SO DID I!

...OKAY!

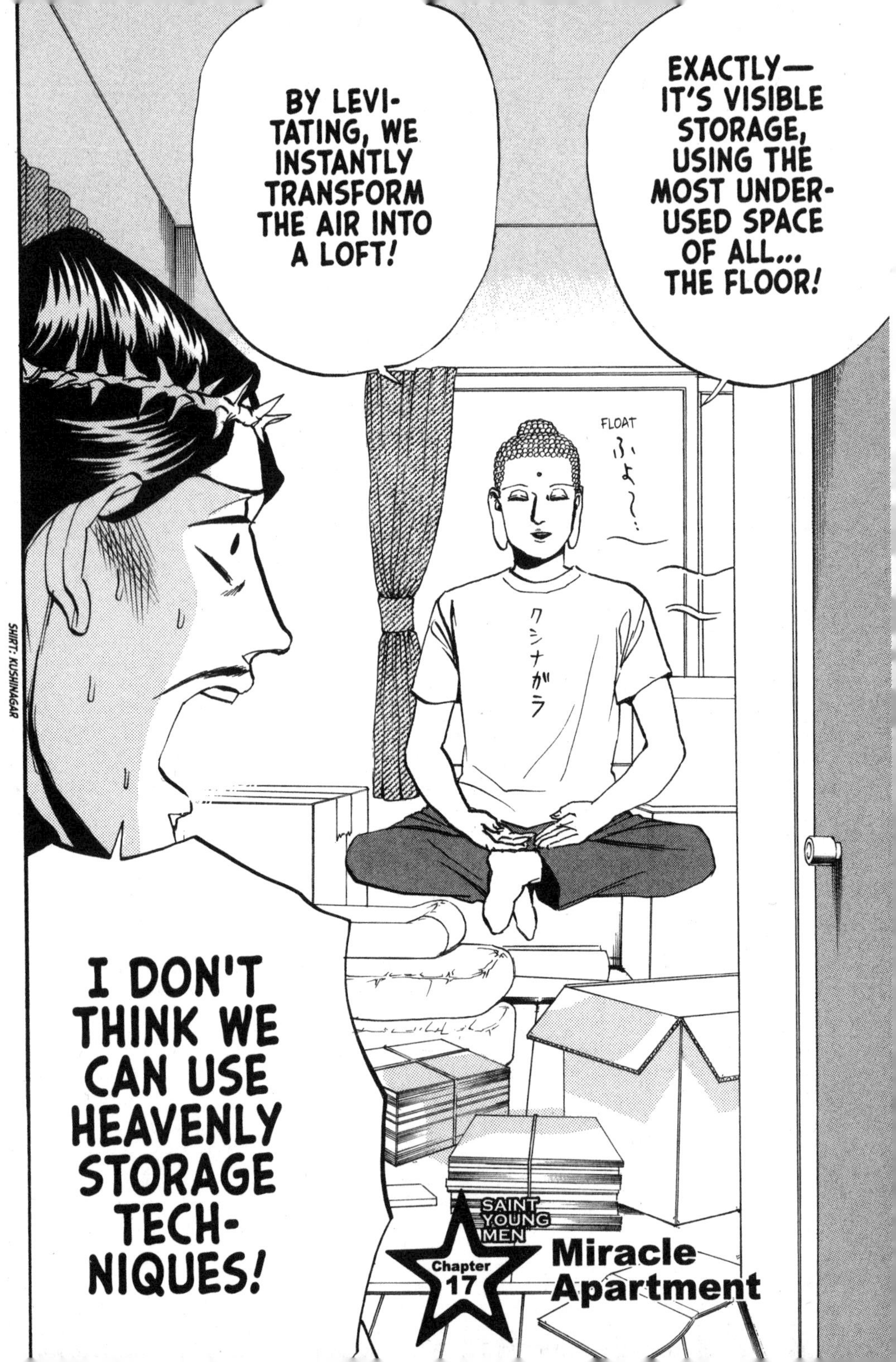
EXACTLY— IT'S VISIBLE STORAGE, USING THE MOST UNDER-USED SPACE OF ALL... THE FLOOR!
BY LEVI-TATING, WE INSTANTLY TRANSFORM THE AIR INTO A LOFT!
FLOAT
ふよ〜…
クシナガラ
SHIRT: KUSHINAGAR
I DON'T THINK WE CAN USE HEAVENLY STORAGE TECH-NIQUES!
SAINT YOUNG MEN
Chapter 17
Miracle Apartment

BUDDHA: FAVORITE GAME IS SHOGI (JAPANESE CHESS). FINDS IT VERY MOVING WHEN A PAWN GETS PROMOTED.

JESUS: FAVORITE GAME IS HIS ONLINE RPG. HAS GOTTEN HIS CHARACTER SO STRONG, IT CAN SHOOT AN ARROW FROM TOKYO TO PHUKET.

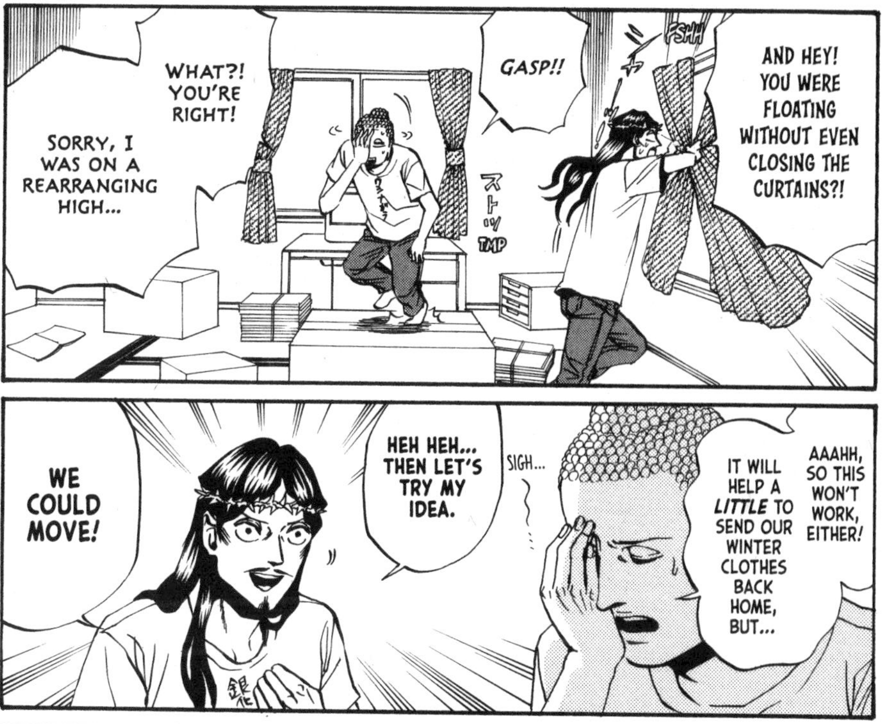
AND HEY! YOU WERE FLOATING WITHOUT EVEN CLOSING THE CURTAINS?!
FSHH
GASP!!
WHAT?! YOU'RE RIGHT!
SORRY, I WAS ON A REARRANGING HIGH...
TMP
AAAHH, SO THIS WON'T WORK, EITHER!
IT WILL HELP A *LITTLE* TO SEND OUR WINTER CLOTHES BACK HOME, BUT...
SIGH...
HEH HEH... THEN LET'S TRY MY IDEA.
WE COULD MOVE!

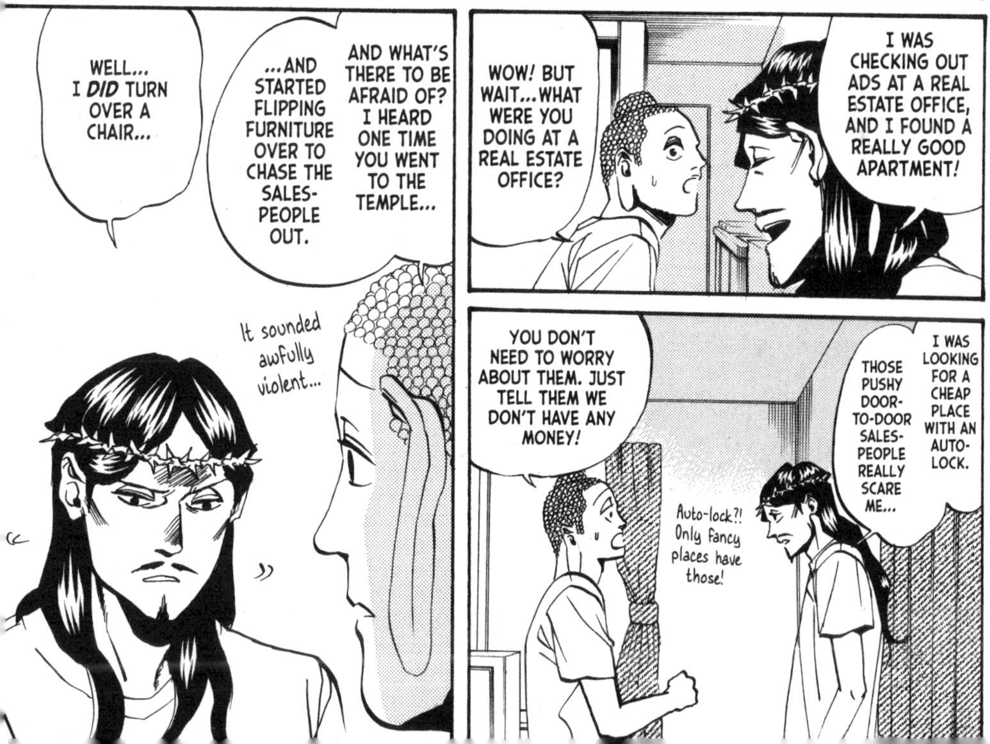
I WAS CHECKING OUT ADS AT A REAL ESTATE OFFICE, AND I FOUND A REALLY GOOD APARTMENT!
WOW! BUT WAIT... WHAT WERE YOU DOING AT A REAL ESTATE OFFICE?
I WAS LOOKING FOR A CHEAP PLACE WITH AN AUTO-LOCK.
THOSE PUSHY DOOR-TO-DOOR SALES-PEOPLE REALLY SCARE ME...
YOU DON'T NEED TO WORRY ABOUT THEM. JUST TELL THEM WE DON'T HAVE ANY MONEY!
Auto-lock?! Only fancy places have those!
AND WHAT'S THERE TO BE AFRAID OF? I HEARD ONE TIME YOU WENT TO THE TEMPLE...
...AND STARTED FLIPPING FURNITURE OVER TO CHASE THE SALES-PEOPLE OUT.
WELL... I *DID* TURN OVER A CHAIR...
It sounded awfully violent...

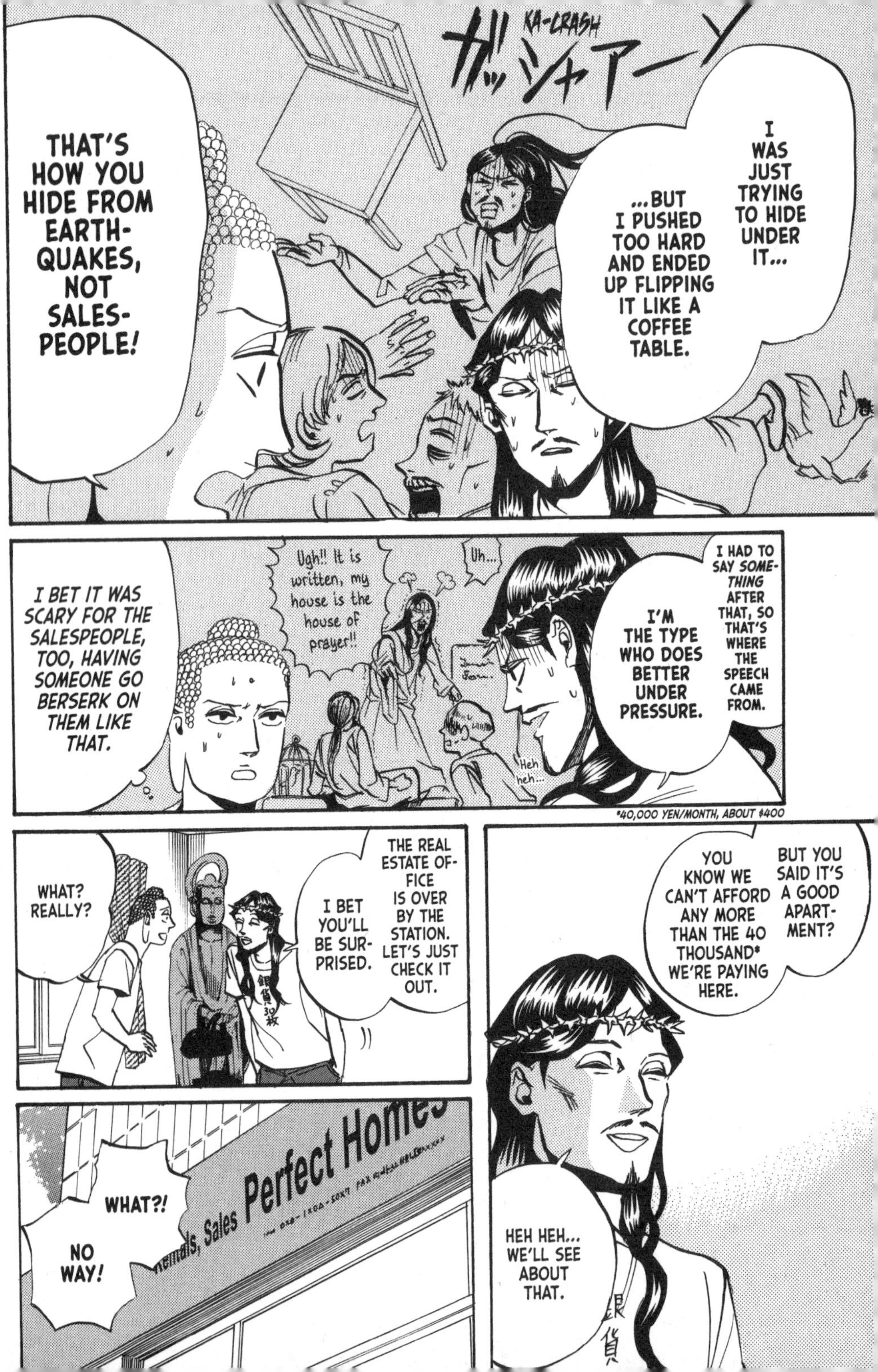
KA-CRASH
ガッシャアーン
I WAS JUST TRYING TO HIDE UNDER IT...
...BUT I PUSHED TOO HARD AND ENDED UP FLIPPING IT LIKE A COFFEE TABLE.
THAT'S HOW YOU HIDE FROM EARTH-QUAKES, NOT SALES-PEOPLE!
I HAD TO SAY *SOMETHING* AFTER THAT, SO THAT'S WHERE THE SPEECH CAME FROM.
I'M THE TYPE WHO DOES BETTER UNDER PRESSURE.
Heh heh...
Uh...
Ugh!! It is written, my house is the house of prayer!!
I BET IT WAS SCARY FOR THE SALESPEOPLE, TOO, HAVING SOMEONE GO BERSERK ON THEM LIKE THAT.
*40,000 YEN/MONTH, ABOUT $400
BUT YOU SAID IT'S A GOOD APART-MENT?
YOU KNOW WE CAN'T AFFORD ANY MORE THAN THE 40 THOUSAND* WE'RE PAYING HERE.
HEH HEH... WE'LL SEE ABOUT THAT.
THE REAL ESTATE OF-FICE IS OVER BY THE STATION. LET'S JUST CHECK IT OUT.
I BET YOU'LL BE SUR-PRISED.
WHAT? REALLY?
Rentals, Sales Perfect Homes
WHAT?!
NO WAY!

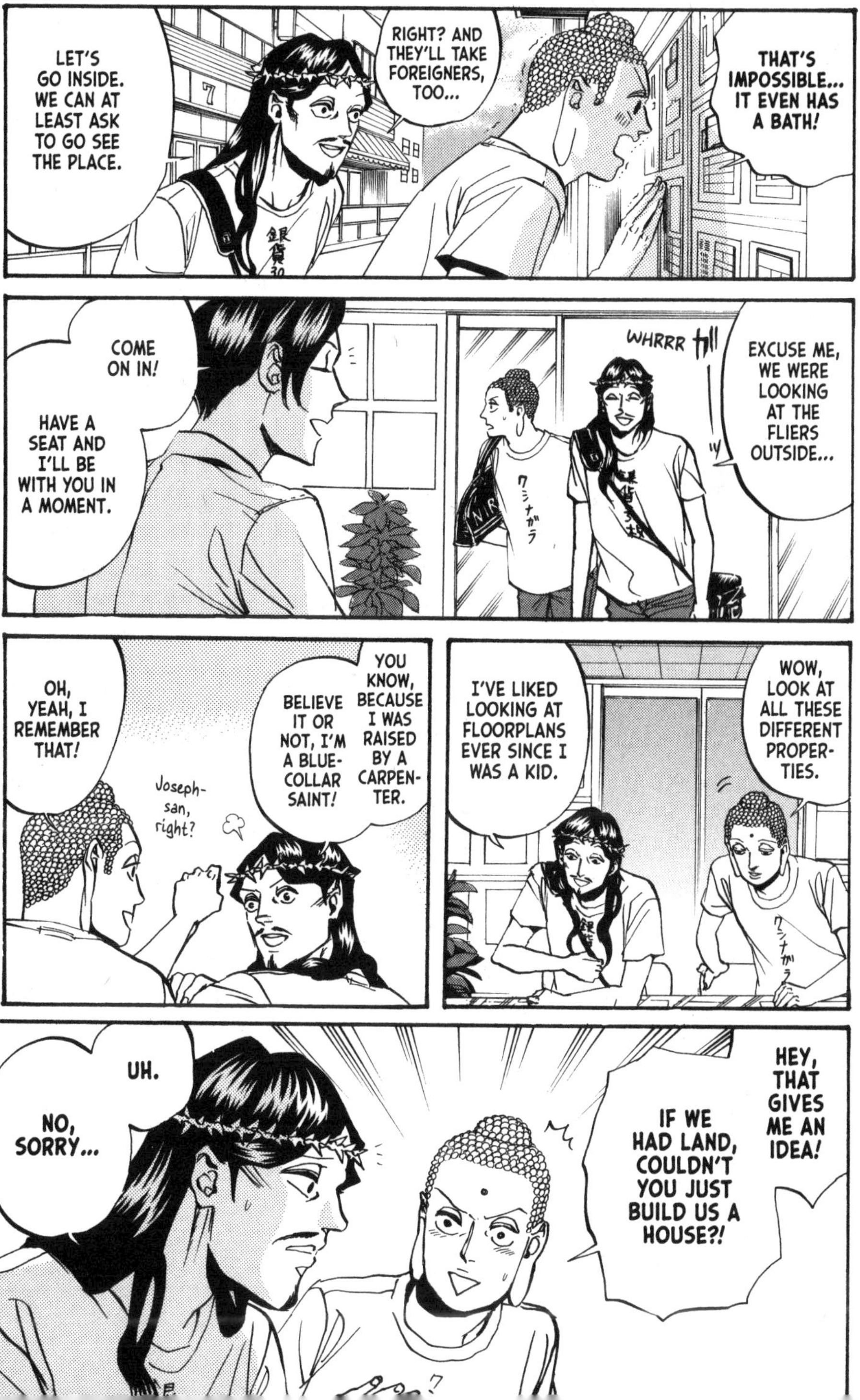
THAT'S IMPOSSIBLE... IT EVEN HAS A BATH!
RIGHT? AND THEY'LL TAKE FOREIGNERS, TOO...
LET'S GO INSIDE. WE CAN AT LEAST ASK TO GO SEE THE PLACE.
EXCUSE ME, WE WERE LOOKING AT THE FLIERS OUTSIDE...
WHRRR
COME ON IN!
HAVE A SEAT AND I'LL BE WITH YOU IN A MOMENT.
WOW, LOOK AT ALL THESE DIFFERENT PROPERTIES.
I'VE LIKED LOOKING AT FLOORPLANS EVER SINCE I WAS A KID.
YOU KNOW, BECAUSE I WAS RAISED BY A CARPENTER.
BELIEVE IT OR NOT, I'M A BLUE-COLLAR SAINT!
OH, YEAH, I REMEMBER THAT!
Joseph-san, right?
HEY, THAT GIVES ME AN IDEA!
IF WE HAD LAND, COULDN'T YOU JUST BUILD US A HOUSE?!
UH.
NO, SORRY...

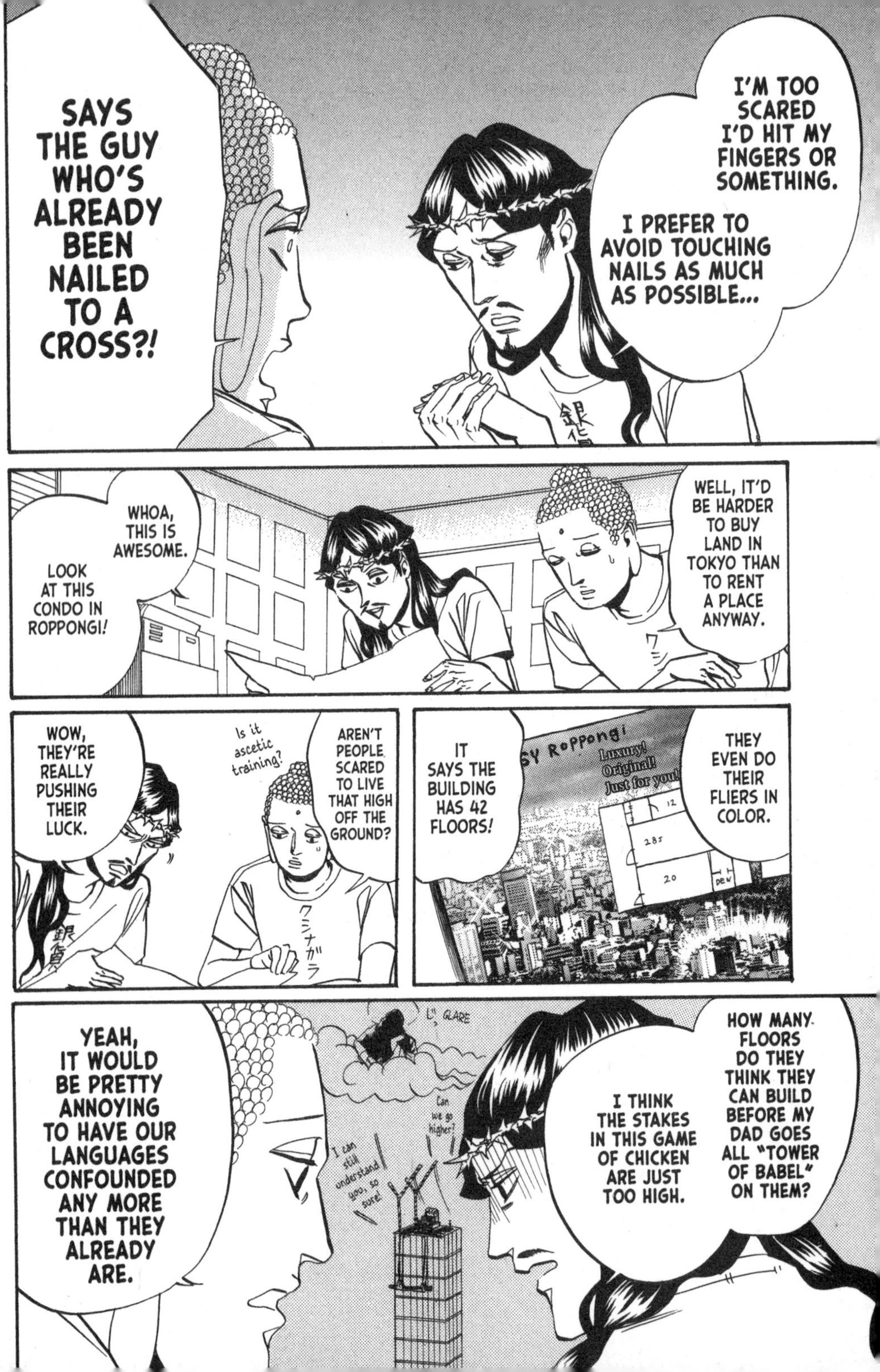
I'M TOO SCARED I'D HIT MY FINGERS OR SOMETHING.
I PREFER TO AVOID TOUCHING NAILS AS MUCH AS POSSIBLE...
SAYS THE GUY WHO'S ALREADY BEEN NAILED TO A CROSS?!
WELL, IT'D BE HARDER TO BUY LAND IN TOKYO THAN TO RENT A PLACE ANYWAY.
WHOA, THIS IS AWESOME.
LOOK AT THIS CONDO IN ROPPONGI!
THEY EVEN DO THEIR FLIERS IN COLOR.
SY Roppongi
Luxury! Original! Just for you!
12
285
20
DEN
IT SAYS THE BUILDING HAS 42 FLOORS!
AREN'T PEOPLE SCARED TO LIVE THAT HIGH OFF THE GROUND?
Is it ascetic training?
クシナガラ
WOW, THEY'RE REALLY PUSHING THEIR LUCK.
HOW MANY FLOORS DO THEY THINK THEY CAN BUILD BEFORE MY DAD GOES ALL "TOWER OF BABEL" ON THEM?
I THINK THE STAKES IN THIS GAME OF CHICKEN ARE JUST TOO HIGH.
GLARE
Can we go higher?
I can still understand you, so sure!
YEAH, IT WOULD BE PRETTY ANNOYING TO HAVE OUR LANGUAGES CONFOUNDED ANY MORE THAN THEY ALREADY ARE.

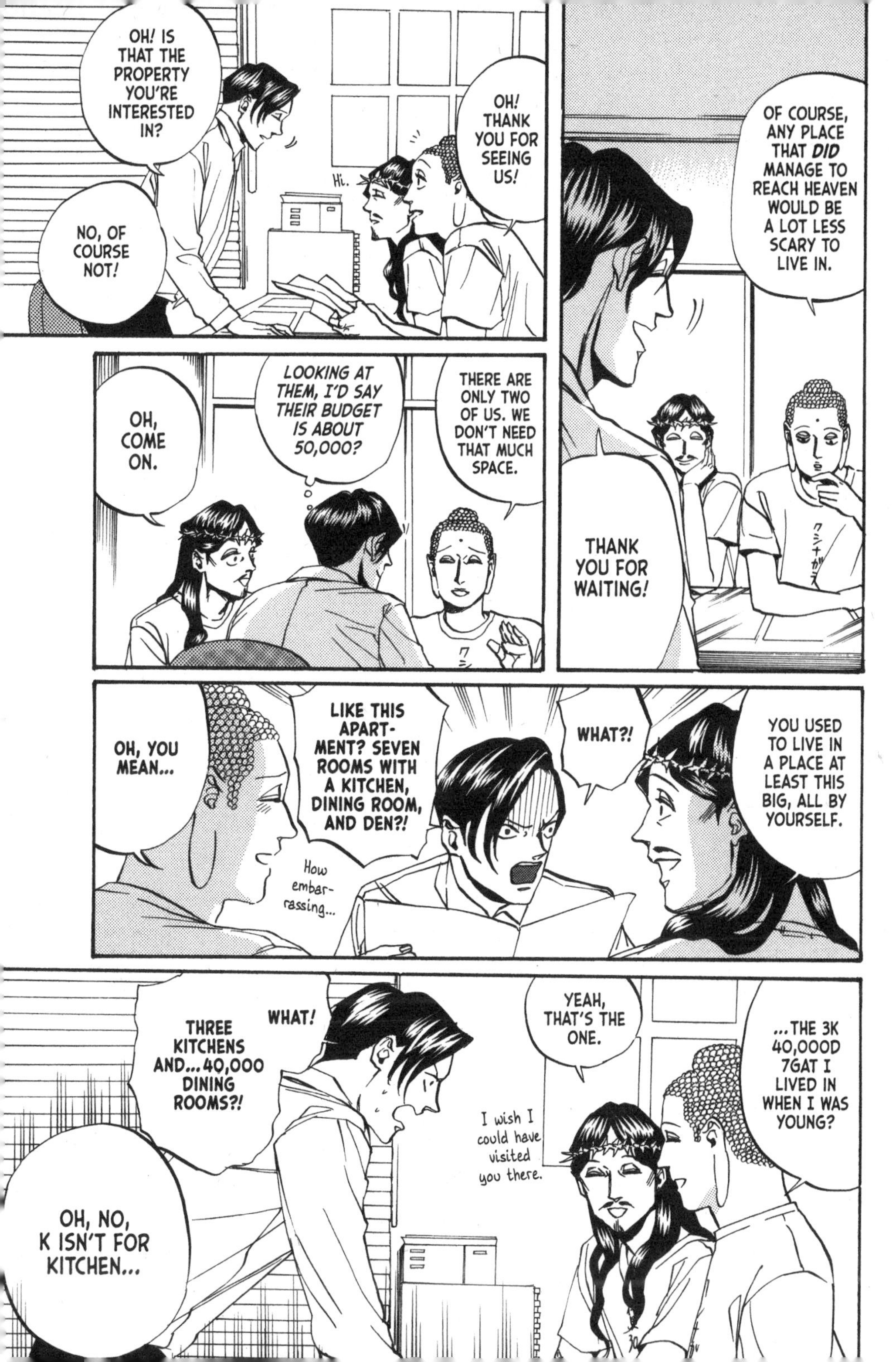
OF COURSE, ANY PLACE THAT *DID* MANAGE TO REACH HEAVEN WOULD BE A LOT LESS SCARY TO LIVE IN.
THANK YOU FOR WAITING!
OH! THANK YOU FOR SEEING US!
Hi.
OH! IS THAT THE PROPERTY YOU'RE INTERESTED IN?
NO, OF COURSE NOT!
THERE ARE ONLY TWO OF US. WE DON'T NEED THAT MUCH SPACE.
LOOKING AT THEM, I'D SAY THEIR BUDGET IS ABOUT 50,000?
OH, COME ON.
YOU USED TO LIVE IN A PLACE AT LEAST THIS BIG, ALL BY YOURSELF.
WHAT?!
LIKE THIS APART-MENT? SEVEN ROOMS WITH A KITCHEN, DINING ROOM, AND DEN?!
How embar-rassing...
OH, YOU MEAN...
...THE 3K 40,000D 7GAT I LIVED IN WHEN I WAS YOUNG?
YEAH, THAT'S THE ONE.
I wish I could have visited you there.
WHAT!
THREE KITCHENS AND...40,000 DINING ROOMS?!
OH, NO, K ISN'T FOR KITCHEN...

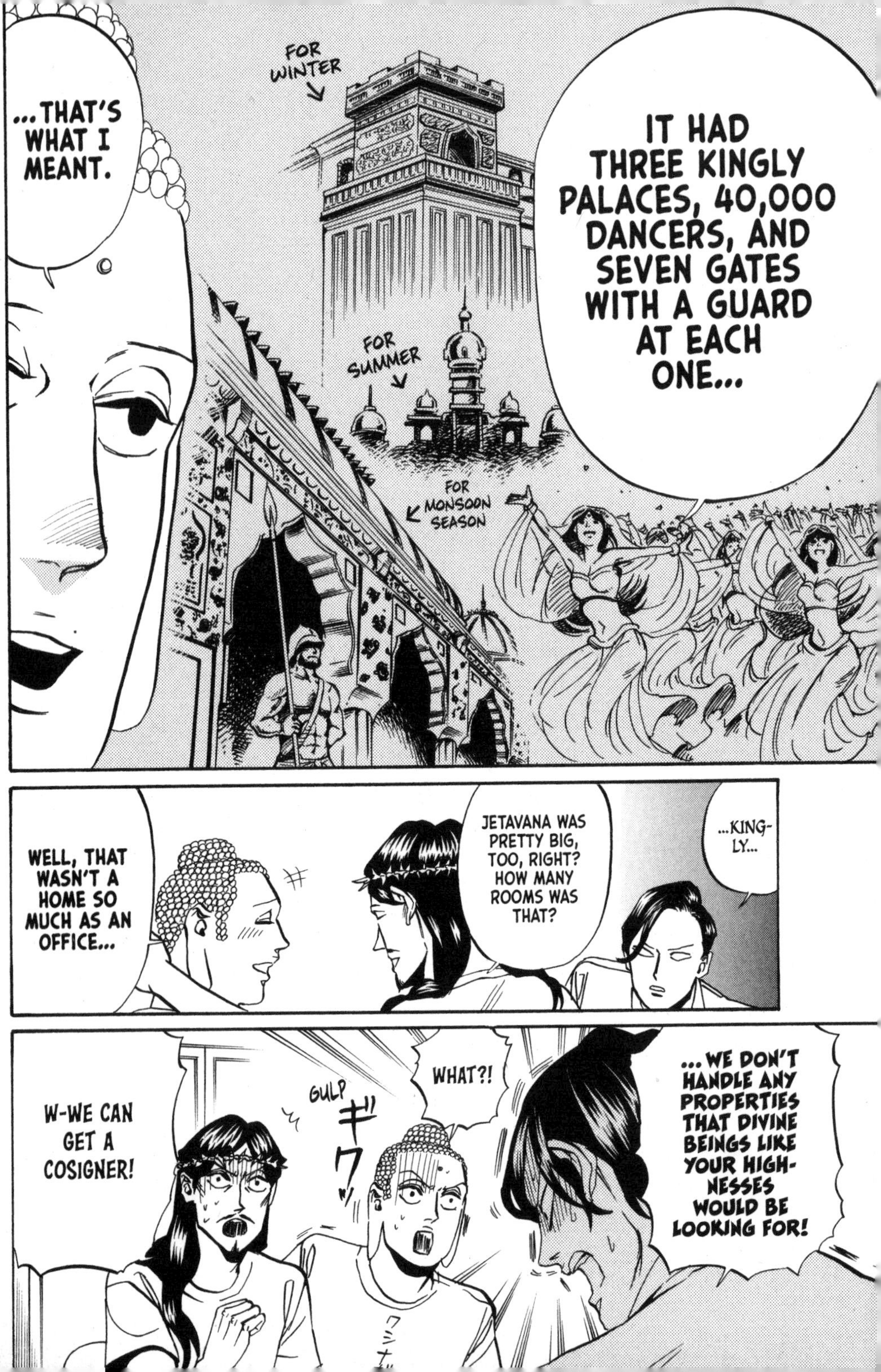
IT HAD THREE KINGLY PALACES, 40,000 DANCERS, AND SEVEN GATES WITH A GUARD AT EACH ONE...
FOR WINTER
FOR SUMMER
FOR MONSOON SEASON
...THAT'S WHAT I MEANT.
...KING-LY...
JETAVANA WAS PRETTY BIG, TOO, RIGHT? HOW MANY ROOMS WAS THAT?
WELL, THAT WASN'T A HOME SO MUCH AS AN OFFICE...
...WE DON'T HANDLE ANY PROPERTIES THAT DIVINE BEINGS LIKE YOUR HIGH-NESSES WOULD BE LOOKING FOR!
WHAT?!
GULP
W-WE CAN GET A COSIGNER!

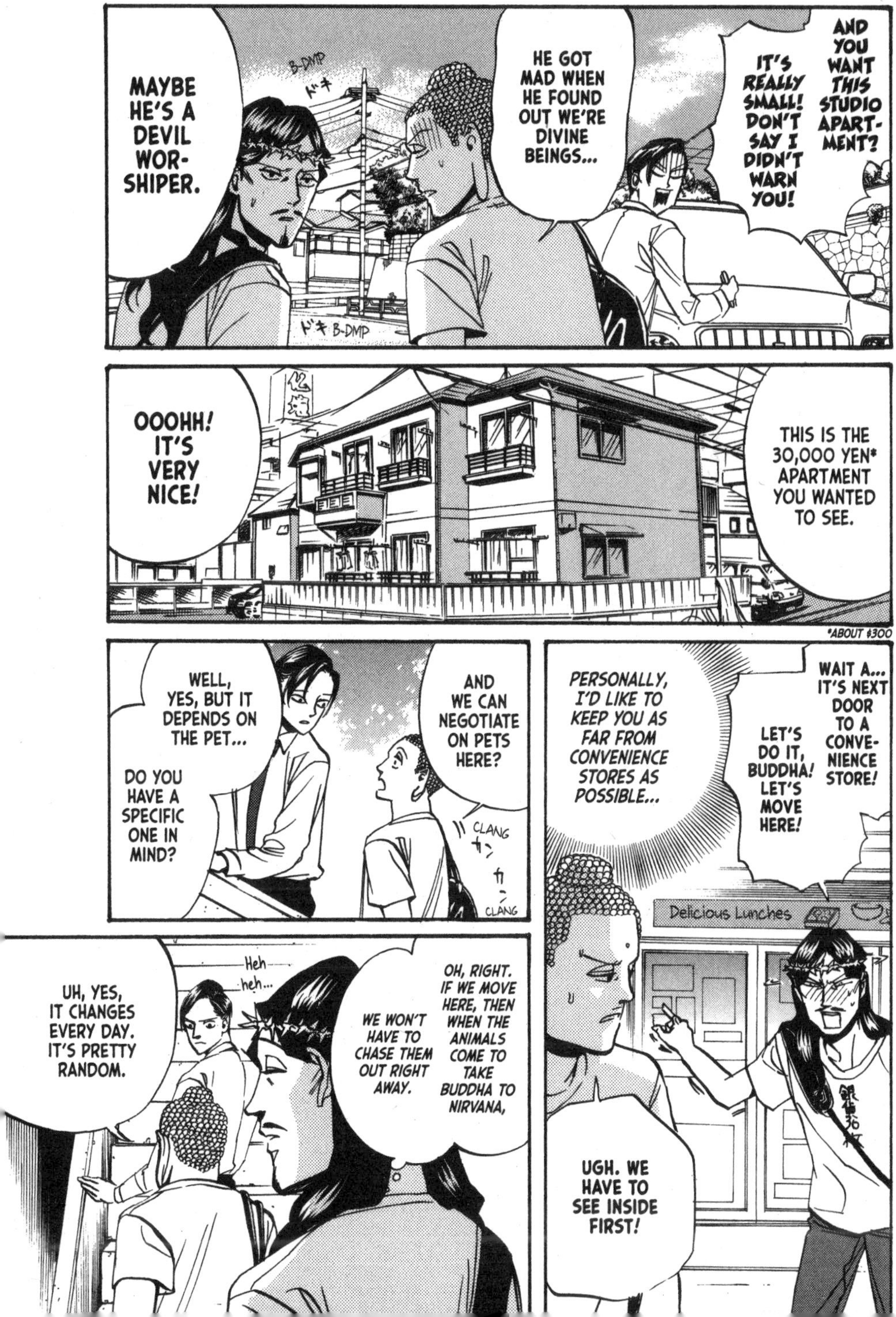
AND YOU WANT THIS STUDIO APARTMENT?
IT'S REALLY SMALL! DON'T SAY I DIDN'T WARN YOU!
HE GOT MAD WHEN HE FOUND OUT WE'RE DIVINE BEINGS...
B-DMP ドキ
MAYBE HE'S A DEVIL WORSHIPER.
ドキ B-DMP
THIS IS THE 30,000 YEN* APARTMENT YOU WANTED TO SEE.
OOOHH! IT'S VERY NICE!
*ABOUT $300
WAIT A... IT'S NEXT DOOR TO A CONVENIENCE STORE!
LET'S DO IT, BUDDHA! LET'S MOVE HERE!
PERSONALLY, I'D LIKE TO KEEP YOU AS FAR FROM CONVENIENCE STORES AS POSSIBLE...
Delicious Lunches
UGH. WE HAVE TO SEE INSIDE FIRST!
AND WE CAN NEGOTIATE ON PETS HERE?
CLANG カン
カン CLANG
WELL, YES, BUT IT DEPENDS ON THE PET...
DO YOU HAVE A SPECIFIC ONE IN MIND?
OH, RIGHT. IF WE MOVE HERE, THEN WHEN THE ANIMALS COME TO TAKE BUDDHA TO NIRVANA,
WE WON'T HAVE TO CHASE THEM OUT RIGHT AWAY.
Heh heh...
UH, YES, IT CHANGES EVERY DAY. IT'S PRETTY RANDOM.

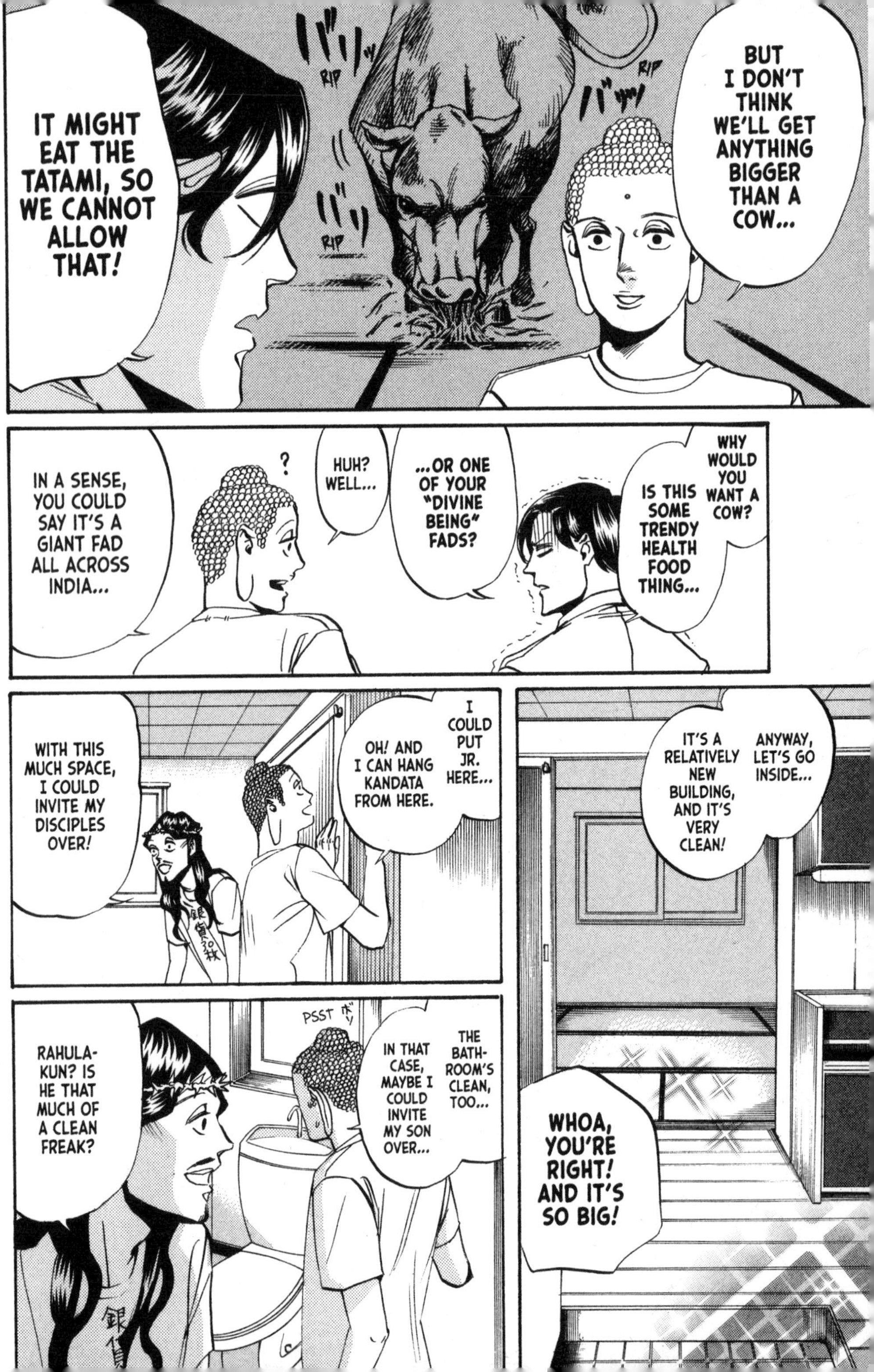
BUT I DON'T THINK WE'LL GET ANYTHING BIGGER THAN A COW...
RIP
RIP
RIP
IT MIGHT EAT THE TATAMI, SO WE CANNOT ALLOW THAT!
WHY WOULD YOU WANT A COW?
IS THIS SOME TRENDY HEALTH FOOD THING...
...OR ONE OF YOUR "DIVINE BEING" FADS?
HUH? WELL...
?
IN A SENSE, YOU COULD SAY IT'S A GIANT FAD ALL ACROSS INDIA...
ANYWAY, LET'S GO INSIDE...
IT'S A RELATIVELY NEW BUILDING, AND IT'S VERY CLEAN!
WHOA, YOU'RE RIGHT! AND IT'S SO BIG!
I COULD PUT JR. HERE...
OH! AND I CAN HANG KANDATA FROM HERE.
WITH THIS MUCH SPACE, I COULD INVITE MY DISCIPLES OVER!
PSST
THE BATH-ROOM'S CLEAN, TOO...
IN THAT CASE, MAYBE I COULD INVITE MY SON OVER...
RAHULA-KUN? IS HE THAT MUCH OF A CLEAN FREAK?

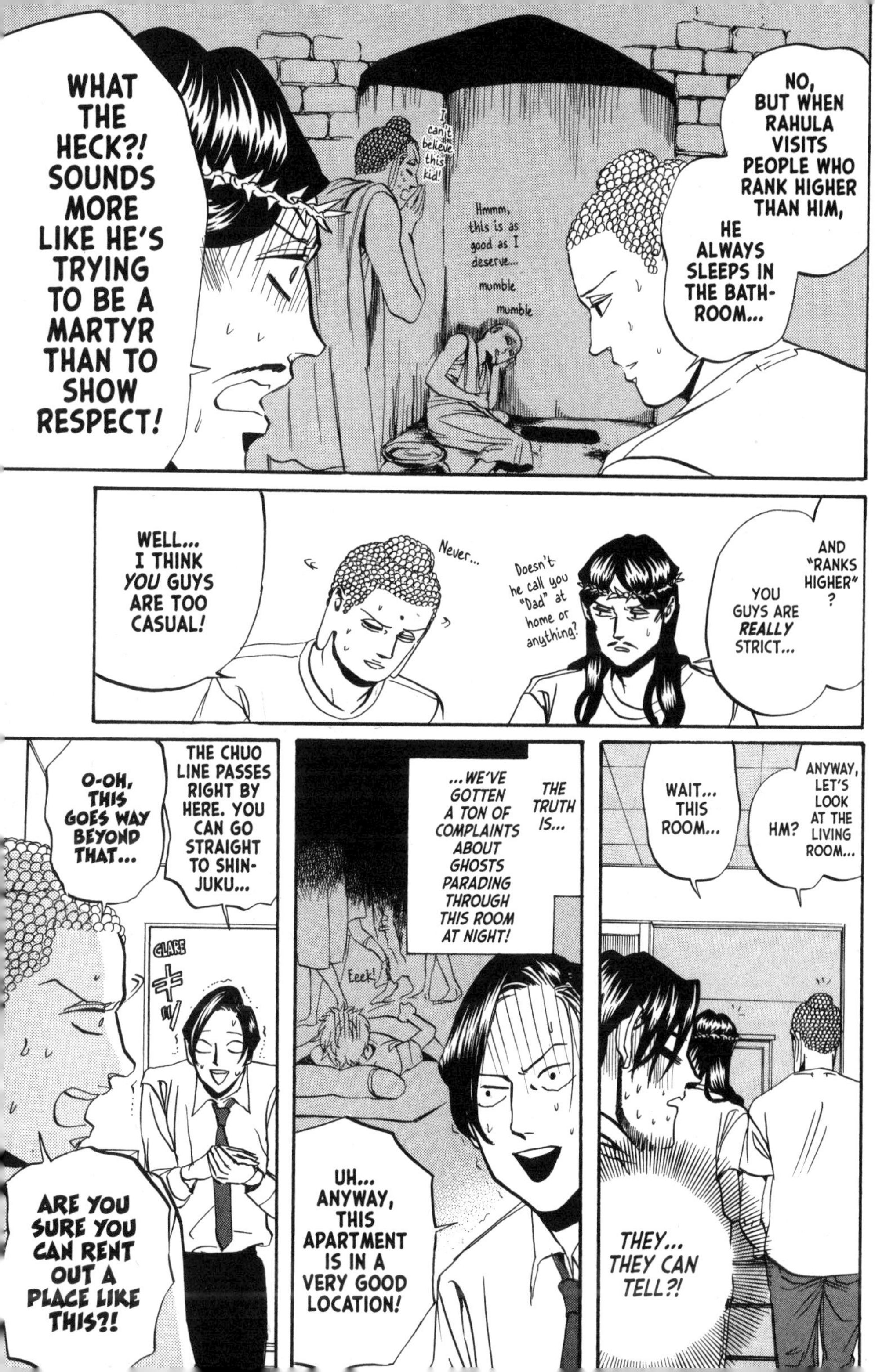
NO, BUT WHEN RAHULA VISITS PEOPLE WHO RANK HIGHER THAN HIM,
HE ALWAYS SLEEPS IN THE BATH-ROOM...
Hmmm, this is as good as I deserve... mumble mumble
I can't believe this kid!
WHAT THE HECK?! SOUNDS MORE LIKE HE'S TRYING TO BE A MARTYR THAN TO SHOW RESPECT!
AND "RANKS HIGHER"?
YOU GUYS ARE REALLY STRICT...
Doesn't he call you "Dad" at home or anything?
Never...
WELL... I THINK YOU GUYS ARE TOO CASUAL!
ANYWAY, LET'S LOOK AT THE LIVING ROOM...
HM?
WAIT... THIS ROOM...
THEY... THEY CAN TELL?!
THE TRUTH IS...
...WE'VE GOTTEN A TON OF COMPLAINTS ABOUT GHOSTS PARADING THROUGH THIS ROOM AT NIGHT!
Eeek!
UH... ANYWAY, THIS APARTMENT IS IN A VERY GOOD LOCATION!
THE CHUO LINE PASSES RIGHT BY HERE. YOU CAN GO STRAIGHT TO SHIN-JUKU...
O-OH, THIS GOES WAY BEYOND THAT...
GLARE
ARE YOU SURE YOU CAN RENT OUT A PLACE LIKE THIS?!

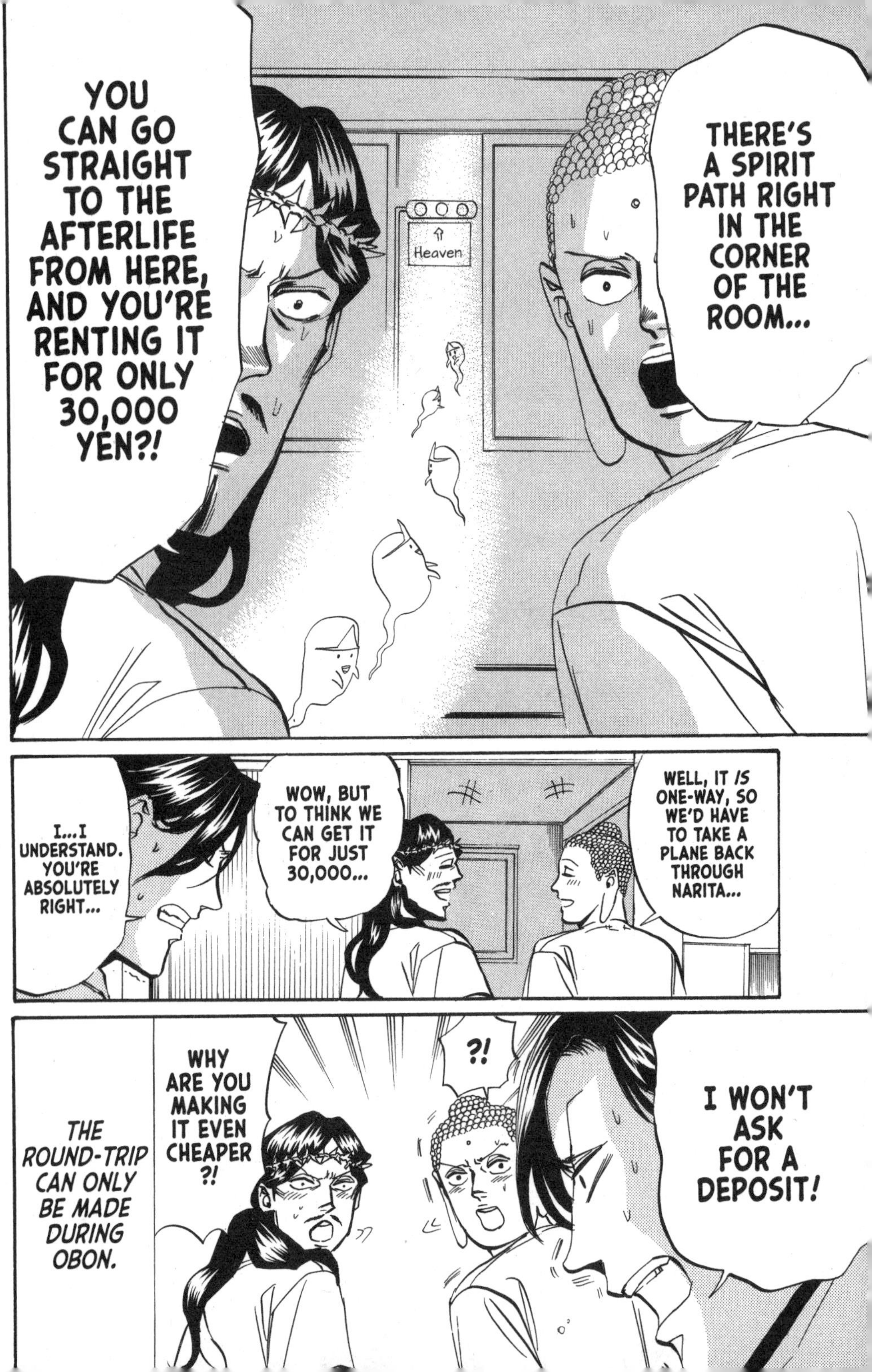
THERE'S A SPIRIT PATH RIGHT IN THE CORNER OF THE ROOM...
Heaven
YOU CAN GO STRAIGHT TO THE AFTERLIFE FROM HERE, AND YOU'RE RENTING IT FOR ONLY 30,000 YEN?!
WELL, IT *IS* ONE-WAY, SO WE'D HAVE TO TAKE A PLANE BACK THROUGH NARITA...
WOW, BUT TO THINK WE CAN GET IT FOR JUST 30,000...
I...I UNDERSTAND. YOU'RE ABSOLUTELY RIGHT...
I WON'T ASK FOR A DEPOSIT!
?!
WHY ARE YOU MAKING IT EVEN CHEAPER ?!
THE ROUND-TRIP CAN ONLY BE MADE DURING OBON.

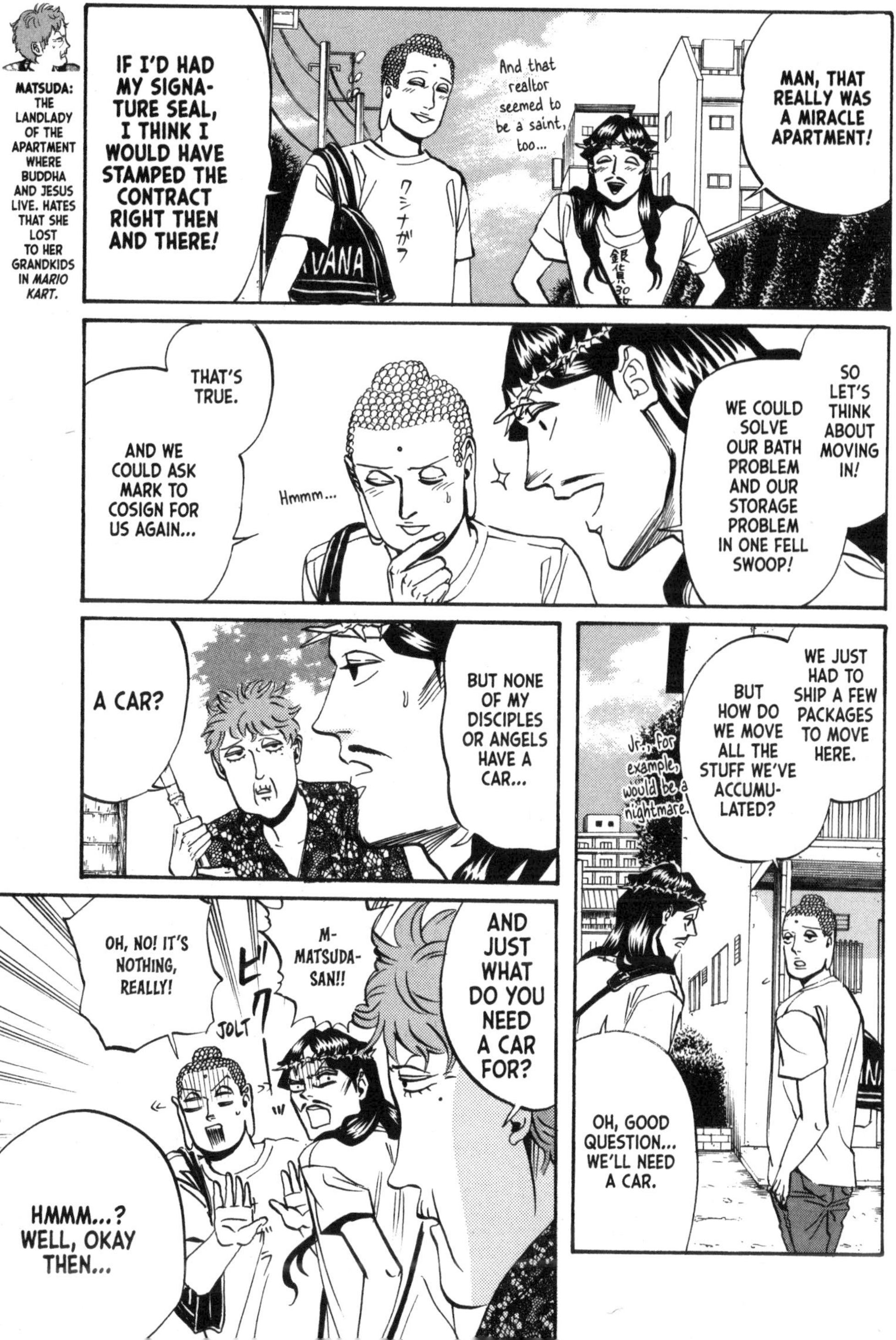
MATSUDA: THE LANDLADY OF THE APARTMENT WHERE BUDDHA AND JESUS LIVE. HATES THAT SHE LOST TO HER GRANDKIDS IN *MARIO KART*.
MAN, THAT REALLY WAS A MIRACLE APARTMENT!
And that realtor seemed to be a saint, too...
IF I'D HAD MY SIGNATURE SEAL, I THINK I WOULD HAVE STAMPED THE CONTRACT RIGHT THEN AND THERE!
SO LET'S THINK ABOUT MOVING IN!
WE COULD SOLVE OUR BATH PROBLEM AND OUR STORAGE PROBLEM IN ONE FELL SWOOP!
Hmmm...
THAT'S TRUE.
AND WE COULD ASK MARK TO COSIGN FOR US AGAIN...
WE JUST HAD TO SHIP A FEW PACKAGES TO MOVE HERE.
BUT HOW DO WE MOVE ALL THE STUFF WE'VE ACCUMULATED?
Jr., for example, would be a nightmare.
OH, GOOD QUESTION... WE'LL NEED A CAR.
BUT NONE OF MY DISCIPLES OR ANGELS HAVE A CAR...
A CAR?
AND JUST WHAT DO YOU NEED A CAR FOR?
M-MATSUDA-SAN!!
OH, NO! IT'S NOTHING, REALLY!
JOLT
HMMM...? WELL, OKAY THEN...

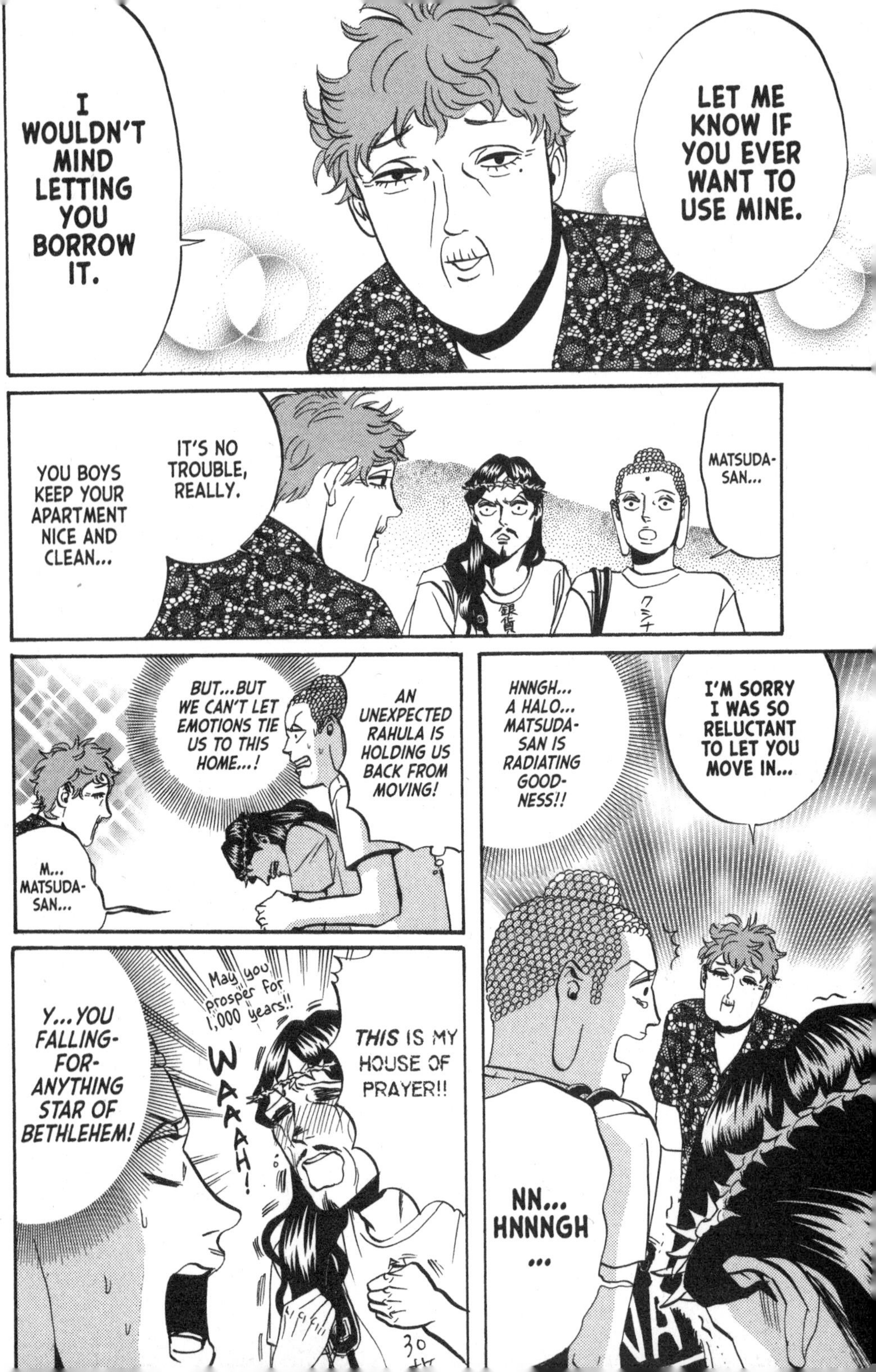

LET ME KNOW IF YOU EVER WANT TO USE MINE.
I WOULDN'T MIND LETTING YOU BORROW IT.
MATSUDA-SAN...
IT'S NO TROUBLE, REALLY.
YOU BOYS KEEP YOUR APARTMENT NICE AND CLEAN...
I'M SORRY I WAS SO RELUCTANT TO LET YOU MOVE IN...
HNNGH... A HALO... MATSUDA-SAN IS RADIATING GOOD-NESS!!
NN... HNNNGH ...
AN UNEXPECTED RAHULA IS HOLDING US BACK FROM MOVING!
BUT...BUT WE CAN'T LET EMOTIONS TIE US TO THIS HOME...!
M... MATSUDA-SAN...
THIS IS MY HOUSE OF PRAYER!!
May you prosper for 1,000 years!!
WAAAH!
Y...YOU FALLING-FOR-ANYTHING STAR OF BETHLEHEM!

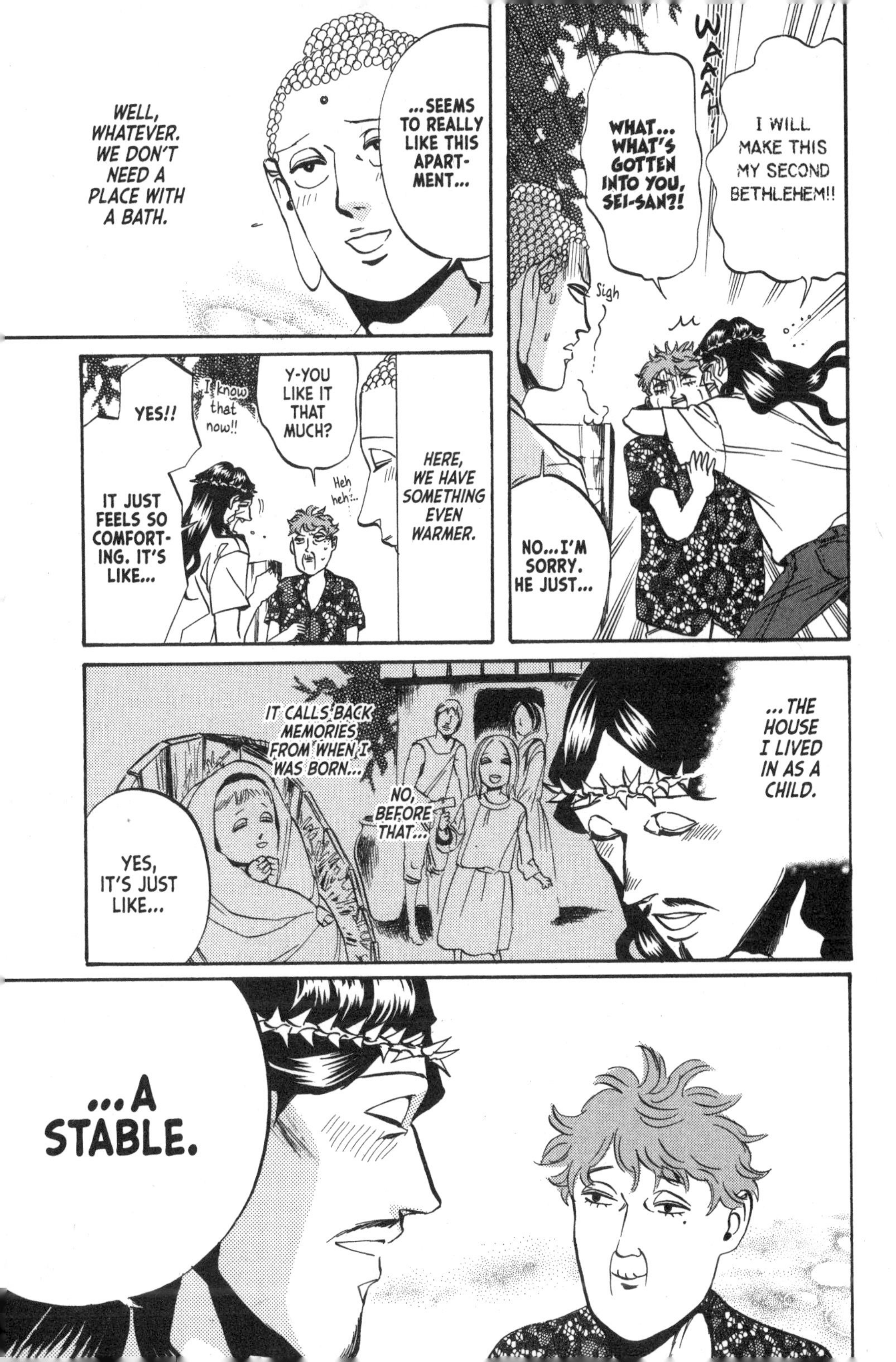
I WILL MAKE THIS MY SECOND BETHLEHEM!!
WAAAH!
WHAT... WHAT'S GOTTEN INTO YOU, SEI-SAN?!
Sigh
NO...I'M SORRY. HE JUST...
...SEEMS TO REALLY LIKE THIS APARTMENT...
WELL, WHATEVER. WE DON'T NEED A PLACE WITH A BATH.
HERE, WE HAVE SOMETHING EVEN WARMER.
Y-YOU LIKE IT THAT MUCH?
Heh heh...
YES!!
I know that now!!
IT JUST FEELS SO COMFORTING. IT'S LIKE...
...THE HOUSE I LIVED IN AS A CHILD.
IT CALLS BACK MEMORIES FROM WHEN I WAS BORN...
NO, BEFORE THAT...
YES, IT'S JUST LIKE...
...A STABLE.

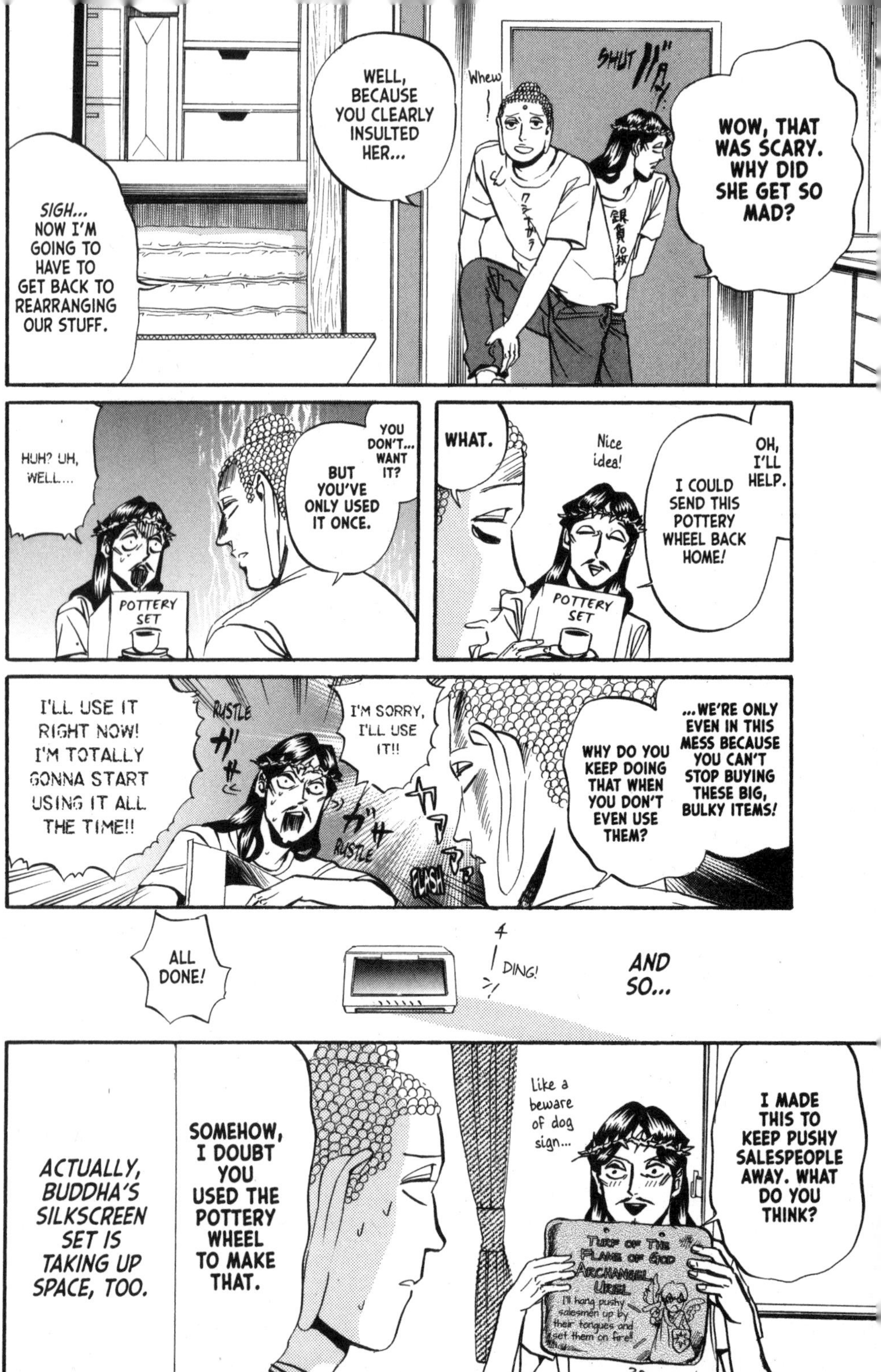
SHUT
WOW, THAT WAS SCARY. WHY DID SHE GET SO MAD?
Whew
WELL, BECAUSE YOU CLEARLY INSULTED HER...
SIGH... NOW I'M GOING TO HAVE TO GET BACK TO REARRANGING OUR STUFF.
OH, I'LL HELP.
I COULD SEND THIS POTTERY WHEEL BACK HOME!
Nice idea!
WHAT.
POTTERY SET
YOU DON'T... WANT IT?
BUT YOU'VE ONLY USED IT ONCE.
HUH? UH, WELL....
POTTERY SET
...WE'RE ONLY EVEN IN THIS MESS BECAUSE YOU CAN'T STOP BUYING THESE BIG, BULKY ITEMS!
WHY DO YOU KEEP DOING THAT WHEN YOU DON'T EVEN USE THEM?
FLASH
I'M SORRY, I'LL USE IT!!
RUSTLE
RUSTLE
I'LL USE IT RIGHT NOW! I'M TOTALLY GONNA START USING IT ALL THE TIME!!
AND SO...
DING!
ALL DONE!
I MADE THIS TO KEEP PUSHY SALESPEOPLE AWAY. WHAT DO YOU THINK?
TURF OF THE FLAME OF GOD ARCHANGEL URIEL
I'll hang pushy salesmen up by their tongues and set them on fire!
Like a beware of dog sign...
SOMEHOW, I DOUBT YOU USED THE POTTERY WHEEL TO MAKE THAT.
ACTUALLY, BUDDHA'S SILKSCREEN SET IS TAKING UP SPACE, TOO.

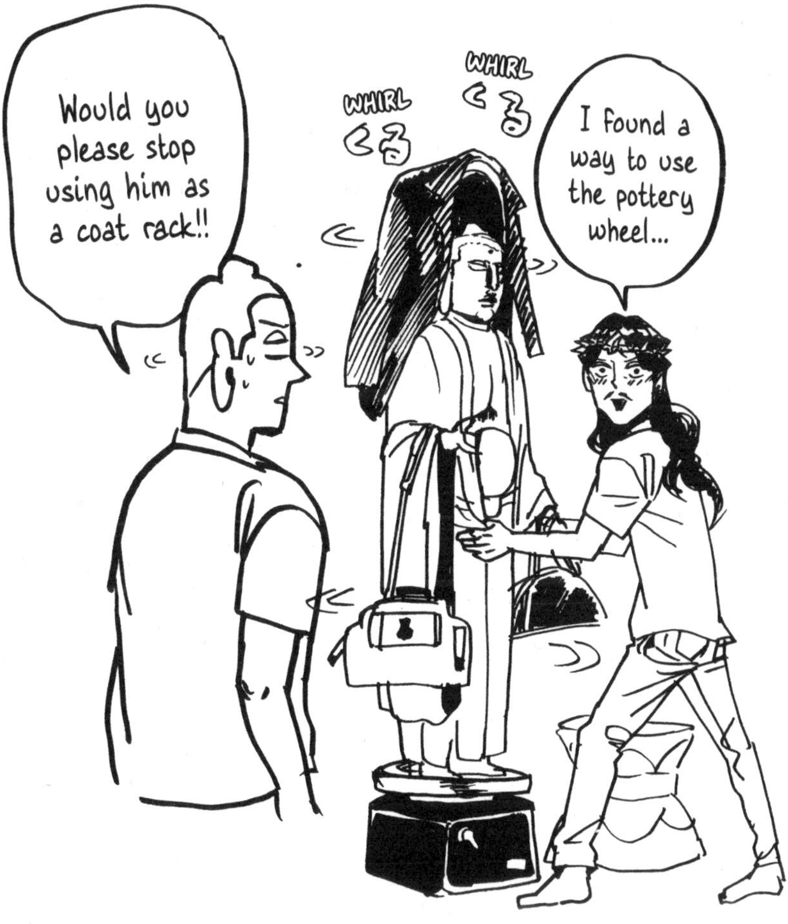
I found a way to use the pottery wheel...
WHIRL
WHIRL
Would you please stop using him as a coat rack!!

CHAPTER 17 TRANSLATION NOTES

30 pieces of silver, page 27

30 pieces of silver is the amount of money Jesus's enemies paid to Judas Iscariot for betraying him. It was the going rate for slaves in that part of the world at that time, as well as the amount foretold in the Old Testament Book of Zechariah as the blood-money paid for betraying God.

Kushinagar, page 28

Kushinagar is a village in India, where the Buddha attained parinirvana, or "nirvana without remainder," meaning that since he had attained enlightenment during his lifetime, he was released from the cycles of rebirth upon his physical death.

Overturning furniture, page 30

In Jesus's day, animals were ritually slaughtered in temples near where he preached. Enterprising people took advantage of this practice and went to the temple to sell ceremonially fit animals to those wishing to worship. In John 2, he notably made an impromptu whip to drive out the barterers, liberated all the animals, and overturned the tables where money was exchanged and said, "Make not my father's house a house of merchandise." It was the second clearing of the temple, toward the end of his ministry, when Jesus reminded the barterers that the temple is a house of prayer.

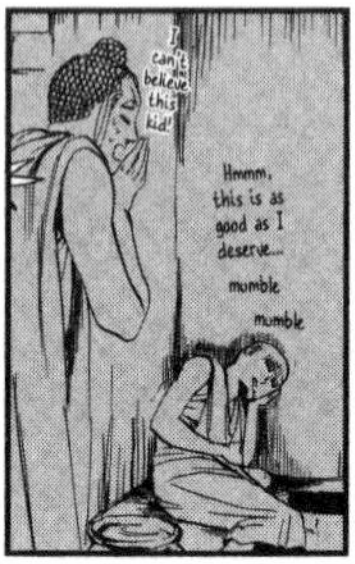
I can't believe this kid!
Hmmm, this is as good as I deserve...
mumble
mumble

Rahula sleeping in the bathroom, page 37

There is a famous story from when the Buddha's son was a novice monk, in which the Buddha made a rule that no novice could sleep in the same room as a fully ordained monk. When he retired to bed and found nowhere to sleep that did not already house ordained monks, Rahula snuck into an outhouse and slept there. When the Buddha realized that this was the sort of treatment novices were receiving, the rule was adjusted.

Obon, page 38

Obon is a festival usually held in August. It is believed that the spirit world is closer to the world of the living during this festival, and that ancestors come back to the mortal world to visit their families.

Just like a stable, page 41

Jesus was born at a time when the Jewish people were returning to their ancestral homes to participate in a census for their Roman rulers. Joseph took his wife Mary to his own ancestral town of Bethlehem, where he would have found lodging with relatives, either close or distant. The homes of his relatives would have had a guest room, or *kataluma* (which is translated to "inn" in familiar versions the Bible), in addition to a family room which also had a space for the animals to come in during the night. Because so many people were coming in from out of town, all the guest rooms were full. Whether Joseph and Mary stayed in the family room with their host family and their animals or whether they stayed in a stable is unclear, but we do know that when Jesus was born, the only bed available for the newborn child was a manger—a feeding trough for the animals.

Uriel, page 42

According to the apocryphal text *The Apocalypse of Peter*, Uriel is the archangel who will supervise the punishment of sinners in hell. One of these punishments is that blasphemers will be hanged by their tongues and set on fire.

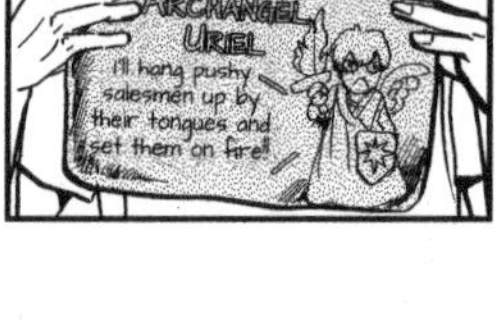
Turf of the Flame of God
Archangel Urel
I'll hang pushy salesmen up by their tongues and set them on fire!!

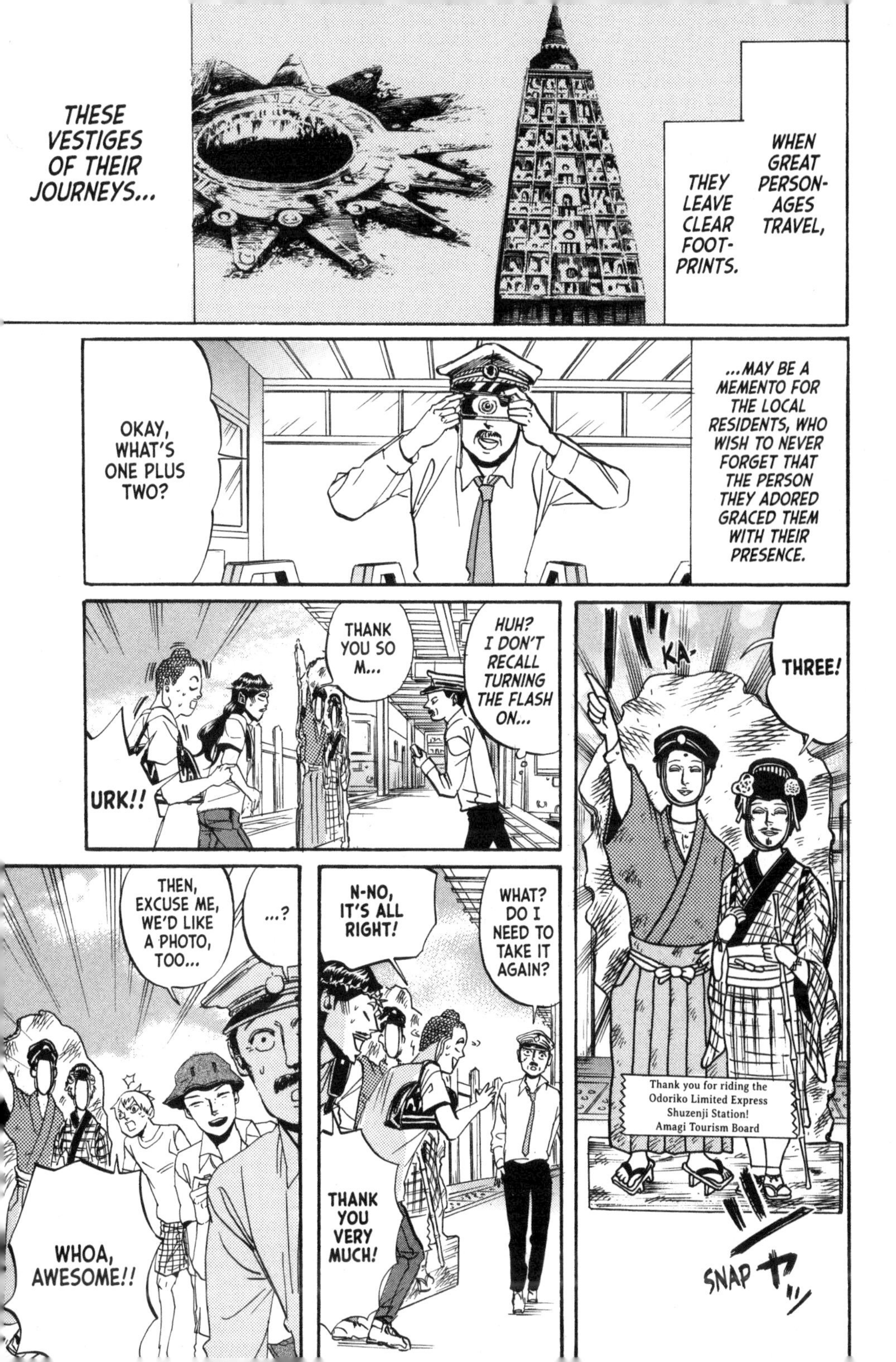

WHEN GREAT PERSONAGES TRAVEL,
THEY LEAVE CLEAR FOOTPRINTS.
THESE VESTIGES OF THEIR JOURNEYS...
...MAY BE A MEMENTO FOR THE LOCAL RESIDENTS, WHO WISH TO NEVER FORGET THAT THE PERSON THEY ADORED GRACED THEM WITH THEIR PRESENCE.
OKAY, WHAT'S ONE PLUS TWO?
THREE!
KA-
Thank you for riding the Odoriko Limited Express Shuzenji Station! Amagi Tourism Board
SNAP
HUH? I DON'T RECALL TURNING THE FLASH ON...
THANK YOU SO M...
URK!!
WHAT? DO I NEED TO TAKE IT AGAIN?
N-NO, IT'S ALL RIGHT!
THANK YOU VERY MUCH!
...?
THEN, EXCUSE ME, WE'D LIKE A PHOTO, TOO...
WHOA, AWESOME!!

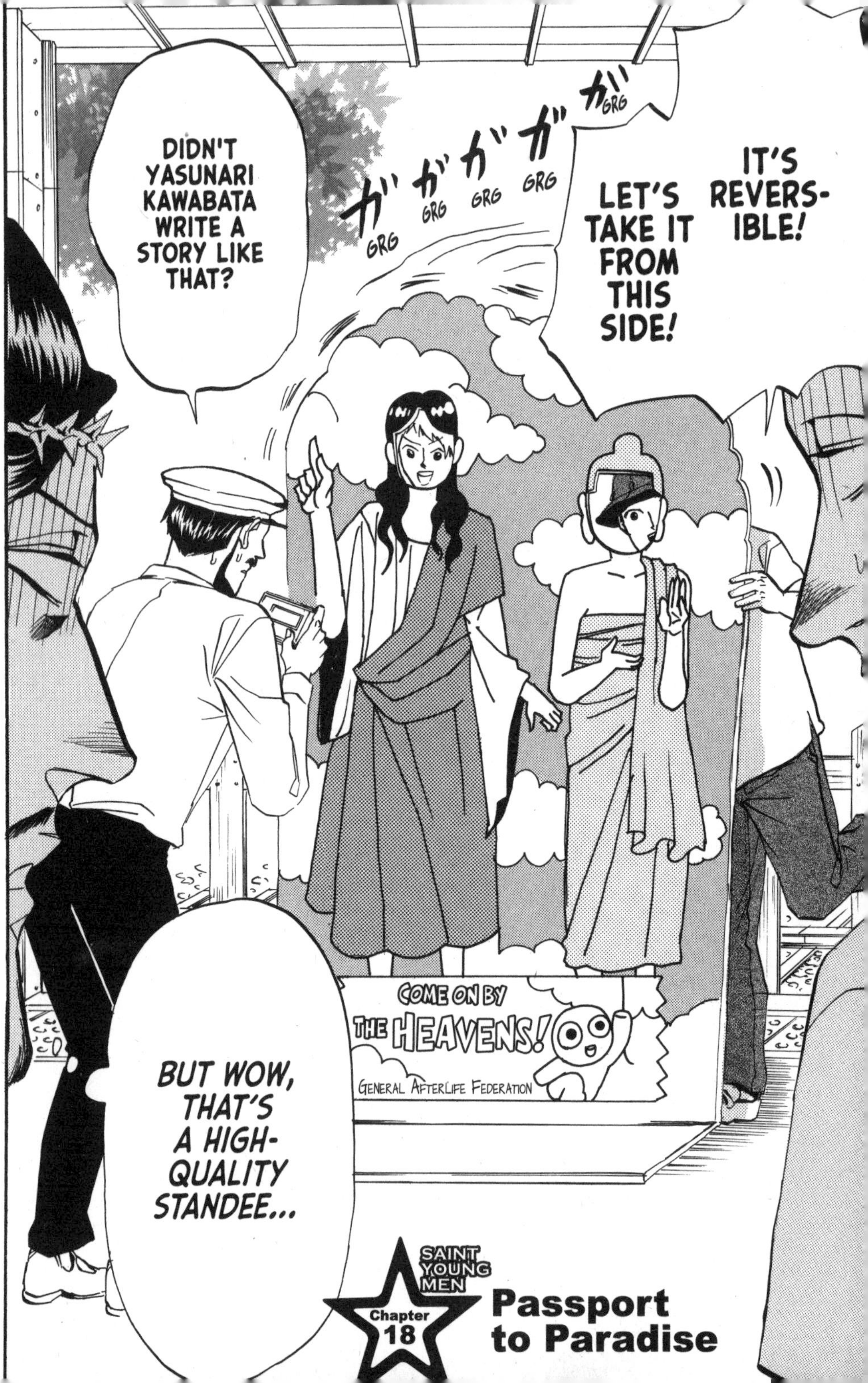
IT'S REVERSIBLE!
LET'S TAKE IT FROM THIS SIDE!
ガガガガガ GRG GRG GRG GRG GRG
DIDN'T YASUNARI KAWABATA WRITE A STORY LIKE THAT?
COME ON BY THE HEAVENS!
GENERAL AFTERLIFE FEDERATION
BUT WOW, THAT'S A HIGH-QUALITY STANDEE...
SAINT YOUNG MEN
Chapter 18
Passport to Paradise

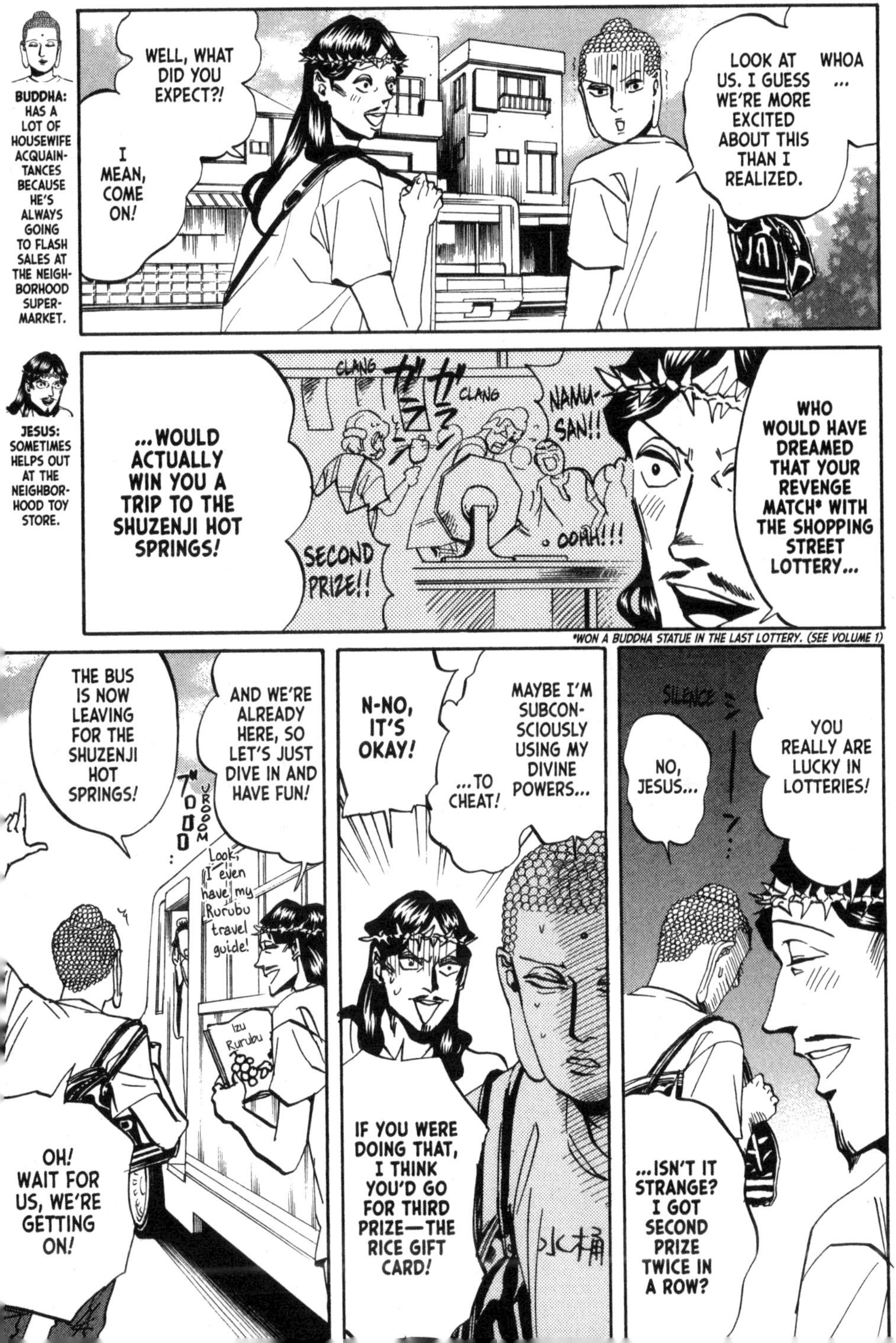
BUDDHA: HAS A LOT OF HOUSEWIFE ACQUAINTANCES BECAUSE HE'S ALWAYS GOING TO FLASH SALES AT THE NEIGHBORHOOD SUPERMARKET.
WHOA ...
LOOK AT US. I GUESS WE'RE MORE EXCITED ABOUT THIS THAN I REALIZED.
WELL, WHAT DID YOU EXPECT?!
I MEAN, COME ON!
JESUS: SOMETIMES HELPS OUT AT THE NEIGHBORHOOD TOY STORE.
WHO WOULD HAVE DREAMED THAT YOUR REVENGE MATCH* WITH THE SHOPPING STREET LOTTERY...
NAMU-SAN!!
CLANG
CLANG
OOHH!!!
SECOND PRIZE!!
...WOULD ACTUALLY WIN YOU A TRIP TO THE SHUZENJI HOT SPRINGS!
SILENCE
YOU REALLY ARE LUCKY IN LOTTERIES!
NO, JESUS...
...ISN'T IT STRANGE? I GOT SECOND PRIZE TWICE IN A ROW?
MAYBE I'M SUBCONSCIOUSLY USING MY DIVINE POWERS...
...TO CHEAT!
N-NO, IT'S OKAY!
IF YOU WERE DOING THAT, I THINK YOU'D GO FOR THIRD PRIZE—THE RICE GIFT CARD!
AND WE'RE ALREADY HERE, SO LET'S JUST DIVE IN AND HAVE FUN!
THE BUS IS NOW LEAVING FOR THE SHUZENJI HOT SPRINGS!
VROOM
Look, I even have my Rurubu travel guide!
Izu Rurubu
OH! WAIT FOR US, WE'RE GETTING ON!

*WON A BUDDHA STATUE IN THE LAST LOTTERY. (SEE VOLUME 1)

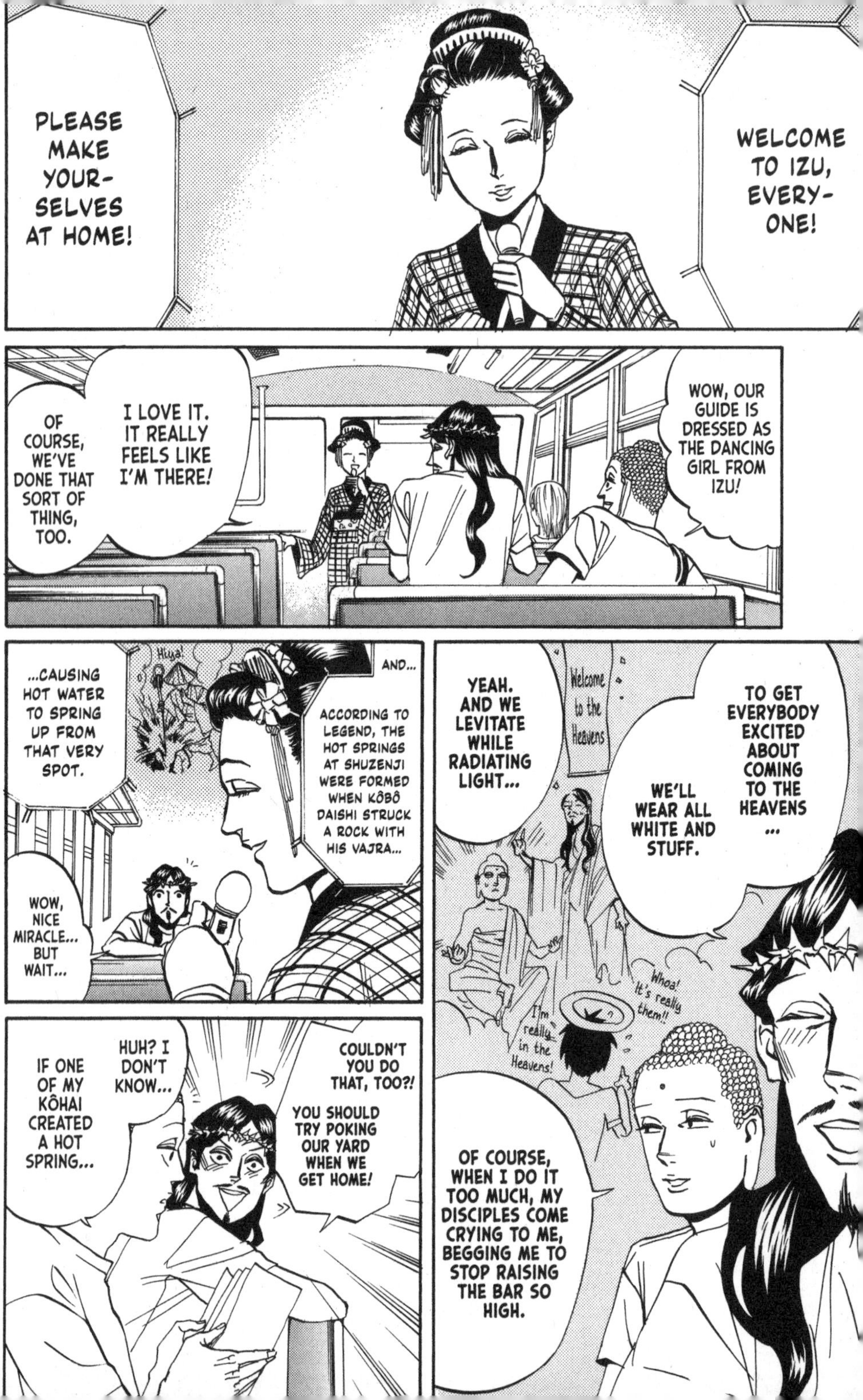
WELCOME TO IZU, EVERYONE!
PLEASE MAKE YOURSELVES AT HOME!
WOW, OUR GUIDE IS DRESSED AS THE DANCING GIRL FROM IZU!
I LOVE IT. IT REALLY FEELS LIKE I'M THERE!
OF COURSE, WE'VE DONE THAT SORT OF THING, TOO.
TO GET EVERYBODY EXCITED ABOUT COMING TO THE HEAVENS...
WE'LL WEAR ALL WHITE AND STUFF.
YEAH. AND WE LEVITATE WHILE RADIATING LIGHT...
Welcome to the Heavens
Whoa! It's really them!!
I'm really in the Heavens!
OF COURSE, WHEN I DO IT TOO MUCH, MY DISCIPLES COME CRYING TO ME, BEGGING ME TO STOP RAISING THE BAR SO HIGH.
AND...
ACCORDING TO LEGEND, THE HOT SPRINGS AT SHUZENJI WERE FORMED WHEN KÔBÔ DAISHI STRUCK A ROCK WITH HIS VAJRA...
...CAUSING HOT WATER TO SPRING UP FROM THAT VERY SPOT.
Hiya!
WOW, NICE MIRACLE... BUT WAIT...
COULDN'T YOU DO THAT, TOO?!
YOU SHOULD TRY POKING OUR YARD WHEN WE GET HOME!
HUH? I DON'T KNOW...
IF ONE OF MY KÔHAI CREATED A HOT SPRING...

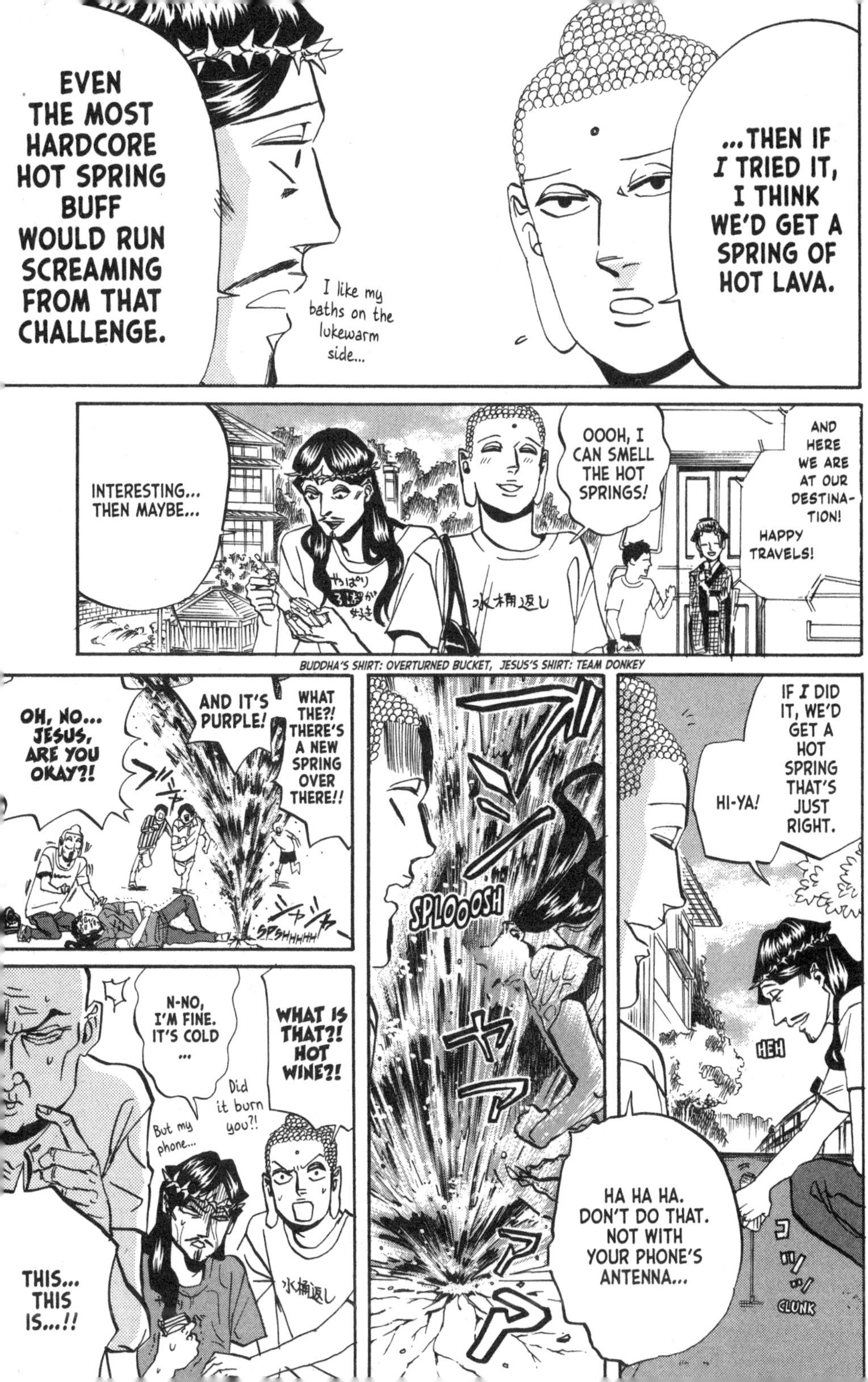
...THEN IF I TRIED IT, I THINK WE'D GET A SPRING OF HOT LAVA.
EVEN THE MOST HARDCORE HOT SPRING BUFF WOULD RUN SCREAMING FROM THAT CHALLENGE.
I like my baths on the lukewarm side...
AND HERE WE ARE AT OUR DESTINATION!
HAPPY TRAVELS!
OOOH, I CAN SMELL THE HOT SPRINGS!
INTERESTING... THEN MAYBE...
水桶返し
BUDDHA'S SHIRT: OVERTURNED BUCKET, JESUS'S SHIRT: TEAM DONKEY
IF I DID IT, WE'D GET A HOT SPRING THAT'S JUST RIGHT.
HI-YA!
HEH
HA HA HA. DON'T DO THAT. NOT WITH YOUR PHONE'S ANTENNA...
CLUNK
SPLOOOSH
WHAT THE?! THERE'S A NEW SPRING OVER THERE!!
AND IT'S PURPLE!
OH, NO... JESUS, ARE YOU OKAY?!
SPSHHHHH
WHAT IS THAT?! HOT WINE?!
Did it burn you?!
N-NO, I'M FINE. IT'S COLD...
But my phone...
THIS... THIS IS...!!
水桶返し

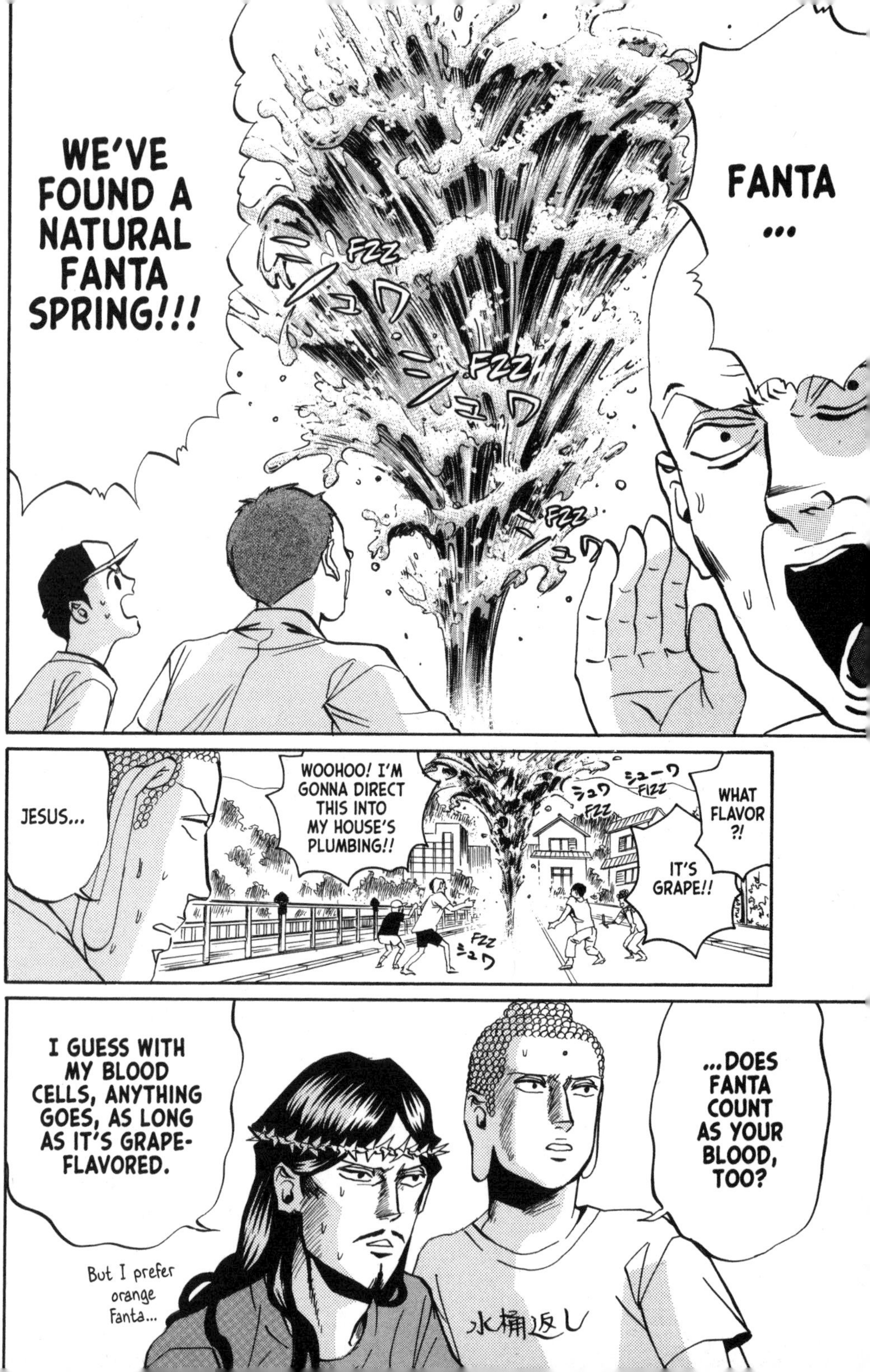
FANTA …
WE'VE FOUND A NATURAL FANTA SPRING!!!
FZZ
FZZ
FZZ
WHAT FLAVOR?!
IT'S GRAPE!!
シューワ FIZZ
シュワ FZZ
WOOHOO! I'M GONNA DIRECT THIS INTO MY HOUSE'S PLUMBING!!
FZZ
JESUS...
...DOES FANTA COUNT AS YOUR BLOOD, TOO?
I GUESS WITH MY BLOOD CELLS, ANYTHING GOES, AS LONG AS IT'S GRAPE-FLAVORED.
But I prefer orange Fanta...
水桶返し

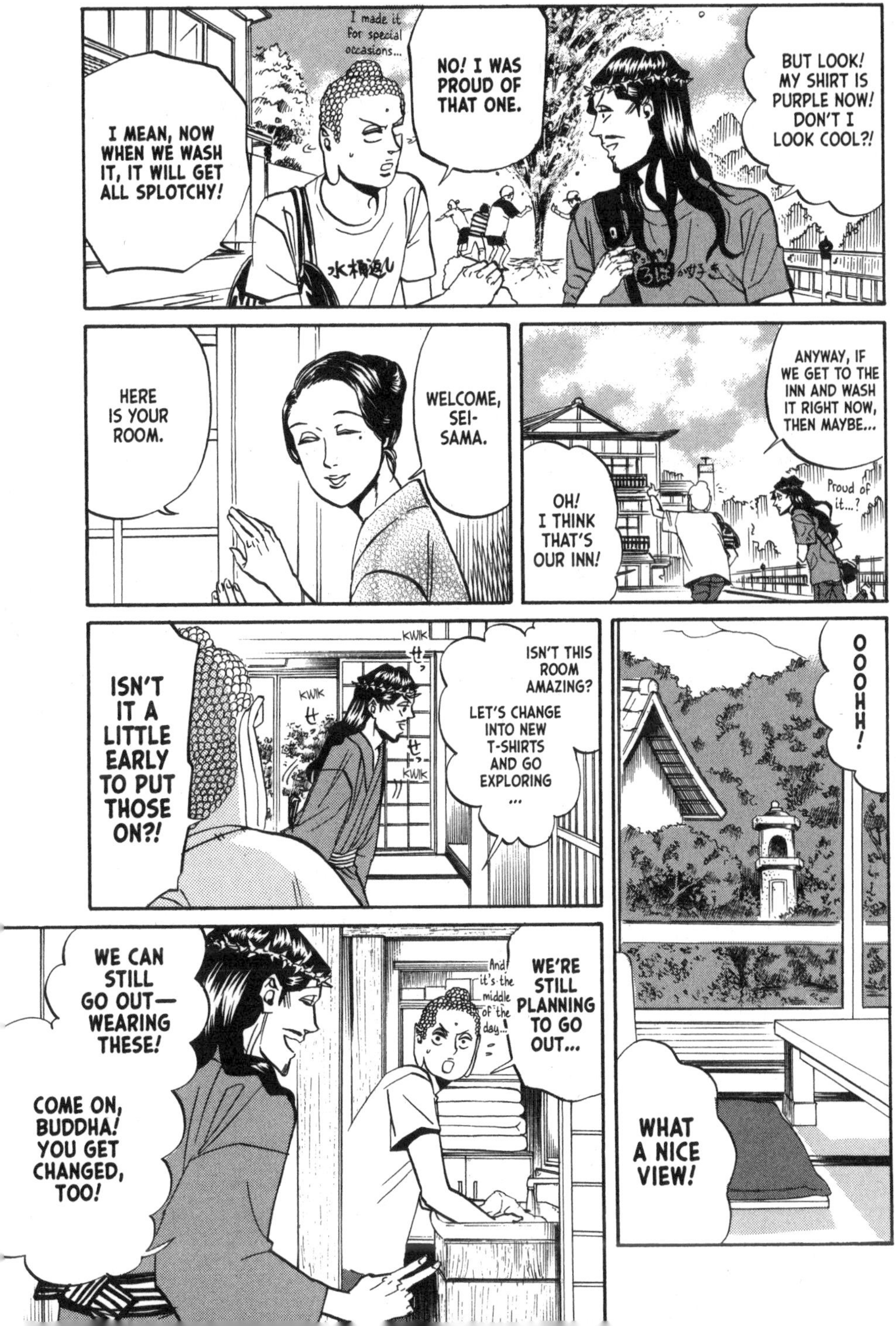
BUT LOOK! MY SHIRT IS PURPLE NOW! DON'T I LOOK COOL?!
NO! I WAS PROUD OF THAT ONE.
I made it for special occasions...
I MEAN, NOW WHEN WE WASH IT, IT WILL GET ALL SPLOTCHY!
ANYWAY, IF WE GET TO THE INN AND WASH IT RIGHT NOW, THEN MAYBE...
Proud of it...?
OH! I THINK THAT'S OUR INN!
WELCOME, SEI-SAMA.
HERE IS YOUR ROOM.
OOOHH!
WHAT A NICE VIEW!
ISN'T THIS ROOM AMAZING?
LET'S CHANGE INTO NEW T-SHIRTS AND GO EXPLORING ...
KWIK
KWIK
KWIK
ISN'T IT A LITTLE EARLY TO PUT THOSE ON?!
WE'RE STILL PLANNING TO GO OUT...
And it's the middle of the day...!
WE CAN STILL GO OUT— WEARING THESE!
COME ON, BUDDHA! YOU GET CHANGED, TOO!

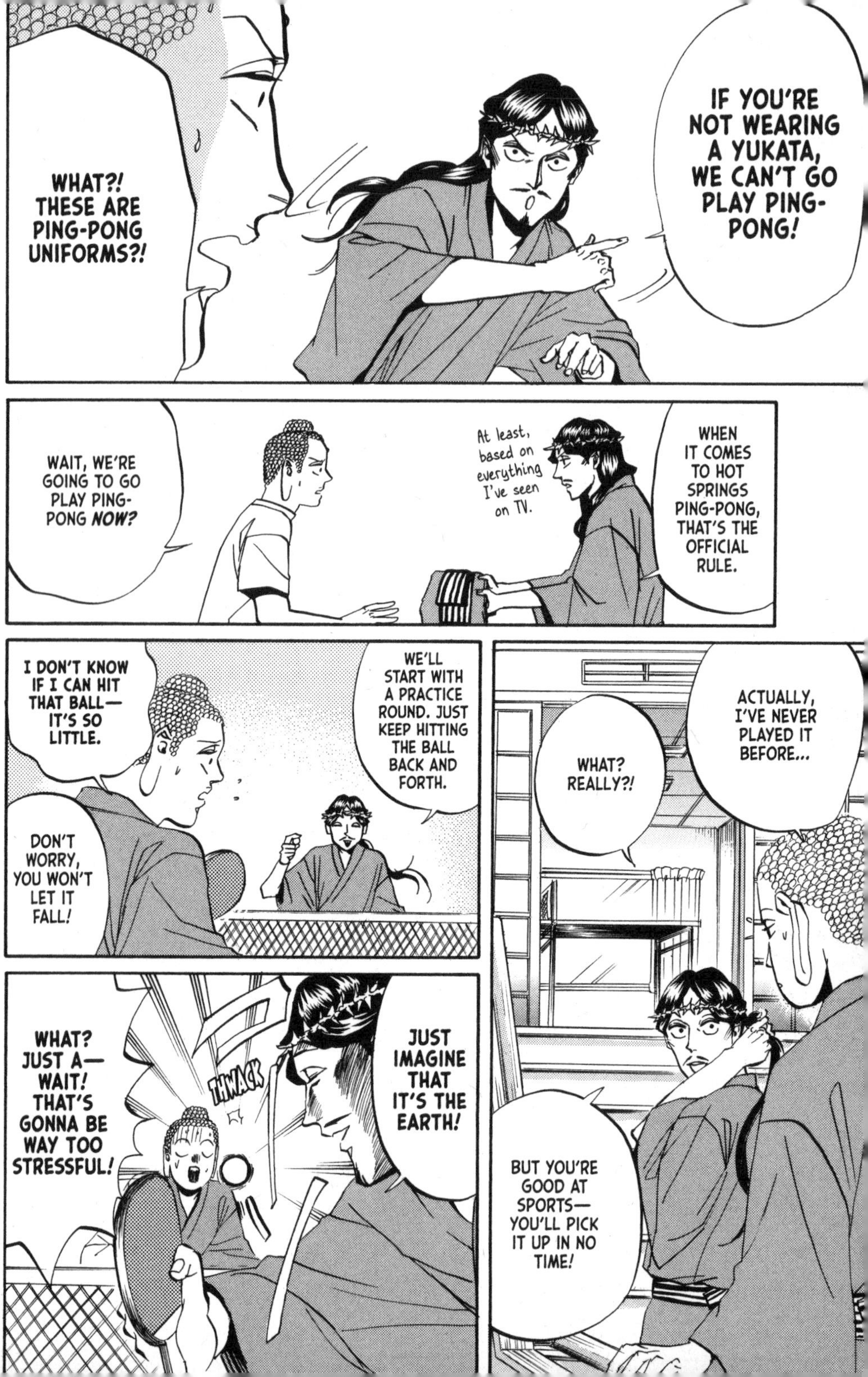
IF YOU'RE NOT WEARING A YUKATA, WE CAN'T GO PLAY PING-PONG!
WHAT?! THESE ARE PING-PONG UNIFORMS?!
WHEN IT COMES TO HOT SPRINGS PING-PONG, THAT'S THE OFFICIAL RULE.
At least, based on everything I've seen on TV.
WAIT, WE'RE GOING TO GO PLAY PING-PONG *NOW?*
ACTUALLY, I'VE NEVER PLAYED IT BEFORE...
WHAT? REALLY?!
BUT YOU'RE GOOD AT SPORTS—YOU'LL PICK IT UP IN NO TIME!
WE'LL START WITH A PRACTICE ROUND. JUST KEEP HITTING THE BALL BACK AND FORTH.
I DON'T KNOW IF I CAN HIT THAT BALL—IT'S SO LITTLE.
DON'T WORRY, YOU WON'T LET IT FALL!
JUST IMAGINE THAT IT'S THE EARTH!
THWACK
WHAT? JUST A—WAIT! THAT'S GONNA BE WAY TOO STRESSFUL!

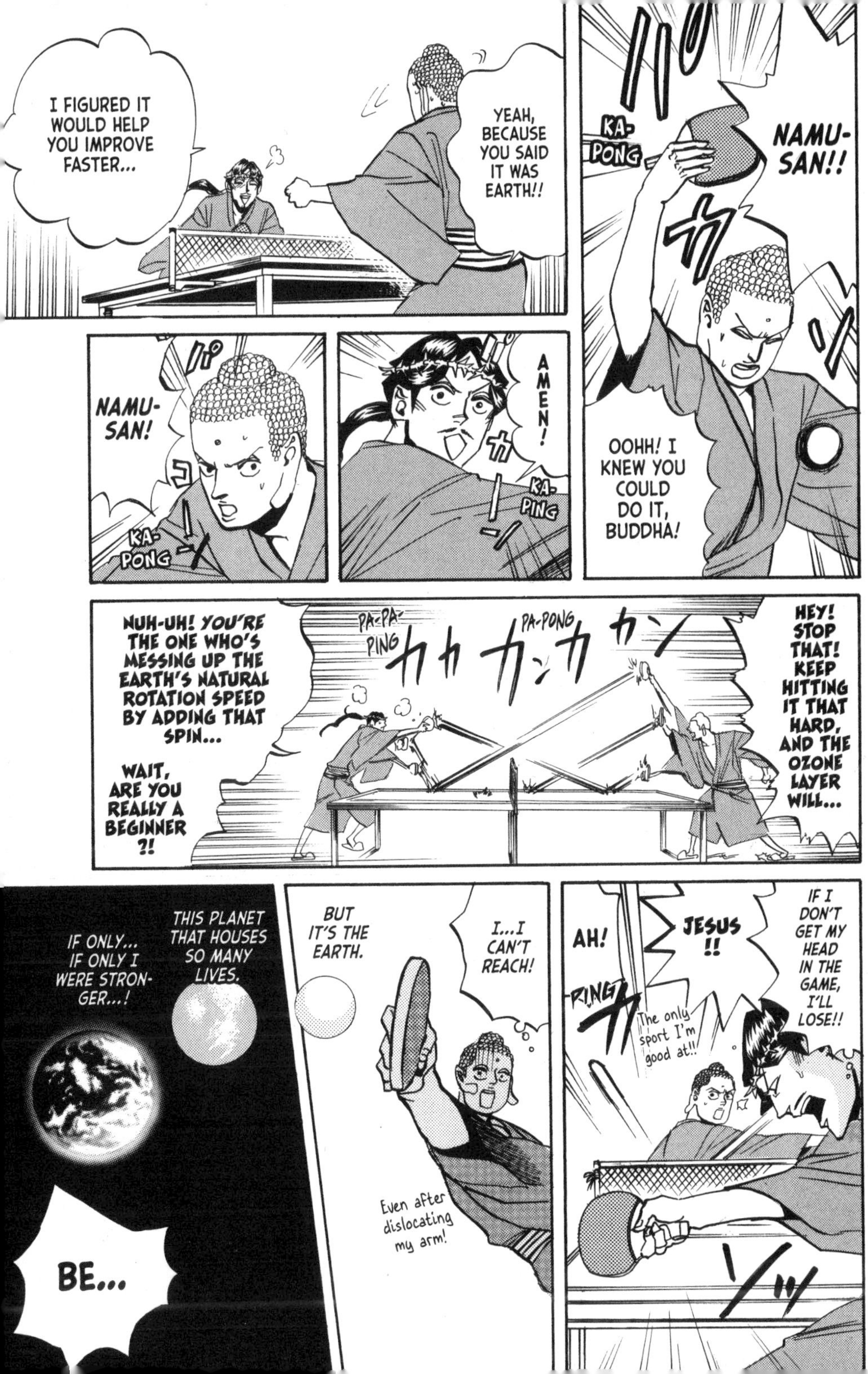

KA-PONG
NAMU-SAN!!
OOHH! I KNEW YOU COULD DO IT, BUDDHA!
YEAH, BECAUSE YOU SAID IT WAS EARTH!!
I FIGURED IT WOULD HELP YOU IMPROVE FASTER...
AMEN!
KA-PING
NAMU-SAN!
KA-PONG
HEY! STOP THAT! KEEP HITTING IT THAT HARD, AND THE OZONE LAYER WILL...
PA-PONG
PA-PA-PING
NUH-UH! YOU'RE THE ONE WHO'S MESSING UP THE EARTH'S NATURAL ROTATION SPEED BY ADDING THAT SPIN...
WAIT, ARE YOU REALLY A BEGINNER?!
IF I DON'T GET MY HEAD IN THE GAME, I'LL LOSE!!
JESUS!!
AH!
PING
The only sport I'm good at!!
I...I CAN'T REACH!
BUT IT'S THE EARTH.
Even after dislocating my arm!
THIS PLANET THAT HOUSES SO MANY LIVES.
IF ONLY... IF ONLY I WERE STRONGER...!
BE...

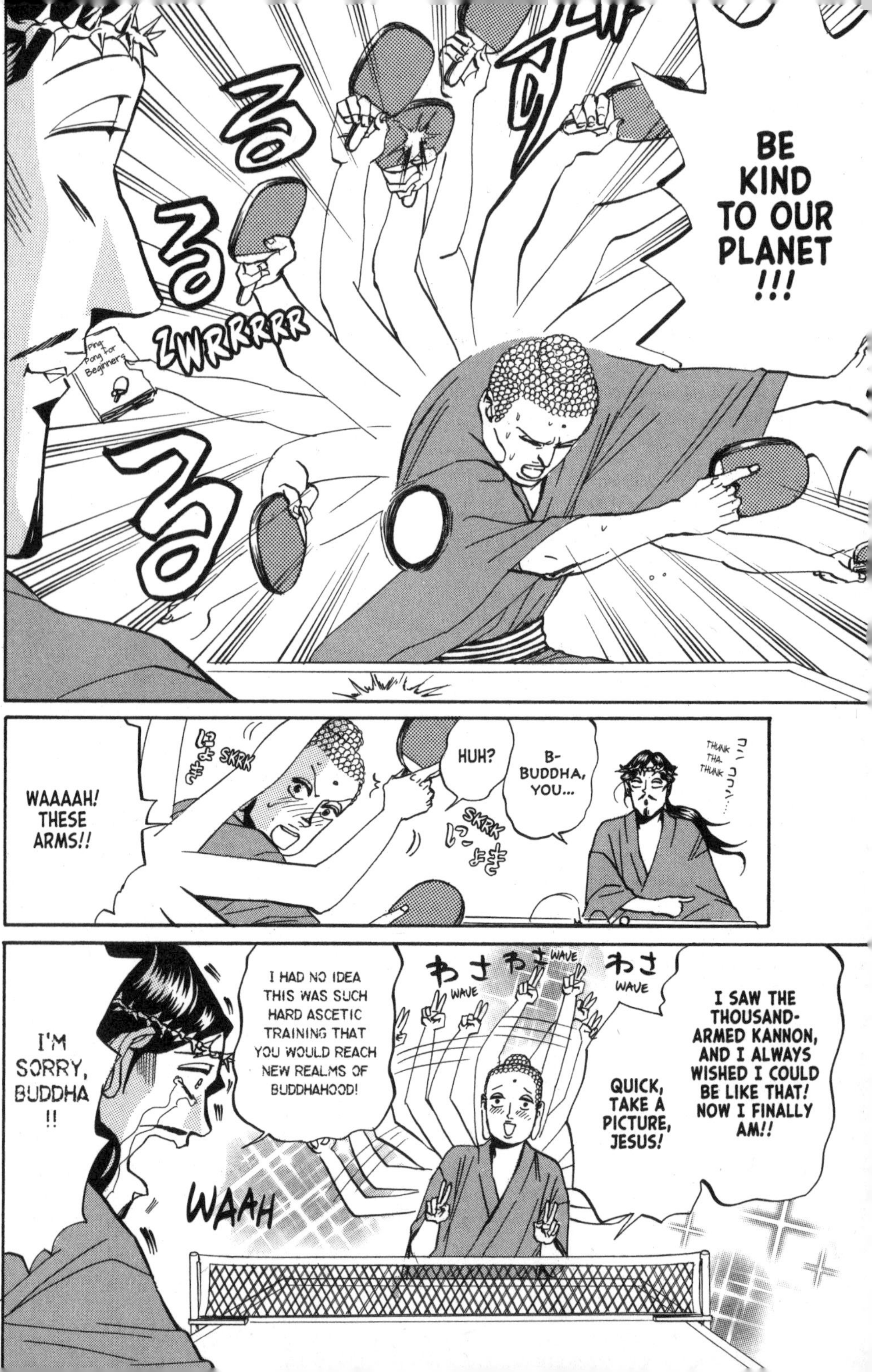
BE KIND TO OUR PLANET!!!
ZWRRRRR
Ping-Pong for Beginners
THUNK THA-THUNK
B-BUDDHA, YOU...
HUH?
SKRK
SKRK
WAAAAH! THESE ARMS!!
I SAW THE THOUSAND-ARMED KANNON, AND I ALWAYS WISHED I COULD BE LIKE THAT! NOW I FINALLY AM!!
QUICK, TAKE A PICTURE, JESUS!
WAVE
WAVE
WAVE
I HAD NO IDEA THIS WAS SUCH HARD ASCETIC TRAINING THAT YOU WOULD REACH NEW REALMS OF BUDDHAHOOD!
I'M SORRY, BUDDHA!!
WAAH

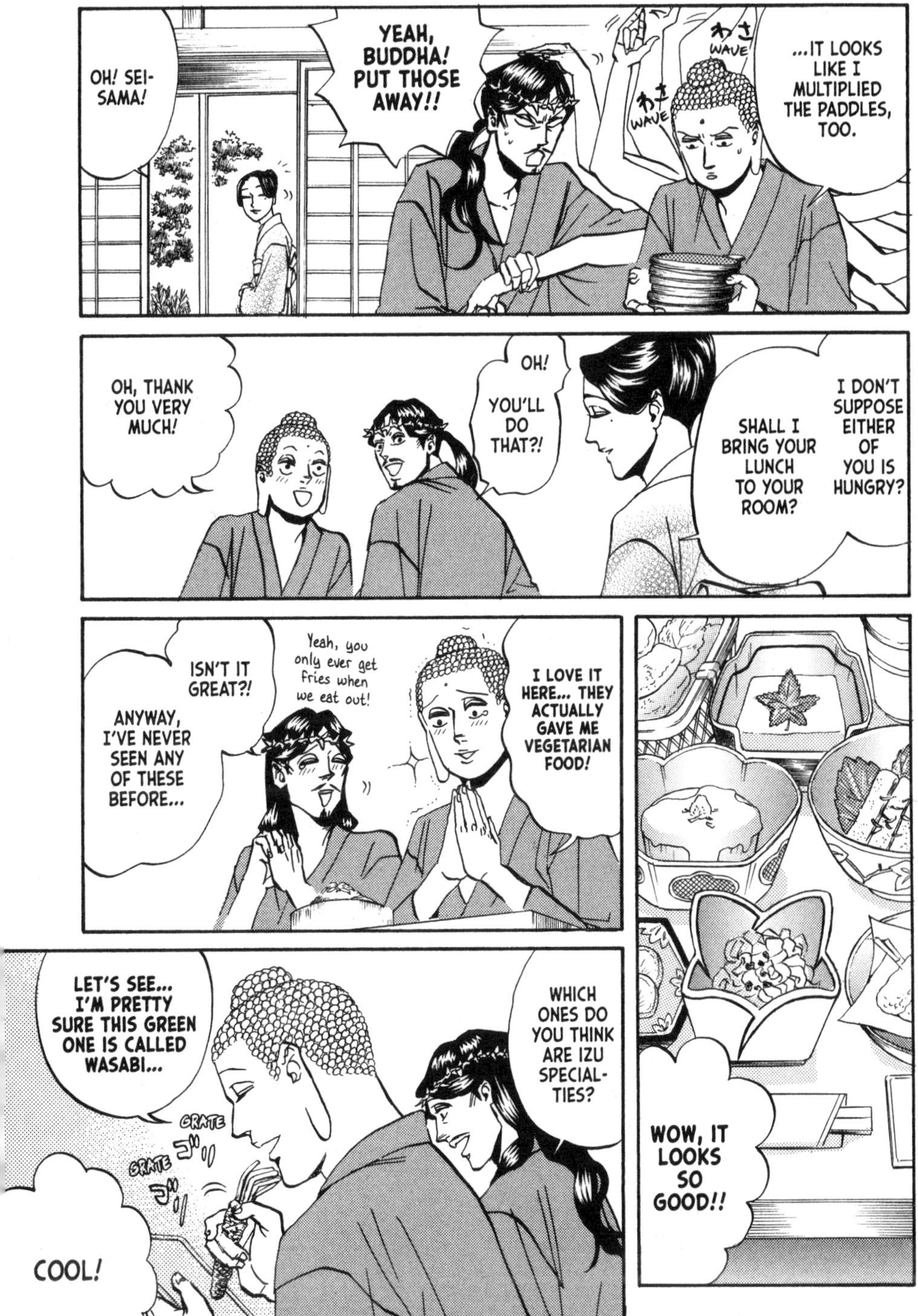
...IT LOOKS LIKE I MULTIPLIED THE PADDLES, TOO.
わさ WAVE
わさ WAVE
YEAH, BUDDHA! PUT THOSE AWAY!!
OH! SEI-SAMA!
I DON'T SUPPOSE EITHER OF YOU IS HUNGRY?
SHALL I BRING YOUR LUNCH TO YOUR ROOM?
OH! YOU'LL DO THAT?!
OH, THANK YOU VERY MUCH!
WOW, IT LOOKS SO GOOD!!
I LOVE IT HERE... THEY ACTUALLY GAVE ME VEGETARIAN FOOD!
Yeah, you only ever get fries when we eat out!
ISN'T IT GREAT?!
ANYWAY, I'VE NEVER SEEN ANY OF THESE BEFORE...
WHICH ONES DO YOU THINK ARE IZU SPECIAL-TIES?
LET'S SEE... I'M PRETTY SURE THIS GREEN ONE IS CALLED WASABI...
GRATE ゴリ
GRATE ゴリ
COOL!

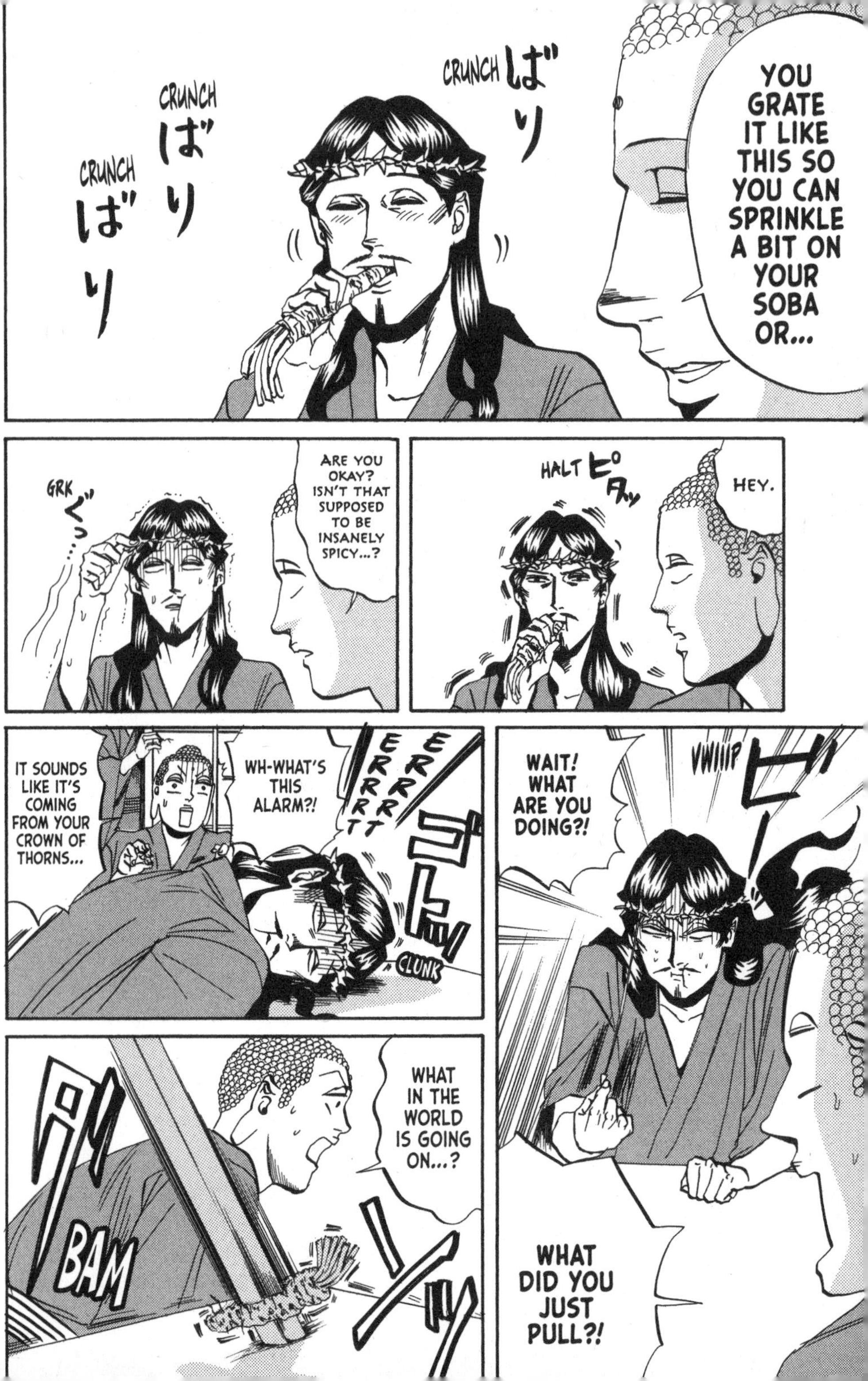
YOU GRATE IT LIKE THIS SO YOU CAN SPRINKLE A BIT ON YOUR SOBA OR...
CRUNCH ばり
CRUNCH ばり
CRUNCH ばり
HEY.
HALT ピタッ
ARE YOU OKAY? ISN'T THAT SUPPOSED TO BE INSANELY SPICY...?
GRK ぐっ
WAIT! WHAT ARE YOU DOING?!
VWIIIP ビー!
WHAT DID YOU JUST PULL?!
WH-WHAT'S THIS ALARM?!
ERRRT
ERRRT
IT SOUNDS LIKE IT'S COMING FROM YOUR CROWN OF THORNS...
ゴトッ
CLUNK
WHAT IN THE WORLD IS GOING ON...?
ダッ
BAM

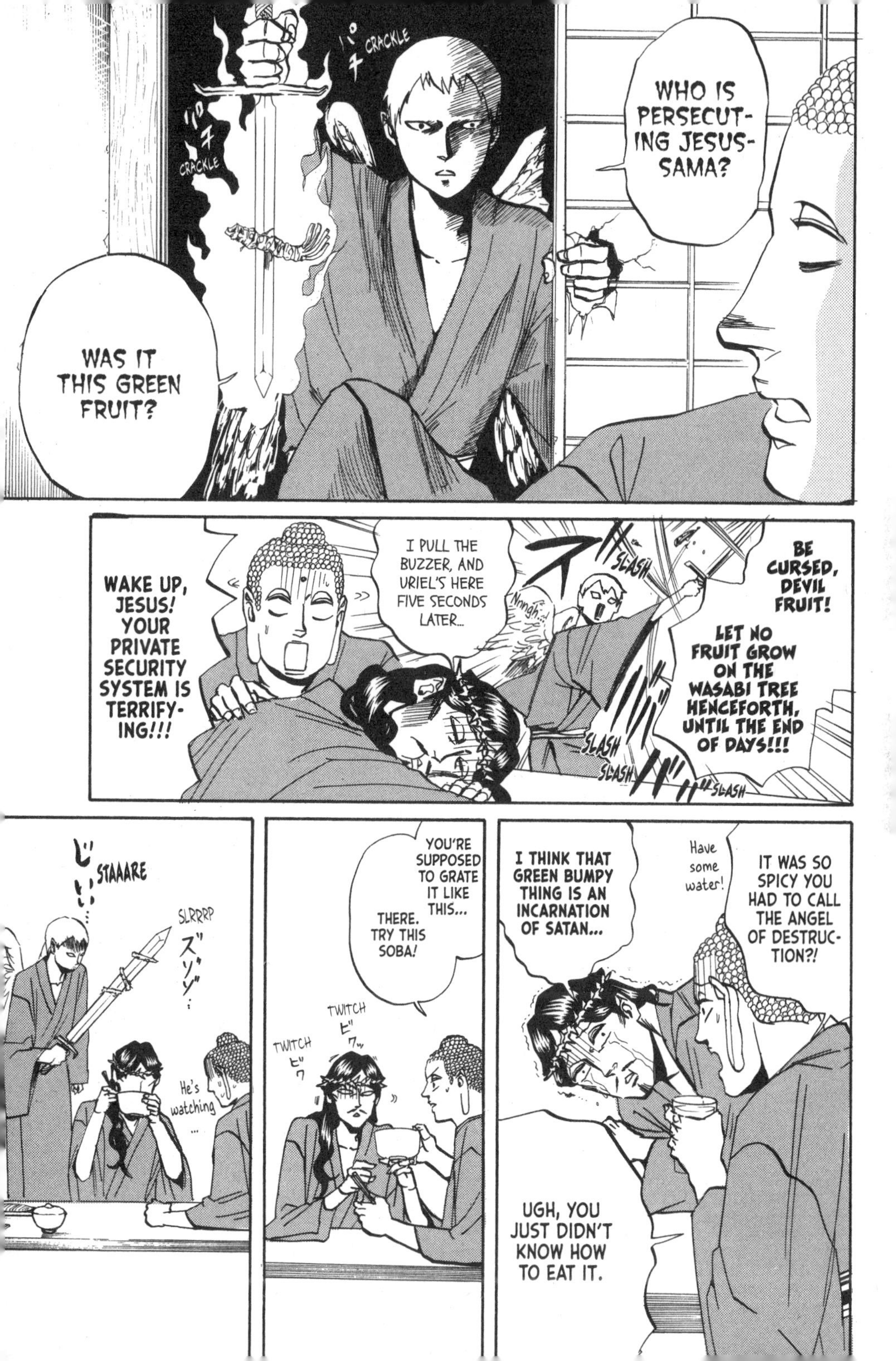
パチ CRACKLE
パチ CRACKLE
WHO IS PERSECUTING JESUS-SAMA?
WAS IT THIS GREEN FRUIT?
BE CURSED, DEVIL FRUIT!
LET NO FRUIT GROW ON THE WASABI TREE HENCEFORTH, UNTIL THE END OF DAYS!!!
ズ SLASH
SLASH SLASH SLASH
Nnngh...!
I PULL THE BUZZER, AND URIEL'S HERE FIVE SECONDS LATER...
WAKE UP, JESUS! YOUR PRIVATE SECURITY SYSTEM IS TERRIFYING!!!
IT WAS SO SPICY YOU HAD TO CALL THE ANGEL OF DESTRUCTION?!
Have some water!
I THINK THAT GREEN BUMPY THING IS AN INCARNATION OF SATAN...
UGH, YOU JUST DIDN'T KNOW HOW TO EAT IT.
YOU'RE SUPPOSED TO GRATE IT LIKE THIS...
THERE. TRY THIS SOBA!
ビクッ TWITCH
ビク TWITCH
じーっ STAAARE
SLRRRP ズゾゾ
He's watching...

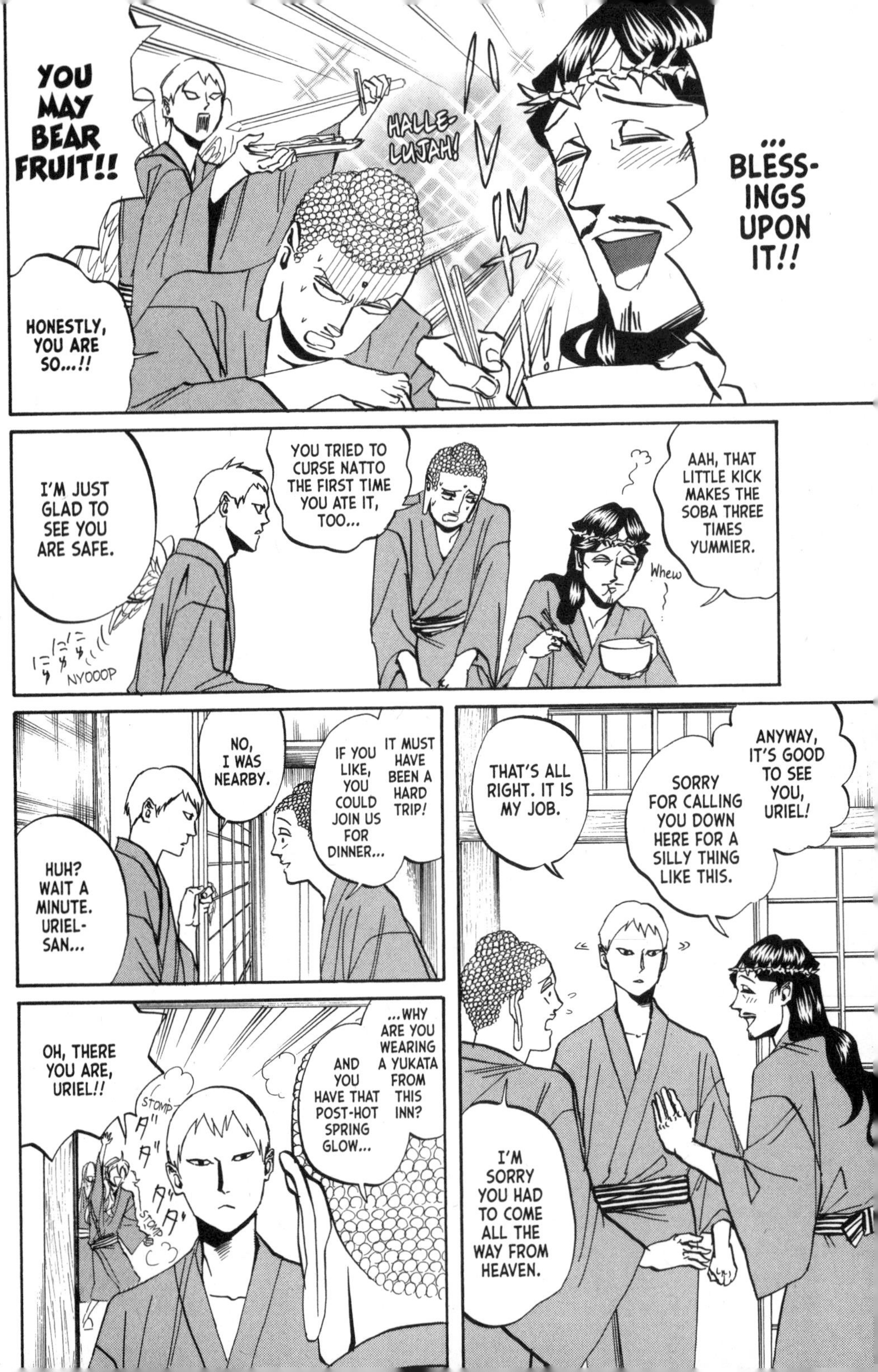
...BLESSINGS UPON IT!!
HALLELUJAH!
YOU MAY BEAR FRUIT!!
HONESTLY, YOU ARE SO...!!
AAH, THAT LITTLE KICK MAKES THE SOBA THREE TIMES YUMMIER.
Whew
YOU TRIED TO CURSE NATTO THE FIRST TIME YOU ATE IT, TOO...
I'M JUST GLAD TO SEE YOU ARE SAFE.
NYOOOP
ANYWAY, IT'S GOOD TO SEE YOU, URIEL!
SORRY FOR CALLING YOU DOWN HERE FOR A SILLY THING LIKE THIS.
THAT'S ALL RIGHT. IT IS MY JOB.
I'M SORRY YOU HAD TO COME ALL THE WAY FROM HEAVEN.
IT MUST HAVE BEEN A HARD TRIP!
IF YOU LIKE, YOU COULD JOIN US FOR DINNER...
NO, I WAS NEARBY.
HUH? WAIT A MINUTE. URIEL-SAN...
...WHY ARE YOU WEARING A YUKATA FROM THIS INN?
AND YOU HAVE THAT POST-HOT SPRING GLOW...
OH, THERE YOU ARE, URIEL!!
STOMP
STOMP

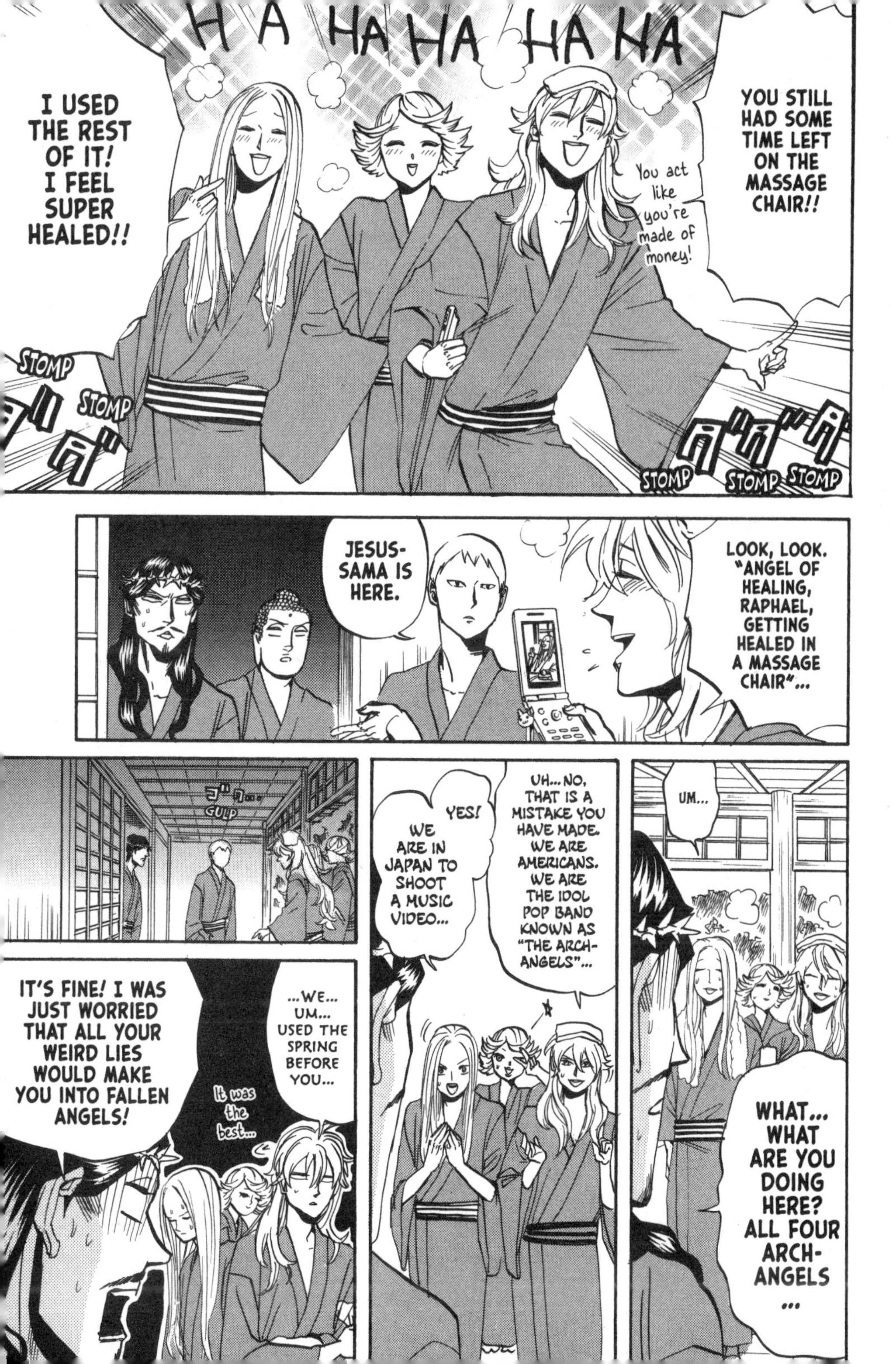
HA HA HA HA HA HA
YOU STILL HAD SOME TIME LEFT ON THE MASSAGE CHAIR!!
You act like you're made of money!
I USED THE REST OF IT! I FEEL SUPER HEALED!!
STOMP STOMP STOMP
STOMP STOMP
LOOK, LOOK. "ANGEL OF HEALING, RAPHAEL, GETTING HEALED IN A MASSAGE CHAIR"...
JESUS-SAMA IS HERE.
UM...
WHAT... WHAT ARE YOU DOING HERE? ALL FOUR ARCH-ANGELS...
UH... NO, THAT IS A MISTAKE YOU HAVE MADE. WE ARE AMERICANS. WE ARE THE IDOL POP BAND KNOWN AS "THE ARCH-ANGELS"...
YES! WE ARE IN JAPAN TO SHOOT A MUSIC VIDEO...
GULP
...WE... UM... USED THE SPRING BEFORE YOU...
It was the best...
IT'S FINE! I WAS JUST WORRIED THAT ALL YOUR WEIRD LIES WOULD MAKE YOU INTO FALLEN ANGELS!

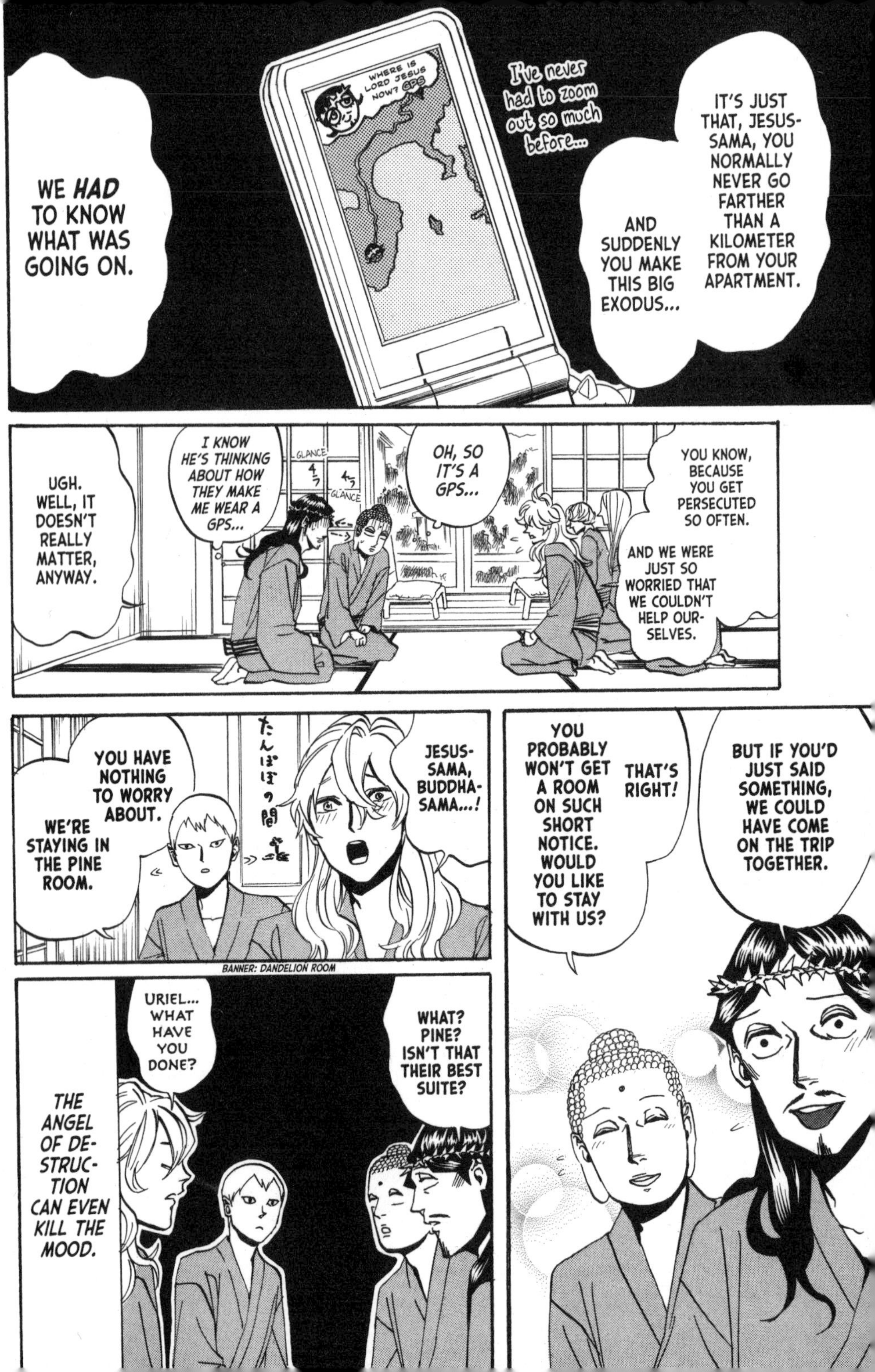
IT'S JUST THAT, JESUS-SAMA, YOU NORMALLY NEVER GO FARTHER THAN A KILOMETER FROM YOUR APARTMENT.
AND SUDDENLY YOU MAKE THIS BIG EXODUS...
I've never had to zoom out so much before...
WHERE IS LORD JESUS NOW? GPS
WE *HAD* TO KNOW WHAT WAS GOING ON.
YOU KNOW, BECAUSE YOU GET PERSECUTED SO OFTEN.
AND WE WERE JUST SO WORRIED THAT WE COULDN'T HELP OUR-SELVES.
OH, SO IT'S A GPS...
GLANCE
GLANCE
I KNOW HE'S THINKING ABOUT HOW THEY MAKE ME WEAR A GPS...
UGH. WELL, IT DOESN'T REALLY MATTER, ANYWAY.
BUT IF YOU'D JUST SAID SOMETHING, WE COULD HAVE COME ON THE TRIP TOGETHER.
THAT'S RIGHT!
YOU PROBABLY WON'T GET A ROOM ON SUCH SHORT NOTICE. WOULD YOU LIKE TO STAY WITH US?
JESUS-SAMA, BUDDHA-SAMA...!
たんぽぽの間
YOU HAVE NOTHING TO WORRY ABOUT.
WE'RE STAYING IN THE PINE ROOM.
BANNER: DANDELION ROOM
WHAT? PINE? ISN'T THAT THEIR BEST SUITE?
URIEL... WHAT HAVE YOU DONE?
THE ANGEL OF DE-STRUC-TION CAN EVEN KILL THE MOOD.

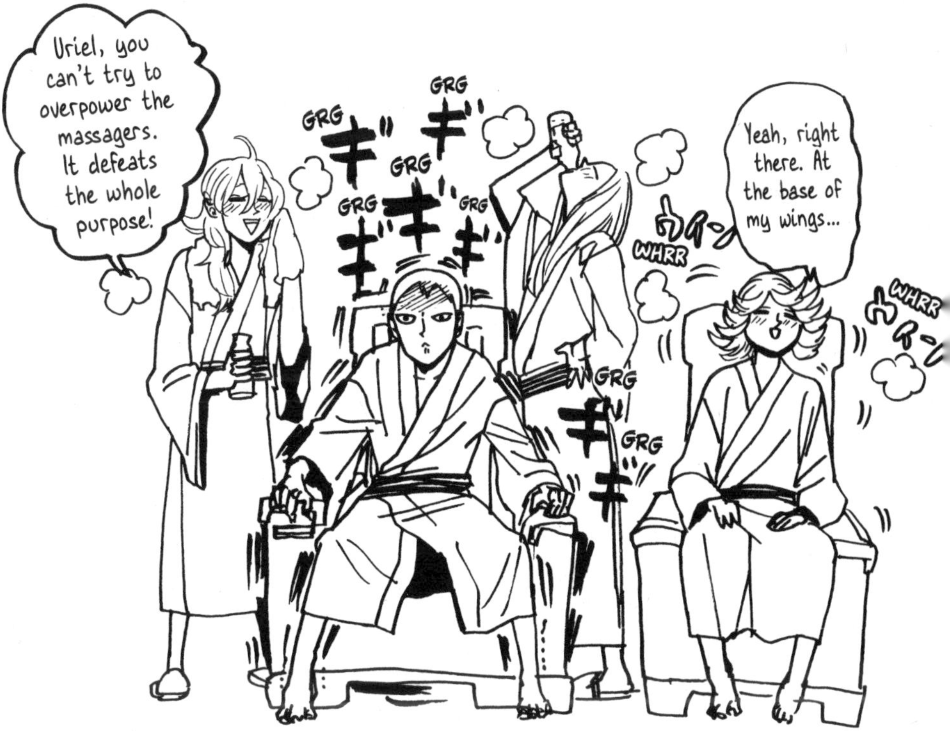
Yeah, right there. At the base of my wings...
WHRR
WHRR
GRG
GRG
GRG
GRG
GRG
GRG
GRG
Uriel, you can't try to overpower the massagers. It defeats the whole purpose!

CHAPTER 18 TRANSLATION NOTES

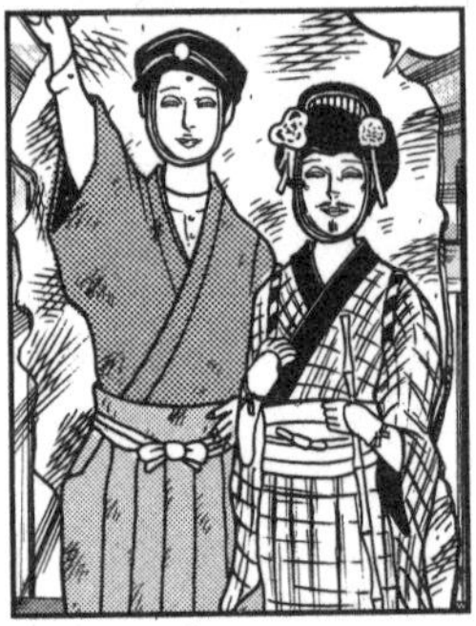

Yasunari Kawabata, page 46
Yasunari Kawabata was the first Japanese author to win the Nobel Prize for literature in 1968. One of his more famous stories is "The Dancing Girl of Izu" (*Izu no odoriko*), which is represented in the photo-op standee. Jesus and Buddha are visiting Shuzenji, which is on the Izu Peninsula where the story takes place, and the Odoriko Limited Express is named for the dancing girl.

Passport to Paradise, page 46
The Japanese title of this chapter is *Ii Tabi, Gokuraku Kibun,* meaning "good travels, feels like paradise." This is a play on *Ii Tabi, Yume Kibun* (good travels, feels like a dream), the title of a Japanese travel show.

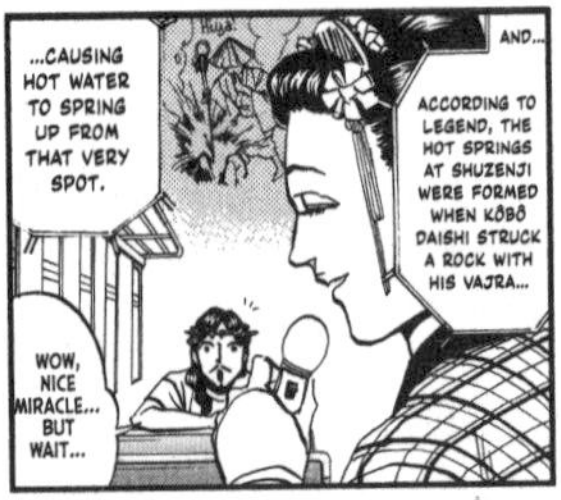
AND...
ACCORDING TO LEGEND, THE HOT SPRINGS AT SHUZENJI WERE FORMED WHEN KŌBŌ DAISHI STRUCK A ROCK WITH HIS VAJRA...
...CAUSING HOT WATER TO SPRING UP FROM THAT VERY SPOT.
WOW, NICE MIRACLE... BUT WAIT...

Kōbō Daishi, page 48
Kōbō Daishi, also known as Kūkai, is one of the most prominent Buddhist figures of Japan, and the founder of the Esoteric Shingon sect of Buddhism. The *vajra* he used to strike the rock and form the hot spring is a weapon and ritual object used in Buddhism to symbolize the indestructibility of diamond and the irresistible force of thunder.

The most hardcore hot springs buff, page 49
To be specific, Jesus names *Edokko,* or Tokyoites. Natives of Tokyo have a reputation for liking their baths extra hot.

Overturned Bucket, page 49
This is a reference to a lecture the Buddha gave to his son Rahula, using a bucket and water as an object lesson to teach him not to lie or harm others, or his training will be overturned and empty like a bucket that once held water.

Team Donkey, page 49
Before Jesus was born, his mother, Mary, rode to Bethlehem on a donkey, as opposed to a horse or a camel. Soon before he was crucified, he entered Jerusalem while riding a donkey, in accordance with prophecy.

Anything goes, page 50
Many Christian churches regularly participate in a rite known variously as the Eucharist, the Holy Communion, the Lord's Supper, or the Sacrament. While the specifics vary according to denomination, the general practice is to eat a piece of bread or wafer and drink a bit of wine, in remembrance of Jesus Christ and his sacrifice, and to show their commitment to make him and his teachings a part of themselves. The bread is his flesh, and the wine is his blood—some denominations believe it literally becomes these things, while others believe his flesh and blood are present "in, with, and under" the bread and wine. Still other denominations think of the bread and wine as symbols to commemorate the flesh and blood of Christ. Not all congregations use wine—many use grape juice, or even simply water, believing that the important thing is not the liquid itself, but that it be blessed with the right authority and partaken of properly.

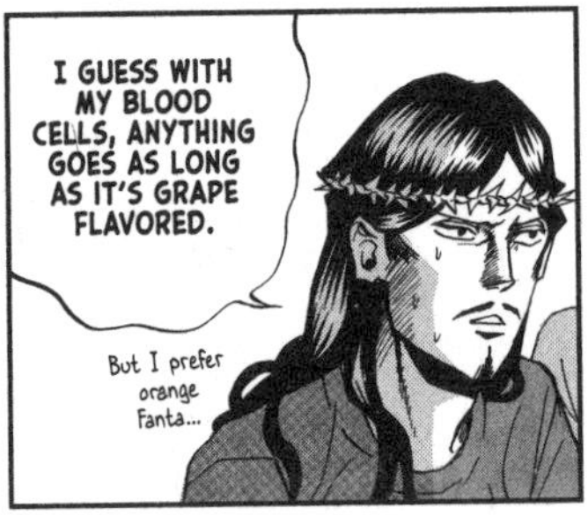
I GUESS WITH MY BLOOD CELLS, ANYTHING GOES AS LONG AS IT'S GRAPE FLAVORED.
But I prefer orange Fanta...

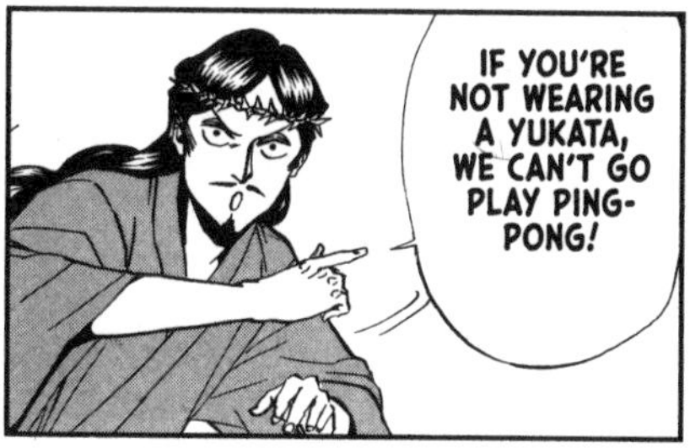
IF YOU'RE NOT WEARING A YUKATA, WE CAN'T GO PLAY PING-PONG!

Yukata, page 52
Traditional Japanese inns (and some hotels) provide *yukata* for their guests. These hotel *yukata* are a kind of lightweight, cotton *kimono* that is more like regular clothes than a bathrobe, but still used more as loungewear. Nevertheless, it's a common tourist activity to explore a hot springs resort town while wearing the *yukata* provided by one's lodgings.

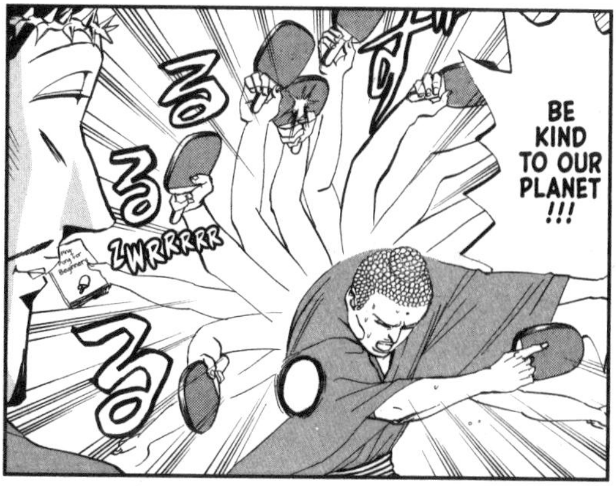
BE KIND TO OUR PLANET !!!
ZWRRRRR

Thousand-Armed Kannon, page 54
Kannon, also known as Guan Yin or Avalokiteshvara, is the Bodhisattva personifying perfect compassion. Kannon is often depicted with a thousand arms in painting and sculpture, which is generally thought to show a dedication towards helping all those who seek compassion.

Let no fruit grow, page 57
This line closely resembles one spoken by Jesus on his way to the temple in Jerusalem. He came upon a fig tree that was covered in leaves, but there was no fruit, he cursed it to an eternity of barrenness for its hypocrisy, and before long the tree withered away and died.

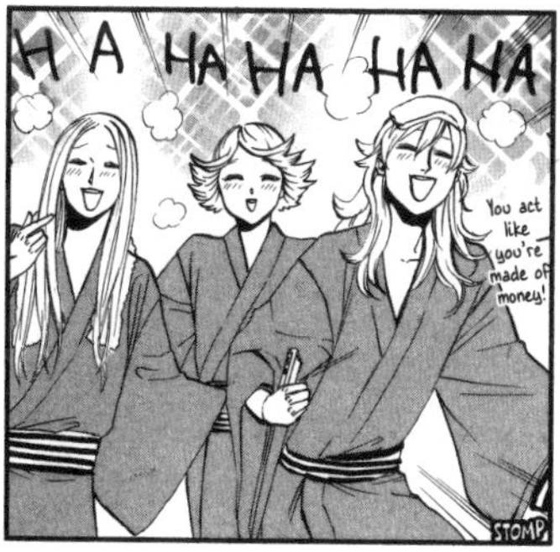
HA HA HA HA HA HA
You act like you're made of money!
STOMP

All four archangels, page 59
Archangels are the highest-ranking angels in the service of God. The number of archangels varies according to religion, but for the purposes of this story, there are four.

SAINT☆YOUNG MEN

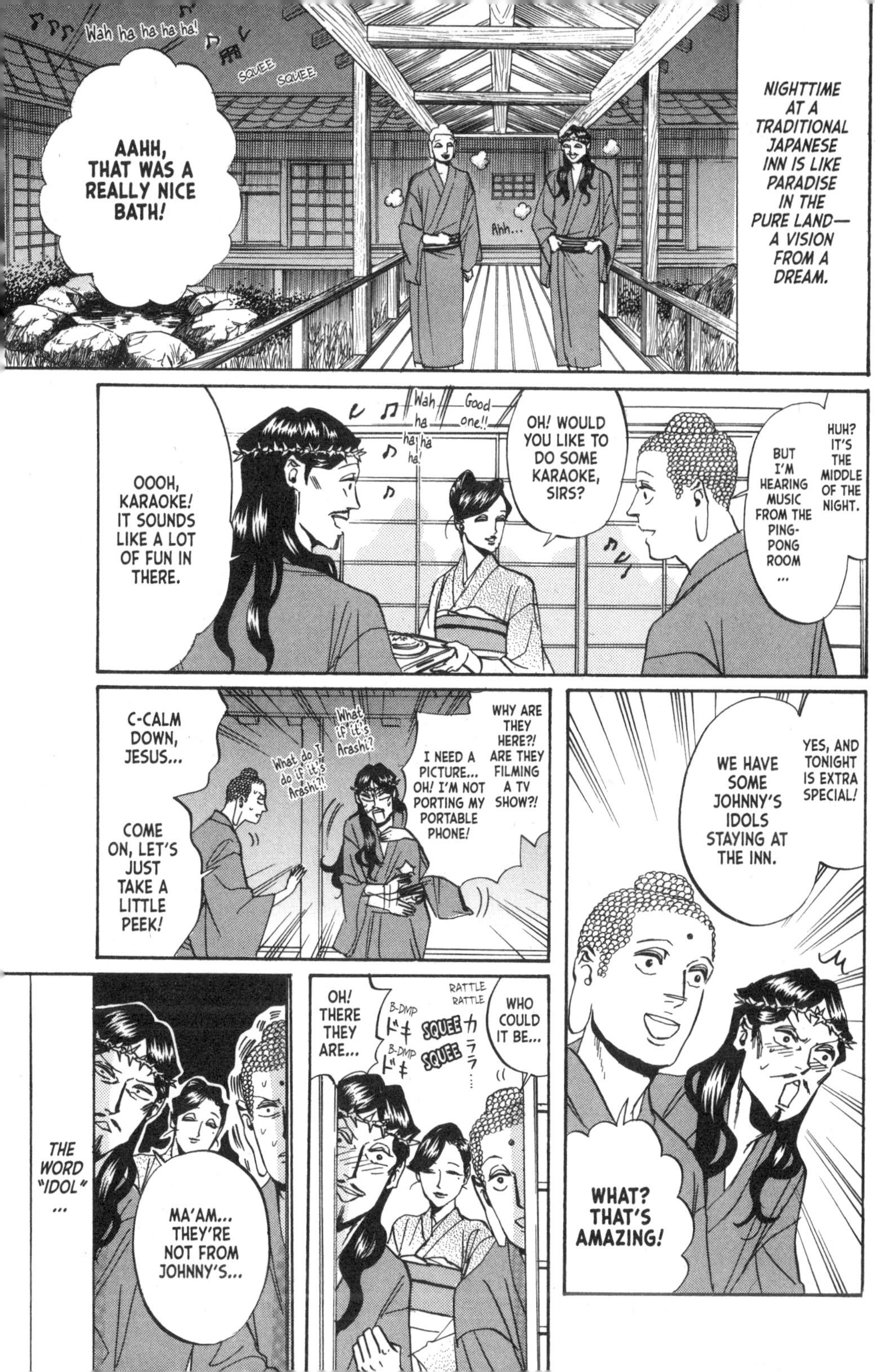
NIGHTTIME AT A TRADITIONAL JAPANESE INN IS LIKE PARADISE IN THE PURE LAND—A VISION FROM A DREAM.
Ahh...
AAHH, THAT WAS A REALLY NICE BATH!
Wah ha ha ha ha!
SQUEE SQUEE
HUH? IT'S THE MIDDLE OF THE NIGHT.
BUT I'M HEARING MUSIC FROM THE PING-PONG ROOM...
OH! WOULD YOU LIKE TO DO SOME KARAOKE, SIRS?
Good one!!
Wah ha ha ha ha!
OOOH, KARAOKE! IT SOUNDS LIKE A LOT OF FUN IN THERE.
YES, AND TONIGHT IS EXTRA SPECIAL!
WE HAVE SOME JOHNNY'S IDOLS STAYING AT THE INN.
WHAT? THAT'S AMAZING!
WHY ARE THEY HERE?! ARE THEY FILMING A TV SHOW?!
I NEED A PICTURE... OH! I'M NOT PORTING MY PORTABLE PHONE!
What if it's Arashi?
What do I do if it's Arashi?!
C-CALM DOWN, JESUS...
COME ON, LET'S JUST TAKE A LITTLE PEEK!
WHO COULD IT BE...
RATTLE RATTLE
カララ...
SQUEE SQUEE
B-DMP ドキ
B-DMP ドキ
OH! THERE THEY ARE...
MA'AM... THEY'RE NOT FROM JOHNNY'S...
THE WORD "IDOL"...

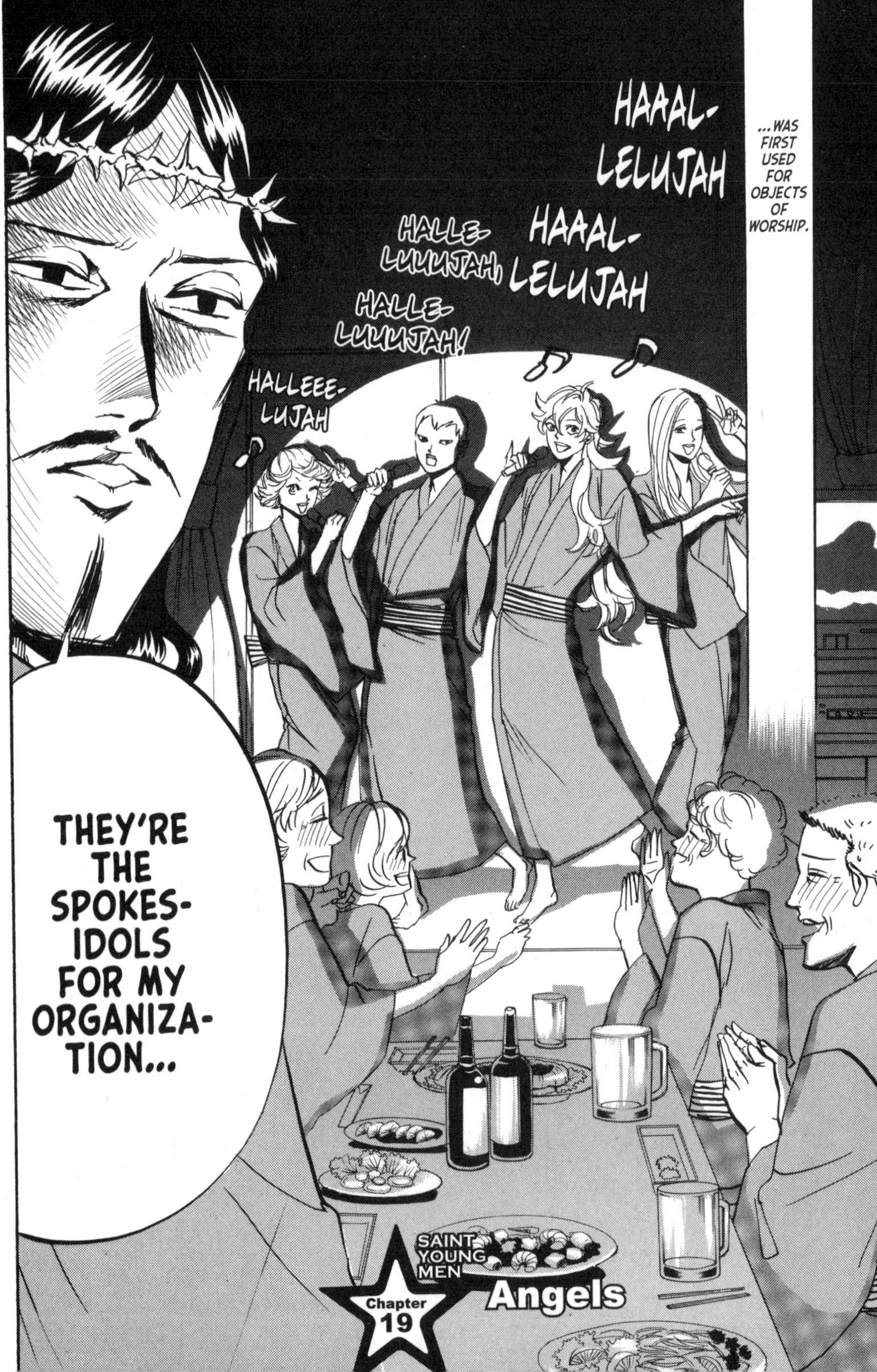
...WAS FIRST USED FOR OBJECTS OF WORSHIP.
HAAAL-LELUJAH
HAAAL-LELUJAH
HALLE-LUUUJAH,
HALLE-LUUUJAH!
HALLEEE-LUJAH
THEY'RE THE SPOKES-IDOLS FOR MY ORGANIZA-TION...
SAINT YOUNG MEN
Chapter 19
Angels

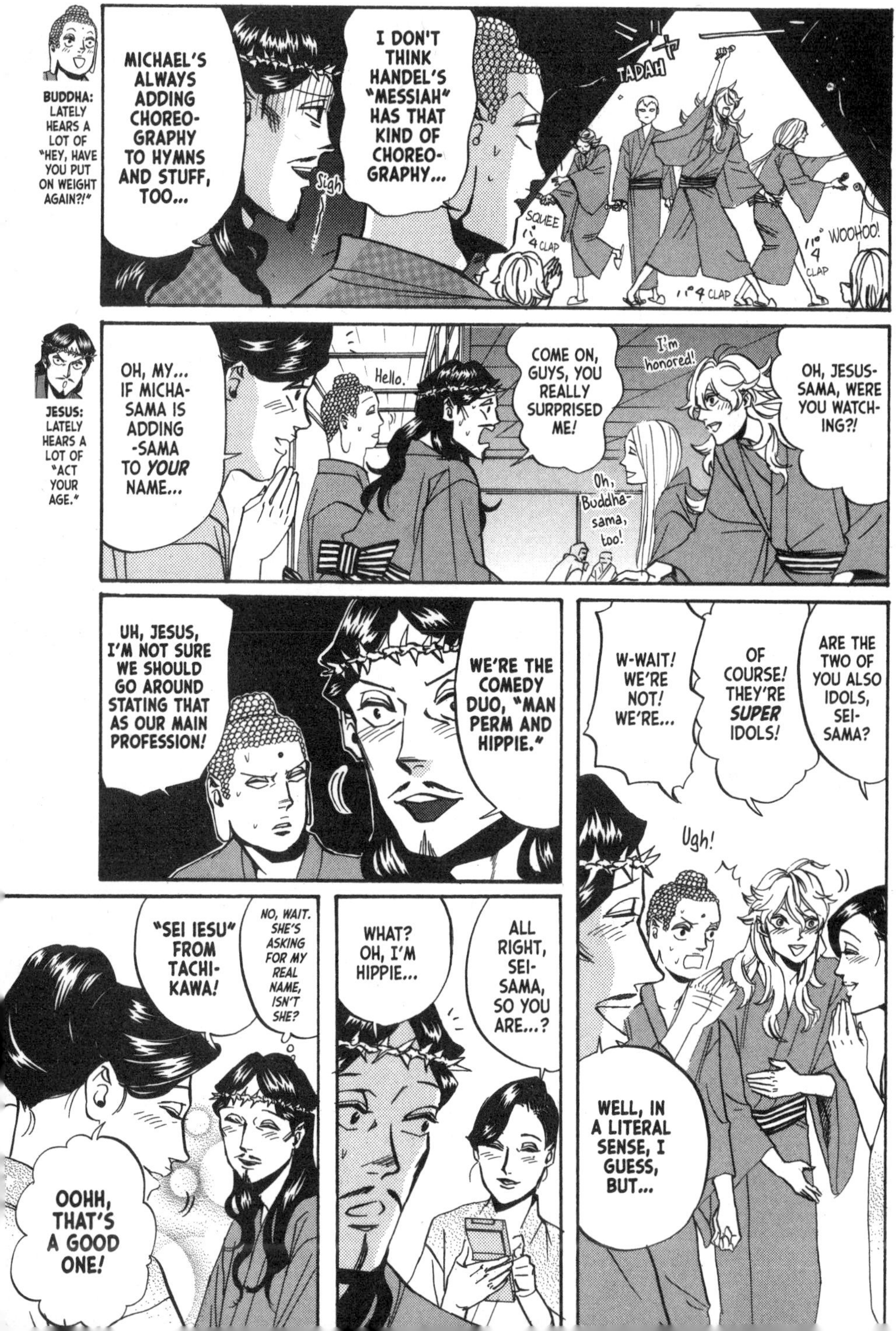
TADAH
WOOHOO!
CLAP
CLAP
SQUEE
CLAP
I DON'T THINK HANDEL'S "MESSIAH" HAS THAT KIND OF CHOREOGRAPHY...
Sigh
MICHAEL'S ALWAYS ADDING CHOREOGRAPHY TO HYMNS AND STUFF, TOO...
BUDDHA: LATELY HEARS A LOT OF "HEY, HAVE YOU PUT ON WEIGHT AGAIN?!"
OH, JESUS-SAMA, WERE YOU WATCHING?!
I'm honored!
COME ON, GUYS, YOU REALLY SURPRISED ME!
Oh, Buddha-sama, too!
Hello.
OH, MY... IF MICHA-SAMA IS ADDING -SAMA TO YOUR NAME...
JESUS: LATELY HEARS A LOT OF "ACT YOUR AGE."
ARE THE TWO OF YOU ALSO IDOLS, SEI-SAMA?
OF COURSE! THEY'RE SUPER IDOLS!
W-WAIT! WE'RE NOT! WE'RE...
Ugh!
WELL, IN A LITERAL SENSE, I GUESS, BUT...
WE'RE THE COMEDY DUO, "MAN PERM AND HIPPIE."
UH, JESUS, I'M NOT SURE WE SHOULD GO AROUND STATING THAT AS OUR MAIN PROFESSION!
ALL RIGHT, SEI-SAMA, SO YOU ARE...?
WHAT? OH, I'M HIPPIE...
NO, WAIT. SHE'S ASKING FOR MY REAL NAME, ISN'T SHE?
"SEI IESU" FROM TACHIKAWA!
OOHH, THAT'S A GOOD ONE!

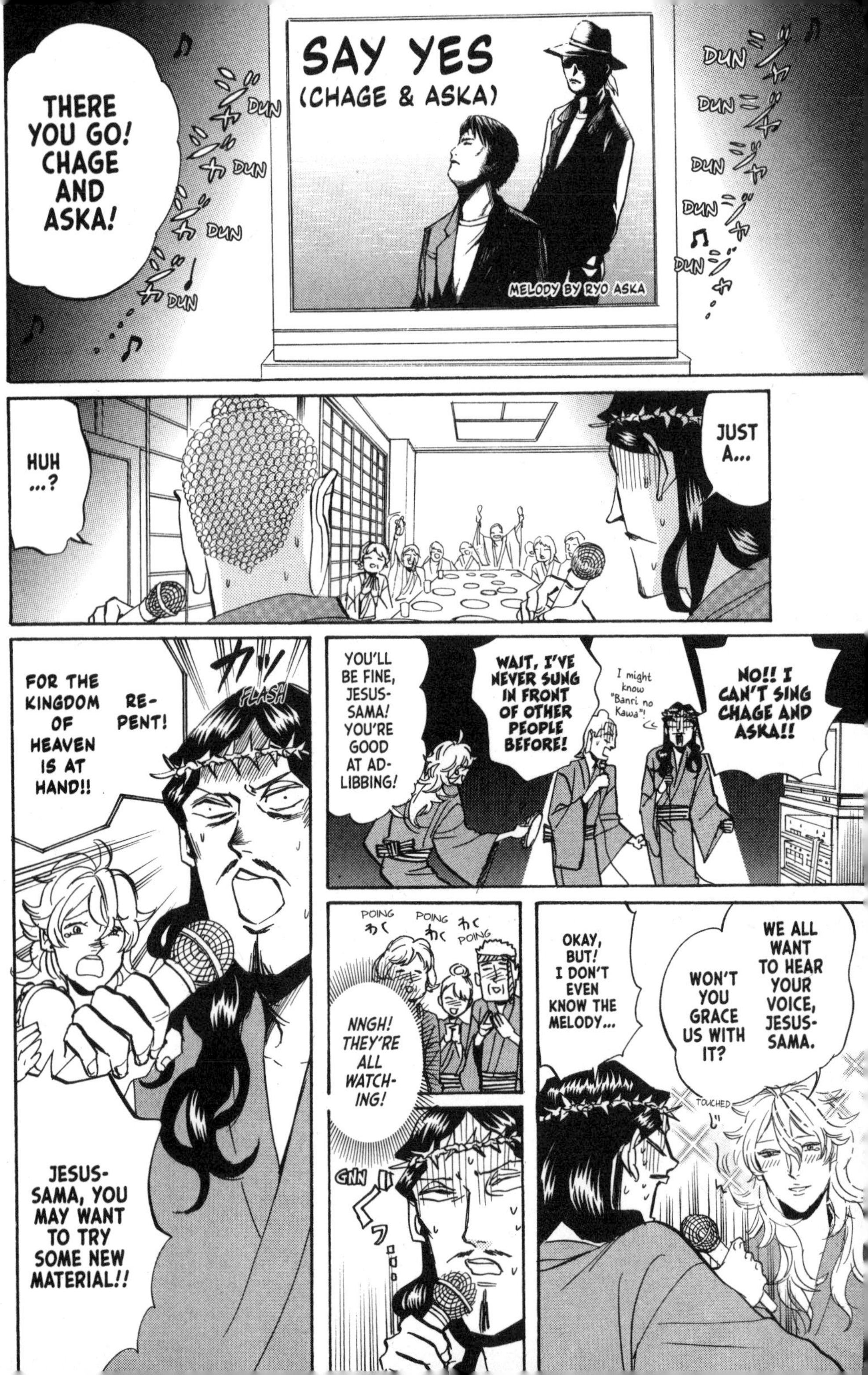
DUN DUN DUN DUN DUN
SAY YES
(CHAGE & ASKA)
MELODY BY RYO ASKA
DUN DUN DUN DUN
THERE YOU GO! CHAGE AND ASKA!
JUST A...
HUH ...?
NO!! I CAN'T SING CHAGE AND ASKA!!
I might know "Banri no Kawa"!
WAIT, I'VE NEVER SUNG IN FRONT OF OTHER PEOPLE BEFORE!
YOU'LL BE FINE, JESUS-SAMA! YOU'RE GOOD AT AD-LIBBING!
WE ALL WANT TO HEAR YOUR VOICE, JESUS-SAMA.
WON'T YOU GRACE US WITH IT?
TOUCHED
OKAY, BUT! I DON'T EVEN KNOW THE MELODY...
POING POING POING
NNGH! THEY'RE ALL WATCHING!
GNN
FLASH
REPENT!
FOR THE KINGDOM OF HEAVEN IS AT HAND!!
JESUS-SAMA, YOU MAY WANT TO TRY SOME NEW MATERIAL!!

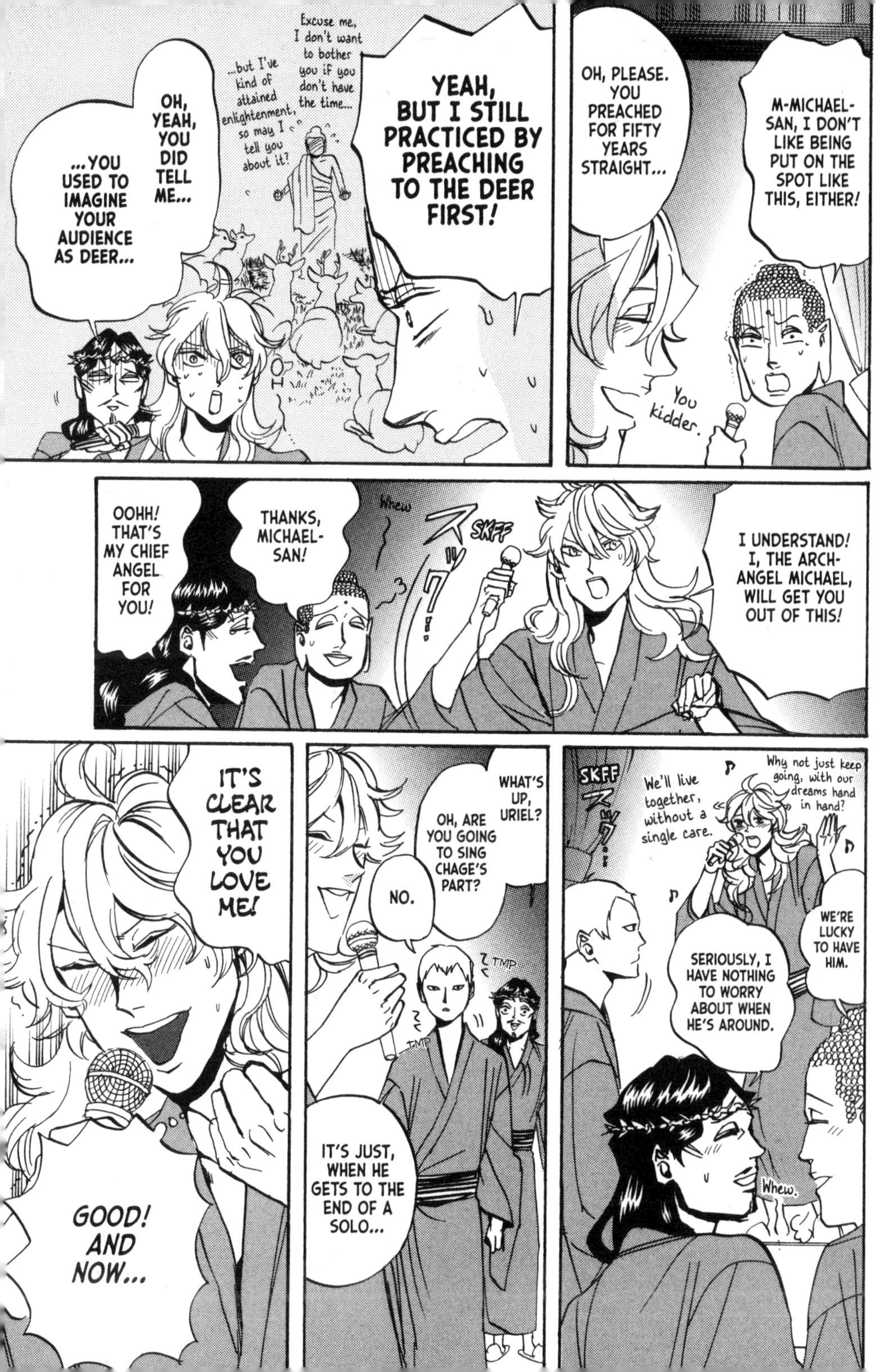

M-MICHAEL-SAN, I DON'T LIKE BEING PUT ON THE SPOT LIKE THIS, EITHER!
OH, PLEASE. YOU PREACHED FOR FIFTY YEARS STRAIGHT...
You kidder.
YEAH, BUT I STILL PRACTICED BY PREACHING TO THE DEER FIRST!
Excuse me, I don't want to bother you if you don't have the time...
...but I've kind of attained enlightenment, so may I tell you about it?
OH, YEAH, YOU DID TELL ME...
...YOU USED TO IMAGINE YOUR AUDIENCE AS DEER...
I UNDERSTAND! I, THE ARCH-ANGEL MICHAEL, WILL GET YOU OUT OF THIS!
SKFF
Whew
THANKS, MICHAEL-SAN!
OOHH! THAT'S MY CHIEF ANGEL FOR YOU!
SKFF
Why not just keep going, with our dreams hand in hand?
We'll live together, without a single care.
WE'RE LUCKY TO HAVE HIM.
SERIOUSLY, I HAVE NOTHING TO WORRY ABOUT WHEN HE'S AROUND.
Whew.
WHAT'S UP, URIEL?
OH, ARE YOU GOING TO SING CHAGE'S PART?
NO.
TMP
TMP
IT'S JUST, WHEN HE GETS TO THE END OF A SOLO...
IT'S CLEAR THAT YOU LOVE ME!
GOOD! AND NOW...

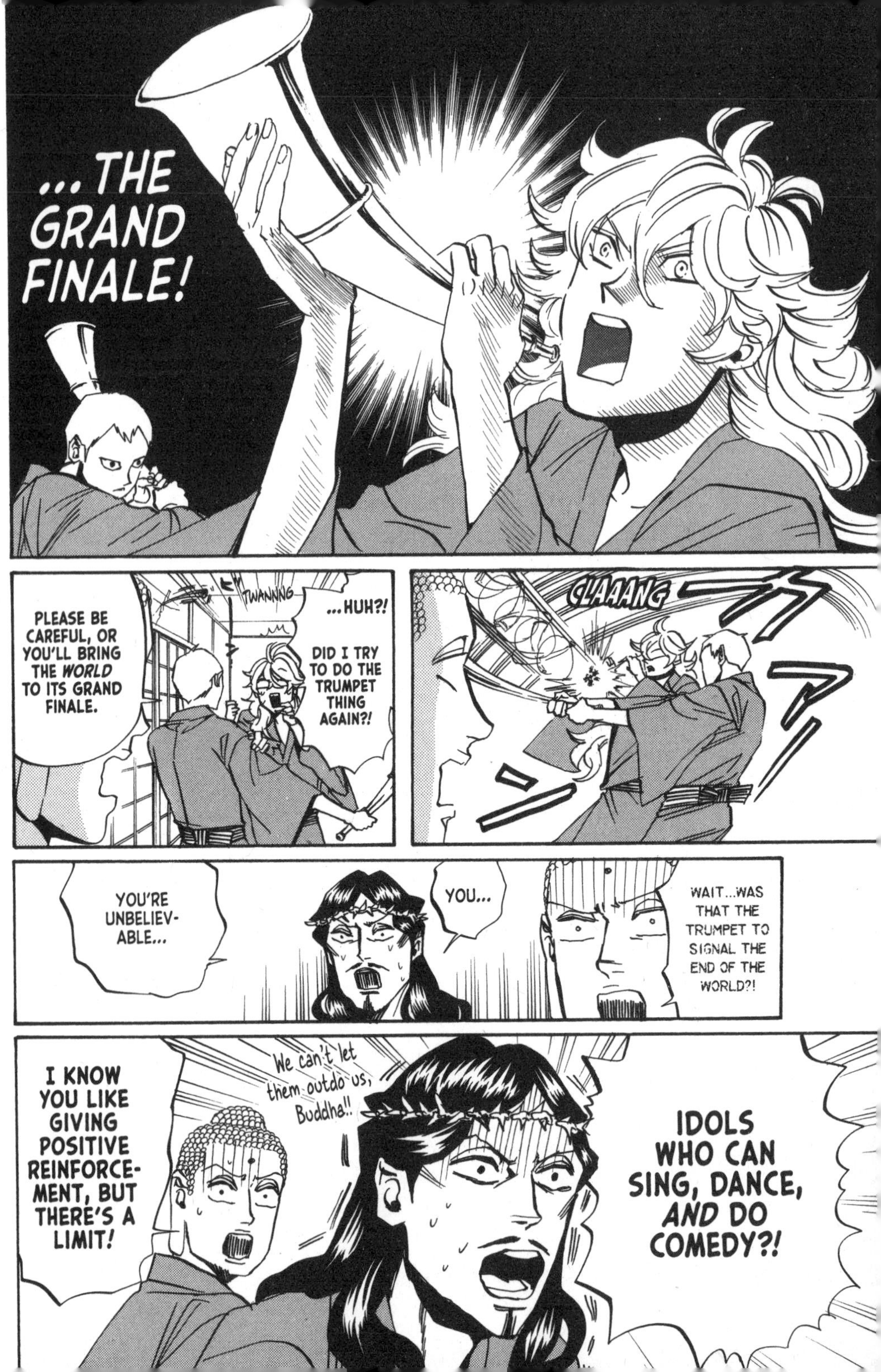
...THE GRAND FINALE!
CLAAANG
...HUH?!
DID I TRY TO DO THE TRUMPET THING AGAIN?!
TWANNNG
PLEASE BE CAREFUL, OR YOU'LL BRING THE *WORLD* TO ITS GRAND FINALE.
WAIT...WAS THAT THE TRUMPET TO SIGNAL THE END OF THE WORLD?!
YOU...
YOU'RE UNBELIEV-ABLE...
IDOLS WHO CAN SING, DANCE, *AND* DO COMEDY?!
We can't let them outdo us, Buddha!!
I KNOW YOU LIKE GIVING POSITIVE REINFORCE-MENT, BUT THERE'S A LIMIT!

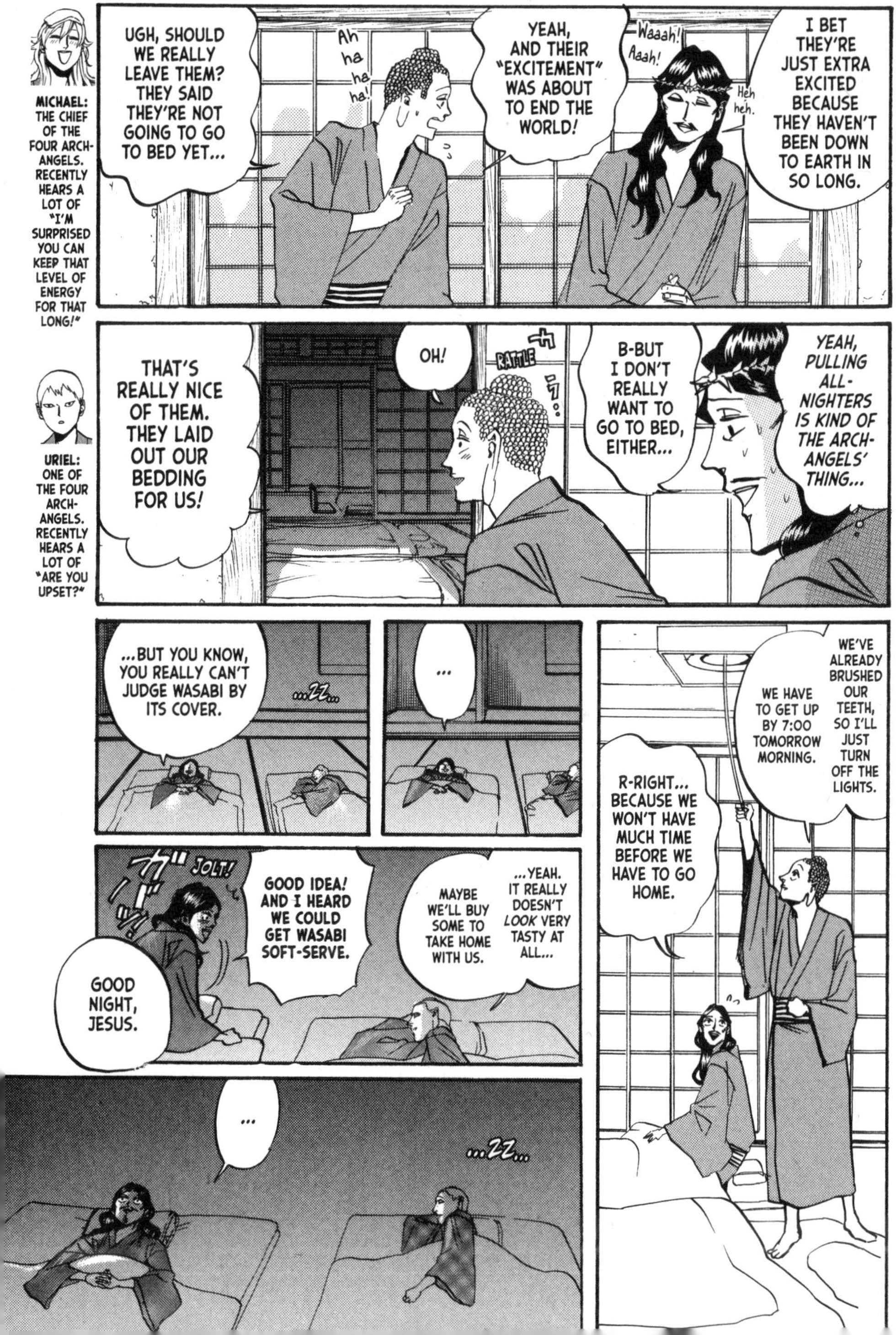
I BET THEY'RE JUST EXTRA EXCITED BECAUSE THEY HAVEN'T BEEN DOWN TO EARTH IN SO LONG.
Heh heh.
Waaah! Aaah!
YEAH, AND THEIR "EXCITEMENT" WAS ABOUT TO END THE WORLD!
Ah ha ha ha!
UGH, SHOULD WE REALLY LEAVE THEM? THEY SAID THEY'RE NOT GOING TO GO TO BED YET...
MICHAEL: THE CHIEF OF THE FOUR ARCH-ANGELS. RECENTLY HEARS A LOT OF "I'M SURPRISED YOU CAN KEEP THAT LEVEL OF ENERGY FOR THAT LONG!"
YEAH, PULLING ALL-NIGHTERS IS KIND OF THE ARCH-ANGELS' THING...
B-BUT I DON'T REALLY WANT TO GO TO BED, EITHER...
RATTLE
OH!
THAT'S REALLY NICE OF THEM. THEY LAID OUT OUR BEDDING FOR US!
URIEL: ONE OF THE FOUR ARCH-ANGELS. RECENTLY HEARS A LOT OF "ARE YOU UPSET?"
WE'VE ALREADY BRUSHED OUR TEETH, SO I'LL JUST TURN OFF THE LIGHTS.
WE HAVE TO GET UP BY 7:00 TOMORROW MORNING.
R-RIGHT... BECAUSE WE WON'T HAVE MUCH TIME BEFORE WE HAVE TO GO HOME.
...
...BUT YOU KNOW, YOU REALLY CAN'T JUDGE WASABI BY ITS COVER.
...zz...
...YEAH. IT REALLY DOESN'T LOOK VERY TASTY AT ALL...
MAYBE WE'LL BUY SOME TO TAKE HOME WITH US.
GOOD IDEA! AND I HEARD WE COULD GET WASABI SOFT-SERVE.
JOLT!
GOOD NIGHT, JESUS.
...zz...
...

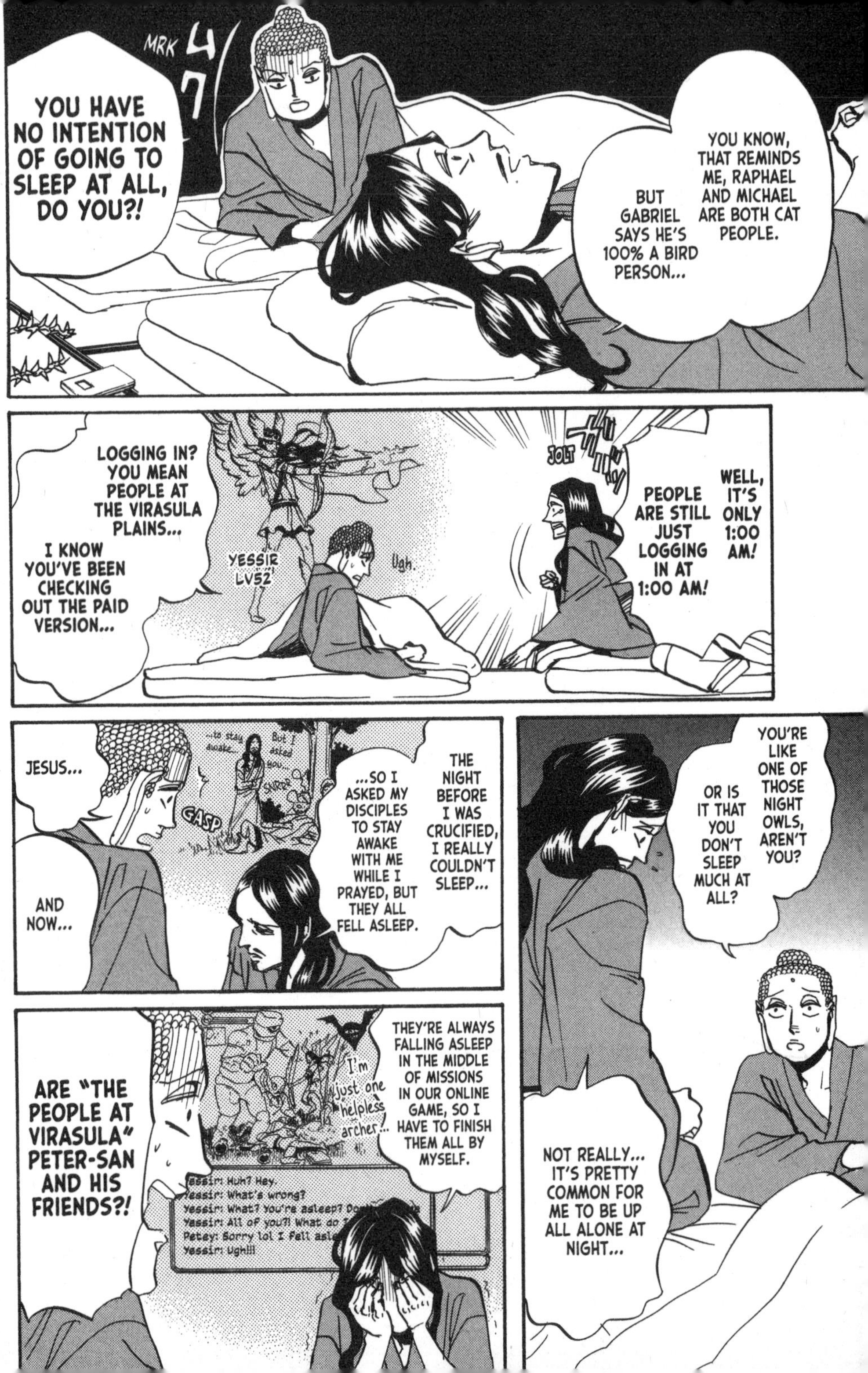

YOU KNOW, THAT REMINDS ME, RAPHAEL AND MICHAEL ARE BOTH CAT PEOPLE.
BUT GABRIEL SAYS HE'S 100% A BIRD PERSON...
MRK
YOU HAVE NO INTENTION OF GOING TO SLEEP AT ALL, DO YOU?!
WELL, IT'S ONLY 1:00 AM!
PEOPLE ARE STILL JUST LOGGING IN AT 1:00 AM!
JOLT
Ugh.
YESSIR LV52
LOGGING IN? YOU MEAN PEOPLE AT THE VIRASULA PLAINS...
I KNOW YOU'VE BEEN CHECKING OUT THE PAID VERSION...
YOU'RE LIKE ONE OF THOSE NIGHT OWLS, AREN'T YOU?
OR IS IT THAT YOU DON'T SLEEP MUCH AT ALL?
NOT REALLY... IT'S PRETTY COMMON FOR ME TO BE UP ALL ALONE AT NIGHT...
THE NIGHT BEFORE I WAS CRUCIFIED, I REALLY COULDN'T SLEEP...
...SO I ASKED MY DISCIPLES TO STAY AWAKE WITH ME WHILE I PRAYED, BUT THEY ALL FELL ASLEEP.
But I asked you...
...to stay awake...
SNRRR
GASP
JESUS...
AND NOW...
THEY'RE ALWAYS FALLING ASLEEP IN THE MIDDLE OF MISSIONS IN OUR ONLINE GAME, SO I HAVE TO FINISH THEM ALL BY MYSELF.
I'm just one helpless archer...
Yessir: Huh? Hey.
Yessir: What's wrong?
Yessir: What? You're asleep?
Yessir: All of you?! What do
Petey: Sorry lol I fell asle
Yessir: Ugh!!!
ARE "THE PEOPLE AT VIRASULA" PETER-SAN AND HIS FRIENDS?!

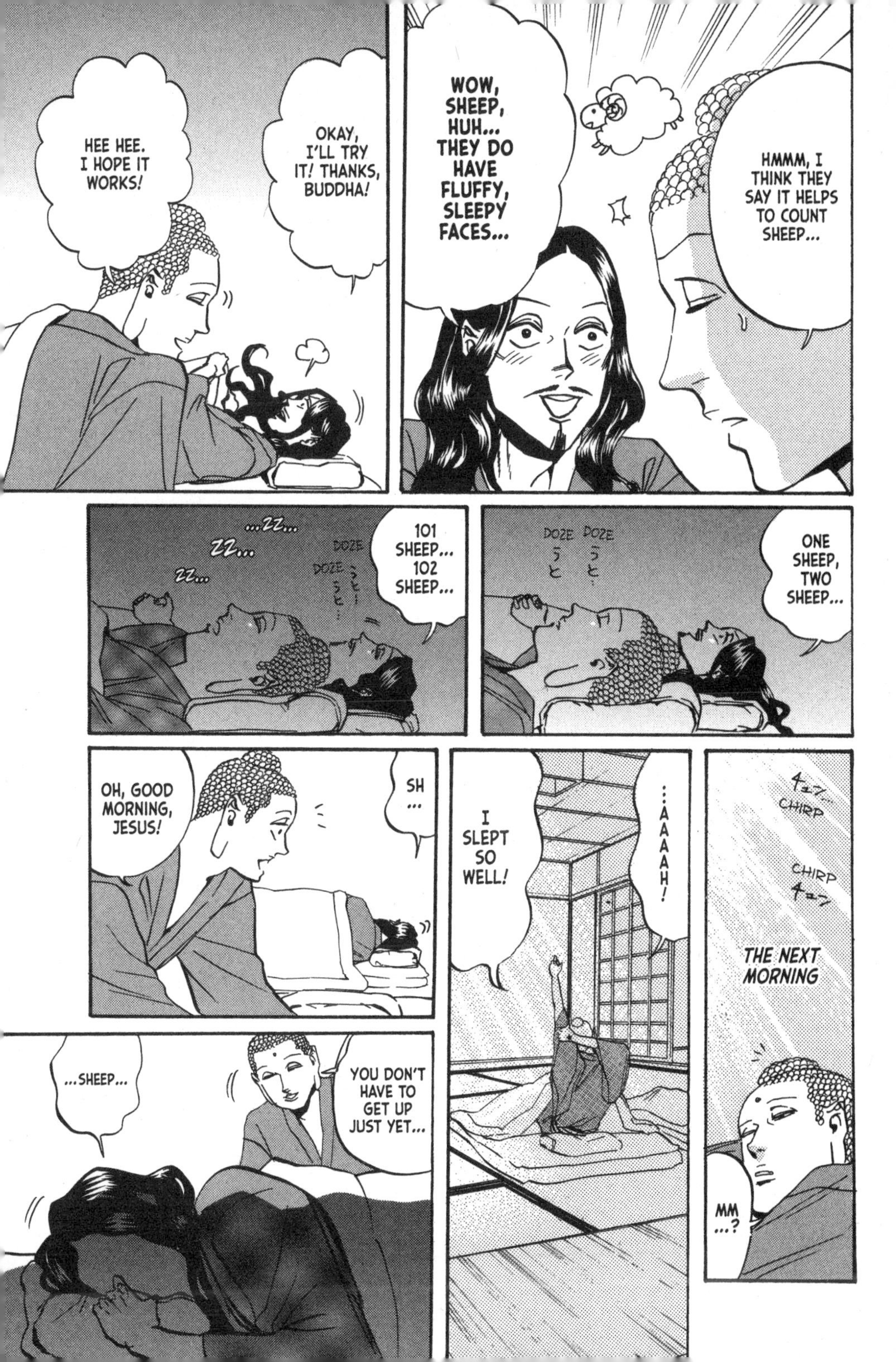
HMMM, I THINK THEY SAY IT HELPS TO COUNT SHEEP...
WOW, SHEEP, HUH... THEY DO HAVE FLUFFY, SLEEPY FACES...
OKAY, I'LL TRY IT! THANKS, BUDDHA!
HEE HEE. I HOPE IT WORKS!
DOZE DOZE
ONE SHEEP, TWO SHEEP...
101 SHEEP... 102 SHEEP...
DOZE DOZE
ZZ...
ZZ...
...ZZ...
CHIRP
CHIRP
THE NEXT MORNING
MM ...?
...AAAAAH!
I SLEPT SO WELL!
SH ...
OH, GOOD MORNING, JESUS!
YOU DON'T HAVE TO GET UP JUST YET...
...SHEEP...

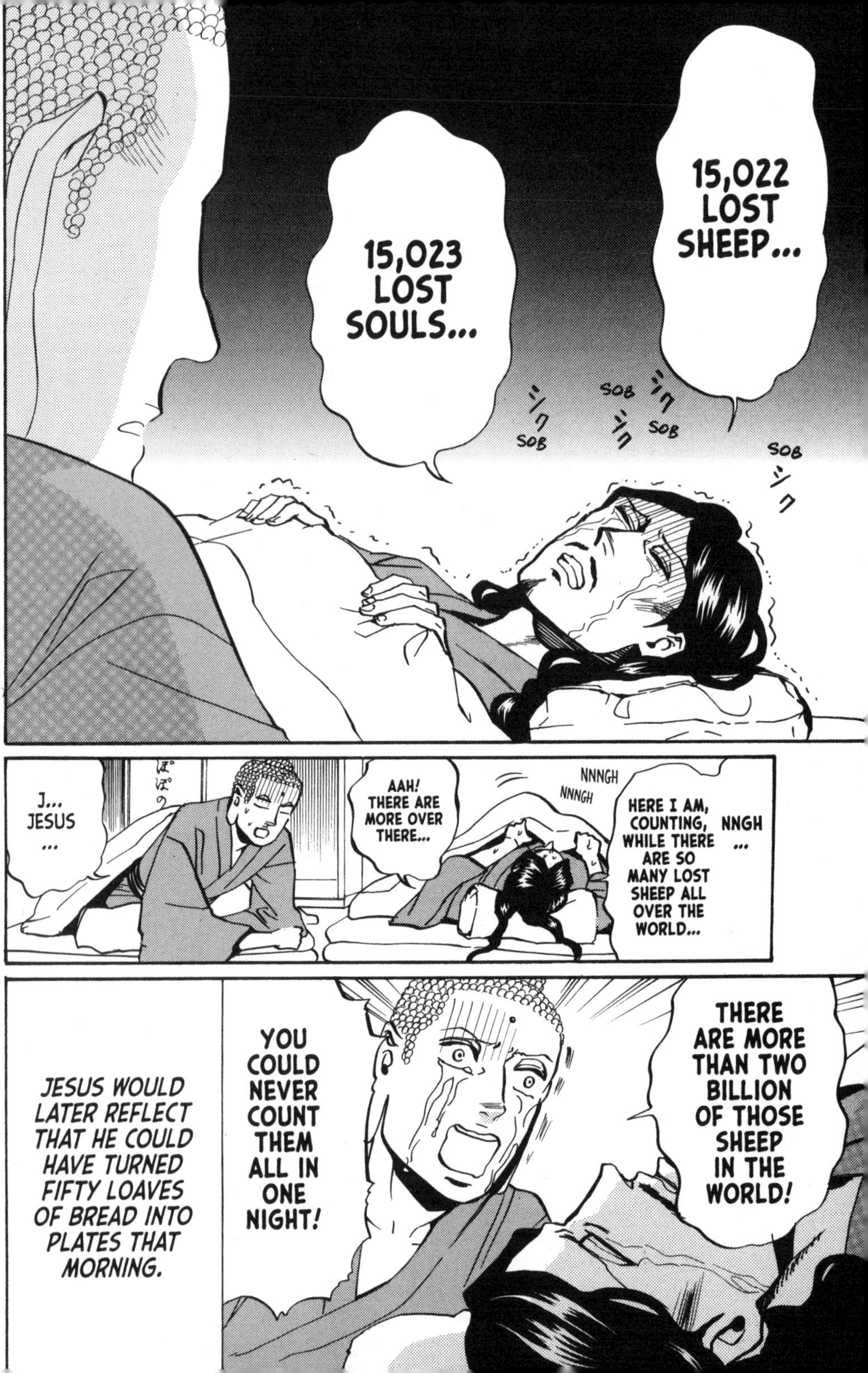
15,022 LOST SHEEP...
15,023 LOST SOULS...
SOB シク
SOB シク SOB シク
シク SOB
NNGH ...
HERE I AM, COUNTING, WHILE THERE ARE SO MANY LOST SHEEP ALL OVER THE WORLD...
NNNGH NNNGH
AAH! THERE ARE MORE OVER THERE...
J... JESUS ...
THERE ARE MORE THAN TWO BILLION OF THOSE SHEEP IN THE WORLD!
YOU COULD NEVER COUNT THEM ALL IN ONE NIGHT!
JESUS WOULD LATER REFLECT THAT HE COULD HAVE TURNED FIFTY LOAVES OF BREAD INTO PLATES THAT MORNING.

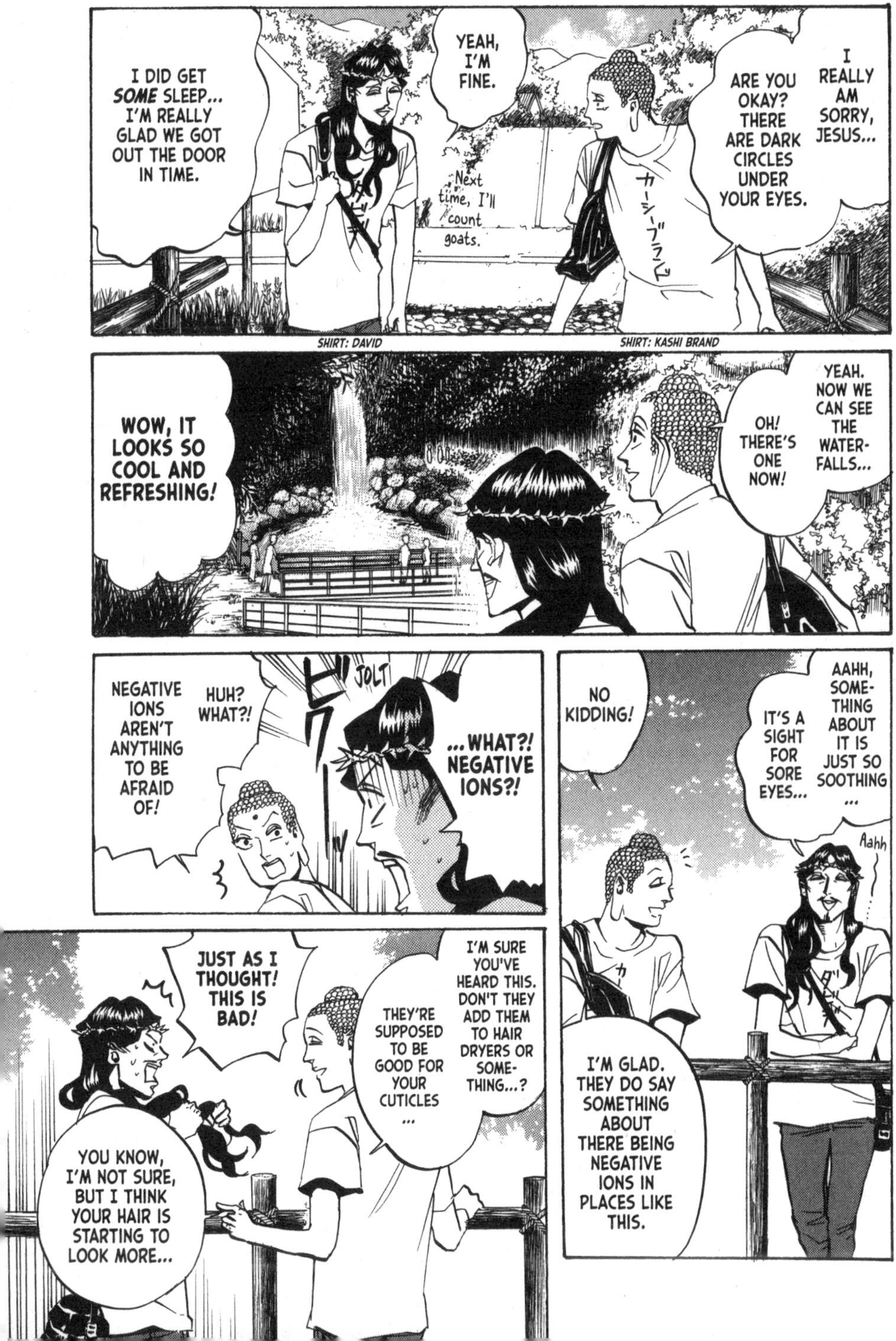
I REALLY AM SORRY, JESUS...
ARE YOU OKAY? THERE ARE DARK CIRCLES UNDER YOUR EYES.
YEAH, I'M FINE.
Next time, I'll count goats.
I DID GET SOME SLEEP... I'M REALLY GLAD WE GOT OUT THE DOOR IN TIME.
SHIRT: KASHI BRAND
SHIRT: DAVID
YEAH. NOW WE CAN SEE THE WATERFALLS...
OH! THERE'S ONE NOW!
WOW, IT LOOKS SO COOL AND REFRESHING!
AAHH, SOMETHING ABOUT IT IS JUST SO SOOTHING...
IT'S A SIGHT FOR SORE EYES...
NO KIDDING!
Aahh
I'M GLAD. THEY DO SAY SOMETHING ABOUT THERE BEING NEGATIVE IONS IN PLACES LIKE THIS.
JOLT
...WHAT?! NEGATIVE IONS?!
HUH? WHAT?!
NEGATIVE IONS AREN'T ANYTHING TO BE AFRAID OF!
I'M SURE YOU'VE HEARD THIS. DON'T THEY ADD THEM TO HAIR DRYERS OR SOMETHING...?
THEY'RE SUPPOSED TO BE GOOD FOR YOUR CUTICLES...
JUST AS I THOUGHT! THIS IS BAD!
YOU KNOW, I'M NOT SURE, BUT I THINK YOUR HAIR IS STARTING TO LOOK MORE...

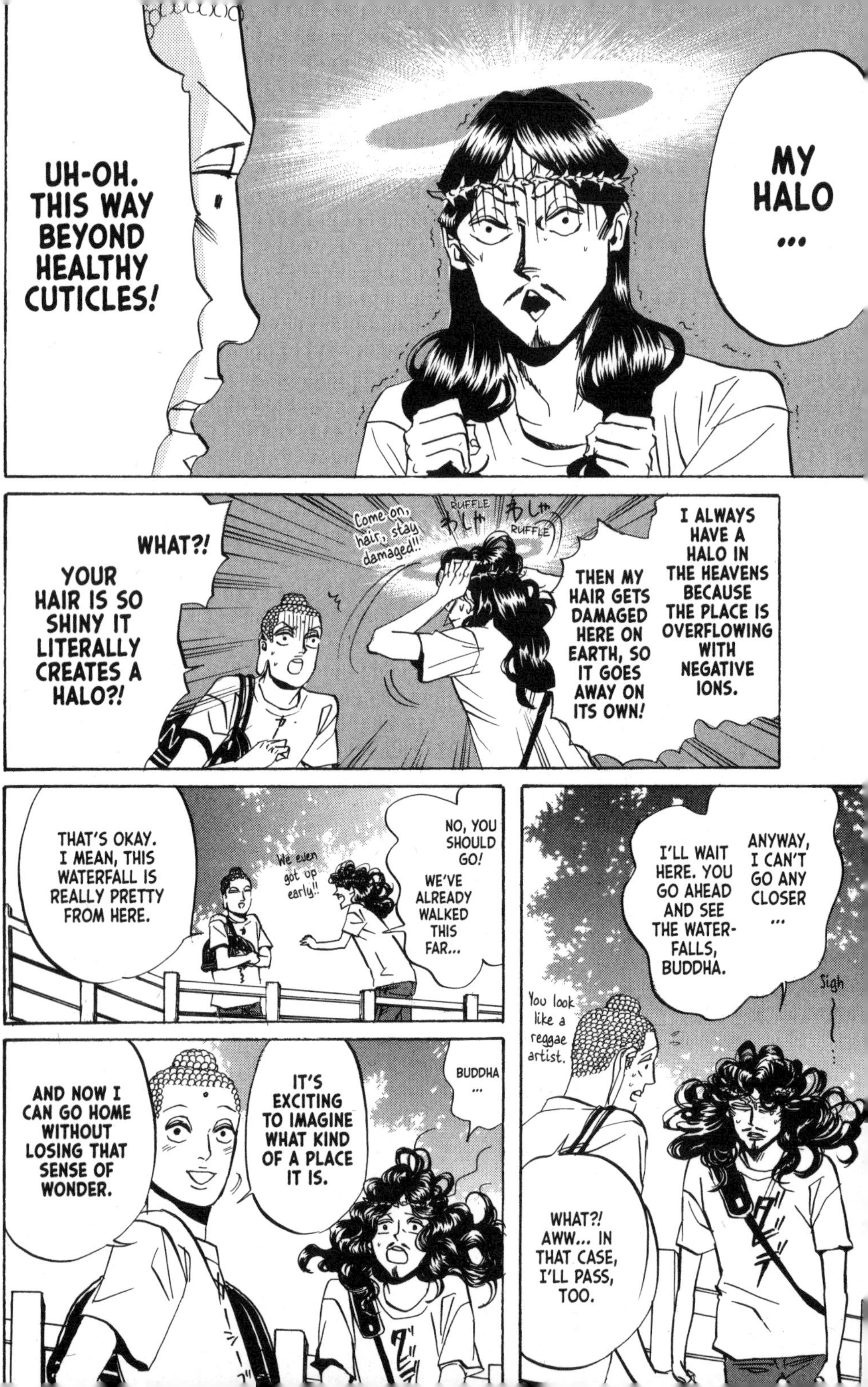

MY HALO ...
UH-OH. THIS WAY BEYOND HEALTHY CUTICLES!
I ALWAYS HAVE A HALO IN THE HEAVENS BECAUSE THE PLACE IS OVERFLOWING WITH NEGATIVE IONS.
THEN MY HAIR GETS DAMAGED HERE ON EARTH, SO IT GOES AWAY ON ITS OWN!
RUFFLE
RUFFLE
Come on, hair, stay damaged!!
WHAT?!
YOUR HAIR IS SO SHINY IT LITERALLY CREATES A HALO?!
ANYWAY, I CAN'T GO ANY CLOSER ...
Sigh
I'LL WAIT HERE. YOU GO AHEAD AND SEE THE WATER-FALLS, BUDDHA.
You look like a reggae artist.
WHAT?! AWW... IN THAT CASE, I'LL PASS, TOO.
NO, YOU SHOULD GO! WE'VE ALREADY WALKED THIS FAR...
We even got up early!!
THAT'S OKAY. I MEAN, THIS WATERFALL IS REALLY PRETTY FROM HERE.
BUDDHA ...
IT'S EXCITING TO IMAGINE WHAT KIND OF A PLACE IT IS.
AND NOW I CAN GO HOME WITHOUT LOSING THAT SENSE OF WONDER.

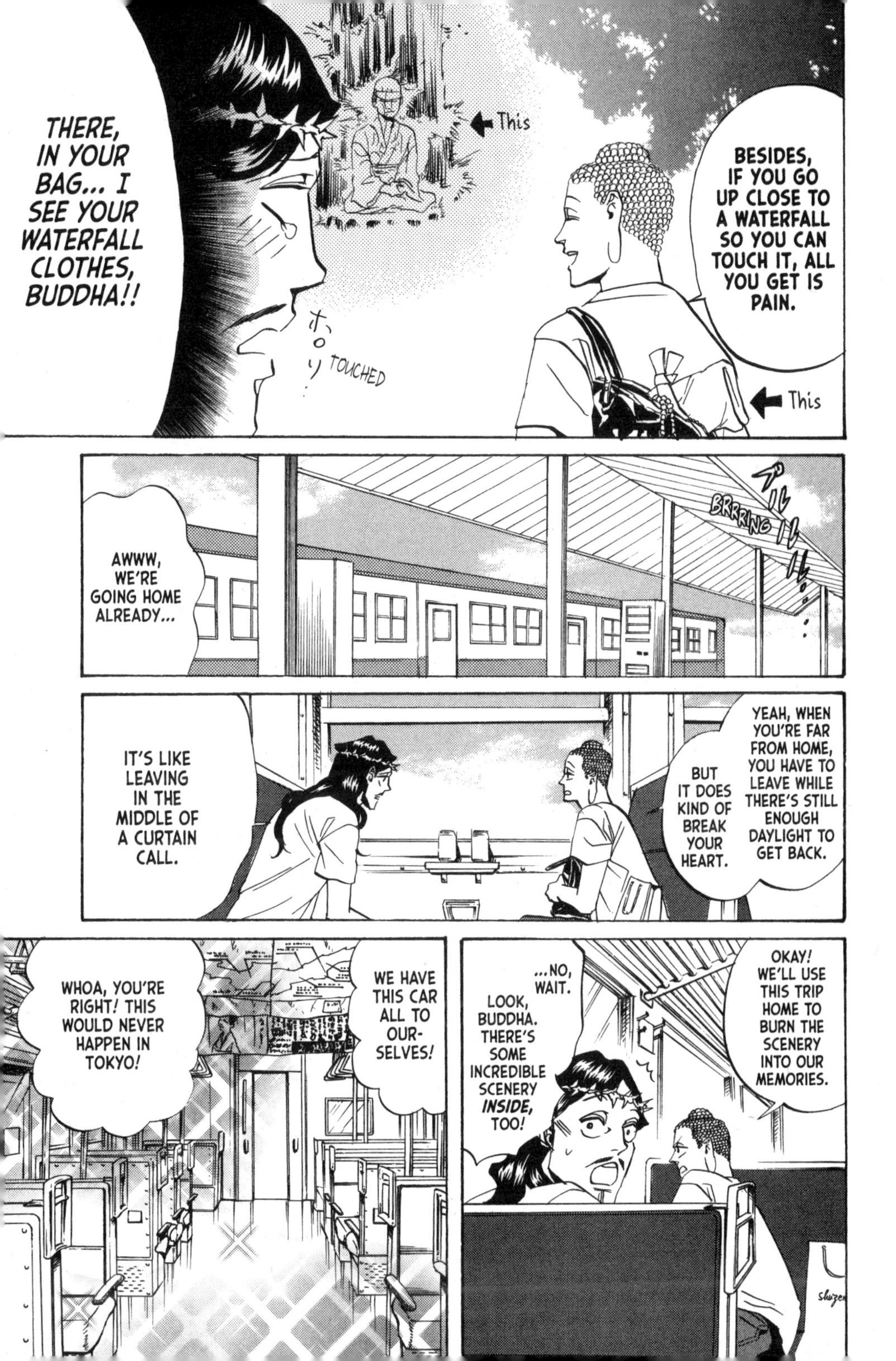

BESIDES, IF YOU GO UP CLOSE TO A WATERFALL SO YOU CAN TOUCH IT, ALL YOU GET IS PAIN.
This
THERE, IN YOUR BAG... I SEE YOUR WATERFALL CLOTHES, BUDDHA!!
This
TOUCHED
BRRRING
AWWW, WE'RE GOING HOME ALREADY...
YEAH, WHEN YOU'RE FAR FROM HOME, YOU HAVE TO LEAVE WHILE THERE'S STILL ENOUGH DAYLIGHT TO GET BACK.
BUT IT DOES KIND OF BREAK YOUR HEART.
IT'S LIKE LEAVING IN THE MIDDLE OF A CURTAIN CALL.
OKAY! WE'LL USE THIS TRIP HOME TO BURN THE SCENERY INTO OUR MEMORIES.
...NO, WAIT.
LOOK, BUDDHA. THERE'S SOME INCREDIBLE SCENERY *INSIDE*, TOO!
WE HAVE THIS CAR ALL TO OURSELVES!
WHOA, YOU'RE RIGHT! THIS WOULD NEVER HAPPEN IN TOKYO!

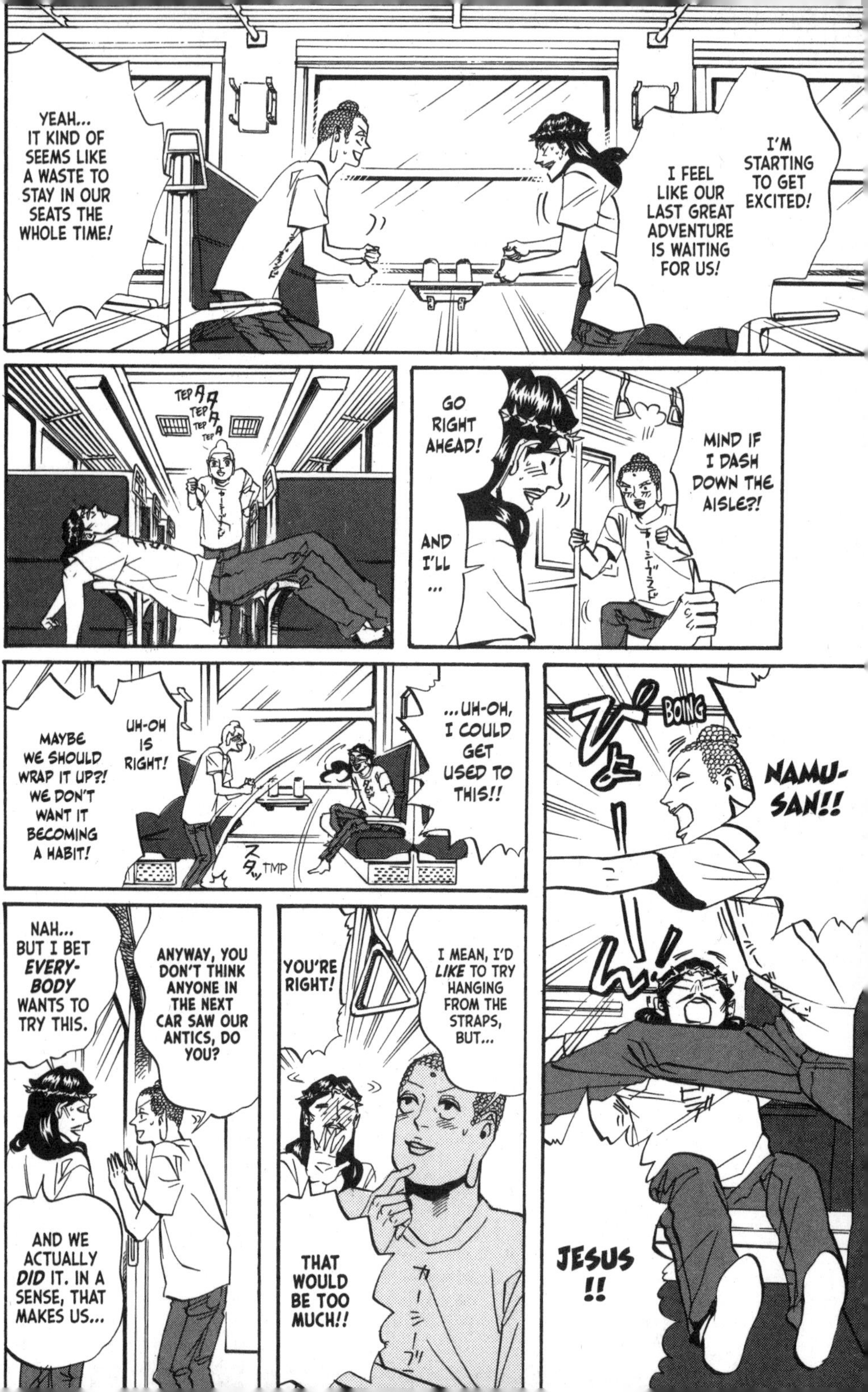
I'M STARTING TO GET EXCITED!
I FEEL LIKE OUR LAST GREAT ADVENTURE IS WAITING FOR US!
YEAH... IT KIND OF SEEMS LIKE A WASTE TO STAY IN OUR SEATS THE WHOLE TIME!
MIND IF I DASH DOWN THE AISLE?!
GO RIGHT AHEAD!
AND I'LL ...
TEP TEP TEP TEP
BOING
NAMU-SAN!!
JESUS !!
...UH-OH, I COULD GET USED TO THIS!!
UH-OH IS RIGHT!
MAYBE WE SHOULD WRAP IT UP?! WE DON'T WANT IT BECOMING A HABIT!
TMP
I MEAN, I'D LIKE TO TRY HANGING FROM THE STRAPS, BUT...
YOU'RE RIGHT!
THAT WOULD BE TOO MUCH!!
ANYWAY, YOU DON'T THINK ANYONE IN THE NEXT CAR SAW OUR ANTICS, DO YOU?
NAH... BUT I BET EVERYBODY WANTS TO TRY THIS.
AND WE ACTUALLY DID IT. IN A SENSE, THAT MAKES US...

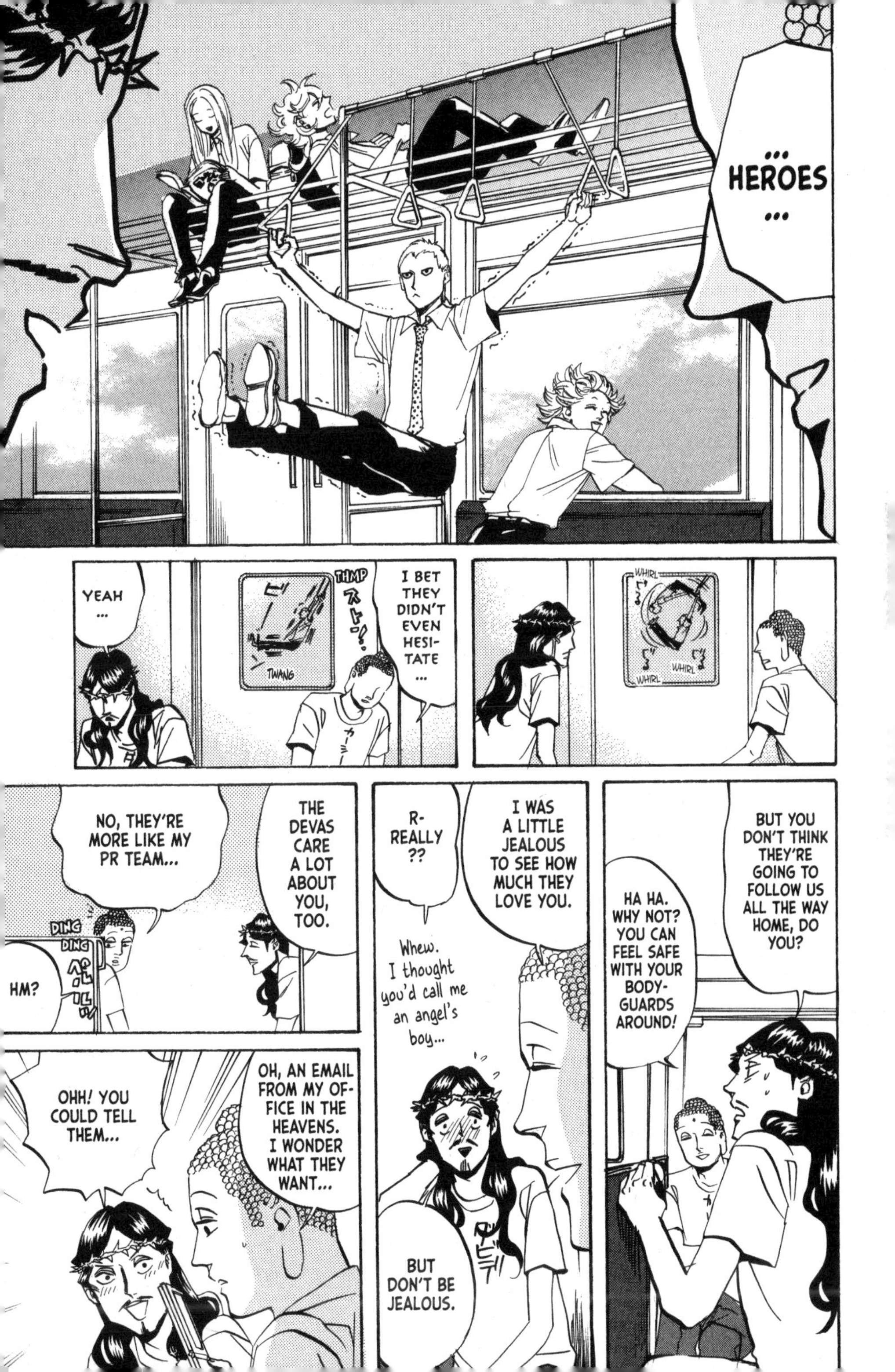
...HEROES...
WHIRL
WHIRL
WHIRL
I BET THEY DIDN'T EVEN HESITATE...
THMP
TWANG
YEAH...
BUT YOU DON'T THINK THEY'RE GOING TO FOLLOW US ALL THE WAY HOME, DO YOU?
HA HA. WHY NOT? YOU CAN FEEL SAFE WITH YOUR BODY-GUARDS AROUND!
I WAS A LITTLE JEALOUS TO SEE HOW MUCH THEY LOVE YOU.
R-REALLY??
Whew. I thought you'd call me an angel's boy...
BUT DON'T BE JEALOUS.
THE DEVAS CARE A LOT ABOUT YOU, TOO.
NO, THEY'RE MORE LIKE MY PR TEAM...
DING
DING
HM?
OH, AN EMAIL FROM MY OFFICE IN THE HEAVENS. I WONDER WHAT THEY WANT...
OHH! YOU COULD TELL THEM...

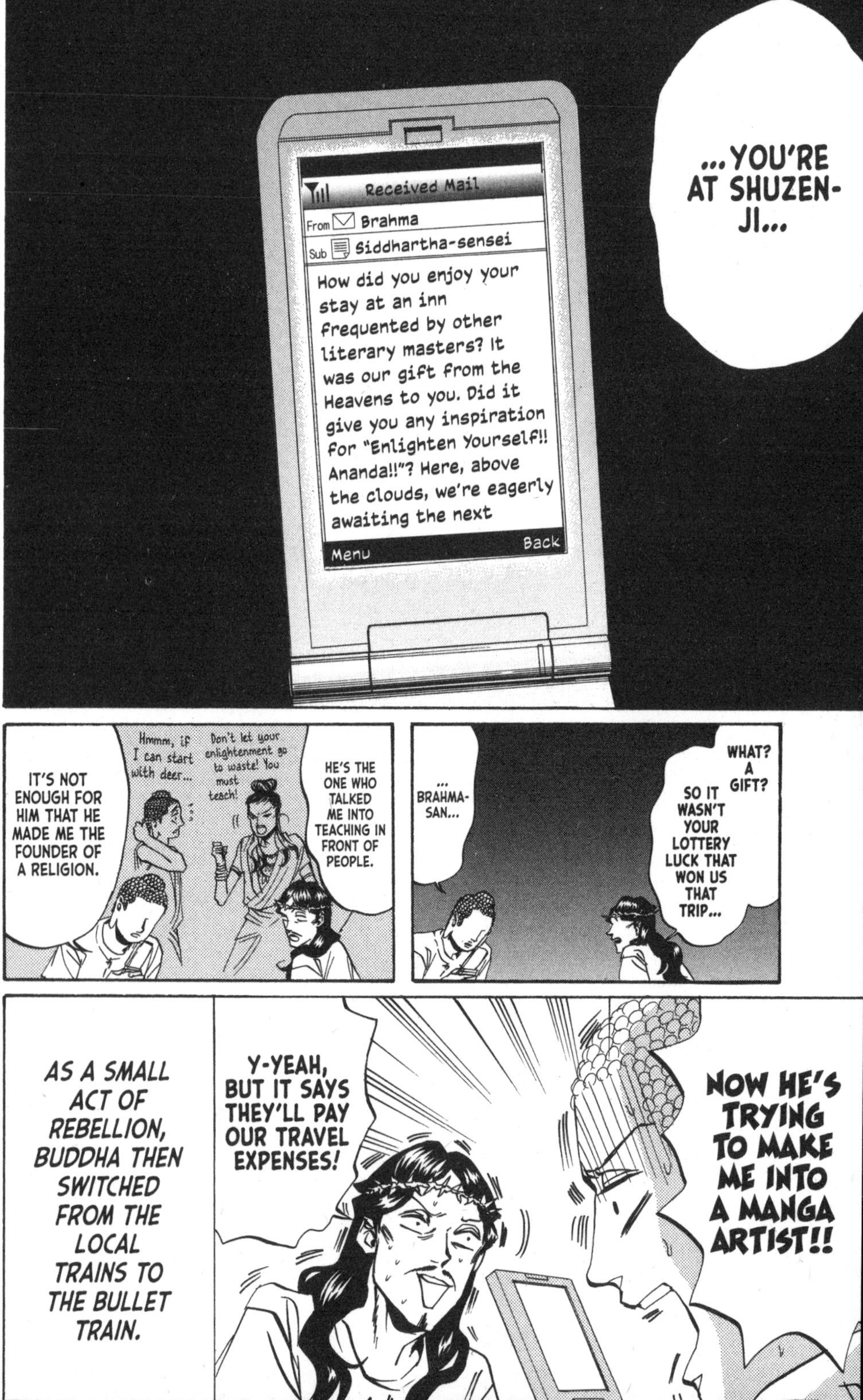
...YOU'RE AT SHUZEN-JI...
Received Mail
From Brahma
Sub Siddhartha-sensei
How did you enjoy your stay at an inn frequented by other literary masters? It was our gift from the Heavens to you. Did it give you any inspiration for "Enlighten Yourself!! Ananda!!"? Here, above the clouds, we're eagerly awaiting the next
Menu
Back
WHAT? A GIFT?
SO IT WASN'T YOUR LOTTERY LUCK THAT WON US THAT TRIP...
...BRAHMA-SAN...
HE'S THE ONE WHO TALKED ME INTO TEACHING IN FRONT OF PEOPLE.
Don't let your enlightenment go to waste! You must teach!
Hmmm, if I can start with deer...
IT'S NOT ENOUGH FOR HIM THAT HE MADE ME THE FOUNDER OF A RELIGION.
NOW HE'S TRYING TO MAKE ME INTO A MANGA ARTIST!!
Y-YEAH, BUT IT SAYS THEY'LL PAY OUR TRAVEL EXPENSES!
AS A SMALL ACT OF REBELLION, BUDDHA THEN SWITCHED FROM THE LOCAL TRAINS TO THE BULLET TRAIN.

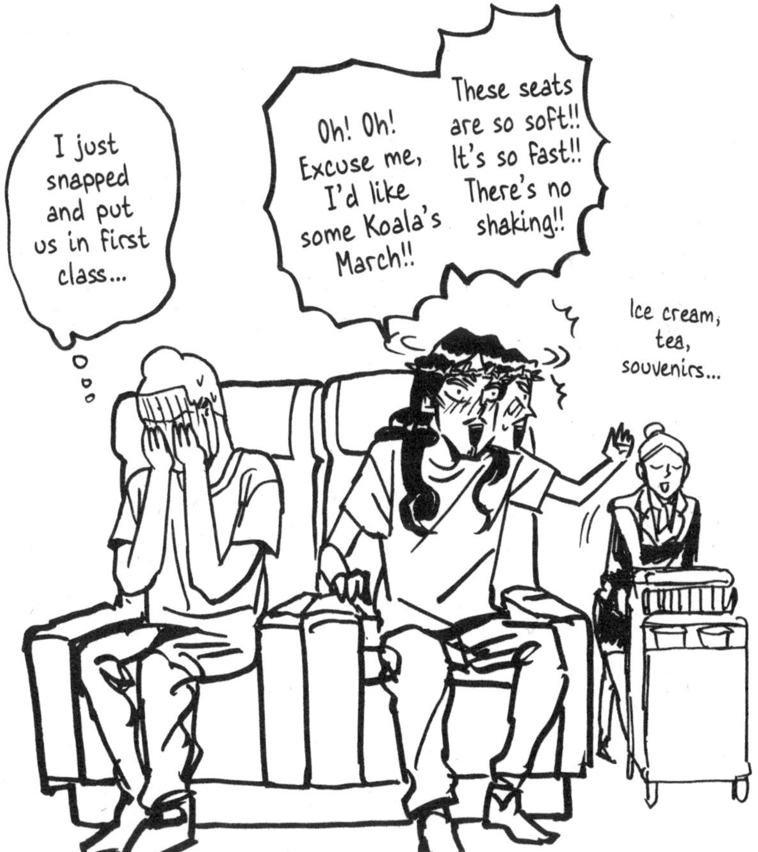
Ice cream, tea, souvenirs...
These seats are so soft!! It's so fast!! There's no shaking!!
Oh! Oh! Excuse me, I'd like some Koala's March!!
I just snapped and put us in first class...

CHAPTER 19 TRANSLATION NOTES

Johnny's idols, page 65
Johnny's is a collection of male pop star idols represented by a famous talent agency called Johnny & Associates. They manage many different boy bands, including the famous Arashi.

Sei Iesu from Tachikawa, page 67
In Japan, Jesus's name is pronounced Iesu. This is because Christianity was first brought to Japan by the Portuguese in 1549, when they were pronouncing the J like a Y, and did not use the final S. As a result, the Japanese pronunciation of the name sounds exactly like the Japanese pronunciation of the English word "yes."

Chage and Aska, page 68
Chage and Aska are a Japanese pop duo. Their first hit was "*Banri no Kara* (Thousand-Mile River)" in 1980, and "Say Yes" spent 13 consecutive weeks at the top of the charts when it came out in 1991.

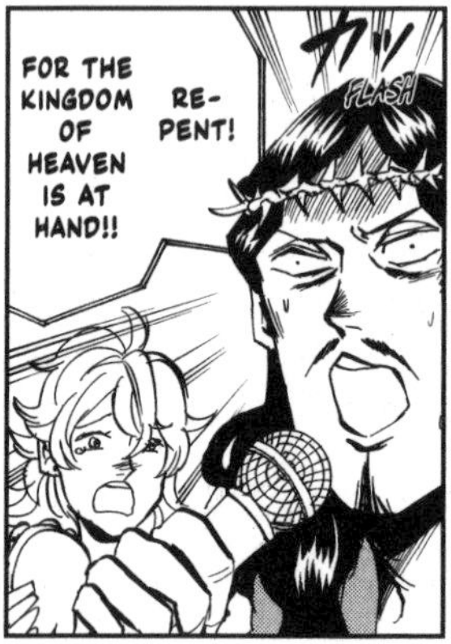
カッ
FLASH
RE-PENT!
FOR THE KINGDOM OF HEAVEN IS AT HAND!!

Your old standby, page 68
This is a reference to the Bible verse (Matthew 4:17) which states: "From that time Jesus began to preach, and to say, Repent: for the Kingdom of Heaven is at hand."

Preaching to deer, page 69
Shortly after becoming enlightened, the Buddha was hesitant to teach. After some persuasion, he went to the Deer Park at Sarnath, where he taught his first sermon to the same men who had practiced asceticism with him before his enlightenment. They first mocked him, but after they heard his teachings, they became his disciples. In the Osamu Tezuka telling of the tale, after their first encounter in the park, the ascetics walked away and Buddha taught the deer instead until the men returned to hear him.

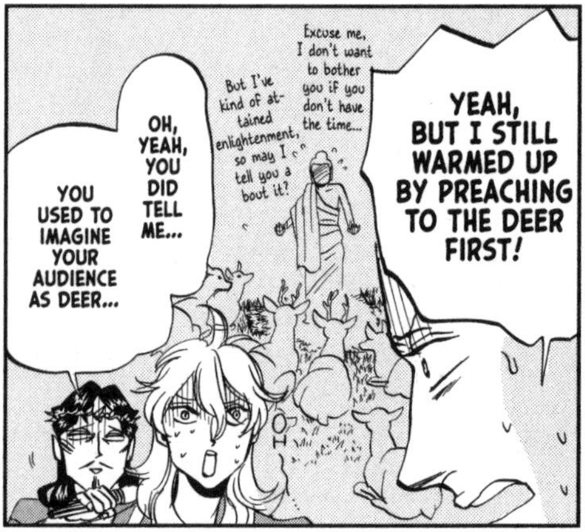
YEAH, BUT I STILL WARMED UP BY PREACHING TO THE DEER FIRST!
Excuse me, I don't want to bother you if you don't have the time...
But I've kind of attained enlightenment, so may I tell you a bout it?
OH, YEAH, YOU DID TELL ME...
YOU USED TO IMAGINE YOUR AUDIENCE AS DEER...

Imagine an audience as deer, page 70

The original Japanese text had Jesus describe a Japanese superstition for overcoming stage fright, which is to mime writing the Chinese character for "person" on your hand and then put your hand to your mouth to "swallow" the writing, but in Buddha's case, he would write the character for "deer." This image is replaced here with a different trick for overcoming stage fright, which is to imagine the audience as something less intimidating, usually the same people but dressed in only their underwear, but in this case, again, the image is deer.

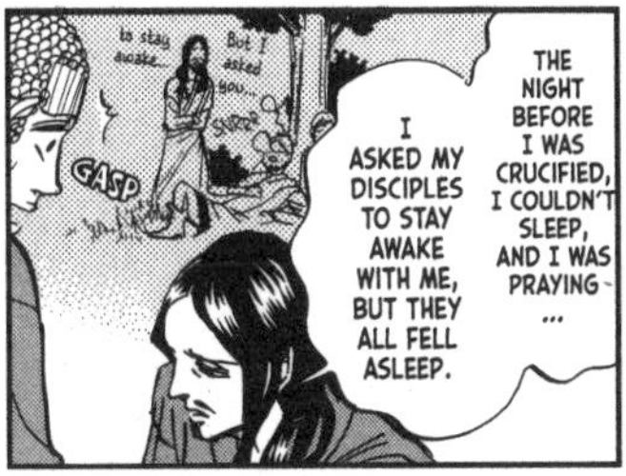
THE NIGHT BEFORE I WAS CRUCIFIED, I COULDN'T SLEEP, AND I WAS PRAYING...
I ASKED MY DISCIPLES TO STAY AWAKE WITH ME, BUT THEY ALL FELL ASLEEP.
GASP

The night before the crucifixion, page 72

Before Jesus was arrested, he went with his apostles to the Garden of Gethsemane to pray. Leaving most of them at the entrance to the garden, he took Peter, James, and John with him and told them to wait at a particular spot and watch him. He then went a little farther away, where he suffered for the sins of all humankind—a pain so great that "his sweat was as it were great drops of blood falling down to the ground" (Luke 22:44). Three times he returned to his apostles and found them asleep, because "the spirit indeed is willing, but the flesh is weak" (Matthew 26:41).

Kashi Brand, page 75

The Kingdom of Kashi is an ancient Indian kingdom known for being very wealthy. It was in this kingdom that the Buddha began teaching.

David, page 75

David was chosen by God to be the king of Israel, and Jesus Christ was descended from him through Mary.

The waterfalls, page 75

One of the tourist attractions near Shuzenji is the Kawazu Waterfalls—a pleasant walking trail that goes past seven waterfalls.

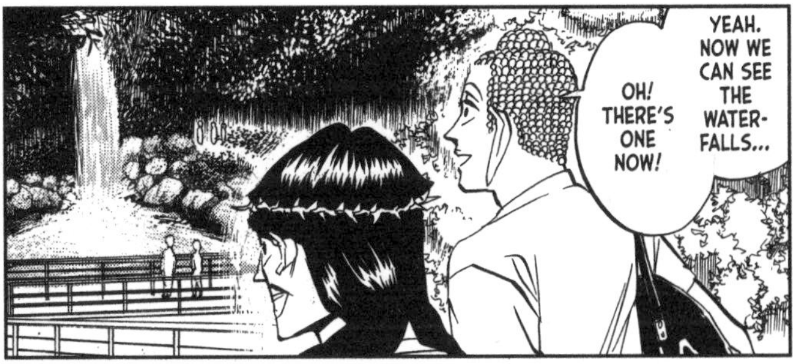
YEAH. NOW WE CAN SEE THE WATER-FALLS...
OH! THERE'S ONE NOW!

Negative ions, page 75

Negative ions—molecules with a negative electric charge—can be found in abundance out in nature, and are believed by some to have a positive effect on people's moods. These ions can also help hair to lock in moisture and be smoother and shinier.

Waterfall clothes, page 77

A form of ascetic training famous in Japan is *takigyô*, the practice of meditating under a waterfall.

SAINT☆YOUNG MEN

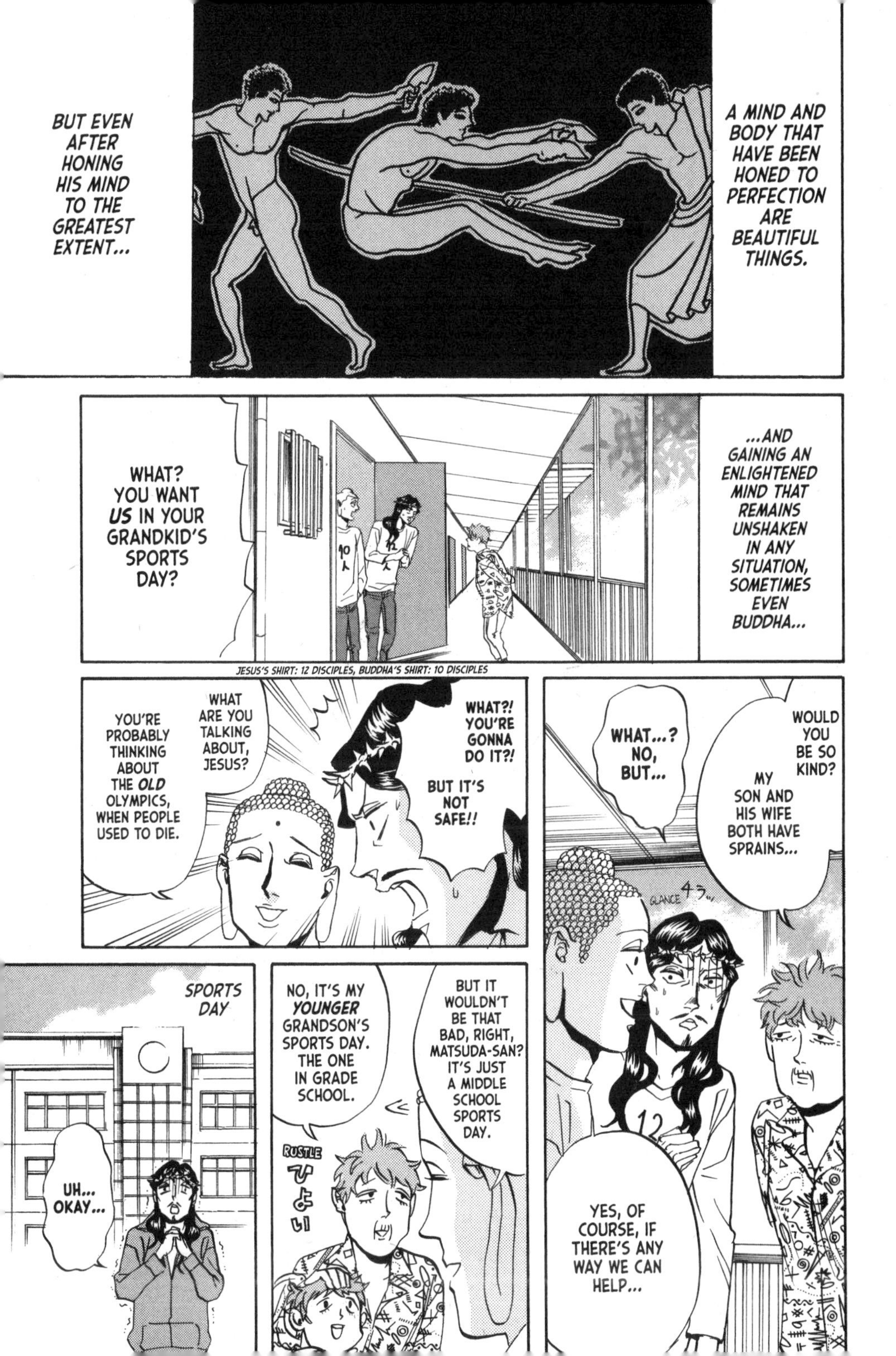
A MIND AND BODY THAT HAVE BEEN HONED TO PERFECTION ARE BEAUTIFUL THINGS.
BUT EVEN AFTER HONING HIS MIND TO THE GREATEST EXTENT...
...AND GAINING AN ENLIGHTENED MIND THAT REMAINS UNSHAKEN IN ANY SITUATION, SOMETIMES EVEN BUDDHA...
WHAT? YOU WANT *US* IN YOUR GRANDKID'S SPORTS DAY?
JESUS'S SHIRT: 12 DISCIPLES, BUDDHA'S SHIRT: 10 DISCIPLES
WOULD YOU BE SO KIND?
MY SON AND HIS WIFE BOTH HAVE SPRAINS...
WHAT...? NO, BUT...
GLANCE
YES, OF COURSE, IF THERE'S ANY WAY WE CAN HELP...
WHAT?! YOU'RE GONNA DO IT?!
BUT IT'S NOT SAFE!!
WHAT ARE YOU TALKING ABOUT, JESUS?
YOU'RE PROBABLY THINKING ABOUT THE *OLD* OLYMPICS, WHEN PEOPLE USED TO DIE.
BUT IT WOULDN'T BE THAT BAD, RIGHT, MATSUDA-SAN? IT'S JUST A MIDDLE SCHOOL SPORTS DAY.
NO, IT'S MY *YOUNGER* GRANDSON'S SPORTS DAY. THE ONE IN GRADE SCHOOL.
RUSTLE
SPORTS DAY
UH... OKAY...

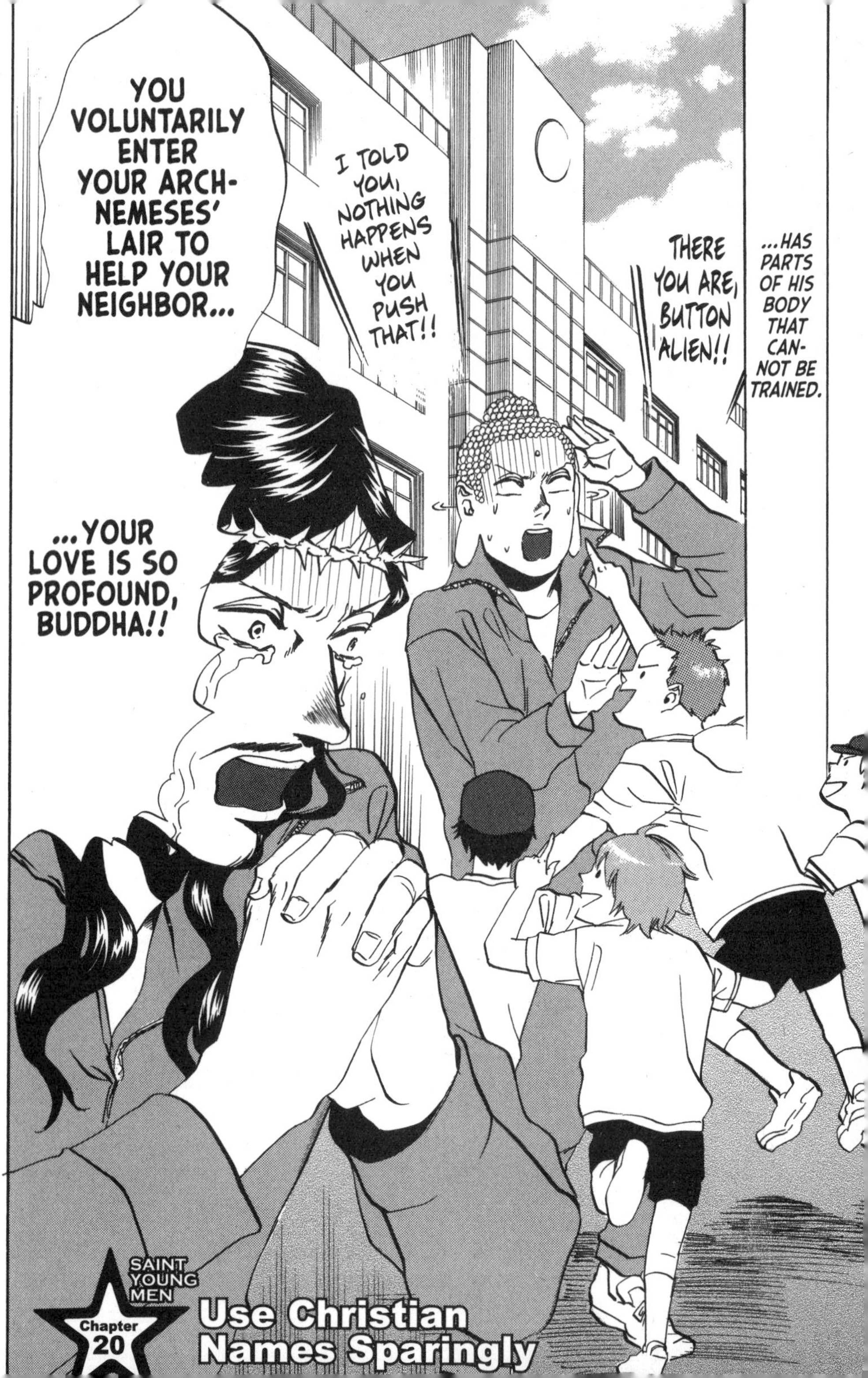
...HAS PARTS OF HIS BODY THAT CAN-NOT BE TRAINED.
THERE YOU ARE, BUTTON ALIEN!!
I TOLD YOU, NOTHING HAPPENS WHEN YOU PUSH THAT!!
YOU VOLUNTARILY ENTER YOUR ARCH-NEMESES' LAIR TO HELP YOUR NEIGHBOR...
...YOUR LOVE IS SO PROFOUND, BUDDHA!!
SAINT YOUNG MEN
Chapter 20
Use Christian Names Sparingly

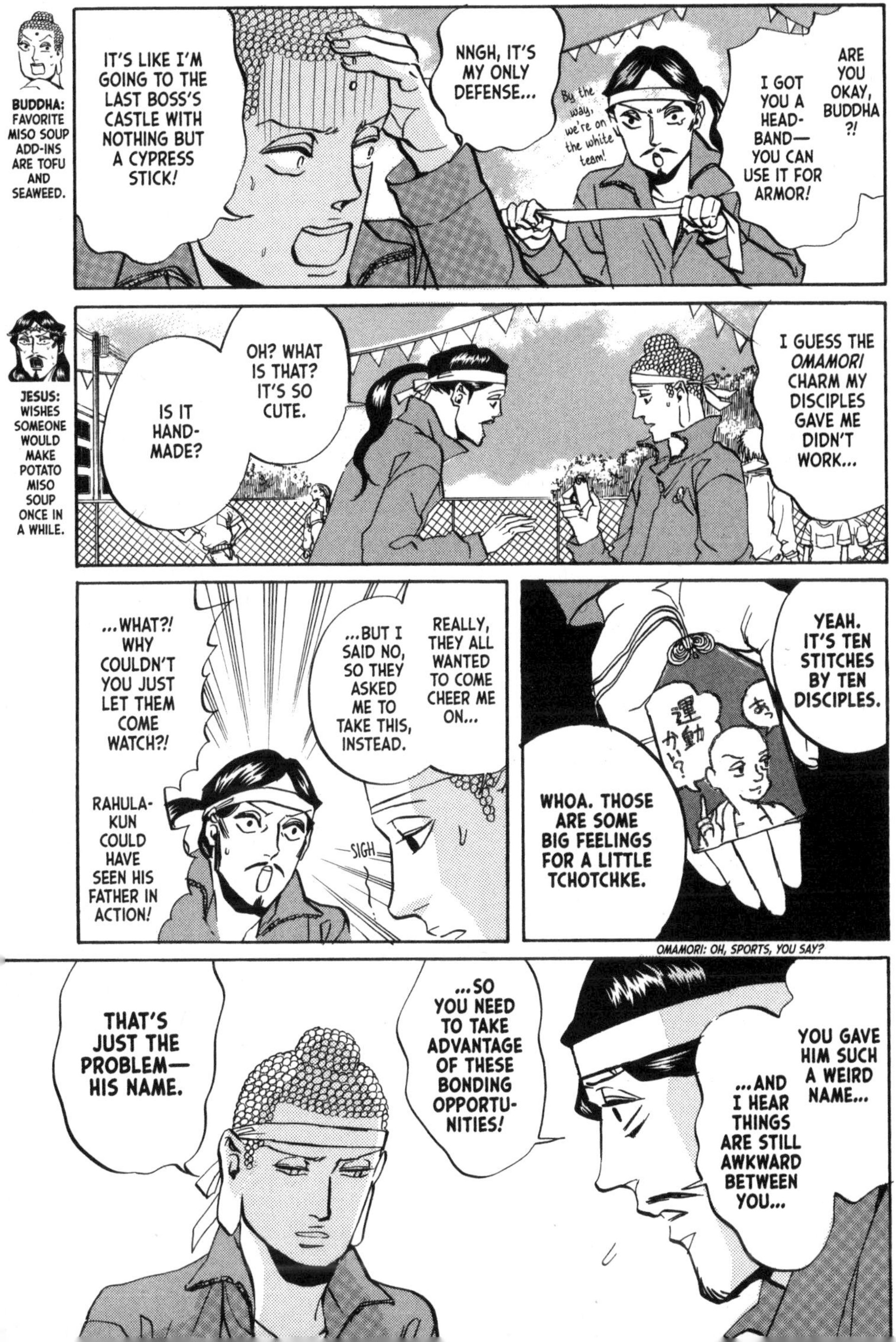
BUDDHA: FAVORITE MISO SOUP ADD-INS ARE TOFU AND SEAWEED.
ARE YOU OKAY, BUDDHA?!
I GOT YOU A HEAD-BAND—YOU CAN USE IT FOR ARMOR!
By the way, we're on the white team!
NNGH, IT'S MY ONLY DEFENSE...
IT'S LIKE I'M GOING TO THE LAST BOSS'S CASTLE WITH NOTHING BUT A CYPRESS STICK!
JESUS: WISHES SOMEONE WOULD MAKE POTATO MISO SOUP ONCE IN A WHILE.
I GUESS THE *OMAMORI* CHARM MY DISCIPLES GAVE ME DIDN'T WORK...
OH? WHAT IS THAT? IT'S SO CUTE.
IS IT HAND-MADE?
YEAH. IT'S TEN STITCHES BY TEN DISCIPLES.
あっ
運動かい？
WHOA. THOSE ARE SOME BIG FEELINGS FOR A LITTLE TCHOTCHKE.
REALLY, THEY ALL WANTED TO COME CHEER ME ON...
...BUT I SAID NO, SO THEY ASKED ME TO TAKE THIS, INSTEAD.
...WHAT?! WHY COULDN'T YOU JUST LET THEM COME WATCH?!
RAHULA-KUN COULD HAVE SEEN HIS FATHER IN ACTION!
SIGH
YOU GAVE HIM SUCH A WEIRD NAME...
...AND I HEAR THINGS ARE STILL AWKWARD BETWEEN YOU...
...SO YOU NEED TO TAKE ADVANTAGE OF THESE BONDING OPPORTU-NITIES!
THAT'S JUST THE PROBLEM—HIS NAME.
OMAMORI: OH, SPORTS, YOU SAY?

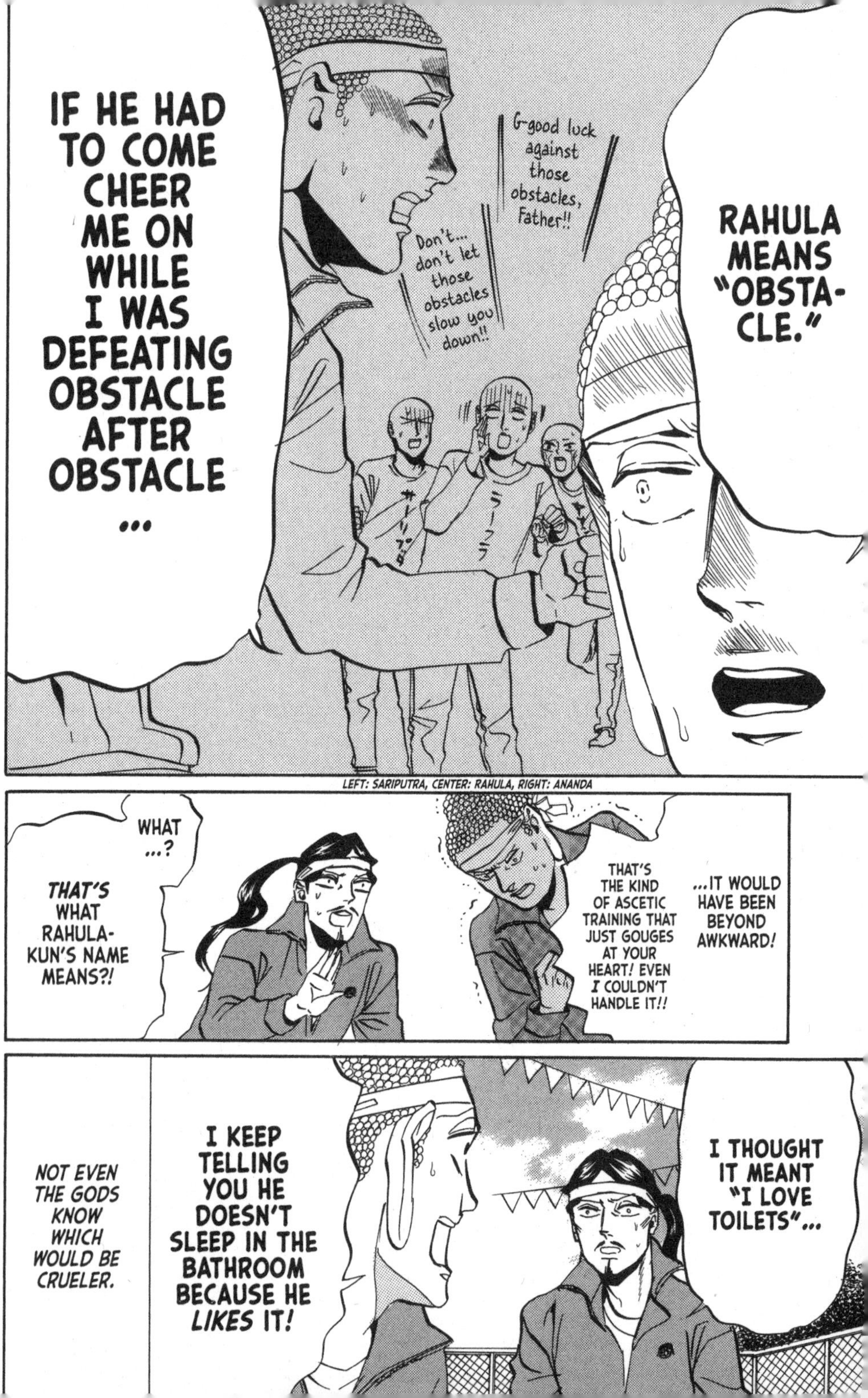

RAHULA MEANS "OBSTACLE."
G-good luck against those obstacles, Father!!
Don't... don't let those obstacles slow you down!!
IF HE HAD TO COME CHEER ME ON WHILE I WAS DEFEATING OBSTACLE AFTER OBSTACLE...
LEFT: SARIPUTRA, CENTER: RAHULA, RIGHT: ANANDA
...IT WOULD HAVE BEEN BEYOND AWKWARD!
THAT'S THE KIND OF ASCETIC TRAINING THAT JUST GOUGES AT YOUR HEART! EVEN *I* COULDN'T HANDLE IT!!
WHAT ...?
THAT'S WHAT RAHULA-KUN'S NAME MEANS?!
I THOUGHT IT MEANT "I LOVE TOILETS"...
I KEEP TELLING YOU HE DOESN'T SLEEP IN THE BATHROOM BECAUSE HE *LIKES* IT!
NOT EVEN THE GODS KNOW WHICH WOULD BE CRUELER.

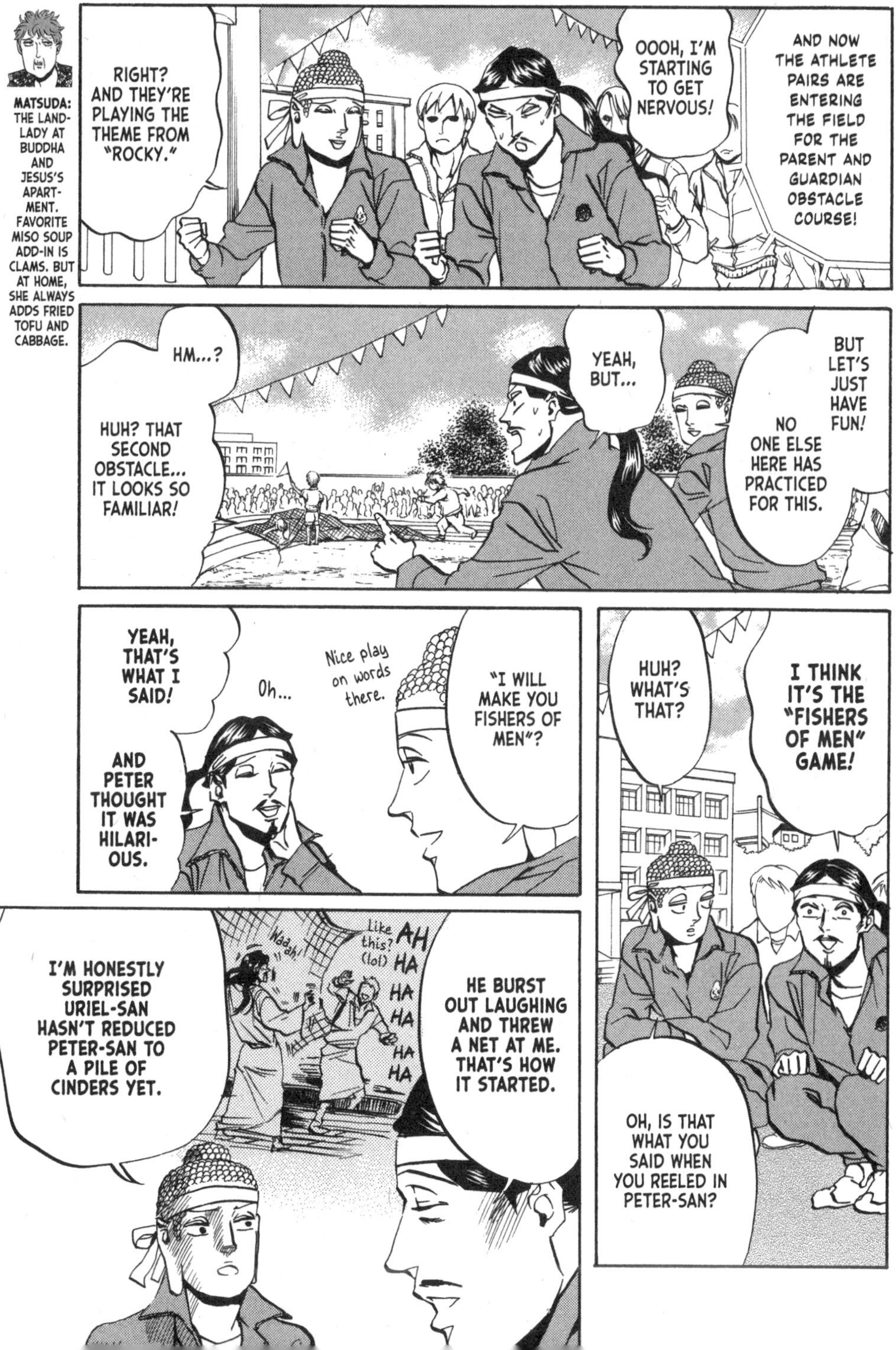
MATSUDA: THE LANDLADY AT BUDDHA AND JESUS'S APARTMENT. FAVORITE MISO SOUP ADD-IN IS CLAMS. BUT AT HOME, SHE ALWAYS ADDS FRIED TOFU AND CABBAGE.
AND NOW THE ATHLETE PAIRS ARE ENTERING THE FIELD FOR THE PARENT AND GUARDIAN OBSTACLE COURSE!
OOOH, I'M STARTING TO GET NERVOUS!
RIGHT? AND THEY'RE PLAYING THE THEME FROM "ROCKY."
BUT LET'S JUST HAVE FUN!
NO ONE ELSE HERE HAS PRACTICED FOR THIS.
YEAH, BUT...
HM...?
HUH? THAT SECOND OBSTACLE... IT LOOKS SO FAMILIAR!
I THINK IT'S THE "FISHERS OF MEN" GAME!
HUH? WHAT'S THAT?
OH, IS THAT WHAT YOU SAID WHEN YOU REELED IN PETER-SAN?
"I WILL MAKE YOU FISHERS OF MEN"?
Nice play on words there.
Oh...
YEAH, THAT'S WHAT I SAID!
AND PETER THOUGHT IT WAS HILARIOUS.
HE BURST OUT LAUGHING AND THREW A NET AT ME. THAT'S HOW IT STARTED.
Like this? (lol)
AH HA HA HA HA HA
Waah
I'M HONESTLY SURPRISED URIEL-SAN HASN'T REDUCED PETER-SAN TO A PILE OF CINDERS YET.

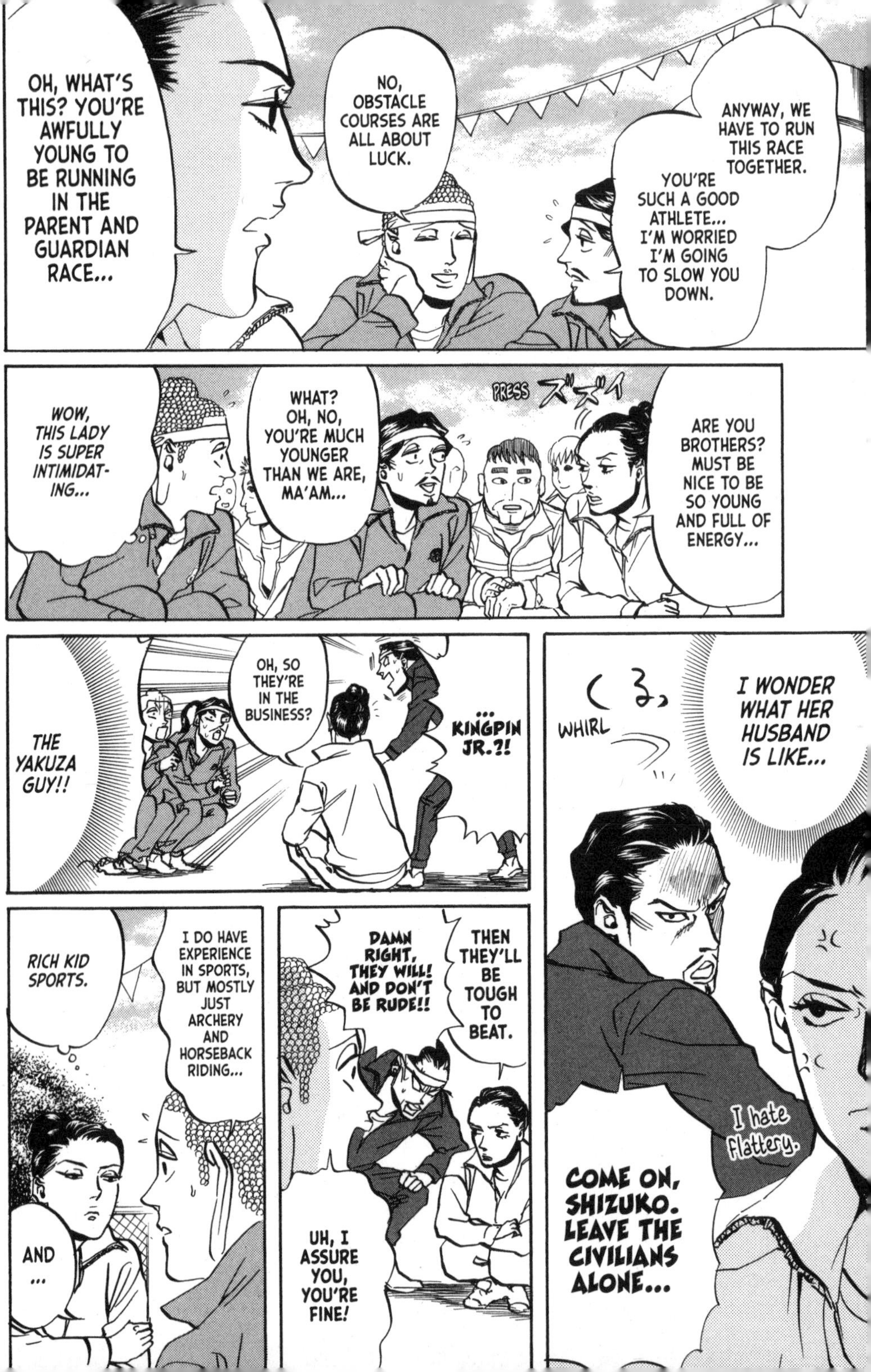
ANYWAY, WE HAVE TO RUN THIS RACE TOGETHER.
YOU'RE SUCH A GOOD ATHLETE... I'M WORRIED I'M GOING TO SLOW YOU DOWN.
NO, OBSTACLE COURSES ARE ALL ABOUT LUCK.
OH, WHAT'S THIS? YOU'RE AWFULLY YOUNG TO BE RUNNING IN THE PARENT AND GUARDIAN RACE...
ARE YOU BROTHERS? MUST BE NICE TO BE SO YOUNG AND FULL OF ENERGY...
PRESS ズズイ
WHAT? OH, NO, YOU'RE MUCH YOUNGER THAN WE ARE, MA'AM...
WOW, THIS LADY IS SUPER INTIMIDAT-ING...
I WONDER WHAT HER HUSBAND IS LIKE...
くる。
WHIRL
I hate Flattery.
COME ON, SHIZUKO. LEAVE THE CIVILIANS ALONE...
...KINGPIN JR.?!
OH, SO THEY'RE IN THE BUSINESS?
THE YAKUZA GUY!!
THEN THEY'LL BE TOUGH TO BEAT.
DAMN RIGHT, THEY WILL! AND DON'T BE RUDE!!
UH, I ASSURE YOU, YOU'RE FINE!
I DO HAVE EXPERIENCE IN SPORTS, BUT MOSTLY JUST ARCHERY AND HORSEBACK RIDING...
RICH KID SPORTS.
AND ...

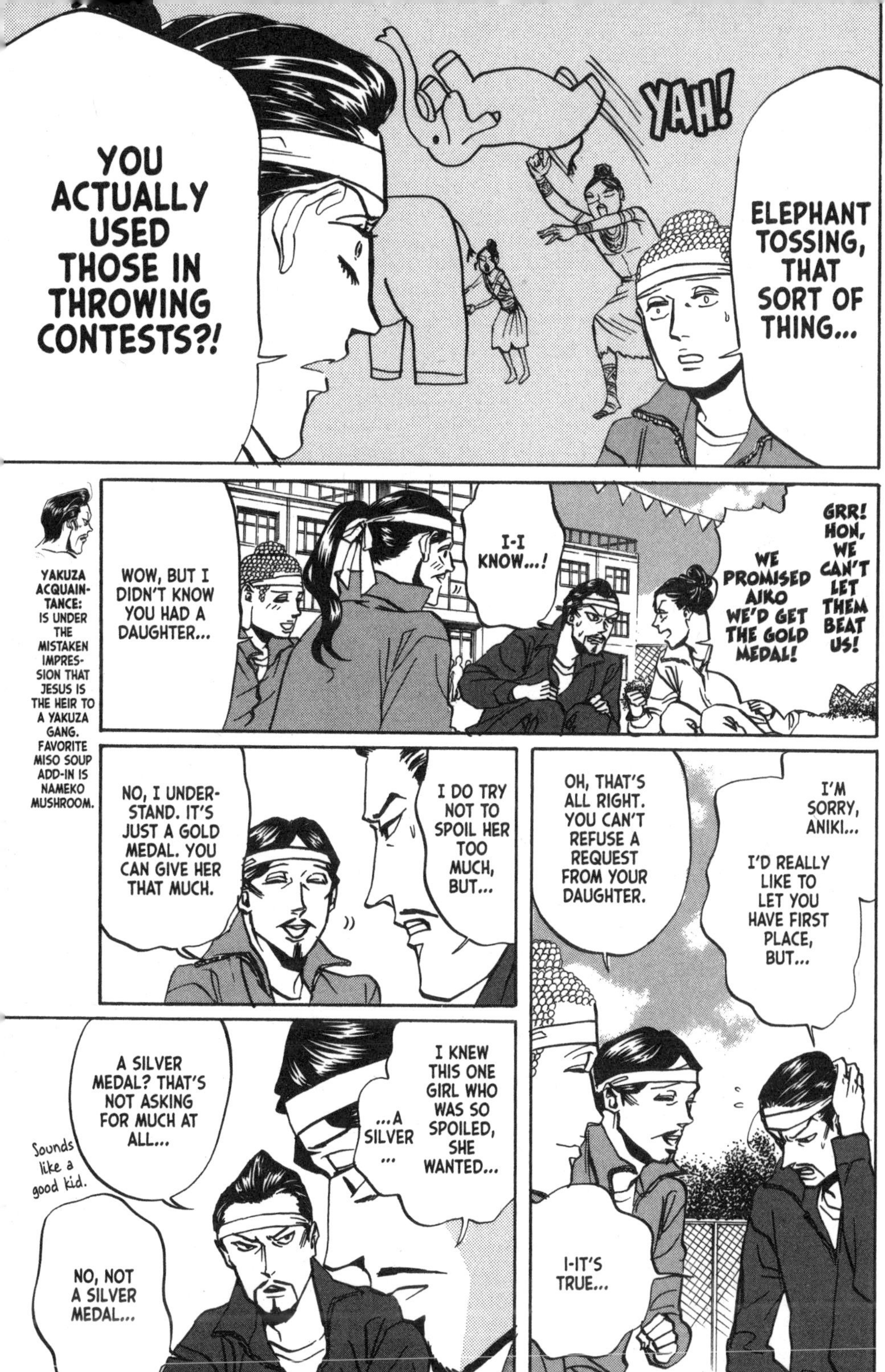
ELEPHANT TOSSING, THAT SORT OF THING...
YAH!
YOU ACTUALLY USED THOSE IN THROWING CONTESTS?!
GRR! HON, WE CAN'T LET THEM BEAT US!
WE PROMISED AIKO WE'D GET THE GOLD MEDAL!
I-I KNOW...!
WOW, BUT I DIDN'T KNOW YOU HAD A DAUGHTER...
YAKUZA ACQUAINTANCE: IS UNDER THE MISTAKEN IMPRESSION THAT JESUS IS THE HEIR TO A YAKUZA GANG. FAVORITE MISO SOUP ADD-IN IS NAMEKO MUSHROOM.
I'M SORRY, ANIKI...
I'D REALLY LIKE TO LET YOU HAVE FIRST PLACE, BUT...
OH, THAT'S ALL RIGHT. YOU CAN'T REFUSE A REQUEST FROM YOUR DAUGHTER.
I-IT'S TRUE...
I DO TRY NOT TO SPOIL HER TOO MUCH, BUT...
NO, I UNDERSTAND. IT'S JUST A GOLD MEDAL. YOU CAN GIVE HER THAT MUCH.
I KNEW THIS ONE GIRL WHO WAS SO SPOILED, SHE WANTED...
...A SILVER...
A SILVER MEDAL? THAT'S NOT ASKING FOR MUCH AT ALL...
Sounds like a good kid.
NO, NOT A SILVER MEDAL...

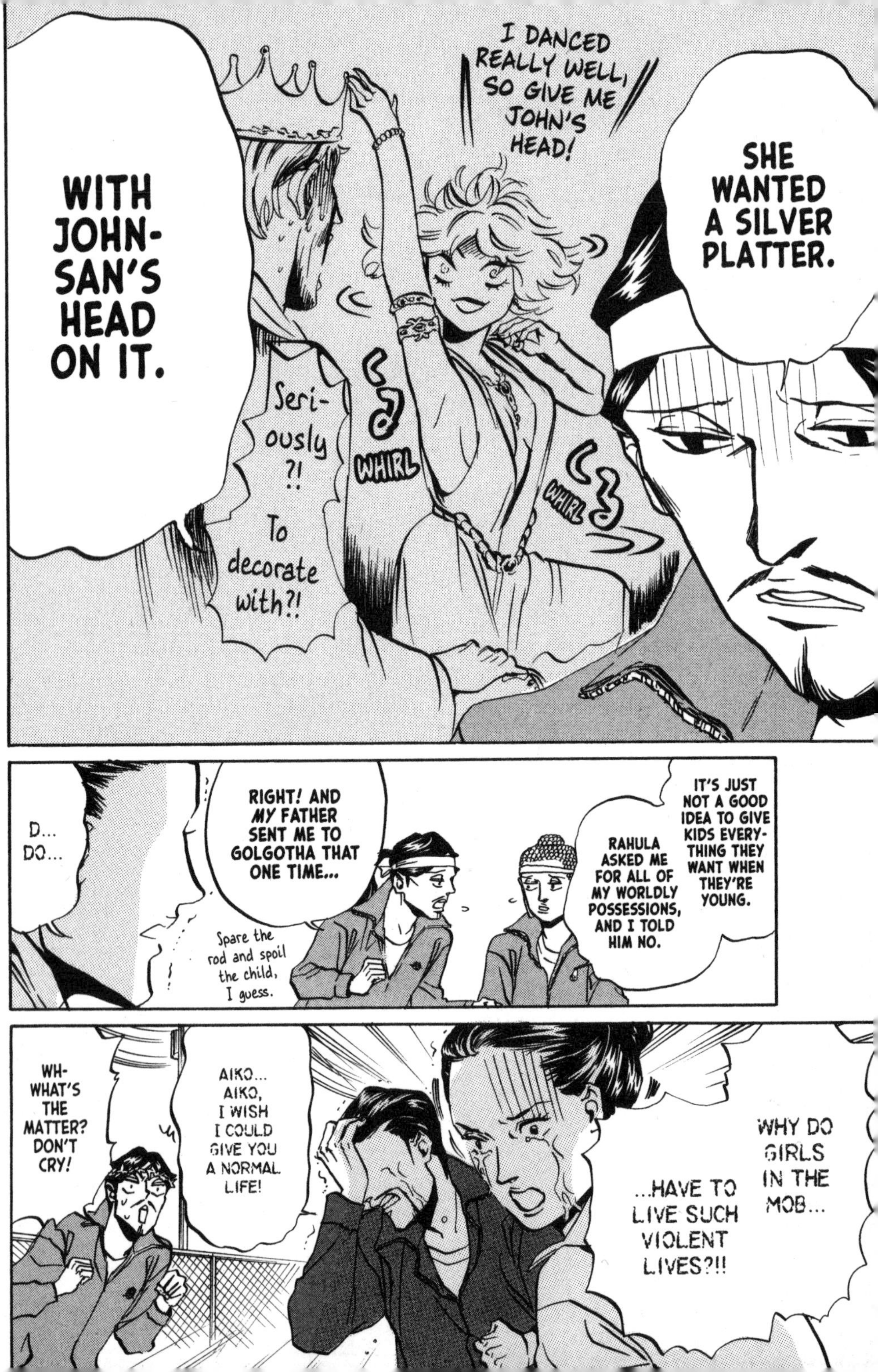
I DANCED REALLY WELL, SO GIVE ME JOHN'S HEAD!
SHE WANTED A SILVER PLATTER.
WITH JOHN-SAN'S HEAD ON IT.
WHIRL
WHIRL
Seri-ously?! To decorate with?!
IT'S JUST NOT A GOOD IDEA TO GIVE KIDS EVERY-THING THEY WANT WHEN THEY'RE YOUNG.
RAHULA ASKED ME FOR ALL OF MY WORLDLY POSSESSIONS, AND I TOLD HIM NO.
RIGHT! AND MY FATHER SENT ME TO GOLGOTHA THAT ONE TIME...
Spare the rod and spoil the child, I guess.
D... DO...
WHY DO GIRLS IN THE MOB...
...HAVE TO LIVE SUCH VIOLENT LIVES?!!
AIKO... AIKO, I WISH I COULD GIVE YOU A NORMAL LIFE!
WH-WHAT'S THE MATTER? DON'T CRY!

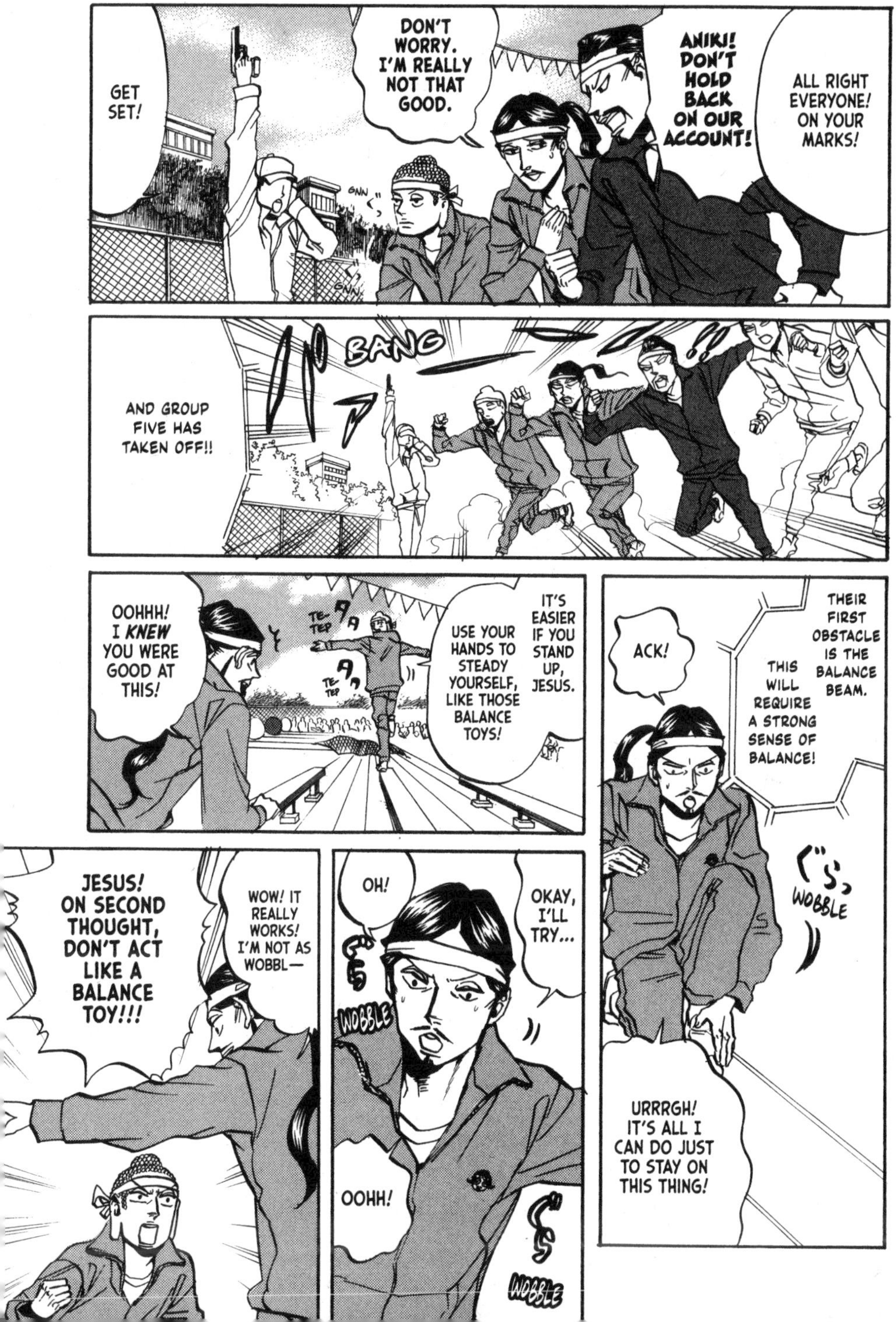
ALL RIGHT EVERYONE! ON YOUR MARKS!
ANIKI! DON'T HOLD BACK ON OUR ACCOUNT!
DON'T WORRY. I'M REALLY NOT THAT GOOD.
GET SET!
GNN
GNN
BANG
AND GROUP FIVE HAS TAKEN OFF!!
THEIR FIRST OBSTACLE IS THE BALANCE BEAM.
THIS WILL REQUIRE A STRONG SENSE OF BALANCE!
ACK!
WOBBLE
URRRGH! IT'S ALL I CAN DO JUST TO STAY ON THIS THING!
IT'S EASIER IF YOU STAND UP, JESUS.
USE YOUR HANDS TO STEADY YOURSELF, LIKE THOSE BALANCE TOYS!
TE-TEP
TE-TEP
OOHHH! I *KNEW* YOU WERE GOOD AT THIS!
OKAY, I'LL TRY...
OH!
WOBBLE
OOHH!
WOBBLE
WOW! IT REALLY WORKS! I'M NOT AS WOBBL—
JESUS! ON SECOND THOUGHT, DON'T ACT LIKE A BALANCE TOY!!!

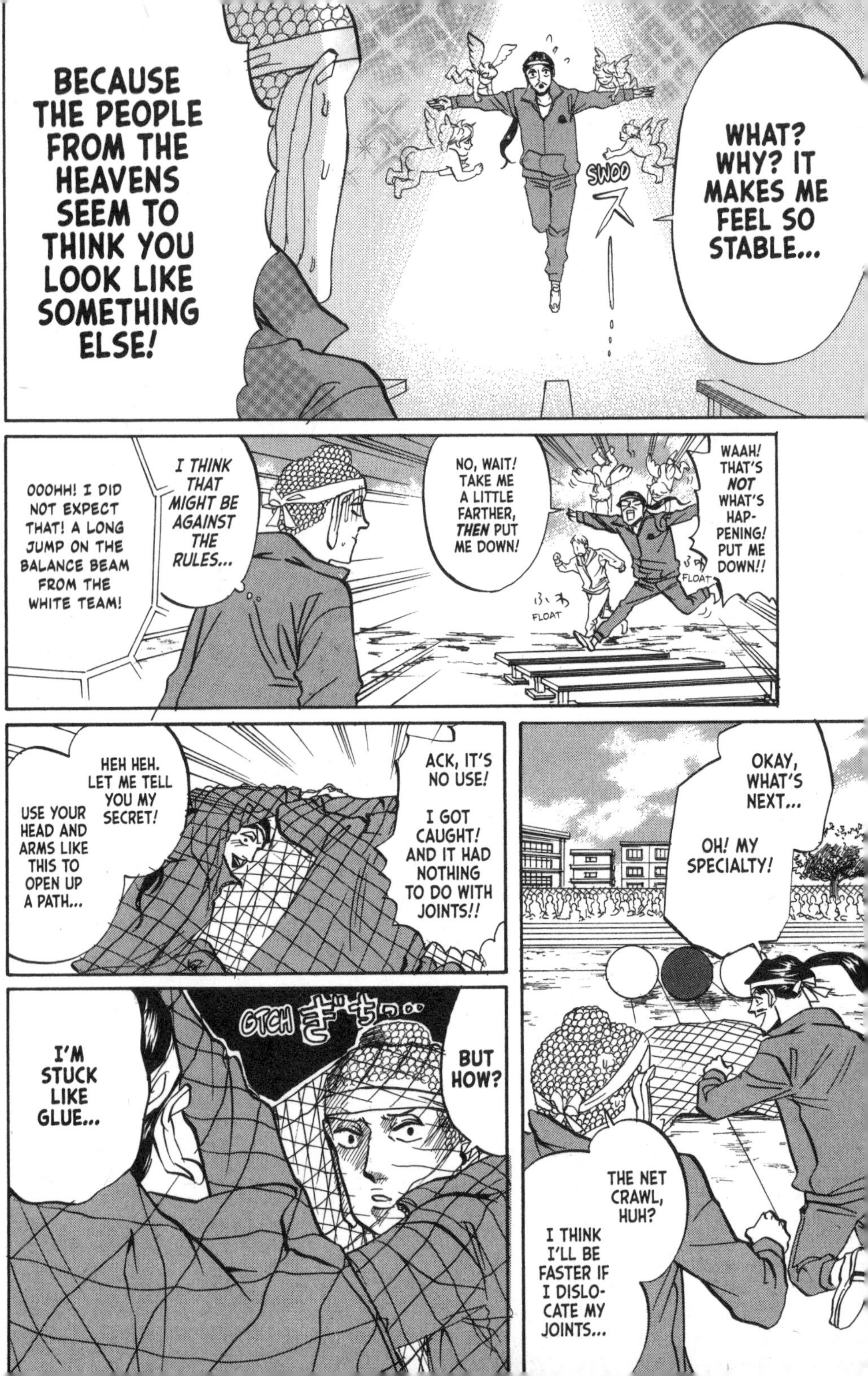
WHAT? WHY? IT MAKES ME FEEL SO STABLE...
SWOO
BECAUSE THE PEOPLE FROM THE HEAVENS SEEM TO THINK YOU LOOK LIKE SOMETHING ELSE!
WAAH! THAT'S NOT WHAT'S HAP-PENING! PUT ME DOWN!!
FLOAT
NO, WAIT! TAKE ME A LITTLE FARTHER, THEN PUT ME DOWN!
ふわ
FLOAT
I THINK THAT MIGHT BE AGAINST THE RULES...
OOOHH! I DID NOT EXPECT THAT! A LONG JUMP ON THE BALANCE BEAM FROM THE WHITE TEAM!
OKAY, WHAT'S NEXT...
OH! MY SPECIALTY!
THE NET CRAWL, HUH?
I THINK I'LL BE FASTER IF I DISLO-CATE MY JOINTS...
ACK, IT'S NO USE!
I GOT CAUGHT! AND IT HAD NOTHING TO DO WITH JOINTS!!
HEH HEH. LET ME TELL YOU MY SECRET!
USE YOUR HEAD AND ARMS LIKE THIS TO OPEN UP A PATH...
GTCH
BUT HOW?
I'M STUCK LIKE GLUE...

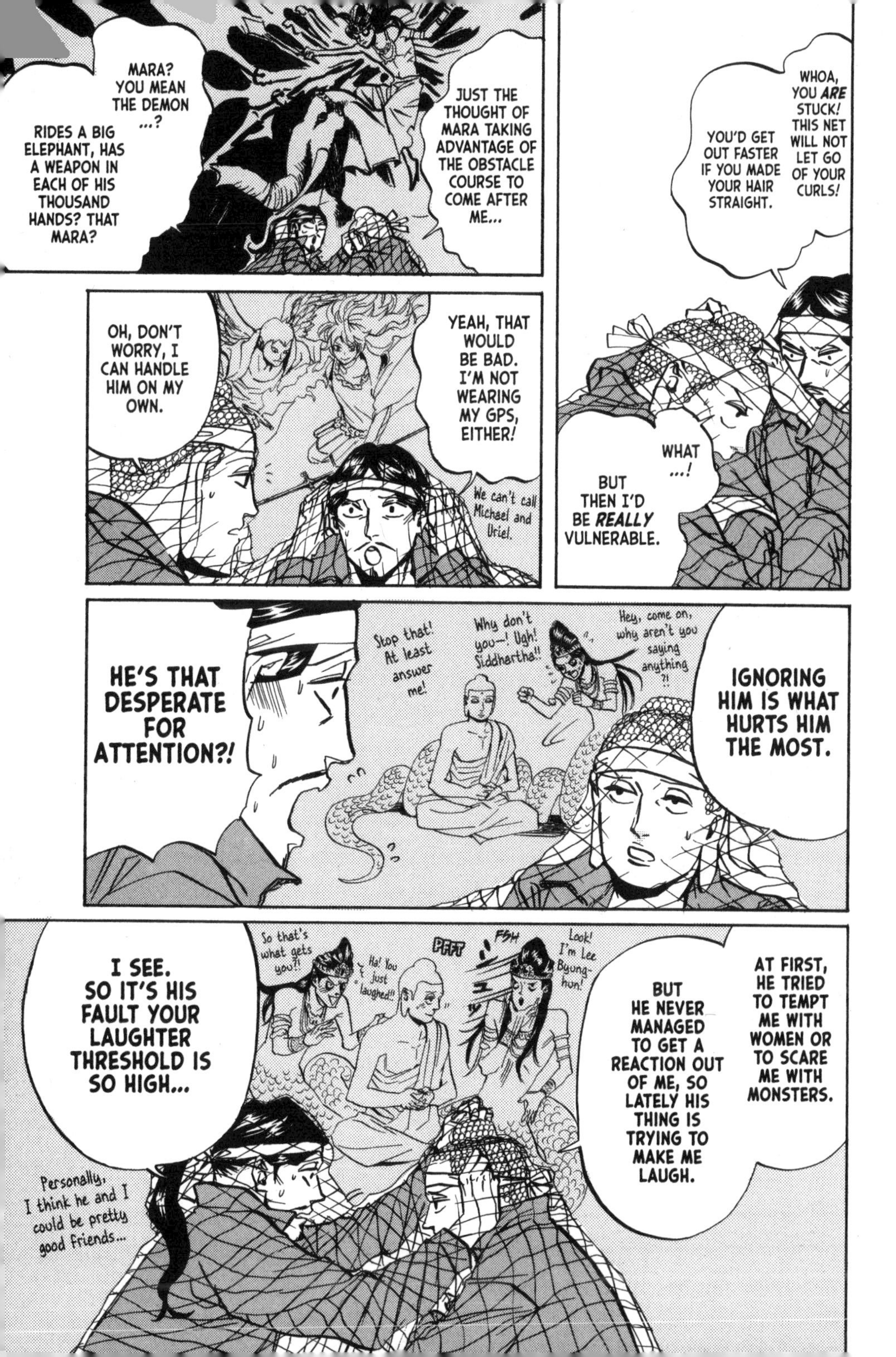
WHOA, YOU ***ARE*** STUCK! THIS NET WILL NOT LET GO OF YOUR CURLS!
YOU'D GET OUT FASTER IF YOU MADE YOUR HAIR STRAIGHT.
WHAT ...!
BUT THEN I'D BE ***REALLY*** VULNERABLE.
JUST THE THOUGHT OF MARA TAKING ADVANTAGE OF THE OBSTACLE COURSE TO COME AFTER ME...
MARA? YOU MEAN THE DEMON ...?
RIDES A BIG ELEPHANT, HAS A WEAPON IN EACH OF HIS THOUSAND HANDS? THAT MARA?
YEAH, THAT WOULD BE BAD. I'M NOT WEARING MY GPS, EITHER!
We can't call Michael and Uriel.
OH, DON'T WORRY, I CAN HANDLE HIM ON MY OWN.
IGNORING HIM IS WHAT HURTS HIM THE MOST.
Hey, come on, why aren't you saying anything ?!
Why don't you—! Ugh! Siddhartha!!
Stop that! At least answer me!
HE'S THAT DESPERATE FOR ATTENTION?!
AT FIRST, HE TRIED TO TEMPT ME WITH WOMEN OR TO SCARE ME WITH MONSTERS.
BUT HE NEVER MANAGED TO GET A REACTION OUT OF ME, SO LATELY HIS THING IS TRYING TO MAKE ME LAUGH.
Look! I'm Lee Byung-hun!
FSH
PFFT
Ha! You just laughed!!
So that's what gets you?!
I SEE. SO IT'S HIS FAULT YOUR LAUGHTER THRESHOLD IS SO HIGH...
Personally, I think he and I could be pretty good friends...

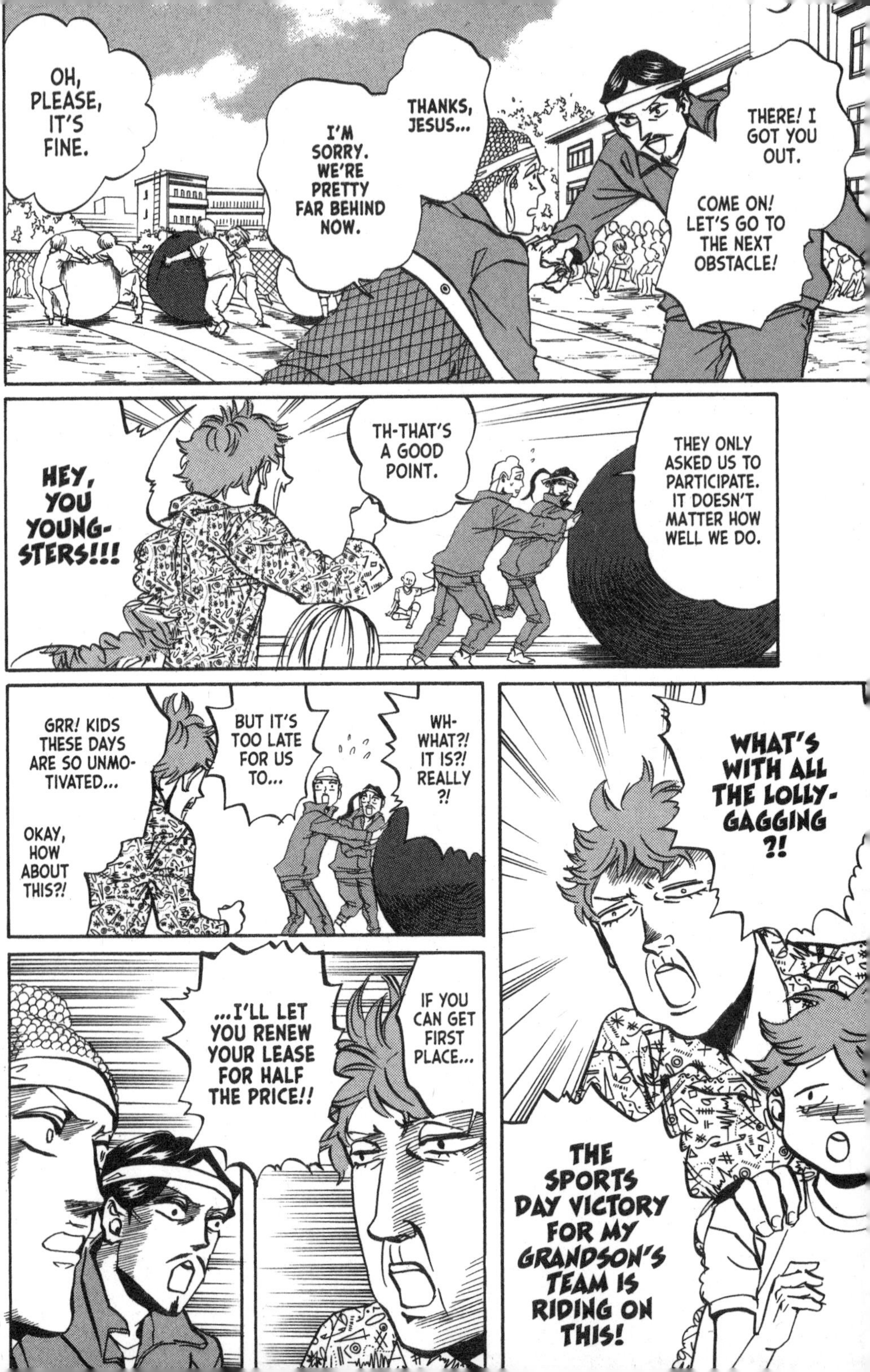
THERE! I GOT YOU OUT.
COME ON! LET'S GO TO THE NEXT OBSTACLE!
THANKS, JESUS...
I'M SORRY. WE'RE PRETTY FAR BEHIND NOW.
OH, PLEASE, IT'S FINE.
THEY ONLY ASKED US TO PARTICIPATE. IT DOESN'T MATTER HOW WELL WE DO.
TH-THAT'S A GOOD POINT.
HEY, YOU YOUNG-STERS!!!
WHAT'S WITH ALL THE LOLLY-GAGGING?!
THE SPORTS DAY VICTORY FOR MY GRANDSON'S TEAM IS RIDING ON THIS!
WH-WHAT?! IT IS?! REALLY?!
BUT IT'S TOO LATE FOR US TO...
GRR! KIDS THESE DAYS ARE SO UNMO-TIVATED...
OKAY, HOW ABOUT THIS?!
IF YOU CAN GET FIRST PLACE...
...I'LL LET YOU RENEW YOUR LEASE FOR HALF THE PRICE!!

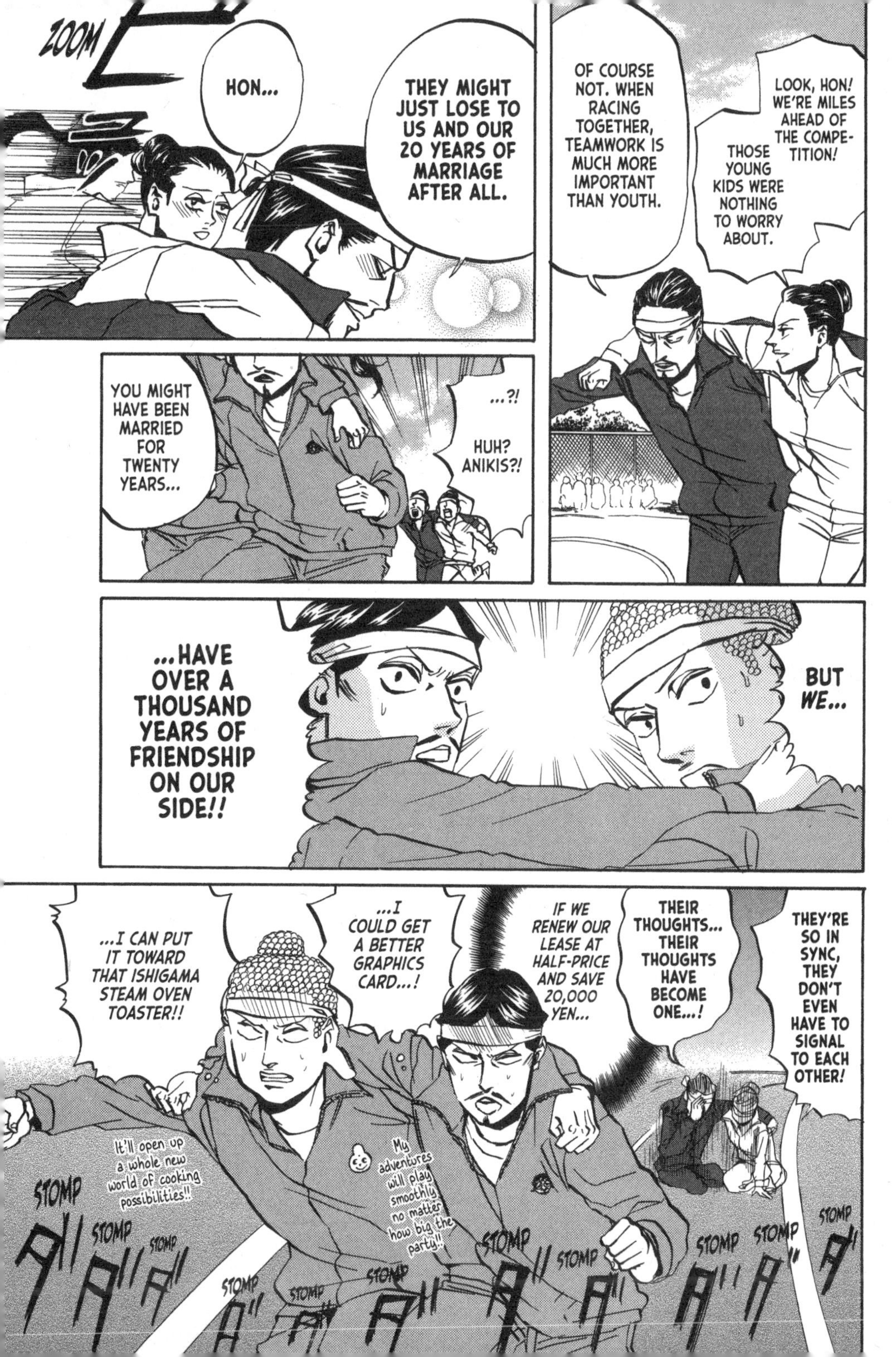
LOOK, HON! WE'RE MILES AHEAD OF THE COMPE-TITION!
THOSE YOUNG KIDS WERE NOTHING TO WORRY ABOUT.
OF COURSE NOT. WHEN RACING TOGETHER, TEAMWORK IS MUCH MORE IMPORTANT THAN YOUTH.
THEY MIGHT JUST LOSE TO US AND OUR 20 YEARS OF MARRIAGE AFTER ALL.
HON...
ZOOM
...?!
HUH? ANIKIS?!
YOU MIGHT HAVE BEEN MARRIED FOR TWENTY YEARS...
BUT WE...
...HAVE OVER A THOUSAND YEARS OF FRIENDSHIP ON OUR SIDE!!
THEY'RE SO IN SYNC, THEY DON'T EVEN HAVE TO SIGNAL TO EACH OTHER!
THEIR THOUGHTS... THEIR THOUGHTS HAVE BECOME ONE...!
IF WE RENEW OUR LEASE AT HALF-PRICE AND SAVE 20,000 YEN...
...I COULD GET A BETTER GRAPHICS CARD...!
My adventures will play smoothly no matter how big the party!!
...I CAN PUT IT TOWARD THAT ISHIGAMA STEAM OVEN TOASTER!!
It'll open up a whole new world of cooking possibilities!!
STOMP STOMP STOMP STOMP STOMP STOMP STOMP STOMP STOMP STOMP STOMP

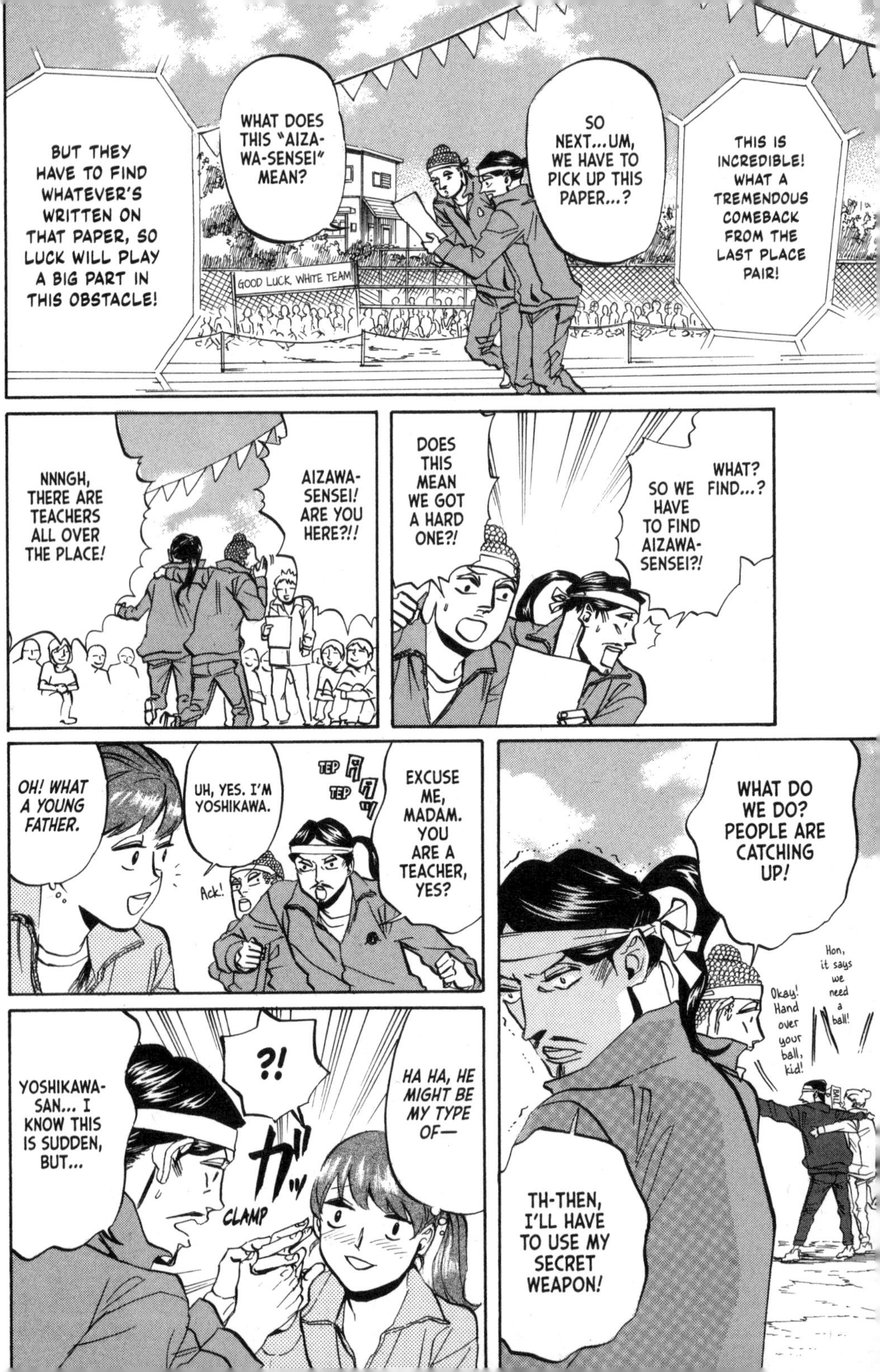
THIS IS INCREDIBLE! WHAT A TREMENDOUS COMEBACK FROM THE LAST PLACE PAIR!
SO NEXT...UM, WE HAVE TO PICK UP THIS PAPER...?
WHAT DOES THIS "AIZAWA-SENSEI" MEAN?
GOOD LUCK, WHITE TEAM
BUT THEY HAVE TO FIND WHATEVER'S WRITTEN ON THAT PAPER, SO LUCK WILL PLAY A BIG PART IN THIS OBSTACLE!
WHAT? FIND...?
SO WE HAVE TO FIND AIZAWA-SENSEI?!
DOES THIS MEAN WE GOT A HARD ONE?!
AIZAWA-SENSEI! ARE YOU HERE?!!
NNNGH, THERE ARE TEACHERS ALL OVER THE PLACE!
WHAT DO WE DO? PEOPLE ARE CATCHING UP!
Hon, it says we need a ball!
Okay! Hand over your ball, kid!
TH-THEN, I'LL HAVE TO USE MY SECRET WEAPON!
EXCUSE ME, MADAM. YOU ARE A TEACHER, YES?
TEP TEP
UH, YES. I'M YOSHIKAWA.
Ack!
OH! WHAT A YOUNG FATHER.
HA HA, HE MIGHT BE MY TYPE OF—
?!
YOSHIKAWA-SAN... I KNOW THIS IS SUDDEN, BUT...
CLAMP

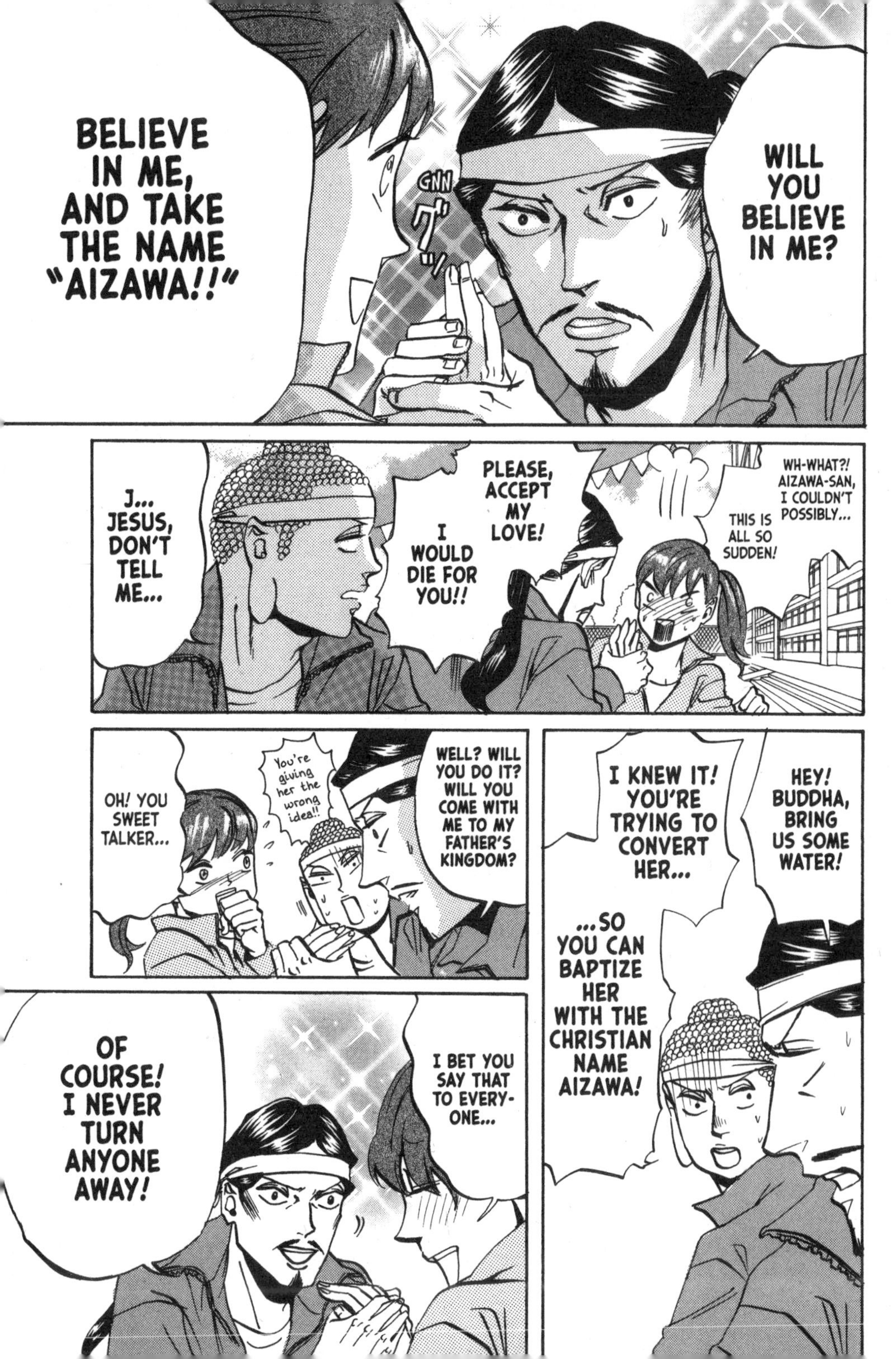
WILL YOU BELIEVE IN ME?
GNN
BELIEVE IN ME, AND TAKE THE NAME "AIZAWA!!"
WH-WHAT?! AIZAWA-SAN, I COULDN'T POSSIBLY...
THIS IS ALL SO SUDDEN!
PLEASE, ACCEPT MY LOVE!
I WOULD DIE FOR YOU!!
J... JESUS, DON'T TELL ME...
HEY! BUDDHA, BRING US SOME WATER!
I KNEW IT! YOU'RE TRYING TO CONVERT HER...
...SO YOU CAN BAPTIZE HER WITH THE CHRISTIAN NAME AIZAWA!
WELL? WILL YOU DO IT? WILL YOU COME WITH ME TO MY FATHER'S KINGDOM?
You're giving her the wrong idea!!
OH! YOU SWEET TALKER...
I BET YOU SAY THAT TO EVERY-ONE...
OF COURSE! I NEVER TURN ANYONE AWAY!

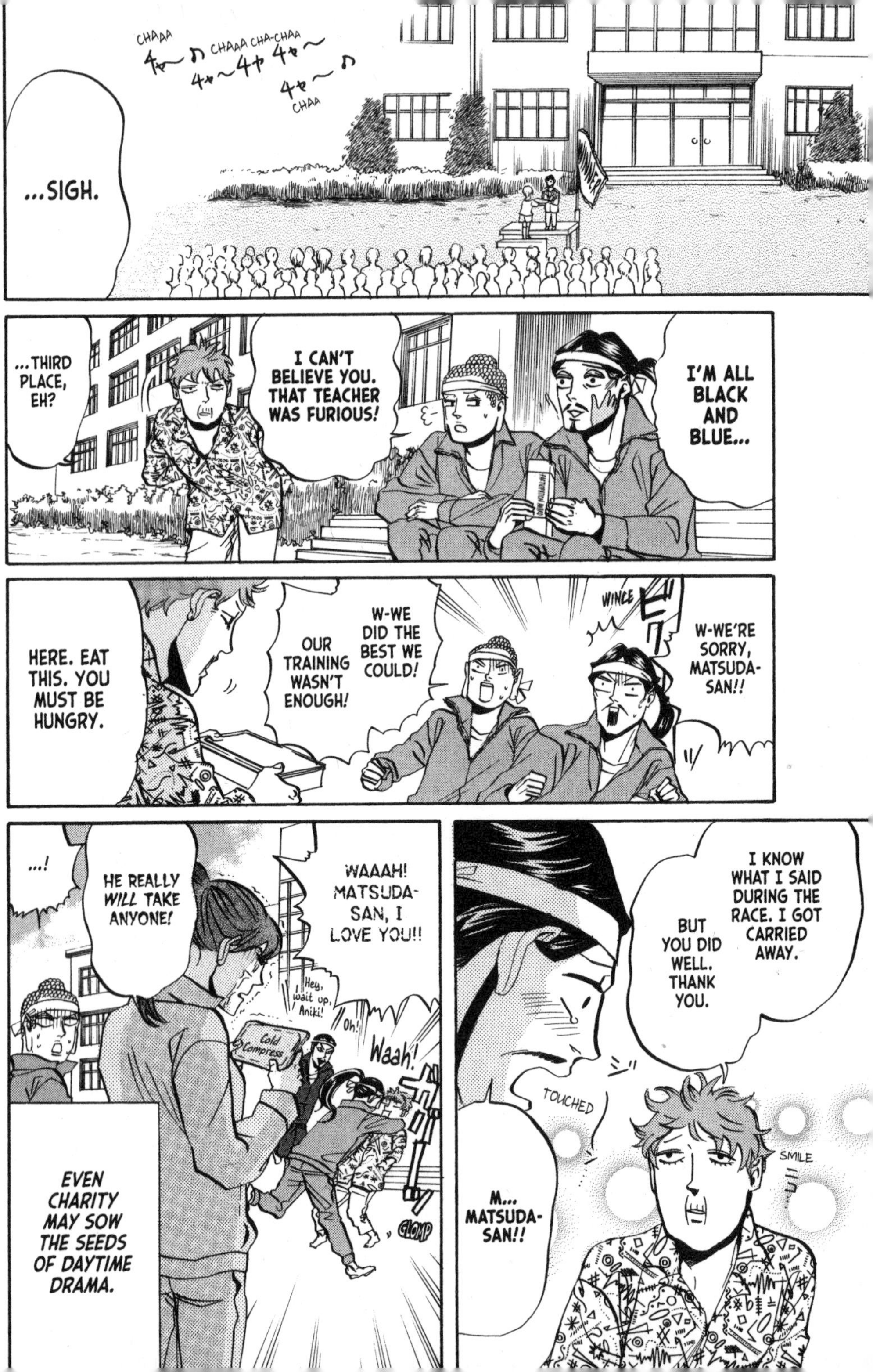
CHAAA
CHAAA CHA-CHAA
CHAA
...SIGH.
I'M ALL BLACK AND BLUE...
I CAN'T BELIEVE YOU. THAT TEACHER WAS FURIOUS!
...THIRD PLACE, EH?
WINCE
W-WE'RE SORRY, MATSUDA-SAN!!
W-WE DID THE BEST WE COULD!
OUR TRAINING WASN'T ENOUGH!
HERE. EAT THIS. YOU MUST BE HUNGRY.
I KNOW WHAT I SAID DURING THE RACE. I GOT CARRIED AWAY.
BUT YOU DID WELL. THANK YOU.
TOUCHED
SMILE
M... MATSUDA-SAN!!
WAAAH! MATSUDA-SAN, I LOVE YOU!!
Hey, wait up, Aniki!
Oh!
Waah!
GLOMP
Cold Compress
HE REALLY WILL TAKE ANYONE!
...!
EVEN CHARITY MAY SOW THE SEEDS OF DAYTIME DRAMA.

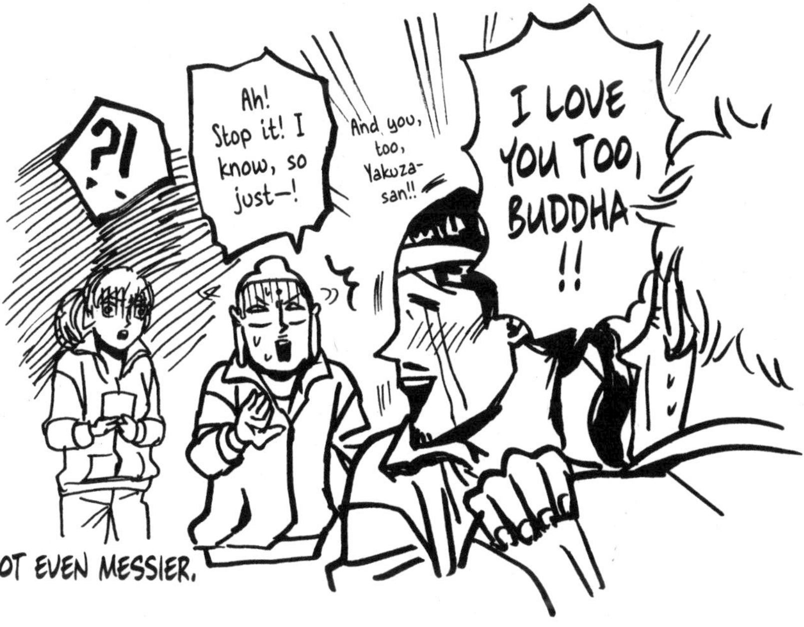
I LOVE YOU TOO, BUDDHA!!
And you, too, Yakuza-san!!
Ah! Stop it! I know, so just—!
?!

THINGS GOT EVEN MESSIER.

CHAPTER 20 TRANSLATION NOTES

10 and 12 disciples, page 85
Of all their disciples, Jesus Christ and the Buddha both had a core group that was closest to them. Jesus had 12 apostles, and Buddha had 10 principal disciples.

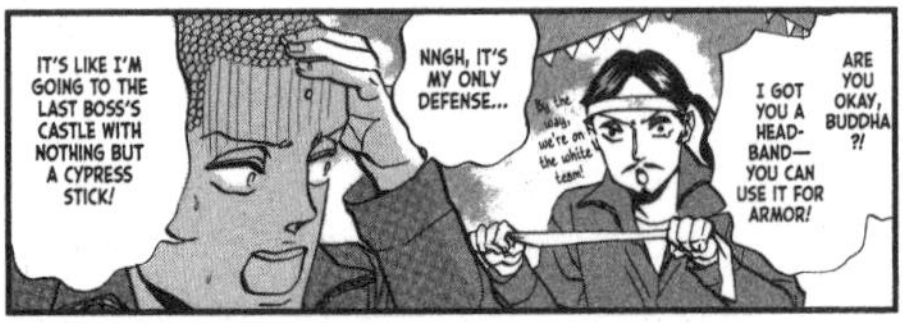

ARE YOU OKAY, BUDDHA?!
I GOT YOU A HEAD-BAND— YOU CAN USE IT FOR ARMOR!
By the way, we're on the white team!
NNGH, IT'S MY ONLY DEFENSE...
IT'S LIKE I'M GOING TO THE LAST BOSS'S CASTLE WITH NOTHING BUT A CYPRESS STICK!

Cypress stick, page 87
In the *Dragon Quest* franchise of video games, the "cypress stick" is a simple wooden stick, and usually the weakest weapon in the game.

Omamori charm, page 87
This is a generic term for any kind of good luck charm meant to provide some kind of protection, but in this case, it refers specifically to the type of amulet seen in Buddha's hand. This type of *omamori* can be purchased at Shinto shrines and Buddhist temples all over Japan, and is made in all types of colors and fabrics. Inside the fabric is a prayer for safety or some other blessing, and the owner is to carry the amulet with them so it can protect them at all times. In this case, the charm was handmade by Buddha's disciples.

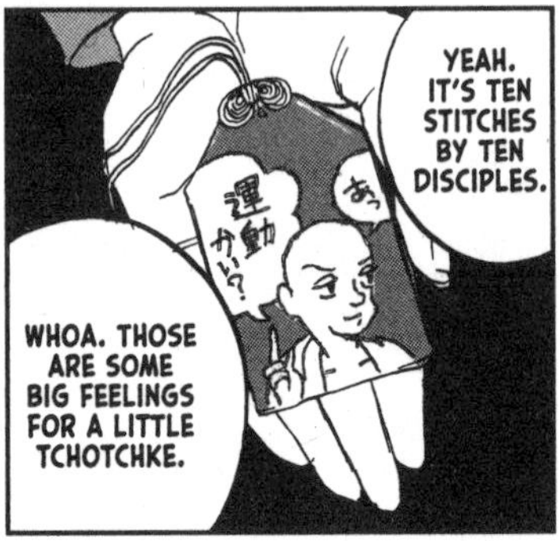

YEAH. IT'S TEN STITCHES BY TEN DISCIPLES.
あっ
WHOA. THOSE ARE SOME BIG FEELINGS FOR A LITTLE TCHOTCHKE.

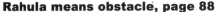

Ten Stitches by Ten Disciples, page 87
This refers to a *Senninbari* or one-thousand stitch charm that was giving to soldiers on their way to war. This charm was a belt or sash that had one thousand knots or stitches, where ideally each stitch was made by a different embroiderer.

Rahula means obstacle, page 88
According to some Buddhist traditions, Rahula was born the day Siddhartha Gautama had determined to leave his palace and kingdom in his quest for enlightenment. He received news of the birth as he was preparing to go, and said, "A *rahu* (obstacle) is born, a fetter has arisen." In other words, because the child might tempt him to stay and give up on his quest, his new son was an obstacle, holding him back from enlightenment.

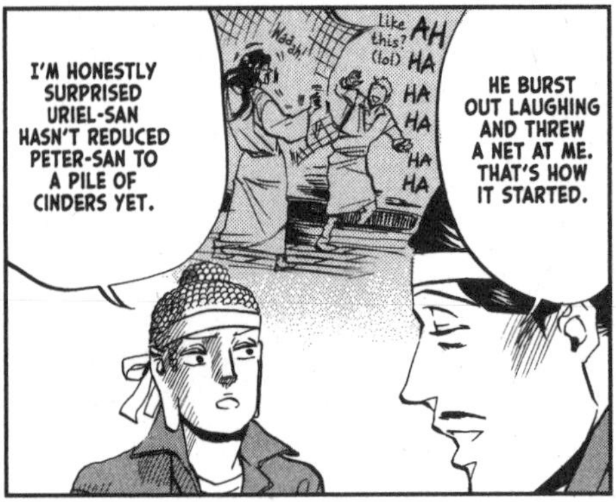

HE BURST OUT LAUGHING AND THREW A NET AT ME. THAT'S HOW IT STARTED.
AH HA HA HA HA HA HA
Like this? (lol)
I'M HONESTLY SURPRISED URIEL-SAN HASN'T REDUCED PETER-SAN TO A PILE OF CINDERS YET.

Fishers of men, page 89
When Jesus called Peter and his brother Andrew to the ministry, he went to them while they were busy at their trade of fishing. He told them, "Follow me, and I will make you fishers of men," indicating that they would bring people into the Kingdom of Heaven.

Buddha's sports career, page 91
As the prince of a kingdom that was constantly at war, Siddhartha Gautama trained in all the martial arts, including archery, horseback riding, and wrestling. According to legend, he once participated in a martial arts tournament, during which his rival killed an elephant. Siddhartha then took the elephant and threw it outside the city.

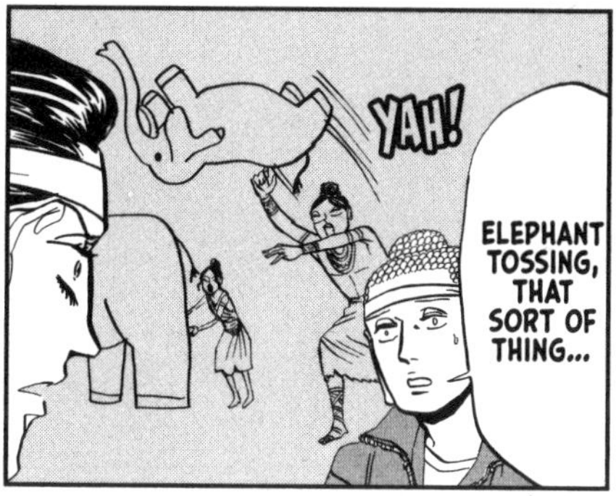
ELEPHANT TOSSING, THAT SORT OF THING...
YAH!

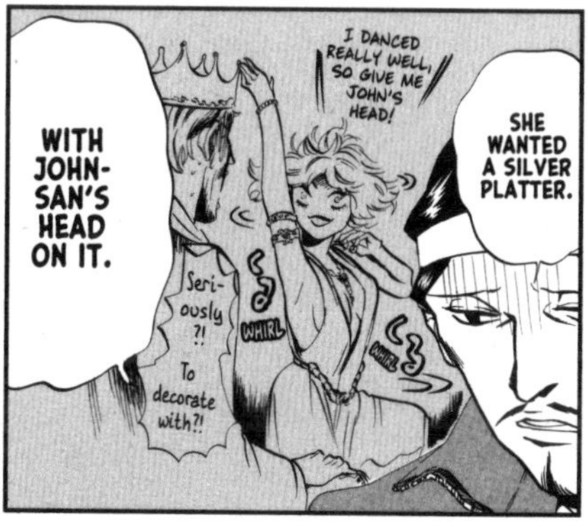
SHE WANTED A SILVER PLATTER.
I DANCED REALLY WELL, SO GIVE ME JOHN'S HEAD!
WITH JOHN-SAN'S HEAD ON IT.
WHIRL
WHIRL
Seriously ?!
To decorate with?!

A silver platter, page 92
The daughter of Herodias danced before King Herod, pleasing him enough that he promised to give her anything she wanted. Under her mother's instructions, she asked for the head of John the Baptist on a silver platter, and he was subsequently beheaded. Herodias was married to Herod (an unlawful state of affairs that was condemned by John the Baptist), which would make Salome Herod's stepdaughter.

Rahula's request for wealth, page 92
After attaining enlightenment, the Buddha returned to visit his old home. This is when Rahula met his father, and, on his mother's instructions, asked the Buddha for his inheritance of riches and royal crown. The Buddha knew these things would not bring true happiness to his son. He decided to instead give Rahula the inheritance of the knowledge he had gained on his path to enlightenment, and had him ordained.

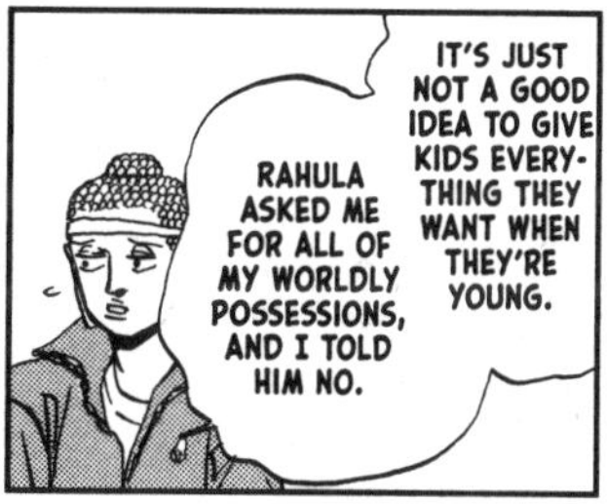
IT'S JUST NOT A GOOD IDEA TO GIVE KIDS EVERY-THING THEY WANT WHEN THEY'RE YOUNG.
RAHULA ASKED ME FOR ALL OF MY WORLDLY POSSESSIONS, AND I TOLD HIM NO.

Spare the rod and spoil the child, page 92
The Japanese version of this idiom (which is what was used in the original text) more literally translates to, "if you love your child, send them on a journey," meaning that if a parent really cares about their child, they will let them experience the pain of the world instead of keeping them sheltered.

Baptize her with the Christian name Aizawa, page 99
A Christian name, or baptismal name, is a name given to, or taken by, a person at their baptism or christening. In Christian cultures, the term is synonymous with "first name" or "given name."

SAINT☆YOUNG MEN

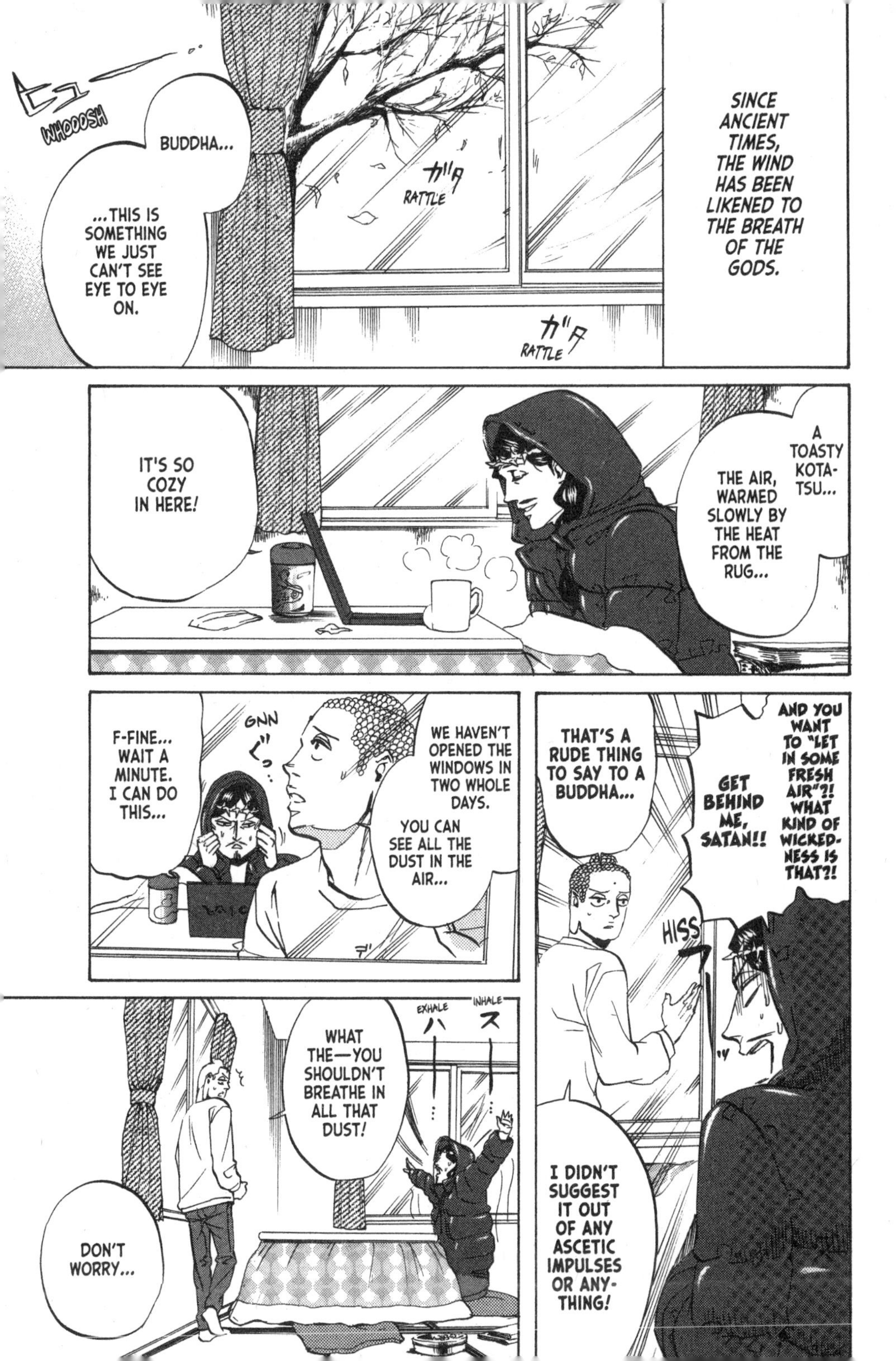
SINCE ANCIENT TIMES, THE WIND HAS BEEN LIKENED TO THE BREATH OF THE GODS.
ガタ RATTLE
ガタ RATTLE
BUDDHA...
...THIS IS SOMETHING WE JUST CAN'T SEE EYE TO EYE ON.
WHOOOSH
A TOASTY KOTATSU...
THE AIR, WARMED SLOWLY BY THE HEAT FROM THE RUG...
IT'S SO COZY IN HERE!
AND YOU WANT TO "LET IN SOME FRESH AIR"?! WHAT KIND OF WICKEDNESS IS THAT?!
GET BEHIND ME, SATAN!!
THAT'S A RUDE THING TO SAY TO A BUDDHA...
HISS
I DIDN'T SUGGEST IT OUT OF ANY ASCETIC IMPULSES OR ANY-THING!
WE HAVEN'T OPENED THE WINDOWS IN TWO WHOLE DAYS.
YOU CAN SEE ALL THE DUST IN THE AIR...
GNN
F-FINE... WAIT A MINUTE. I CAN DO THIS...
INHALE
EXHALE
WHAT THE—YOU SHOULDN'T BREATHE IN ALL THAT DUST!
DON'T WORRY...

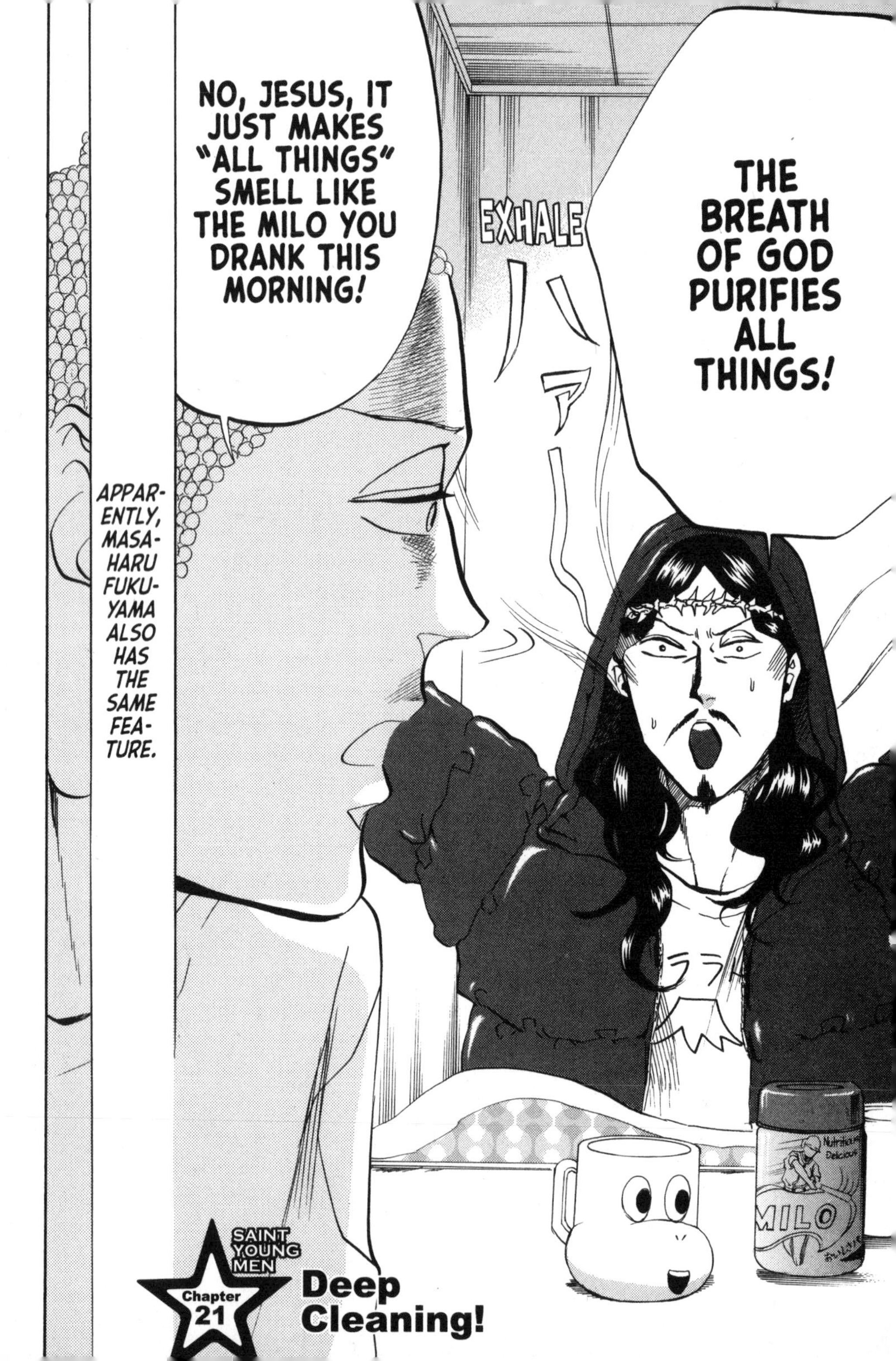
THE BREATH OF GOD PURIFIES ALL THINGS!
EXHALE
NO, JESUS, IT JUST MAKES "ALL THINGS" SMELL LIKE THE MILO YOU DRANK THIS MORNING!
APPARENTLY, MASAHARU FUKUYAMA ALSO HAS THE SAME FEATURE.
MILO
SAINT YOUNG MEN
Chapter 21
Deep Cleaning!

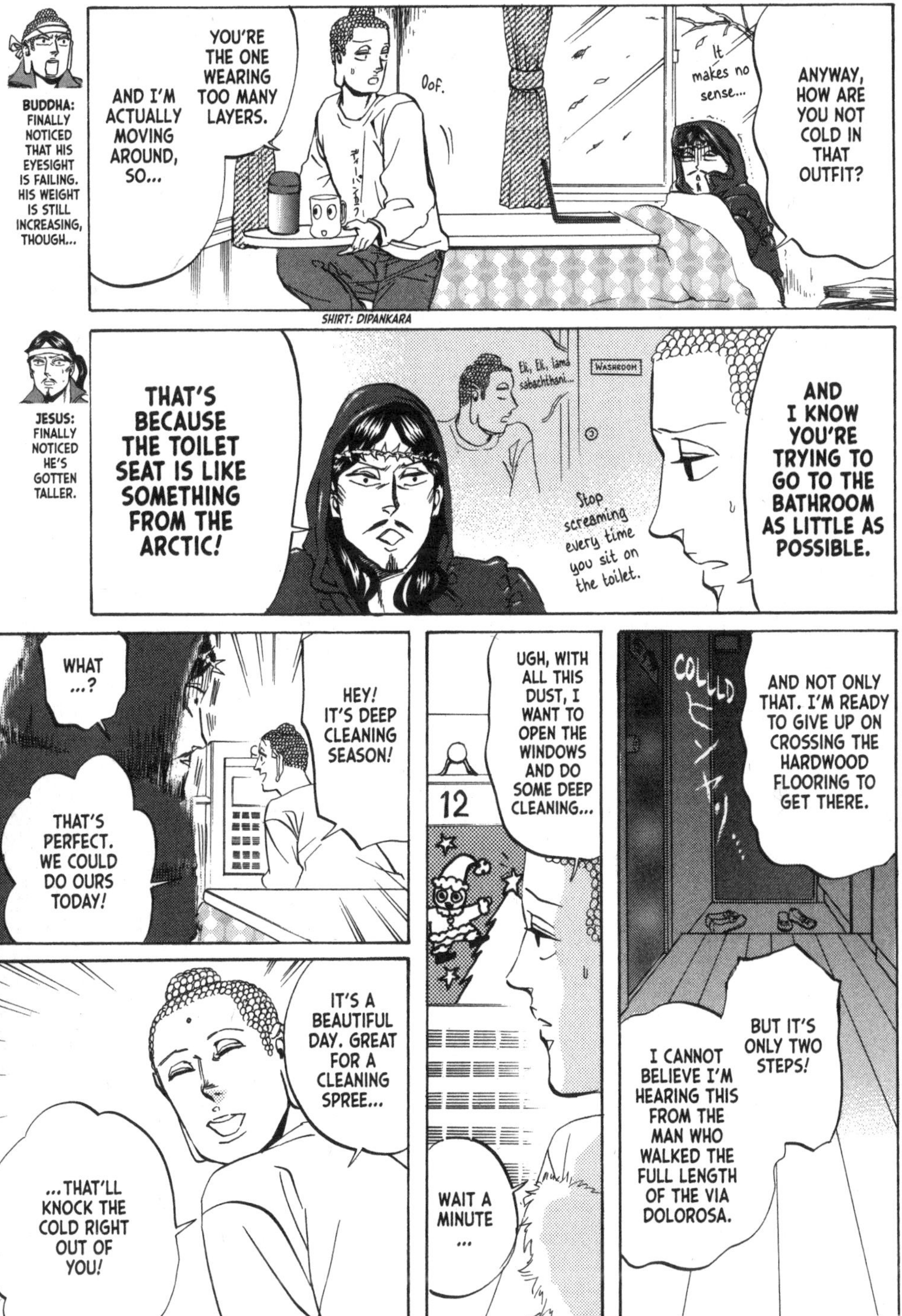
BUDDHA: FINALLY NOTICED THAT HIS EYESIGHT IS FAILING. HIS WEIGHT IS STILL INCREASING, THOUGH...
ANYWAY, HOW ARE YOU NOT COLD IN THAT OUTFIT?
It makes no sense...
Oof.
YOU'RE THE ONE WEARING TOO MANY LAYERS.
AND I'M ACTUALLY MOVING AROUND, SO...
SHIRT: DIPANKARA
JESUS: FINALLY NOTICED HE'S GOTTEN TALLER.
AND I KNOW YOU'RE TRYING TO GO TO THE BATHROOM AS LITTLE AS POSSIBLE.
WASHROOM
Eli, Eli, lama sabachthani...
Stop screaming every time you sit on the toilet.
THAT'S BECAUSE THE TOILET SEAT IS LIKE SOMETHING FROM THE ARCTIC!
AND NOT ONLY THAT. I'M READY TO GIVE UP ON CROSSING THE HARDWOOD FLOORING TO GET THERE.
COLD
BUT IT'S ONLY TWO STEPS!
I CANNOT BELIEVE I'M HEARING THIS FROM THE MAN WHO WALKED THE FULL LENGTH OF THE VIA DOLOROSA.
UGH, WITH ALL THIS DUST, I WANT TO OPEN THE WINDOWS AND DO SOME DEEP CLEANING...
12
WAIT A MINUTE ...
HEY! IT'S DEEP CLEANING SEASON!
WHAT ...?
THAT'S PERFECT. WE COULD DO OURS TODAY!
IT'S A BEAUTIFUL DAY. GREAT FOR A CLEANING SPREE...
...THAT'LL KNOCK THE COLD RIGHT OUT OF YOU!

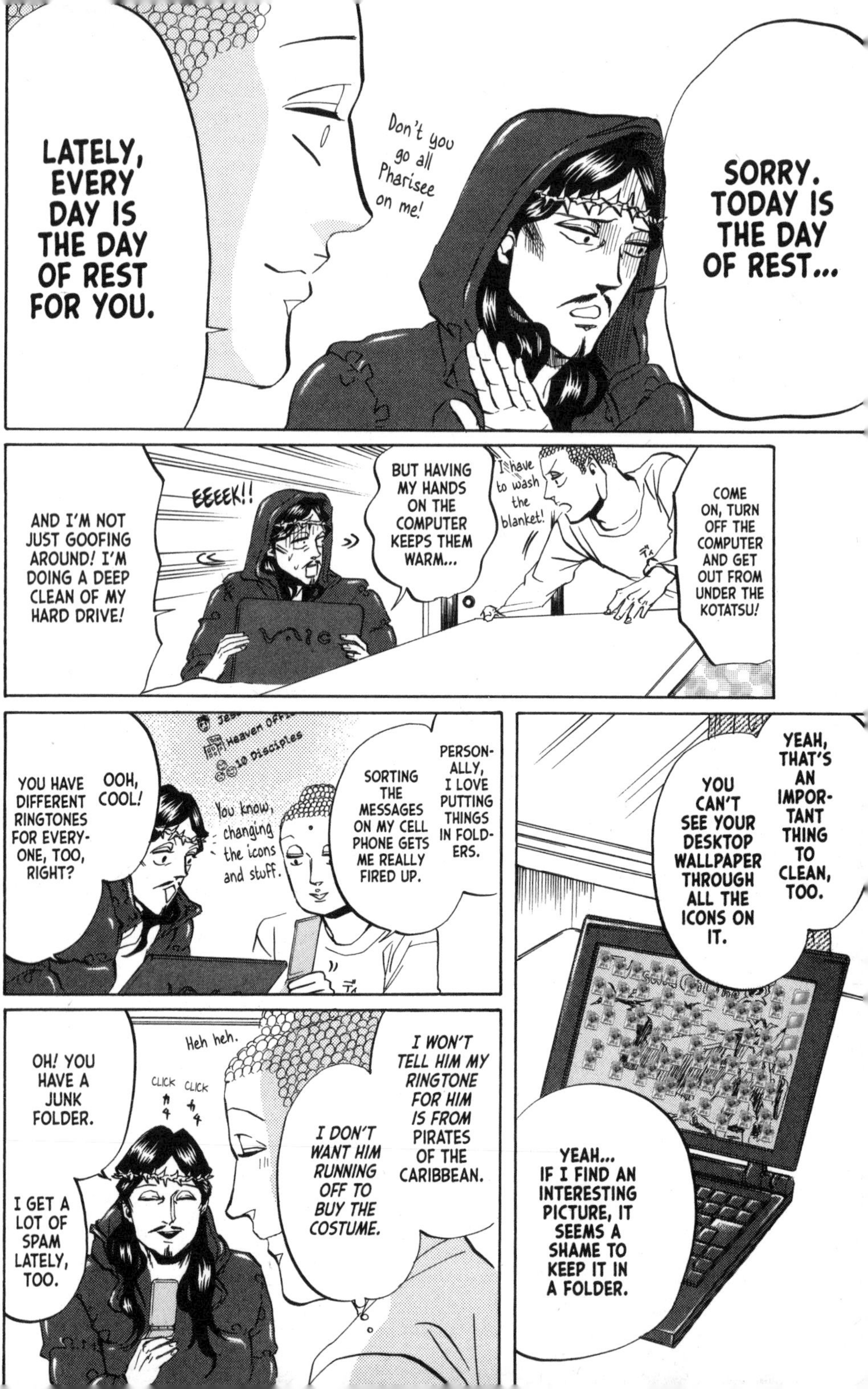
SORRY. TODAY IS THE DAY OF REST...
Don't you go all Pharisee on me!
LATELY, EVERY DAY IS THE DAY OF REST FOR YOU.
COME ON, TURN OFF THE COMPUTER AND GET OUT FROM UNDER THE KOTATSU!
I have to wash the blanket!
BUT HAVING MY HANDS ON THE COMPUTER KEEPS THEM WARM...
EEEEK!!
AND I'M NOT JUST GOOFING AROUND! I'M DOING A DEEP CLEAN OF MY HARD DRIVE!
YEAH, THAT'S AN IMPORTANT THING TO CLEAN, TOO.
YOU CAN'T SEE YOUR DESKTOP WALLPAPER THROUGH ALL THE ICONS ON IT.
YEAH... IF I FIND AN INTERESTING PICTURE, IT SEEMS A SHAME TO KEEP IT IN A FOLDER.
PERSONALLY, I LOVE PUTTING THINGS IN FOLDERS.
SORTING THE MESSAGES ON MY CELL PHONE GETS ME REALLY FIRED UP.
You know, changing the icons and stuff.
10 Disciples
OOH, COOL!
YOU HAVE DIFFERENT RINGTONES FOR EVERYONE, TOO, RIGHT?
I WON'T TELL HIM MY RINGTONE FOR HIM IS FROM PIRATES OF THE CARIBBEAN.
I DON'T WANT HIM RUNNING OFF TO BUY THE COSTUME.
Heh heh.
CLICK CLICK
OH! YOU HAVE A JUNK FOLDER.
I GET A LOT OF SPAM LATELY, TOO.

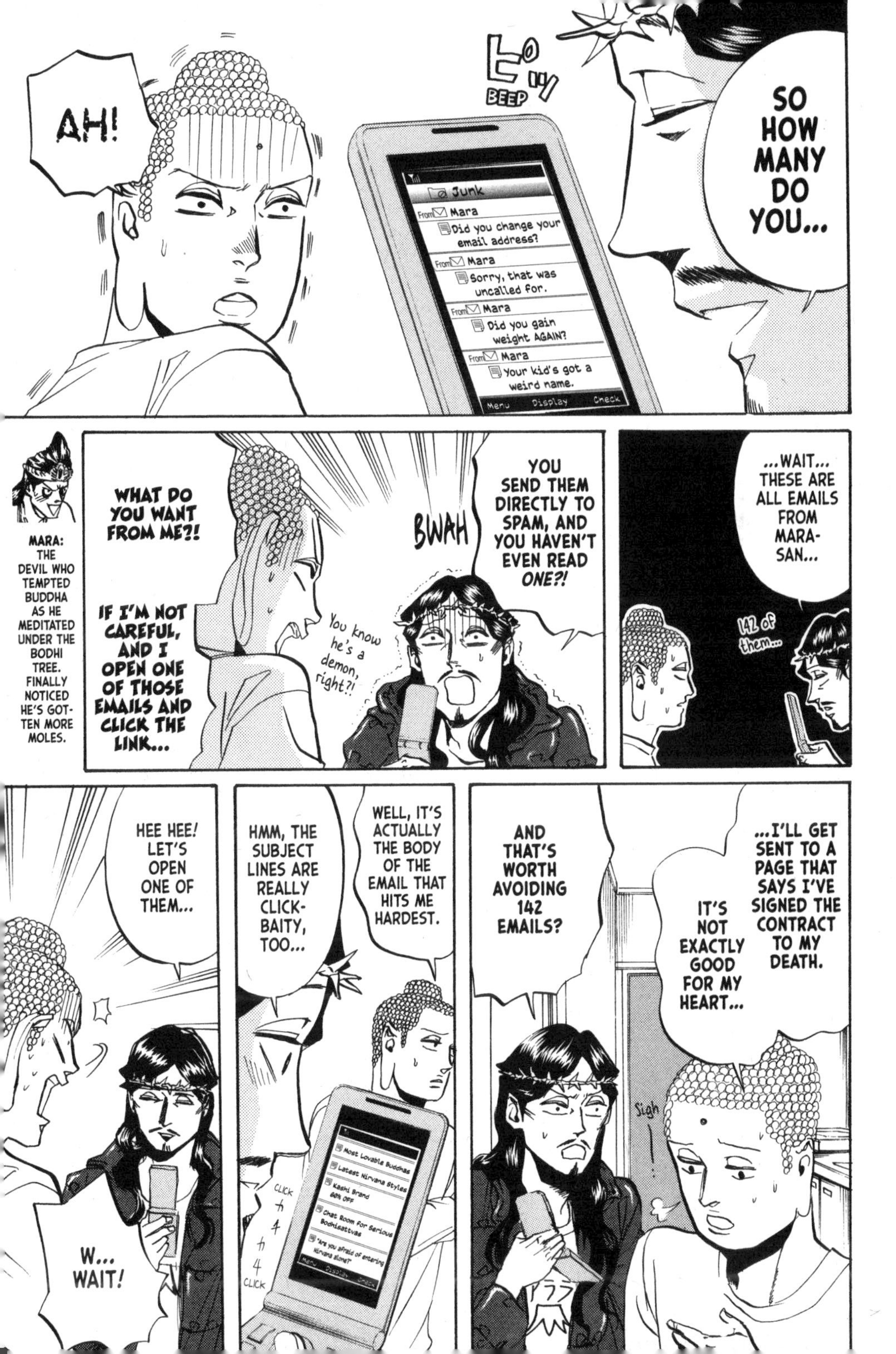
SO HOW MANY DO YOU...
BEEP
Junk
From Mara
Did you change your email address?
From Mara
Sorry, that was uncalled for.
From Mara
Did you gain weight AGAIN?
From Mara
Your kid's got a weird name.
Menu Display Check
AH!
...WAIT... THESE ARE ALL EMAILS FROM MARA-SAN...
142 of them...
YOU SEND THEM DIRECTLY TO SPAM, AND YOU HAVEN'T EVEN READ ONE?!
BWAH
You know he's a demon, right?!
WHAT DO YOU WANT FROM ME?!
IF I'M NOT CAREFUL, AND I OPEN ONE OF THOSE EMAILS AND CLICK THE LINK...
MARA: THE DEVIL WHO TEMPTED BUDDHA AS HE MEDITATED UNDER THE BODHI TREE. FINALLY NOTICED HE'S GOTTEN MORE MOLES.
...I'LL GET SENT TO A PAGE THAT SAYS I'VE SIGNED THE CONTRACT TO MY DEATH.
IT'S NOT EXACTLY GOOD FOR MY HEART...
AND THAT'S WORTH AVOIDING 142 EMAILS?
Sigh
WELL, IT'S ACTUALLY THE BODY OF THE EMAIL THAT HITS ME HARDEST.
HMM, THE SUBJECT LINES ARE REALLY CLICK-BAITY, TOO...
Most Lovable Buddhas
Latest Nirvana Styles
Kashi Brand 66% OFF
Chat Room For Serious Bodhisattvas
"Are you afraid of entering Nirvana alone?"
Menu Display Check
CLICK
CLICK
HEE HEE! LET'S OPEN ONE OF THEM...
W... WAIT!

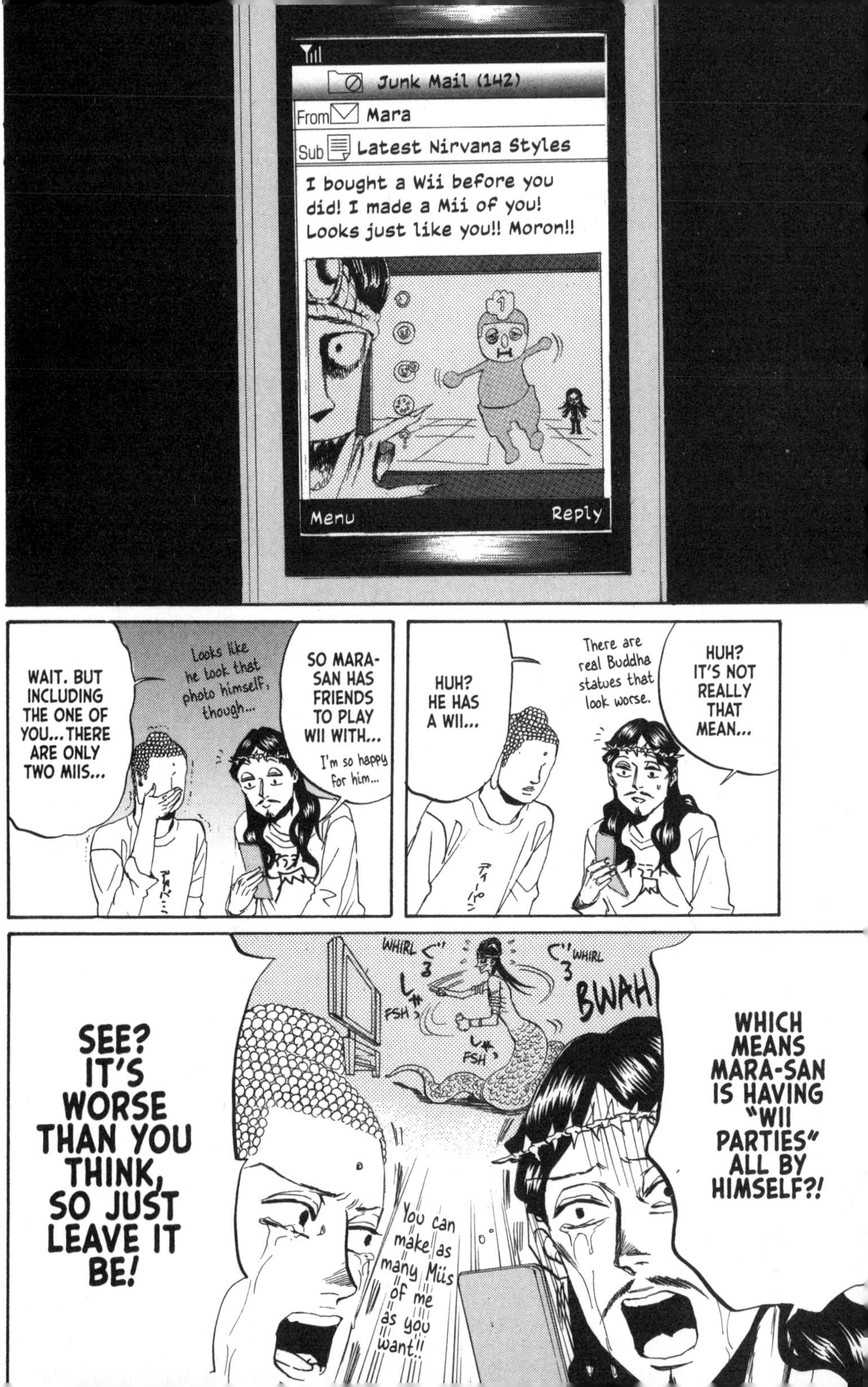
Junk Mail (142)
From Mara
Sub Latest Nirvana Styles
I bought a Wii before you did! I made a Mii of you! Looks just like you!! Moron!!
Menu
Reply
HUH? IT'S NOT REALLY THAT MEAN...
There are real Buddha statues that look worse.
HUH? HE HAS A WII...
SO MARA-SAN HAS FRIENDS TO PLAY WII WITH...
I'm so happy for him...
Looks like he took that photo himself, though...
WAIT. BUT INCLUDING THE ONE OF YOU...THERE ARE ONLY TWO MIIS...
WHICH MEANS MARA-SAN IS HAVING "WII PARTIES" ALL BY HIMSELF?!
BWAH
WHIRL
WHIRL
FSH
FSH
You can make as many Miis of me as you want!!
SEE? IT'S WORSE THAN YOU THINK, SO JUST LEAVE IT BE!

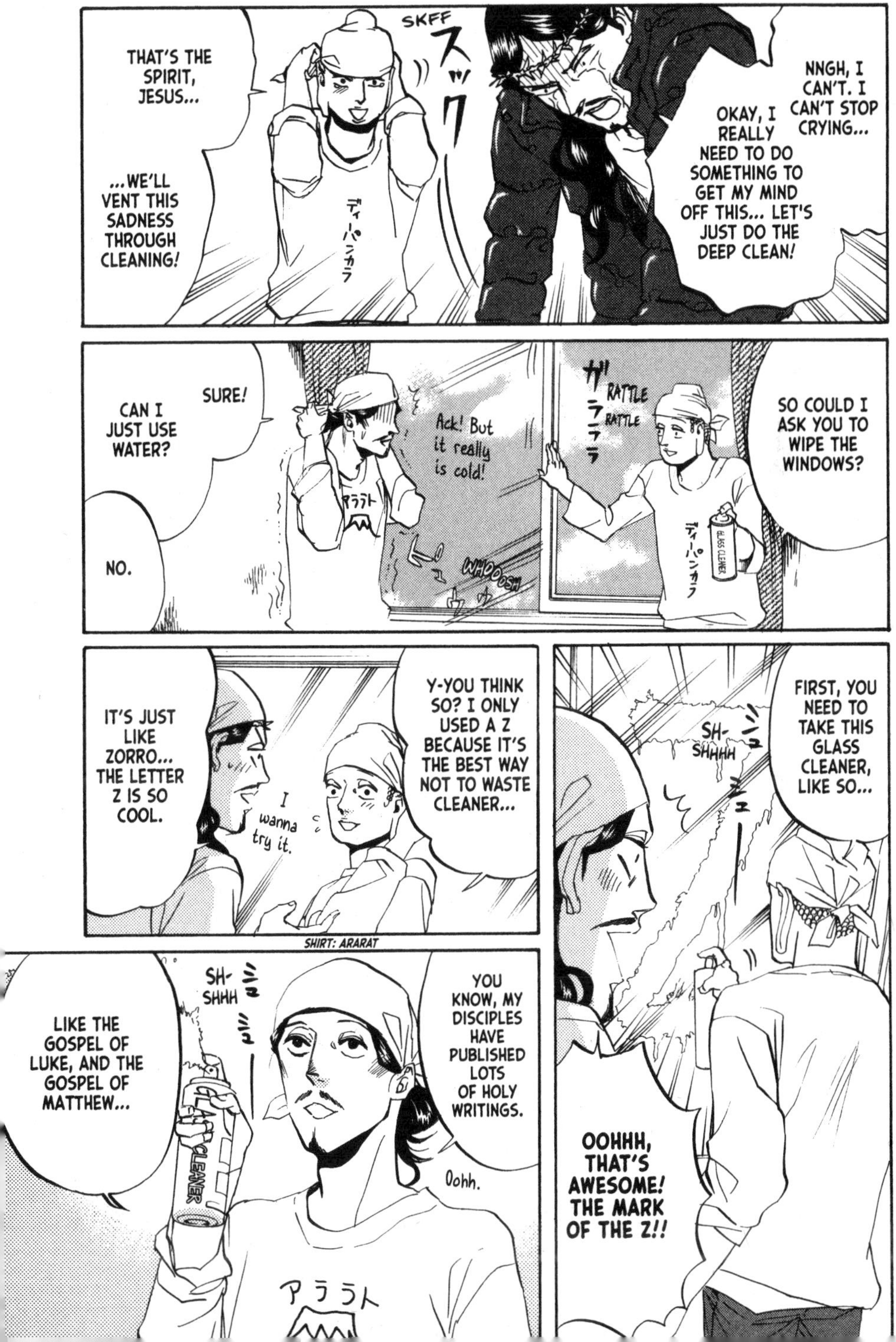
NNGH, I CAN'T. I CAN'T STOP CRYING...
OKAY, I REALLY NEED TO DO SOMETHING TO GET MY MIND OFF THIS... LET'S JUST DO THE DEEP CLEAN!
SKFF
スック
THAT'S THE SPIRIT, JESUS...
...WE'LL VENT THIS SADNESS THROUGH CLEANING!
ディーパンカラ
SO COULD I ASK YOU TO WIPE THE WINDOWS?
ガラララ
RATTLE RATTLE
GLASS CLEANER
ディーパンカラ
Ack! But it really is cold!
WHOOOSH
アララト
SURE!
CAN I JUST USE WATER?
NO.
FIRST, YOU NEED TO TAKE THIS GLASS CLEANER, LIKE SO...
SH-SHHHH
OOHHH, THAT'S AWESOME! THE MARK OF THE Z!!
Y-YOU THINK SO? I ONLY USED A Z BECAUSE IT'S THE BEST WAY NOT TO WASTE CLEANER...
I wanna try it.
IT'S JUST LIKE ZORRO... THE LETTER Z IS SO COOL.
SHIRT: ARARAT
YOU KNOW, MY DISCIPLES HAVE PUBLISHED LOTS OF HOLY WRITINGS.
Oohh.
SH-SHHH
LIKE THE GOSPEL OF LUKE, AND THE GOSPEL OF MATTHEW...
GLASS CLEANER
アララト

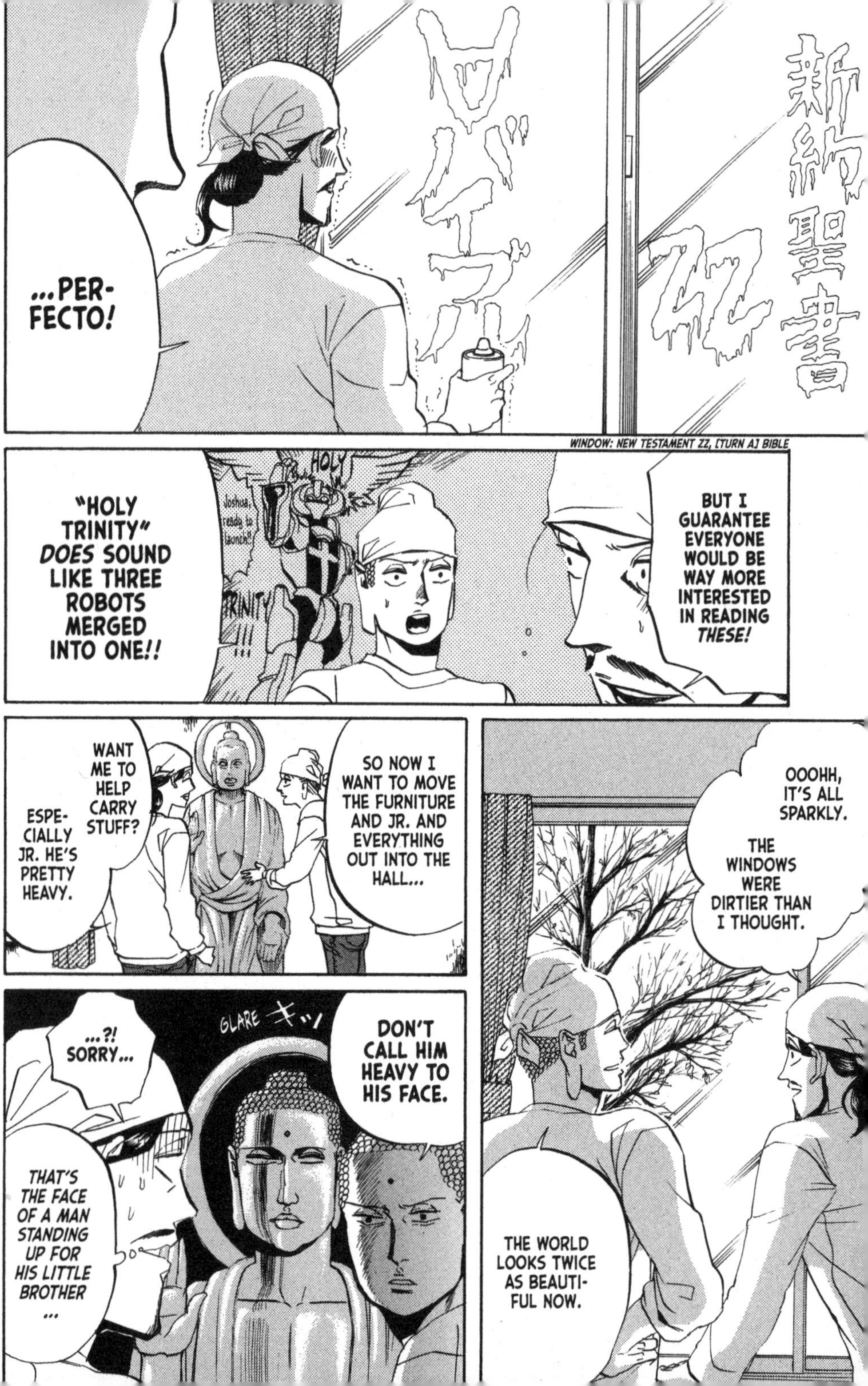
新約聖書
ZZ
∀バイブル
...PER-FECTO!
WINDOW: NEW TESTAMENT ZZ, [TURN A] BIBLE
BUT I GUARANTEE EVERYONE WOULD BE WAY MORE INTERESTED IN READING *THESE!*
HOLY
Joshua, ready to launch!!
TRINITY!!!
"HOLY TRINITY" *DOES* SOUND LIKE THREE ROBOTS MERGED INTO ONE!!
OOOHH, IT'S ALL SPARKLY.
THE WINDOWS WERE DIRTIER THAN I THOUGHT.
THE WORLD LOOKS TWICE AS BEAUTI-FUL NOW.
SO NOW I WANT TO MOVE THE FURNITURE AND JR. AND EVERYTHING OUT INTO THE HALL...
WANT ME TO HELP CARRY STUFF?
ESPE-CIALLY JR. HE'S PRETTY HEAVY.
DON'T CALL HIM HEAVY TO HIS FACE.
GLARE キッ
...?! SORRY...
THAT'S THE FACE OF A MAN STANDING UP FOR HIS LITTLE BROTHER ...

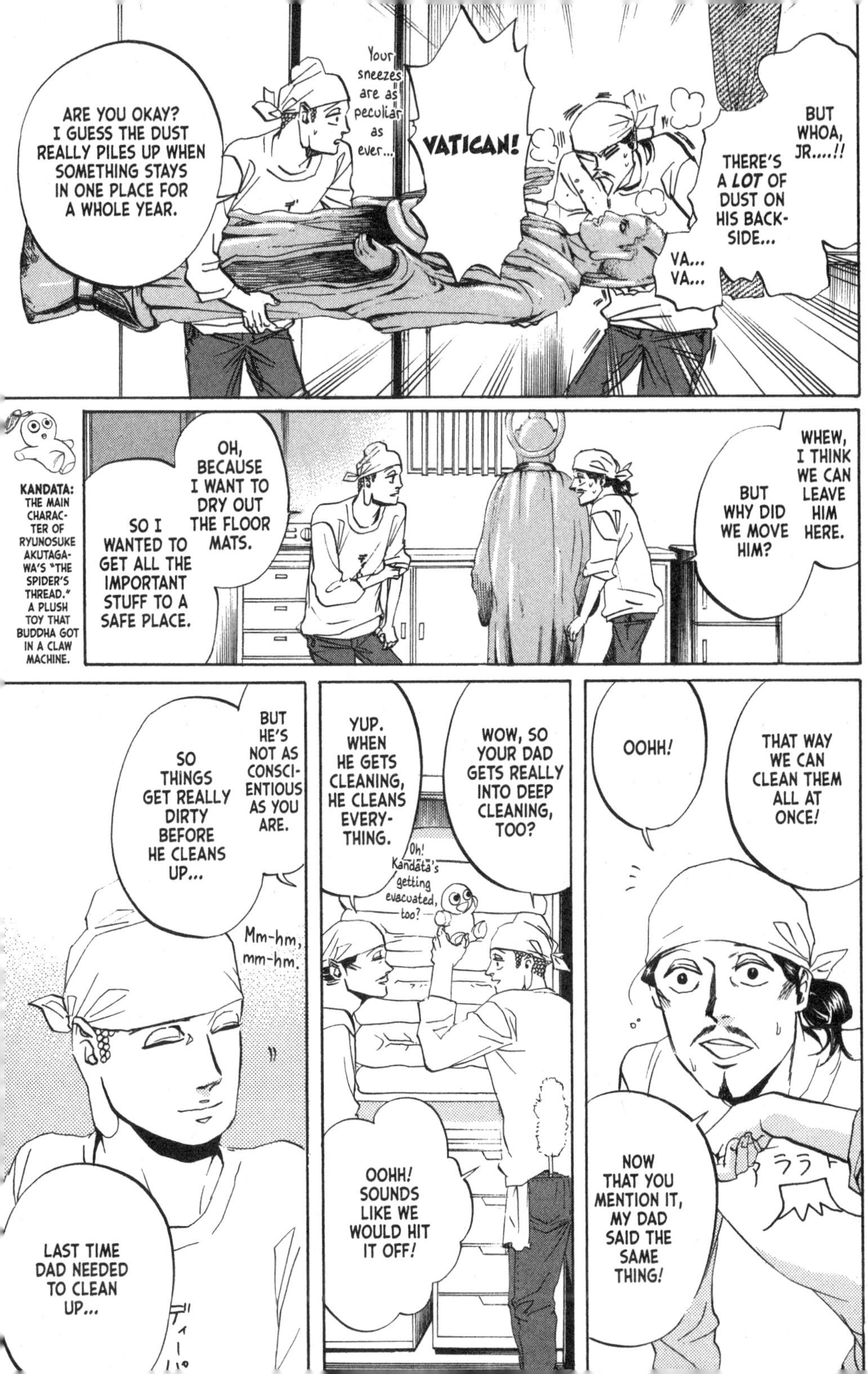
BUT WHOA, JR....!!
THERE'S A *LOT* OF DUST ON HIS BACK-SIDE...
VA... VA...
VATICAN!
Your sneezes are as peculiar as ever...
ARE YOU OKAY? I GUESS THE DUST REALLY PILES UP WHEN SOMETHING STAYS IN ONE PLACE FOR A WHOLE YEAR.
WHEW, I THINK WE CAN LEAVE HIM HERE.
BUT WHY DID WE MOVE HIM?
OH, BECAUSE I WANT TO DRY OUT THE FLOOR MATS.
SO I WANTED TO GET ALL THE IMPORTANT STUFF TO A SAFE PLACE.
THAT WAY WE CAN CLEAN THEM ALL AT ONCE!
OOHH!
NOW THAT YOU MENTION IT, MY DAD SAID THE SAME THING!
WOW, SO YOUR DAD GETS REALLY INTO DEEP CLEANING, TOO?
YUP. WHEN HE GETS CLEANING, HE CLEANS EVERY-THING.
Oh! Kandata's getting evacuated, too?
OOHH! SOUNDS LIKE WE WOULD HIT IT OFF!
BUT HE'S NOT AS CONSCI-ENTIOUS AS YOU ARE.
SO THINGS GET REALLY DIRTY BEFORE HE CLEANS UP...
Mm-hm, mm-hm.
LAST TIME DAD NEEDED TO CLEAN UP...

KANDATA: THE MAIN CHARACTER OF RYUNOSUKE AKUTAGAWA'S "THE SPIDER'S THREAD." A PLUSH TOY THAT BUDDHA GOT IN A CLAW MACHINE.

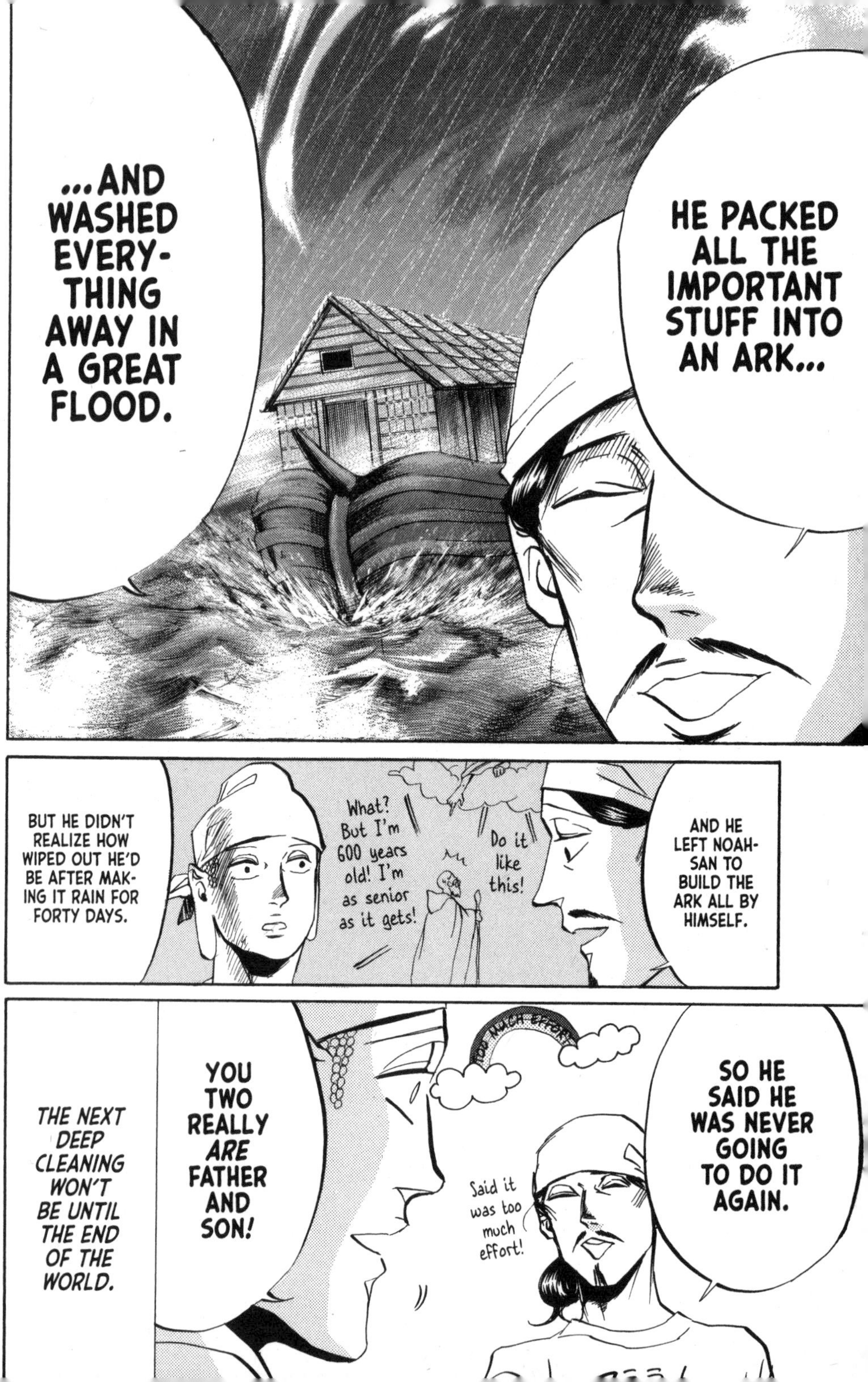
HE PACKED ALL THE IMPORTANT STUFF INTO AN ARK...
...AND WASHED EVERY-THING AWAY IN A GREAT FLOOD.
AND HE LEFT NOAH-SAN TO BUILD THE ARK ALL BY HIMSELF.
Do it like this!
What? But I'm 600 years old! I'm as senior as it gets!
BUT HE DIDN'T REALIZE HOW WIPED OUT HE'D BE AFTER MAK-ING IT RAIN FOR FORTY DAYS.
SO HE SAID HE WAS NEVER GOING TO DO IT AGAIN.
TOO MUCH EFFORT
Said it was too much effort!
YOU TWO REALLY *ARE* FATHER AND SON!
THE NEXT DEEP CLEANING WON'T BE UNTIL THE END OF THE WORLD.

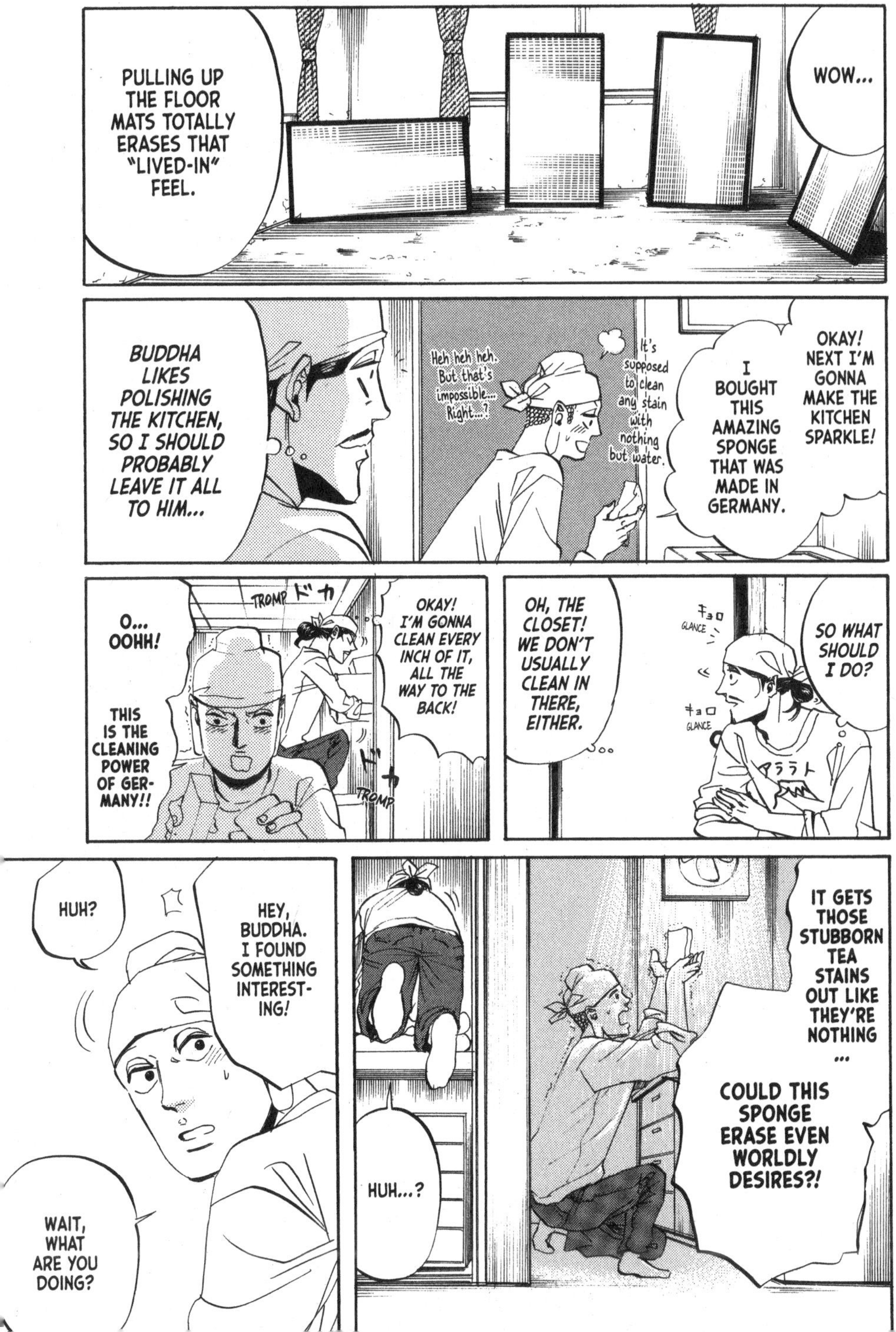
WOW...
PULLING UP THE FLOOR MATS TOTALLY ERASES THAT "LIVED-IN" FEEL.
OKAY! NEXT I'M GONNA MAKE THE KITCHEN SPARKLE!
I BOUGHT THIS AMAZING SPONGE THAT WAS MADE IN GERMANY.
It's supposed to clean any stain with nothing but water.
Heh heh heh. But that's impossible... Right...?
BUDDHA LIKES POLISHING THE KITCHEN, SO I SHOULD PROBABLY LEAVE IT ALL TO HIM...
SO WHAT SHOULD I DO?
キョロ GLANCE
キョロ GLANCE
アララト
OH, THE CLOSET! WE DON'T USUALLY CLEAN IN THERE, EITHER.
OKAY! I'M GONNA CLEAN EVERY INCH OF IT, ALL THE WAY TO THE BACK!
TROMP ドカ
O... OOHH!
THIS IS THE CLEANING POWER OF GERMANY!!
ドカ TROMP
IT GETS THOSE STUBBORN TEA STAINS OUT LIKE THEY'RE NOTHING...
COULD THIS SPONGE ERASE EVEN WORLDLY DESIRES?!
HUH...?
HEY, BUDDHA. I FOUND SOMETHING INTERESTING!
HUH?
WAIT, WHAT ARE YOU DOING?

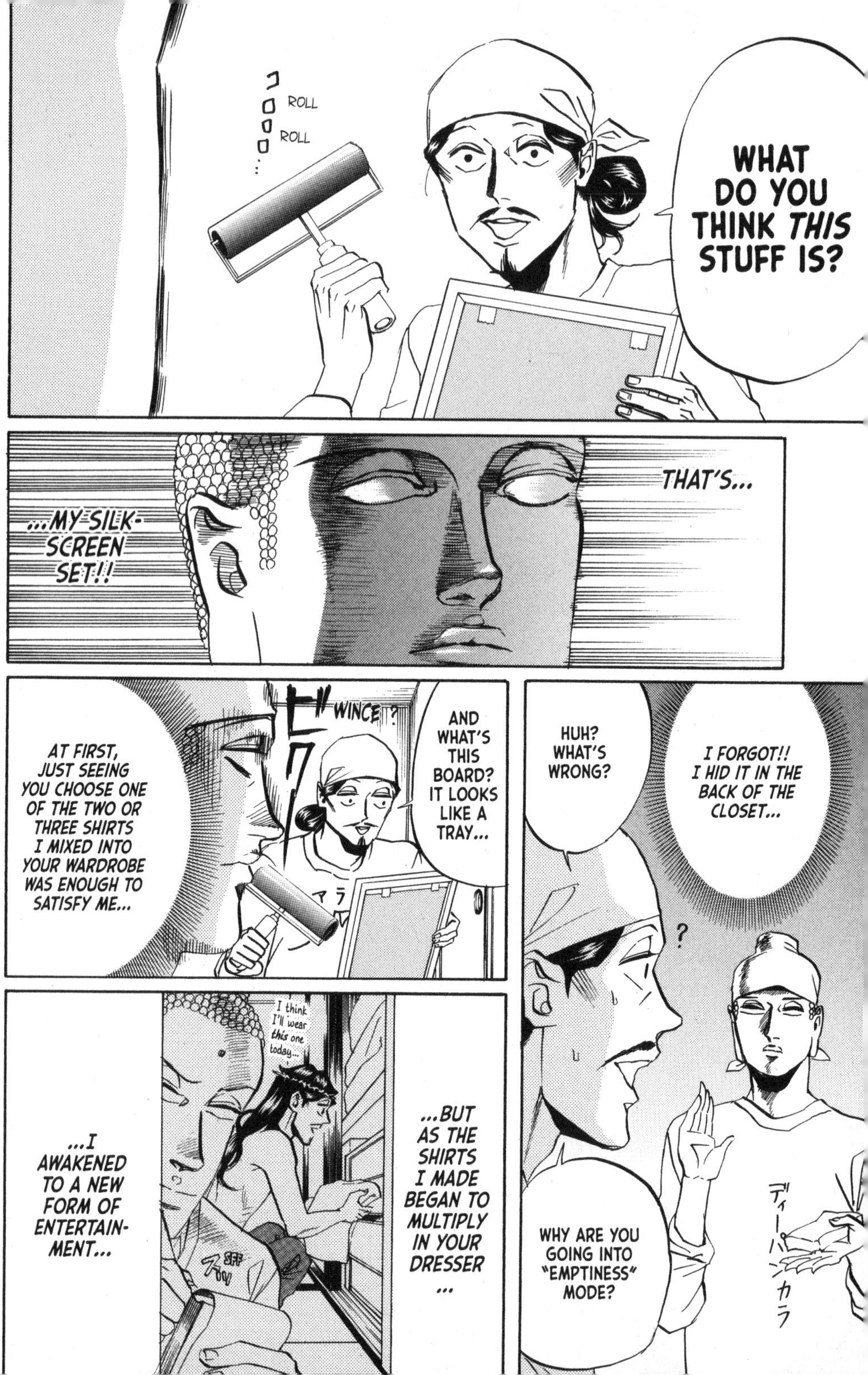
ROLL
ROLL
WHAT DO YOU THINK *THIS* STUFF IS?
THAT'S...
...MY SILK-SCREEN SET!!
I FORGOT!! I HID IT IN THE BACK OF THE CLOSET...
HUH? WHAT'S WRONG?
?
WHY ARE YOU GOING INTO "EMPTINESS" MODE?
WINCE
?
AND WHAT'S THIS BOARD? IT LOOKS LIKE A TRAY...
AT FIRST, JUST SEEING YOU CHOOSE ONE OF THE TWO OR THREE SHIRTS I MIXED INTO YOUR WARDROBE WAS ENOUGH TO SATISFY ME...
...BUT AS THE SHIRTS I MADE BEGAN TO MULTIPLY IN YOUR DRESSER ...
I think I'll wear *this* one today...
...I AWAKENED TO A NEW FORM OF ENTERTAIN-MENT...

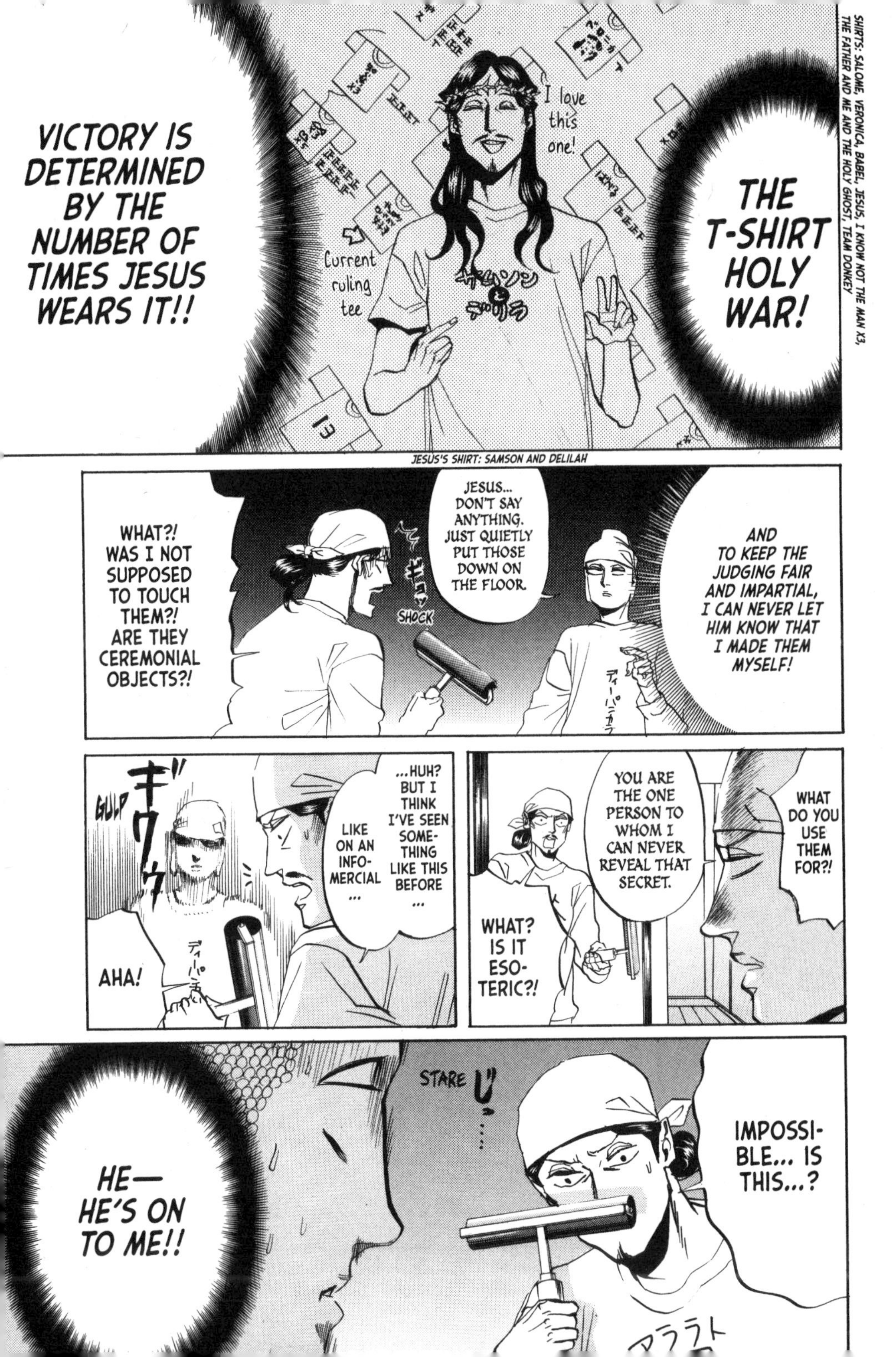
SHIRTS: SALOME, VERONICA, BABEL, JESUS, I KNOW NOT THE MAN X3, THE FATHER AND ME AND THE HOLY GHOST, TEAM DONKEY
THE T-SHIRT HOLY WAR!
I love this one!
Current ruling tee
VICTORY IS DETERMINED BY THE NUMBER OF TIMES JESUS WEARS IT!!
JESUS'S SHIRT: SAMSON AND DELILAH
AND TO KEEP THE JUDGING FAIR AND IMPARTIAL, I CAN NEVER LET HIM KNOW THAT I MADE THEM MYSELF!
JESUS... DON'T SAY ANYTHING. JUST QUIETLY PUT THOSE DOWN ON THE FLOOR.
SHOCK
WHAT?! WAS I NOT SUPPOSED TO TOUCH THEM?! ARE THEY CEREMONIAL OBJECTS?!
WHAT DO YOU USE THEM FOR?!
YOU ARE THE ONE PERSON TO WHOM I CAN NEVER REVEAL THAT SECRET.
WHAT? IS IT ESOTERIC?!
...HUH? BUT I THINK I'VE SEEN SOMETHING LIKE THIS BEFORE...
LIKE ON AN INFOMERCIAL...
GULP
AHA!
IMPOSSIBLE... IS THIS...?
STARE
HE— HE'S ON TO ME!!

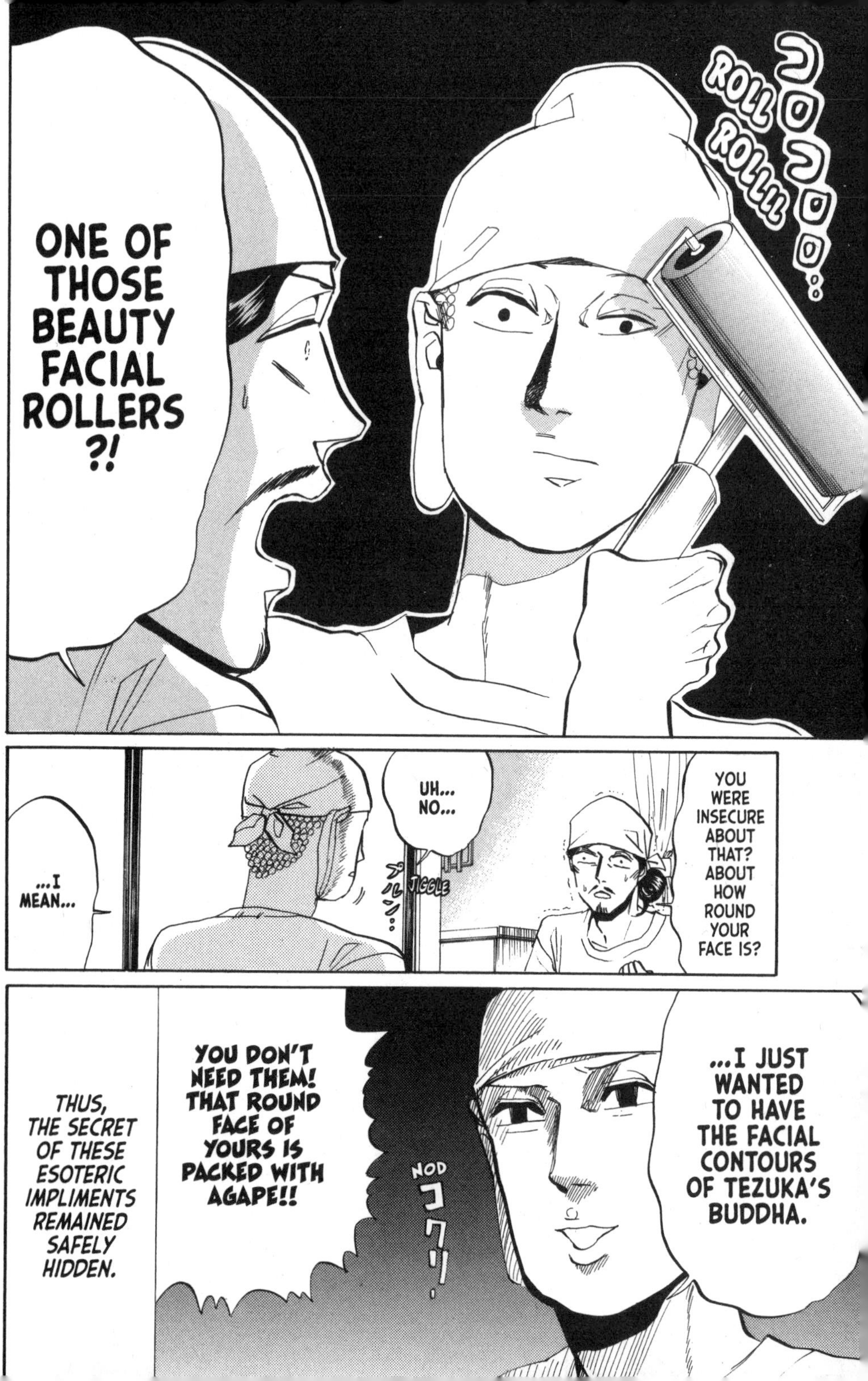
ROLL ROLL
ONE OF THOSE BEAUTY FACIAL ROLLERS ?!
YOU WERE INSECURE ABOUT THAT? ABOUT HOW ROUND YOUR FACE IS?
UH... NO...
JIGGLE
...I MEAN...
...I JUST WANTED TO HAVE THE FACIAL CONTOURS OF TEZUKA'S BUDDHA.
NOD
YOU DON'T NEED THEM! THAT ROUND FACE OF YOURS IS PACKED WITH AGAPE!!
THUS, THE SECRET OF THESE ESOTERIC IMPLIMENTS REMAINED SAFELY HIDDEN.

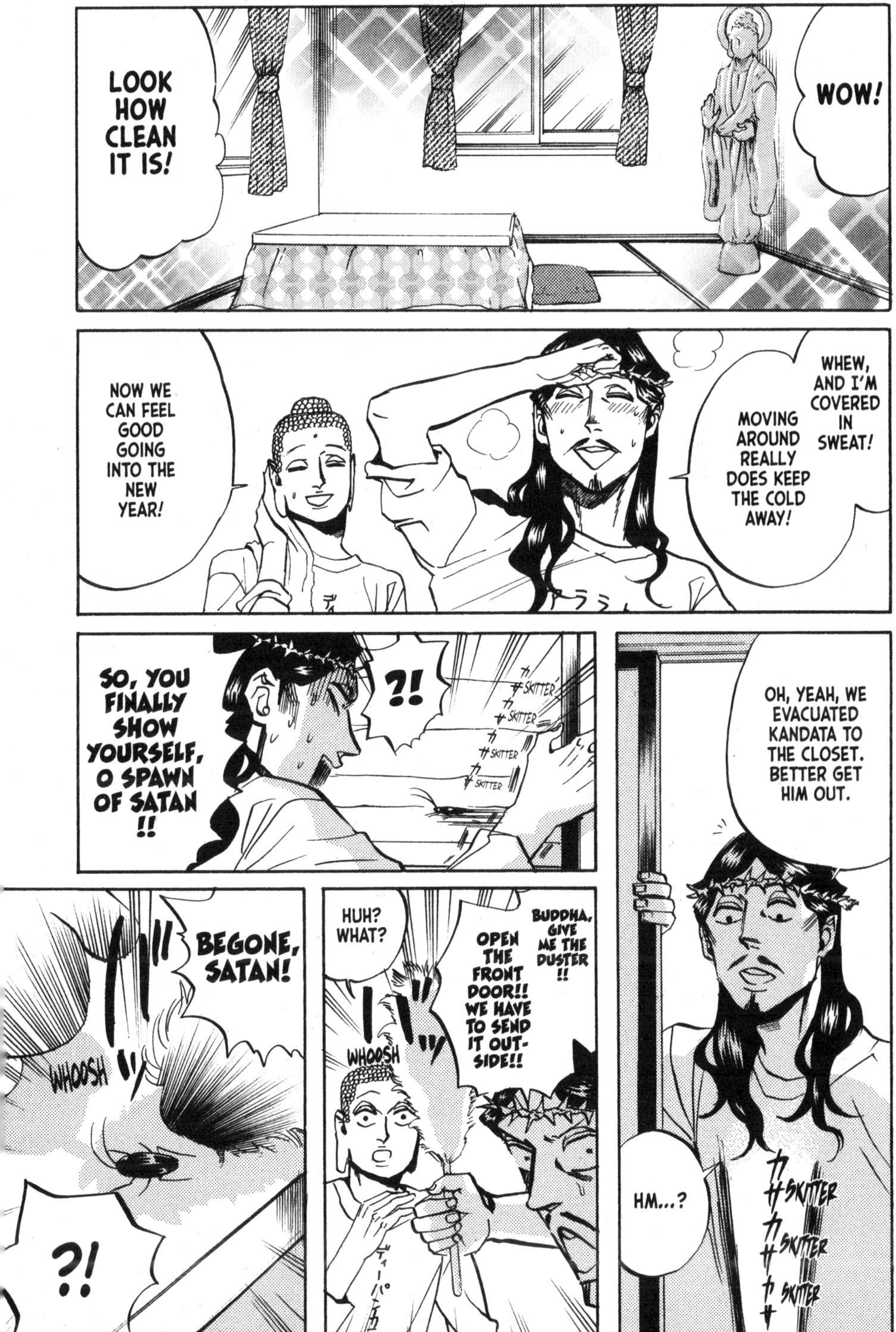
WOW!
LOOK HOW CLEAN IT IS!
WHEW, AND I'M COVERED IN SWEAT!
MOVING AROUND REALLY DOES KEEP THE COLD AWAY!
NOW WE CAN FEEL GOOD GOING INTO THE NEW YEAR!
OH, YEAH, WE EVACUATED KANDATA TO THE CLOSET. BETTER GET HIM OUT.
HM...?
SKITTER
SKITTER
SKITTER
SKITTER
SKITTER
SKITTER
SKITTER
?!
SO, YOU FINALLY SHOW YOURSELF, O SPAWN OF SATAN!!
BUDDHA, GIVE ME THE DUSTER!!
OPEN THE FRONT DOOR!! WE HAVE TO SEND IT OUT-SIDE!!
HUH? WHAT?
WHOOSH
BEGONE, SATAN!
WHOOSH
?!

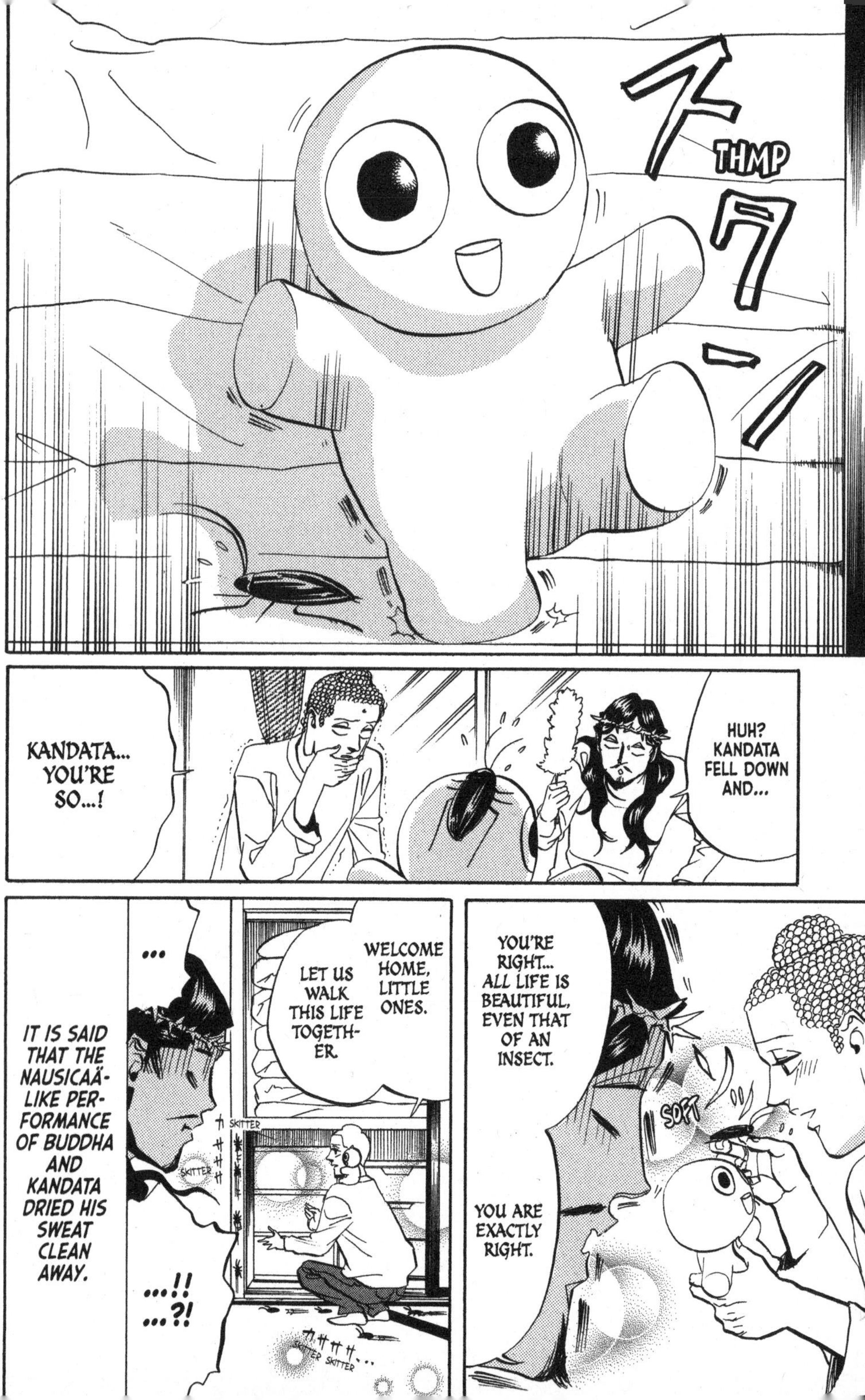
THMP
HUH? KANDATA FELL DOWN AND...
KANDATA... YOU'RE SO...!
YOU'RE RIGHT... *ALL* LIFE IS BEAUTIFUL, EVEN THAT OF AN INSECT.
SOFT
YOU ARE EXACTLY RIGHT.
WELCOME HOME, LITTLE ONES.
LET US WALK THIS LIFE TOGETHER.
SKITTER
SKITTER
SKITTER SKITTER
...
...!!
...?!
IT IS SAID THAT THE NAUSICAÄ-LIKE PERFORMANCE OF BUDDHA AND KANDATA DRIED HIS SWEAT CLEAN AWAY.

• THE ONE EMAIL OF MARA'S THAT BUDDHA REPLIED TO •

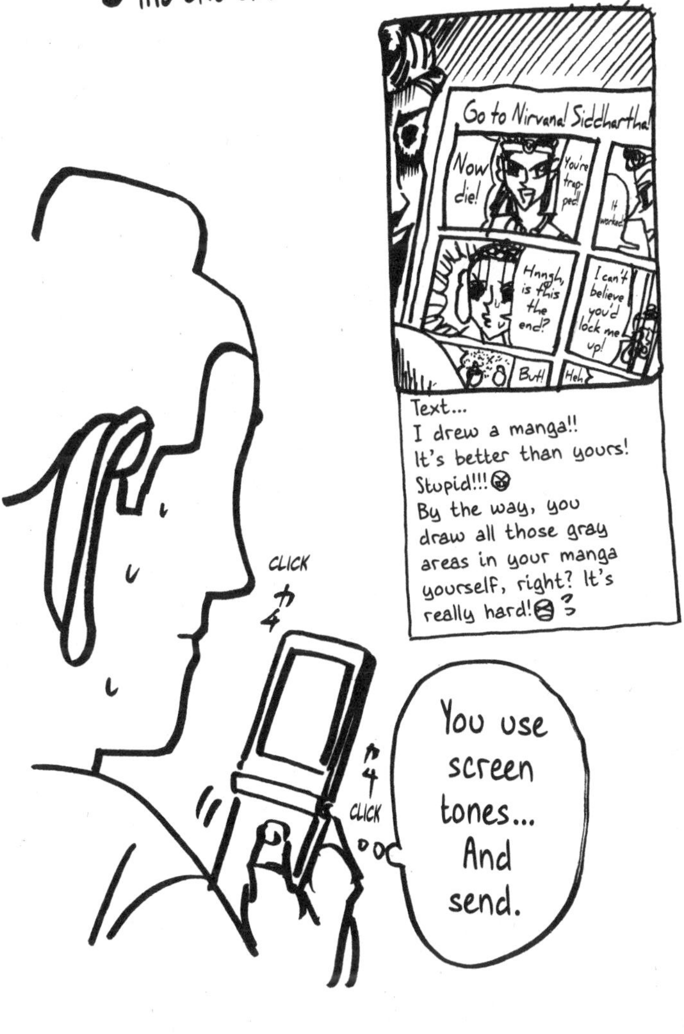
Go to Nirvana! Siddhartha!
You're trap-ped!
Now die!
It worked!
I can't believe you'd lock me up!
Hnngh, is this the end?
Heh
But!
Text...
I drew a manga!!
It's better than yours!
Stupid!!!
By the way, you draw all those gray areas in your manga yourself, right? It's really hard!
CLICK
CLICK
You use screen tones... And send.

CHAPTER 21 TRANSLATION NOTES

Milo, page 106
Milo is a drink mix used to make malted chocolate milk.

Masaharu Fukuyama, page 106
Masaharu Fukuyama is a famous Japanese singer who starred in several gum commercials.

Dipankara, page 107
Dipankara is a Buddha of the past, who was the Buddha eons before Gautama Buddha. There is a story in which Dipankara prophesied to Sumedha, a past incarnation of Siddhartha Gautama, that he would become a Buddha in a future life.

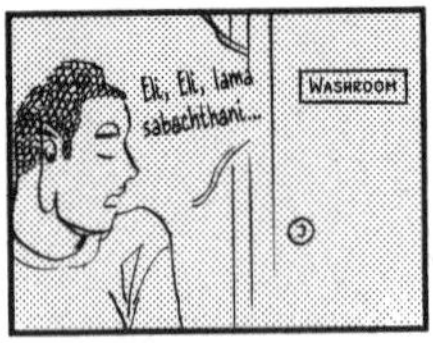
WASHROOM
Eli, Eli, lama sabachthani...

Eli, Eli, lama sabachthani, page 107
"My God, My God, why hast thou forsaken me?" This is what Jesus said on the cross right before he died.

Deep cleaning season, page 107
Instead of spring cleaning, it's traditional in Japan to do deep cleaning in December, to make sure everything is fresh and tidy for the new year.

Pharisees and the day of rest, page 108
The day of rest, also known as the Sabbath, is a weekly holy day used to rest from work and to recharge spiritually, which was originally observed on Saturday—the seventh day of the week—to commemorate the seventh day of the creation of the Earth, during which God rested. After Christ's Ascension into Heaven, Christians began to observe the Sabbath on Sunday to commemorate the Resurrection. The Pharisees were a group of Jewish people who were known for their strict observance of the law, which included very rigid rules for the Sabbath, dictating even a limit to the number of steps that were allowed to be taken that day. They often accused Jesus of breaking the Sabbath when they learned he had healed someone on the day of rest.

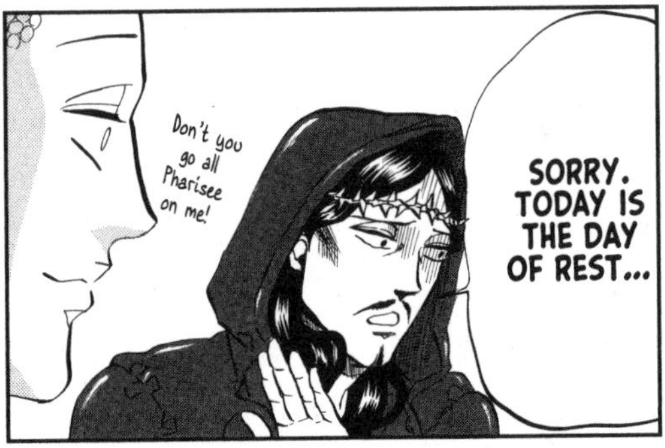
SORRY. TODAY IS THE DAY OF REST...
Don't you go all Pharisee on me!

The Gospel of Luke, the Gospel of Matthew, and Ararat, page 111
The Gospel According to Luke and *The Gospel According to Matthew* are two of the books in the New Testament of the Bible. Each of them is an account of the life and teachings of Jesus. These two books are supplemented by *The Gospel According to Mark* and *The Gospel According to John*. Ararat is the name of the mountain where Noah's ark landed when the waters from the Great Flood began to recede.

***New Testament ZZ* and *[TURN A] Bible*, page 112**
These title adjustments to the Bible were inspired by the *Gundam* franchise, a series of anime series about giant robots called Gundams. These series include *Gundam ZZ* and *Turn A Gundam*.

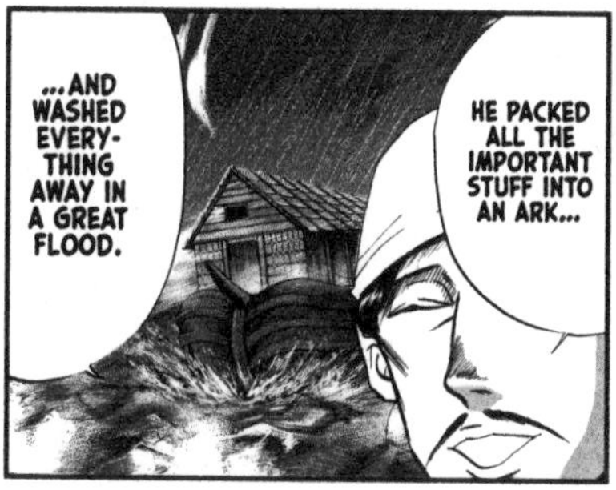
HE PACKED ALL THE IMPORTANT STUFF INTO AN ARK...
...AND WASHED EVERY-THING AWAY IN A GREAT FLOOD.

The Great Flood and the rainbow, page 114

Many people are familiar with the story of Noah and the Ark, when Noah builds an ark, fills it with animals, and he and his family are spared when the rains come for 40 days and 40 nights, flooding the whole Earth, and thus destroying the wicked. Genesis does state that Noah was 600 years old at the time. The rainbow was given by God after the flood as a sign of mercy—a promise that the world would never again be destroyed by flooding.

Tally marks, page 117

The marks next to the t-shirts are Japanese tally marks. The Chinese character for "right" or "correct" has exactly five strokes, so by writing one stroke of the character as you count, it's easy to look back at the marks and count them by fives.

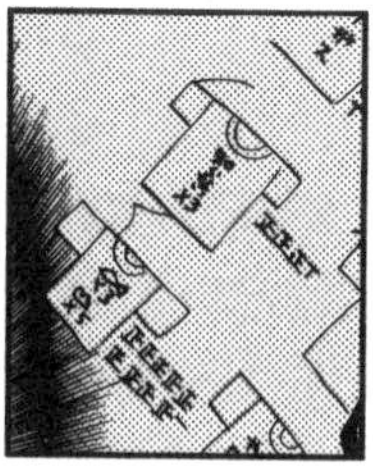

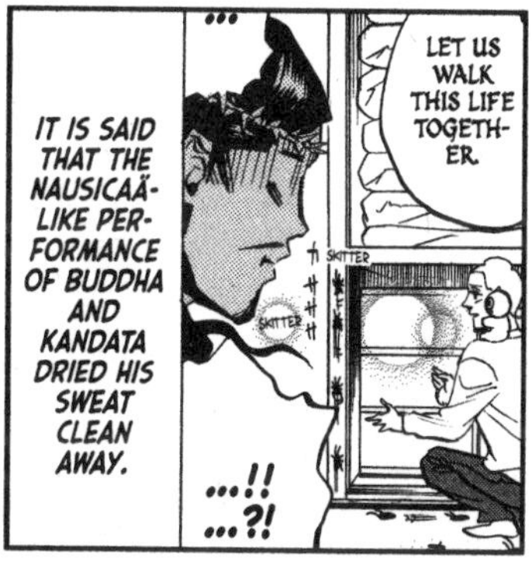
LET US WALK THIS LIFE TOGETH-ER.
SKITTER
SKITTER
...
...!!
...?!
IT IS SAID THAT THE NAUSICAÄ-LIKE PER-FORMANCE OF BUDDHA AND KANDATA DRIED HIS SWEAT CLEAN AWAY.

Nausicaä, page 120

The heroine of *Nausicaä of the Valley of the Wind,* Nausicaä, is the princess of the Valley of the Wind in a post-apocalyptic world, and she communicates with many creatures, including the mutant insects that infest the Earth.

Screen tone, page 121

Screen tones are what manga artists use to "color" their manga. Any area that isn't black or white is made gray or given a texture or pattern with screen tone. It works like a sticker, and comes in sheets, or screens. The manga artist (or their assistants) will cut out a piece of screen tone roughly the size of the area that needs to be covered, then he'll lay it over the drawing and use a small blade to cut away the pieces that don't fit inside the lines. These days, this process can be done digitally.

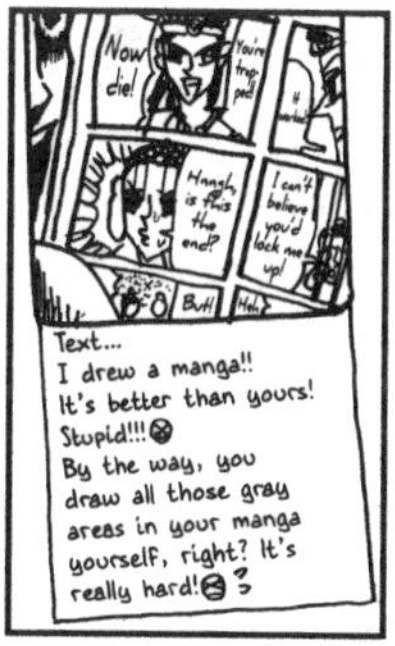
Now die!
Text...
I drew a manga!!
It's better than yours!
Stupid!!!
By the way, you draw all those gray areas in your manga yourself, right? It's really hard!

SAINT☆YOUNG MEN

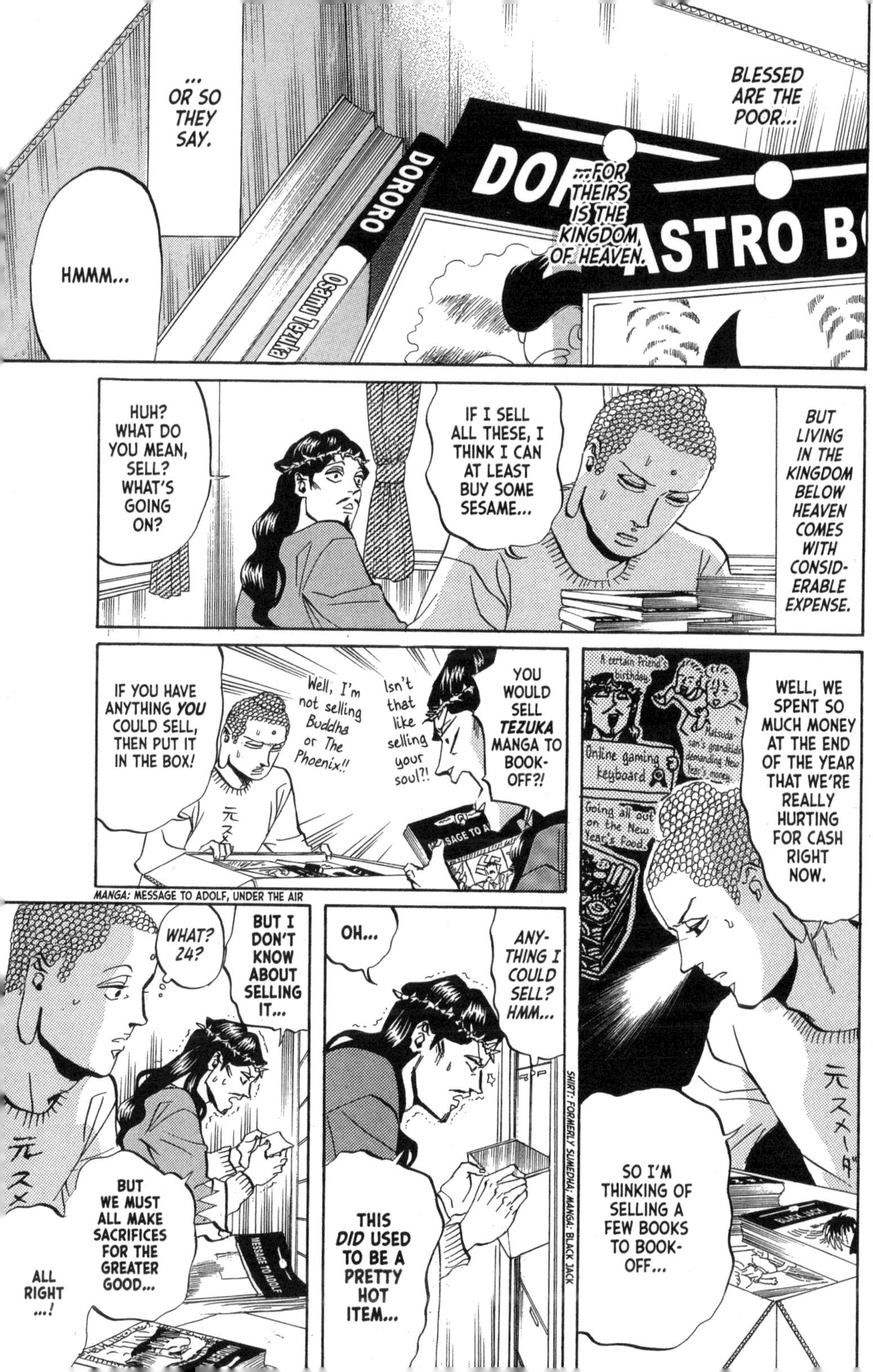
BLESSED ARE THE POOR...
...FOR THEIRS IS THE KINGDOM OF HEAVEN.
...OR SO THEY SAY.
DORORO
Osamu Tezuka
HMMM...
BUT LIVING IN THE KINGDOM BELOW HEAVEN COMES WITH CONSIDERABLE EXPENSE.
IF I SELL ALL THESE, I THINK I CAN AT LEAST BUY SOME SESAME...
HUH? WHAT DO YOU MEAN, SELL? WHAT'S GOING ON?
WELL, WE SPENT SO MUCH MONEY AT THE END OF THE YEAR THAT WE'RE REALLY HURTING FOR CASH RIGHT NOW.
A certain Friend's birthday
Matsuda-san's grandkids demanding New Year's money
Online gaming keyboard
Going all out on the New Year's Food.
SO I'M THINKING OF SELLING A FEW BOOKS TO BOOK-OFF...
YOU WOULD SELL *TEZUKA* MANGA TO BOOK-OFF?!
Isn't that like selling your soul?!
Well, I'm not selling Buddha or The Phoenix!!
IF YOU HAVE ANYTHING *YOU* COULD SELL, THEN PUT IT IN THE BOX!
MANGA: MESSAGE TO ADOLF, UNDER THE AIR
ANYTHING I COULD SELL? HMMM...
OH...
THIS *DID* USED TO BE A PRETTY HOT ITEM...
SHIRT: FORMERLY SUMEDHA; MANGA: BLACK JACK
BUT I DON'T KNOW ABOUT SELLING IT...
WHAT? 24?
MESSAGE TO ADOLF
BUT WE MUST ALL MAKE SACRIFICES FOR THE GREATER GOOD...
ALL RIGHT ...!

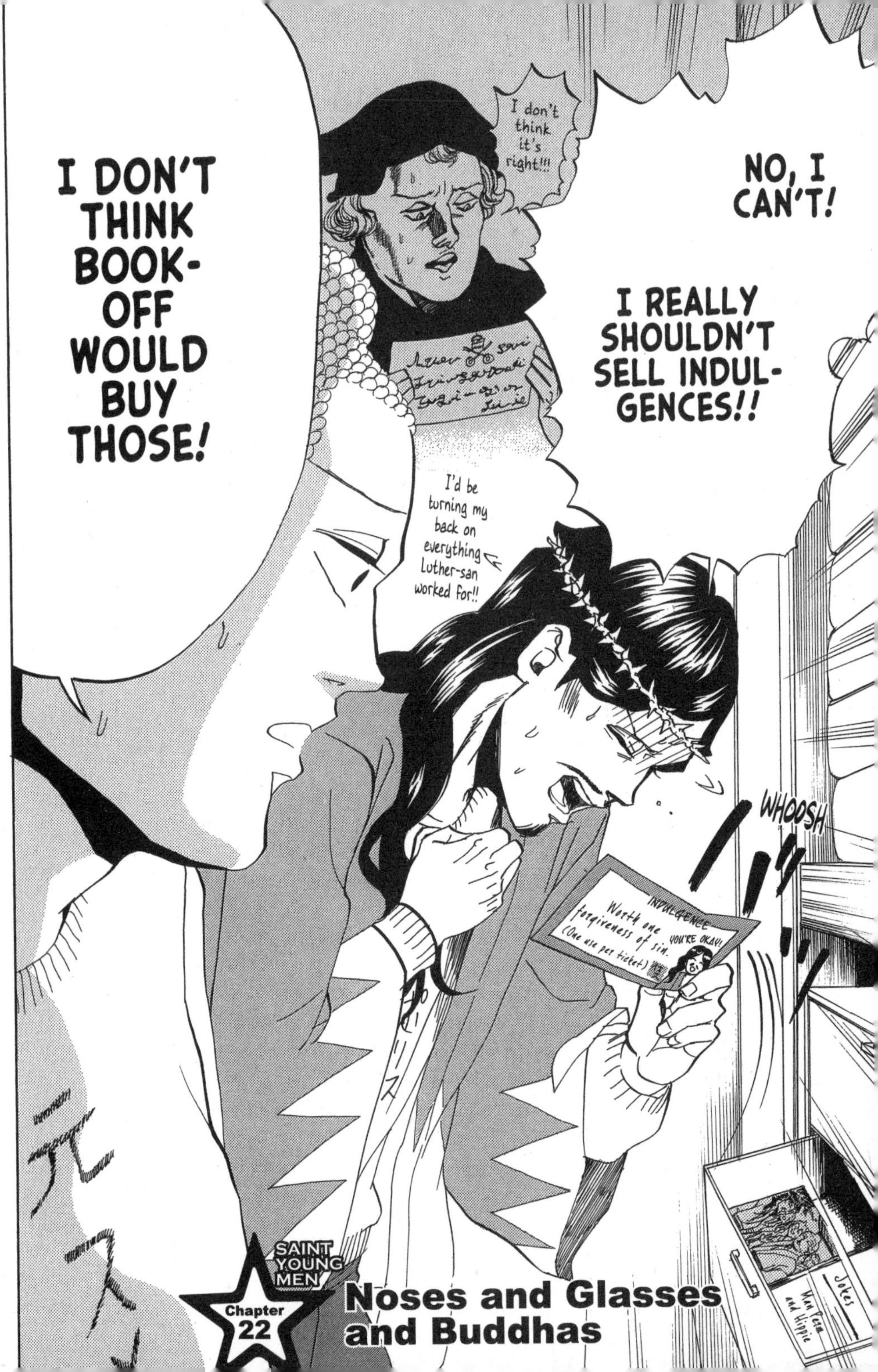
NO, I CAN'T!
I REALLY SHOULDN'T SELL INDUL-GENCES!!
I don't think it's right!!
I'd be turning my back on everything Luther-san worked for!!
I DON'T THINK BOOK-OFF WOULD BUY THOSE!
WHOOSH
INDULGENCE
Worth one forgiveness of sin. (One use per ticket)
YOU'RE OKAY!
Jokes
Man Perm and Hippie
SAINT YOUNG MEN
Chapter 22
Noses and Glasses and Buddhas

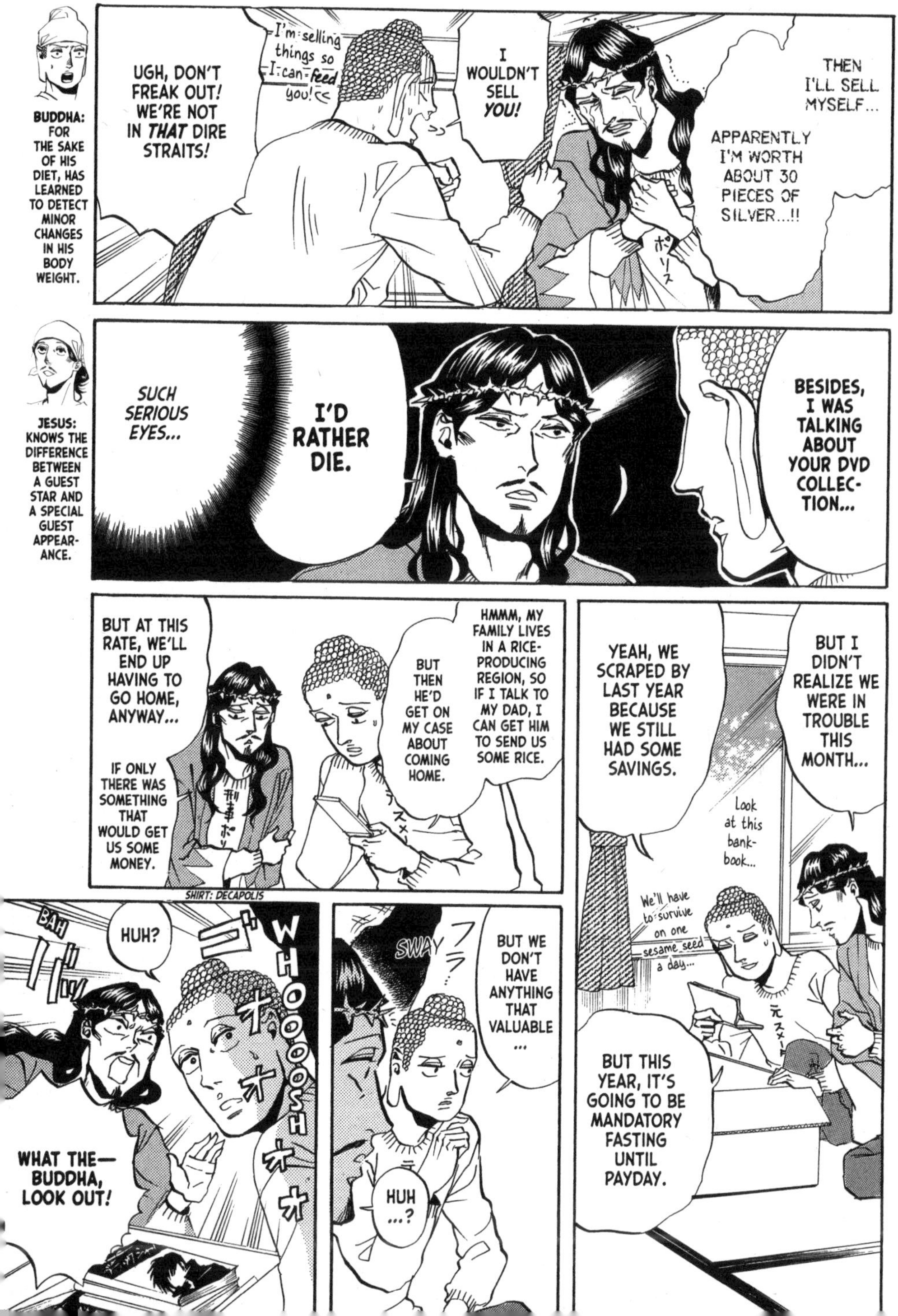
THEN I'LL SELL MYSELF...
APPARENTLY I'M WORTH ABOUT 30 PIECES OF SILVER...!!
I WOULDN'T SELL *YOU!*
I'm selling things so I can *feed* you!
UGH, DON'T FREAK OUT! WE'RE NOT IN *THAT* DIRE STRAITS!
BUDDHA: FOR THE SAKE OF HIS DIET, HAS LEARNED TO DETECT MINOR CHANGES IN HIS BODY WEIGHT.
BESIDES, I WAS TALKING ABOUT YOUR DVD COLLECTION...
I'D RATHER DIE.
SUCH SERIOUS EYES...
JESUS: KNOWS THE DIFFERENCE BETWEEN A GUEST STAR AND A SPECIAL GUEST APPEARANCE.
BUT I DIDN'T REALIZE WE WERE IN TROUBLE THIS MONTH...
YEAH, WE SCRAPED BY LAST YEAR BECAUSE WE STILL HAD SOME SAVINGS.
Look at this bankbook...
We'll have to survive on one sesame seed a day...
BUT THIS YEAR, IT'S GOING TO BE MANDATORY FASTING UNTIL PAYDAY.
HMMM, MY FAMILY LIVES IN A RICE-PRODUCING REGION, SO IF I TALK TO MY DAD, I CAN GET HIM TO SEND US SOME RICE.
BUT THEN HE'D GET ON MY CASE ABOUT COMING HOME.
BUT AT THIS RATE, WE'LL END UP HAVING TO GO HOME, ANYWAY...
IF ONLY THERE WAS SOMETHING THAT WOULD GET US SOME MONEY.
SHIRT: DECAPOLIS
BUT WE DON'T HAVE ANYTHING THAT VALUABLE...
SWAY
HUH ...?
WHOOOOOSH
HUH?
BAH
WHAT THE— BUDDHA, LOOK OUT!

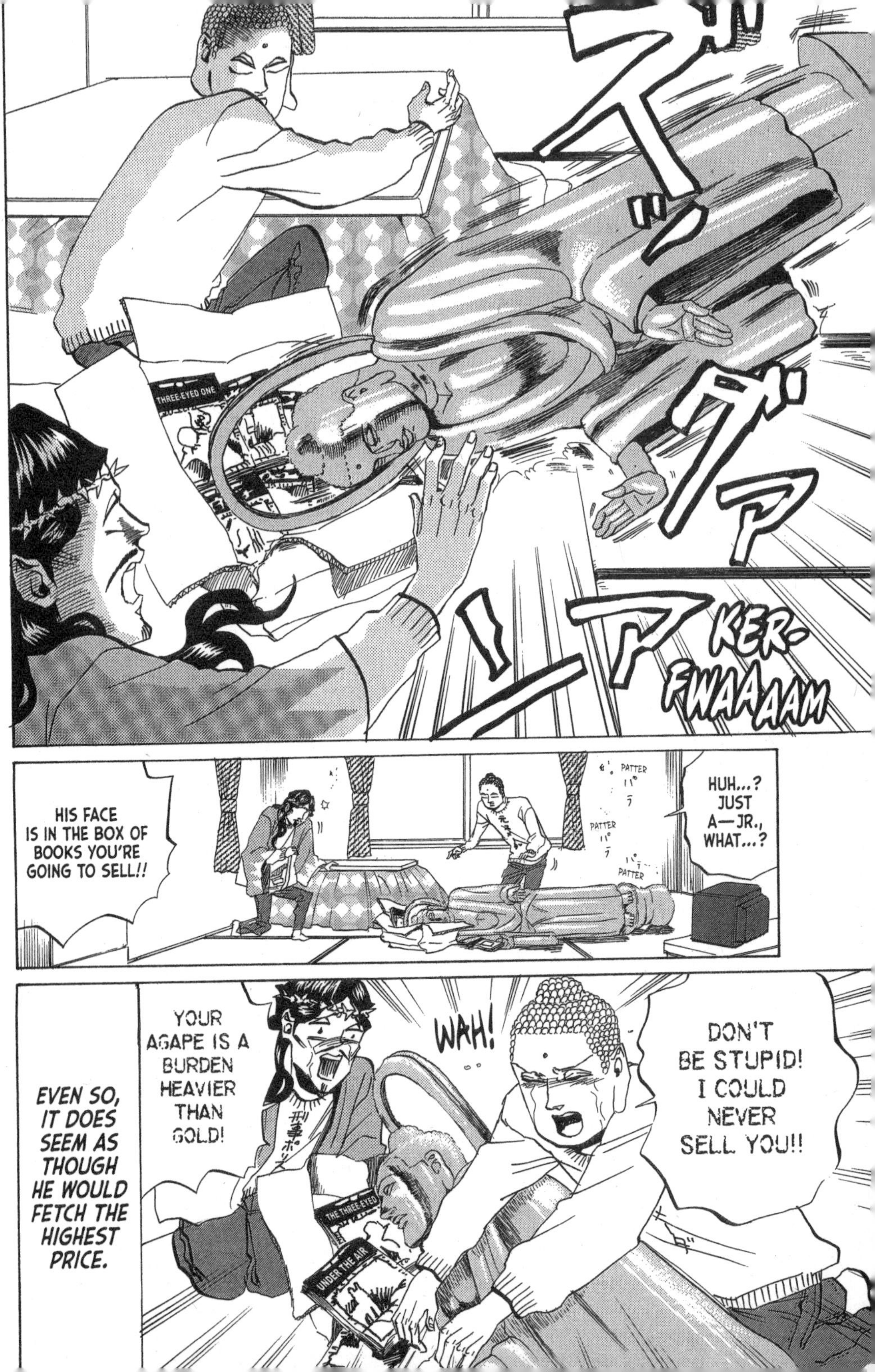
THREE-EYED ONE
KER-FWAAAAM
HUH...? JUST A—JR., WHAT...?
PATTER
PATTER
PATTER
HIS FACE IS IN THE BOX OF BOOKS YOU'RE GOING TO SELL!!
DON'T BE STUPID! I COULD NEVER SELL YOU!!
WAH!
YOUR AGAPE IS A BURDEN HEAVIER THAN GOLD!
EVEN SO, IT DOES SEEM AS THOUGH HE WOULD FETCH THE HIGHEST PRICE.
THE THREE-EYED
UNDER THE AIR

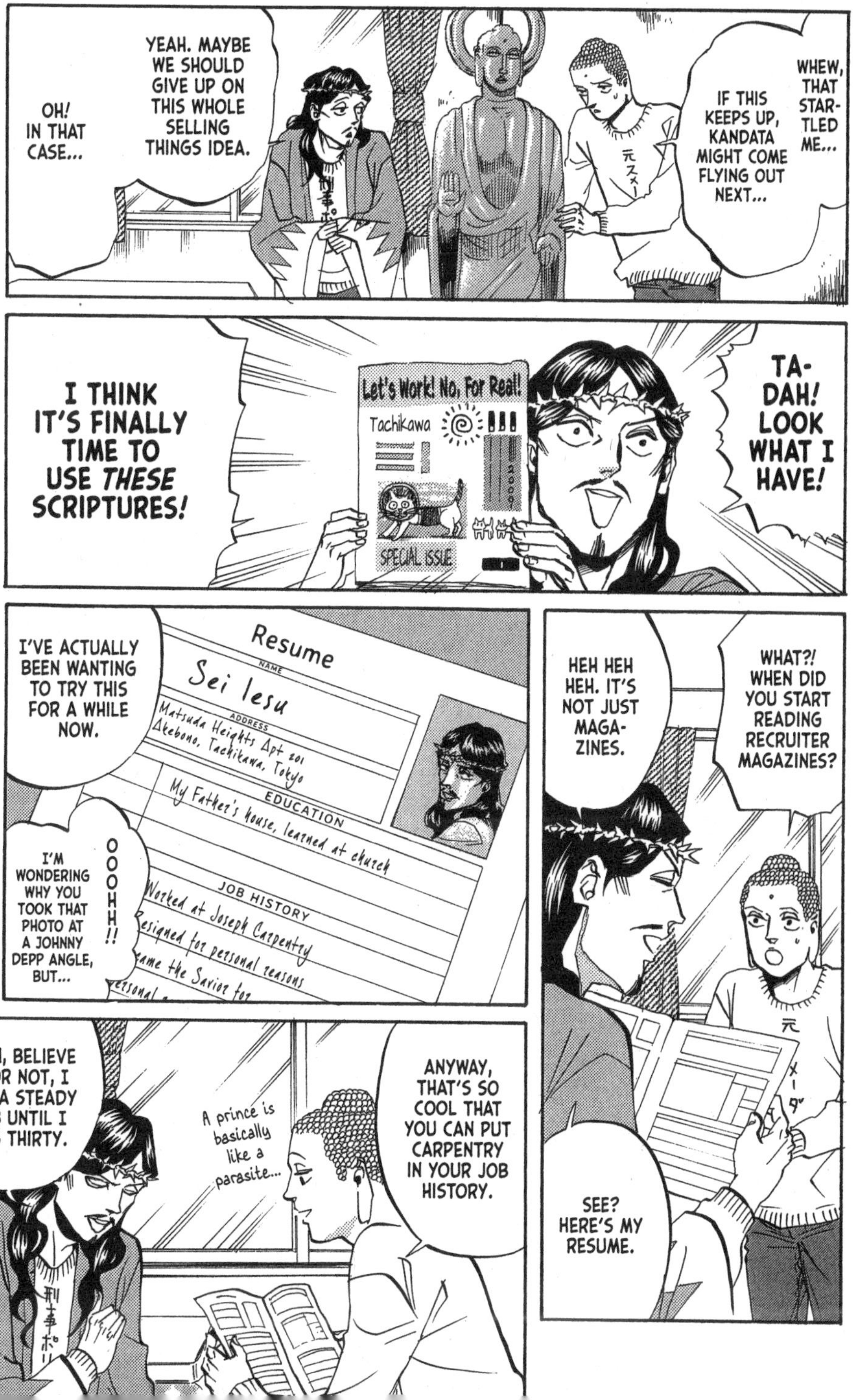
WHEW, THAT STARTLED ME...
IF THIS KEEPS UP, KANDATA MIGHT COME FLYING OUT NEXT...
YEAH. MAYBE WE SHOULD GIVE UP ON THIS WHOLE SELLING THINGS IDEA.
OH! IN THAT CASE...
TA-DAH! LOOK WHAT I HAVE!
Let's Work! No, For Real!
Tachikawa
2009
SPECIAL ISSUE
I THINK IT'S FINALLY TIME TO USE *THESE* SCRIPTURES!
WHAT?! WHEN DID YOU START READING RECRUITER MAGAZINES?
HEH HEH HEH. IT'S NOT JUST MAGA-ZINES.
SEE? HERE'S MY RESUME.
I'VE ACTUALLY BEEN WANTING TO TRY THIS FOR A WHILE NOW.
Resume
NAME
Sei Iesu
ADDRESS
Matsuda Heights Apt 201 Akebono, Tachikawa, Tokyo
EDUCATION
My Father's house, learned at church
JOB HISTORY
Worked at Joseph Carpentry
Resigned for personal reasons
OOOHH!!
I'M WONDERING WHY YOU TOOK THAT PHOTO AT A JOHNNY DEPP ANGLE, BUT...
ANYWAY, THAT'S SO COOL THAT YOU CAN PUT CARPENTRY IN YOUR JOB HISTORY.
A prince is basically like a parasite...
YEAH, BELIEVE IT OR NOT, I HAD A STEADY JOB UNTIL I WAS THIRTY.

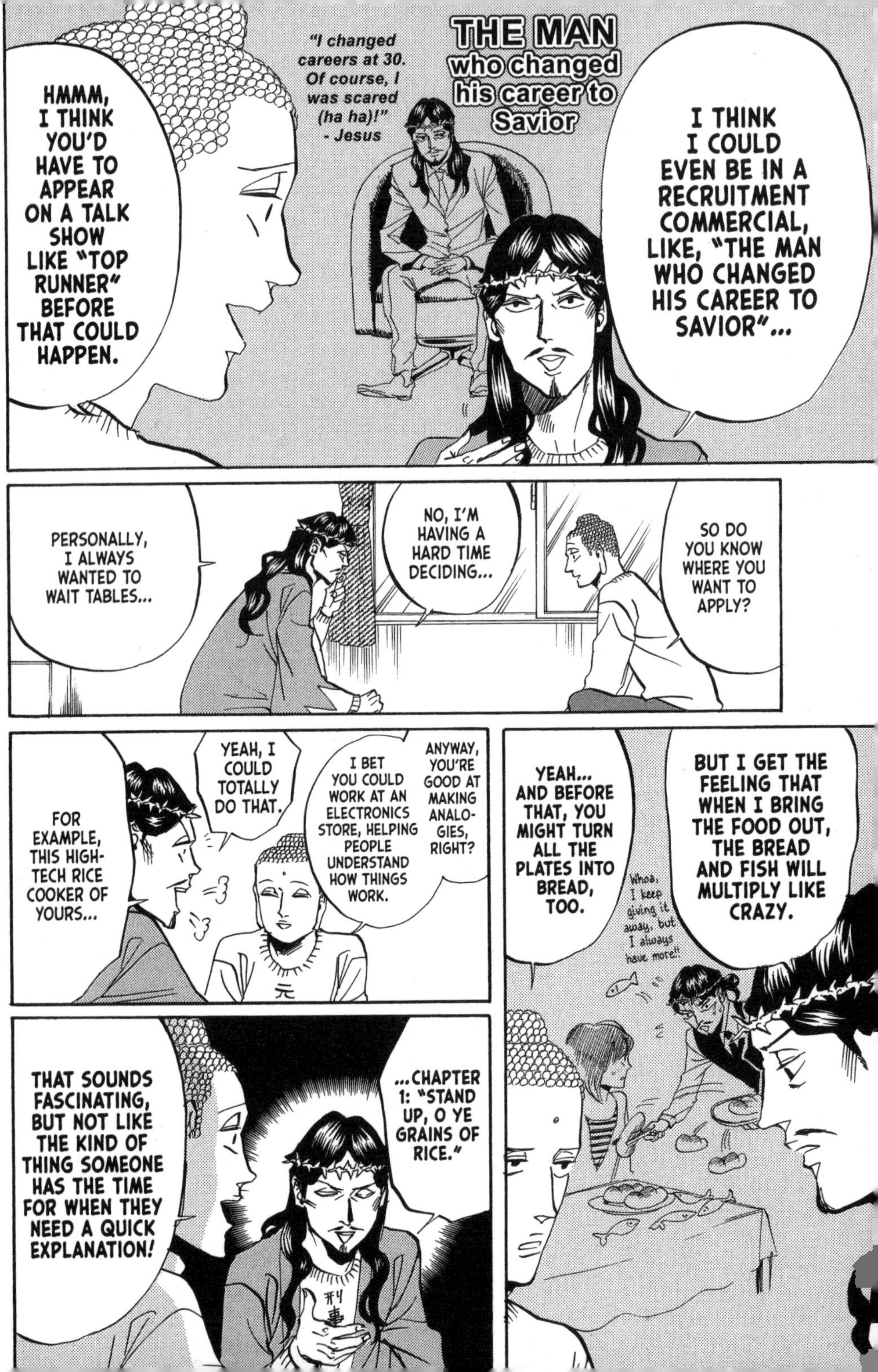
I THINK I COULD EVEN BE IN A RECRUITMENT COMMERCIAL, LIKE, "THE MAN WHO CHANGED HIS CAREER TO SAVIOR"...
THE MAN who changed his career to Savior
"I changed careers at 30. Of course, I was scared (ha ha)!" - Jesus
HMMM, I THINK YOU'D HAVE TO APPEAR ON A TALK SHOW LIKE "TOP RUNNER" BEFORE THAT COULD HAPPEN.
SO DO YOU KNOW WHERE YOU WANT TO APPLY?
NO, I'M HAVING A HARD TIME DECIDING...
PERSONALLY, I ALWAYS WANTED TO WAIT TABLES...
BUT I GET THE FEELING THAT WHEN I BRING THE FOOD OUT, THE BREAD AND FISH WILL MULTIPLY LIKE CRAZY.
YEAH... AND BEFORE THAT, YOU MIGHT TURN ALL THE PLATES INTO BREAD, TOO.
Whoa, I keep giving it away, but I always have more!!
ANYWAY, YOU'RE GOOD AT MAKING ANALOGIES, RIGHT?
I BET YOU COULD WORK AT AN ELECTRONICS STORE, HELPING PEOPLE UNDERSTAND HOW THINGS WORK.
YEAH, I COULD TOTALLY DO THAT.
FOR EXAMPLE, THIS HIGH-TECH RICE COOKER OF YOURS...
...CHAPTER 1: "STAND UP, O YE GRAINS OF RICE."
THAT SOUNDS FASCINATING, BUT NOT LIKE THE KIND OF THING SOMEONE HAS THE TIME FOR WHEN THEY NEED A QUICK EXPLANATION!

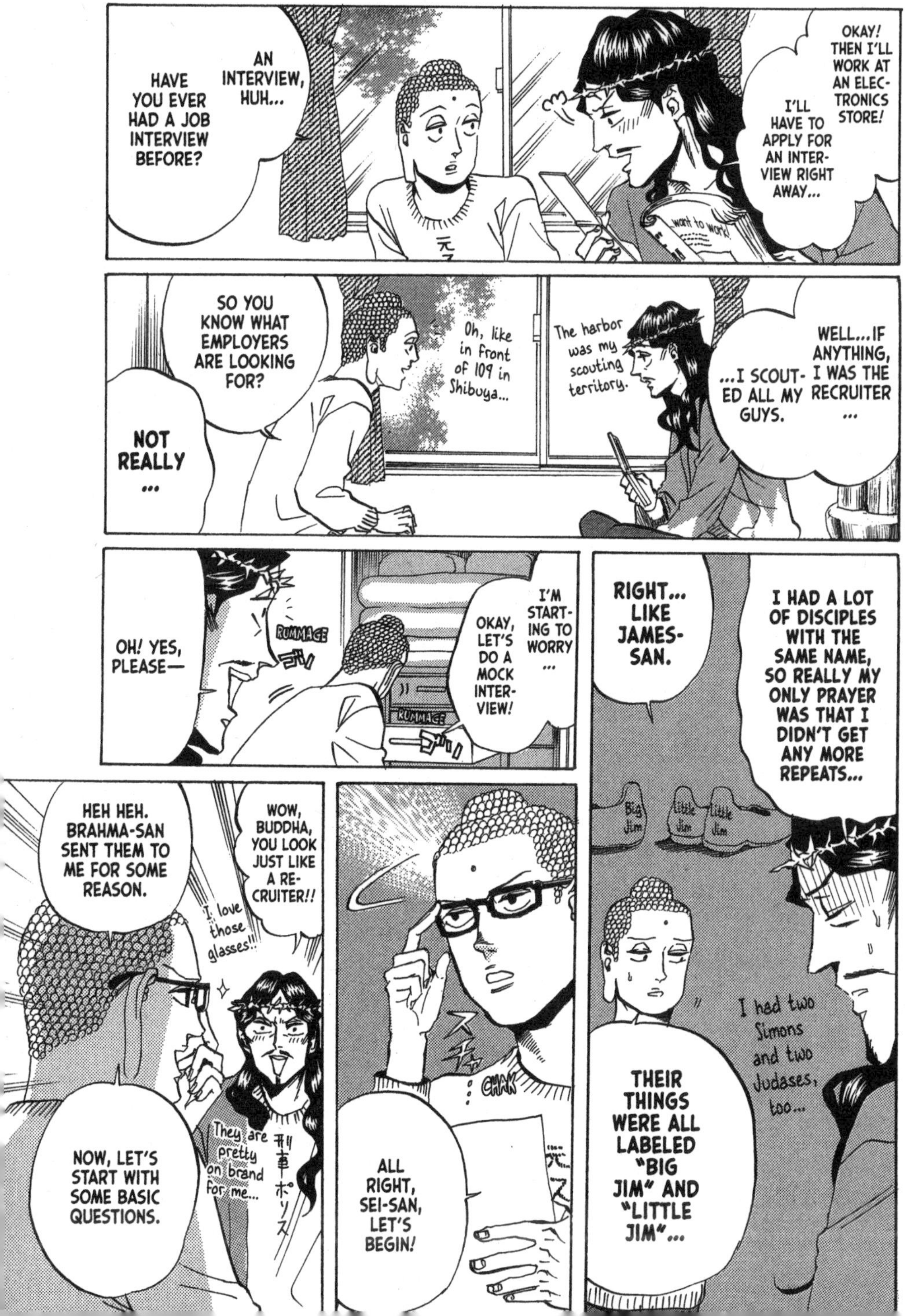
OKAY! THEN I'LL WORK AT AN ELECTRONICS STORE!
I'LL HAVE TO APPLY FOR AN INTERVIEW RIGHT AWAY...
want to work!
AN INTERVIEW, HUH...
HAVE YOU EVER HAD A JOB INTERVIEW BEFORE?
WELL...IF ANYTHING, I WAS THE RECRUITER...
...I SCOUTED ALL MY GUYS.
The harbor was my scouting territory.
Oh, like in front of 109 in Shibuya...
SO YOU KNOW WHAT EMPLOYERS ARE LOOKING FOR?
NOT REALLY...
I HAD A LOT OF DISCIPLES WITH THE SAME NAME, SO REALLY MY ONLY PRAYER WAS THAT I DIDN'T GET ANY MORE REPEATS...
RIGHT... LIKE JAMES-SAN.
Big Jim
Little Jim
Little Jim
I had two Simons and two Judases, too...
THEIR THINGS WERE ALL LABELED "BIG JIM" AND "LITTLE JIM"...
I'M STARTING TO WORRY...
OKAY, LET'S DO A MOCK INTERVIEW!
RUMMAGE
RUMMAGE
OH! YES, PLEASE—
CHAK
ALL RIGHT, SEI-SAN, LET'S BEGIN!
WOW, BUDDHA, YOU LOOK JUST LIKE A RECRUITER!!
I love those glasses!!
HEH HEH. BRAHMA-SAN SENT THEM TO ME FOR SOME REASON.
They are pretty on brand for me...
NOW, LET'S START WITH SOME BASIC QUESTIONS.

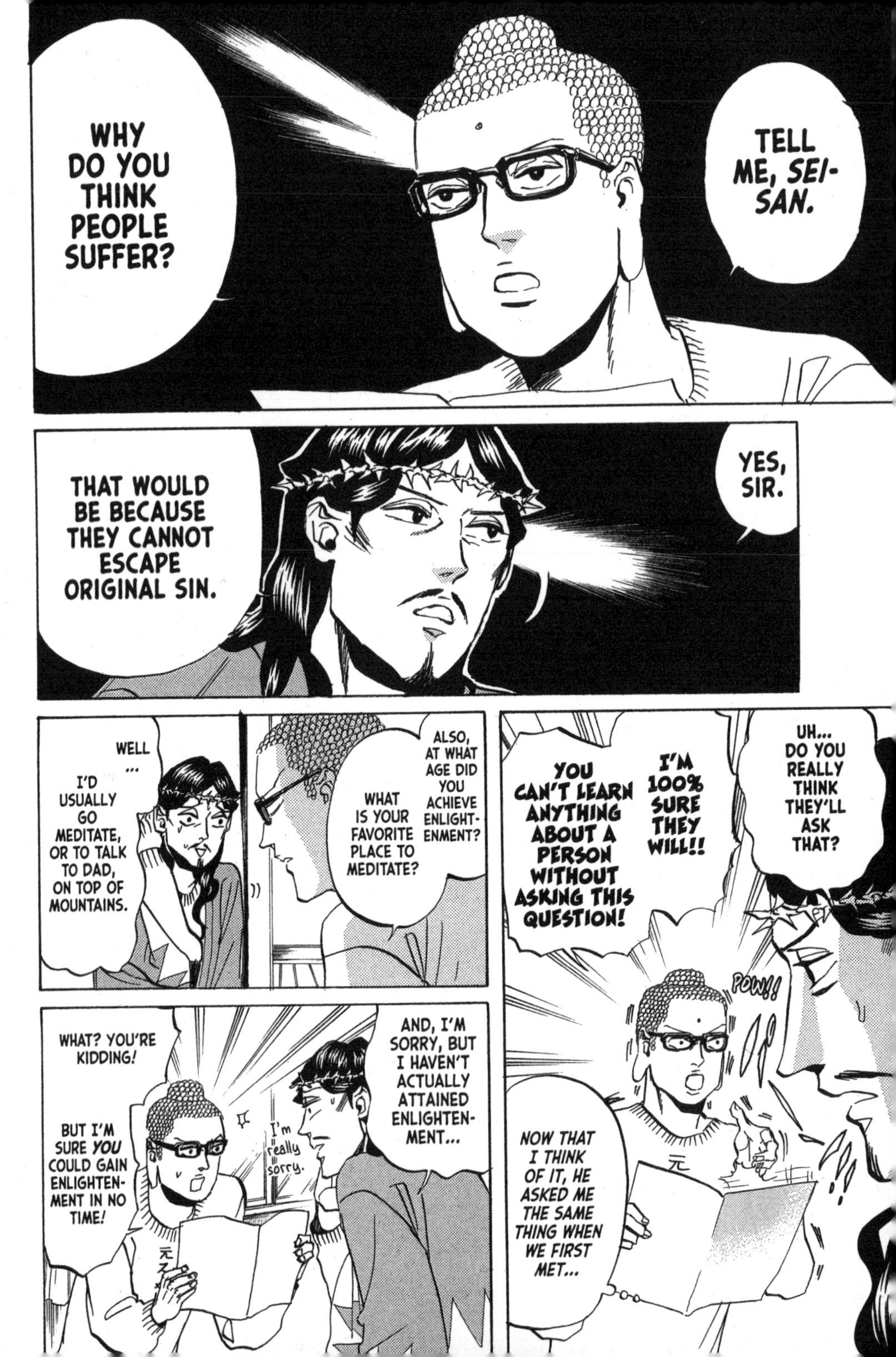
TELL ME, SEI-SAN.
WHY DO YOU THINK PEOPLE SUFFER?
YES, SIR.
THAT WOULD BE BECAUSE THEY CANNOT ESCAPE ORIGINAL SIN.
UH... DO YOU REALLY THINK THEY'LL ASK THAT?
I'M 100% SURE THEY WILL!!
YOU CAN'T LEARN ANYTHING ABOUT A PERSON WITHOUT ASKING THIS QUESTION!
POW!!
NOW THAT I THINK OF IT, HE ASKED ME THE SAME THING WHEN WE FIRST MET...
ALSO, AT WHAT AGE DID YOU ACHIEVE ENLIGHTENMENT?
WHAT IS YOUR FAVORITE PLACE TO MEDITATE?
WELL ...
I'D USUALLY GO MEDITATE, OR TO TALK TO DAD, ON TOP OF MOUNTAINS.
AND, I'M SORRY, BUT I HAVEN'T ACTUALLY ATTAINED ENLIGHTENMENT...
I'm really sorry.
WHAT? YOU'RE KIDDING!
BUT I'M SURE YOU COULD GAIN ENLIGHTENMENT IN NO TIME!

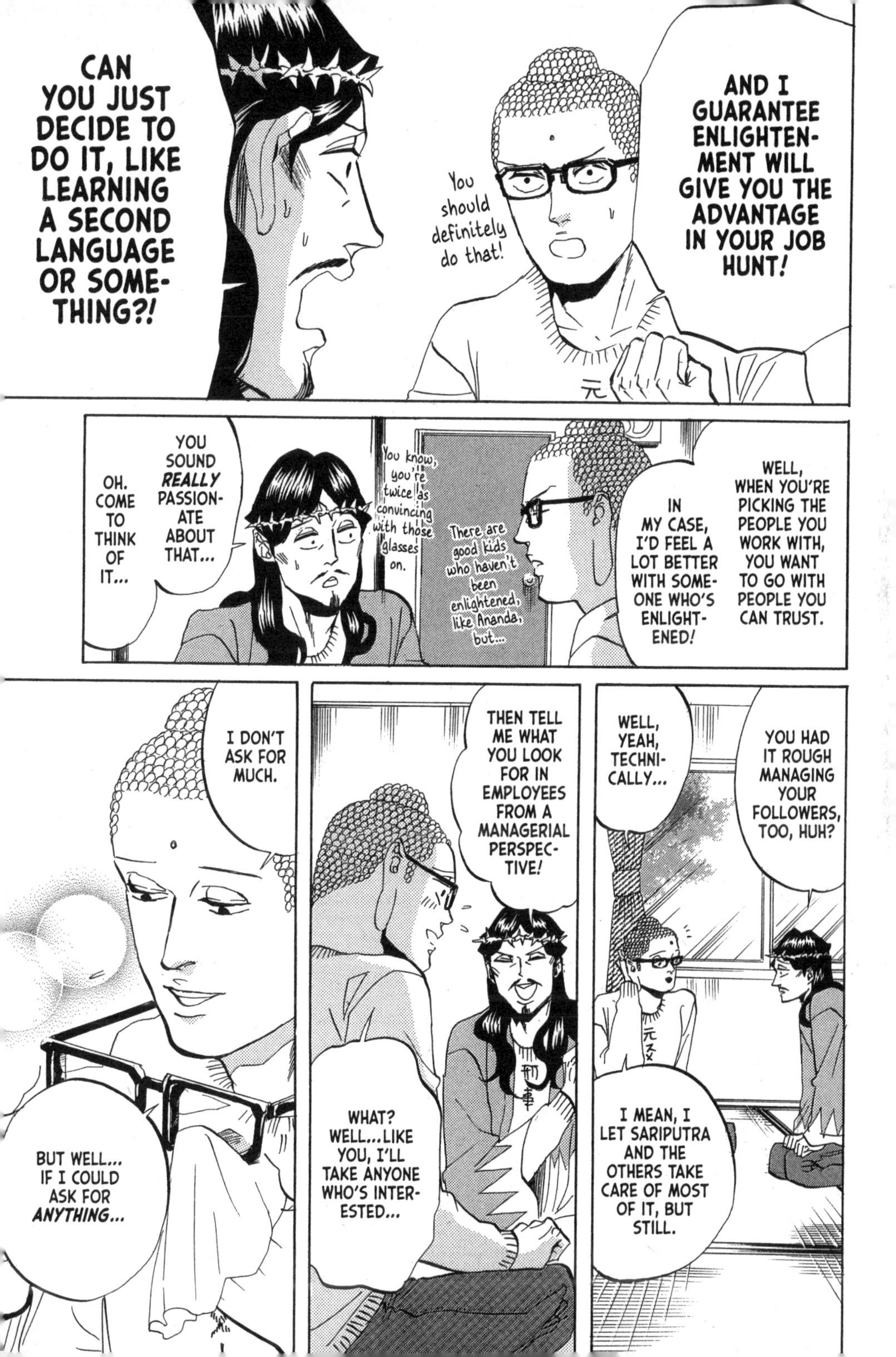
AND I GUARANTEE ENLIGHTENMENT WILL GIVE YOU THE ADVANTAGE IN YOUR JOB HUNT!
You should definitely do that!
CAN YOU JUST DECIDE TO DO IT, LIKE LEARNING A SECOND LANGUAGE OR SOMETHING?!
WELL, WHEN YOU'RE PICKING THE PEOPLE YOU WORK WITH, YOU WANT TO GO WITH PEOPLE YOU CAN TRUST.
IN MY CASE, I'D FEEL A LOT BETTER WITH SOMEONE WHO'S ENLIGHTENED!
There are good kids who haven't been enlightened, like Ananda, but...
You know, you're twice as convincing with those glasses on.
YOU SOUND *REALLY* PASSIONATE ABOUT THAT...
OH. COME TO THINK OF IT...
YOU HAD IT ROUGH MANAGING YOUR FOLLOWERS, TOO, HUH?
WELL, YEAH, TECHNICALLY...
I MEAN, I LET SARIPUTRA AND THE OTHERS TAKE CARE OF MOST OF IT, BUT STILL.
THEN TELL ME WHAT YOU LOOK FOR IN EMPLOYEES FROM A MANAGERIAL PERSPECTIVE!
WHAT? WELL...LIKE YOU, I'LL TAKE ANYONE WHO'S INTERESTED...
I DON'T ASK FOR MUCH.
BUT WELL... IF I COULD ASK FOR *ANYTHING*...

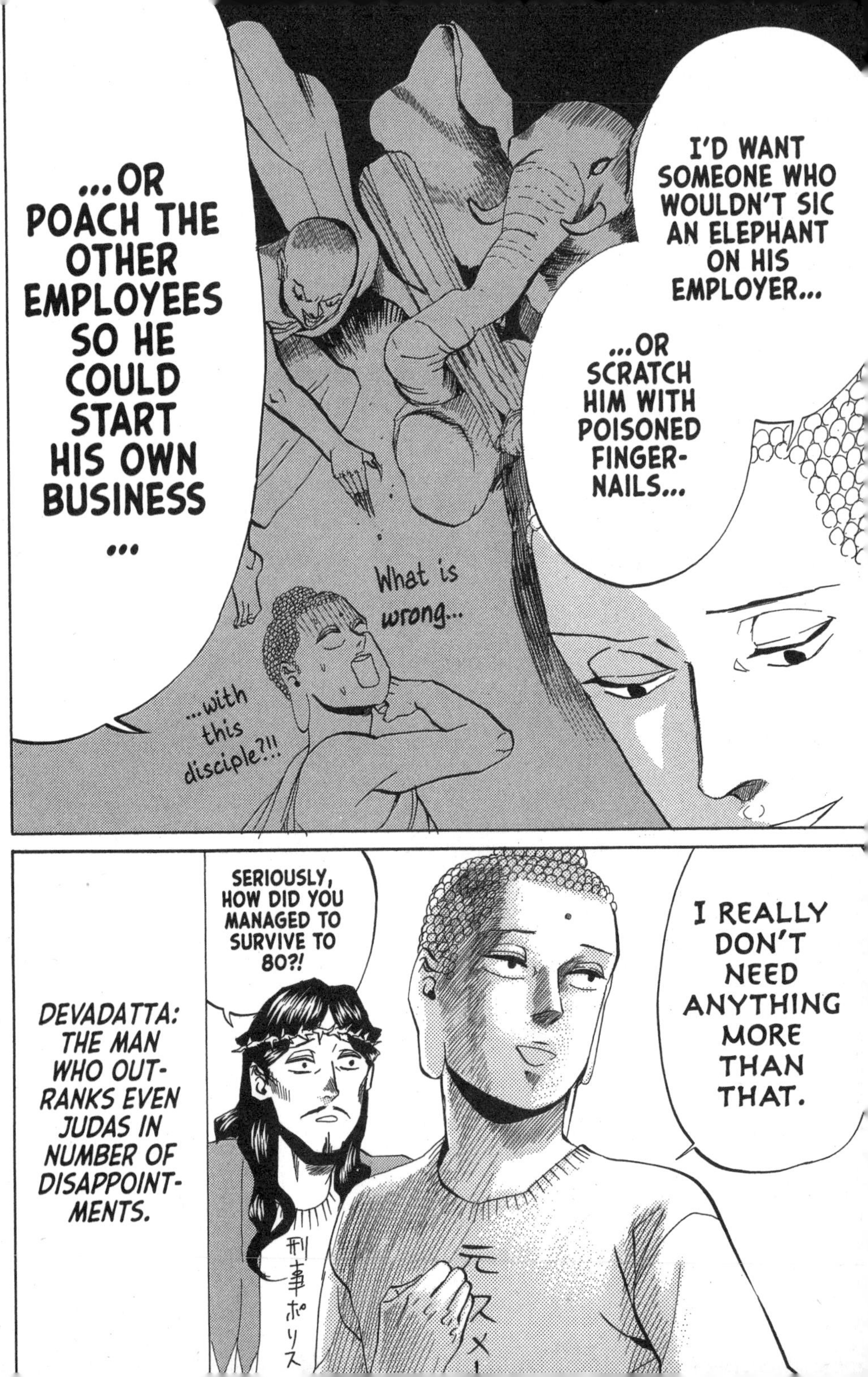
I'D WANT SOMEONE WHO WOULDN'T SIC AN ELEPHANT ON HIS EMPLOYER...
...OR SCRATCH HIM WITH POISONED FINGER-NAILS...
...OR POACH THE OTHER EMPLOYEES SO HE COULD START HIS OWN BUSINESS...
What is wrong...
...with this disciple?!!
I REALLY DON'T NEED ANYTHING MORE THAN THAT.
SERIOUSLY, HOW DID YOU MANAGED TO SURVIVE TO 80?!
DEVADATTA: THE MAN WHO OUT-RANKS EVEN JUDAS IN NUMBER OF DISAPPOINT-MENTS.
刑事ポリス

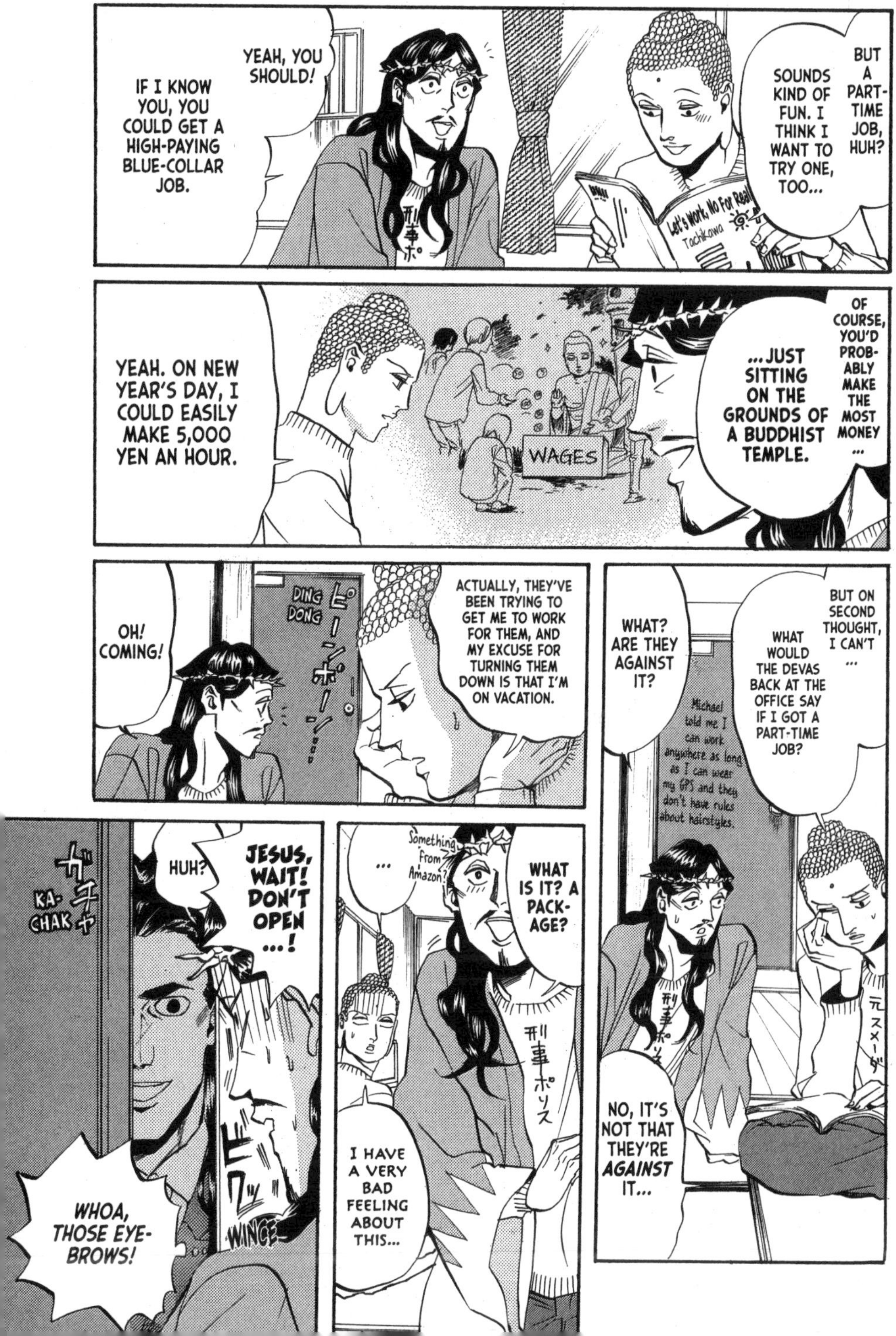
BUT A PART-TIME JOB, HUH?
SOUNDS KIND OF FUN. I THINK I WANT TO TRY ONE, TOO...
Let's work, No For Real
Tachikawa
YEAH, YOU SHOULD!
IF I KNOW YOU, YOU COULD GET A HIGH-PAYING BLUE-COLLAR JOB.
OF COURSE, YOU'D PROBABLY MAKE THE MOST MONEY...
...JUST SITTING ON THE GROUNDS OF A BUDDHIST TEMPLE.
WAGES
YEAH. ON NEW YEAR'S DAY, I COULD EASILY MAKE 5,000 YEN AN HOUR.
BUT ON SECOND THOUGHT, I CAN'T...
WHAT WOULD THE DEVAS BACK AT THE OFFICE SAY IF I GOT A PART-TIME JOB?
WHAT? ARE THEY AGAINST IT?
Michael told me I can work anywhere as long as I can wear my GPS and they don't have rules about hairstyles.
NO, IT'S NOT THAT THEY'RE *AGAINST* IT...
ACTUALLY, THEY'VE BEEN TRYING TO GET ME TO WORK FOR THEM, AND MY EXCUSE FOR TURNING THEM DOWN IS THAT I'M ON VACATION.
DING DONG
OH! COMING!
WHAT IS IT? A PACKAGE?
Something from Amazon?
...
I HAVE A VERY BAD FEELING ABOUT THIS...
JESUS, WAIT! DON'T OPEN...!
HUH?
KA-CHAK
WINCE
WHOA, THOSE EYE-BROWS!

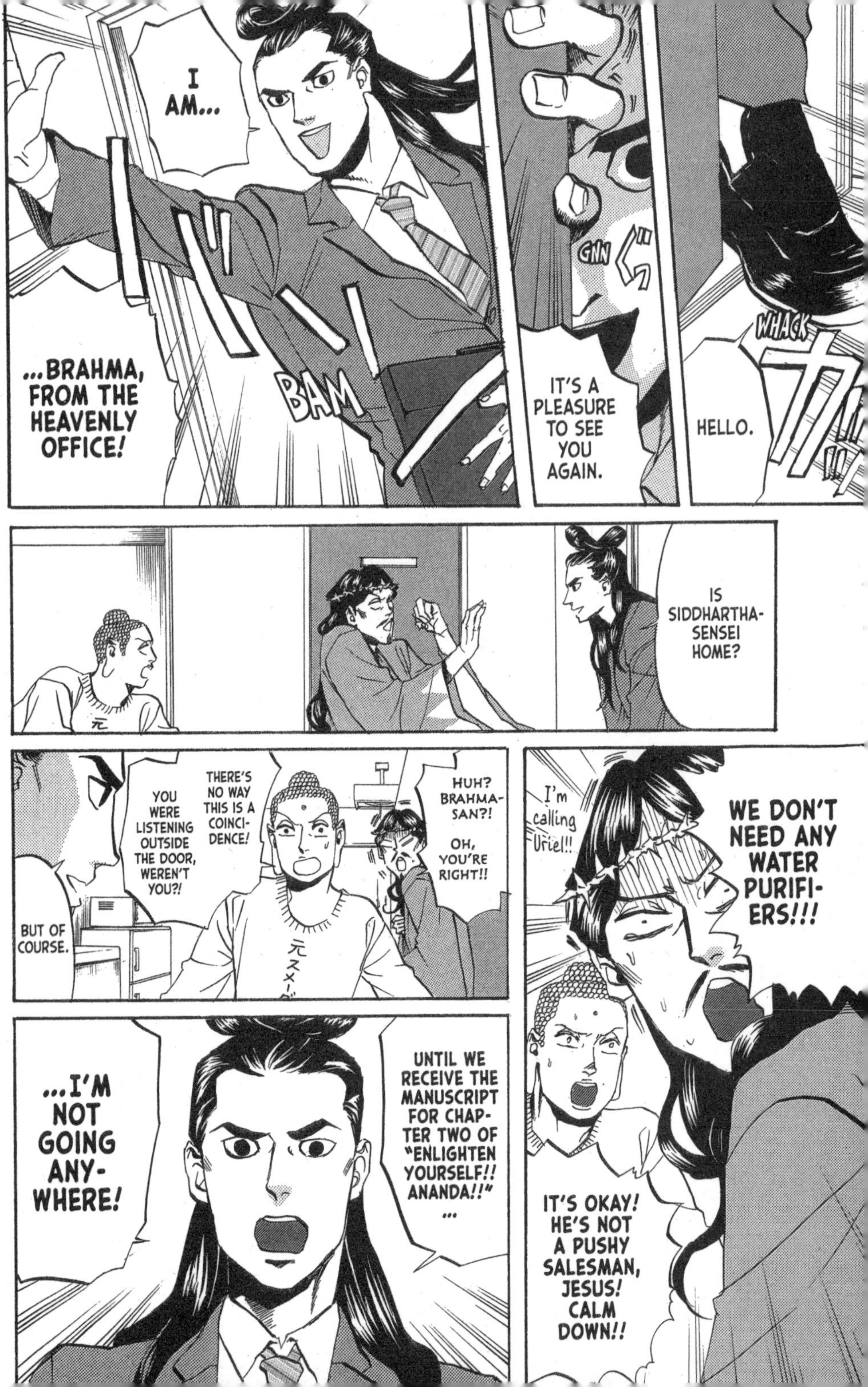
WHACK
HELLO.
GNN
IT'S A PLEASURE TO SEE YOU AGAIN.
I AM...
...BRAHMA, FROM THE HEAVENLY OFFICE!
BAM
IS SIDDHARTHA-SENSEI HOME?
WE DON'T NEED ANY WATER PURIFIERS!!!
I'm calling Uriel!!
IT'S OKAY! HE'S NOT A PUSHY SALESMAN, JESUS! CALM DOWN!!
HUH? BRAHMA-SAN?!
OH, YOU'RE RIGHT!!
THERE'S NO WAY THIS IS A COINCIDENCE!
YOU WERE LISTENING OUTSIDE THE DOOR, WEREN'T YOU?!
BUT OF COURSE.
UNTIL WE RECEIVE THE MANUSCRIPT FOR CHAPTER TWO OF "ENLIGHTEN YOURSELF!! ANANDA!!"...
...I'M NOT GOING ANYWHERE!

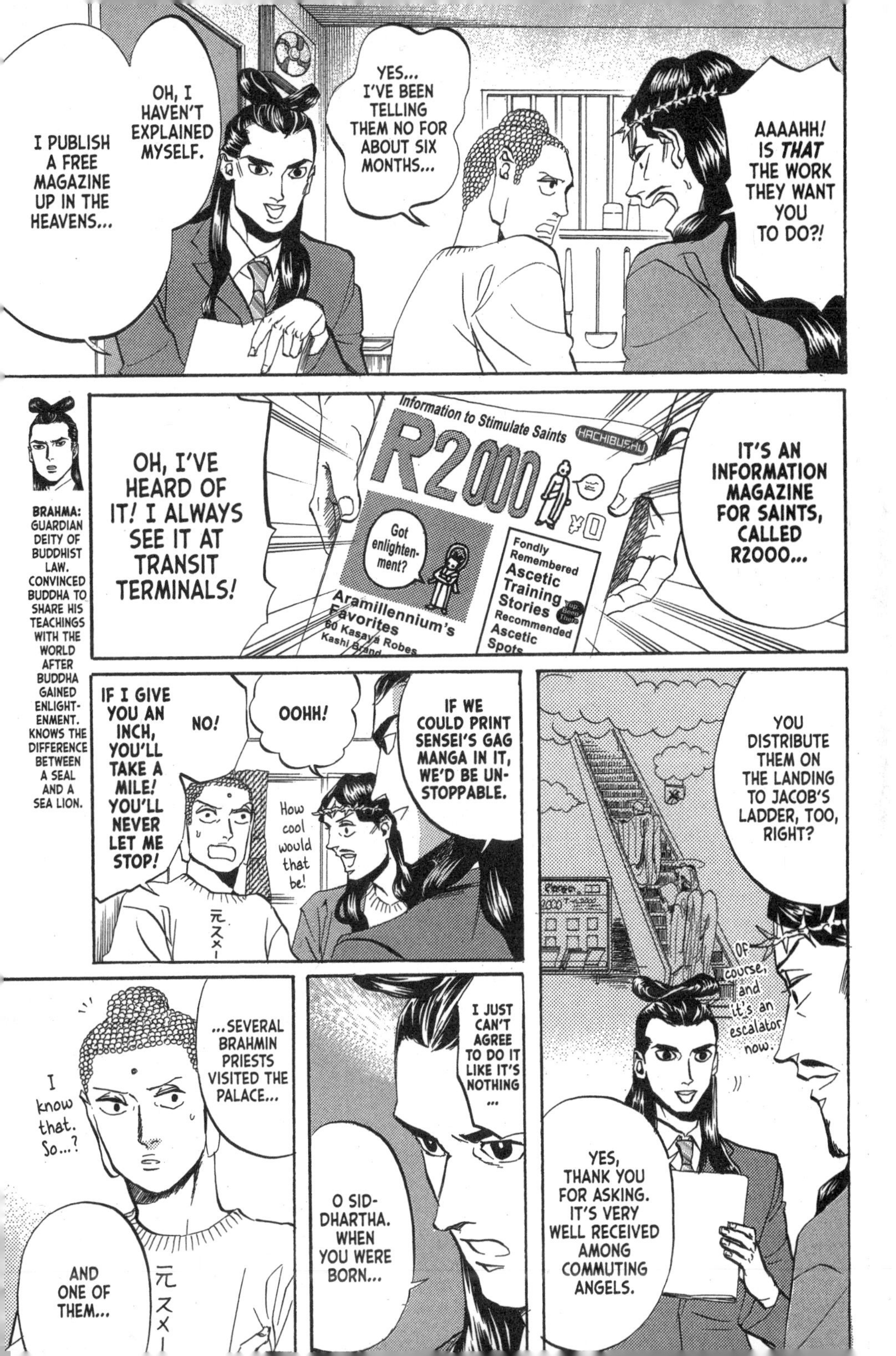
AAAAHH! IS THAT THE WORK THEY WANT YOU TO DO?!
YES... I'VE BEEN TELLING THEM NO FOR ABOUT SIX MONTHS...
OH, I HAVEN'T EXPLAINED MYSELF.
I PUBLISH A FREE MAGAZINE UP IN THE HEAVENS...
IT'S AN INFORMATION MAGAZINE FOR SAINTS, CALLED R2000...
Information to Stimulate Saints
HACHIBUSHU
R2000
¥0
Got enlighten-ment?
Aramillennium's Favorites
60 Kasaya Robes
Kashi Brand
Fondly Remembered Ascetic Training Stories
Yup, Been There
Recommended Ascetic Spots
OH, I'VE HEARD OF IT! I ALWAYS SEE IT AT TRANSIT TERMINALS!
BRAHMA: GUARDIAN DEITY OF BUDDHIST LAW. CONVINCED BUDDHA TO SHARE HIS TEACHINGS WITH THE WORLD AFTER BUDDHA GAINED ENLIGHT-ENMENT. KNOWS THE DIFFERENCE BETWEEN A SEAL AND A SEA LION.
YOU DISTRIBUTE THEM ON THE LANDING TO JACOB'S LADDER, TOO, RIGHT?
Of course, and it's an escalator now.
YES, THANK YOU FOR ASKING. IT'S VERY WELL RECEIVED AMONG COMMUTING ANGELS.
IF WE COULD PRINT SENSEI'S GAG MANGA IN IT, WE'D BE UN-STOPPABLE.
OOHH!
How cool would that be!
NO!
IF I GIVE YOU AN INCH, YOU'LL TAKE A MILE! YOU'LL NEVER LET ME STOP!
元スメー
I JUST CAN'T AGREE TO DO IT LIKE IT'S NOTHING...
O SID-DHARTHA. WHEN YOU WERE BORN...
...SEVERAL BRAHMIN PRIESTS VISITED THE PALACE...
I know that. So...?
AND ONE OF THEM...
元スメー

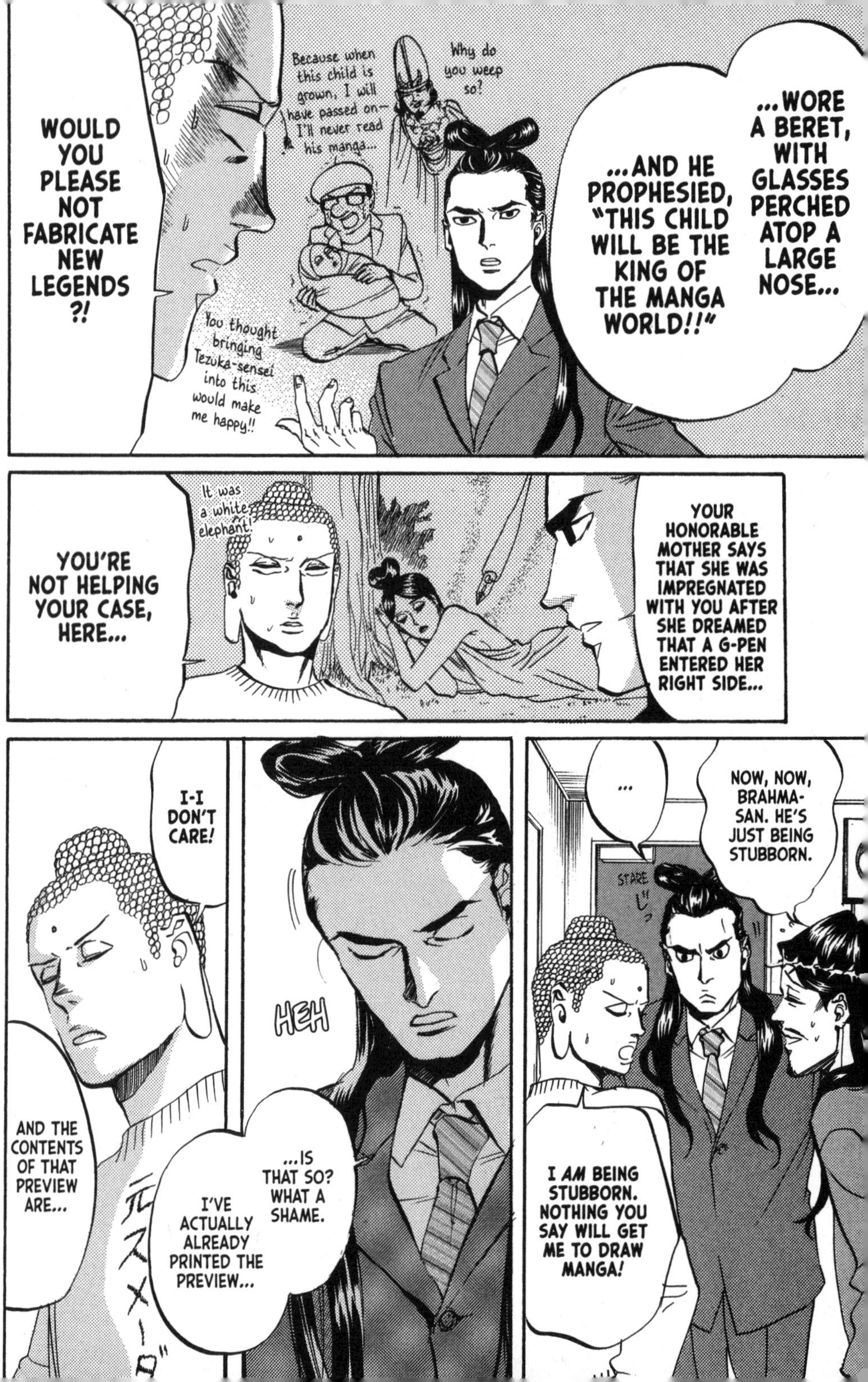
...WORE A BERET, WITH GLASSES PERCHED ATOP A LARGE NOSE...
...AND HE PROPHESIED, "THIS CHILD WILL BE THE KING OF THE MANGA WORLD!!"
Why do you weep so?
Because when this child is grown, I will have passed on— I'll never read his manga...
WOULD YOU PLEASE NOT FABRICATE NEW LEGENDS?!
You thought bringing Tezuka-sensei into this would make me happy!!
YOUR HONORABLE MOTHER SAYS THAT SHE WAS IMPREGNATED WITH YOU AFTER SHE DREAMED THAT A G-PEN ENTERED HER RIGHT SIDE...
It was a white elephant!
YOU'RE NOT HELPING YOUR CASE, HERE...
NOW, NOW, BRAHMA-SAN. HE'S JUST BEING STUBBORN.
...
STARE
I *AM* BEING STUBBORN. NOTHING YOU SAY WILL GET ME TO DRAW MANGA!
HEH
...IS THAT SO? WHAT A SHAME.
I'VE ACTUALLY ALREADY PRINTED THE PREVIEW...
I-I DON'T CARE!
AND THE CONTENTS OF THAT PREVIEW ARE...

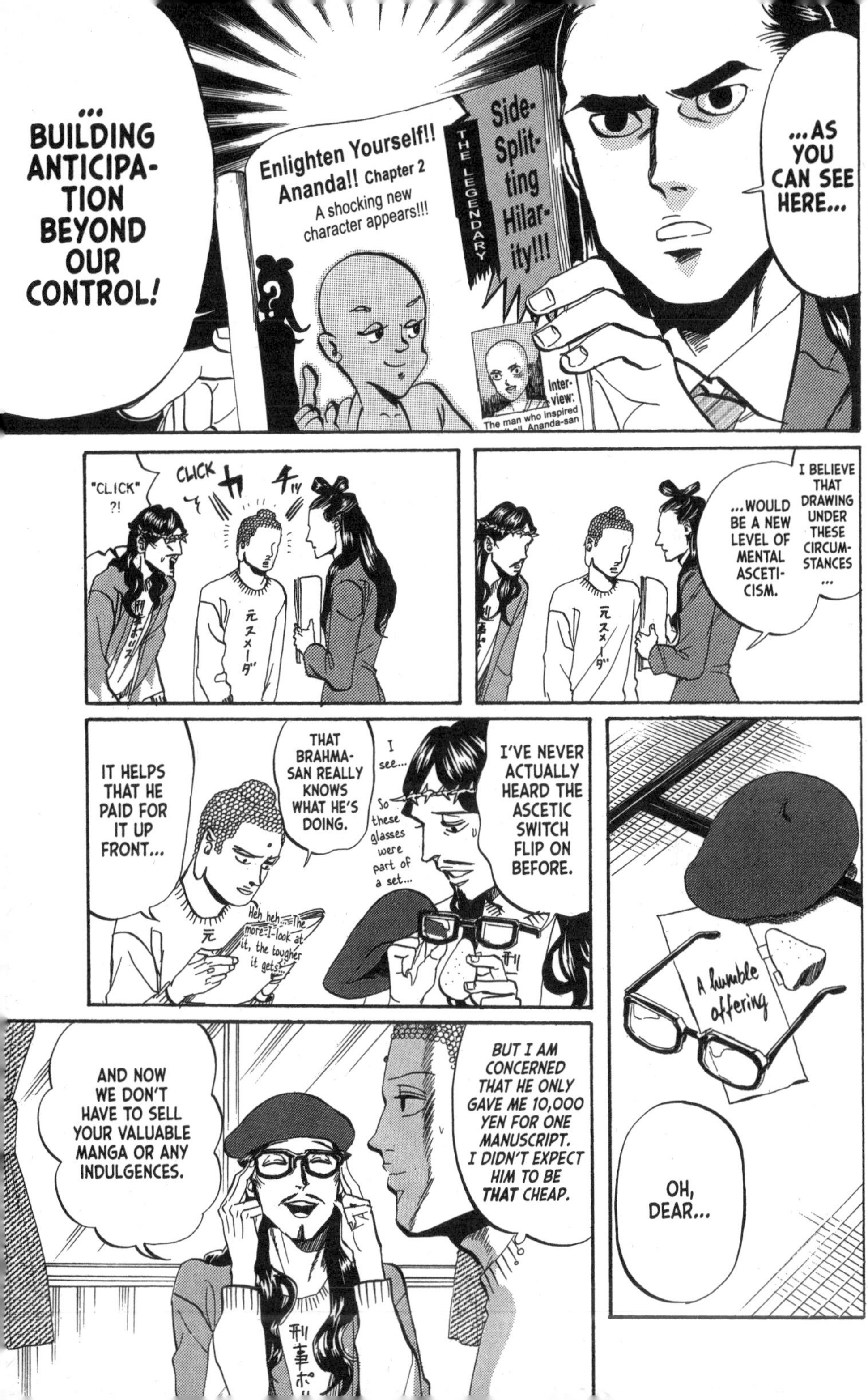

...AS YOU CAN SEE HERE...
Side-Splitting Hilarity!!!
THE LEGENDARY
Enlighten Yourself!! Ananda!! Chapter 2
A shocking new character appears!!!
Interview:
The man who inspired
...BUILDING ANTICIPATION BEYOND OUR CONTROL!
I BELIEVE THAT DRAWING UNDER THESE CIRCUMSTANCES...
...WOULD BE A NEW LEVEL OF MENTAL ASCETICISM.
CLICK
"CLICK"?!
A humble offering
OH, DEAR...
I'VE NEVER ACTUALLY HEARD THE ASCETIC SWITCH FLIP ON BEFORE.
I see...
So these glasses were part of a set...
THAT BRAHMA-SAN REALLY KNOWS WHAT HE'S DOING.
Heh heh... The more I look at it, the tougher it gets...
IT HELPS THAT HE PAID FOR IT UP FRONT...
BUT I AM CONCERNED THAT HE ONLY GAVE ME 10,000 YEN FOR ONE MANUSCRIPT. I DIDN'T EXPECT HIM TO BE THAT CHEAP.
AND NOW WE DON'T HAVE TO SELL YOUR VALUABLE MANGA OR ANY INDULGENCES.

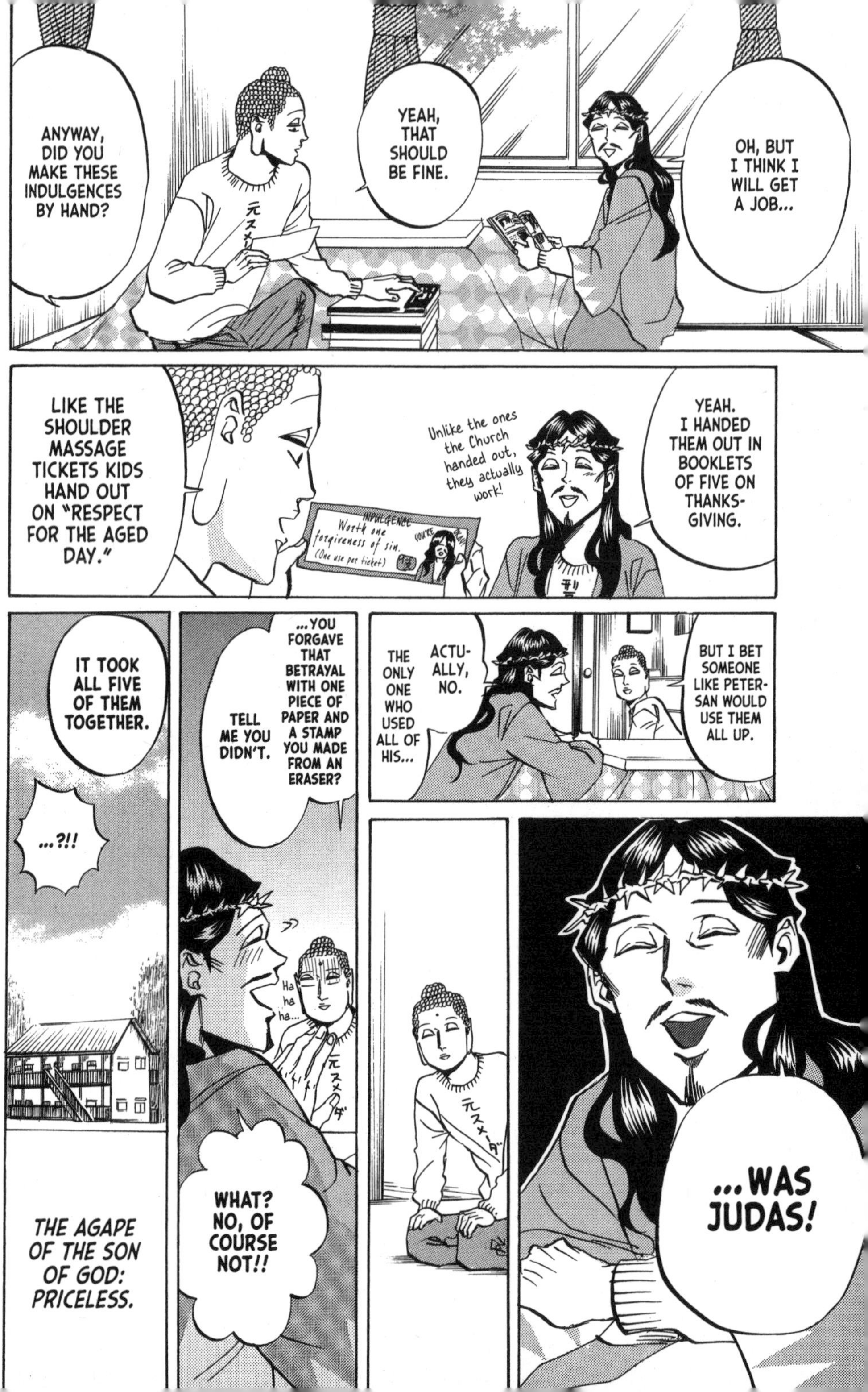

OH, BUT I THINK I WILL GET A JOB...
YEAH, THAT SHOULD BE FINE.
ANYWAY, DID YOU MAKE THESE INDULGENCES BY HAND?
YEAH. I HANDED THEM OUT IN BOOKLETS OF FIVE ON THANKSGIVING.
Unlike the ones the Church handed out, they actually work!
INDULGENCE
Worth one forgiveness of sin.
(One use per ticket)
LIKE THE SHOULDER MASSAGE TICKETS KIDS HAND OUT ON "RESPECT FOR THE AGED DAY."
BUT I BET SOMEONE LIKE PETER-SAN WOULD USE THEM ALL UP.
ACTUALLY, NO.
THE ONLY ONE WHO USED ALL OF HIS...
...WAS JUDAS!
...YOU FORGAVE THAT BETRAYAL WITH ONE PIECE OF PAPER AND A STAMP YOU MADE FROM AN ERASER?
TELL ME YOU DIDN'T.
Ha ha ha...
WHAT? NO, OF COURSE NOT!!
IT TOOK ALL FIVE OF THEM TOGETHER.
...?!!
THE AGAPE OF THE SON OF GOD: PRICELESS.

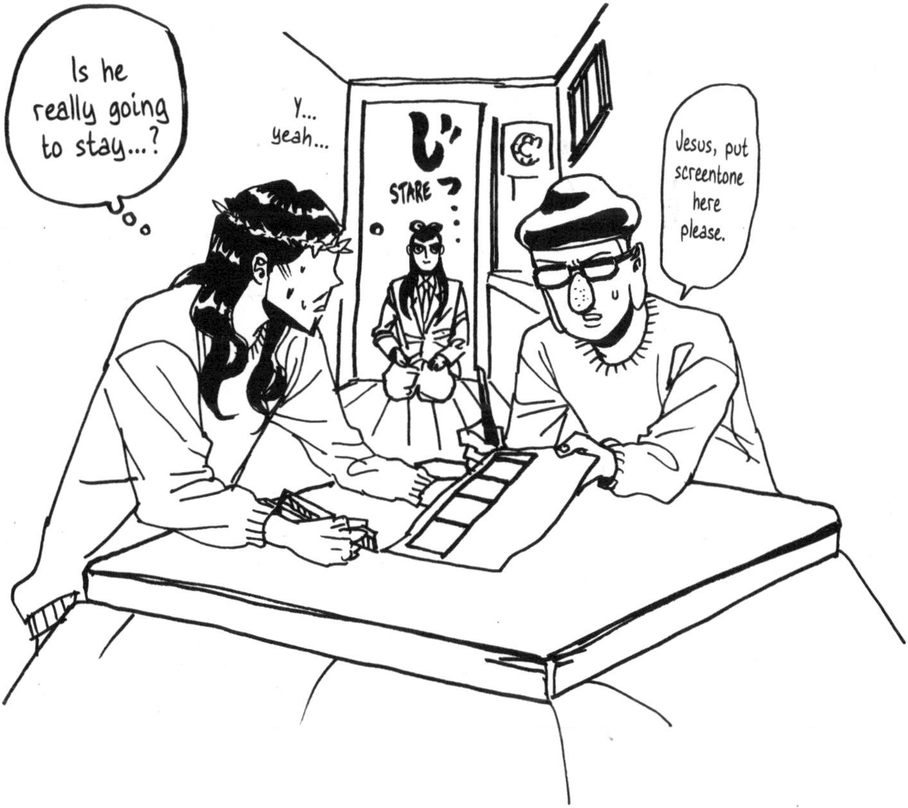
Jesus, put screentone here please.
Y... yeah...
じっ...
STARE
Is he really going to stay...?

CHAPTER 22 TRANSLATION NOTES

Blessed are the poor, page 125
This is a reference to Jesus's famous Sermon on the Mount, specifically the part known as the Beatitudes, where Jesus lists several virtues and the blessings that will reward them. The quotation as found in the King James version of the gospel of Matthew is, "Blessed are the poor in spirit: for theirs is the Kingdom of Heaven," where "poor in spirit" doesn't necessarily refer to literal poverty, but something more like humility. The gospel of Luke records a similar sermon of Jesus's that Luke records as having been given on a plain, which states, "Blessed be ye poor: for yours is the kingdom of God."

Book-Off, page 125
Book-Off is a Japanese chain of used book stores that is so popular it has hundreds of stores and a few overseas.

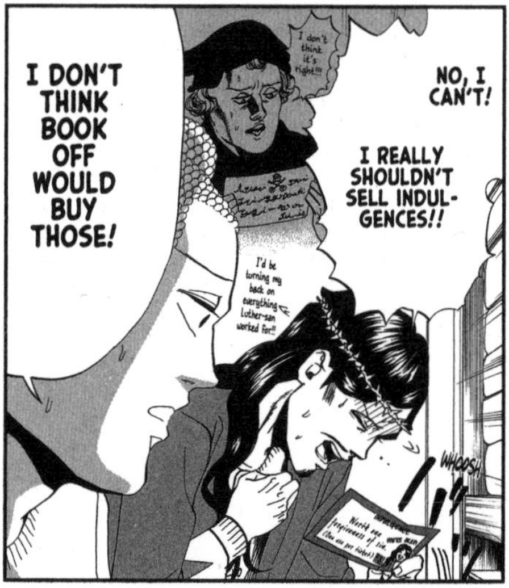
NO, I CAN'T!
I REALLY SHOULDN'T SELL INDUL-GENCES!!
I don't think it's right!!!
I DON'T THINK BOOK OFF WOULD BUY THOSE!
I'd be turning my back on everything Luther-san worked for!!
WHOOSH

Indulgences, page 126
In the Roman Catholic church, an indulgence is a way to reduce the punishment brought about by sin. This can be done through all manner of good deeds, including donating money to a good cause. This particular method of earning an indulgence is notable for having elicited the protest of Martin Luther, a priest from Germany who came to disagree with many practices of the Roman Catholic church, in particular the sale of indulgences. He is one of the most well-known figures in the Protestant Reformation in which many Christians left the Catholic church.

Decapolis, page 127
Decapolis is a region of ten cities that was part of the Roman Empire, and much of Jesus Christ's ministry took place there. Here, the name of the area is given in a pun, using characters that spell *Deka Porisu* and could also mean "Detective Police."

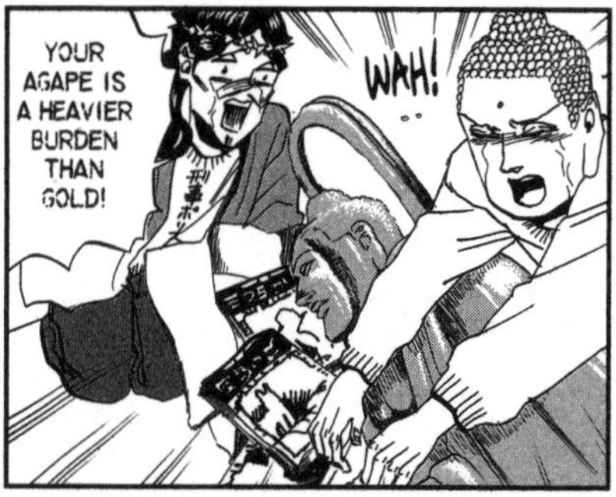
WAH!
YOUR AGAPE IS A HEAVIER BURDEN THAN GOLD!

Heavier burden than gold, page 128
In Japanese, the word "heavy" is used to describe something that weighs a lot, as well as a personality type that is often described as "clingy" or "smothering"—the kind of person with a martyr complex.

Good at analogies, page 130
For a large part of his ministry, Jesus taught using parables and analogies, explaining religious concepts using everyday imagery. These analogies vary in length—some were short stories, some were as short as a sentence.

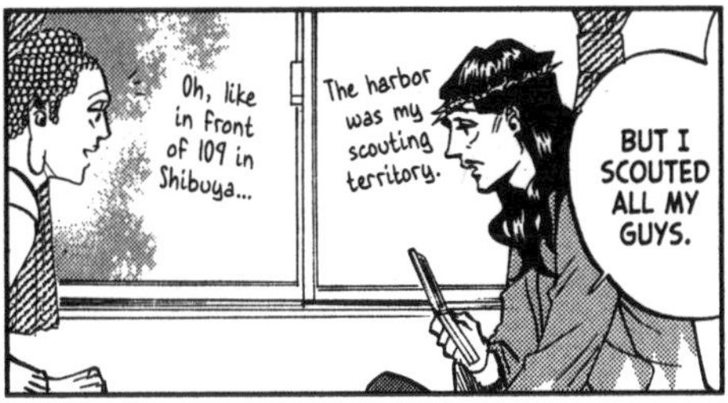
BUT I SCOUTED ALL MY GUYS.
The harbor was my scouting territory.
Oh, like in front of 109 in Shibuya...

Scouting in front of 109, page 131
109 is a department store in Shibuya and a very popular shopping destination. As such, it's a good place for talent scouts to look for young new potential stars.

Original sin, page 132
Original sin is a concept in many Christian denominations that states that humans are prone to sin by nature because Adam and Eve partook of the forbidden fruit in the Garden of Eden, and that Christ came to the world to free humankind from sin, original and otherwise, through his suffering and death.

Devadatta, page 134
Devadatta was a disciple of the Buddha's who was eager to succeed him and become leader of the community. In his jealousy of the Buddha, he tried twice to have an elephant "accidentally" kill him, and failing that, tried to recruit his own followers. Eventually he was taken to the Buddha to be punished for his various crimes, and he pretended to repent, but dipped his hand in poison and tried to scratch the Buddha's foot. The Buddha pushed him away, at which point the ground opened up and Devadatta was swallowed in the flames that sprang out of the earth.

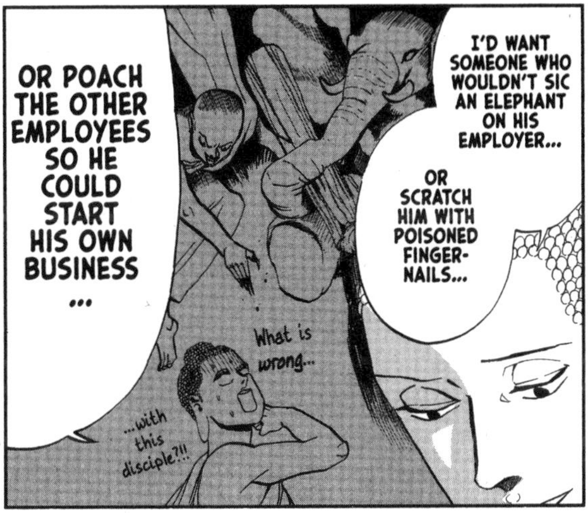
I'D WANT SOMEONE WHO WOULDN'T SIC AN ELEPHANT ON HIS EMPLOYER...
OR SCRATCH HIM WITH POISONED FINGER-NAILS...
OR POACH THE OTHER EMPLOYEES SO HE COULD START HIS OWN BUSINESS ...
What is wrong...
...with this disciple?!!

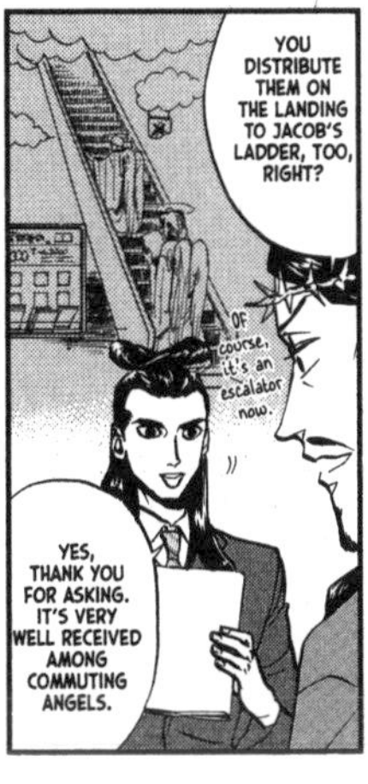
YOU DISTRIBUTE THEM ON THE LANDING TO JACOB'S LADDER, TOO, RIGHT?
Of course, it's an escalator now.
YES, THANK YOU FOR ASKING. IT'S VERY WELL RECEIVED AMONG COMMUTING ANGELS.

Jacob's Ladder, page 137
In the Old Testament, Jacob, the father of the Twelve Tribes of Israel, had a dream in which he saw a ladder extending from the Earth all the way to Heaven, with angels going up and down it.

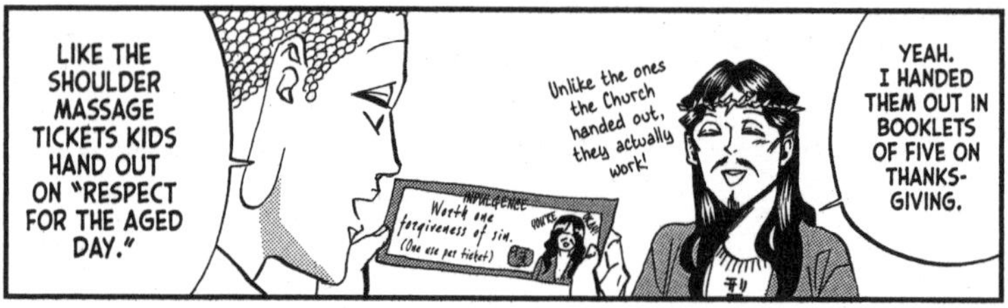
LIKE THE SHOULDER MASSAGE TICKETS KIDS HAND OUT ON "RESPECT FOR THE AGED DAY."
Unlike the ones the Church handed out, they actually work!
INDULGENCE
Worth one forgiveness of sin.
(One use per ticket)
YEAH. I HANDED THEM OUT IN BOOKLETS OF FIVE ON THANKSGIVING.

Thanksgiving and Respect for the Aged Day, page 126

Here, Jesus is probably talking about the Japanese holiday, more specifically known as Labor Thanksgiving Day. It happens around the same time as Thanksgiving in the United States, but is more specifically geared toward thanking laborers for the work they do. Sometimes people will literally give thanks to the workers in their lives by giving them cards or gifts.

Respect for the Aged Day is very much like it sounds—a day for appreciating the senior citizens in one's life. It is celebrated by going home to spend time with one's elders, or by providing services and entertainment to elderly folk in the community.

SAINT☆YOUNG MEN

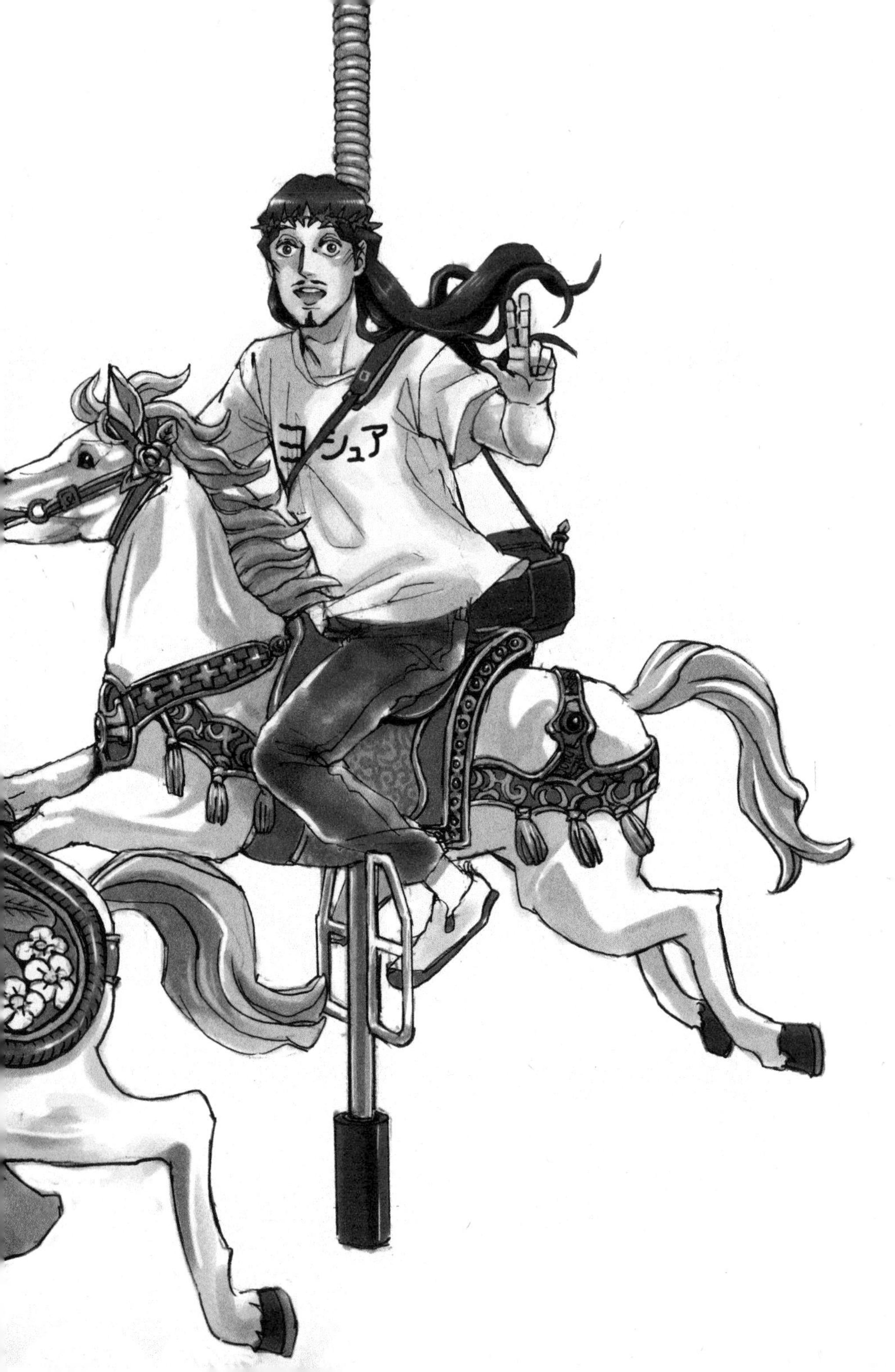
ヨシュア

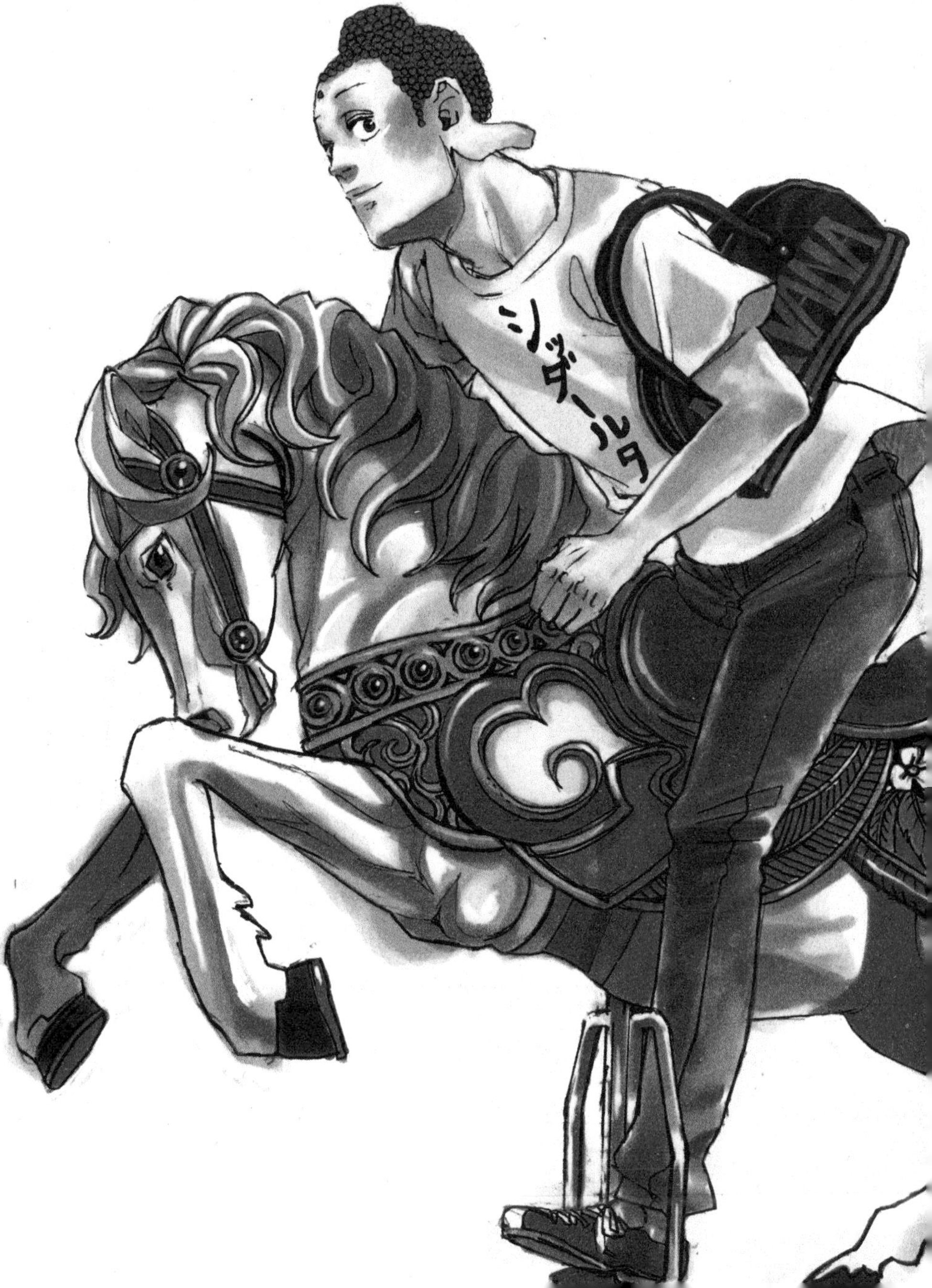
シッダールタ

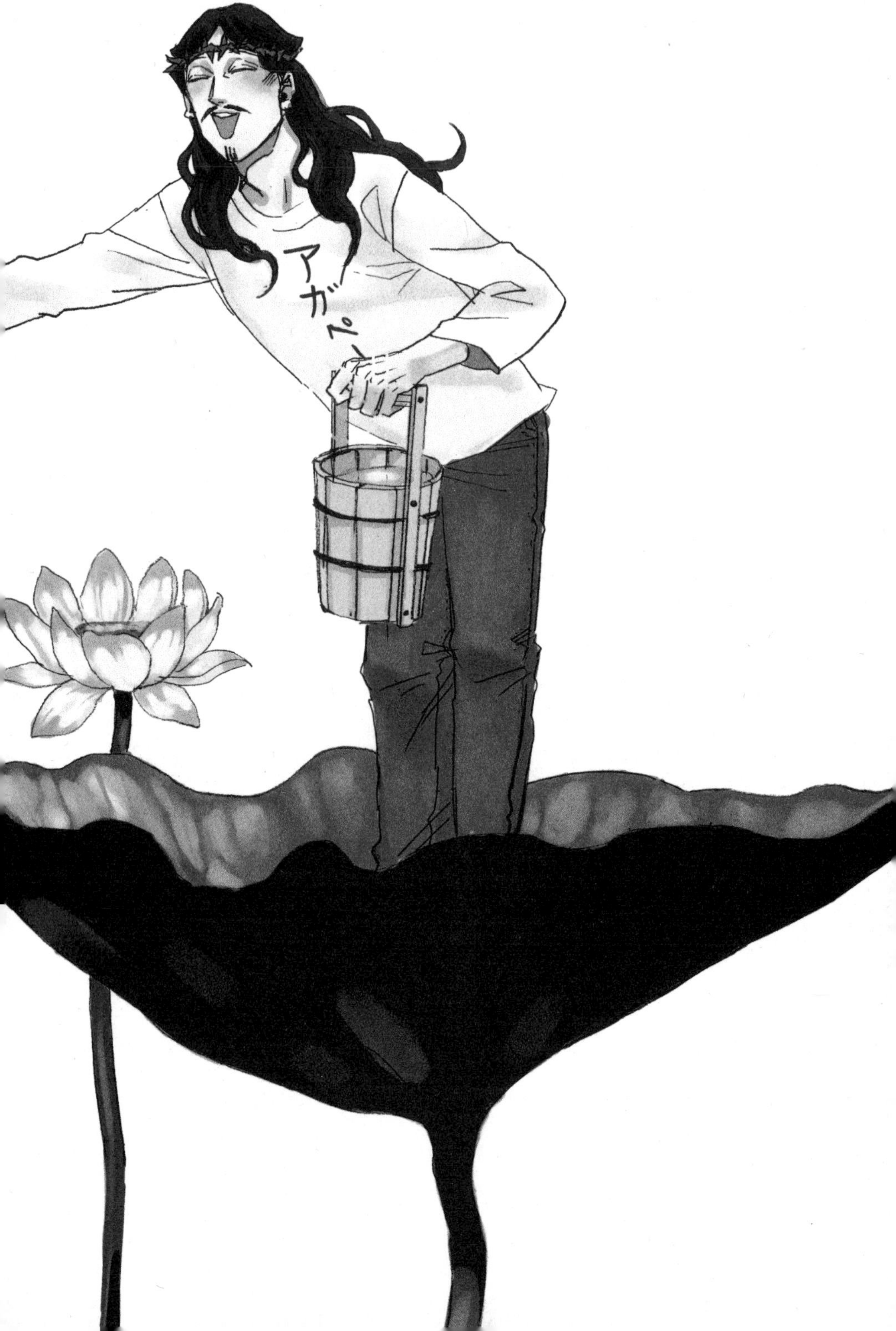
アガペー

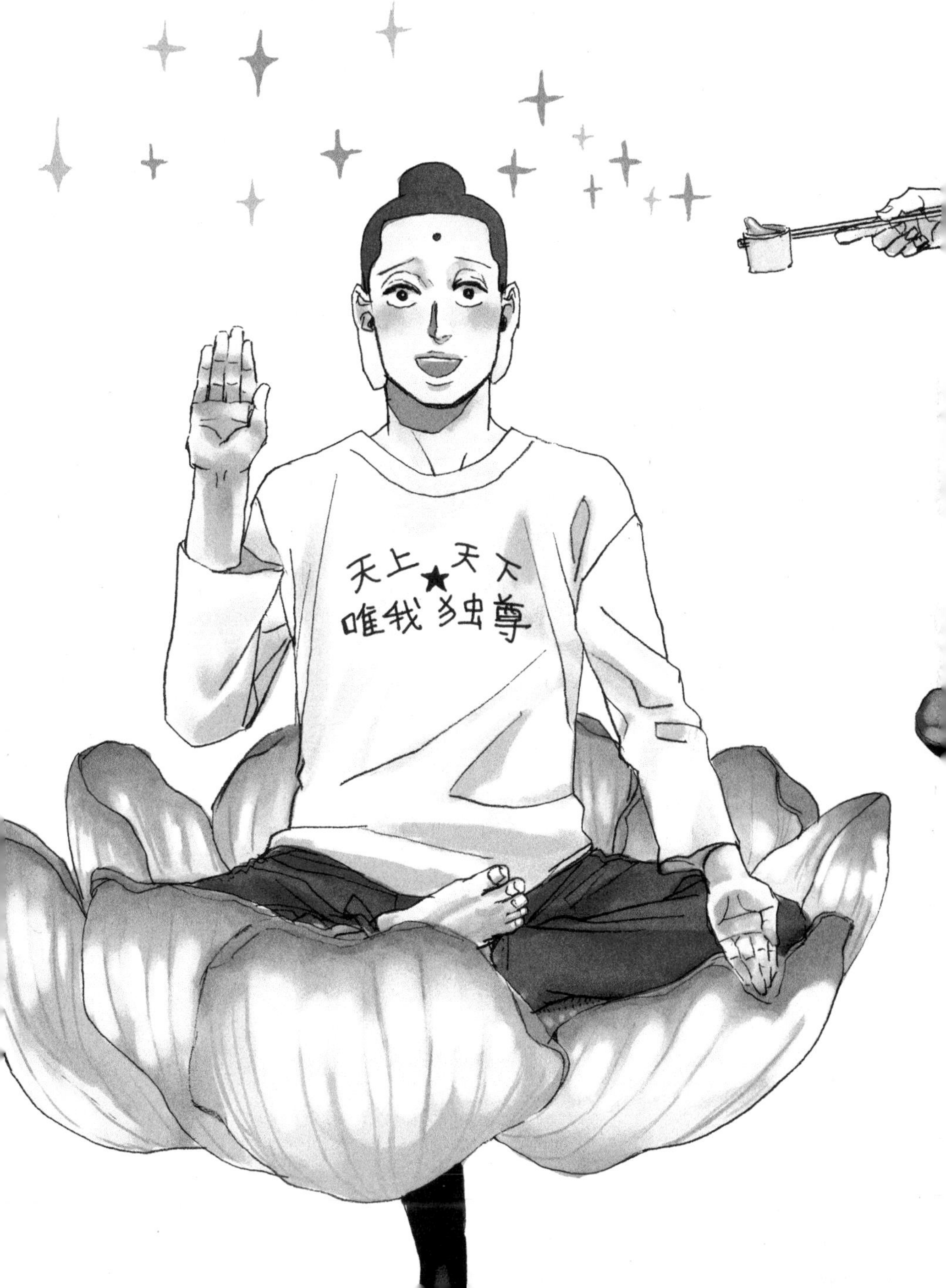
天上★天下
唯我独尊

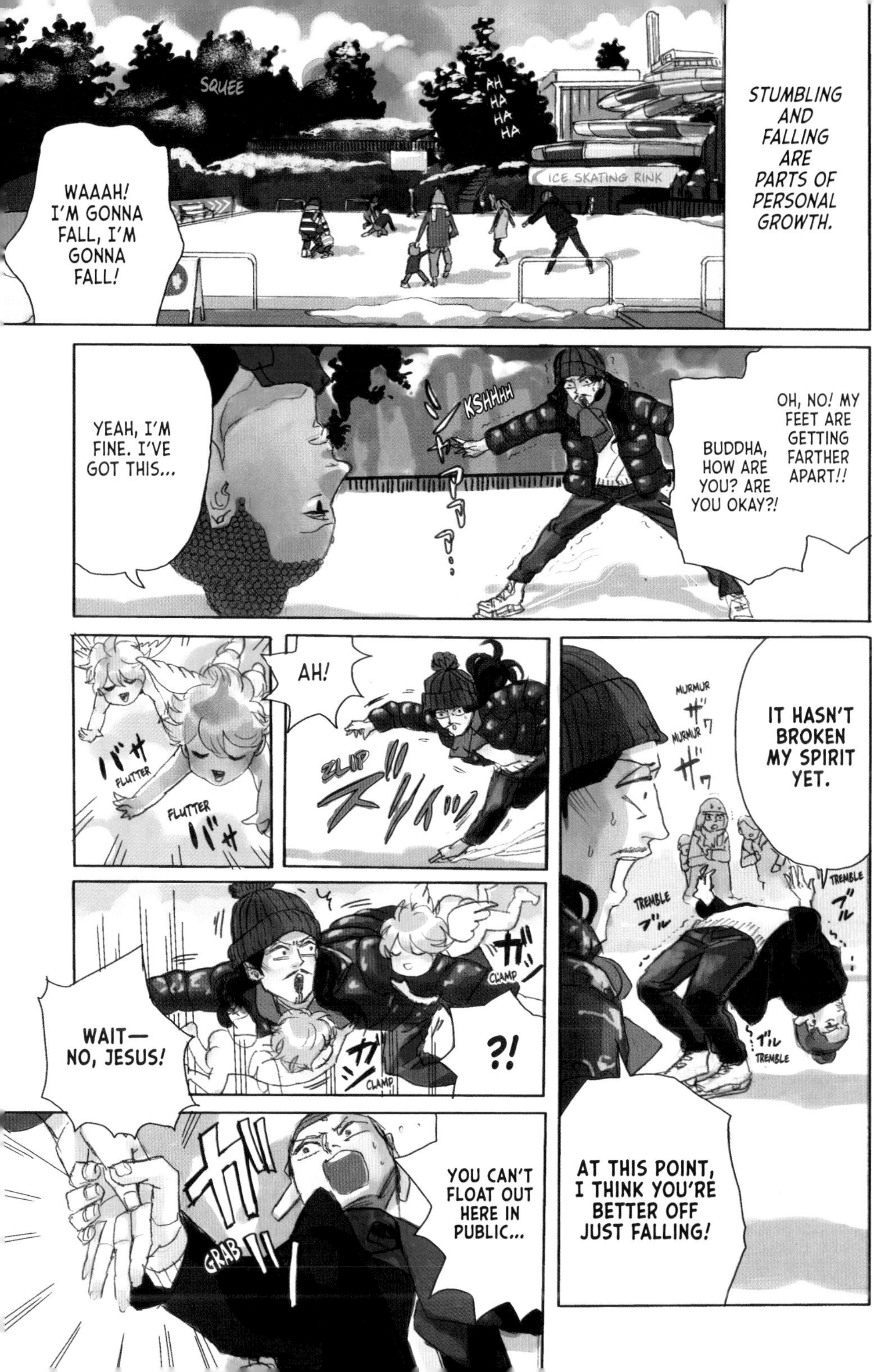
STUMBLING AND FALLING ARE PARTS OF PERSONAL GROWTH.
ICE SKATING RINK
AH HA HA HA
SQUEE
WAAAH! I'M GONNA FALL, I'M GONNA FALL!
OH, NO! MY FEET ARE GETTING FARTHER APART!!
BUDDHA, HOW ARE YOU? ARE YOU OKAY?!
KSHHHH
YEAH, I'M FINE. I'VE GOT THIS...
IT HASN'T BROKEN MY SPIRIT YET.
MURMUR
MURMUR
TREMBLE
TREMBLE
TREMBLE
AT THIS POINT, I THINK YOU'RE BETTER OFF JUST FALLING!
AH!
ZLIP
FLUTTER
FLUTTER
?!
CLAMP
CLAMP
WAIT— NO, JESUS!
YOU CAN'T FLOAT OUT HERE IN PUBLIC...
GRAB

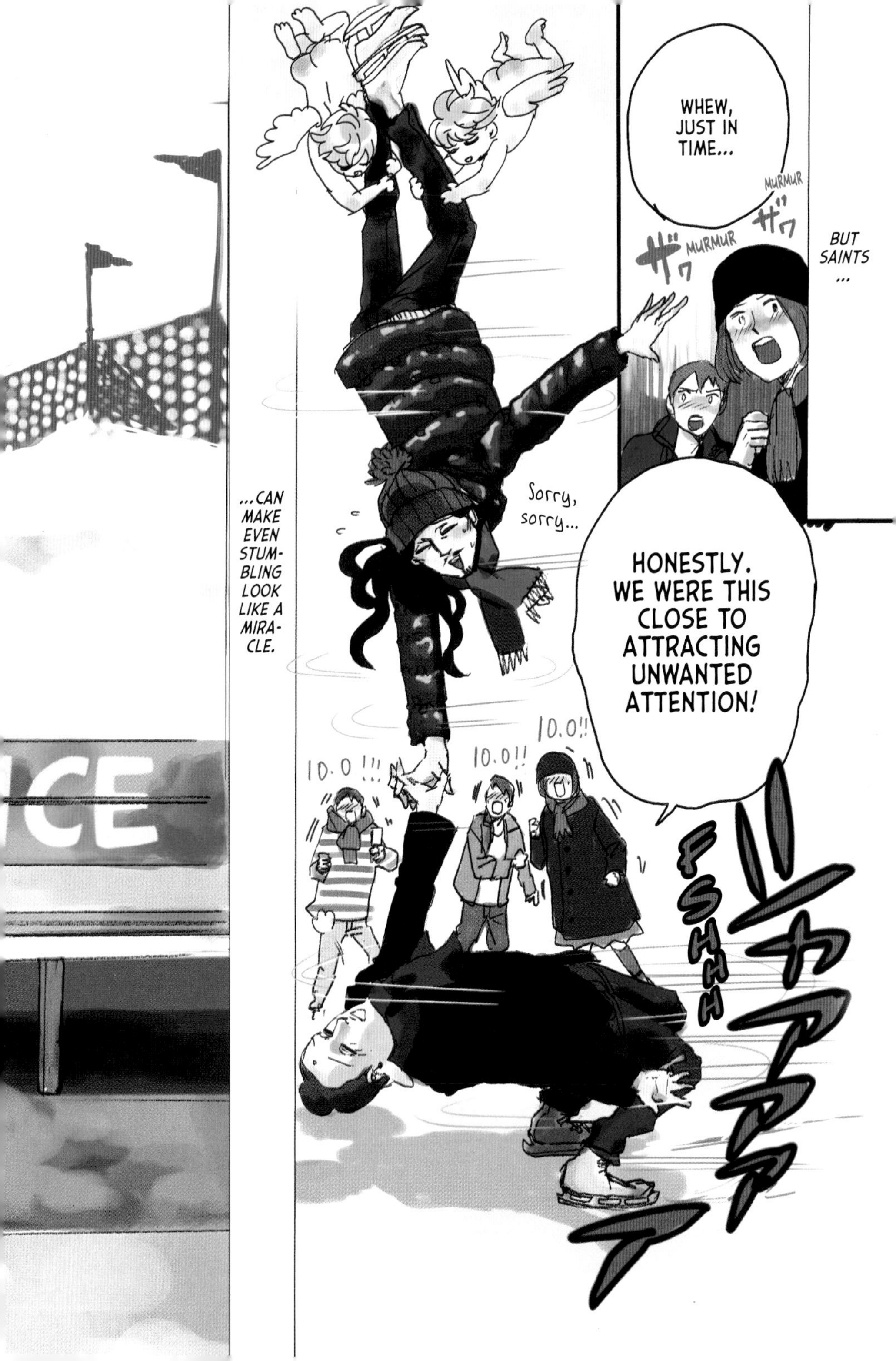
WHEW, JUST IN TIME...
MURMUR
MURMUR
BUT SAINTS...
HONESTLY. WE WERE THIS CLOSE TO ATTRACTING UNWANTED ATTENTION!
Sorry, sorry...
...CAN MAKE EVEN STUMBLING LOOK LIKE A MIRACLE.
10.0!!
10.0!!
10.0!!!
FSHHH
ICE

SAINT YOUNG MEN

Chapter 23
Compulsory Courtesy Chocolate

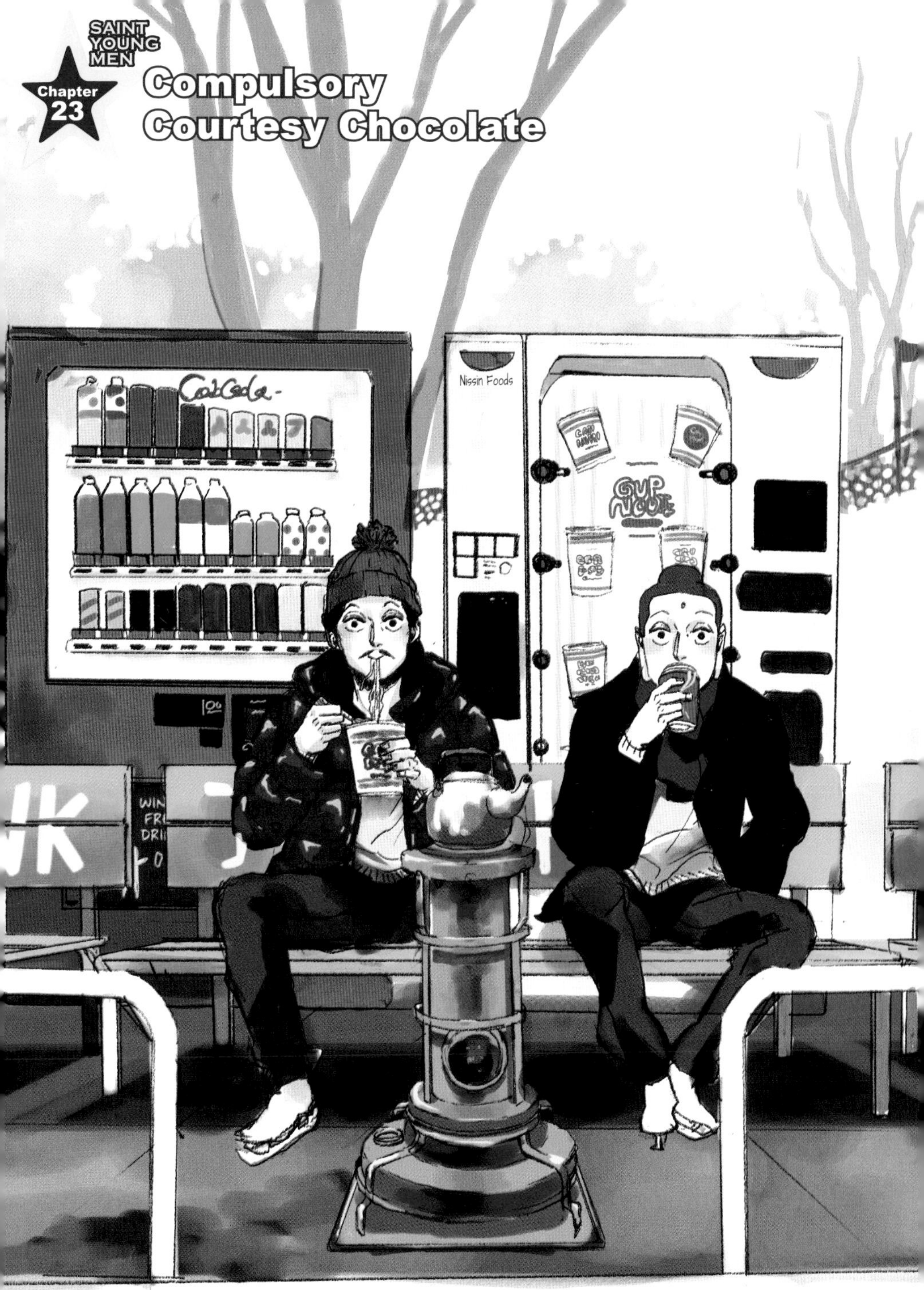
Nissin Foods

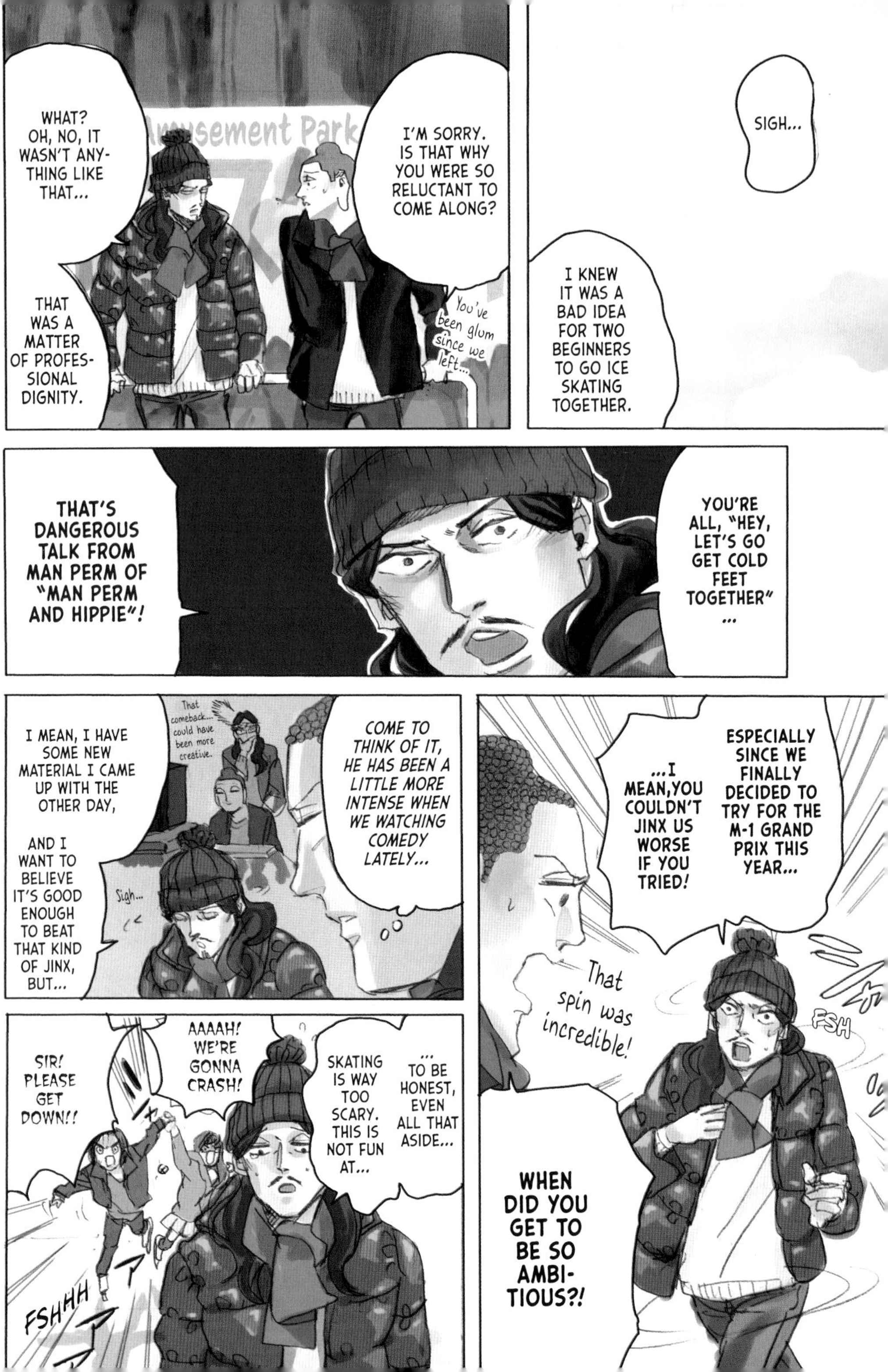
SIGH...
I KNEW IT WAS A BAD IDEA FOR TWO BEGINNERS TO GO ICE SKATING TOGETHER.
I'M SORRY. IS THAT WHY YOU WERE SO RELUCTANT TO COME ALONG?
You've been glum since we left...
WHAT? OH, NO, IT WASN'T ANY-THING LIKE THAT...
THAT WAS A MATTER OF PROFES-SIONAL DIGNITY.
YOU'RE ALL, "HEY, LET'S GO GET COLD FEET TOGETHER"...
THAT'S DANGEROUS TALK FROM MAN PERM OF "MAN PERM AND HIPPIE"!
ESPECIALLY SINCE WE FINALLY DECIDED TO TRY FOR THE M-1 GRAND PRIX THIS YEAR...
...I MEAN, YOU COULDN'T JINX US WORSE IF YOU TRIED!
That spin was incredible!
FSH
WHEN DID YOU GET TO BE SO AMBI-TIOUS?!
COME TO THINK OF IT, HE HAS BEEN A LITTLE MORE INTENSE WHEN WE WATCHING COMEDY LATELY...
That comeback... could have been more creative.
I MEAN, I HAVE SOME NEW MATERIAL I CAME UP WITH THE OTHER DAY,
Sigh...
AND I WANT TO BELIEVE IT'S GOOD ENOUGH TO BEAT THAT KIND OF JINX, BUT...
...TO BE HONEST, EVEN ALL THAT ASIDE...
SKATING IS WAY TOO SCARY. THIS IS NOT FUN AT...
AAAAH! WE'RE GONNA CRASH!
SIR! PLEASE GET DOWN!!
FSHHH

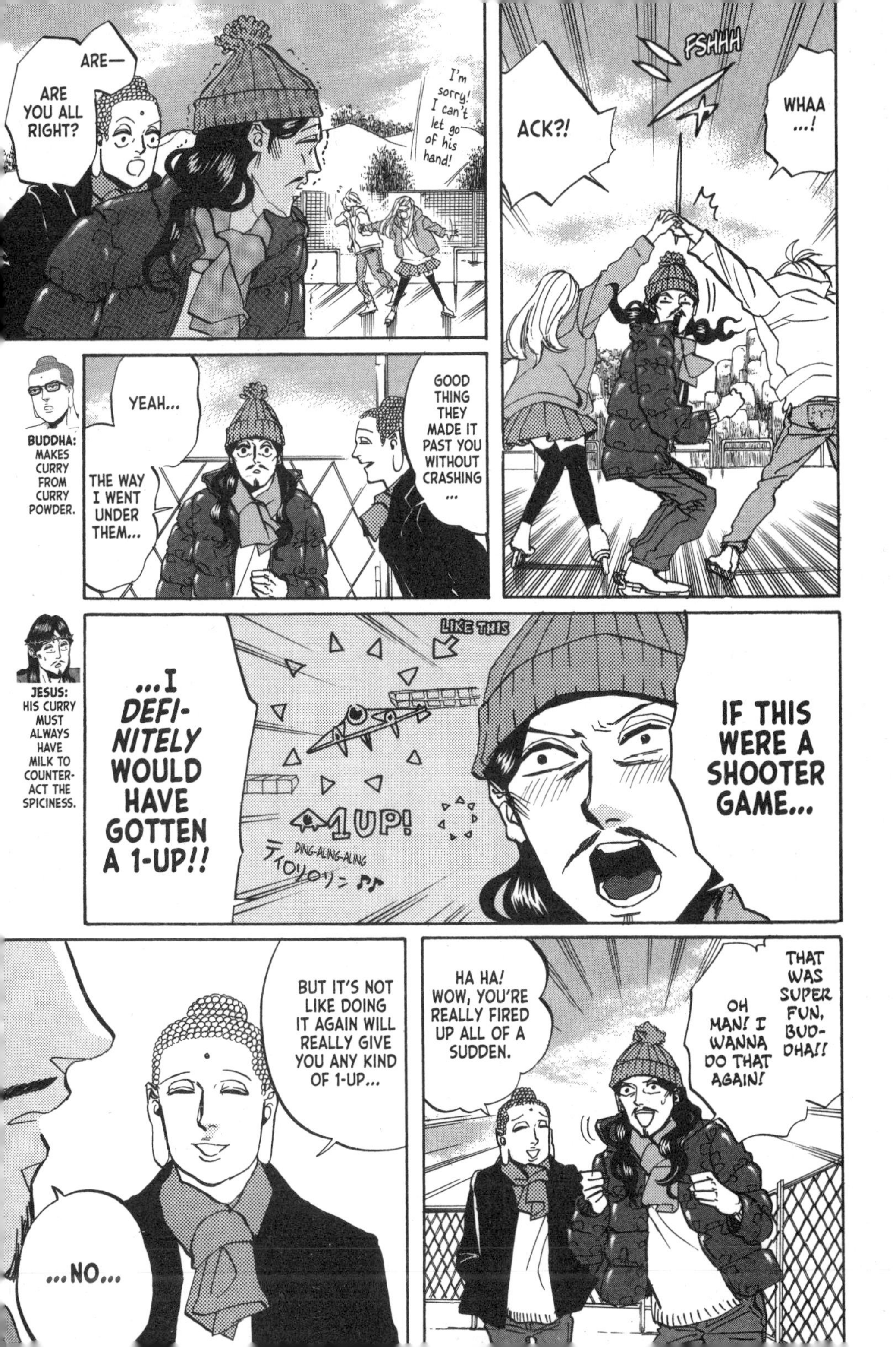
WHAA ...!
FSHHH
ACK?!
I'm sorry! I can't let go of his hand!
ARE— ARE YOU ALL RIGHT?
GOOD THING THEY MADE IT PAST YOU WITHOUT CRASHING ...
YEAH...
THE WAY I WENT UNDER THEM...
BUDDHA: MAKES CURRY FROM CURRY POWDER.
IF THIS WERE A SHOOTER GAME...
LIKE THIS
1UP!
DING-ALING-ALING
ティロリロリン♪♪
...I DEFINITELY WOULD HAVE GOTTEN A 1-UP!!
JESUS: HIS CURRY MUST ALWAYS HAVE MILK TO COUNTERACT THE SPICINESS.
THAT WAS SUPER FUN, BUDDHA!!
OH MAN! I WANNA DO THAT AGAIN!
HA HA! WOW, YOU'RE REALLY FIRED UP ALL OF A SUDDEN.
BUT IT'S NOT LIKE DOING IT AGAIN WILL REALLY GIVE YOU ANY KIND OF 1-UP...
...NO...

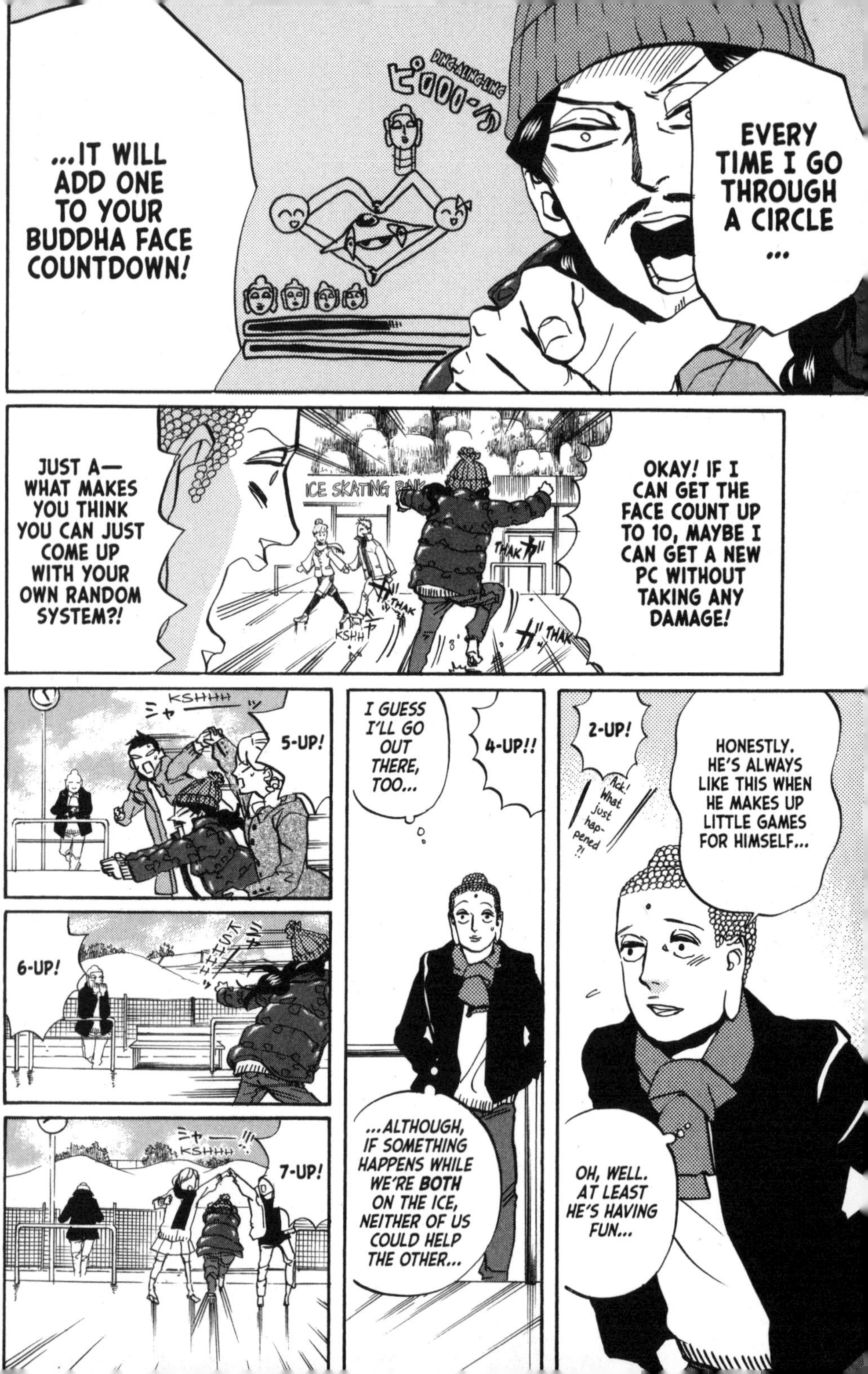
EVERY TIME I GO THROUGH A CIRCLE ...
DING-ALING-LING
...IT WILL ADD ONE TO YOUR BUDDHA FACE COUNTDOWN!
OKAY! IF I CAN GET THE FACE COUNT UP TO 10, MAYBE I CAN GET A NEW PC WITHOUT TAKING ANY DAMAGE!
ICE SKATING
THAK
THAK
KSHH
THAK
JUST A— WHAT MAKES YOU THINK YOU CAN JUST COME UP WITH YOUR OWN RANDOM SYSTEM?!
2-UP!
HONESTLY. HE'S ALWAYS LIKE THIS WHEN HE MAKES UP LITTLE GAMES FOR HIMSELF...
Ack! What just happened?!
OH, WELL. AT LEAST HE'S HAVING FUN...
4-UP!!
I GUESS I'LL GO OUT THERE, TOO...
...ALTHOUGH, IF SOMETHING HAPPENS WHILE WE'RE BOTH ON THE ICE, NEITHER OF US COULD HELP THE OTHER...
KSHHH
5-UP!
6-UP!
KSHHH
7-UP!

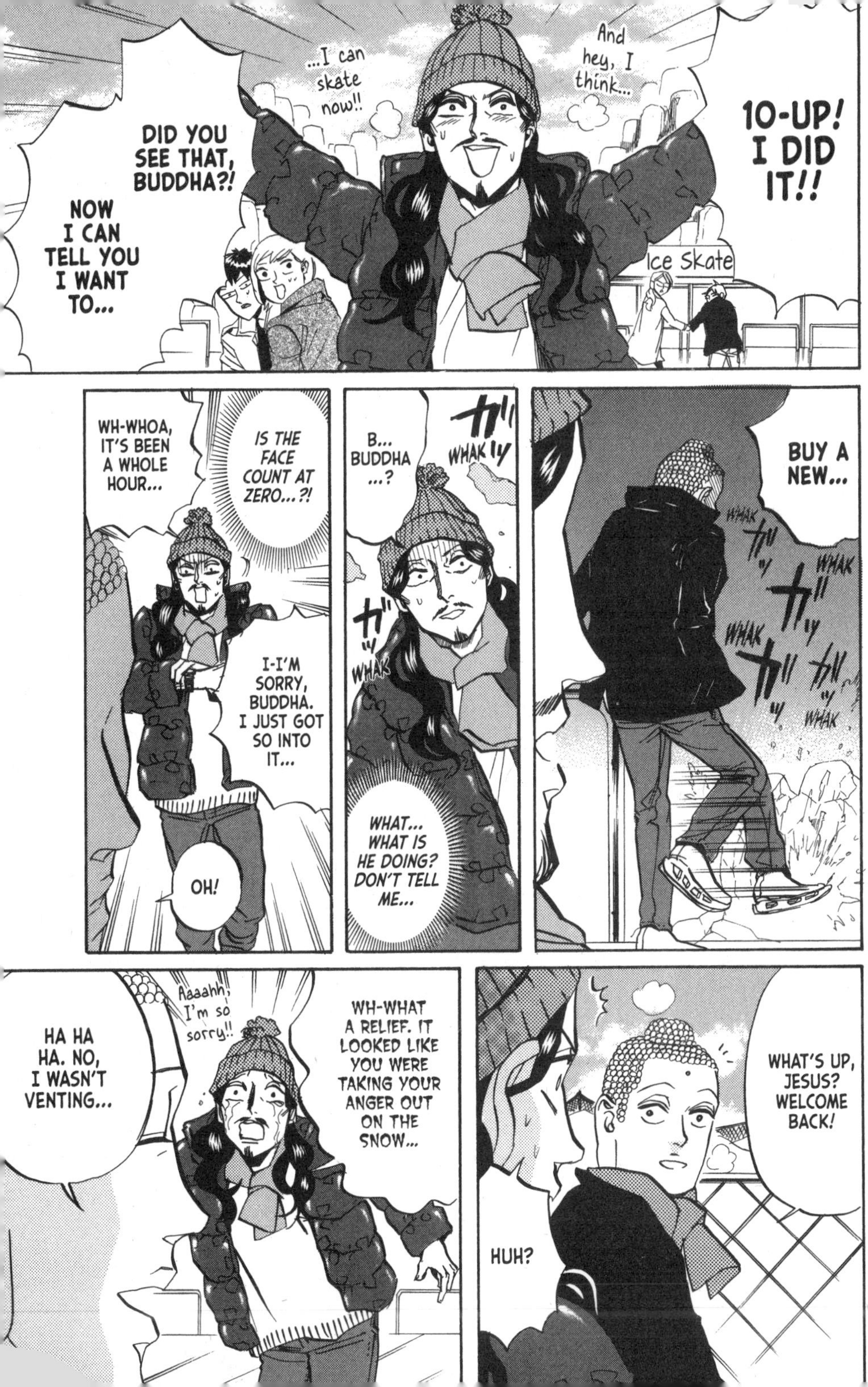

10-UP! I DID IT!!
And hey, I think...
...I can skate now!!
DID YOU SEE THAT, BUDDHA?!
NOW I CAN TELL YOU I WANT TO...
Ice Skate
BUY A NEW...
WHAK
WHAK
WHAK
WHAK
WHAK
B... BUDDHA ...?
WHAK
WHAK
WHAT... WHAT IS HE DOING? DON'T TELL ME...
IS THE FACE COUNT AT ZERO...?!
WH-WHOA, IT'S BEEN A WHOLE HOUR...
I-I'M SORRY, BUDDHA. I JUST GOT SO INTO IT...
OH!
WHAT'S UP, JESUS? WELCOME BACK!
HUH?
WH-WHAT A RELIEF. IT LOOKED LIKE YOU WERE TAKING YOUR ANGER OUT ON THE SNOW...
Aaaahh, I'm so sorry!!
HA HA HA. NO, I WASN'T VENTING...

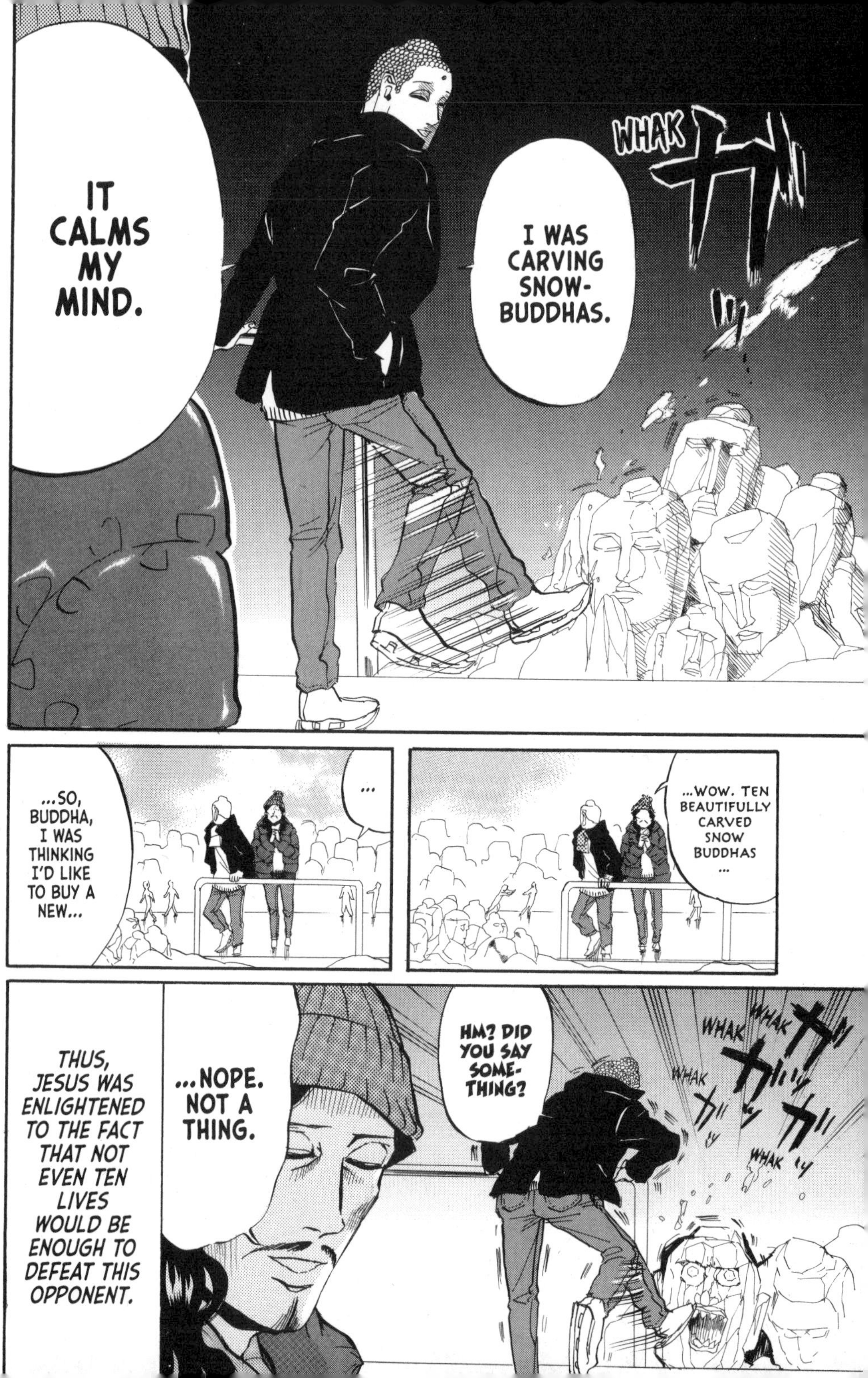
WHAK
I WAS CARVING SNOW-BUDDHAS.
IT CALMS MY MIND.
...WOW. TEN BEAUTIFULLY CARVED SNOW BUDDHAS ...
...
...SO, BUDDHA, I WAS THINKING I'D LIKE TO BUY A NEW...
WHAK WHAK
HM? DID YOU SAY SOME-THING?
WHAK
WHAK
...NOPE. NOT A THING.
THUS, JESUS WAS ENLIGHTENED TO THE FACT THAT NOT EVEN TEN LIVES WOULD BE ENOUGH TO DEFEAT THIS OPPONENT.

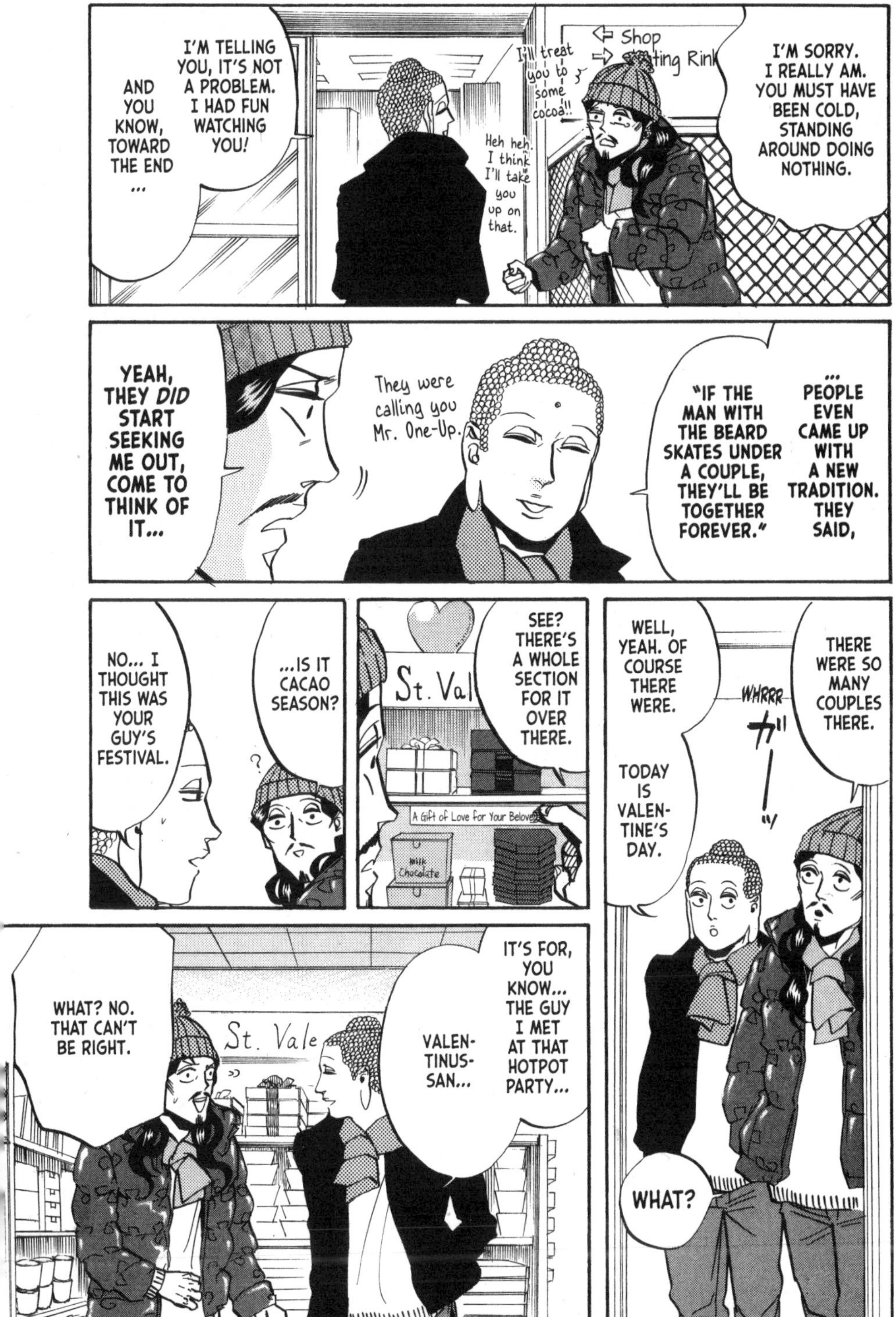
I'M SORRY. I REALLY AM. YOU MUST HAVE BEEN COLD, STANDING AROUND DOING NOTHING.
Shop
ting Rink
I'll treat you to some cocoa!!
Heh heh. I think I'll take you up on that.
I'M TELLING YOU, IT'S NOT A PROBLEM. I HAD FUN WATCHING YOU!
AND YOU KNOW, TOWARD THE END ...
... PEOPLE EVEN CAME UP WITH A NEW TRADITION. THEY SAID,
"IF THE MAN WITH THE BEARD SKATES UNDER A COUPLE, THEY'LL BE TOGETHER FOREVER."
They were calling you Mr. One-Up.
YEAH, THEY *DID* START SEEKING ME OUT, COME TO THINK OF IT...
THERE WERE SO MANY COUPLES THERE.
WELL, YEAH. OF COURSE THERE WERE.
WHRRR
TODAY IS VALEN-TINE'S DAY.
WHAT?
SEE? THERE'S A WHOLE SECTION FOR IT OVER THERE.
St. Val
A Gift of Love for Your Beloved
Milk Chocolate
...IS IT CACAO SEASON?
NO... I THOUGHT THIS WAS YOUR GUY'S FESTIVAL.
IT'S FOR, YOU KNOW... THE GUY I MET AT THAT HOTPOT PARTY...
VALEN-TINUS-SAN...
St. Vale
WHAT? NO. THAT CAN'T BE RIGHT.

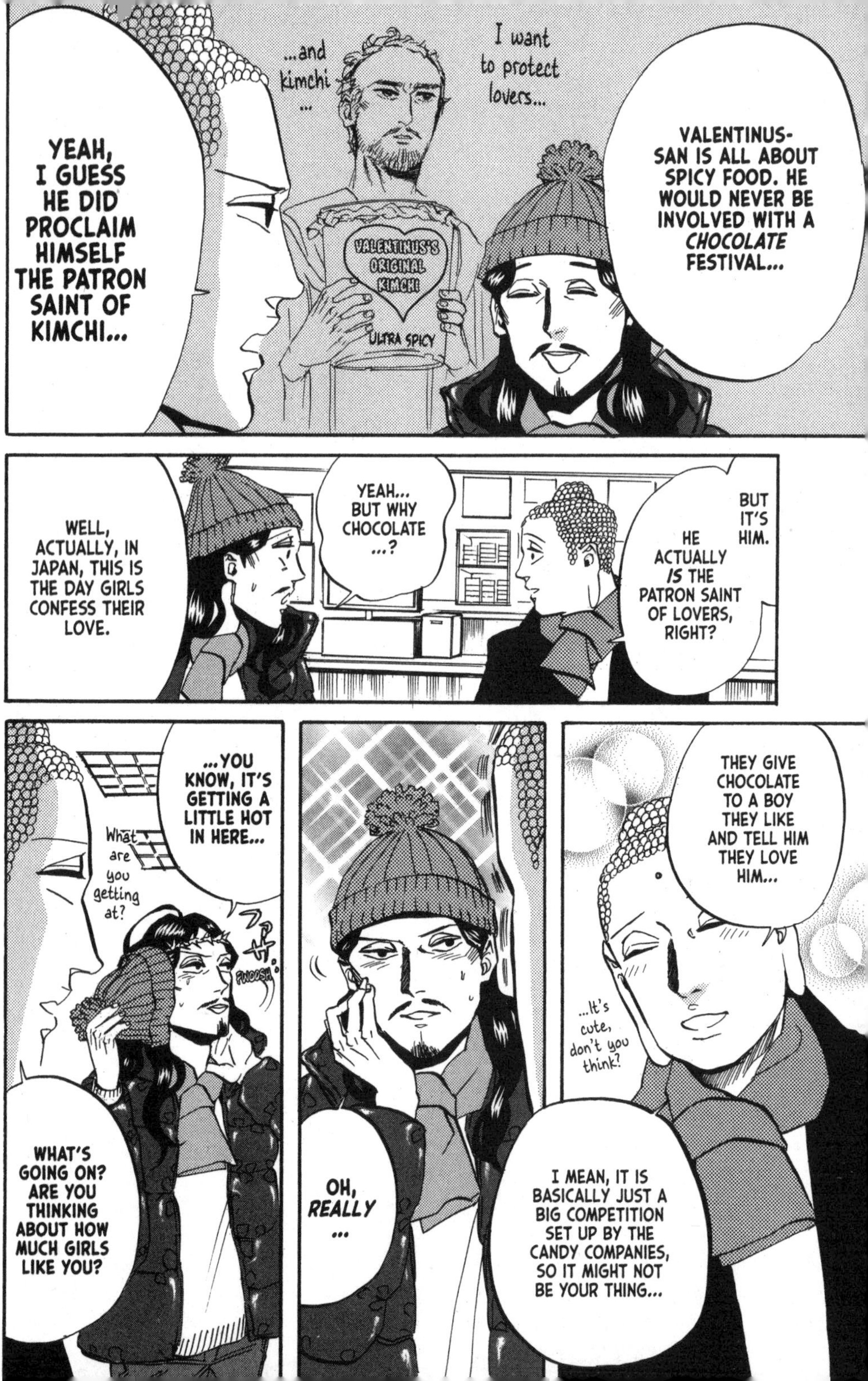
VALENTINUS-SAN IS ALL ABOUT SPICY FOOD. HE WOULD NEVER BE INVOLVED WITH A *CHOCOLATE* FESTIVAL...
I want to protect lovers...
...and kimchi...
VALENTINUS'S ORIGINAL KIMCHI
ULTRA SPICY
YEAH, I GUESS HE DID PROCLAIM HIMSELF THE PATRON SAINT OF KIMCHI...
BUT IT'S HIM.
HE ACTUALLY *IS* THE PATRON SAINT OF LOVERS, RIGHT?
YEAH... BUT WHY CHOCOLATE ...?
WELL, ACTUALLY, IN JAPAN, THIS IS THE DAY GIRLS CONFESS THEIR LOVE.
THEY GIVE CHOCOLATE TO A BOY THEY LIKE AND TELL HIM THEY LOVE HIM...
...It's cute, don't you think?
I MEAN, IT IS BASICALLY JUST A BIG COMPETITION SET UP BY THE CANDY COMPANIES, SO IT MIGHT NOT BE YOUR THING...
OH, *REALLY* ...
...YOU KNOW, IT'S GETTING A LITTLE HOT IN HERE...
What are you getting at?
FWOOSH
WHAT'S GOING ON? ARE YOU THINKING ABOUT HOW MUCH GIRLS LIKE YOU?

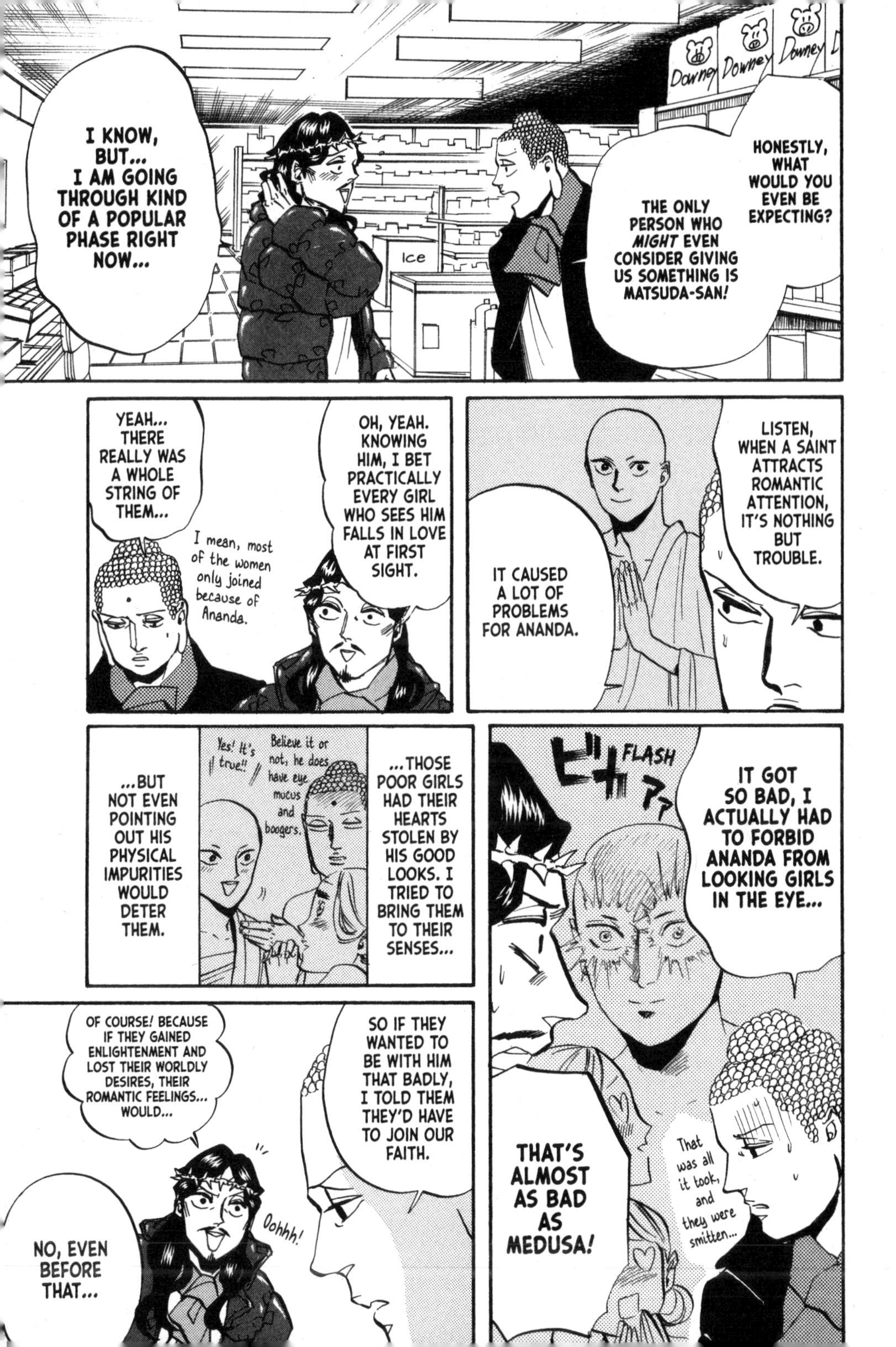

Downey
Downey
Downey
HONESTLY, WHAT WOULD YOU EVEN BE EXPECTING?
THE ONLY PERSON WHO *MIGHT* EVEN CONSIDER GIVING US SOMETHING IS MATSUDA-SAN!
Ice
I KNOW, BUT... I AM GOING THROUGH KIND OF A POPULAR PHASE RIGHT NOW...
LISTEN, WHEN A SAINT ATTRACTS ROMANTIC ATTENTION, IT'S NOTHING BUT TROUBLE.
IT CAUSED A LOT OF PROBLEMS FOR ANANDA.
OH, YEAH. KNOWING HIM, I BET PRACTICALLY EVERY GIRL WHO SEES HIM FALLS IN LOVE AT FIRST SIGHT.
YEAH... THERE REALLY WAS A WHOLE STRING OF THEM...
I mean, most of the women only joined because of Ananda.
FLASH
IT GOT SO BAD, I ACTUALLY HAD TO FORBID ANANDA FROM LOOKING GIRLS IN THE EYE...
That was all it took, and they were smitten...
THAT'S ALMOST AS BAD AS MEDUSA!
...THOSE POOR GIRLS HAD THEIR HEARTS STOLEN BY HIS GOOD LOOKS. I TRIED TO BRING THEM TO THEIR SENSES...
Believe it or not, he does have eye mucus and boogers.
Yes! It's true!!
...BUT NOT EVEN POINTING OUT HIS PHYSICAL IMPURITIES WOULD DETER THEM.
SO IF THEY WANTED TO BE WITH HIM THAT BADLY, I TOLD THEM THEY'D HAVE TO JOIN OUR FAITH.
OF COURSE! BECAUSE IF THEY GAINED ENLIGHTENMENT AND LOST THEIR WORLDLY DESIRES, THEIR ROMANTIC FEELINGS... WOULD...
Oohhh!
NO, EVEN BEFORE THAT...

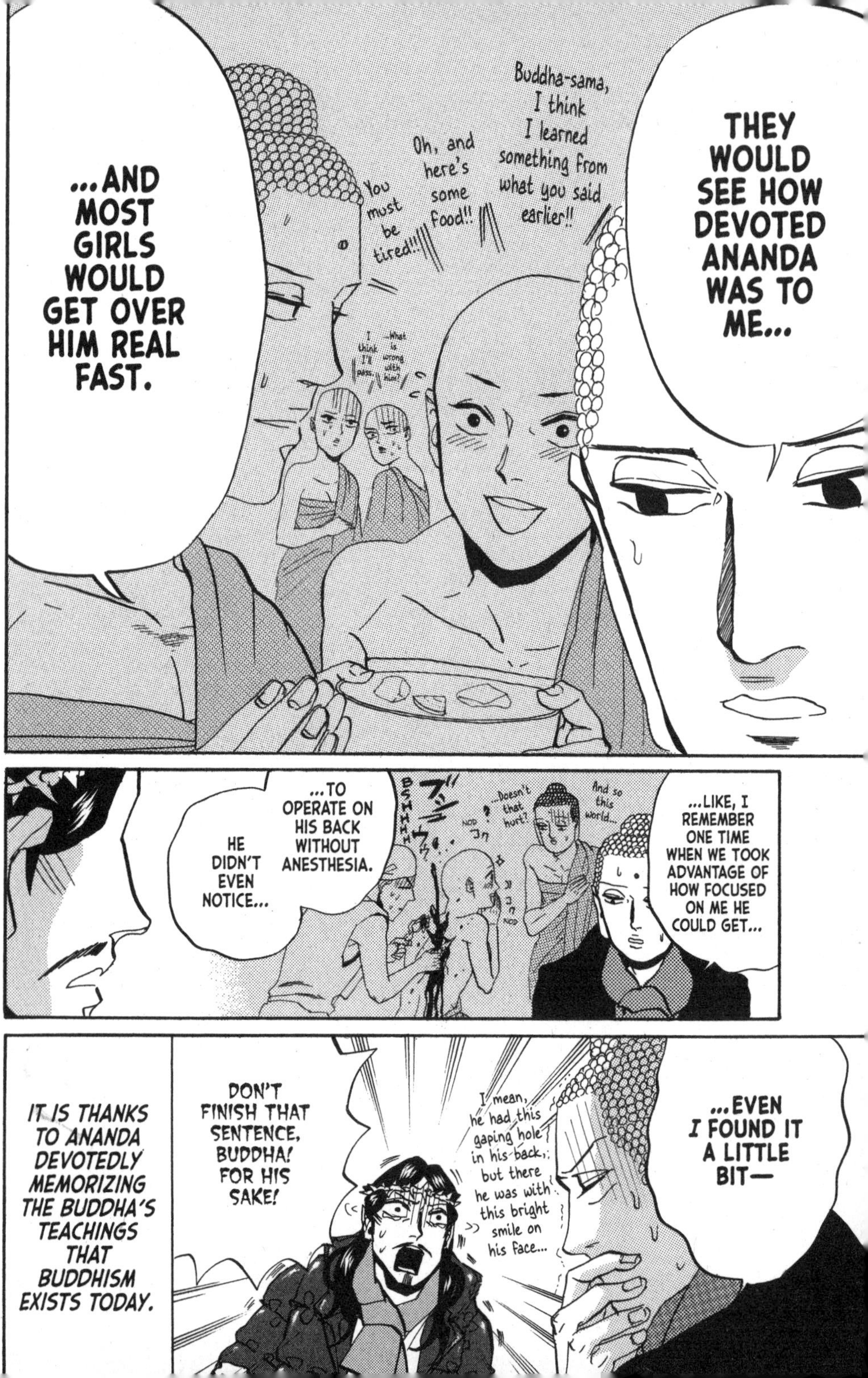
THEY WOULD SEE HOW DEVOTED ANANDA WAS TO ME...
Buddha-sama, I think I learned something from what you said earlier!!
Oh, and here's some food!!
You must be tired!!
...What is wrong with him?
I think I'll pass.
...AND MOST GIRLS WOULD GET OVER HIM REAL FAST.
...LIKE, I REMEMBER ONE TIME WHEN WE TOOK ADVANTAGE OF HOW FOCUSED ON ME HE COULD GET...
And so this world...
...Doesn't that hurt?
NOD
NOD
BSHHHHH
...TO OPERATE ON HIS BACK WITHOUT ANESTHESIA.
HE DIDN'T EVEN NOTICE...
...EVEN I FOUND IT A LITTLE BIT—
I mean, he had this gaping hole in his back, but there he was with this bright smile on his face...
DON'T FINISH THAT SENTENCE, BUDDHA! FOR HIS SAKE!
IT IS THANKS TO ANANDA DEVOTEDLY MEMORIZING THE BUDDHA'S TEACHINGS THAT BUDDHISM EXISTS TODAY.

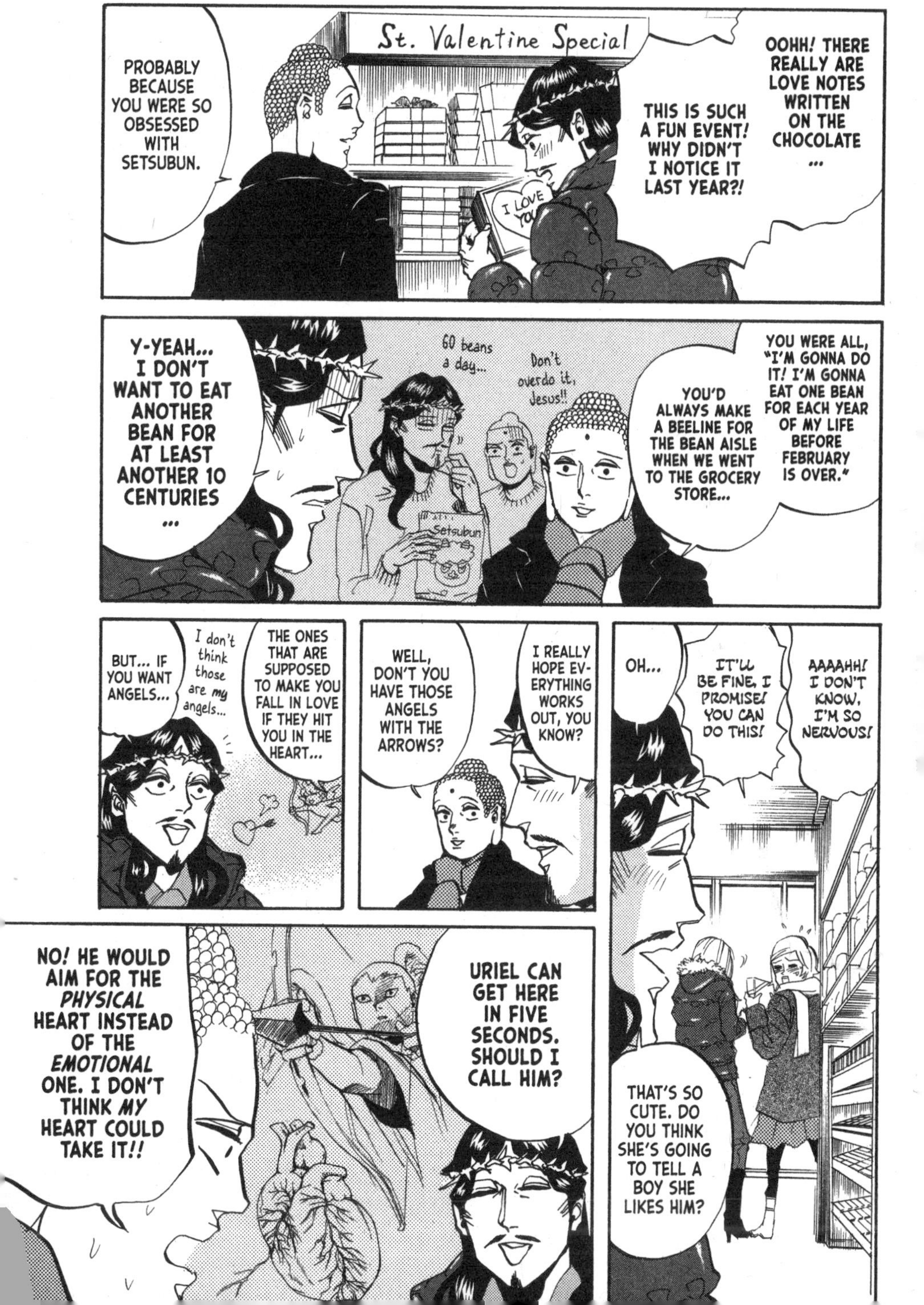
OOHH! THERE REALLY ARE LOVE NOTES WRITTEN ON THE CHOCOLATE ...
THIS IS SUCH A FUN EVENT! WHY DIDN'T I NOTICE IT LAST YEAR?!
St. Valentine Special
I LOVE YOU
PROBABLY BECAUSE YOU WERE SO OBSESSED WITH SETSUBUN.
YOU WERE ALL, "I'M GONNA DO IT! I'M GONNA EAT ONE BEAN FOR EACH YEAR OF MY LIFE BEFORE FEBRUARY IS OVER."
YOU'D ALWAYS MAKE A BEELINE FOR THE BEAN AISLE WHEN WE WENT TO THE GROCERY STORE...
Don't overdo it, Jesus!!
60 beans a day...
Setsubun
Y-YEAH... I DON'T WANT TO EAT ANOTHER BEAN FOR AT LEAST ANOTHER 10 CENTURIES ...
AAAAHH! I DON'T KNOW, I'M SO NERVOUS!
IT'LL BE FINE, I PROMISE! YOU CAN DO THIS!
OH...
THAT'S SO CUTE. DO YOU THINK SHE'S GOING TO TELL A BOY SHE LIKES HIM?
I REALLY HOPE EV-ERYTHING WORKS OUT, YOU KNOW?
WELL, DON'T YOU HAVE THOSE ANGELS WITH THE ARROWS?
THE ONES THAT ARE SUPPOSED TO MAKE YOU FALL IN LOVE IF THEY HIT YOU IN THE HEART...
I don't think those are *my* angels...
BUT... IF YOU WANT ANGELS...
URIEL CAN GET HERE IN FIVE SECONDS. SHOULD I CALL HIM?
NO! HE WOULD AIM FOR THE *PHYSICAL* HEART INSTEAD OF THE *EMOTIONAL* ONE. I DON'T THINK *MY* HEART COULD TAKE IT!!

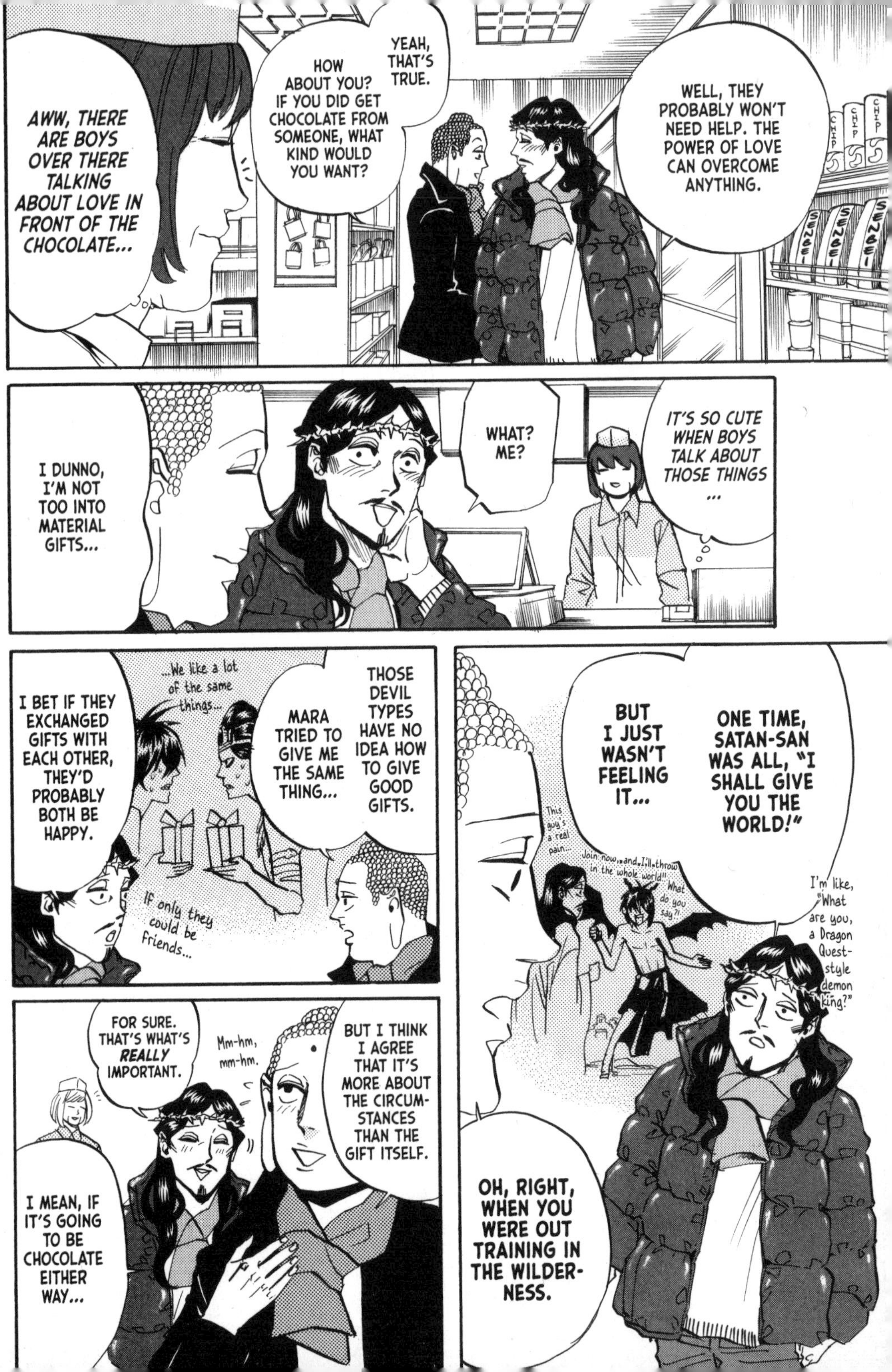
WELL, THEY PROBABLY WON'T NEED HELP. THE POWER OF LOVE CAN OVERCOME ANYTHING.
CHIP
SENBEI
YEAH, THAT'S TRUE.
HOW ABOUT YOU? IF YOU DID GET CHOCOLATE FROM SOMEONE, WHAT KIND WOULD YOU WANT?
AWW, THERE ARE BOYS OVER THERE TALKING ABOUT LOVE IN FRONT OF THE CHOCOLATE...
IT'S SO CUTE WHEN BOYS TALK ABOUT THOSE THINGS ...
WHAT? ME?
I DUNNO, I'M NOT TOO INTO MATERIAL GIFTS...
ONE TIME, SATAN-SAN WAS ALL, "I SHALL GIVE YOU THE WORLD!"
BUT I JUST WASN'T FEELING IT...
I'm like, "What are you, a Dragon Quest-style demon king?"
Join now, and I'll throw in the whole world!!
What do you say?!
This guy's a real pain...
OH, RIGHT, WHEN YOU WERE OUT TRAINING IN THE WILDER-NESS.
THOSE DEVIL TYPES HAVE NO IDEA HOW TO GIVE GOOD GIFTS.
MARA TRIED TO GIVE ME THE SAME THING...
...We like a lot of the same things...
I BET IF THEY EXCHANGED GIFTS WITH EACH OTHER, THEY'D PROBABLY BOTH BE HAPPY.
If only they could be friends...
BUT I THINK I AGREE THAT IT'S MORE ABOUT THE CIRCUM-STANCES THAN THE GIFT ITSELF.
Mm-hm, mm-hm.
FOR SURE. THAT'S WHAT'S *REALLY* IMPORTANT.
I MEAN, IF IT'S GOING TO BE CHOCOLATE EITHER WAY...

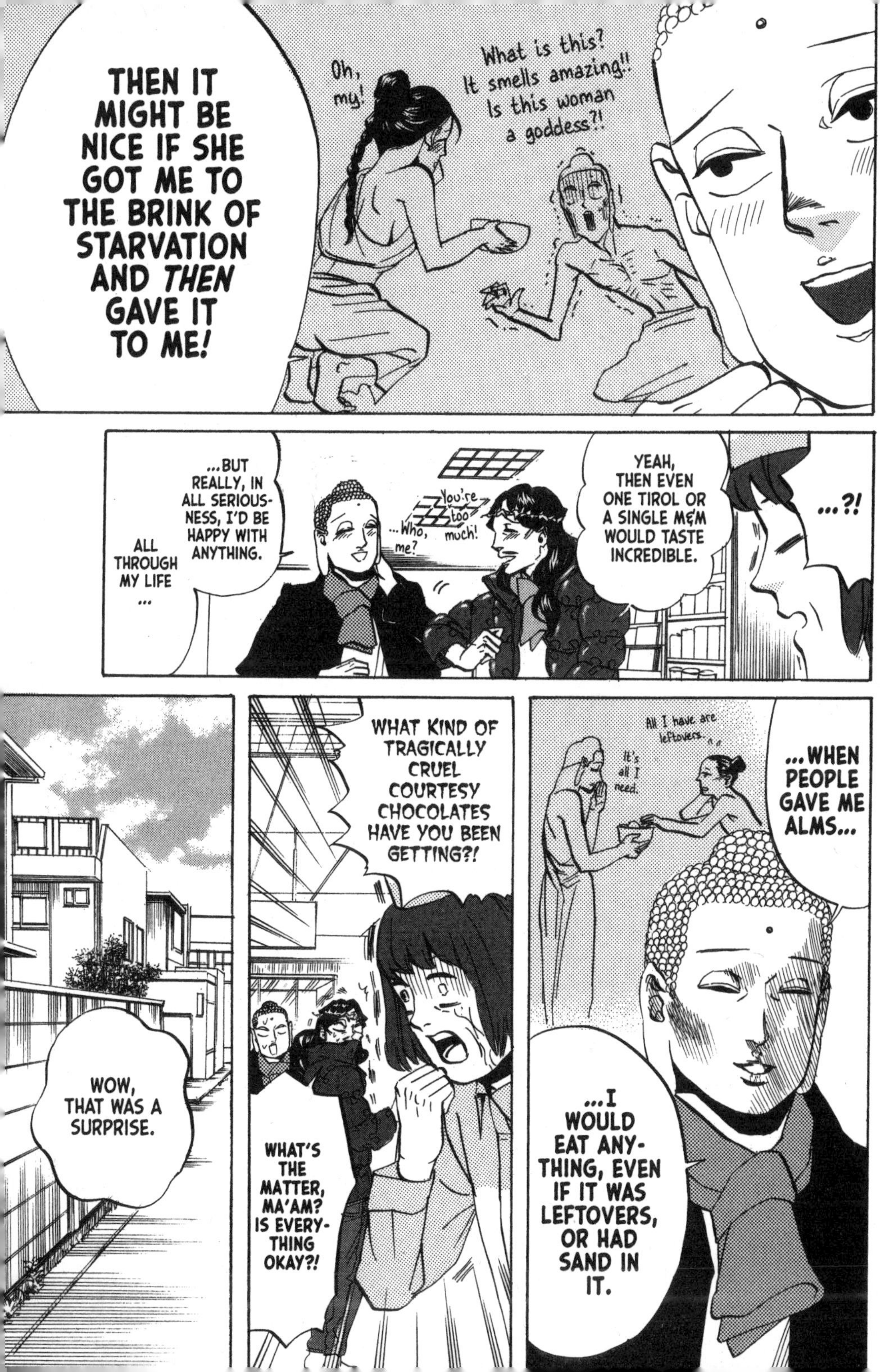
What is this? It smells amazing!! Is this woman a goddess?!
Oh, my!
THEN IT MIGHT BE NICE IF SHE GOT ME TO THE BRINK OF STARVATION AND *THEN* GAVE IT TO ME!
...?!
YEAH, THEN EVEN ONE TIROL OR A SINGLE M&M WOULD TASTE INCREDIBLE.
You're too much!
...Who, me?
...BUT REALLY, IN ALL SERIOUSNESS, I'D BE HAPPY WITH ANYTHING.
ALL THROUGH MY LIFE ...
...WHEN PEOPLE GAVE ME ALMS...
All I have are leftovers.
It's all I need.
...I WOULD EAT ANYTHING, EVEN IF IT WAS LEFTOVERS, OR HAD SAND IN IT.
WHAT KIND OF TRAGICALLY CRUEL COURTESY CHOCOLATES HAVE YOU BEEN GETTING?!
WHAT'S THE MATTER, MA'AM? IS EVERYTHING OKAY?!
WOW, THAT WAS A SURPRISE.

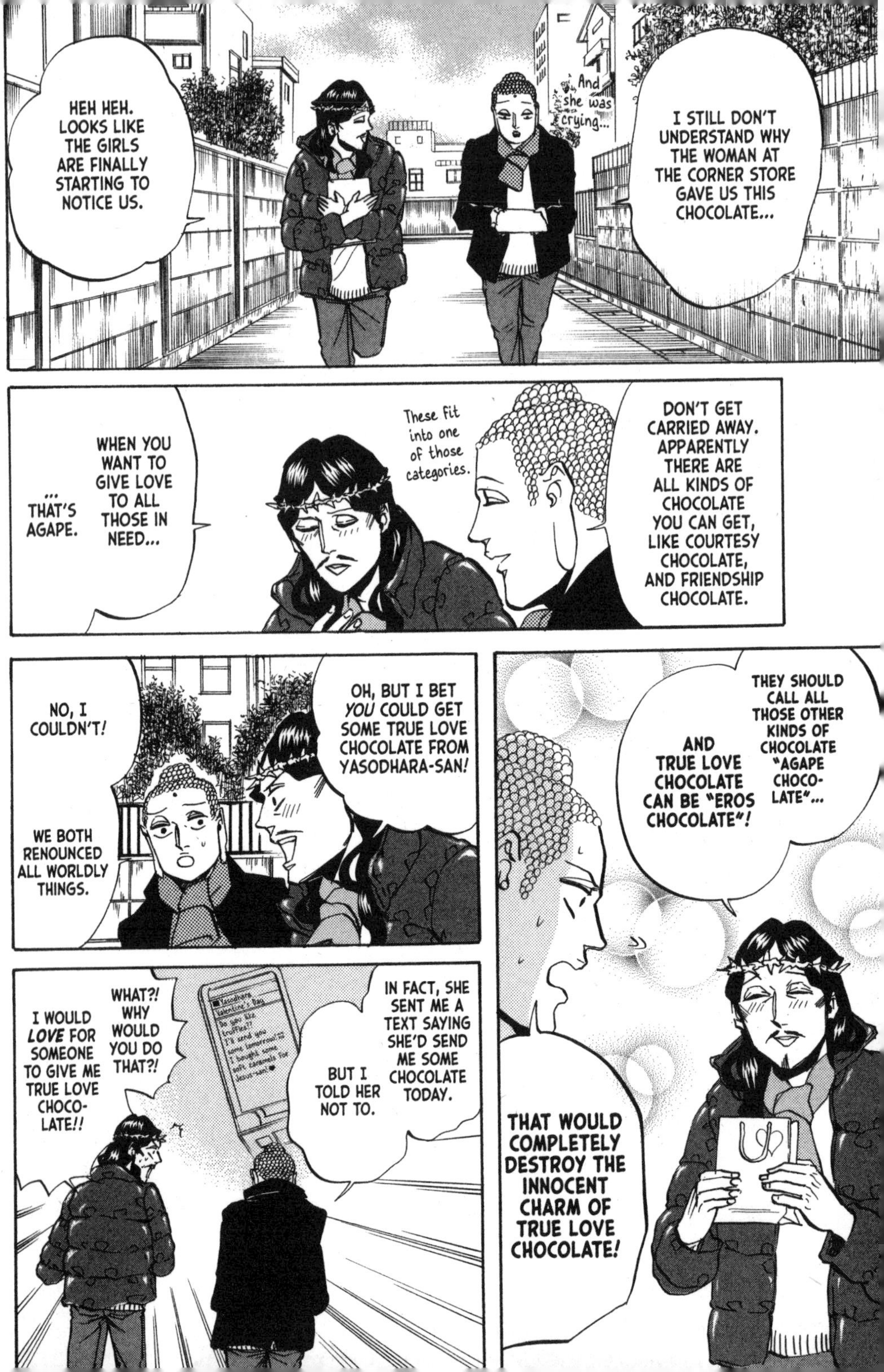
I STILL DON'T UNDERSTAND WHY THE WOMAN AT THE CORNER STORE GAVE US THIS CHOCOLATE...
And she was crying...
HEH HEH. LOOKS LIKE THE GIRLS ARE FINALLY STARTING TO NOTICE US.
DON'T GET CARRIED AWAY. APPARENTLY THERE ARE ALL KINDS OF CHOCOLATE YOU CAN GET, LIKE COURTESY CHOCOLATE, AND FRIENDSHIP CHOCOLATE.
These fit into one of those categories.
WHEN YOU WANT TO GIVE LOVE TO ALL THOSE IN NEED...
...THAT'S AGAPE.
THEY SHOULD CALL ALL THOSE OTHER KINDS OF CHOCOLATE "AGAPE CHOCO-LATE"...
AND TRUE LOVE CHOCOLATE CAN BE "EROS CHOCOLATE"!
THAT WOULD COMPLETELY DESTROY THE INNOCENT CHARM OF TRUE LOVE CHOCOLATE!
OH, BUT I BET *YOU* COULD GET SOME TRUE LOVE CHOCOLATE FROM YASODHARA-SAN!
NO, I COULDN'T!
WE BOTH RENOUNCED ALL WORLDLY THINGS.
IN FACT, SHE SENT ME A TEXT SAYING SHE'D SEND ME SOME CHOCOLATE TODAY.
BUT I TOLD HER NOT TO.
WHAT?! WHY WOULD YOU DO THAT?!
I WOULD *LOVE* FOR SOMEONE TO GIVE ME TRUE LOVE CHOCO-LATE!!

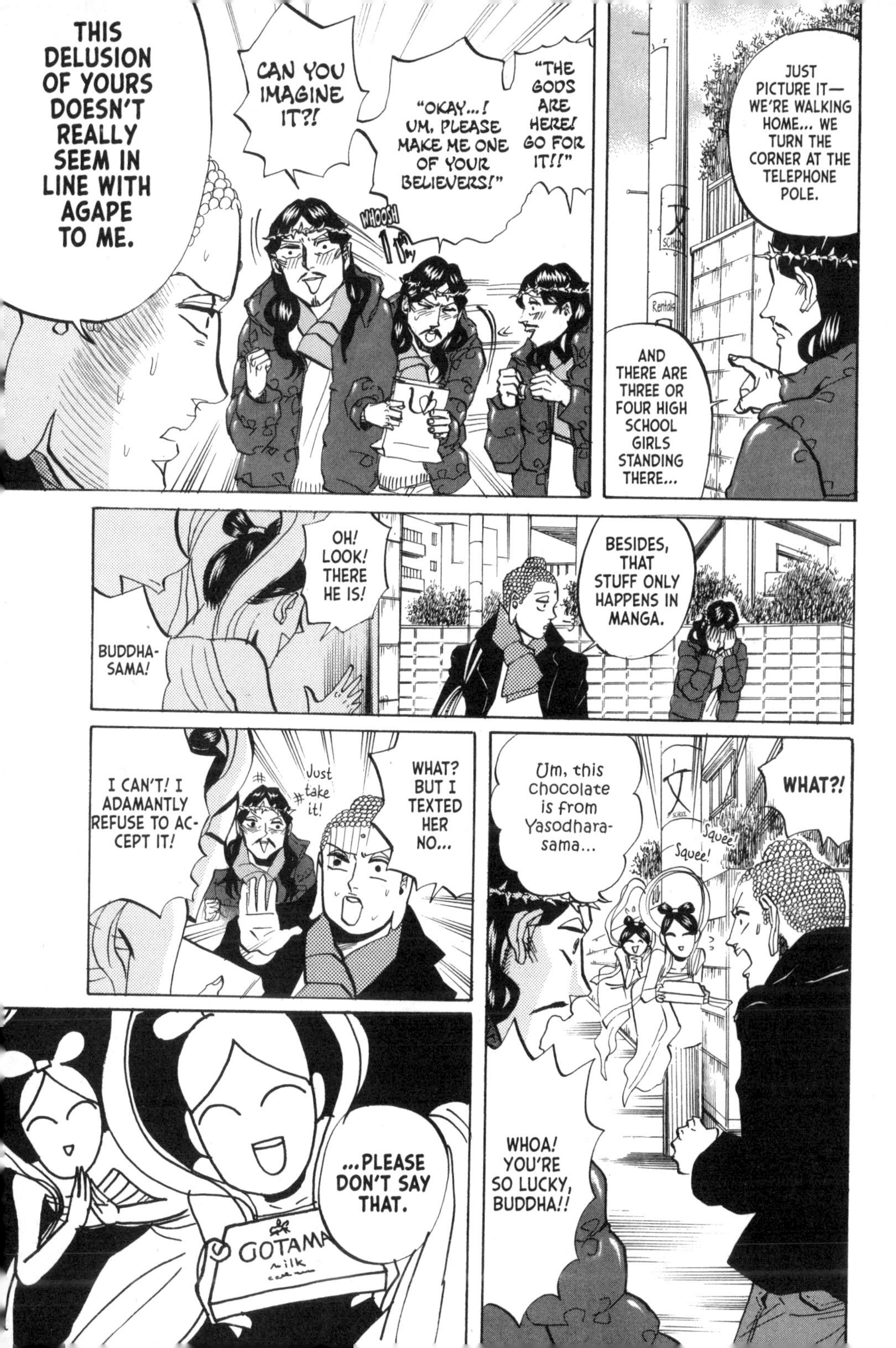
JUST PICTURE IT—WE'RE WALKING HOME... WE TURN THE CORNER AT THE TELEPHONE POLE.
AND THERE ARE THREE OR FOUR HIGH SCHOOL GIRLS STANDING THERE...
SCHOOL
Rentals
"THE GODS ARE HERE! GO FOR IT!!"
"OKAY...! UM, PLEASE MAKE ME ONE OF YOUR BELIEVERS!"
CAN YOU IMAGINE IT?!
WHOOSH
THIS DELUSION OF YOURS DOESN'T REALLY SEEM IN LINE WITH AGAPE TO ME.
BESIDES, THAT STUFF ONLY HAPPENS IN MANGA.
OH! LOOK! THERE HE IS!
BUDDHA-SAMA!
WHAT?!
Um, this chocolate is from Yasodhara-sama...
Squee!
Squee!
SCHOOL
WHOA! YOU'RE SO LUCKY, BUDDHA!!
WHAT? BUT I TEXTED HER NO...
Just take it!
I CAN'T! I ADAMANTLY REFUSE TO ACCEPT IT!
...PLEASE DON'T SAY THAT.
GOTAMA
milk

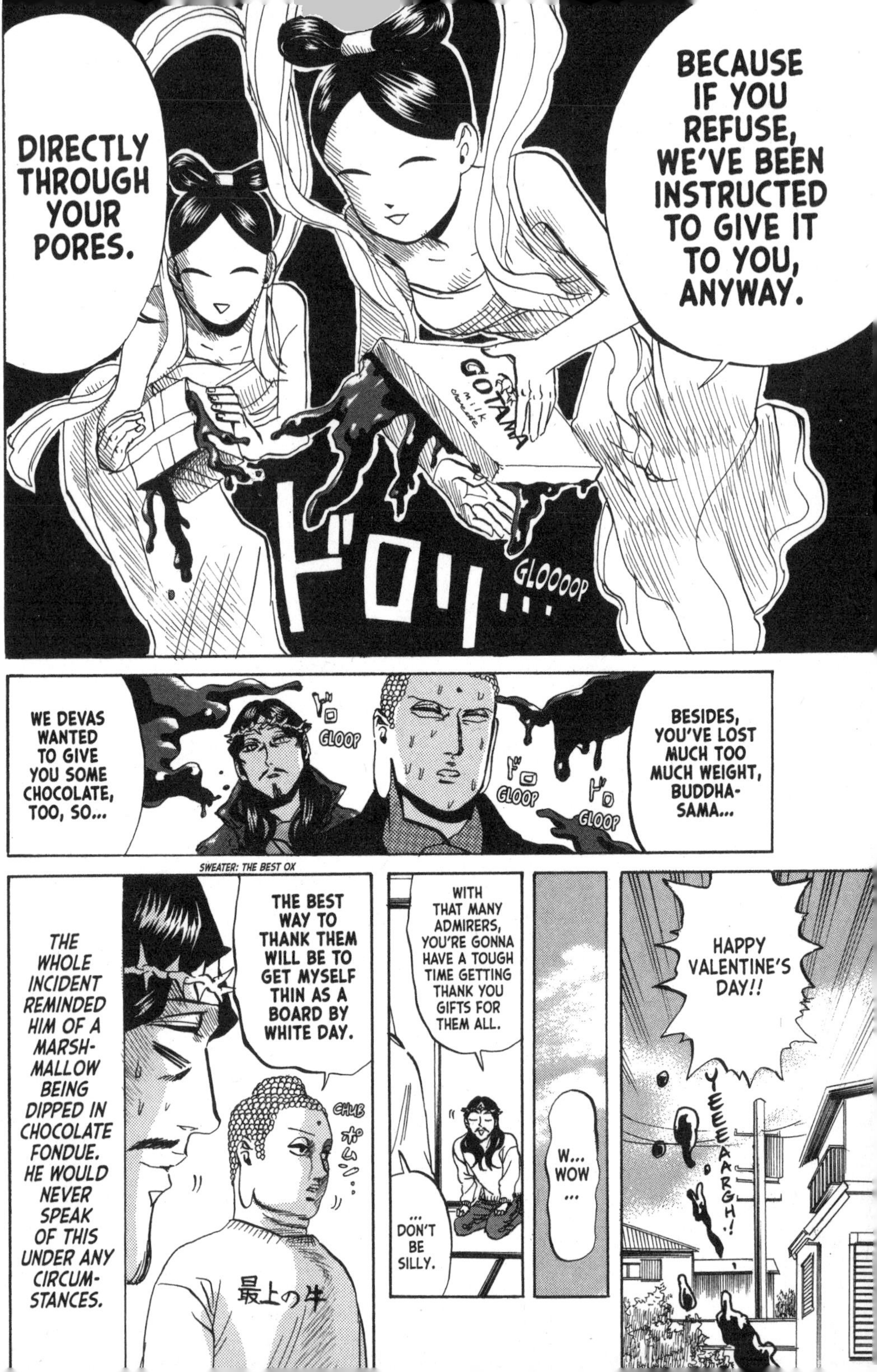
BECAUSE IF YOU REFUSE, WE'VE BEEN INSTRUCTED TO GIVE IT TO YOU, ANYWAY.
DIRECTLY THROUGH YOUR PORES.
GOTANNA milk chocolate
ドロリ…
GLOOOOP
BESIDES, YOU'VE LOST MUCH TOO MUCH WEIGHT, BUDDHA-SAMA...
ドロ
GLOOP
ドロ
GLOOP
ドロ
GLOOP
WE DEVAS WANTED TO GIVE YOU SOME CHOCOLATE, TOO, SO...
SWEATER: THE BEST OX
HAPPY VALENTINE'S DAY!!
YEEEAARGH!
W... WOW ...
WITH THAT MANY ADMIRERS, YOU'RE GONNA HAVE A TOUGH TIME GETTING THANK YOU GIFTS FOR THEM ALL.
... DON'T BE SILLY.
THE BEST WAY TO THANK THEM WILL BE TO GET MYSELF THIN AS A BOARD BY WHITE DAY.
CHUB
ポム
最上の牛
THE WHOLE INCIDENT REMINDED HIM OF A MARSH-MALLOW BEING DIPPED IN CHOCOLATE FONDUE. HE WOULD NEVER SPEAK OF THIS UNDER ANY CIRCUM-STANCES.

WHITE DAY

Diet Notebook
How to Become Like Tezuka's Buddha
Goal
無
Dear Devas
COOKIES: "MU"
離 苦 別
愛
Dear Yasodhara
Here is some tiramisu.
Siddhartha

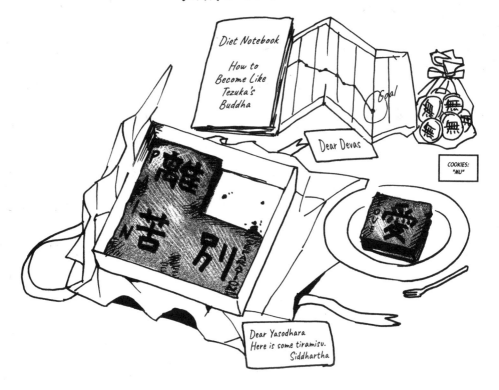

CHAPTER 23 TRANSLATION NOTES

Compulsory Courtesy Chocolate, page 155

The Japanese Valentine's Day tradition is that women give chocolate to the objects of their affection, often as a way to confess their love, or reaffirm their love to their significant other. However, it has also become customary to distribute chocolate among male friends, colleagues, etc. to show appreciation for them. This courtesy chocolate is known as "*giri choco*," and is often translated literally as "obligation chocolate." The title of this chapter takes it even farther, and makes it *girigiri choco*. *Girigiri* is a term used to indicate "just barely"—like how Jesus "just barely" didn't float up into the sky on the previous page. When used to describe chocolate, it can indicate a double obligation, indicating that the giver of the chocolate is truly giving it purely out of a sense of social obligation and otherwise would have totally avoided the tradition. This sort of chocolate usually involves the least amount of thought or effort.

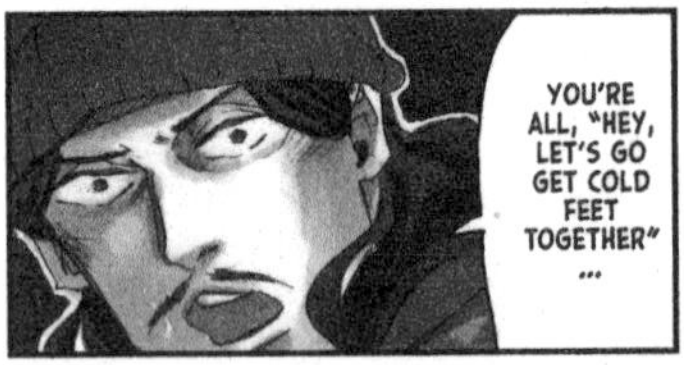
YOU'RE ALL, "HEY, LET'S GO GET COLD FEET TOGETHER"...

Let's go get cold feet, page 156

In Japanese, the word for skating is *suberi,* which means more literally "to glide" or "slide," as across the ice in ice skating. In that same vein, it can mean to "slip," as in "to slip up," as in "to fail utterly," especially with jokes, etc.

Saint Valentine, page 161

Valentine's Day, or Saint Valentine's Day, originated as a festival to commemorate the martyrdom of Saint Valentine (Latin name Valentinus), who is in fact the patron saint of lovers. Legend has it he was imprisoned for secretly performing marriages in order to spare the husbands from being forced to go to war.

Ananda and the ladies, page 162

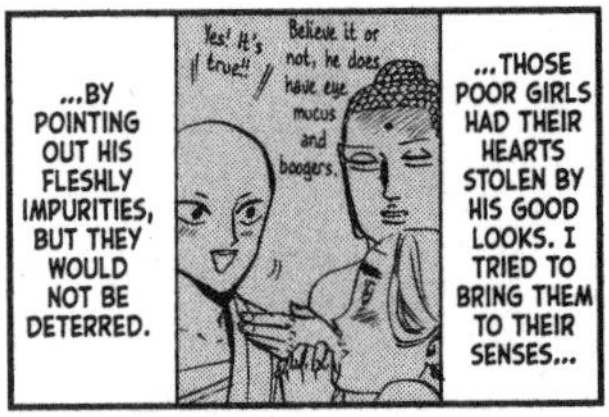
...THOSE POOR GIRLS HAD THEIR HEARTS STOLEN BY HIS GOOD LOOKS. I TRIED TO BRING THEM TO THEIR SENSES...
Believe it or not, he does have eye mucus and boogers.
Yes! It's true!!
...BY POINTING OUT HIS FLESHLY IMPURITIES, BUT THEY WOULD NOT BE DETERRED.

Ananda is famous in Buddhism for being supportive of women. He is the one who convinced the Buddha to allow women to join the Buddhist monastic order, and was so popular that there were even nuns who had to leave the order because they could not overcome their affection for him. Another woman, Matanga, fell in love with Ananda and flirted with him whenever he came to town to beg. The Buddha said she must become a nun for a year before she would be allowed to marry Ananda, and during that year, she learned that her feelings for him were hindering her path to enlightenment, and decided to dedicate her entire life to the Buddha's teachings.

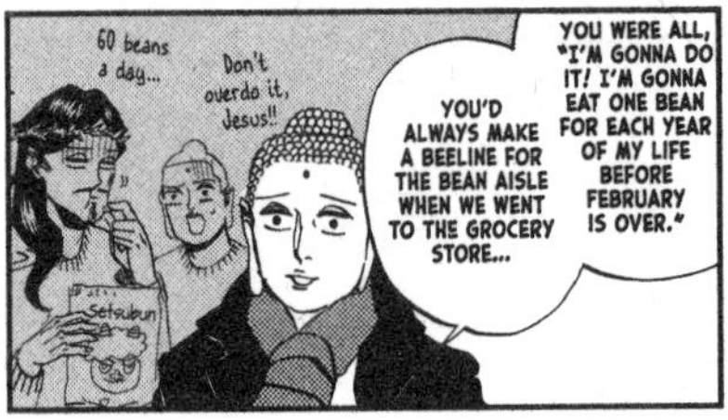
YOU WERE ALL, "I'M GONNA DO IT! I'M GONNA EAT ONE BEAN FOR EACH YEAR OF MY LIFE BEFORE FEBRUARY IS OVER."
YOU'D ALWAYS MAKE A BEELINE FOR THE BEAN AISLE WHEN WE WENT TO THE GROCERY STORE...
Don't overdo it, Jesus!!
60 beans a day...
Setsubun

Setsubun, page 164

On February 3, Setsubun is celebrated in Japan to welcome the coming of spring. It used to be a sort of New Year's celebration, and so was accompanied with traditions to get rid of evil for the coming year. One of these traditions is *mamemaki*, or "bean scattering," a practice that involves chanting, "Demons out! Luck in!" while throwing beans either out the door or at a family member wearing a demon mask. It is also customary to eat roasted soy beans—one for each year of your life.

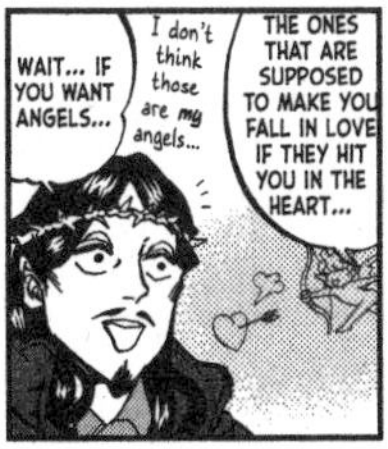
THE ONES THAT ARE SUPPOSED TO MAKE YOU FALL IN LOVE IF THEY HIT YOU IN THE HEART...
I don't think those are my angels...
WAIT... IF YOU WANT ANGELS...

Angels with arrows, page 164

Known most commonly as Cupid in Western entertainment, this angel actually originated from Greek mythology as part of the retinue of Aphrodite, goddess of love. Cupid is the Roman name for Eros, son of Aphrodite and Ares, god of war. He carried magical arrows that could fill their target with desire.

Training in the wilderness, page 165

After his baptism, Jesus went to the wilderness to fast and commune with God. At the end of this period, Satan came tempting him, first trying to get him to change stones into bread. Next, he tempted Jesus to prove that he was the Son of God by jumping from the top of the temple, to see if he was really protected by angels. Finally, Satan offered to give Jesus all the kingdoms and wealth of the world if he would worship Satan. Jesus's response was, "Get thee hence, Satan: for it is written, Thou shalt worship the Lord thy God, and Him only shalt thou serve."

Tirol, page 167

Tirol chocolates are small chocolates that cost 20 or 30 yen, and come in a variety of flavors and packaging, thus making them quite collectible, but are seen to be a cheaper gift.

White Day, page 170

White Day falls one month after Valentine's, on March 14. On White Day, men are expected to give out the gifts, often returning the favor from Valentine's Day. Traditionally the gift involved marshmallows, hence the name White Day, but nowadays anything will do.

The Best Ox, page 170

The Buddha was born into a family whose surname was Gautama, which is Sanskrit for "the best ox."

Mu, page 171

The writing on these cookies is pronounced *mu* in Japanese, and is a reference to a famous parable or *koan* from a Chinese Buddhist collection called *The Gateless Gate*. In this parable, a Zen (or Ch'an in Chinese) master is asked by a disciple if a dog has Buddha-nature, the inherent capacity thought by much of Buddhism there at the time to reside in all living beings, allowing them to become Buddhas. Contrary to the obvious, doctrinally correct answer of "yes," the master answers "no," which has been interpreted many ways—including as a deliberate contradiction of Buddhist teachings in protest of dogmatic thinking, or as a refusal of the premise of the question itself.

Tiramisu, page 171

The writing on this tiramisu, in its undivided form, says *aibetsu riku*, or "separation from loved ones is suffering."

SAINT☆YOUNG MEN

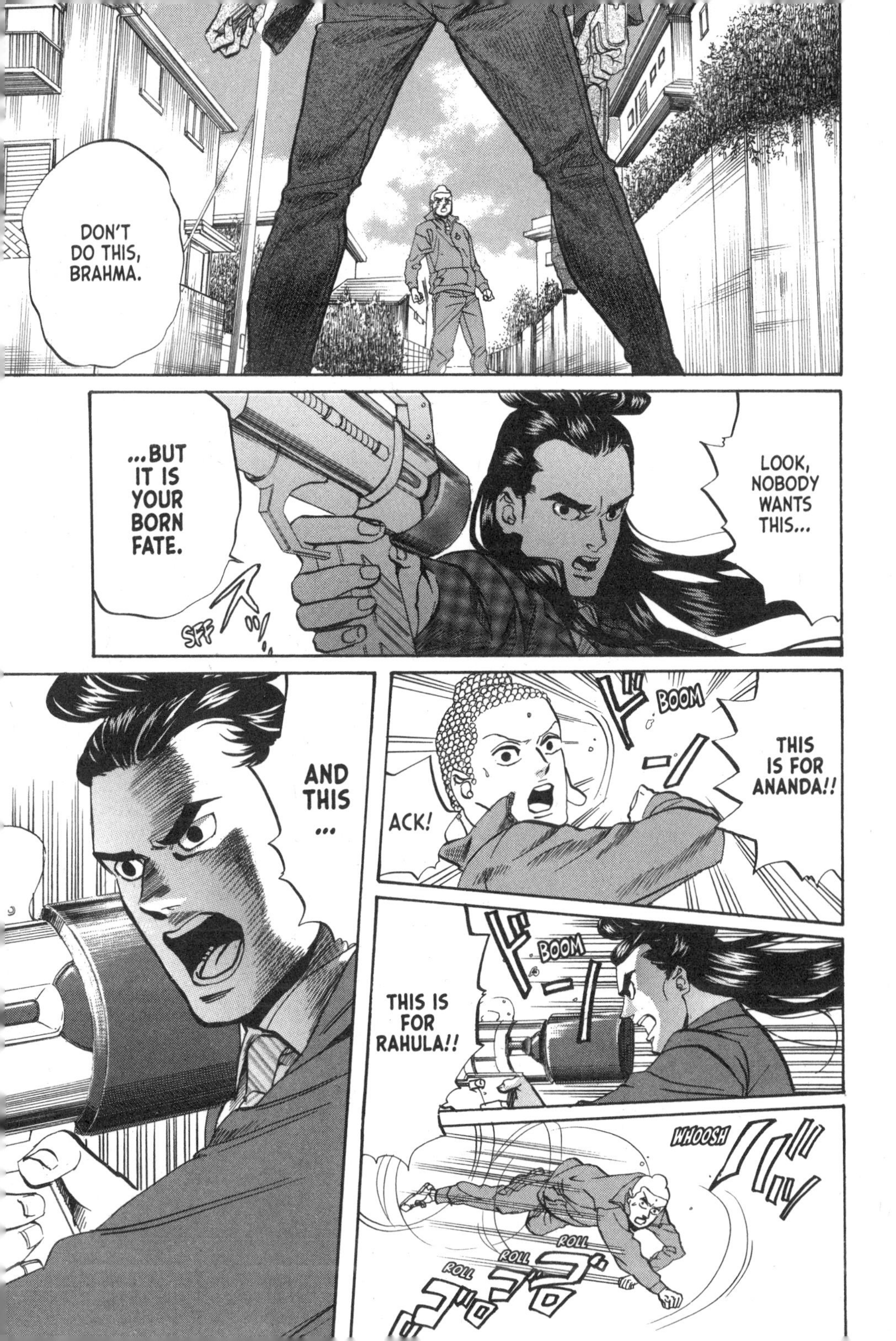
DON'T DO THIS, BRAHMA.
LOOK, NOBODY WANTS THIS...
...BUT IT IS YOUR BORN FATE.
SFF
BOOM
THIS IS FOR ANANDA!!
ACK!
BOOM
THIS IS FOR RAHULA!!
WHOOSH
ROLL
ROLL
ROLL
AND THIS ...

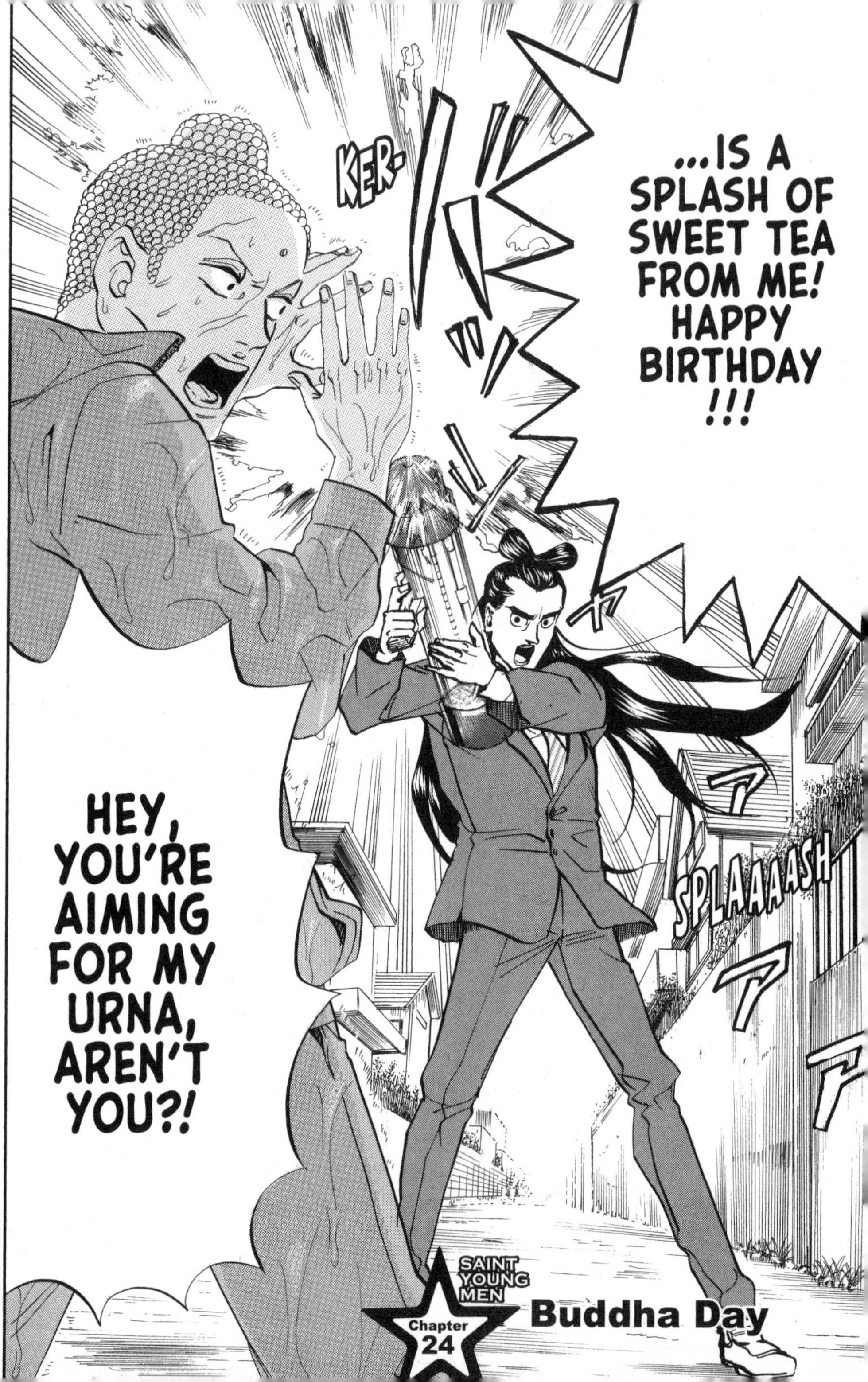
...IS A SPLASH OF SWEET TEA FROM ME! HAPPY BIRTHDAY !!!
KER-
SPLAAAASH
HEY, YOU'RE AIMING FOR MY URNA, AREN'T YOU?!
SAINT YOUNG MEN
Chapter 24
Buddha Day

BUDDHA: WAS APPROACHED FOR AN ON-THE-STREET INTERVIEW AND TOOK IT SERIOUSLY, BUT WAS STUNNED BY THE BEHAVIOR OF HIS ASSOCIATE.

BRAHMA: GUARDIAN DEITY OF BUDDHIST LAW. CONVINCED BUDDHA TO SHARE HIS TEACHINGS WITH THE WORLD AFTER BUDDHA GAINED ENLIGHTENMENT. SPOKE PASSIONATELY ABOUT KAMABOKO FISH CAKE IN AN ON-THE-STREET INTERVIEW.

JESUS: HAPPENED TO CATCH BUDDHA AND BRAHMA'S ON-THE-STREET INTERVIEW WHEN IT WAS ON TV.

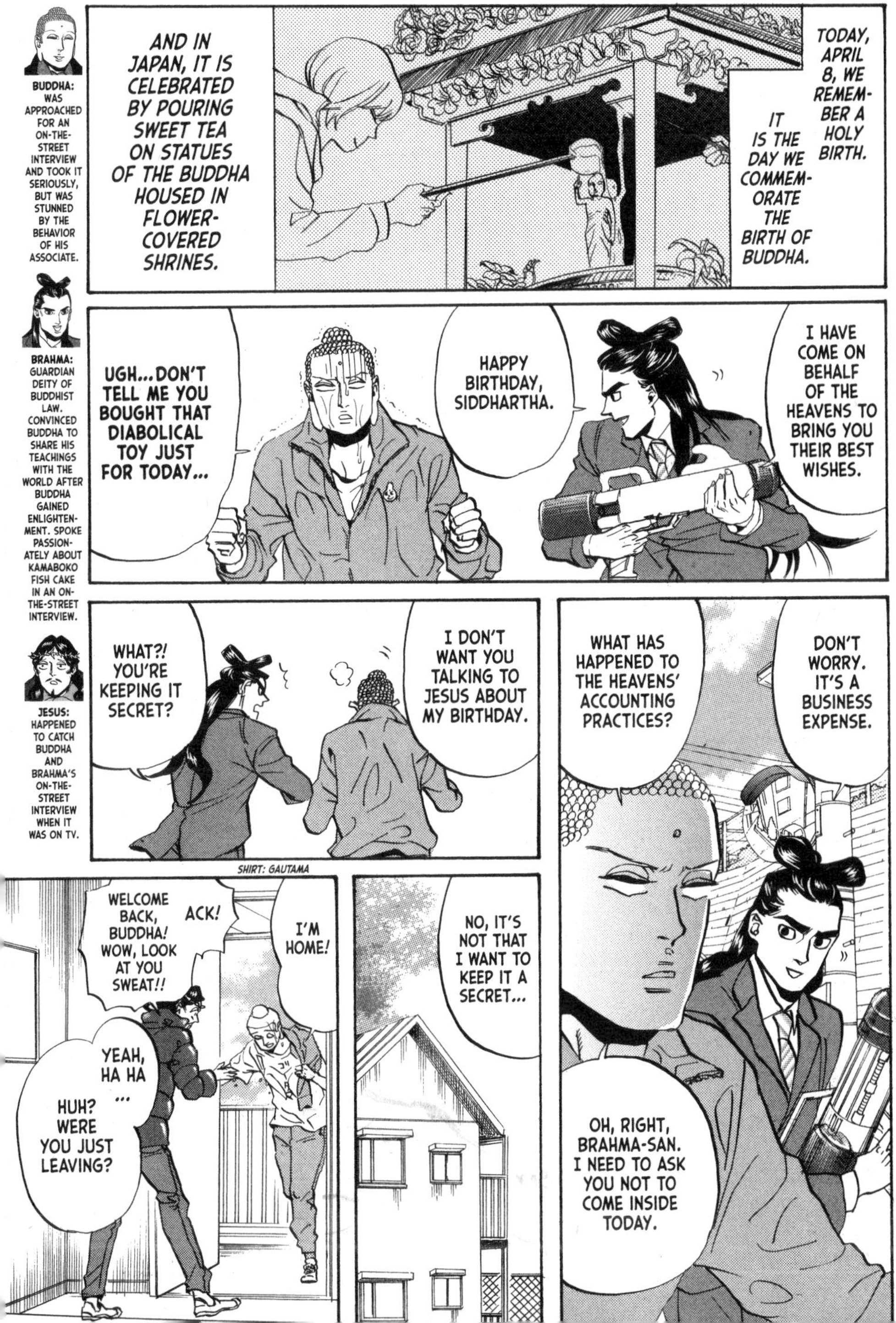
TODAY, APRIL 8, WE REMEMBER A HOLY BIRTH.
IT IS THE DAY WE COMMEMORATE THE BIRTH OF BUDDHA.
AND IN JAPAN, IT IS CELEBRATED BY POURING SWEET TEA ON STATUES OF THE BUDDHA HOUSED IN FLOWER-COVERED SHRINES.
I HAVE COME ON BEHALF OF THE HEAVENS TO BRING YOU THEIR BEST WISHES.
HAPPY BIRTHDAY, SIDDHARTHA.
UGH...DON'T TELL ME YOU BOUGHT THAT DIABOLICAL TOY JUST FOR TODAY...
DON'T WORRY. IT'S A BUSINESS EXPENSE.
WHAT HAS HAPPENED TO THE HEAVENS' ACCOUNTING PRACTICES?
OH, RIGHT, BRAHMA-SAN. I NEED TO ASK YOU NOT TO COME INSIDE TODAY.
I DON'T WANT YOU TALKING TO JESUS ABOUT MY BIRTHDAY.
WHAT?! YOU'RE KEEPING IT SECRET?
SHIRT: GAUTAMA
NO, IT'S NOT THAT I WANT TO KEEP IT A SECRET...
I'M HOME!
WELCOME BACK, BUDDHA! WOW, LOOK AT YOU SWEAT!!
ACK!
YEAH, HA HA ...
HUH? WERE YOU JUST LEAVING?

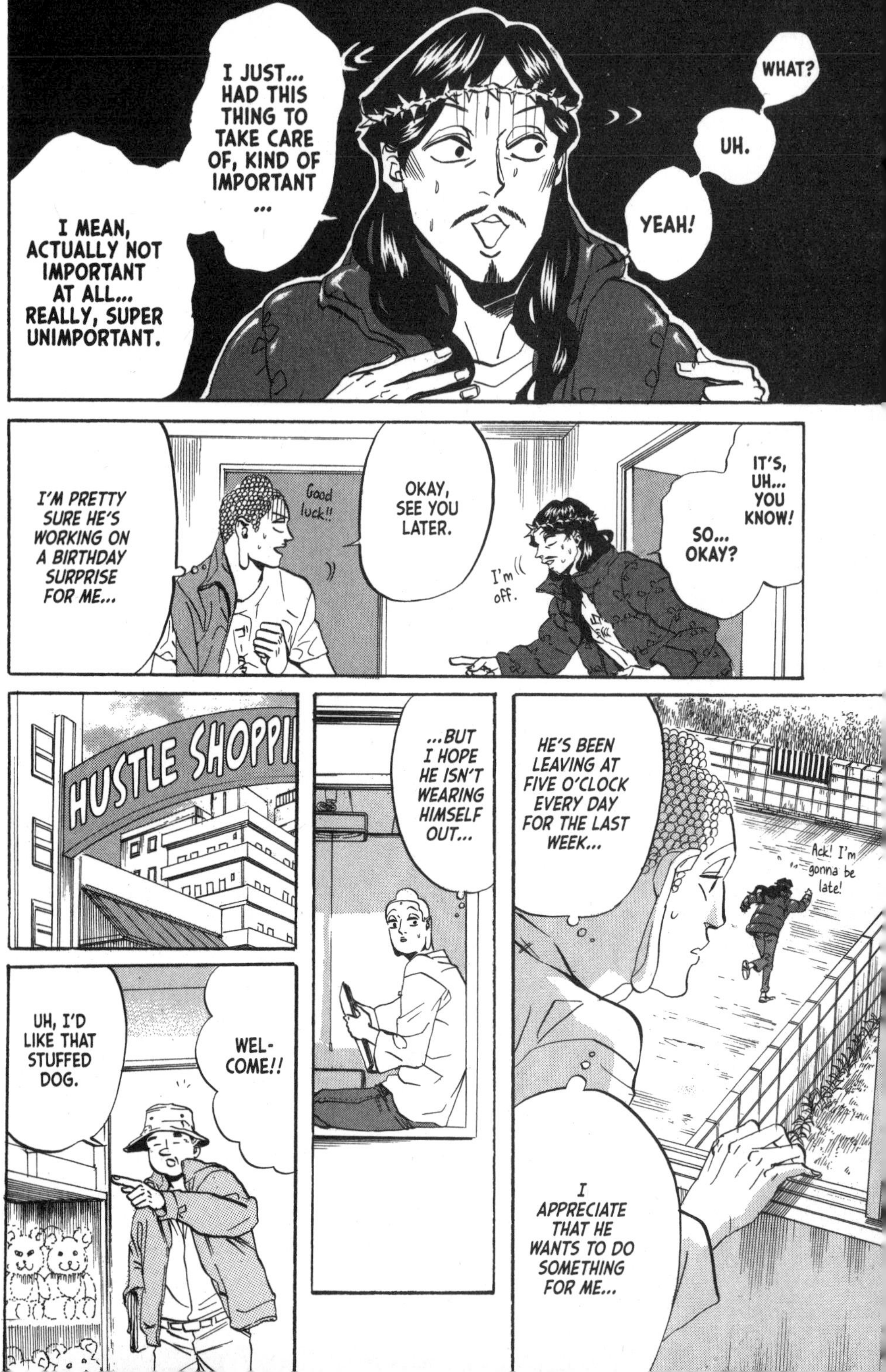
YEAH!
UH.
WHAT?
I JUST... HAD THIS THING TO TAKE CARE OF, KIND OF IMPORTANT ...
I MEAN, ACTUALLY NOT IMPORTANT AT ALL... REALLY, SUPER UNIMPORTANT.
IT'S, UH... YOU KNOW!
SO... OKAY?
I'm off.
OKAY, SEE YOU LATER.
Good luck!!
I'M PRETTY SURE HE'S WORKING ON A BIRTHDAY SURPRISE FOR ME...
HE'S BEEN LEAVING AT FIVE O'CLOCK EVERY DAY FOR THE LAST WEEK...
Ack! I'm gonna be late!
I APPRECIATE THAT HE WANTS TO DO SOMETHING FOR ME...
...BUT I HOPE HE ISN'T WEARING HIMSELF OUT...
HUSTLE SHOPPI
WEL-COME!!
UH, I'D LIKE THAT STUFFED DOG.

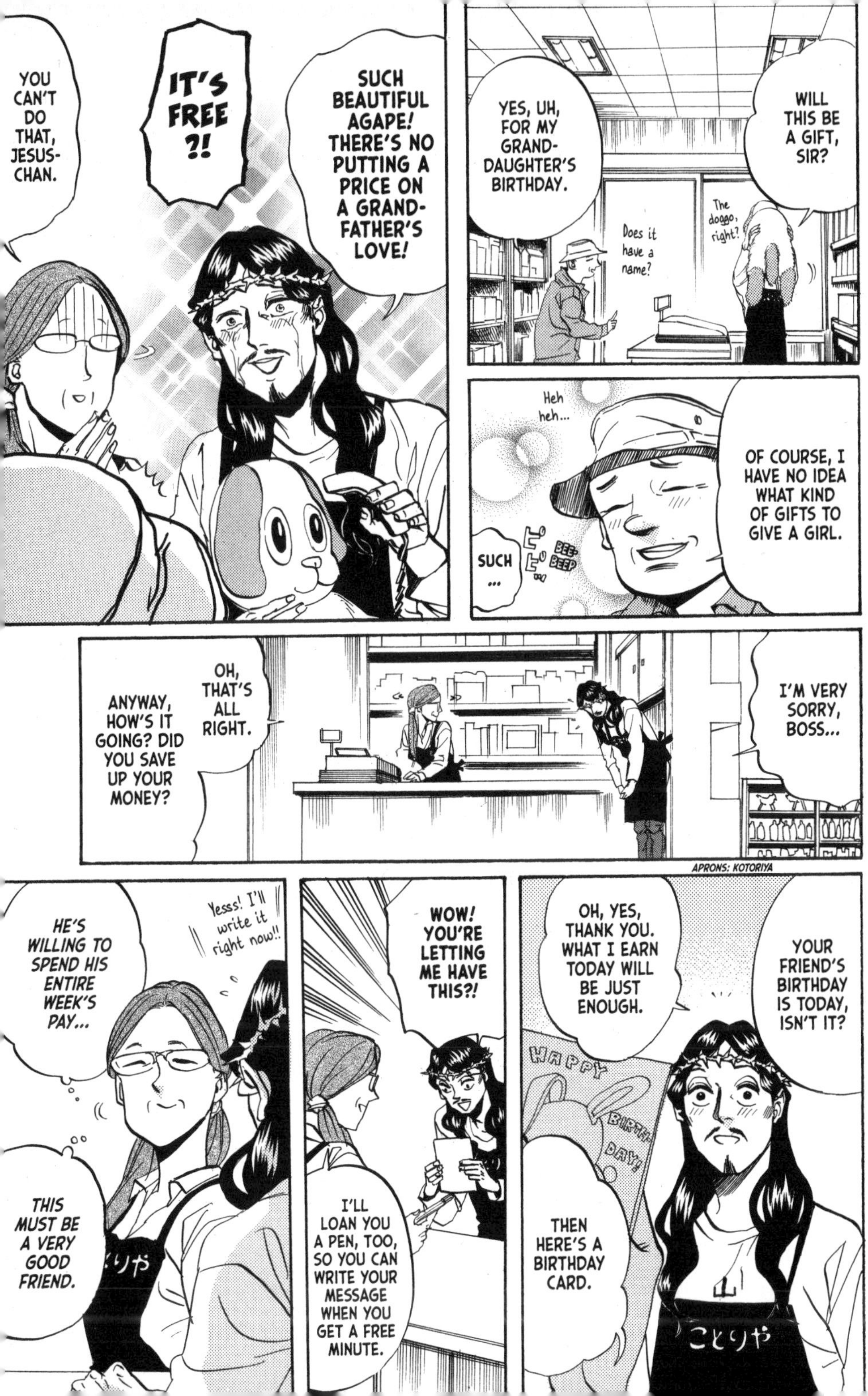
WILL THIS BE A GIFT, SIR?
The doggo, right?
Does it have a name?
YES, UH, FOR MY GRAND-DAUGHTER'S BIRTHDAY.
OF COURSE, I HAVE NO IDEA WHAT KIND OF GIFTS TO GIVE A GIRL.
Heh heh...
BEE-BEEP
SUCH...
SUCH BEAUTIFUL AGAPE! THERE'S NO PUTTING A PRICE ON A GRAND-FATHER'S LOVE!
IT'S FREE?!
YOU CAN'T DO THAT, JESUS-CHAN.
I'M VERY SORRY, BOSS...
OH, THAT'S ALL RIGHT.
ANYWAY, HOW'S IT GOING? DID YOU SAVE UP YOUR MONEY?
APRONS: KOTORIYA
YOUR FRIEND'S BIRTHDAY IS TODAY, ISN'T IT?
OH, YES, THANK YOU. WHAT I EARN TODAY WILL BE JUST ENOUGH.
HAPPY BIRTHDAY!
THEN HERE'S A BIRTHDAY CARD.
ことりや
WOW! YOU'RE LETTING ME HAVE THIS?!
I'LL LOAN YOU A PEN, TOO, SO YOU CAN WRITE YOUR MESSAGE WHEN YOU GET A FREE MINUTE.
Yesss! I'll write it right now!!
HE'S WILLING TO SPEND HIS ENTIRE WEEK'S PAY...
THIS MUST BE A VERY GOOD FRIEND.

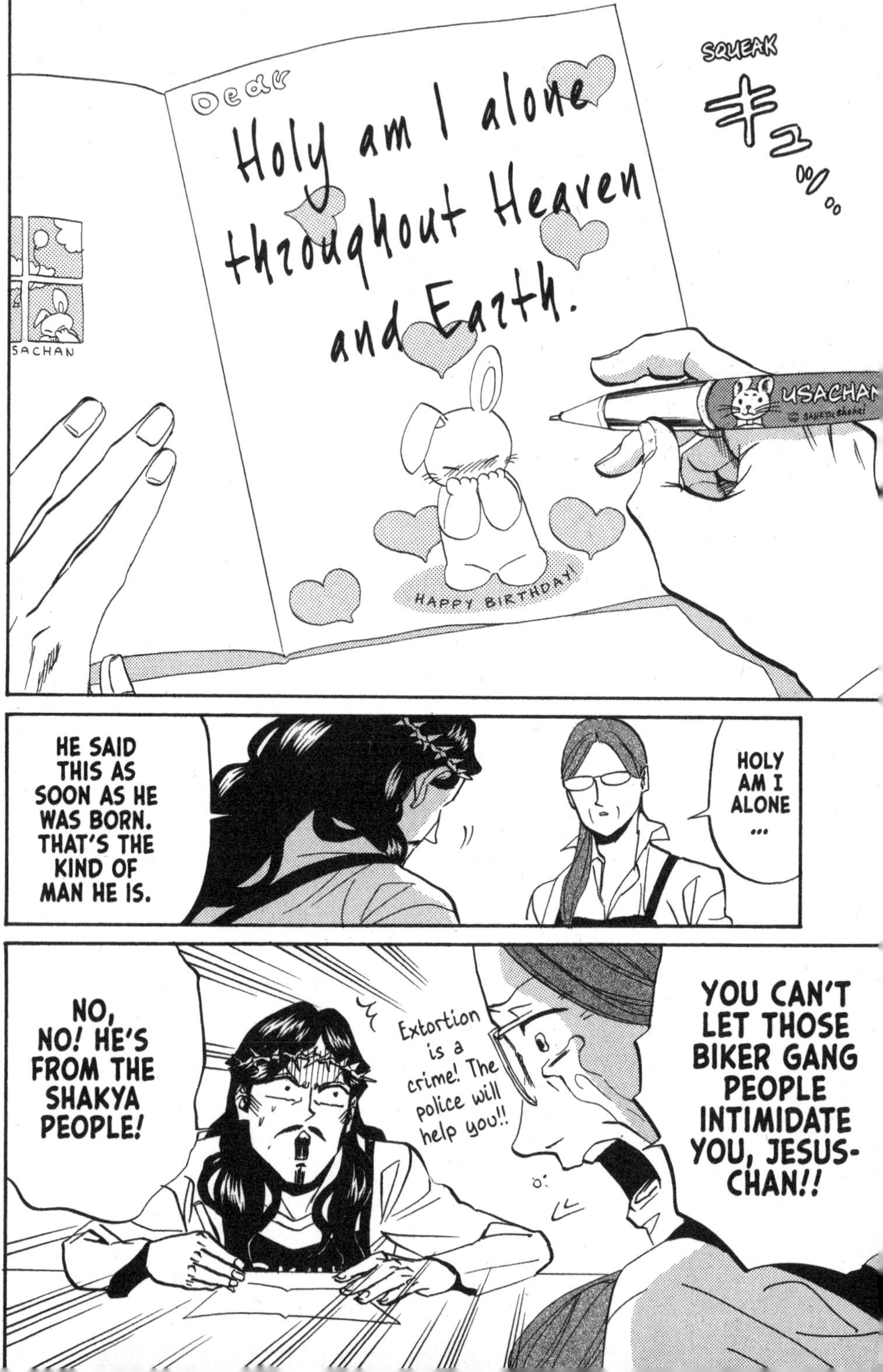
SQUEAK
キュ
Dear
Holy am I alone throughout Heaven and Earth.
HAPPY BIRTHDAY!
USACHAN
SACHAN
HOLY AM I ALONE ...
HE SAID THIS AS SOON AS HE WAS BORN. THAT'S THE KIND OF MAN HE IS.
YOU CAN'T LET THOSE BIKER GANG PEOPLE INTIMIDATE YOU, JESUS-CHAN!!
Extortion is a crime! The police will help you!!
NO, NO! HE'S FROM THE SHAKYA PEOPLE!

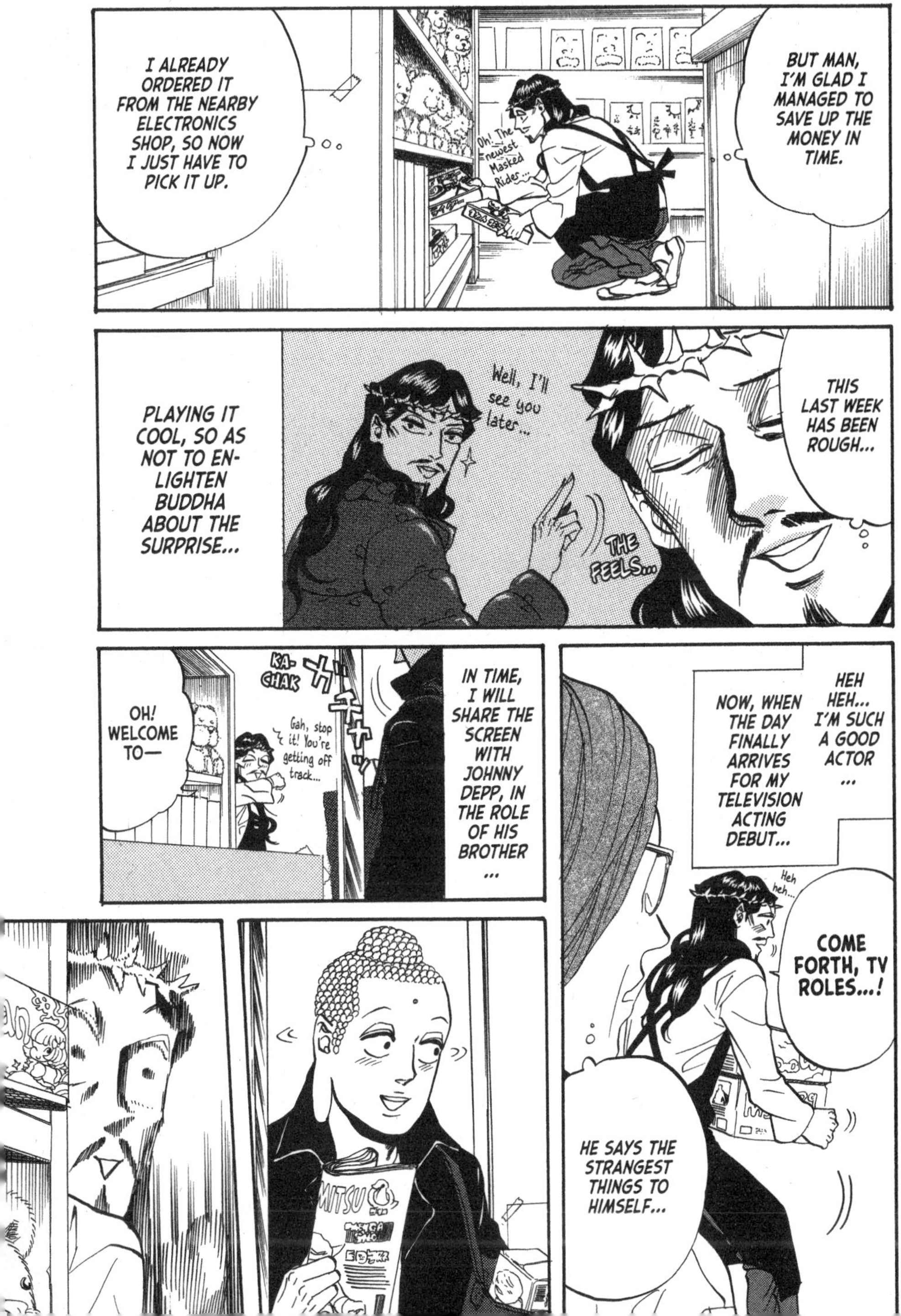
BUT MAN, I'M GLAD I MANAGED TO SAVE UP THE MONEY IN TIME.
Oh! The newest Masked Rider...
I ALREADY ORDERED IT FROM THE NEARBY ELECTRONICS SHOP, SO NOW I JUST HAVE TO PICK IT UP.
THIS LAST WEEK HAS BEEN ROUGH...
THE FEELS...
Well, I'll see you later...
PLAYING IT COOL, SO AS NOT TO EN-LIGHTEN BUDDHA ABOUT THE SURPRISE...
HEH HEH... I'M SUCH A GOOD ACTOR...
NOW, WHEN THE DAY FINALLY ARRIVES FOR MY TELEVISION ACTING DEBUT...
Heh heh...
COME FORTH, TV ROLES...!
HE SAYS THE STRANGEST THINGS TO HIMSELF...
IN TIME, I WILL SHARE THE SCREEN WITH JOHNNY DEPP, IN THE ROLE OF HIS BROTHER...
KA-CHAK
Gah, stop it! You're getting off track...
OH! WELCOME TO—

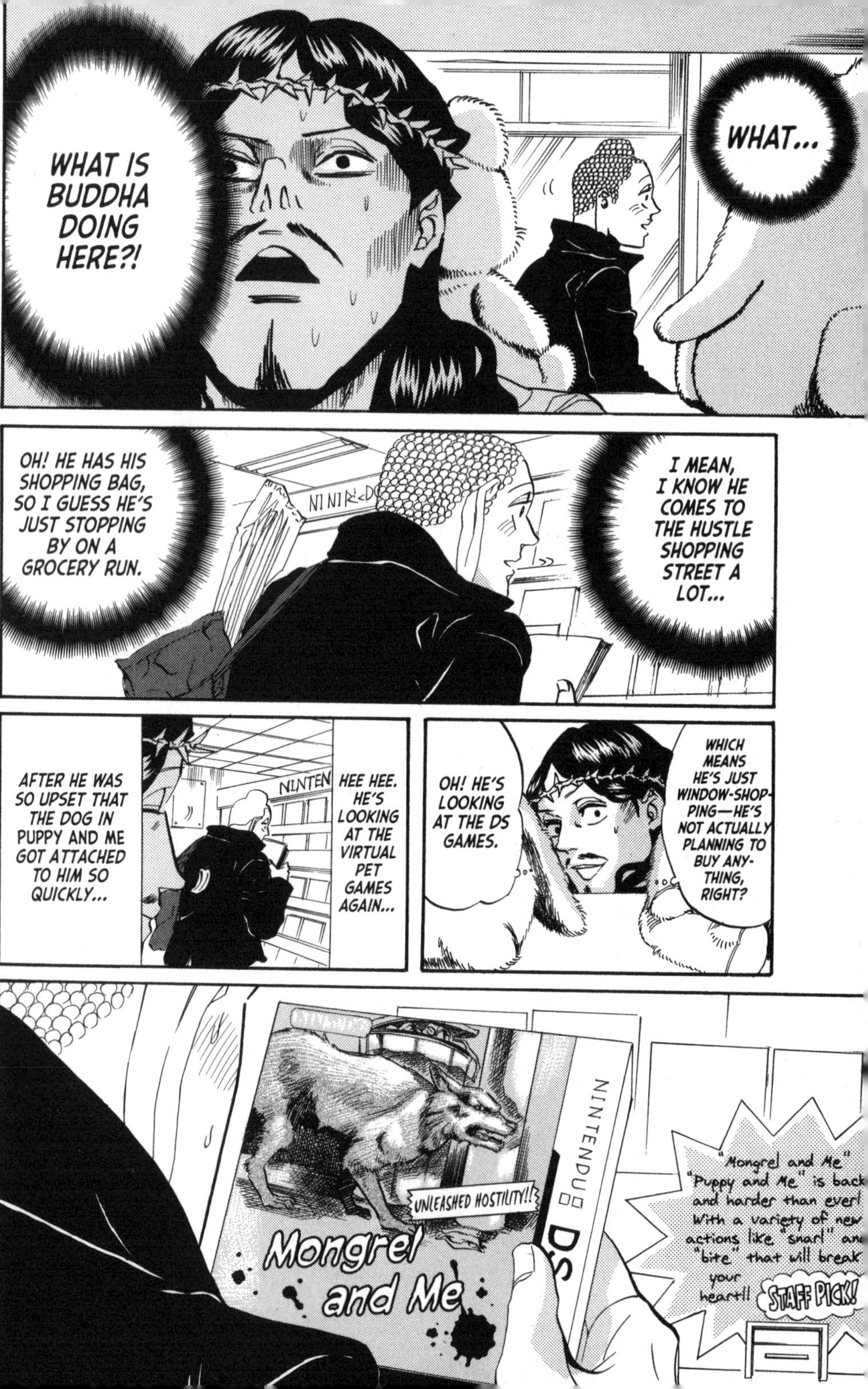
WHAT...
WHAT IS BUDDHA DOING HERE?!
I MEAN, I KNOW HE COMES TO THE HUSTLE SHOPPING STREET A LOT...
OH! HE HAS HIS SHOPPING BAG, SO I GUESS HE'S JUST STOPPING BY ON A GROCERY RUN.
WHICH MEANS HE'S JUST WINDOW-SHOPPING—HE'S NOT ACTUALLY PLANNING TO BUY ANYTHING, RIGHT?
OH! HE'S LOOKING AT THE DS GAMES.
NINTEN
HEE HEE. HE'S LOOKING AT THE VIRTUAL PET GAMES AGAIN...
AFTER HE WAS SO UPSET THAT THE DOG IN PUPPY AND ME GOT ATTACHED TO HIM SO QUICKLY...
"Mongrel and Me" "Puppy and Me" is back and harder than ever! With a variety of new actions like "snarl" an "bite" that will break your heart!!
STAFF PICK!
NINTENDU DS
UNLEASHED HOSTILITY!!
Mongrel and Me

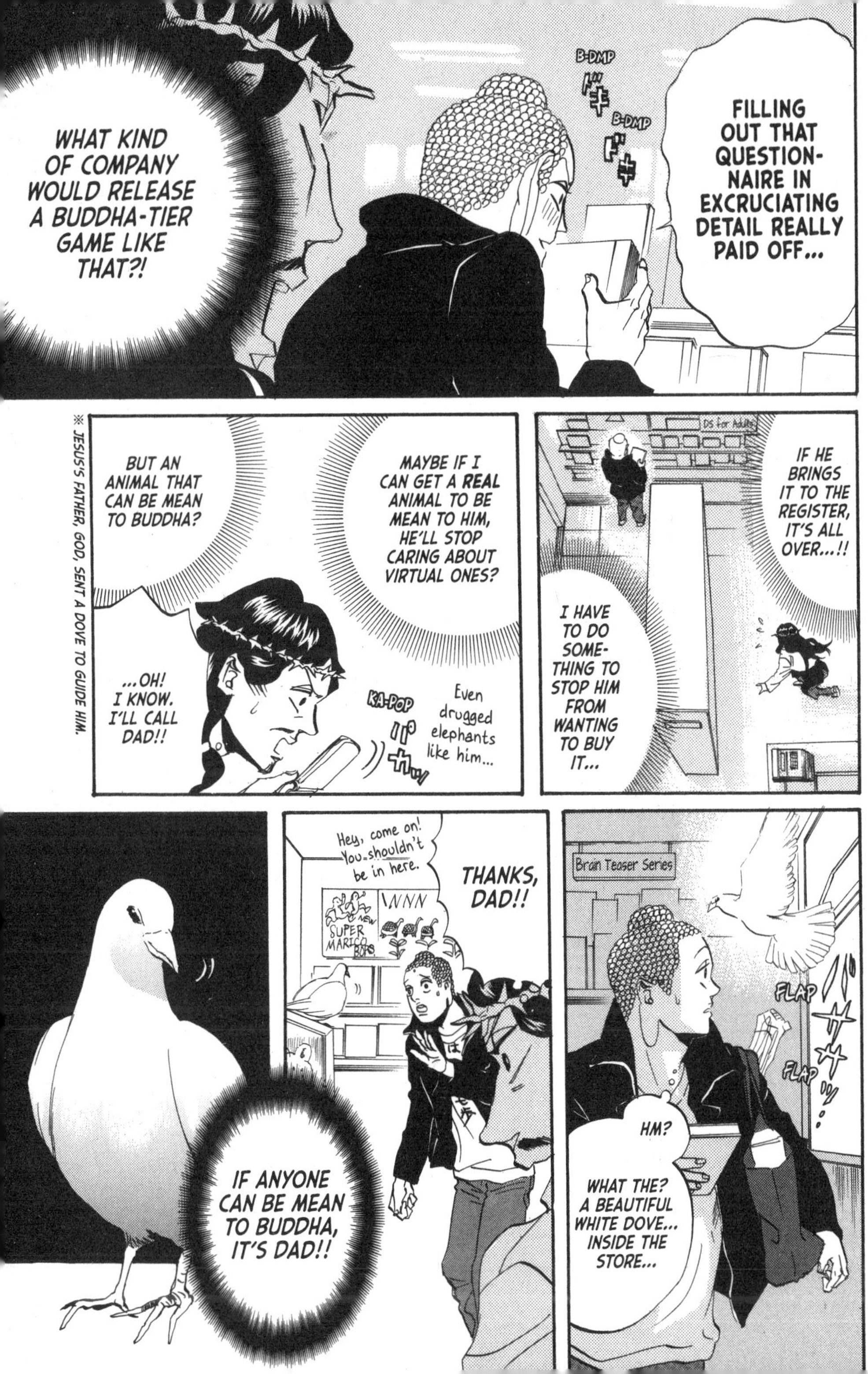

FILLING OUT THAT QUESTION-NAIRE IN EXCRUCIATING DETAIL REALLY PAID OFF...
B-DMP
B-DMP
WHAT KIND OF COMPANY WOULD RELEASE A BUDDHA-TIER GAME LIKE THAT?!
DS for Adults
IF HE BRINGS IT TO THE REGISTER, IT'S ALL OVER...!!
I HAVE TO DO SOME-THING TO STOP HIM FROM WANTING TO BUY IT...
MAYBE IF I CAN GET A REAL ANIMAL TO BE MEAN TO HIM, HE'LL STOP CARING ABOUT VIRTUAL ONES?
BUT AN ANIMAL THAT CAN BE MEAN TO BUDDHA?
Even drugged elephants like him...
KA-POP
...OH! I KNOW. I'LL CALL DAD!!
※ JESUS'S FATHER, GOD, SENT A DOVE TO GUIDE HIM.
Brain Teaser Series
FLAP
FLAP
HM?
WHAT THE? A BEAUTIFUL WHITE DOVE... INSIDE THE STORE...
THANKS, DAD!!
Hey, come on! You shouldn't be in here.
NEW
SUPER MARICO BROS
IF ANYONE CAN BE MEAN TO BUDDHA, IT'S DAD!!

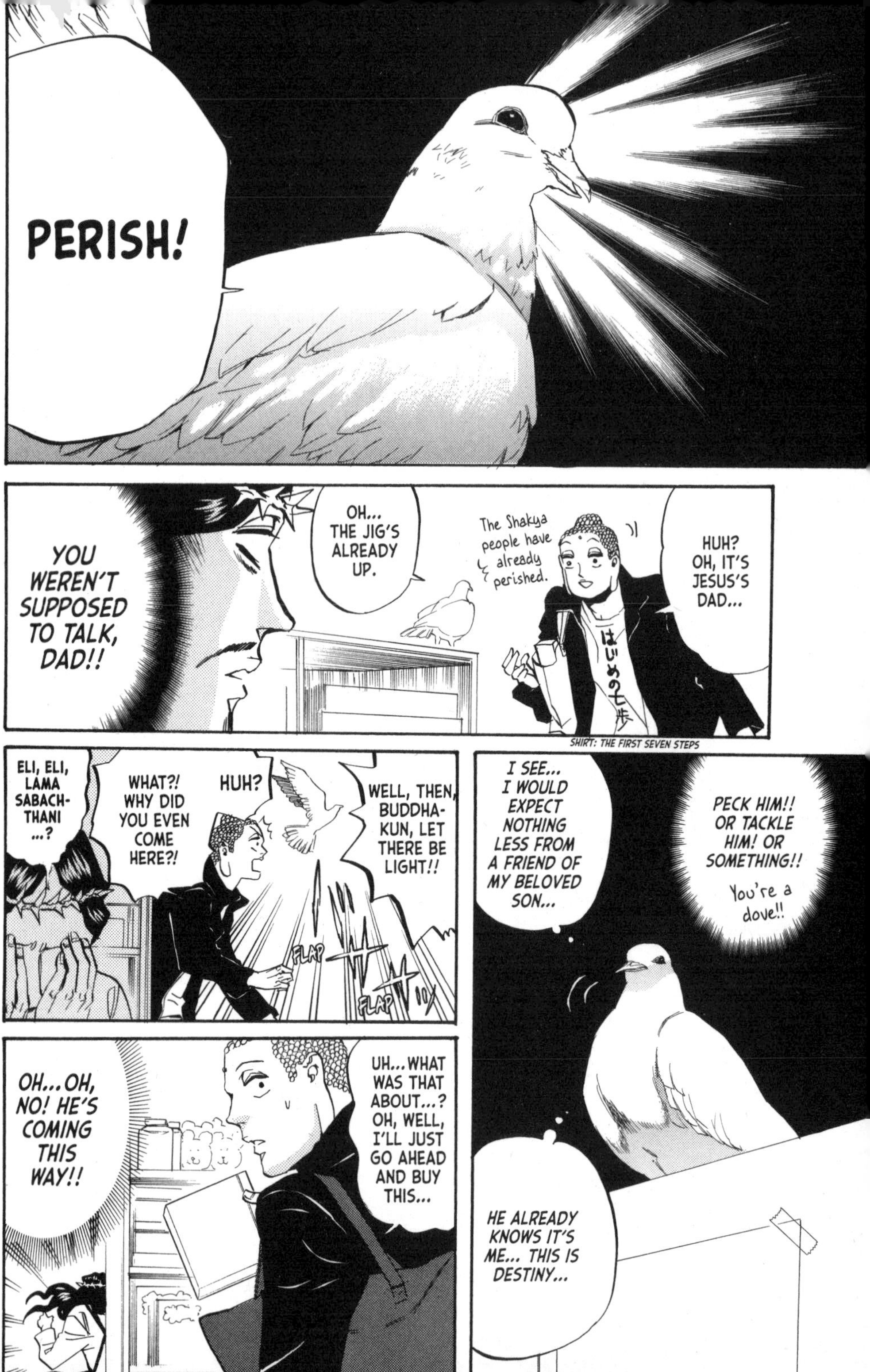
PERISH!
HUH? OH, IT'S JESUS'S DAD...
The Shakya people have already perished.
OH... THE JIG'S ALREADY UP.
YOU WEREN'T SUPPOSED TO TALK, DAD!!
SHIRT: THE FIRST SEVEN STEPS
PECK HIM!! OR TACKLE HIM! OR SOMETHING!!
You're a dove!!
I SEE... I WOULD EXPECT NOTHING LESS FROM A FRIEND OF MY BELOVED SON...
HE ALREADY KNOWS IT'S ME... THIS IS DESTINY...
WELL, THEN, BUDDHA-KUN, LET THERE BE LIGHT!!
HUH?
WHAT?! WHY DID YOU EVEN COME HERE?!
ELI, ELI, LAMA SABACH-THANI ...?
FLAP
FLAP
UH... WHAT WAS THAT ABOUT...? OH, WELL, I'LL JUST GO AHEAD AND BUY THIS...
OH... OH, NO! HE'S COMING THIS WAY!!

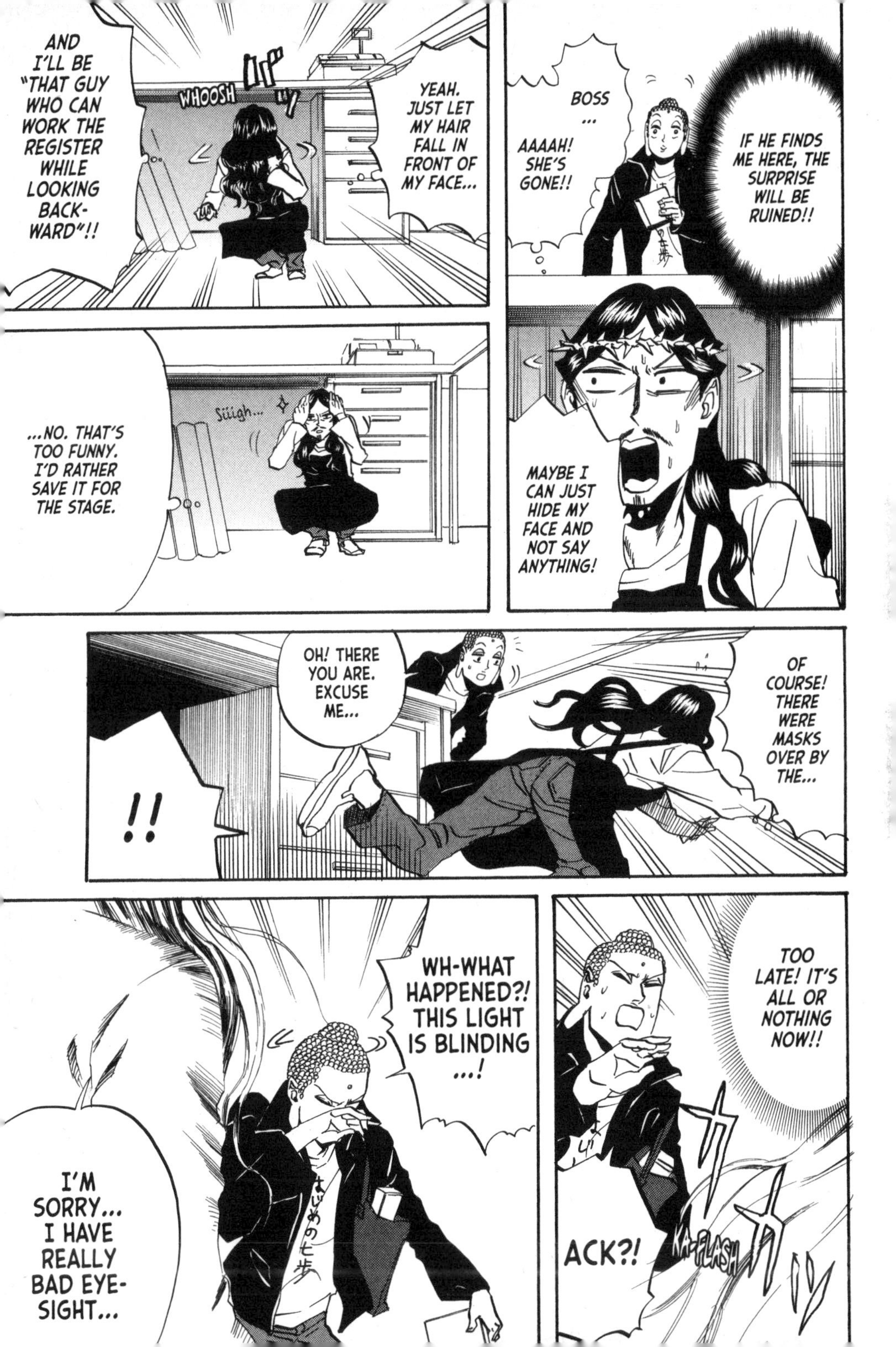
BOSS ...
AAAAH! SHE'S GONE!!
IF HE FINDS ME HERE, THE SURPRISE WILL BE RUINED!!
YEAH. JUST LET MY HAIR FALL IN FRONT OF MY FACE...
WHOOSH
AND I'LL BE "THAT GUY WHO CAN WORK THE REGISTER WHILE LOOKING BACK-WARD"!!
MAYBE I CAN JUST HIDE MY FACE AND NOT SAY ANYTHING!
Siiigh...
...NO. THAT'S TOO FUNNY. I'D RATHER SAVE IT FOR THE STAGE.
OF COURSE! THERE WERE MASKS OVER BY THE...
OH! THERE YOU ARE. EXCUSE ME...
!!
TOO LATE! IT'S ALL OR NOTHING NOW!!
KA-FLASH
ACK?!
WH-WHAT HAPPENED?! THIS LIGHT IS BLINDING ...!
I'M SORRY... I HAVE REALLY BAD EYE-SIGHT...

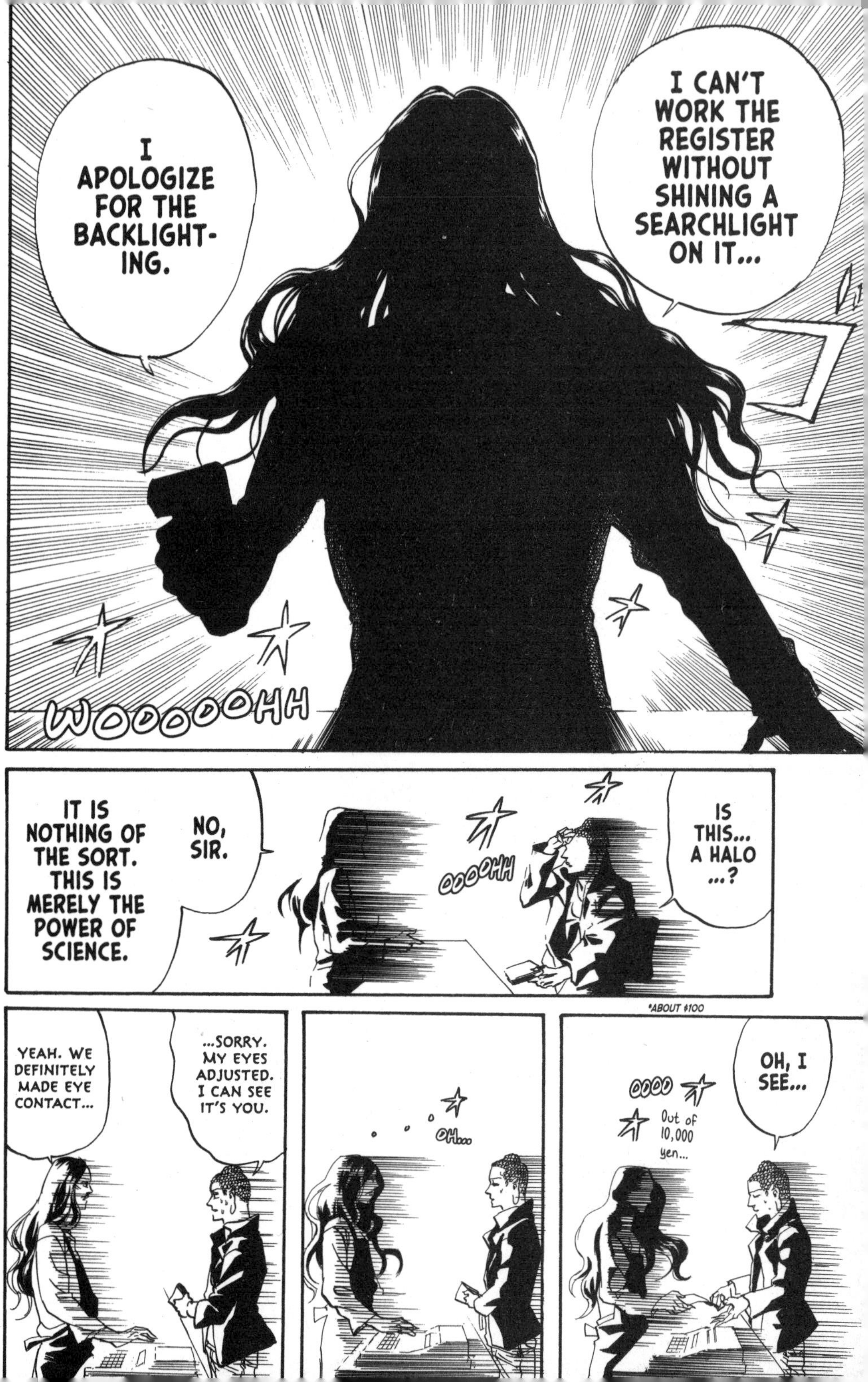
I CAN'T WORK THE REGISTER WITHOUT SHINING A SEARCHLIGHT ON IT...
I APOLOGIZE FOR THE BACKLIGHT-ING.
WOOOOOOHH
IS THIS... A HALO ...?
OOOOHH
NO, SIR.
IT IS NOTHING OF THE SORT. THIS IS MERELY THE POWER OF SCIENCE.
*ABOUT $100
OH, I SEE...
OOOO
Out of 10,000 yen...
OH...
...SORRY. MY EYES ADJUSTED. I CAN SEE IT'S YOU.
YEAH. WE DEFINITELY MADE EYE CONTACT...

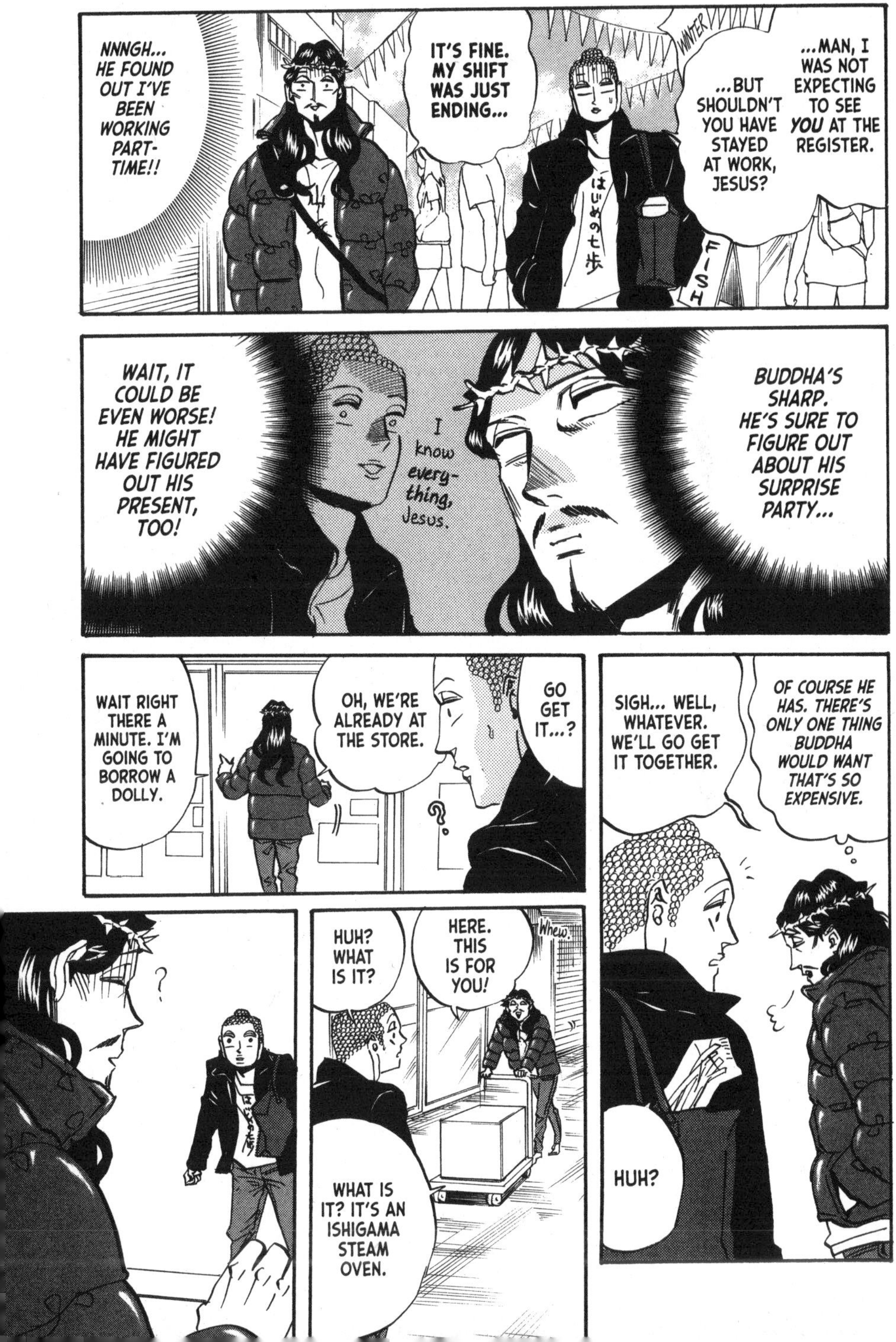
WINTER
...MAN, I WAS NOT EXPECTING TO SEE *YOU* AT THE REGISTER.
...BUT SHOULDN'T YOU HAVE STAYED AT WORK, JESUS?
はじめの七歩
FISH
IT'S FINE. MY SHIFT WAS JUST ENDING...
NNNGH... HE FOUND OUT I'VE BEEN WORKING PART-TIME!!
BUDDHA'S SHARP. HE'S SURE TO FIGURE OUT ABOUT HIS SURPRISE PARTY...
I know everything, Jesus.
WAIT, IT COULD BE EVEN WORSE! HE MIGHT HAVE FIGURED OUT HIS PRESENT, TOO!
OF COURSE HE HAS. THERE'S ONLY ONE THING BUDDHA WOULD WANT THAT'S SO EXPENSIVE.
SIGH... WELL, WHATEVER. WE'LL GO GET IT TOGETHER.
HUH?
GO GET IT...?
OH, WE'RE ALREADY AT THE STORE.
WAIT RIGHT THERE A MINUTE. I'M GOING TO BORROW A DOLLY.
Whew.
HERE. THIS IS FOR YOU!
HUH? WHAT IS IT?
WHAT IS IT? IT'S AN ISHIGAMA STEAM OVEN.
?

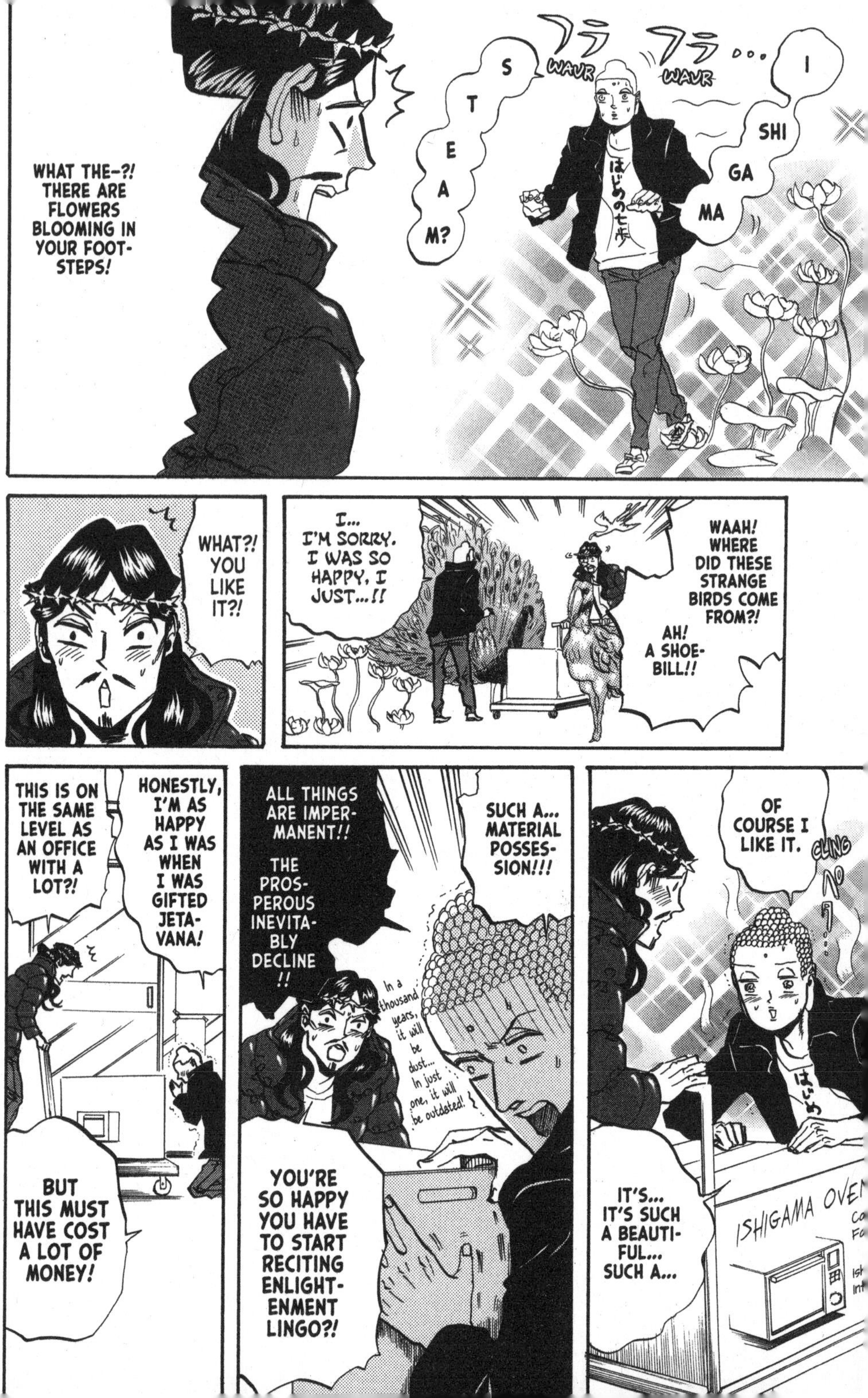
I SHIGAMA
フラ WAUR フラ WAUR...
STEAM?
はじめの七歩
WHAT THE-?! THERE ARE FLOWERS BLOOMING IN YOUR FOOTSTEPS!
WAAH! WHERE DID THESE STRANGE BIRDS COME FROM?!
I... I'M SORRY. I WAS SO HAPPY, I JUST...!!
AH! A SHOEBILL!!
WHAT?! YOU LIKE IT?!
OF COURSE I LIKE IT.
CLING ペタ...
はじめ
IT'S... IT'S SUCH A BEAUTIFUL... SUCH A...
ISHIGAMA OVEN
SUCH A... MATERIAL POSSESSION!!!
ALL THINGS ARE IMPERMANENT!!
THE PROSPEROUS INEVITABLY DECLINE!!
In a thousand years, it will be dust... In just one, it will be outdated!
YOU'RE SO HAPPY YOU HAVE TO START RECITING ENLIGHTENMENT LINGO?!
HONESTLY, I'M AS HAPPY AS I WAS WHEN I WAS GIFTED JETAVANA!
THIS IS ON THE SAME LEVEL AS AN OFFICE WITH A LOT?!
BUT THIS MUST HAVE COST A LOT OF MONEY!

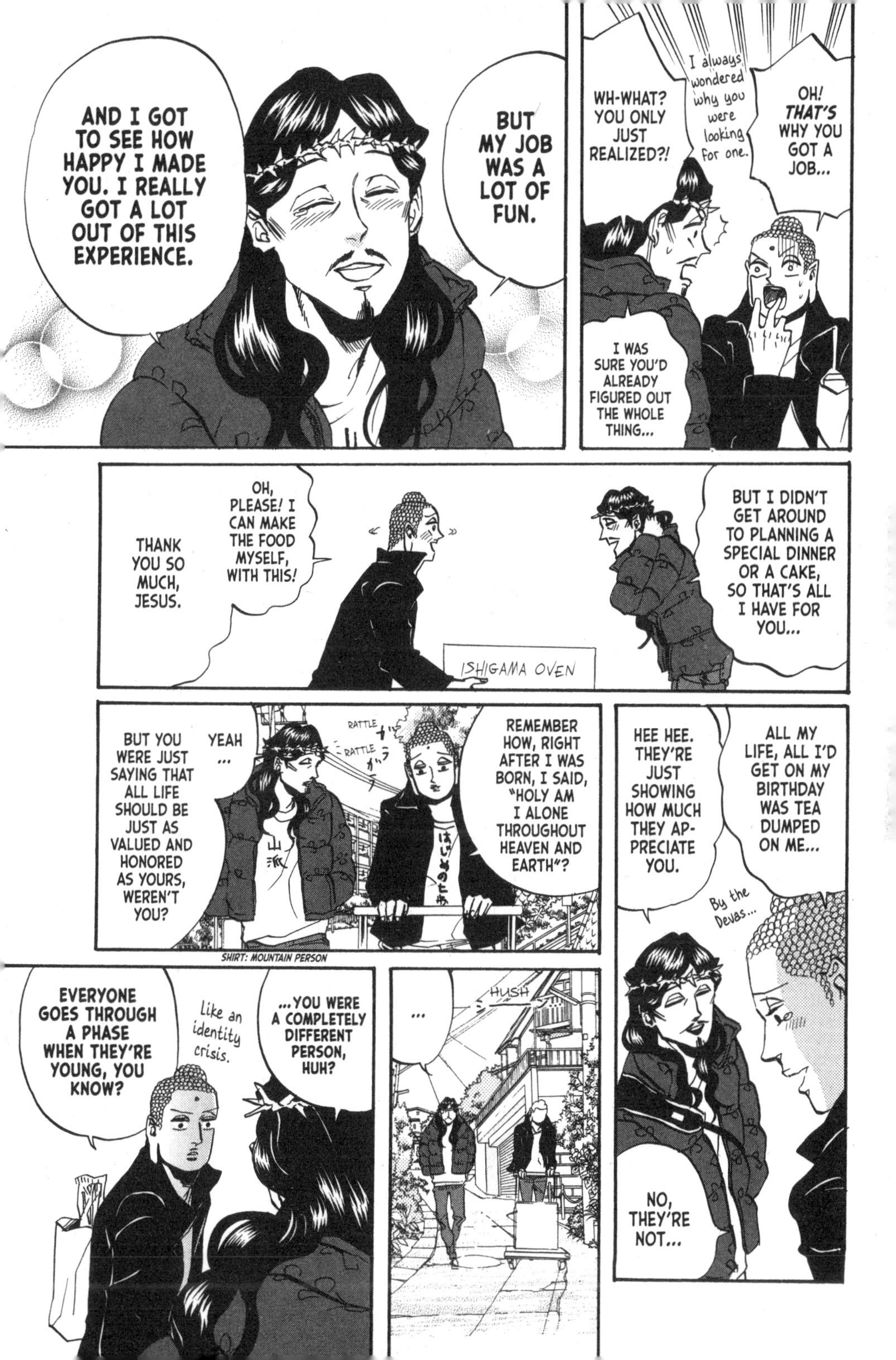
OH! THAT'S WHY YOU GOT A JOB...
I always wondered why you were looking for one.
WH-WHAT? YOU ONLY JUST REALIZED?!
I WAS SURE YOU'D ALREADY FIGURED OUT THE WHOLE THING...
BUT MY JOB WAS A LOT OF FUN.
AND I GOT TO SEE HOW HAPPY I MADE YOU. I REALLY GOT A LOT OUT OF THIS EXPERIENCE.
BUT I DIDN'T GET AROUND TO PLANNING A SPECIAL DINNER OR A CAKE, SO THAT'S ALL I HAVE FOR YOU...
OH, PLEASE! I CAN MAKE THE FOOD MYSELF, WITH THIS!
THANK YOU SO MUCH, JESUS.
ISHIGAMA OVEN
ALL MY LIFE, ALL I'D GET ON MY BIRTHDAY WAS TEA DUMPED ON ME...
HEE HEE. THEY'RE JUST SHOWING HOW MUCH THEY AP-PRECIATE YOU.
By the Devas...
NO, THEY'RE NOT...
REMEMBER HOW, RIGHT AFTER I WAS BORN, I SAID, "HOLY AM I ALONE THROUGHOUT HEAVEN AND EARTH"?
RATTLE
RATTLE
YEAH ...
BUT YOU WERE JUST SAYING THAT ALL LIFE SHOULD BE JUST AS VALUED AND HONORED AS YOURS, WEREN'T YOU?
SHIRT: MOUNTAIN PERSON
...
HUSH
...YOU WERE A COMPLETELY DIFFERENT PERSON, HUH?
Like an identity crisis.
EVERYONE GOES THROUGH A PHASE WHEN THEY'RE YOUNG, YOU KNOW?

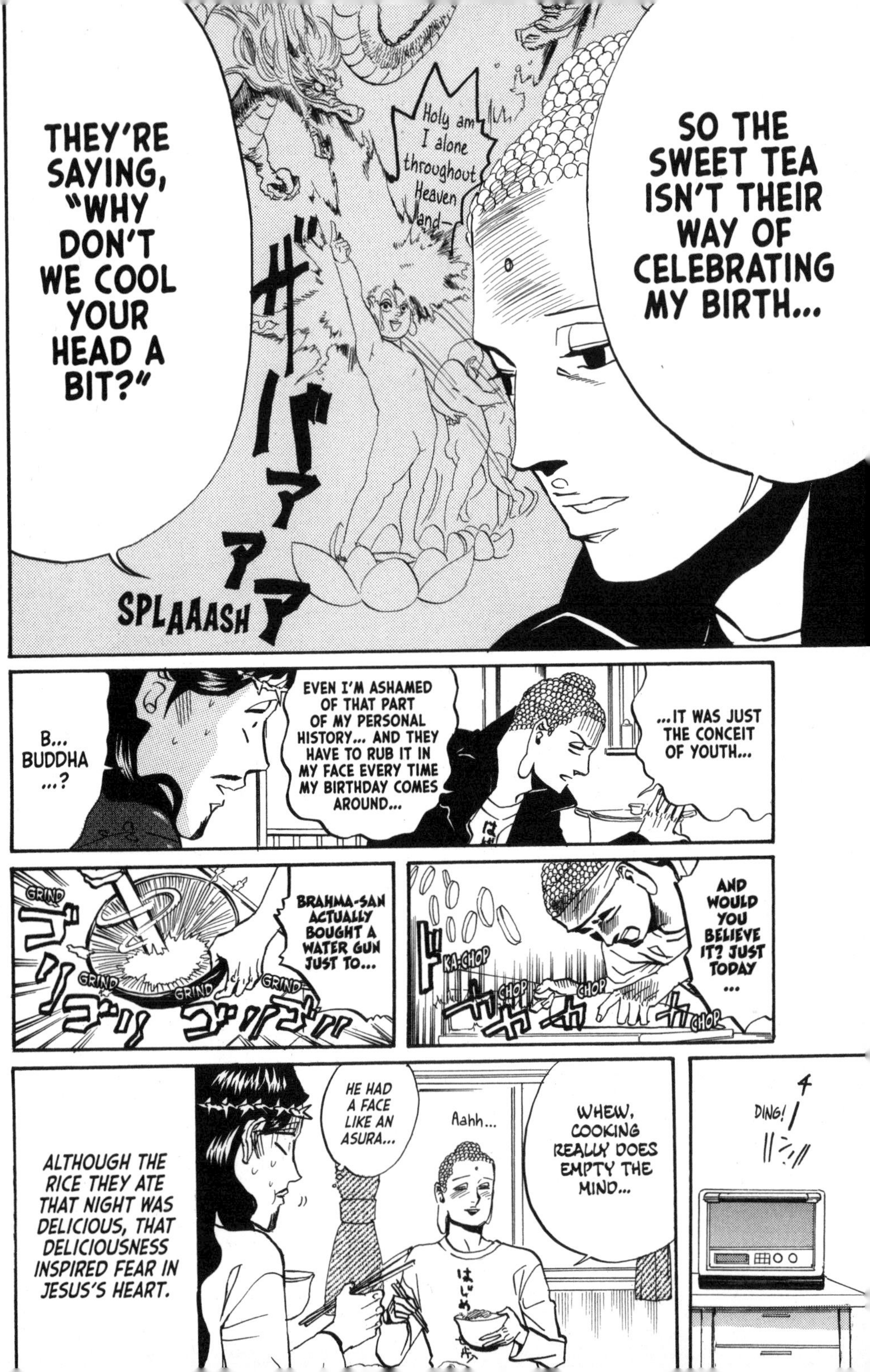
SO THE SWEET TEA ISN'T THEIR WAY OF CELEBRATING MY BIRTH...
Holy am I alone throughout Heaven and–
THEY'RE SAYING, "WHY DON'T WE COOL YOUR HEAD A BIT?"
SPLAAASH
...IT WAS JUST THE CONCEIT OF YOUTH...
EVEN I'M ASHAMED OF THAT PART OF MY PERSONAL HISTORY... AND THEY HAVE TO RUB IT IN MY FACE EVERY TIME MY BIRTHDAY COMES AROUND...
B... BUDDHA ...?
AND WOULD YOU BELIEVE IT? JUST TODAY ...
KA-CHOP
CHOP
CHOP
CHOP
BRAHMA-SAN ACTUALLY BOUGHT A WATER GUN JUST TO...
GRIND
GRIND
GRIND
GRIND
DING!
WHEW, COOKING REALLY DOES EMPTY THE MIND...
Aahh...
HE HAD A FACE LIKE AN ASURA...
ALTHOUGH THE RICE THEY ATE THAT NIGHT WAS DELICIOUS, THAT DELICIOUSNESS INSPIRED FEAR IN JESUS'S HEART.

Nintendu DS Game Software Survey

Q1. Please tell us the game you purchased.

[*Puppy and Me: Shiba Inu*]

Q2. On average, how many games do you play in a year?

❶ (1-2) ❷ 3-4 ❸ 5-6 ❹ 7 or more

Q3. Please tell us what gaming platform you use the most.

[*Nintendu DS*]

Q4. Please give this game a score from 0 to 100, 100 being best.

| | 7 | 0 | points

Q5. Please tell use what you liked about this game.

[*-The graphics were beautiful.*
-I liked that the dog would bark.
-The natural way the puppy moved.]

Q6. Please tell us what you did not like about this game.

[*-The dog got attached to me too quickly.*
-There's no sense of wildness from the dog.
-I wish it wouldn't show me its belly so readily.
-It hesitates before it bites me.]

Q7. Please tell us if you have any other thoughts, opinions, requests, or suggestions in regard to this game.

[*I think that beauty can be found in the eyes of an animal that is not pandering to humans. I would like to see actions from the dog that show me it feels hostility or caution around me (growling, biting like it wants to, breaking its chains and running off, etc.). Why not use a wild dog for a motif? Anyway, I know this game is made for casual gamers, but having the dog come when you call, practically from the start of the game—that's just way too easy. Personally, I think it would feel more real if, at the beginning of the game, you can call it again and again and it won't even look at you, and if you get close to it, it growls and runs away. We're dealing with wild animals here.*]

Thank you for your cooperation.

I know I wrote a lot, but I'm just considering the potential of the software. I have high hopes for a sequel.

CHAPTER 24 TRANSLATION NOTES

Buddha Day, page 177

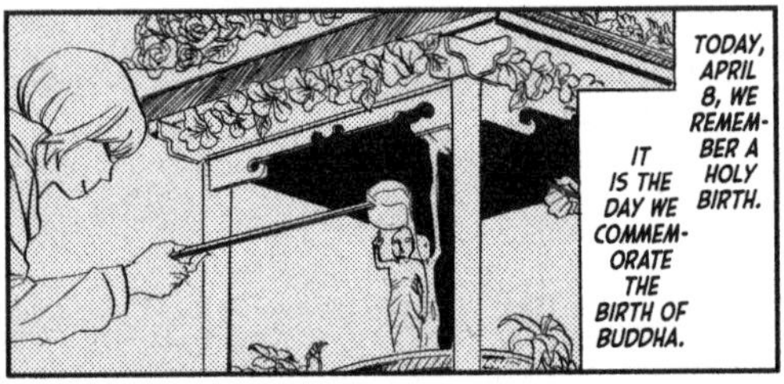
TODAY, APRIL 8, WE REMEMBER A HOLY BIRTH.
IT IS THE DAY WE COMMEMORATE THE BIRTH OF BUDDHA.

Legend has it the exact date of the Buddha's birthday is the eighth day of the fourth month in the lunar calendar. The day is celebrated in Buddhist countries all around the world with festivities that include, but are not limited to, poems, parades, theatrical performances, special decorations, and donating food and clothes to the poor. Every year, this day falls on different dates (usually in May) of the Gregorian calendar, but in Japan, the day is celebrated on April 8 nevertheless. A statue of the Buddha as an infant pointing to the heavens is placed in a small shrine covered with flowers to represent the garden in which he was born, and sweet tea is poured over the statue to represent the sweet rain that fell that day. In some versions of the legend, the sweet rain was either pure water or nectar of immortality that was poured on Baby Buddha by dragons or serpent kings.

Biker gangs, page 180

To the average Japanese person, the phrase "*tenjō tenge yuiga dokuson* (holy am I alone throughout Heaven and Earth)" will likely call to mind a specific, very non-religious image. The saying was commonly embroidered on the backs or sleeves of the long coats worn by members of *bōsōzoku*—violent groups of motorcycle enthusiasts who are given to reckless driving habits.

Drugged elephants like him, page 183

Once, the Buddha's disciple Devadatta tried to kill the Buddha by making an intoxicated elephant attack him. The attempt failed because the elephant would not remain enraged in the Buddha's kind presence.

The First Seven Steps, page 184

While the words on Buddha's t-shirt may put the reader in mind of a classic manga series called *Hajime no Ippo* (The First Step), it is also a reference to the event immediately after his birth, when he took seven steps, pointed up to the Heavens with his right hand and down to the Earth with his left, and proclaimed, "Holy am I alone throughout Heaven and Earth." As he took those seven steps, lotus blossoms bloomed in his footprints.

Mountain Person, page 189

Specifically this refers to preferring mountains over the beach. The Bible contains several accounts of Jesus retiring to the mountains to pray, to commune with God, and so on.

Asura, page 190

An asura is a kind of demon, the opposite of a deva.

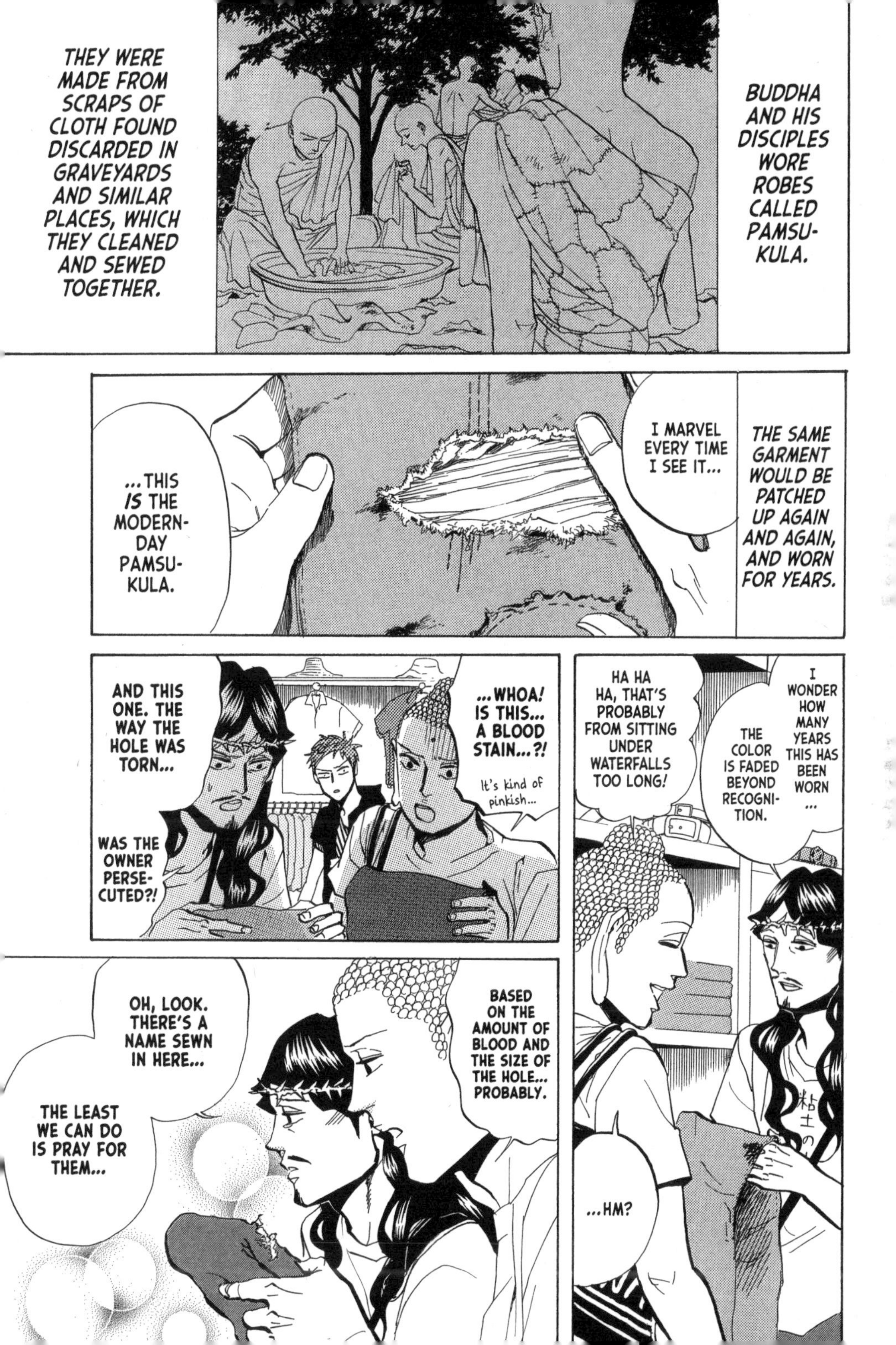
BUDDHA AND HIS DISCIPLES WORE ROBES CALLED PAMSU-KULA.
THEY WERE MADE FROM SCRAPS OF CLOTH FOUND DISCARDED IN GRAVEYARDS AND SIMILAR PLACES, WHICH THEY CLEANED AND SEWED TOGETHER.
THE SAME GARMENT WOULD BE PATCHED UP AGAIN AND AGAIN, AND WORN FOR YEARS.
I MARVEL EVERY TIME I SEE IT...
...THIS *IS* THE MODERN-DAY PAMSU-KULA.
I WONDER HOW MANY YEARS THIS HAS BEEN WORN...
THE COLOR IS FADED BEYOND RECOGNITION.
HA HA HA, THAT'S PROBABLY FROM SITTING UNDER WATERFALLS TOO LONG!
...HM?
...WHOA! IS THIS... A BLOOD STAIN...?!
It's kind of pinkish...
AND THIS ONE. THE WAY THE HOLE WAS TORN...
WAS THE OWNER PERSECUTED?!
BASED ON THE AMOUNT OF BLOOD AND THE SIZE OF THE HOLE... PROBABLY.
OH, LOOK. THERE'S A NAME SEWN IN HERE...
THE LEAST WE CAN DO IS PRAY FOR THEM...

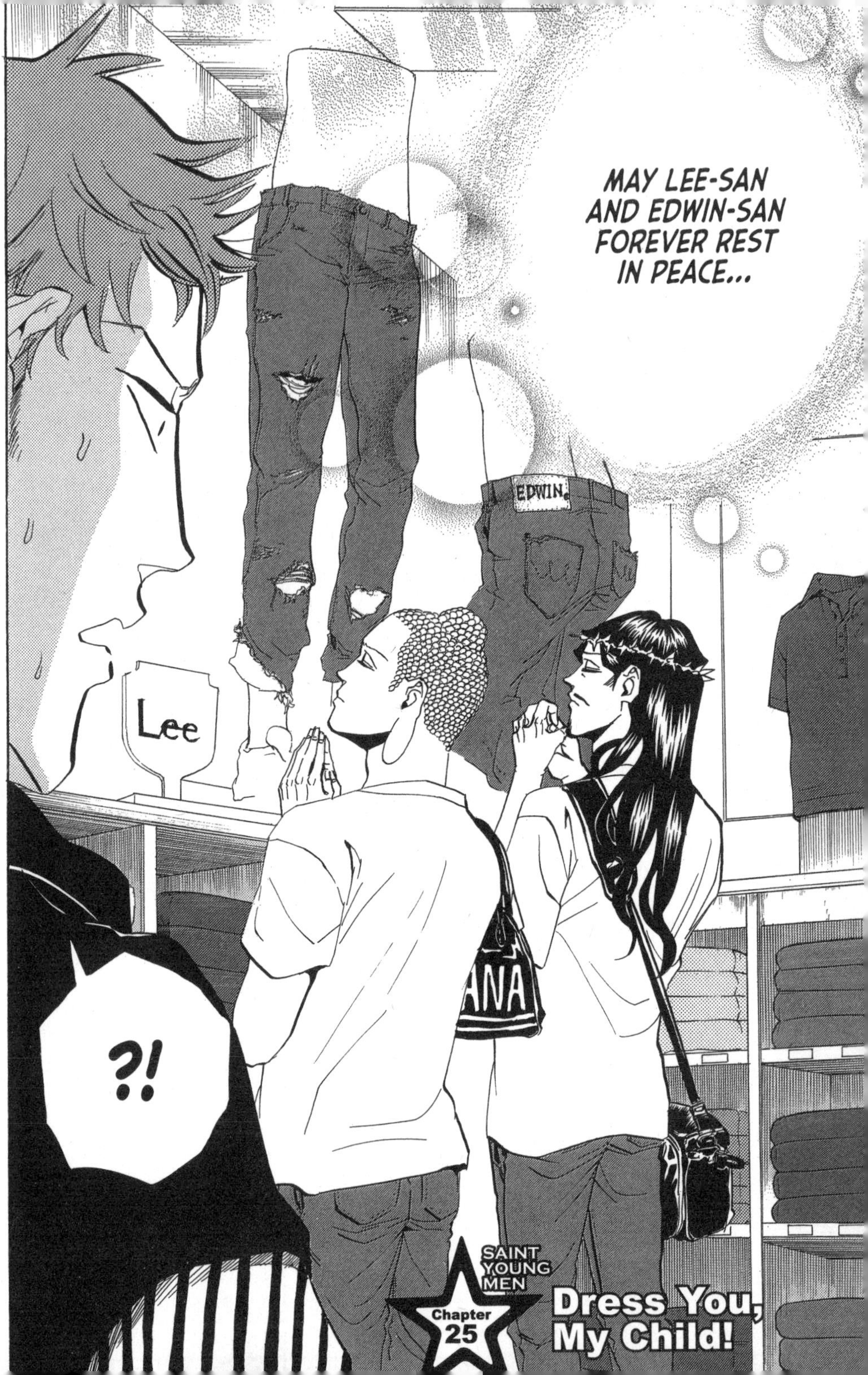
MAY LEE-SAN AND EDWIN-SAN FOREVER REST IN PEACE...
?!
EDWIN
Lee
ANA
SAINT YOUNG MEN
Chapter 25
Dress You, My Child!

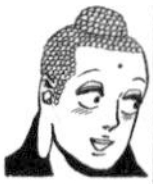

BUDDHA: ALWAYS BRINGS A GLOVE TO WATCH PROFESSIONAL BASEBALL GAMES, SO HE'LL BE READY TO CATCH HOME RUNS.

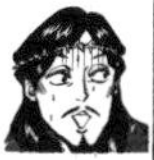

JESUS: WORE A HELMET TO A PROFESSIONAL BASEBALL GAME IN CASE OF FOUL BALLS, BUT HE WORRIED FOR NOTHING.

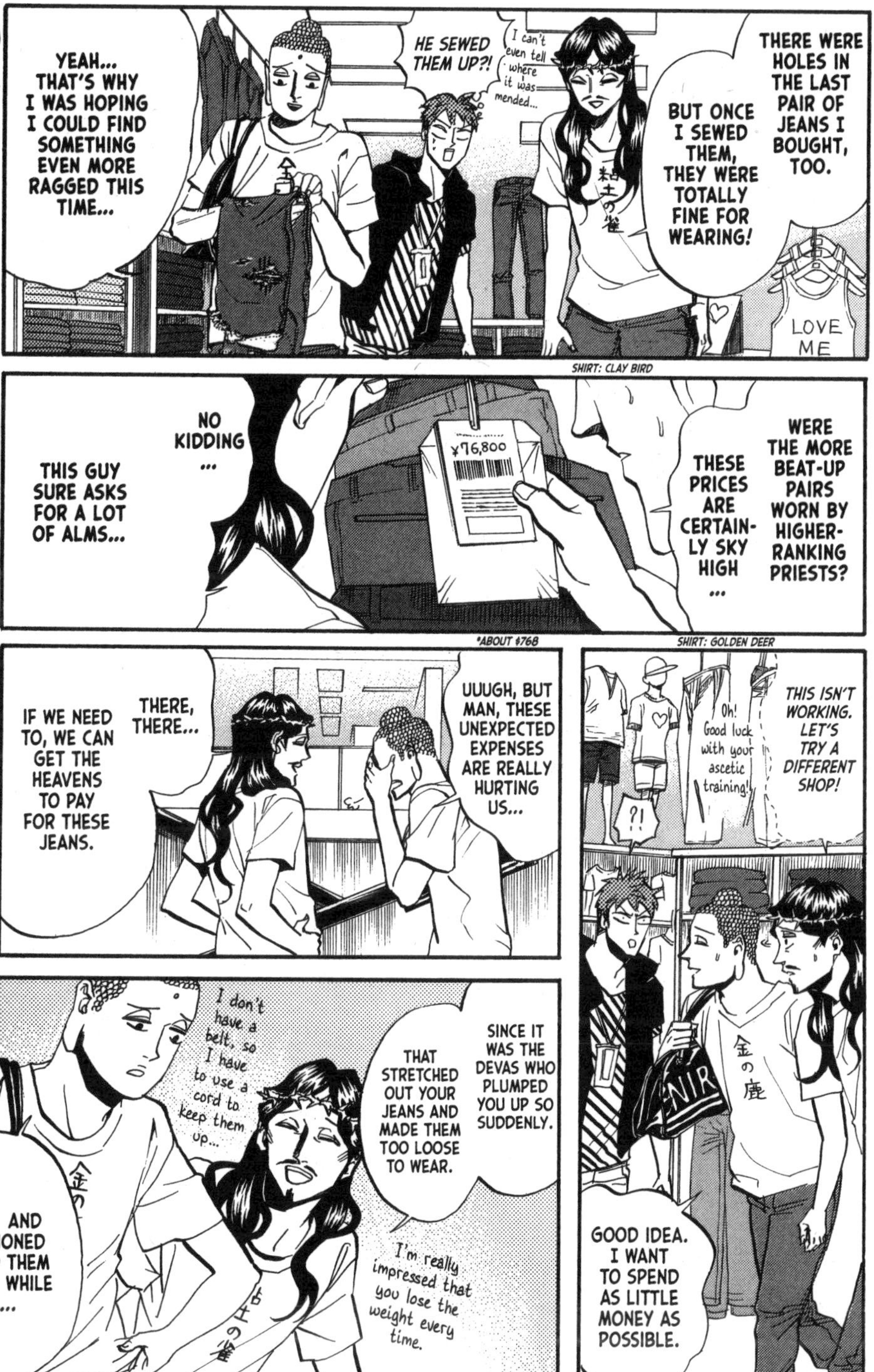
THERE WERE HOLES IN THE LAST PAIR OF JEANS I BOUGHT, TOO.
BUT ONCE I SEWED THEM, THEY WERE TOTALLY FINE FOR WEARING!
HE SEWED THEM UP?!
I can't even tell where it was mended...
YEAH... THAT'S WHY I WAS HOPING I COULD FIND SOMETHING EVEN MORE RAGGED THIS TIME...
LOVE ME
SHIRT: CLAY BIRD
WERE THE MORE BEAT-UP PAIRS WORN BY HIGHER-RANKING PRIESTS?
THESE PRICES ARE CERTAIN-LY SKY HIGH...
¥76,800
NO KIDDING...
THIS GUY SURE ASKS FOR A LOT OF ALMS...
*ABOUT $768
SHIRT: GOLDEN DEER
THIS ISN'T WORKING. LET'S TRY A DIFFERENT SHOP!
Oh! Good luck with your ascetic training!
?!
GOOD IDEA. I WANT TO SPEND AS LITTLE MONEY AS POSSIBLE.
UUUGH, BUT MAN, THESE UNEXPECTED EXPENSES ARE REALLY HURTING US...
THERE, THERE...
IF WE NEED TO, WE CAN GET THE HEAVENS TO PAY FOR THESE JEANS.
SINCE IT WAS THE DEVAS WHO PLUMPED YOU UP SO SUDDENLY.
THAT STRETCHED OUT YOUR JEANS AND MADE THEM TOO LOOSE TO WEAR.
I don't have a belt, so I have to use a cord to keep them up...
I'm really impressed that you lose the weight every time.
YEAH... AND I MENTIONED THAT TO THEM A LITTLE WHILE AGO...

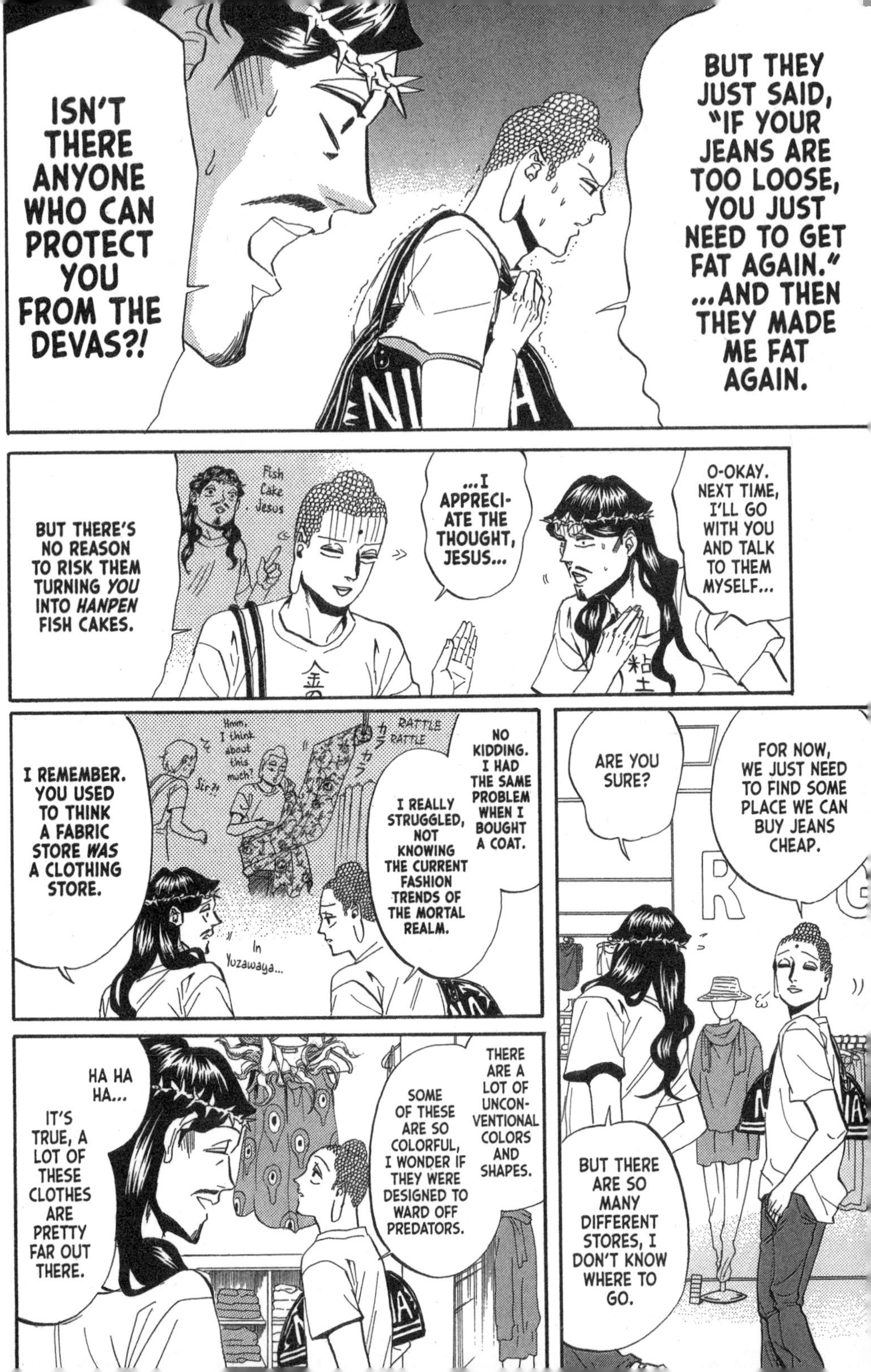
BUT THEY JUST SAID, "IF YOUR JEANS ARE TOO LOOSE, YOU JUST NEED TO GET FAT AGAIN." ...AND THEN THEY MADE ME FAT AGAIN.
ISN'T THERE ANYONE WHO CAN PROTECT YOU FROM THE DEVAS?!
O-OKAY. NEXT TIME, I'LL GO WITH YOU AND TALK TO THEM MYSELF...
...I APPRECIATE THE THOUGHT, JESUS...
Fish Cake Jesus
BUT THERE'S NO REASON TO RISK THEM TURNING *YOU* INTO *HANPEN* FISH CAKES.
FOR NOW, WE JUST NEED TO FIND SOME PLACE WE CAN BUY JEANS CHEAP.
ARE YOU SURE?
BUT THERE ARE SO MANY DIFFERENT STORES, I DON'T KNOW WHERE TO GO.
NO KIDDING. I HAD THE SAME PROBLEM WHEN I BOUGHT A COAT.
I REALLY STRUGGLED, NOT KNOWING THE CURRENT FASHION TRENDS OF THE MORTAL REALM.
RATTLE RATTLE
Hmm, I think about this much?
Sir?!
In Yuzawaya...
I REMEMBER. YOU USED TO THINK A FABRIC STORE *WAS* A CLOTHING STORE.
THERE ARE A LOT OF UNCONVENTIONAL COLORS AND SHAPES.
SOME OF THESE ARE SO COLORFUL, I WONDER IF THEY WERE DESIGNED TO WARD OFF PREDATORS.
HA HA HA...
IT'S TRUE, A LOT OF THESE CLOTHES ARE PRETTY FAR OUT THERE.

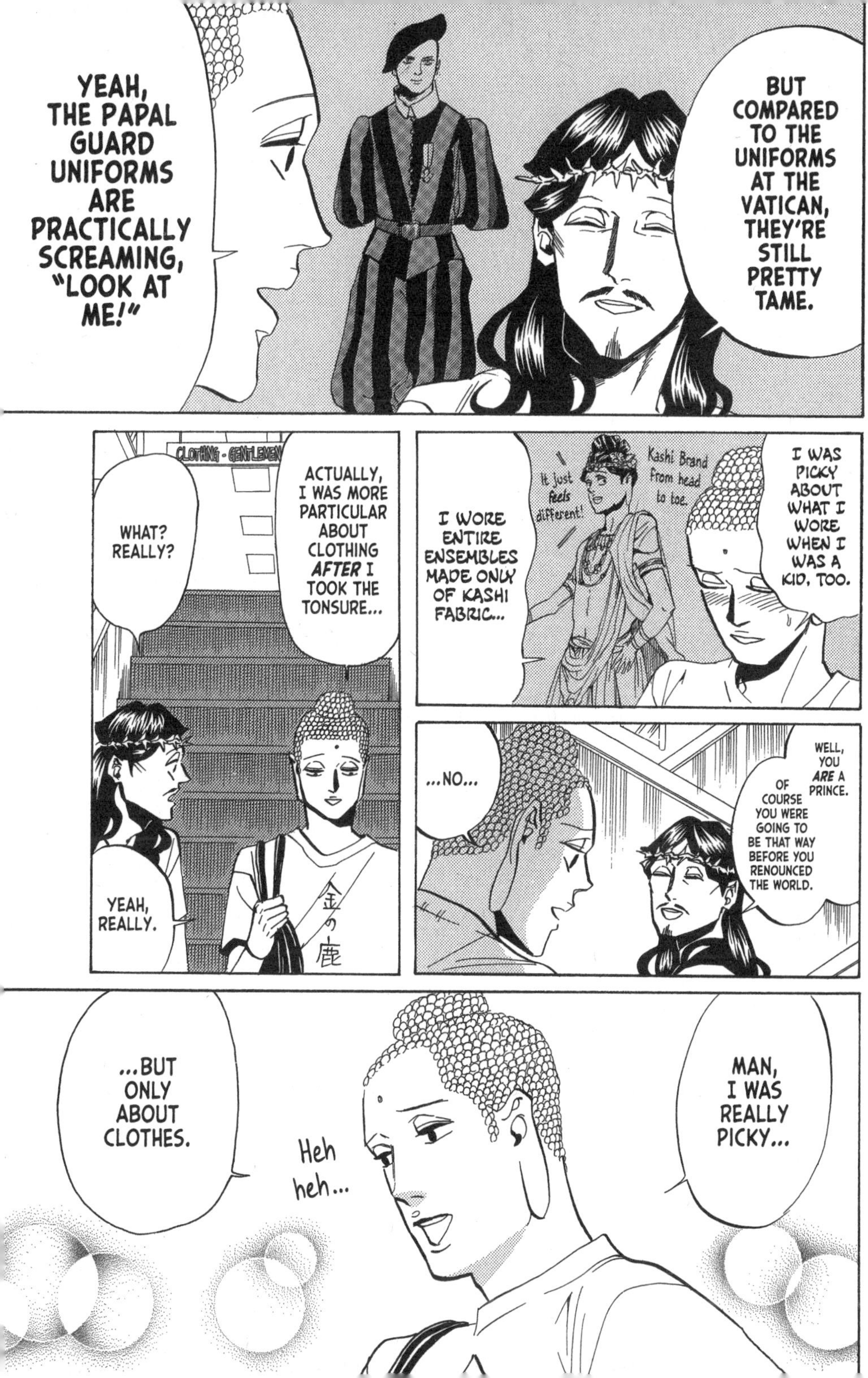
BUT COMPARED TO THE UNIFORMS AT THE VATICAN, THEY'RE STILL PRETTY TAME.
YEAH, THE PAPAL GUARD UNIFORMS ARE PRACTICALLY SCREAMING, "LOOK AT ME!"
I WAS PICKY ABOUT WHAT I WORE WHEN I WAS A KID, TOO.
Kashi Brand from head to toe.
It just *feels* different!
I WORE ENTIRE ENSEMBLES MADE ONLY OF KASHI FABRIC...
WELL, YOU *ARE* A PRINCE.
OF COURSE YOU WERE GOING TO BE THAT WAY BEFORE YOU RENOUNCED THE WORLD.
...NO...
CLOTHING - GENTLEMEN
ACTUALLY, I WAS MORE PARTICULAR ABOUT CLOTHING ***AFTER*** I TOOK THE TONSURE...
WHAT? REALLY?
金の鹿
YEAH, REALLY.
MAN, I WAS REALLY PICKY...
Heh heh...
...BUT ONLY ABOUT CLOTHES.

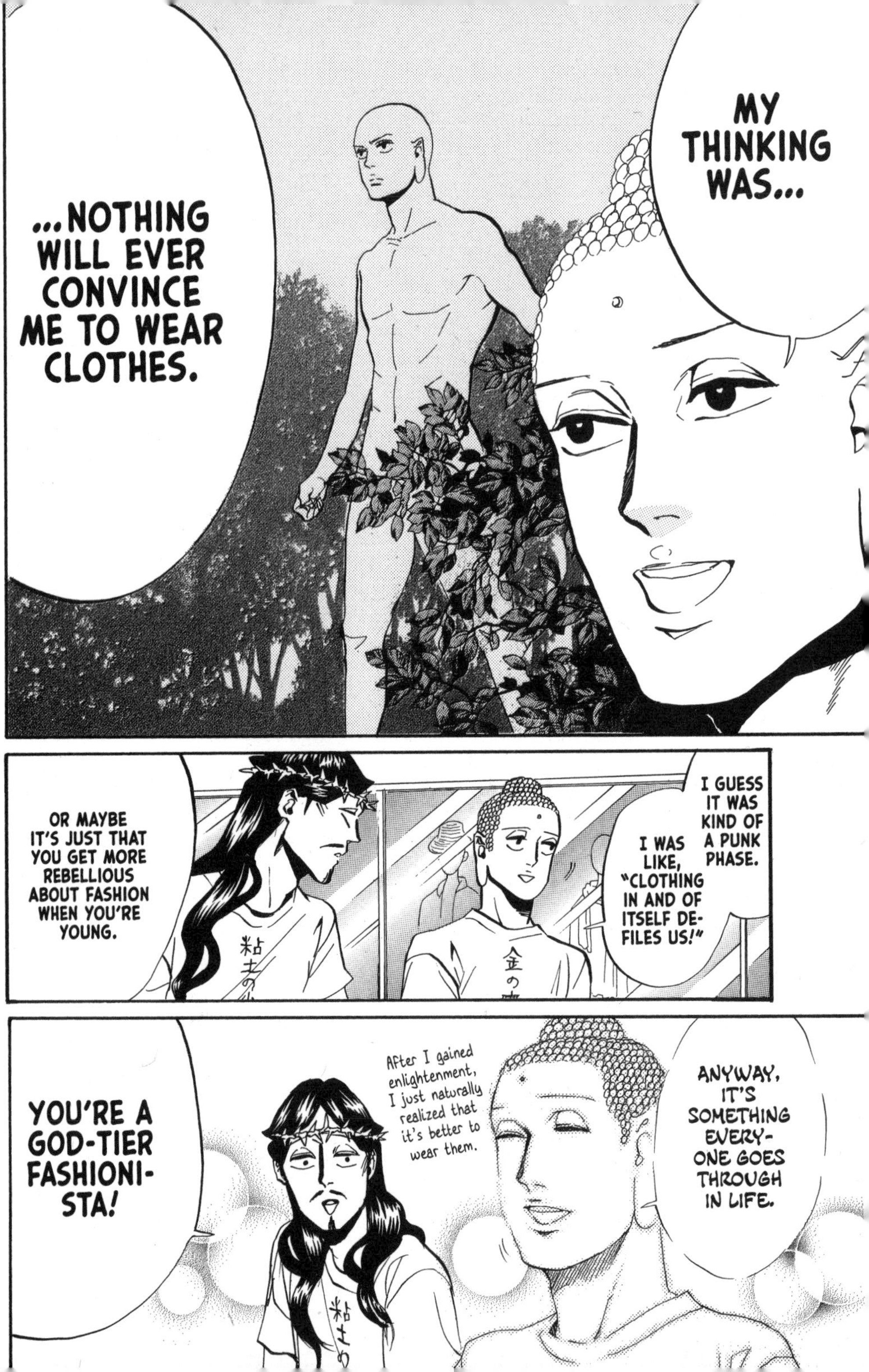
MY THINKING WAS...
...NOTHING WILL EVER CONVINCE ME TO WEAR CLOTHES.
I GUESS IT WAS KIND OF A PUNK PHASE.
I WAS LIKE, "CLOTHING IN AND OF ITSELF DE-FILES US!"
OR MAYBE IT'S JUST THAT YOU GET MORE REBELLIOUS ABOUT FASHION WHEN YOU'RE YOUNG.
ANYWAY, IT'S SOMETHING EVERY-ONE GOES THROUGH IN LIFE.
After I gained enlightenment, I just naturally realized that it's better to wear them.
YOU'RE A GOD-TIER FASHIONI-STA!

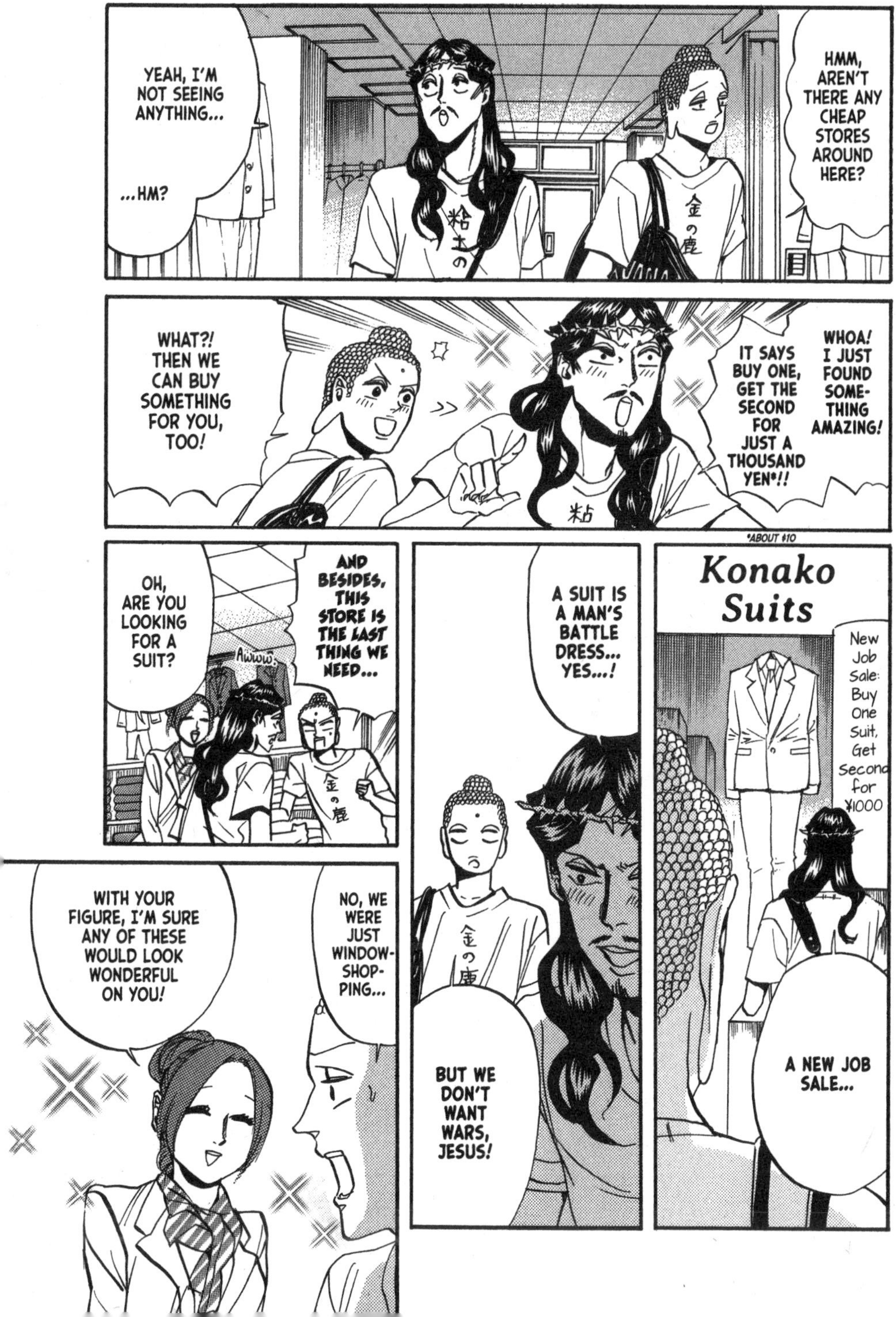
HMM, AREN'T THERE ANY CHEAP STORES AROUND HERE?
YEAH, I'M NOT SEEING ANYTHING...
...HM?
WHOA! I JUST FOUND SOMETHING AMAZING!
IT SAYS BUY ONE, GET THE SECOND FOR JUST A THOUSAND YEN*!!
WHAT?! THEN WE CAN BUY SOMETHING FOR YOU, TOO!
*ABOUT $10
Konako Suits
New Job Sale: Buy One Suit, Get Second for ¥1000
A NEW JOB SALE...
A SUIT IS A MAN'S BATTLE DRESS... YES...!
BUT WE DON'T WANT WARS, JESUS!
AND BESIDES, THIS STORE IS THE LAST THING WE NEED...
OH, ARE YOU LOOKING FOR A SUIT?
Awww.
NO, WE WERE JUST WINDOW-SHOPPING...
WITH YOUR FIGURE, I'M SURE ANY OF THESE WOULD LOOK WONDERFUL ON YOU!

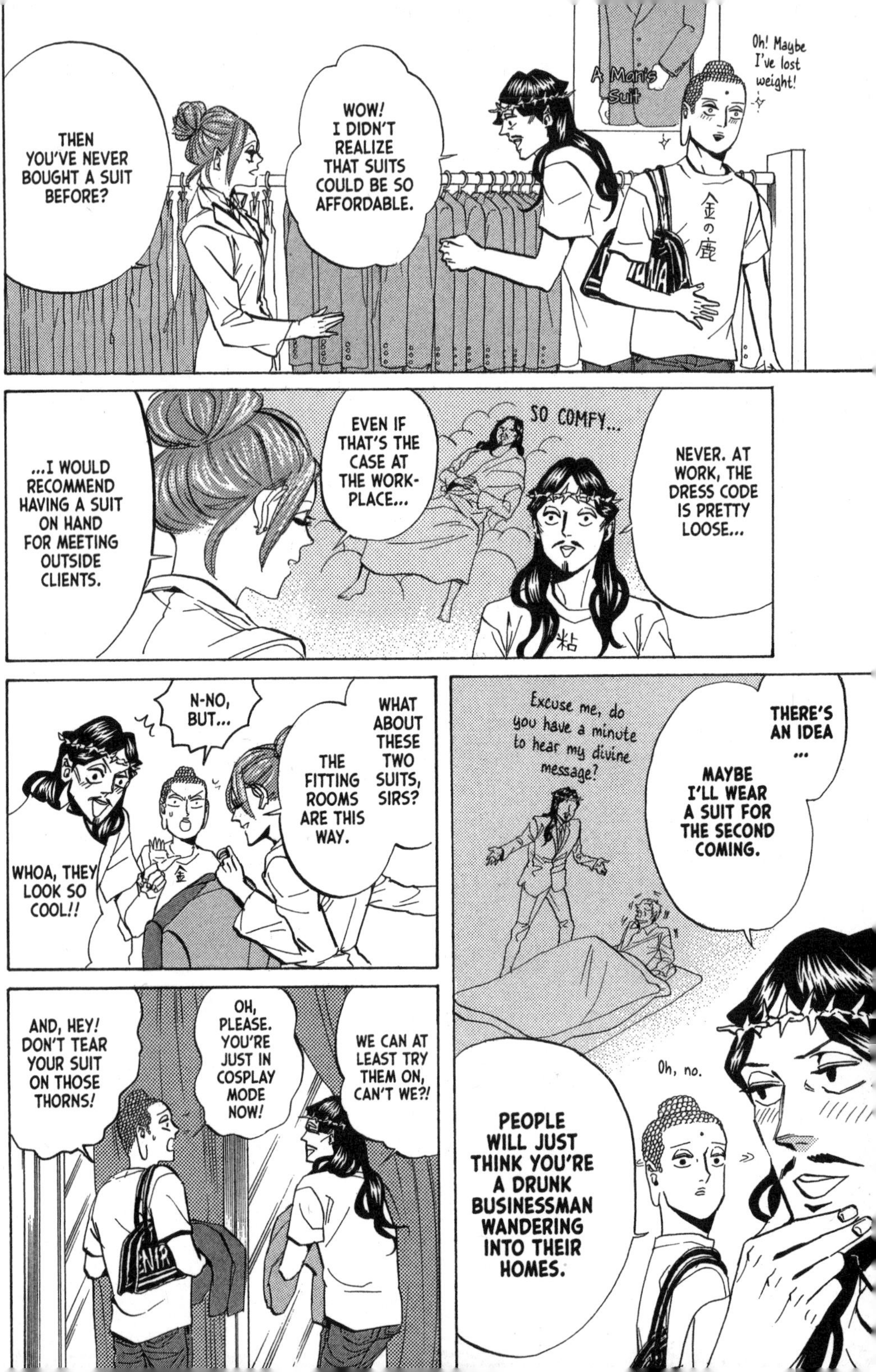
Oh! Maybe I've lost weight!
A Man's Suit
金の鹿
WOW! I DIDN'T REALIZE THAT SUITS COULD BE SO AFFORDABLE.
THEN YOU'VE NEVER BOUGHT A SUIT BEFORE?
NEVER. AT WORK, THE DRESS CODE IS PRETTY LOOSE...
SO COMFY...
EVEN IF THAT'S THE CASE AT THE WORK-PLACE...
...I WOULD RECOMMEND HAVING A SUIT ON HAND FOR MEETING OUTSIDE CLIENTS.
THERE'S AN IDEA ...
MAYBE I'LL WEAR A SUIT FOR THE SECOND COMING.
Excuse me, do you have a minute to hear my divine message?
Oh, no.
PEOPLE WILL JUST THINK YOU'RE A DRUNK BUSINESSMAN WANDERING INTO THEIR HOMES.
WHAT ABOUT THESE TWO SUITS, SIRS?
THE FITTING ROOMS ARE THIS WAY.
N-NO, BUT...
WHOA, THEY LOOK SO COOL!!
WE CAN AT LEAST TRY THEM ON, CAN'T WE?!
OH, PLEASE. YOU'RE JUST IN COSPLAY MODE NOW!
AND, HEY! DON'T TEAR YOUR SUIT ON THOSE THORNS!

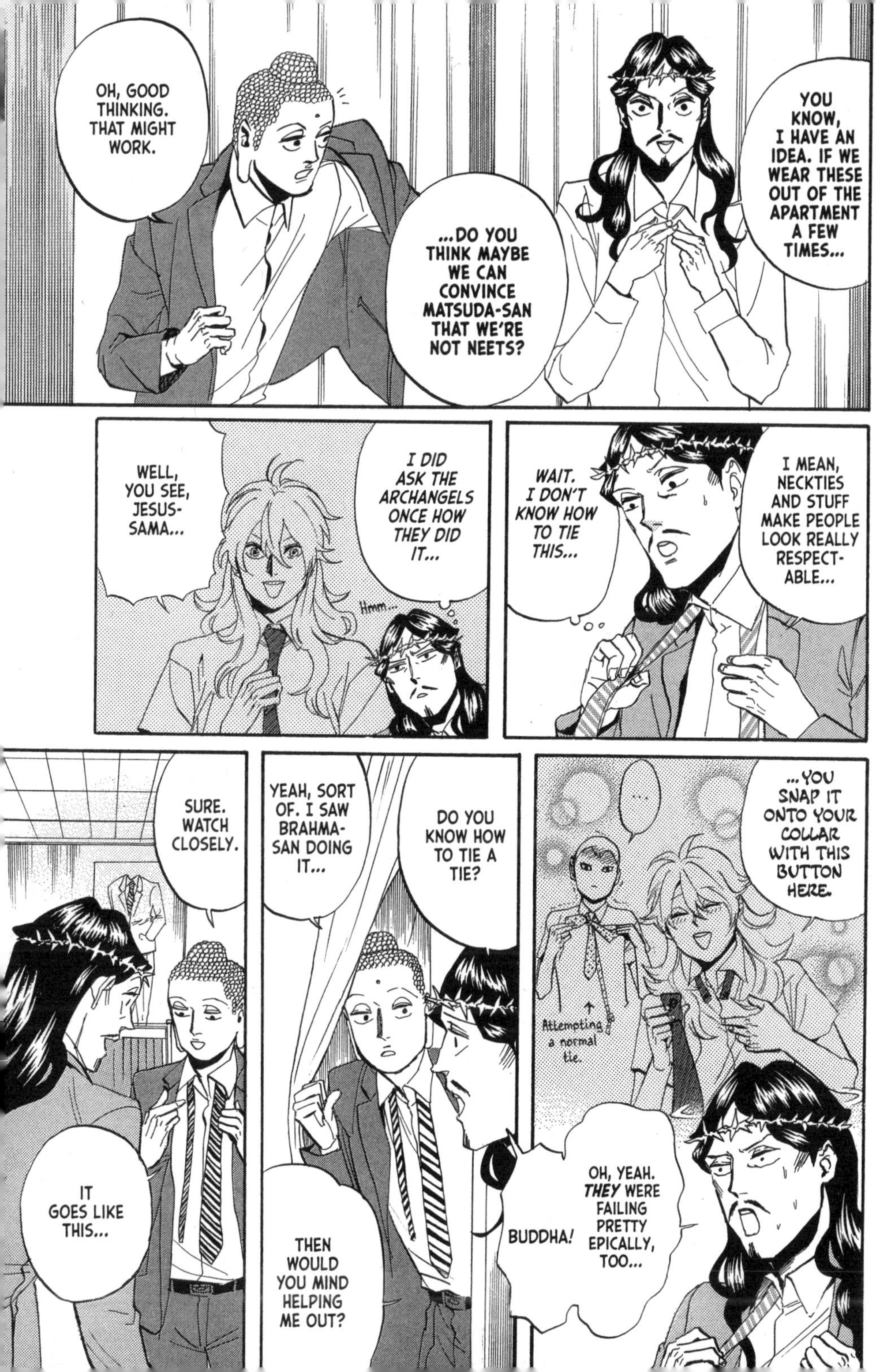
YOU KNOW, I HAVE AN IDEA. IF WE WEAR THESE OUT OF THE APARTMENT A FEW TIMES...
...DO YOU THINK MAYBE WE CAN CONVINCE MATSUDA-SAN THAT WE'RE NOT NEETS?
OH, GOOD THINKING. THAT MIGHT WORK.
I MEAN, NECKTIES AND STUFF MAKE PEOPLE LOOK REALLY RESPECT-ABLE...
WAIT. I DON'T KNOW HOW TO TIE THIS...
I DID ASK THE ARCHANGELS ONCE HOW THEY DID IT...
Hmm...
WELL, YOU SEE, JESUS-SAMA...
...YOU SNAP IT ONTO YOUR COLLAR WITH THIS BUTTON HERE.
...
Attempting a normal tie.
OH, YEAH. *THEY* WERE FAILING PRETTY EPICALLY, TOO...
BUDDHA!
DO YOU KNOW HOW TO TIE A TIE?
YEAH, SORT OF. I SAW BRAHMA-SAN DOING IT...
THEN WOULD YOU MIND HELPING ME OUT?
SURE. WATCH CLOSELY.
IT GOES LIKE THIS...

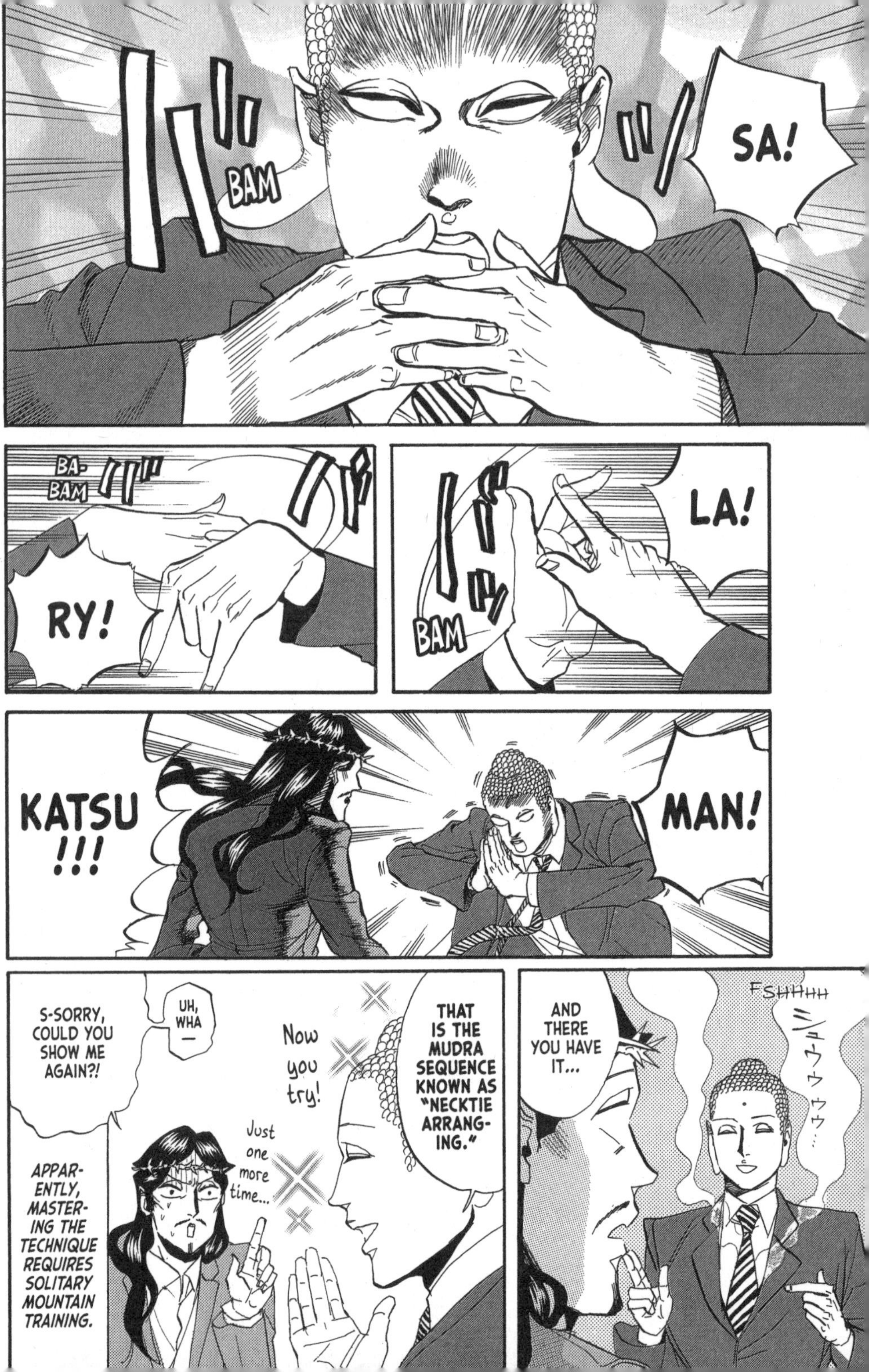
SA!
BAM
LA!
BAM
BA-BAM
RY!
MAN!
KATSU!!!
FSHHHH
シュウウウウ…
AND THERE YOU HAVE IT...
THAT IS THE MUDRA SEQUENCE KNOWN AS "NECKTIE ARRANGING."
Now you try!
UH, WHA—
S-SORRY, COULD YOU SHOW ME AGAIN?!
Just one more time...
APPARENTLY, MASTERING THE TECHNIQUE REQUIRES SOLITARY MOUNTAIN TRAINING.

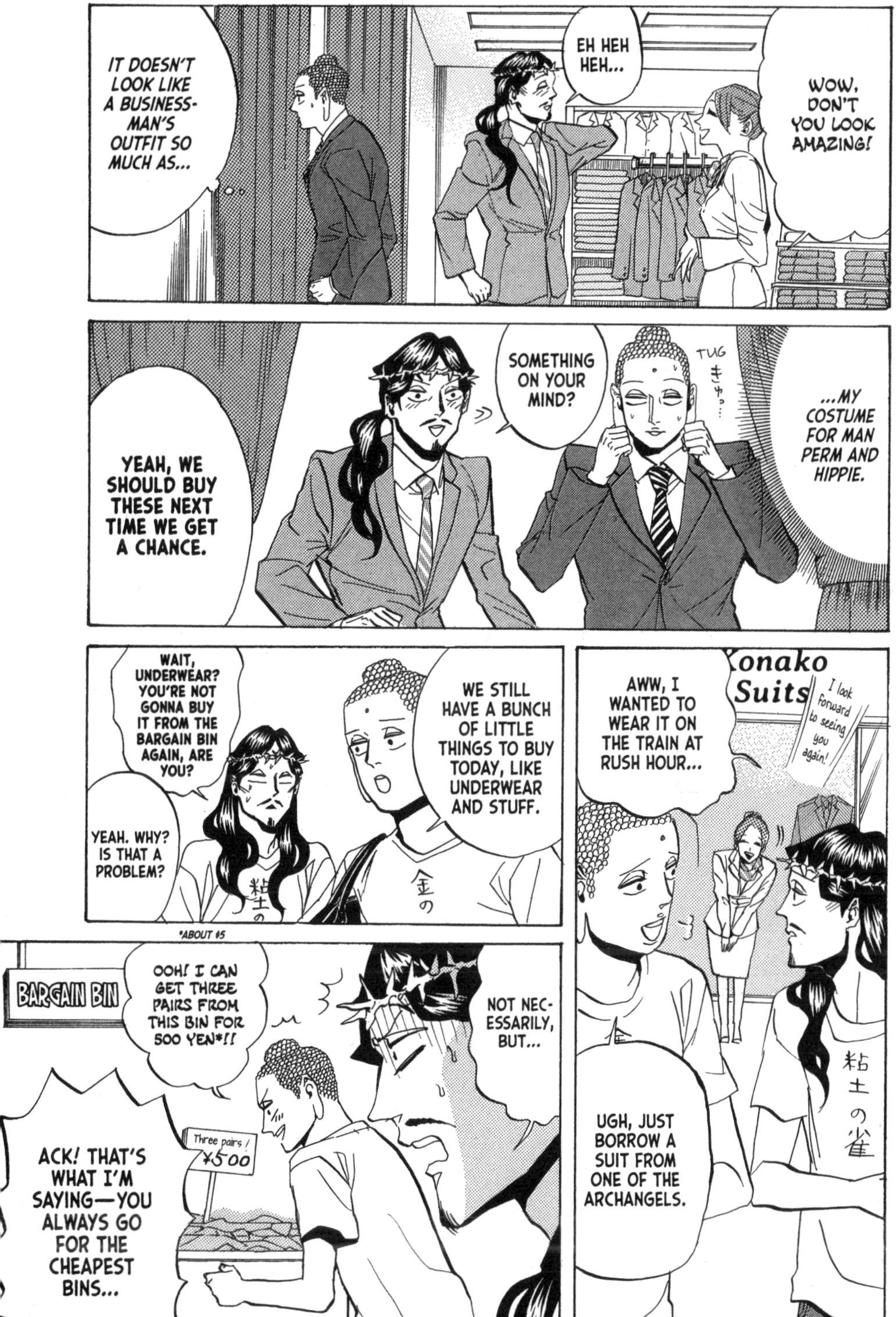
WOW, DON'T YOU LOOK AMAZING!
EH HEH HEH...
IT DOESN'T LOOK LIKE A BUSINESS-MAN'S OUTFIT SO MUCH AS...
...MY COSTUME FOR MAN PERM AND HIPPIE.
TUG
きゅっ
SOMETHING ON YOUR MIND?
YEAH, WE SHOULD BUY THESE NEXT TIME WE GET A CHANCE.
Konako Suits
I look forward to seeing you again!
AWW, I WANTED TO WEAR IT ON THE TRAIN AT RUSH HOUR...
UGH, JUST BORROW A SUIT FROM ONE OF THE ARCHANGELS.
WE STILL HAVE A BUNCH OF LITTLE THINGS TO BUY TODAY, LIKE UNDERWEAR AND STUFF.
WAIT, UNDERWEAR? YOU'RE NOT GONNA BUY IT FROM THE BARGAIN BIN AGAIN, ARE YOU?
YEAH. WHY? IS THAT A PROBLEM?
NOT NEC-ESSARILY, BUT...
OOH! I CAN GET THREE PAIRS FROM THIS BIN FOR 500 YEN*!!
BARGAIN BIN
Three pairs! ¥500
ACK! THAT'S WHAT I'M SAYING—YOU ALWAYS GO FOR THE CHEAPEST BINS...
*ABOUT $5

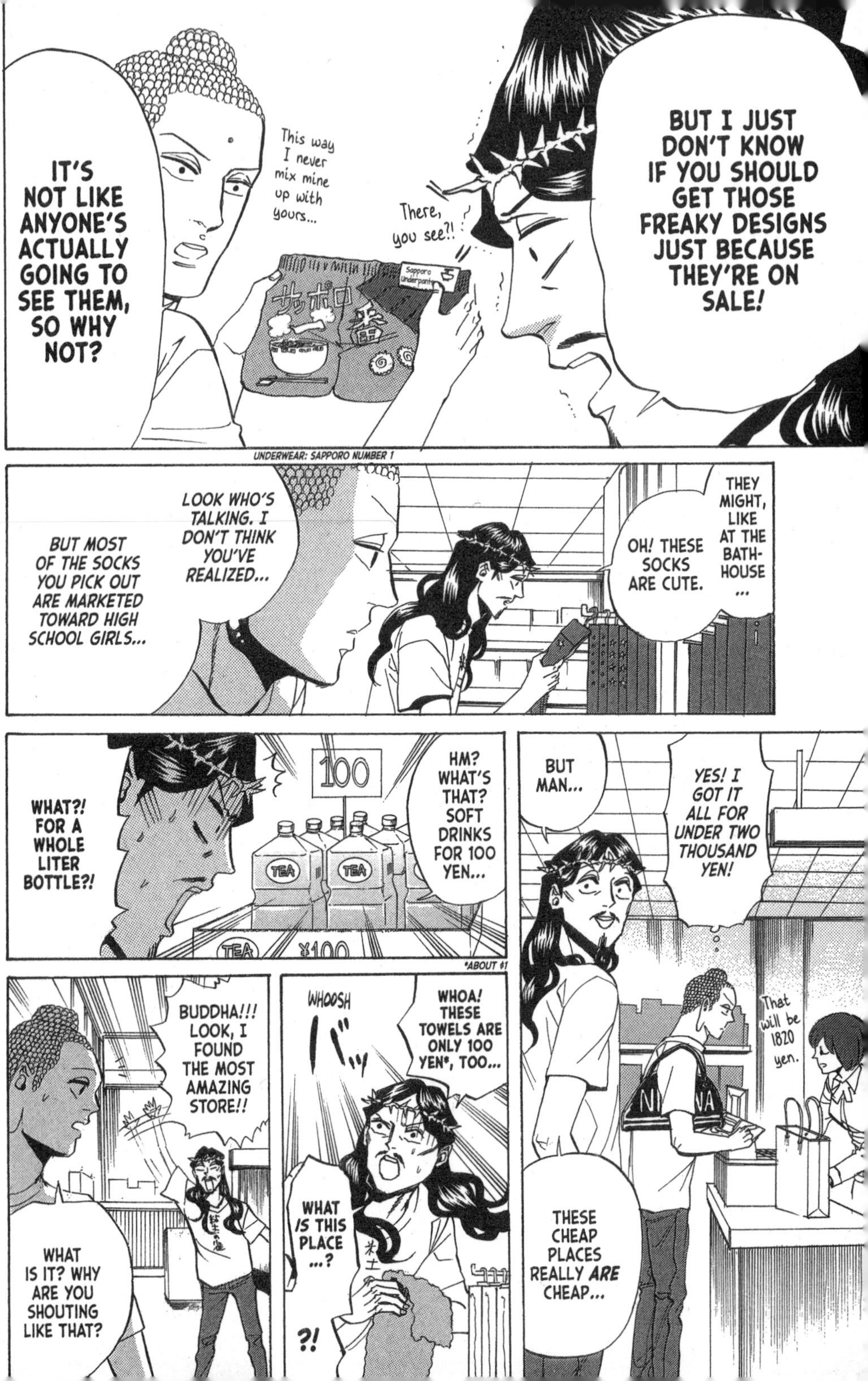

BUT I JUST DON'T KNOW IF YOU SHOULD GET THOSE FREAKY DESIGNS JUST BECAUSE THEY'RE ON SALE!
There, you see?!
Sapporo Underpants
This way I never mix mine up with yours...
IT'S NOT LIKE ANYONE'S ACTUALLY GOING TO SEE THEM, SO WHY NOT?
UNDERWEAR: SAPPORO NUMBER 1
THEY MIGHT, LIKE AT THE BATH-HOUSE ...
OH! THESE SOCKS ARE CUTE.
LOOK WHO'S TALKING. I DON'T THINK YOU'VE REALIZED...
BUT MOST OF THE SOCKS YOU PICK OUT ARE MARKETED TOWARD HIGH SCHOOL GIRLS...
BUT MAN...
YES! I GOT IT ALL FOR UNDER TWO THOUSAND YEN!
That will be 1820 yen.
THESE CHEAP PLACES REALLY *ARE* CHEAP...
HM? WHAT'S THAT? SOFT DRINKS FOR 100 YEN...
100
TEA
¥100
WHAT?! FOR A WHOLE LITER BOTTLE?!
*ABOUT $1
WHOOSH
WHOA! THESE TOWELS ARE ONLY 100 YEN*, TOO...
WHAT *IS* THIS PLACE ...?
?!
BUDDHA!!! LOOK, I FOUND THE MOST AMAZING STORE!!
WHAT IS IT? WHY ARE YOU SHOUTING LIKE THAT?

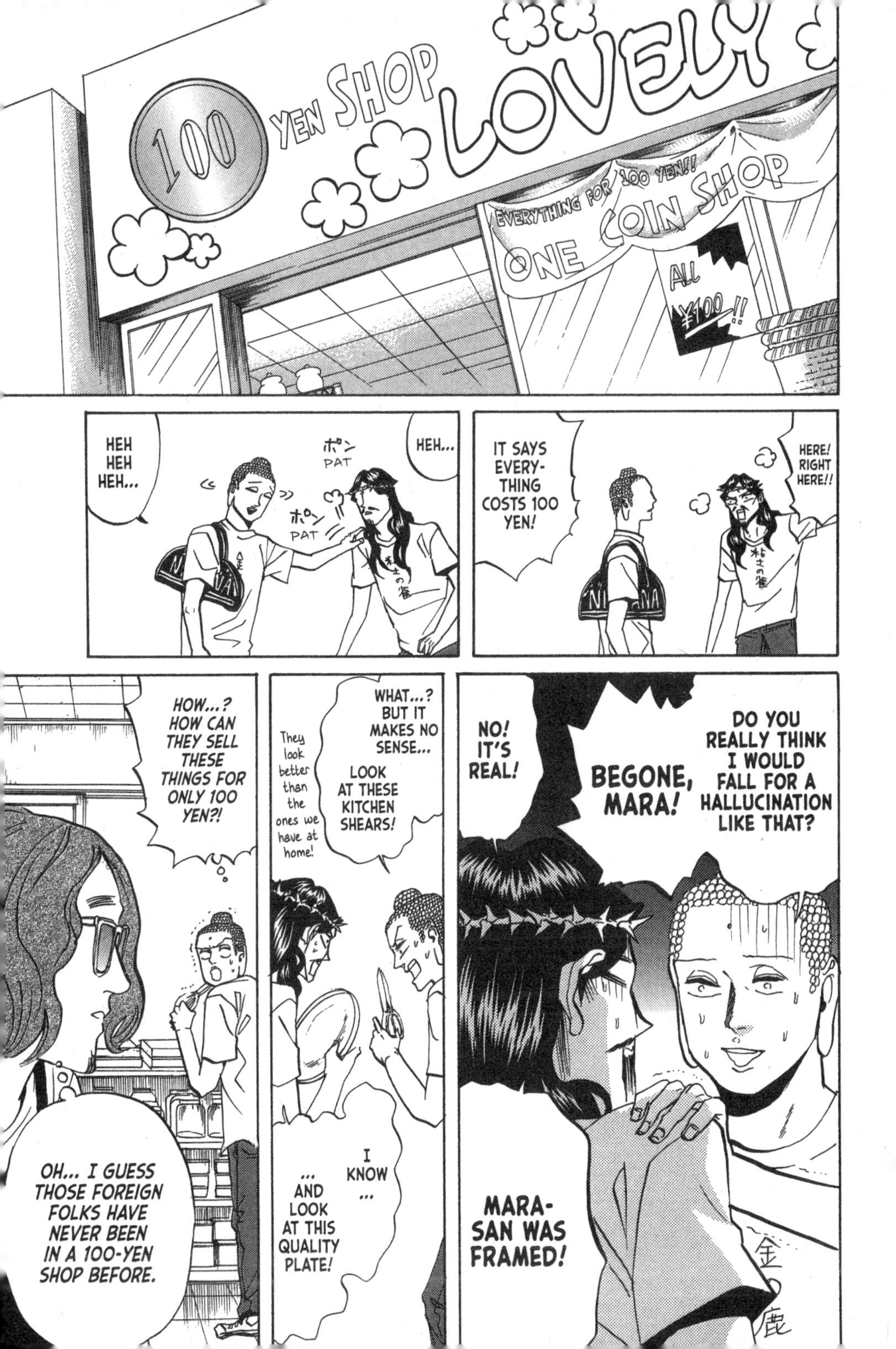
100
YEN SHOP
LOVELY
EVERYTHING FOR 100 YEN!!
ONE COIN SHOP
ALL ¥100!!
HERE! RIGHT HERE!!
IT SAYS EVERY-THING COSTS 100 YEN!
HEH...
ポン PAT
ポン PAT
HEH HEH HEH...
DO YOU REALLY THINK I WOULD FALL FOR A HALLUCINATION LIKE THAT?
BEGONE, MARA!
NO! IT'S REAL!
MARA-SAN WAS FRAMED!
WHAT...? BUT IT MAKES NO SENSE...
LOOK AT THESE KITCHEN SHEARS!
They look better than the ones we have at home!
I KNOW...
...AND LOOK AT THIS QUALITY PLATE!
HOW...? HOW CAN THEY SELL THESE THINGS FOR ONLY 100 YEN?!
OH... I GUESS THOSE FOREIGN FOLKS HAVE NEVER BEEN IN A 100-YEN SHOP BEFORE.

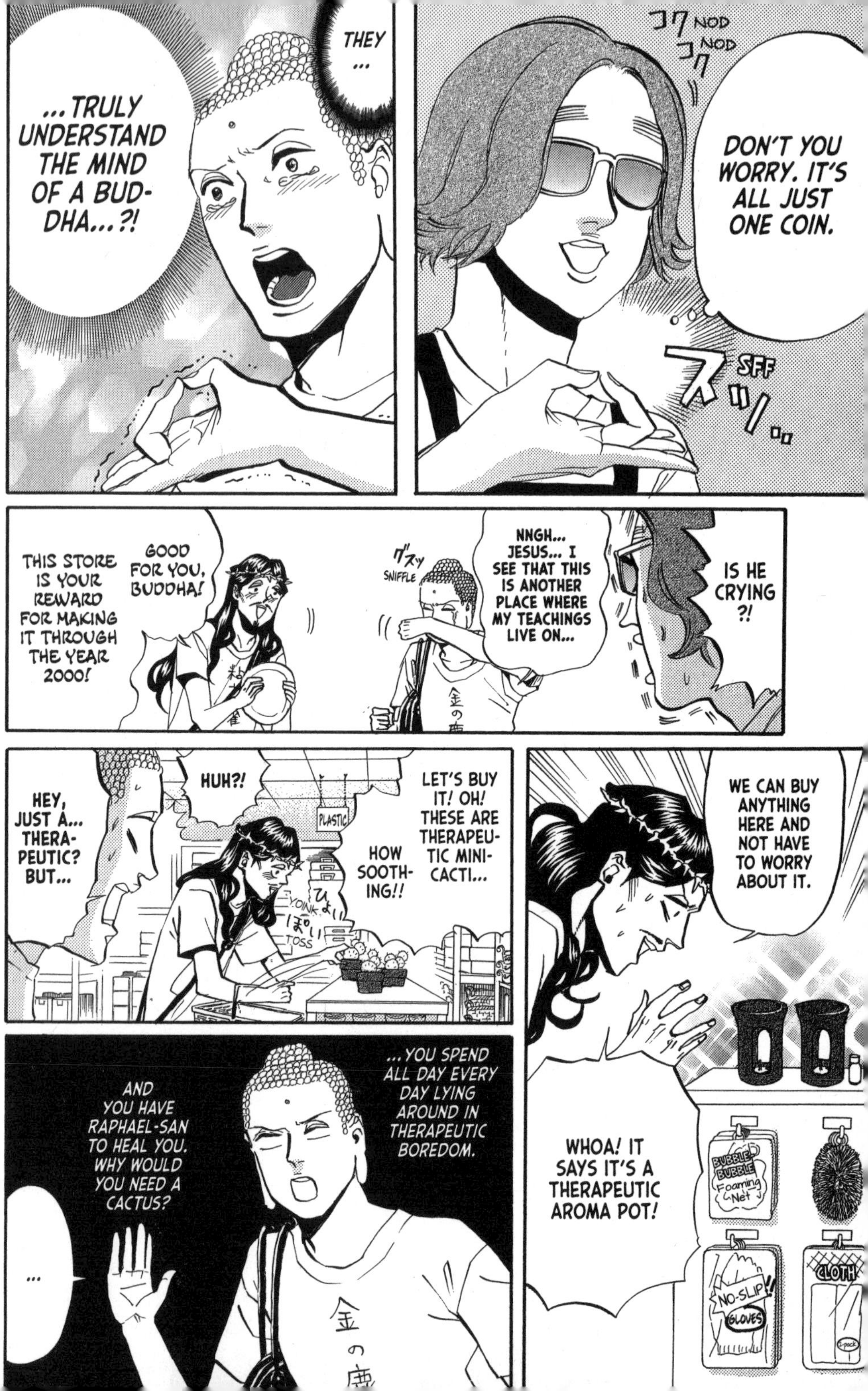
NOD NOD
DON'T YOU WORRY. IT'S ALL JUST ONE COIN.
SFF
THEY...
...TRULY UNDERSTAND THE MIND OF A BUD-DHA...?!
IS HE CRYING?!
NNGH... JESUS... I SEE THAT THIS IS ANOTHER PLACE WHERE MY TEACHINGS LIVE ON...
SNIFFLE
GOOD FOR YOU, BUDDHA!
THIS STORE IS YOUR REWARD FOR MAKING IT THROUGH THE YEAR 2000!
WE CAN BUY ANYTHING HERE AND NOT HAVE TO WORRY ABOUT IT.
WHOA! IT SAYS IT'S A THERAPEUTIC AROMA POT!
BUBBLE BUBBLE Foaming Net
NO-SLIP GLOVES
CLOTH
LET'S BUY IT! OH! THESE ARE THERAPEU-TIC MINI-CACTI...
HOW SOOTH-ING!!
YOINK
TOSS
PLASTIC
HUH?!
HEY, JUST A... THERA-PEUTIC? BUT...
...YOU SPEND ALL DAY EVERY DAY LYING AROUND IN THERAPEUTIC BOREDOM.
AND YOU HAVE RAPHAEL-SAN TO HEAL YOU. WHY WOULD YOU NEED A CACTUS?
...

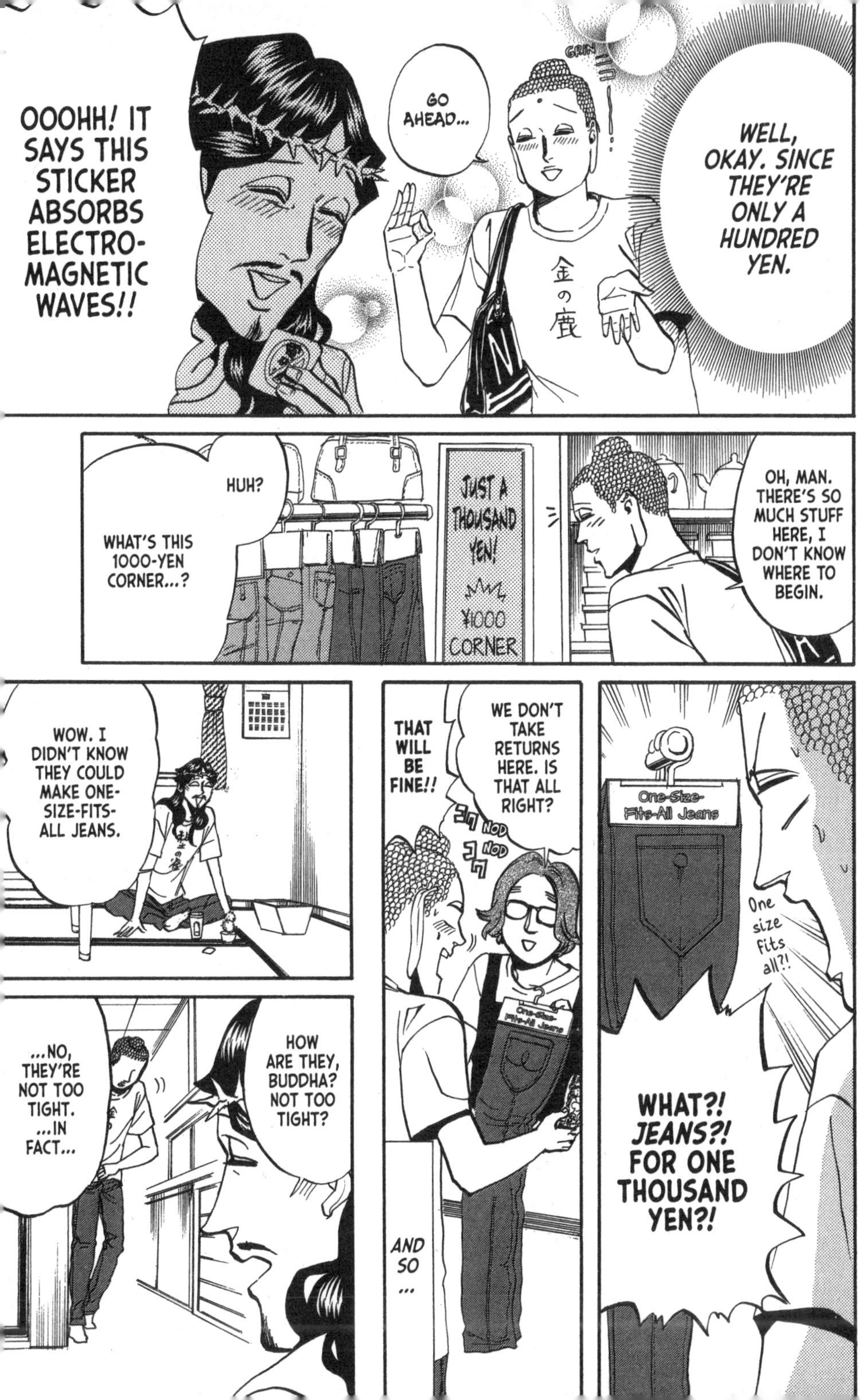
WELL, OKAY. SINCE THEY'RE ONLY A HUNDRED YEN.
GRIN
GO AHEAD...
OOOHH! IT SAYS THIS STICKER ABSORBS ELECTRO-MAGNETIC WAVES!!
OH, MAN. THERE'S SO MUCH STUFF HERE, I DON'T KNOW WHERE TO BEGIN.
JUST A THOUSAND YEN!
¥1000 CORNER
HUH?
WHAT'S THIS 1000-YEN CORNER...?
One-Size-Fits-All Jeans
One size fits all?!
WHAT?! JEANS?! FOR ONE THOUSAND YEN?!
WE DON'T TAKE RETURNS HERE. IS THAT ALL RIGHT?
THAT WILL BE FINE!!
NOD
NOD
One-Size-Fits-All Jeans
AND SO ...
WOW. I DIDN'T KNOW THEY COULD MAKE ONE-SIZE-FITS-ALL JEANS.
HOW ARE THEY, BUDDHA? NOT TOO TIGHT?
...NO, THEY'RE NOT TOO TIGHT. ...IN FACT...

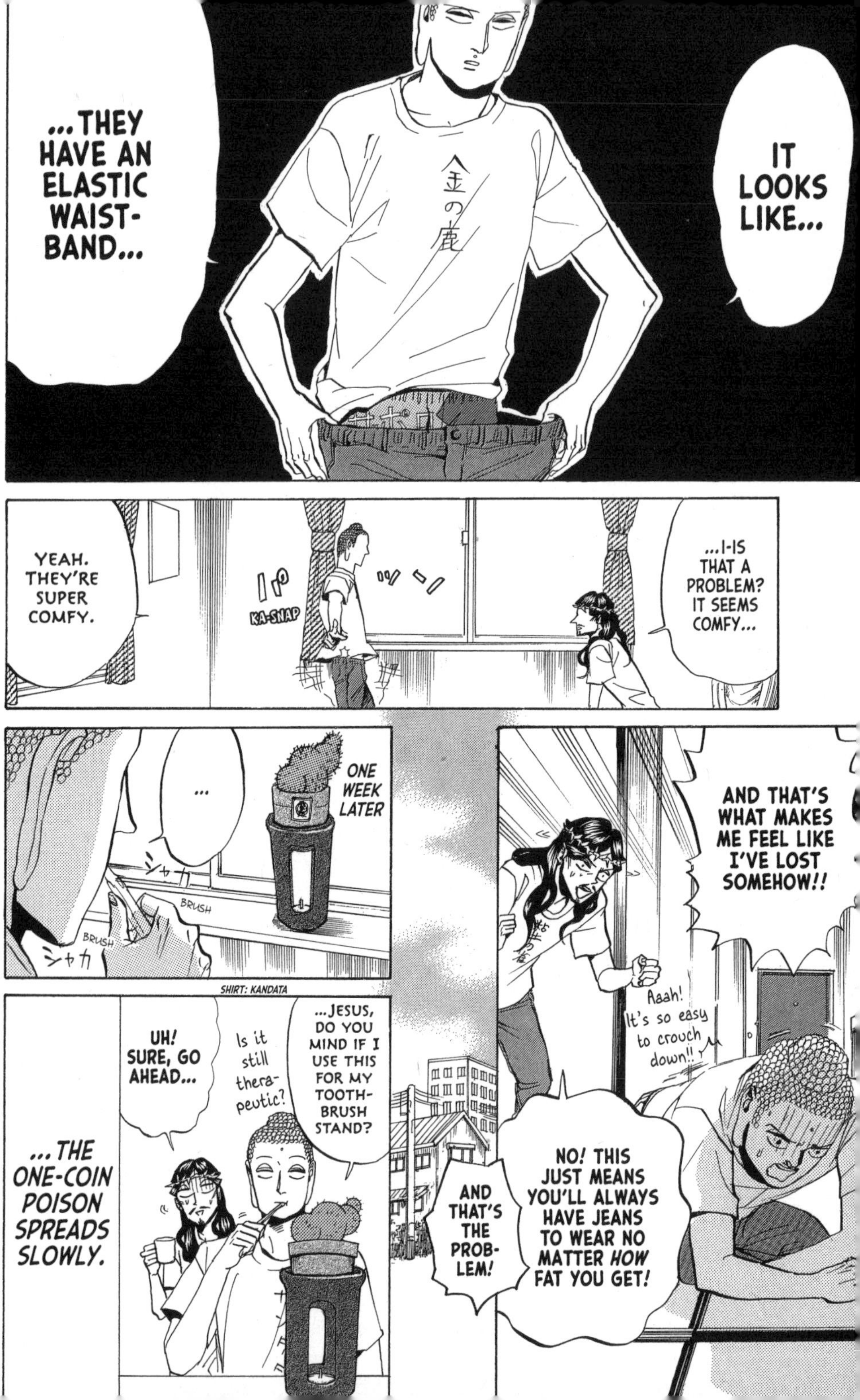
IT LOOKS LIKE...
...THEY HAVE AN ELASTIC WAIST-BAND...
...I-IS THAT A PROBLEM? IT SEEMS COMFY...
KA-SNAP
YEAH. THEY'RE SUPER COMFY.
AND THAT'S WHAT MAKES ME FEEL LIKE I'VE LOST SOMEHOW!!
Aaah! It's so easy to crouch down!!
NO! THIS JUST MEANS YOU'LL ALWAYS HAVE JEANS TO WEAR NO MATTER HOW FAT YOU GET!
AND THAT'S THE PROB-LEM!
ONE WEEK LATER
...
シャカ
BRUSH
BRUSH
シャカ
SHIRT: KANDATA
...JESUS, DO YOU MIND IF I USE THIS FOR MY TOOTH-BRUSH STAND?
Is it still thera-peutic?
UH! SURE, GO AHEAD...
...THE ONE-COIN POISON SPREADS SLOWLY.

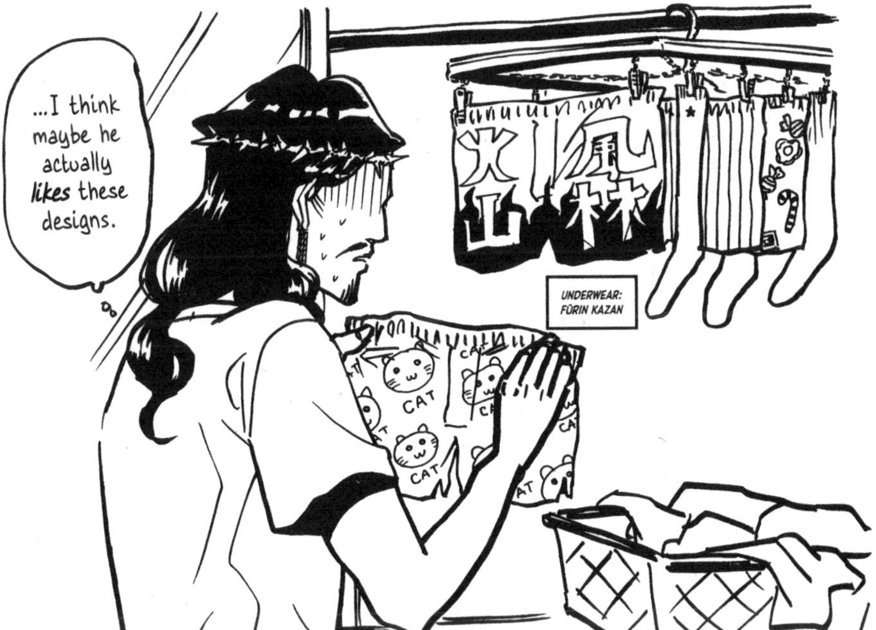
...I think maybe he actually *likes* these designs.
UNDERWEAR: FŪRIN KAZAN
CAT

CHAPTER 25 TRANSLATION NOTES

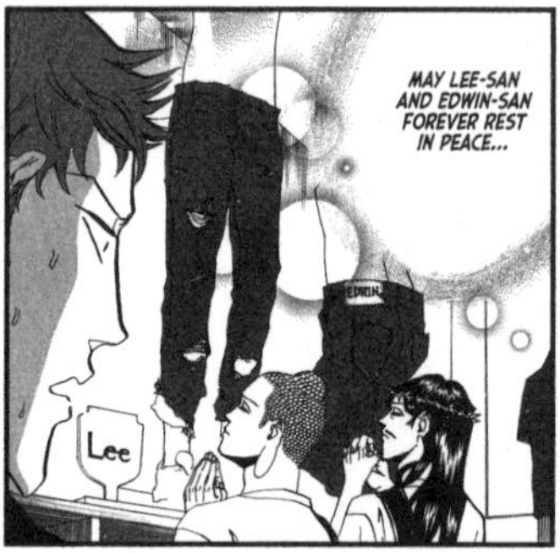
MAY LEE-SAN AND EDWIN-SAN FOREVER REST IN PEACE...
Lee

Lee and Edwin, page 194
Lee and Edwin are both clothing brands that focus mainly on jeans.

Dress You, My Child!, page 194
The Japanese title of this chapter is *Fuku Kitaru!*, which literally means "clothing comes!" However, the Japanese word for "clothing" is pronounced the same as the Japanese word for "blessings," and so the chapter title is a play on "blessings come!"

Clay Bird, page 195
There is an apocryphal account of Jesus as a child making birds out of clay and bringing them to life. There is also a mention in the Qur'an of Jesus forming birds out of clay and breathing life into them with God's permission.

Golden Deer, page 195
In a past life, the Buddha was born as a beautiful golden deer who rescued a man from drowning in a river. He asked only that the man not tell anyone about him, because he did not want to be hunted. But the king learned of a golden deer through the dreams of his wife, and determined to track the deer down, offering a very lavish reward to whoever helped him find the creature. The man who had been rescued by the deer was very poor, and the reward tempted him enough to break his promise and reveal the deer's home to the king. When the king found the deer, the deer told him of the man's promise, and king nearly punished the man instead of killing the deer. But the deer forgave the man and asked the king to have compassion, not only on the man and the deer, but on all creatures.

Yuzawaya, page 196
A craft and art supply store where many cosplayers go to buy fabric.

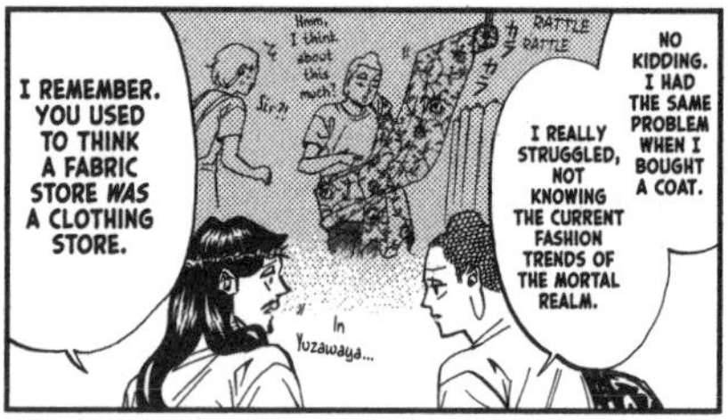
NO KIDDING. I HAD THE SAME PROBLEM WHEN I BOUGHT A COAT.
RATTLE RATTLE
I REALLY STRUGGLED, NOT KNOWING THE CURRENT FASHION TRENDS OF THE MORTAL REALM.
I REMEMBER. YOU USED TO THINK A FABRIC STORE *WAS* A CLOTHING STORE.
In Yuzawaya...

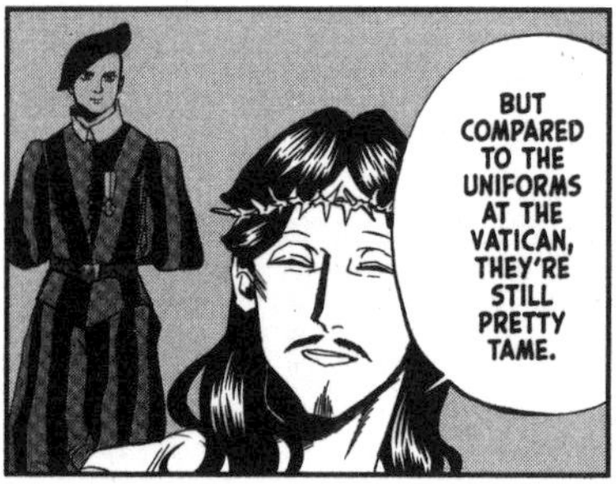
BUT COMPARED TO THE UNIFORMS AT THE VATICAN, THEY'RE STILL PRETTY TAME.

Papal Guard uniforms, page 197
The Papal Guard uniforms are blue, red, orange, and yellow in color. They were designed in the early 20th century and inspired by paintings of the Papal Guard from the Renaissance.

Nothing will ever convince me to wear clothes, page 198

In stories about the Buddha's previous lives, there is mention of a time when he went naked. After he gained enlightenment, he realized that nudity did not serve much purpose in helping one to change for the better, and forbade the practice among his followers.

Katsu, page 202

After Buddha performs a sequence of mudras (accompanied by the appropriate mantra syllable) to tie his tie, he finishes by shouting *katsu.* This word means "to yell" or "shout," and is often shouted by Zen masters at their students to encourage and guide them. It is also used in martial arts contexts to focus energy.

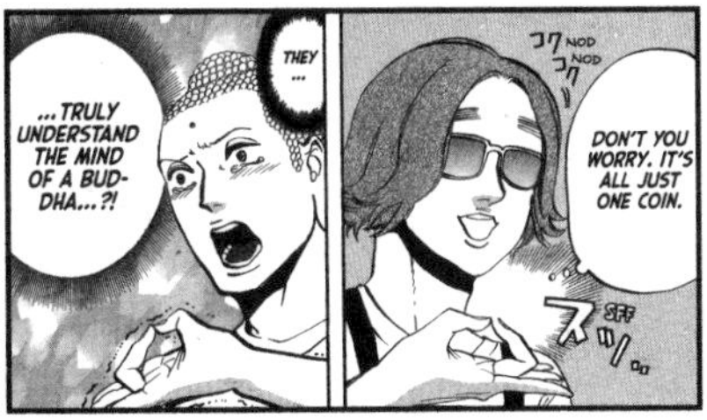
NOD NOD
DON'T YOU WORRY. IT'S ALL JUST ONE COIN.
SFF
THEY ...
...TRULY UNDERSTAND THE MIND OF A BUD-DHA...?!

One-Coin Mudra, page 206

The gesture used by this shop employee to tell Buddha that he really does only need one 100-yen coin to pay for everything resembles the Shuni Mudra, a gesture associated largely with yogic traditions, known as the mudra of patience. It as well is similar to the hand gesture in Japan used to ask how much something costs.

Since it's only 100 yen, page 207

Here, Buddha is forming another mudra with his hands. This one is the Vitarka Mudra, or the teaching mudra.

Fūrin Kazan, page 209

This a slogan used by the famous samurai Takeda Shingen. It means "wind, forest, fire, mountain," and is a reference to Sun Tzu's *The Art of War,* where he advises warriors to be swift as the wind, gentle as the forest, fierce as fire, and unshakable as the mountains.

SAINT☆YOUNG MEN

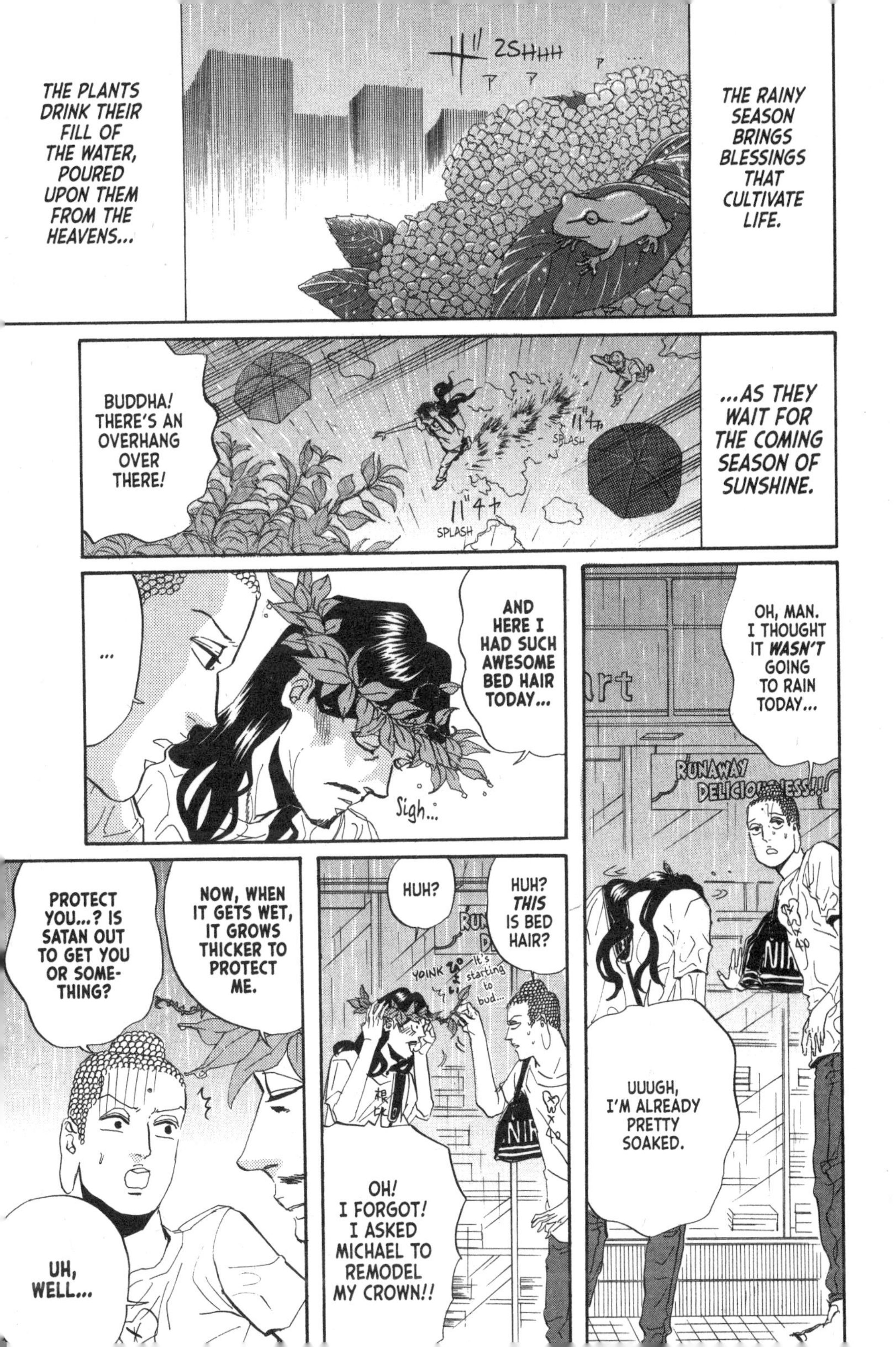
THE RAINY SEASON BRINGS BLESSINGS THAT CULTIVATE LIFE.
ZSHHH
THE PLANTS DRINK THEIR FILL OF THE WATER, POURED UPON THEM FROM THE HEAVENS...
...AS THEY WAIT FOR THE COMING SEASON OF SUNSHINE.
SPLASH
SPLASH
BUDDHA! THERE'S AN OVERHANG OVER THERE!
OH, MAN. I THOUGHT IT *WASN'T* GOING TO RAIN TODAY...
UUUGH, I'M ALREADY PRETTY SOAKED.
AND HERE I HAD SUCH AWESOME BED HAIR TODAY...
Sigh...
...
HUH? *THIS* IS BED HAIR?
HUH?
YOINK
It's starting to bud...
OH! I FORGOT! I ASKED MICHAEL TO REMODEL MY CROWN!!
NOW, WHEN IT GETS WET, IT GROWS THICKER TO PROTECT ME.
PROTECT YOU...? IS SATAN OUT TO GET YOU OR SOME-THING?
UH, WELL...

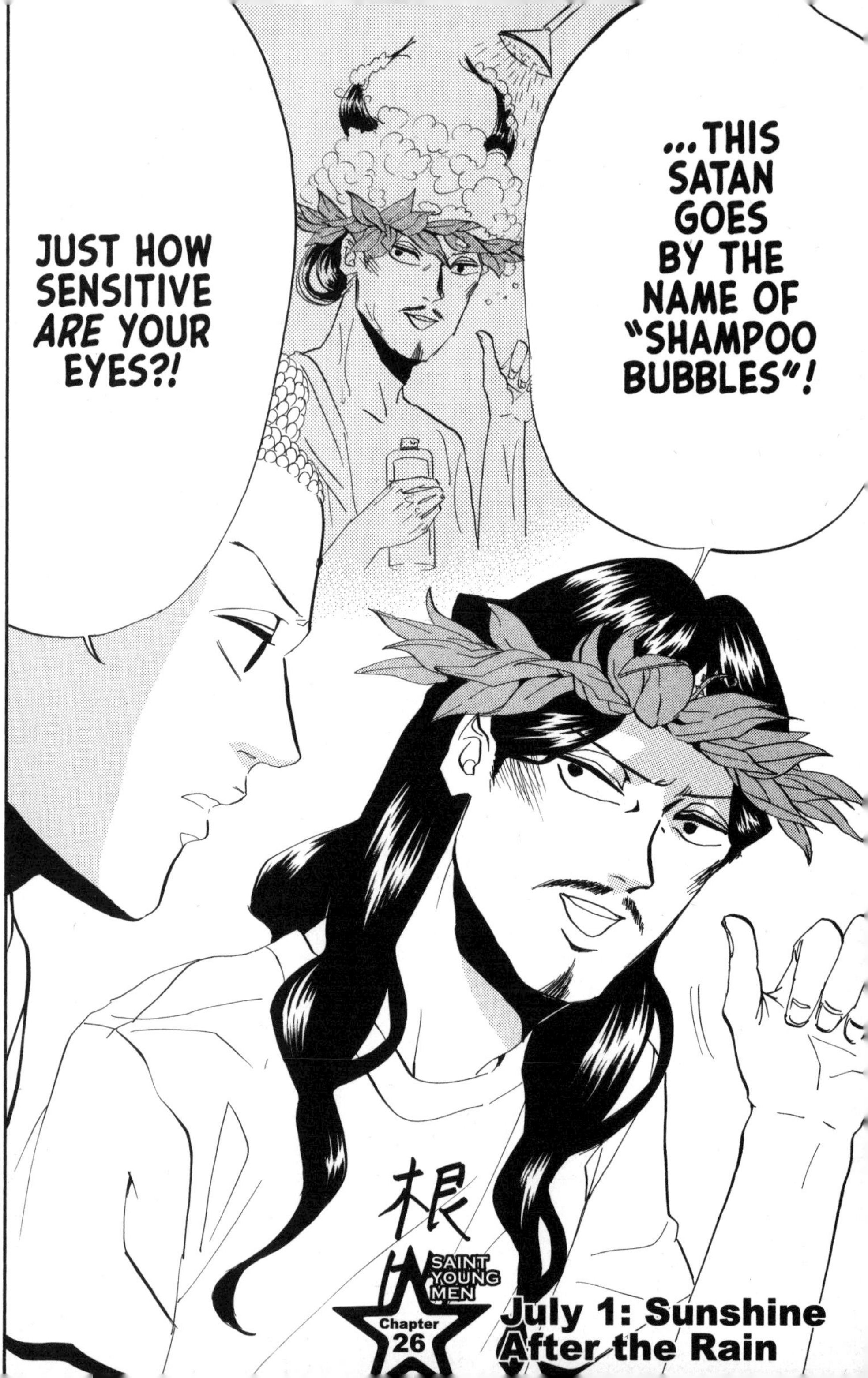
...THIS SATAN GOES BY THE NAME OF "SHAMPOO BUBBLES"!
JUST HOW SENSITIVE *ARE* YOUR EYES?!
根性
SAINT YOUNG MEN
Chapter 26
July 1: Sunshine After the Rain

SHIRT: BATTLE OF WILLS

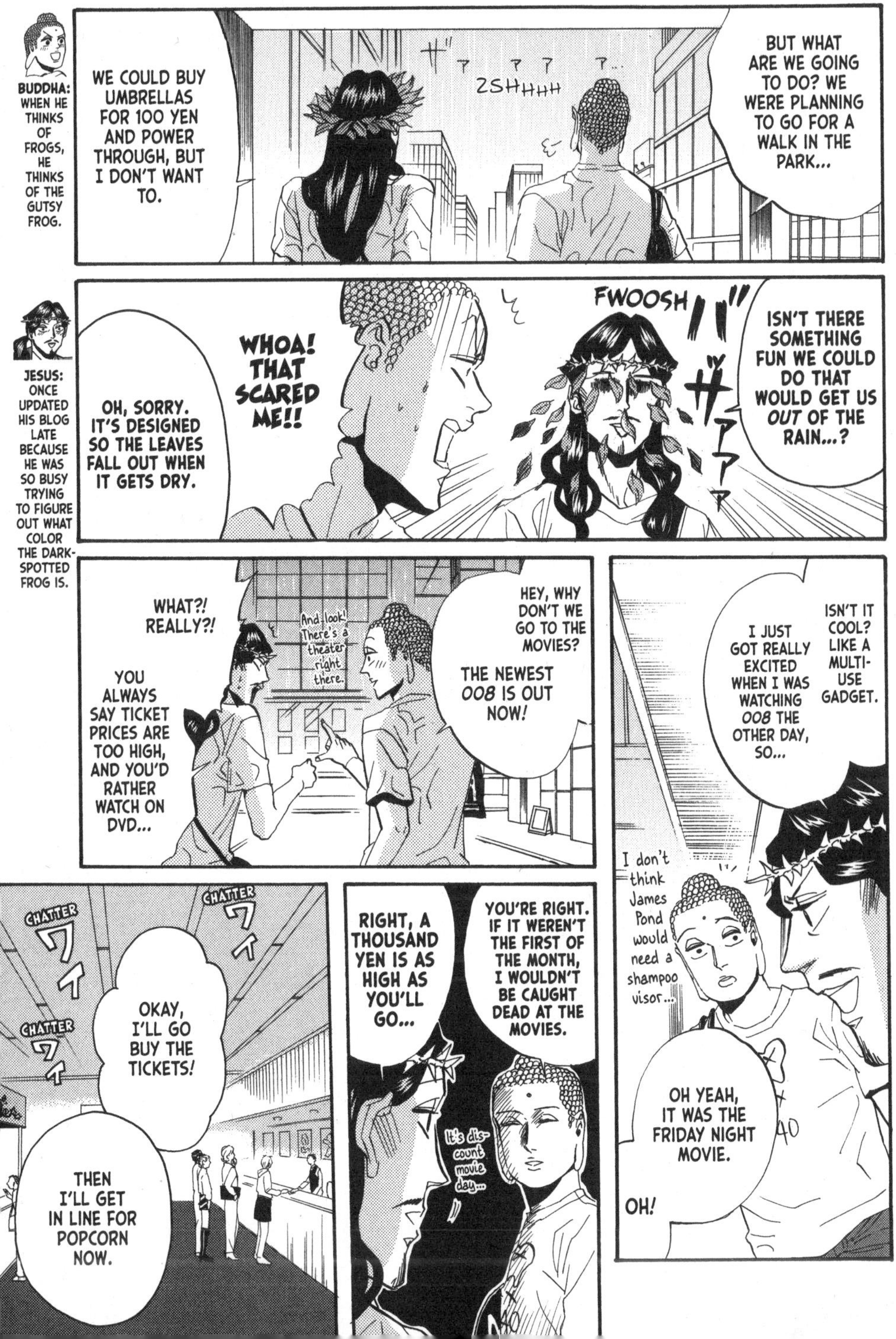
BUT WHAT ARE WE GOING TO DO? WE WERE PLANNING TO GO FOR A WALK IN THE PARK...
ZSHHHHH
WE COULD BUY UMBRELLAS FOR 100 YEN AND POWER THROUGH, BUT I DON'T WANT TO.
BUDDHA: WHEN HE THINKS OF FROGS, HE THINKS OF THE GUTSY FROG.
ISN'T THERE SOMETHING FUN WE COULD DO THAT WOULD GET US *OUT* OF THE RAIN...?
FWOOSH
WHOA! THAT SCARED ME!!
OH, SORRY. IT'S DESIGNED SO THE LEAVES FALL OUT WHEN IT GETS DRY.
JESUS: ONCE UPDATED HIS BLOG LATE BECAUSE HE WAS SO BUSY TRYING TO FIGURE OUT WHAT COLOR THE DARK-SPOTTED FROG IS.
ISN'T IT COOL? LIKE A MULTI-USE GADGET.
I JUST GOT REALLY EXCITED WHEN I WAS WATCHING *008* THE OTHER DAY, SO...
I don't think James Pond would need a shampoo visor...
OH!
OH YEAH, IT WAS THE FRIDAY NIGHT MOVIE.
HEY, WHY DON'T WE GO TO THE MOVIES?
THE NEWEST *008* IS OUT NOW!
And look! There's a theater right there.
WHAT?! REALLY?!
YOU ALWAYS SAY TICKET PRICES ARE TOO HIGH, AND YOU'D RATHER WATCH ON DVD...
YOU'RE RIGHT. IF IT WEREN'T THE FIRST OF THE MONTH, I WOULDN'T BE CAUGHT DEAD AT THE MOVIES.
RIGHT, A THOUSAND YEN IS AS HIGH AS YOU'LL GO...
It's discount movie day...
CHATTER
CHATTER
OKAY, I'LL GO BUY THE TICKETS!
THEN I'LL GET IN LINE FOR POPCORN NOW.

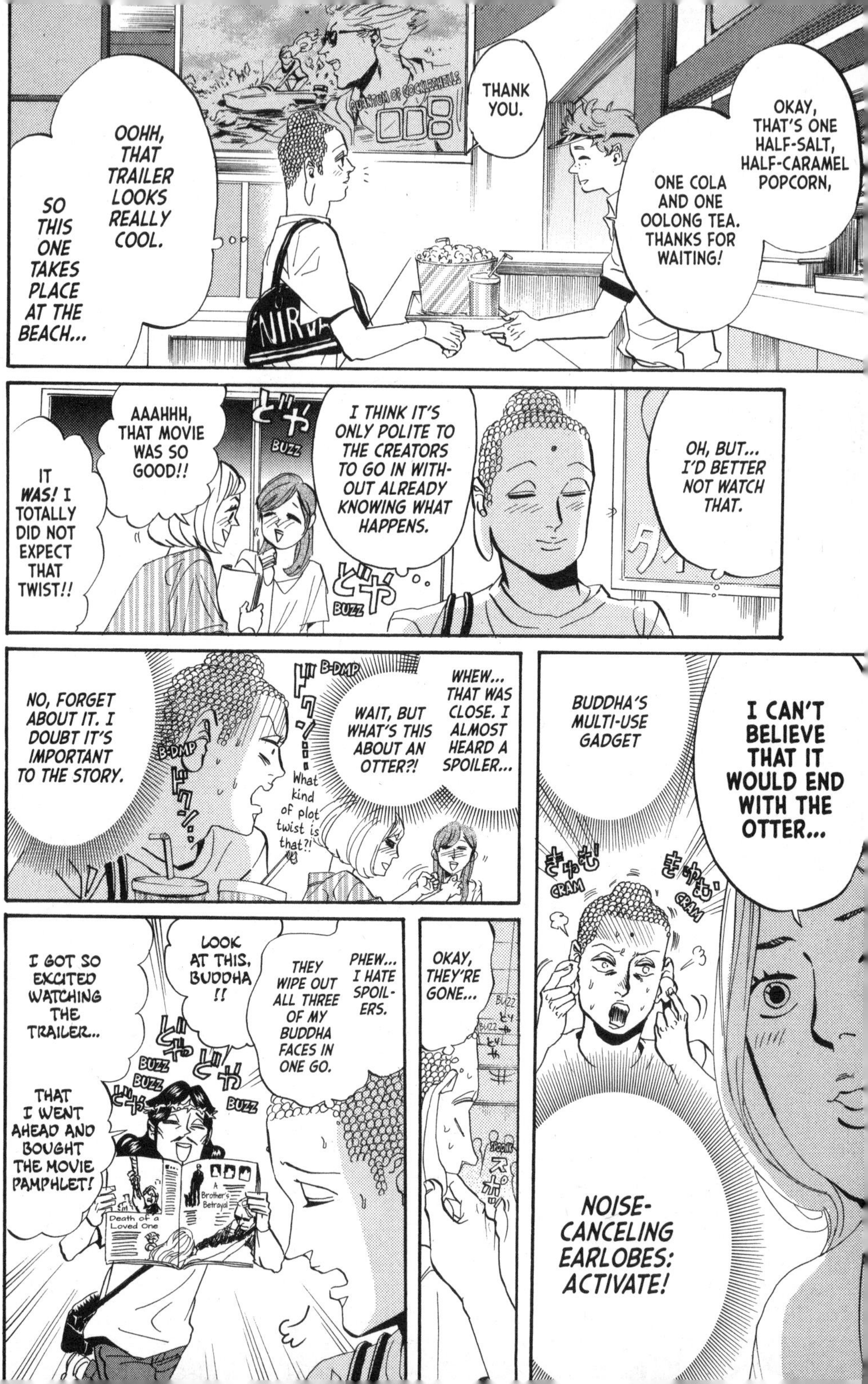
OKAY, THAT'S ONE HALF-SALT, HALF-CARAMEL POPCORN,
ONE COLA AND ONE OOLONG TEA. THANKS FOR WAITING!
THANK YOU.
QUANTUM OF COCKLESHELLS
008
OOHH, THAT TRAILER LOOKS REALLY COOL.
SO THIS ONE TAKES PLACE AT THE BEACH...
OH, BUT... I'D BETTER NOT WATCH THAT.
I THINK IT'S ONLY POLITE TO THE CREATORS TO GO IN WITH-OUT ALREADY KNOWING WHAT HAPPENS.
BUZZ
AAAHHH, THAT MOVIE WAS SO GOOD!!
IT WAS! I TOTALLY DID NOT EXPECT THAT TWIST!!
BUZZ
I CAN'T BELIEVE THAT IT WOULD END WITH THE OTTER...
BUDDHA'S MULTI-USE GADGET
CRAM
CRAM
NOISE-CANCELING EARLOBES: ACTIVATE!
WHEW... THAT WAS CLOSE. I ALMOST HEARD A SPOILER...
WAIT, BUT WHAT'S THIS ABOUT AN OTTER?!
B-DMP
B-DMP
What kind of plot twist is that?!
NO, FORGET ABOUT IT. I DOUBT IT'S IMPORTANT TO THE STORY.
OKAY, THEY'RE GONE...
BUZZ
BUZZ
SPOINK
PHEW... I HATE SPOIL-ERS.
THEY WIPE OUT ALL THREE OF MY BUDDHA FACES IN ONE GO.
LOOK AT THIS, BUDDHA!!
BUZZ
BUZZ
BUZZ
I GOT SO EXCITED WATCHING THE TRAILER..
THAT I WENT AHEAD AND BOUGHT THE MOVIE PAMPHLET!
A Brother's Betrayal
Death of a Loved One

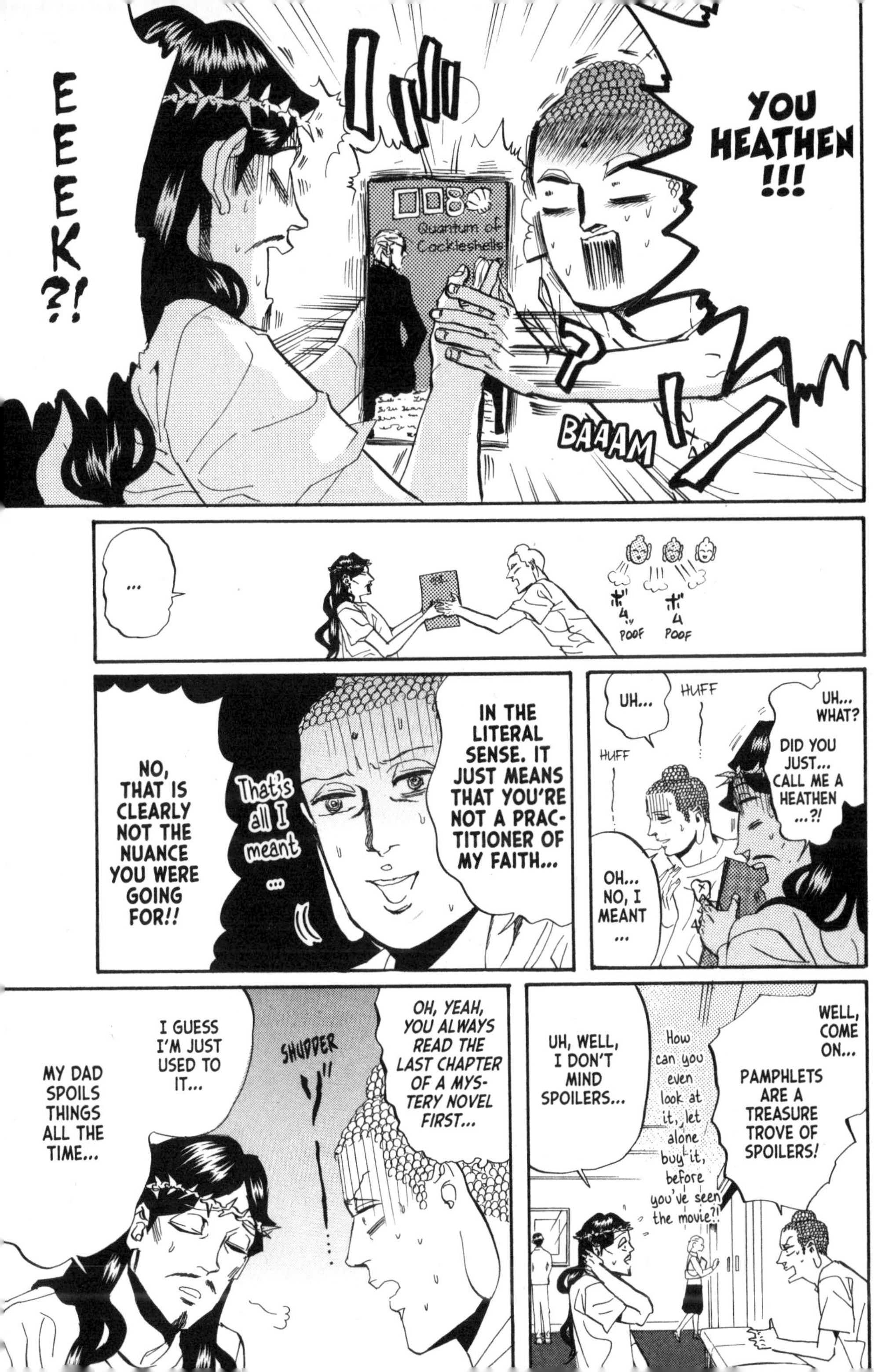
YOU HEATHEN!!!
008
Quantum of Cockleshells
BAAAM
EEEEK?!
POOF
POOF
...
UH... WHAT?
DID YOU JUST... CALL ME A HEATHEN ...?!
HUFF
UH...
HUFF
OH... NO, I MEANT ...
IN THE LITERAL SENSE. IT JUST MEANS THAT YOU'RE NOT A PRACTITIONER OF MY FAITH...
That's all I meant ...
NO, THAT IS CLEARLY NOT THE NUANCE YOU WERE GOING FOR!!
WELL, COME ON...
PAMPHLETS ARE A TREASURE TROVE OF SPOILERS!
How can you even look at it, let alone buy it, before you've seen the movie?!
UH, WELL, I DON'T MIND SPOILERS...
OH, YEAH, YOU ALWAYS READ THE LAST CHAPTER OF A MYSTERY NOVEL FIRST...
SHUDDER
I GUESS I'M JUST USED TO IT...
MY DAD SPOILS THINGS ALL THE TIME...

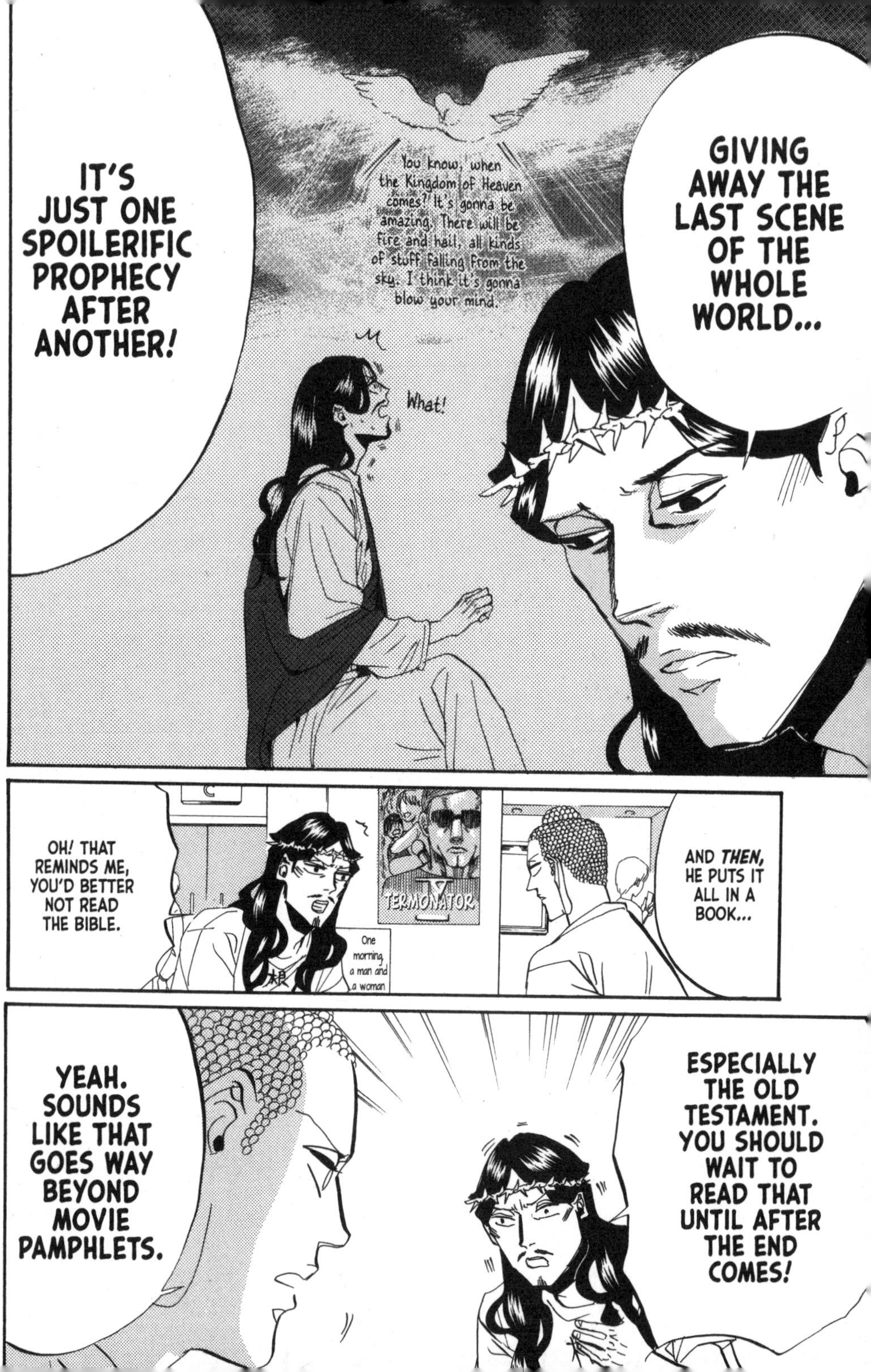
GIVING AWAY THE LAST SCENE OF THE WHOLE WORLD...
You know, when the Kingdom of Heaven comes? It's gonna be amazing. There will be fire and hail, all kinds of stuff falling from the sky. I think it's gonna blow your mind.
What!
IT'S JUST ONE SPOILERIFIC PROPHECY AFTER ANOTHER!
AND *THEN*, HE PUTS IT ALL IN A BOOK...
TERMONATOR
One morning, a man and a woman
OH! THAT REMINDS ME, YOU'D BETTER NOT READ THE BIBLE.
ESPECIALLY THE OLD TESTAMENT. YOU SHOULD WAIT TO READ THAT UNTIL AFTER THE END COMES!
YEAH. SOUNDS LIKE THAT GOES WAY BEYOND MOVIE PAMPHLETS.

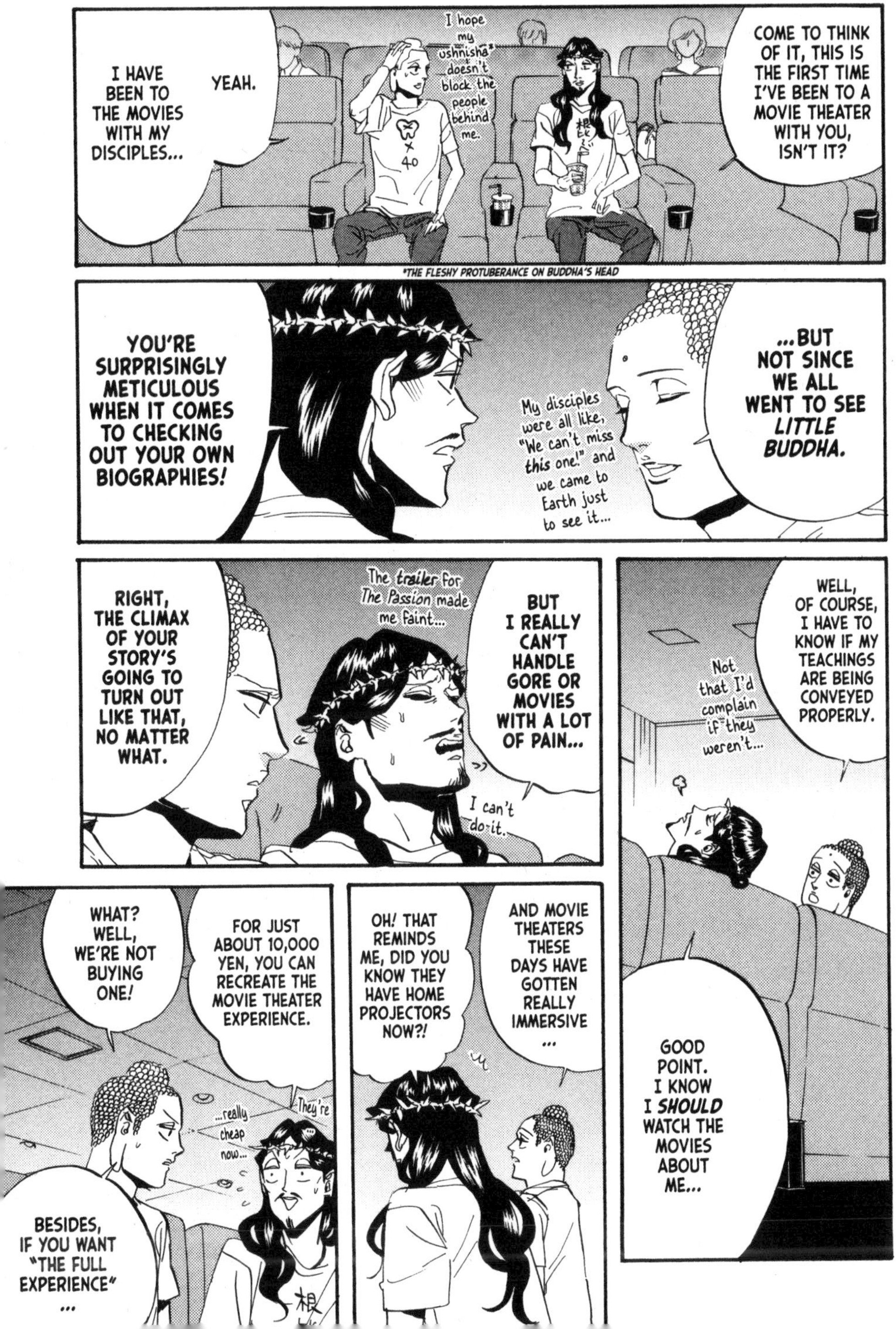
COME TO THINK OF IT, THIS IS THE FIRST TIME I'VE BEEN TO A MOVIE THEATER WITH YOU, ISN'T IT?
I hope my ushnisha* doesn't block the people behind me.
YEAH.
I HAVE BEEN TO THE MOVIES WITH MY DISCIPLES...
*THE FLESHY PROTUBERANCE ON BUDDHA'S HEAD
...BUT NOT SINCE WE ALL WENT TO SEE *LITTLE BUDDHA.*
My disciples were all like, "We can't miss *this* one!" and we came to Earth just to see it...
YOU'RE SURPRISINGLY METICULOUS WHEN IT COMES TO CHECKING OUT YOUR OWN BIOGRAPHIES!
WELL, OF COURSE, I HAVE TO KNOW IF MY TEACHINGS ARE BEING CONVEYED PROPERLY.
Not that I'd complain if they weren't...
GOOD POINT. I KNOW I *SHOULD* WATCH THE MOVIES ABOUT ME...
BUT I REALLY CAN'T HANDLE GORE OR MOVIES WITH A LOT OF PAIN...
I can't do it.
The *trailer* for The Passion made me faint...
RIGHT, THE CLIMAX OF YOUR STORY'S GOING TO TURN OUT LIKE THAT, NO MATTER WHAT.
AND MOVIE THEATERS THESE DAYS HAVE GOTTEN REALLY IMMERSIVE...
OH! THAT REMINDS ME, DID YOU KNOW THEY HAVE HOME PROJECTORS NOW?!
FOR JUST ABOUT 10,000 YEN, YOU CAN RECREATE THE MOVIE THEATER EXPERIENCE.
WHAT? WELL, WE'RE NOT BUYING ONE!
They're ...really cheap now...
BESIDES, IF YOU WANT "THE FULL EXPERIENCE"...

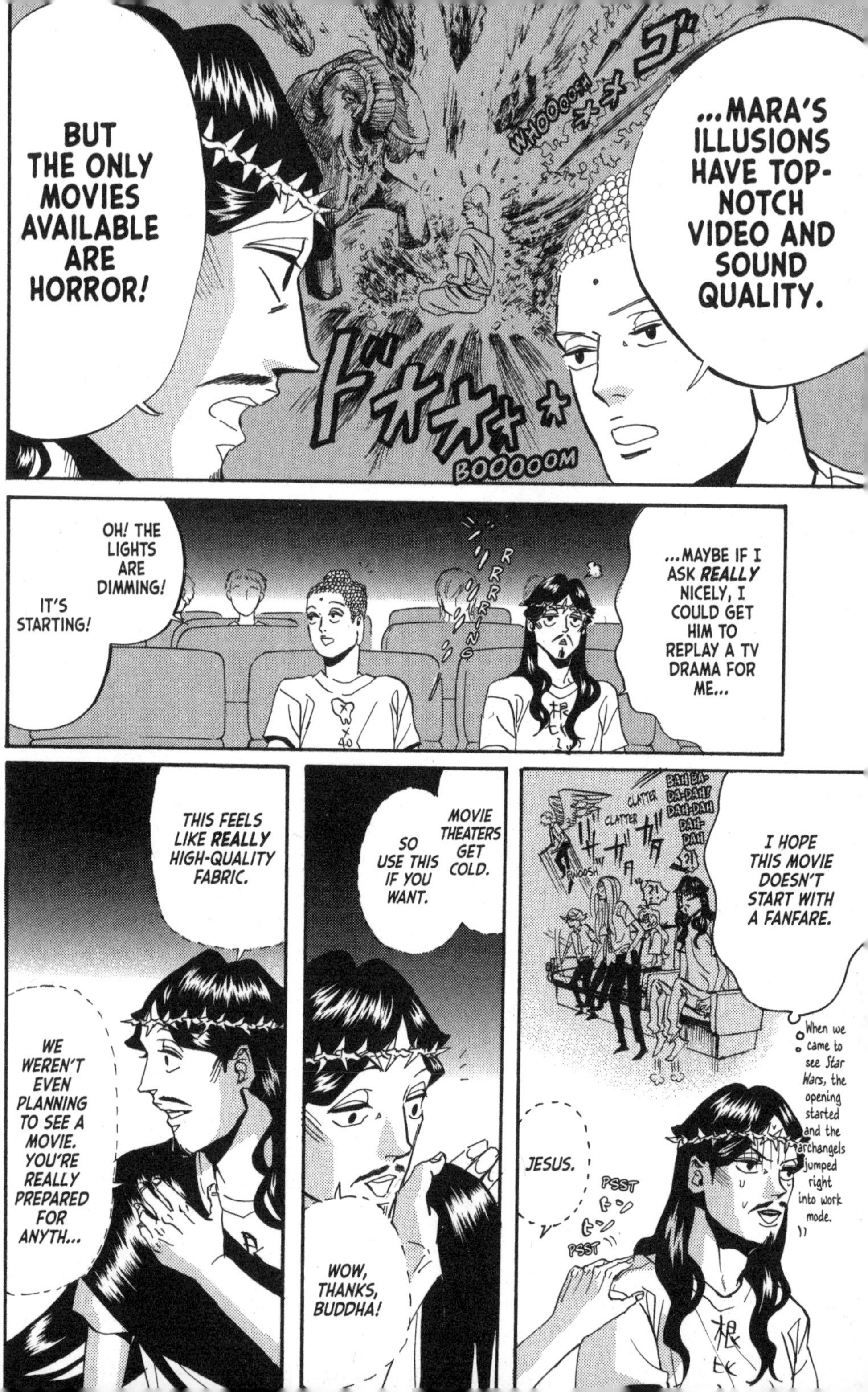
...MARA'S ILLUSIONS HAVE TOP-NOTCH VIDEO AND SOUND QUALITY.
WHOOOOSH
BUT THE ONLY MOVIES AVAILABLE ARE HORROR!
BOOOOOM
...MAYBE IF I ASK REALLY NICELY, I COULD GET HIM TO REPLAY A TV DRAMA FOR ME...
RRRRING
OH! THE LIGHTS ARE DIMMING!
IT'S STARTING!
I HOPE THIS MOVIE DOESN'T START WITH A FANFARE.
BAH BA-DAH! DAH-DAH DAH-DAH
CLATTER
CLATTER
WHOOSH
When we came to see Star Wars, the opening started and the archangels jumped right into work mode.
JESUS.
PSST
PSST
MOVIE THEATERS GET COLD.
SO USE THIS IF YOU WANT.
WOW, THANKS, BUDDHA!
THIS FEELS LIKE REALLY HIGH-QUALITY FABRIC.
WE WEREN'T EVEN PLANNING TO SEE A MOVIE. YOU'RE REALLY PREPARED FOR ANYTH...

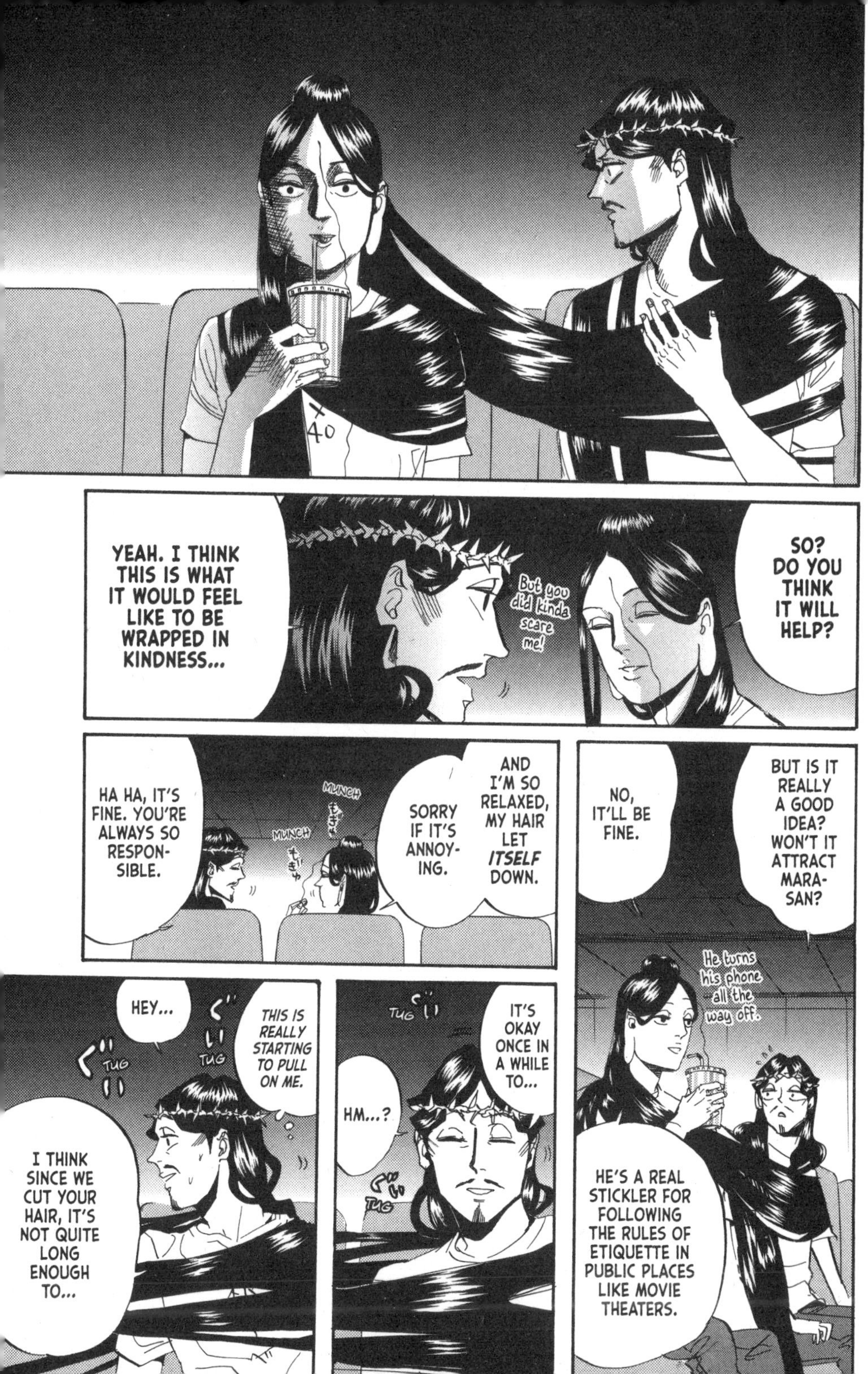
SO? DO YOU THINK IT WILL HELP?
But you did kinda scare me!
YEAH. I THINK THIS IS WHAT IT WOULD FEEL LIKE TO BE WRAPPED IN KINDNESS...
BUT IS IT REALLY A GOOD IDEA? WON'T IT ATTRACT MARA-SAN?
NO, IT'LL BE FINE.
He turns his phone all the way off.
HE'S A REAL STICKLER FOR FOLLOWING THE RULES OF ETIQUETTE IN PUBLIC PLACES LIKE MOVIE THEATERS.
AND I'M SO RELAXED, MY HAIR LET *ITSELF* DOWN.
SORRY IF IT'S ANNOYING.
MUNCH
MUNCH
HA HA, IT'S FINE. YOU'RE ALWAYS SO RESPONSIBLE.
IT'S OKAY ONCE IN A WHILE TO...
TUG
HM...?
TUG
THIS IS REALLY STARTING TO PULL ON ME.
TUG
HEY...
TUG
I THINK SINCE WE CUT YOUR HAIR, IT'S NOT QUITE LONG ENOUGH TO...

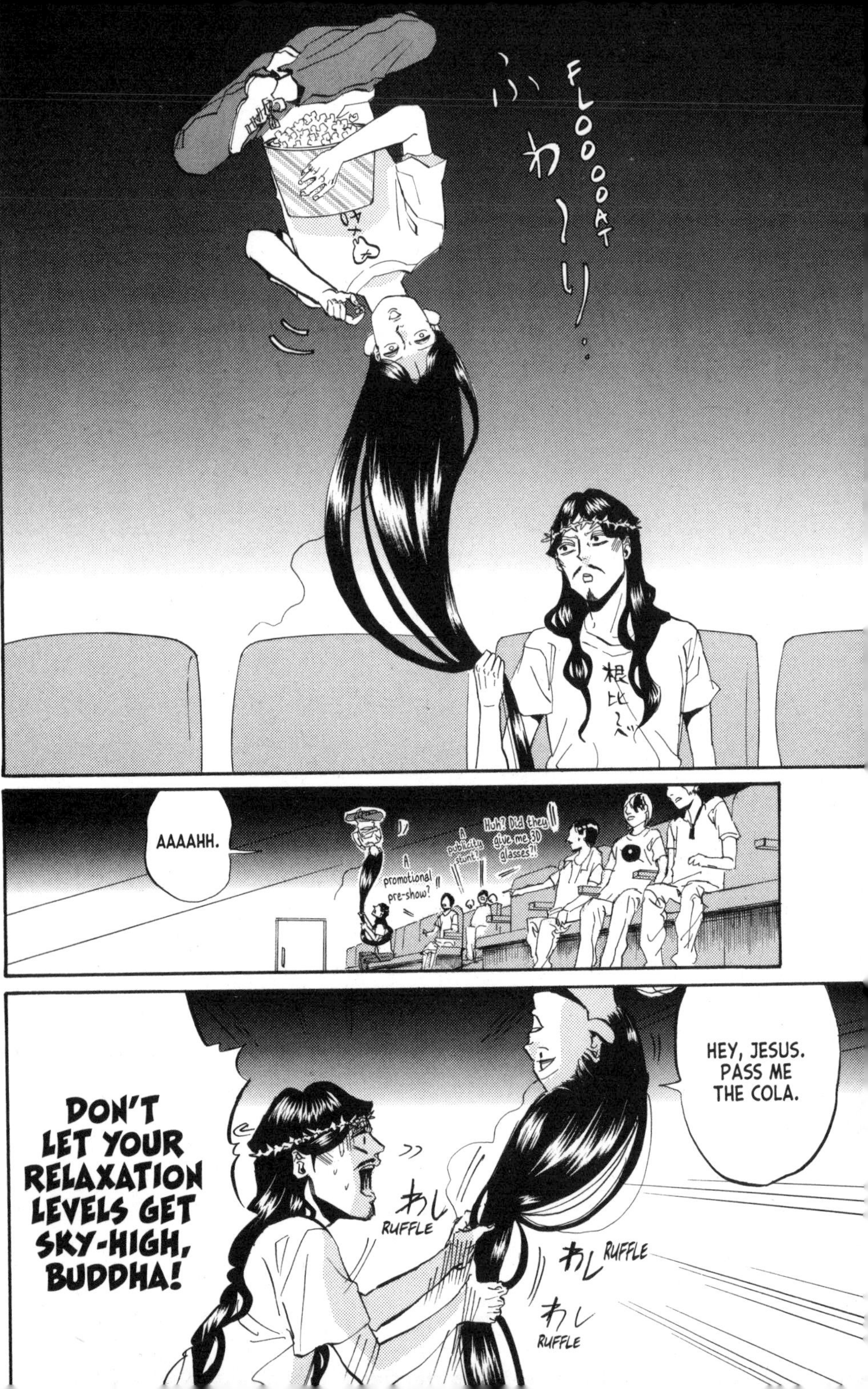
FLOOOOAT
ふわ〜り..
Huh? Did they give me 3D glasses?!
A publicity stunt?
A promotional pre-show?
AAAAHH.
HEY, JESUS. PASS ME THE COLA.
DON'T LET YOUR RELAXATION LEVELS GET SKY-HIGH, BUDDHA!
わし RUFFLE
わし RUFFLE
わし RUFFLE

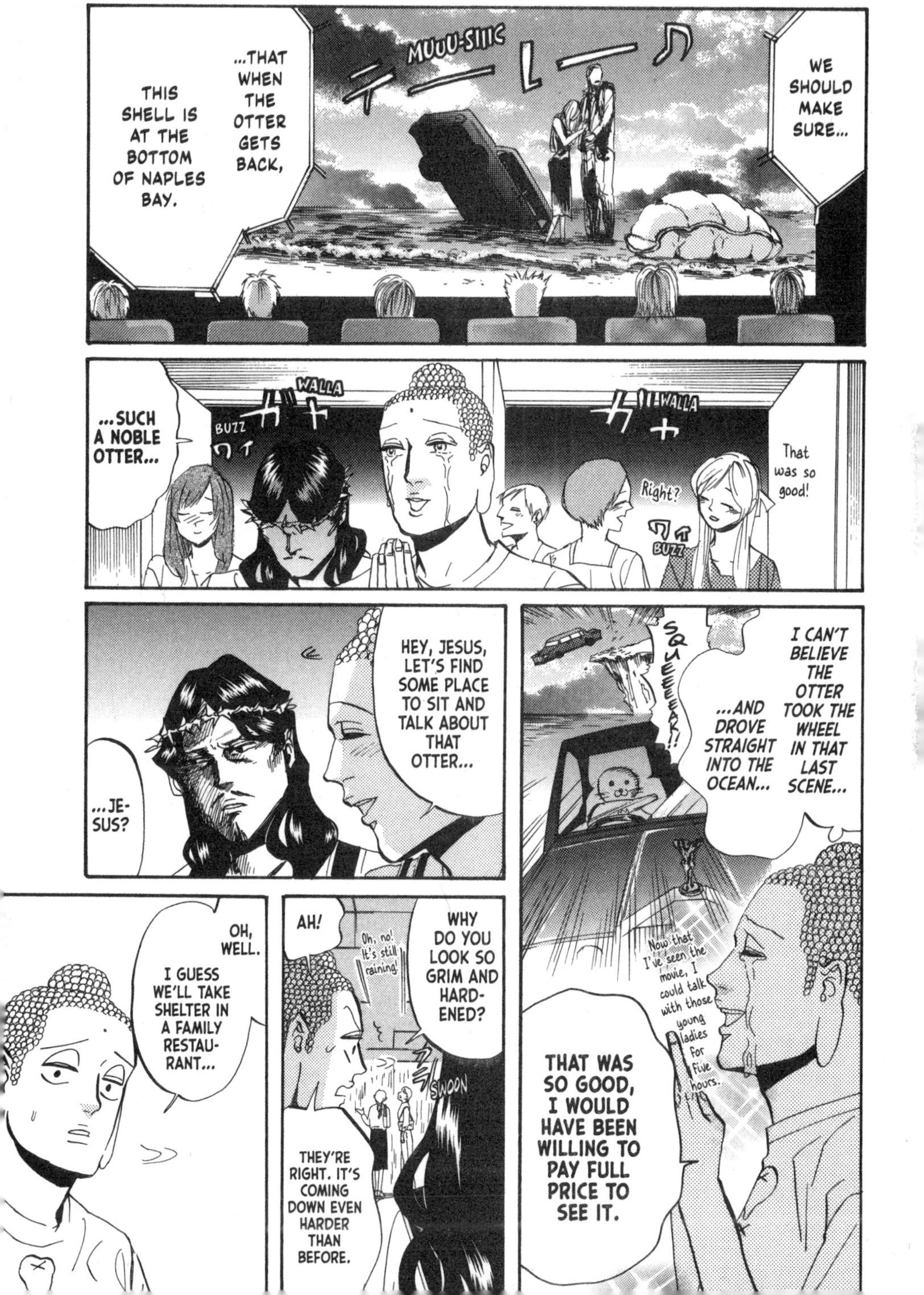
MUUU-SIIIC
WE SHOULD MAKE SURE...
...THAT WHEN THE OTTER GETS BACK,
THIS SHELL IS AT THE BOTTOM OF NAPLES BAY.
WALLA
That was so good!
Right?
BUZZ
WALLA
BUZZ
...SUCH A NOBLE OTTER...
I CAN'T BELIEVE THE OTTER TOOK THE WHEEL IN THAT LAST SCENE...
...AND DROVE STRAIGHT INTO THE OCEAN...
SQUEEEEAK!!
Now that I've seen the movie, I could talk with those young ladies for five hours.
THAT WAS SO GOOD, I WOULD HAVE BEEN WILLING TO PAY FULL PRICE TO SEE IT.
HEY, JESUS, LET'S FIND SOME PLACE TO SIT AND TALK ABOUT THAT OTTER...
...JE-SUS?
WHY DO YOU LOOK SO GRIM AND HARD-ENED?
AH!
Oh, no! It's still raining!
SWOON
THEY'RE RIGHT. IT'S COMING DOWN EVEN HARDER THAN BEFORE.
OH, WELL.
I GUESS WE'LL TAKE SHELTER IN A FAMILY RESTAU-RANT...

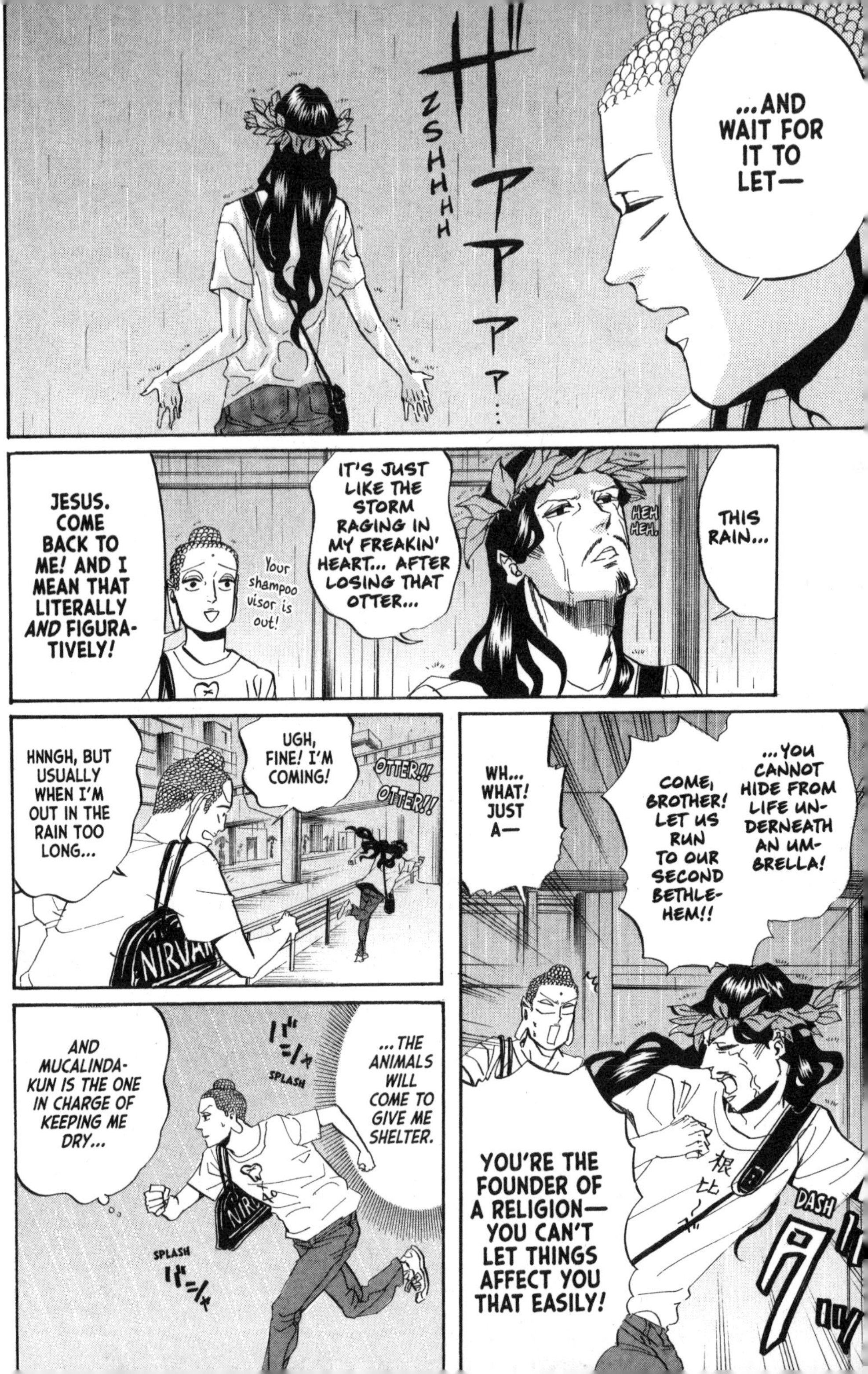
...AND WAIT FOR IT TO LET—
ザァァァ…
ZSHHHH
THIS RAIN...
HEH HEH.
IT'S JUST LIKE THE STORM RAGING IN MY FREAKIN' HEART... AFTER LOSING THAT OTTER...
Your shampoo visor is out!
JESUS. COME BACK TO ME! AND I MEAN THAT LITERALLY *AND* FIGURATIVELY!
...YOU CANNOT HIDE FROM LIFE UNDERNEATH AN UMBRELLA!
COME, BROTHER! LET US RUN TO OUR SECOND BETHLEHEM!!
WH... WHAT! JUST A—
YOU'RE THE FOUNDER OF A RELIGION— YOU CAN'T LET THINGS AFFECT YOU THAT EASILY!
DASH
UGH, FINE! I'M COMING!
OTTER!!
OTTER!!
HNNGH, BUT USUALLY WHEN I'M OUT IN THE RAIN TOO LONG...
...THE ANIMALS WILL COME TO GIVE ME SHELTER.
SPLASH
AND MUCALINDA-KUN IS THE ONE IN CHARGE OF KEEPING ME DRY...
SPLASH

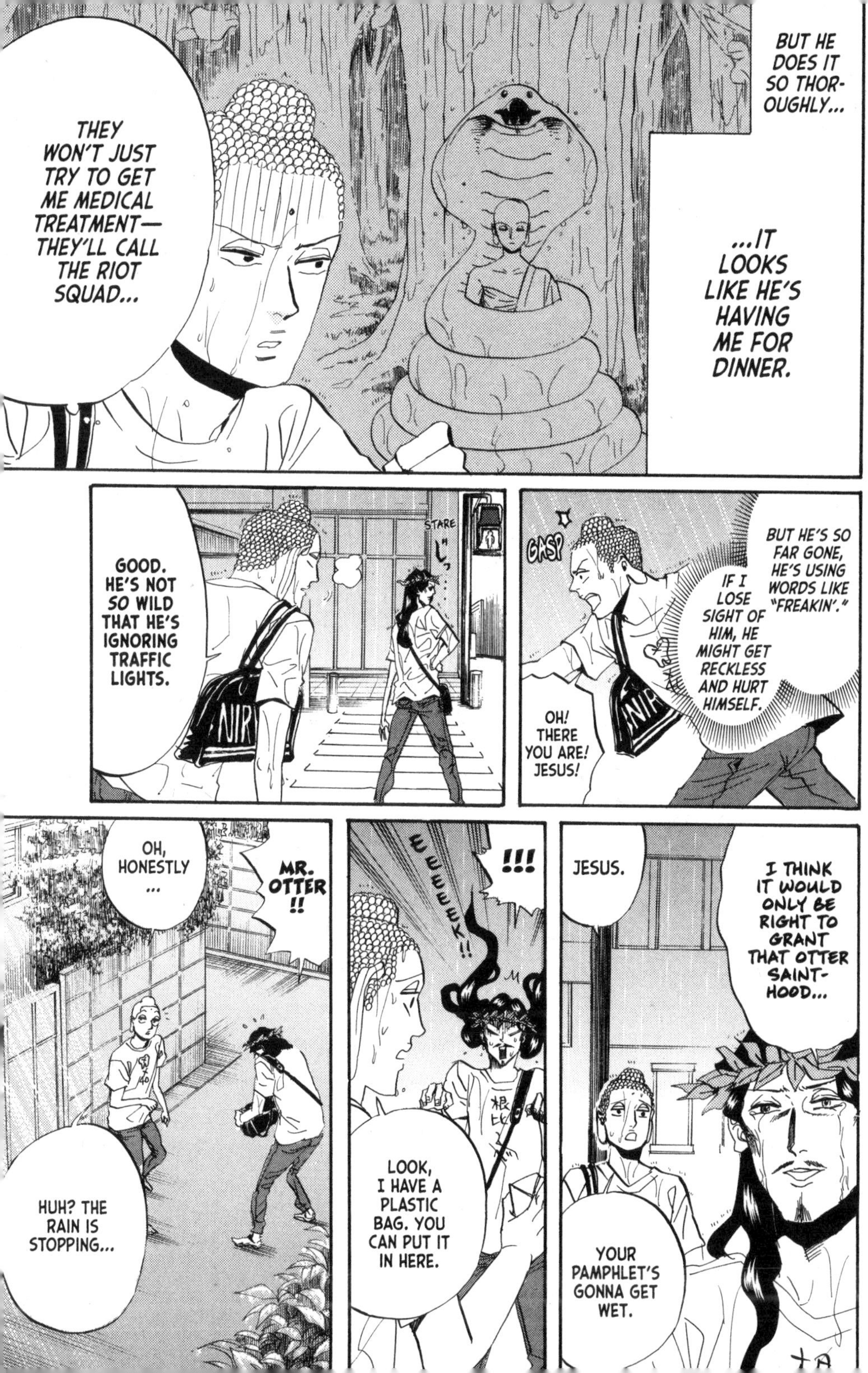

BUT HE DOES IT SO THOROUGHLY...
...IT LOOKS LIKE HE'S HAVING ME FOR DINNER.
THEY WON'T JUST TRY TO GET ME MEDICAL TREATMENT—THEY'LL CALL THE RIOT SQUAD...
GASP
BUT HE'S SO FAR GONE, HE'S USING WORDS LIKE "FREAKIN'."
IF I LOSE SIGHT OF HIM, HE MIGHT GET RECKLESS AND HURT HIMSELF.
OH! THERE YOU ARE! JESUS!
STARE
GOOD. HE'S NOT SO WILD THAT HE'S IGNORING TRAFFIC LIGHTS.
I THINK IT WOULD ONLY BE RIGHT TO GRANT THAT OTTER SAINTHOOD...
JESUS.
YOUR PAMPHLET'S GONNA GET WET.
!!!
EEEEEEK!!
LOOK, I HAVE A PLASTIC BAG. YOU CAN PUT IT IN HERE.
MR. OTTER!!
OH, HONESTLY...
HUH? THE RAIN IS STOPPING...

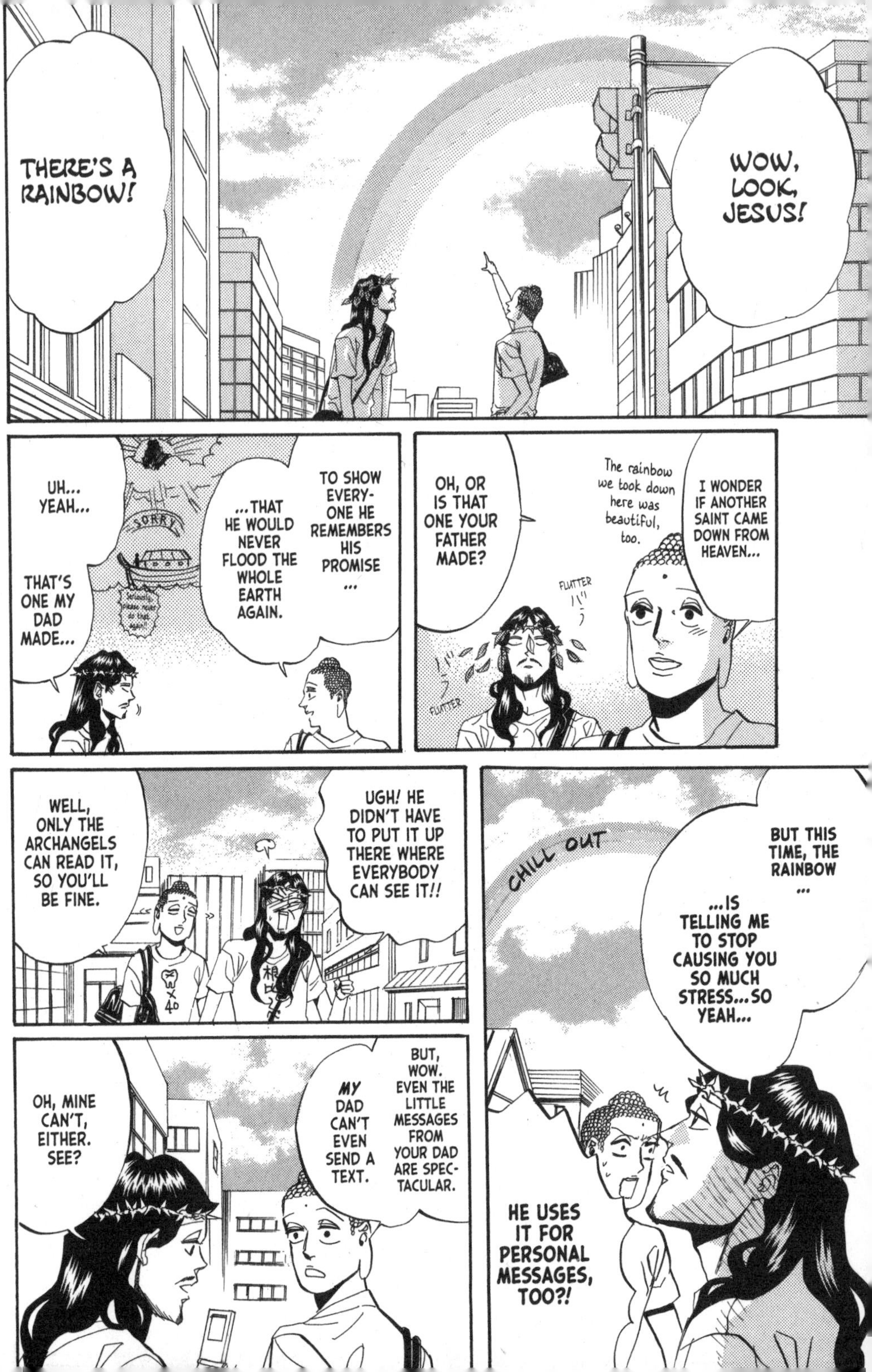
WOW, LOOK, JESUS!
THERE'S A RAINBOW!
I WONDER IF ANOTHER SAINT CAME DOWN FROM HEAVEN...
The rainbow we took down here was beautiful, too.
FLUTTER
FLUTTER
OH, OR IS THAT ONE YOUR FATHER MADE?
TO SHOW EVERY-ONE HE REMEMBERS HIS PROMISE...
...THAT HE WOULD NEVER FLOOD THE WHOLE EARTH AGAIN.
SORRY
UH... YEAH...
THAT'S ONE MY DAD MADE...
BUT THIS TIME, THE RAINBOW...
...IS TELLING ME TO STOP CAUSING YOU SO MUCH STRESS...SO YEAH...
CHILL OUT
HE USES IT FOR PERSONAL MESSAGES, TOO?!
UGH! HE DIDN'T HAVE TO PUT IT UP THERE WHERE EVERYBODY CAN SEE IT!!
WELL, ONLY THE ARCHANGELS CAN READ IT, SO YOU'LL BE FINE.
BUT, WOW. EVEN THE LITTLE MESSAGES FROM YOUR DAD ARE SPEC-TACULAR.
MY DAD CAN'T EVEN SEND A TEXT.
OH, MINE CAN'T, EITHER. SEE?

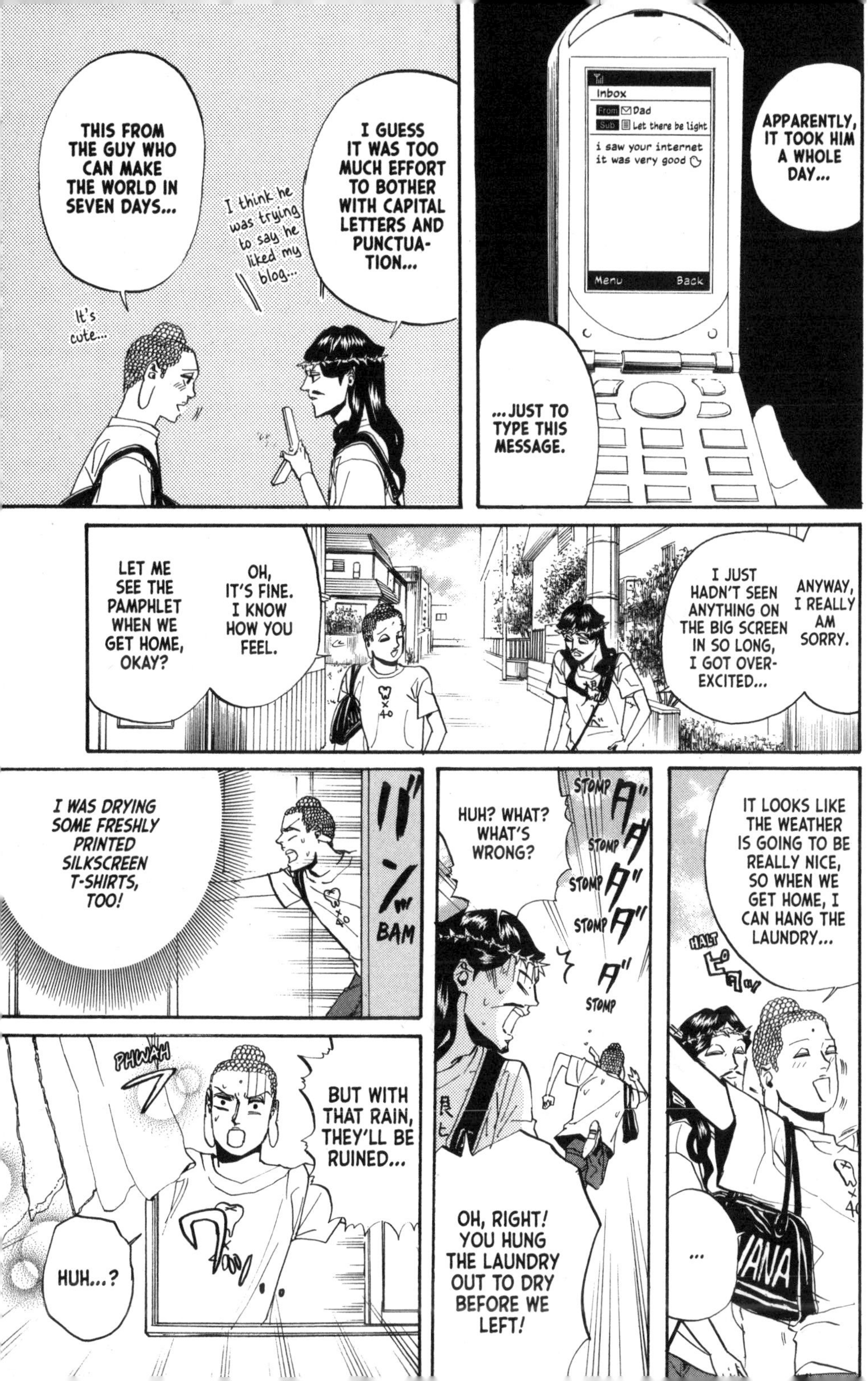
Inbox
From Dad
Sub Let there be light
i saw your internet
it was very good
Menu
Back
APPARENTLY, IT TOOK HIM A WHOLE DAY...
...JUST TO TYPE THIS MESSAGE.
I GUESS IT WAS TOO MUCH EFFORT TO BOTHER WITH CAPITAL LETTERS AND PUNCTUATION...
I think he was trying to say he liked my blog...
THIS FROM THE GUY WHO CAN MAKE THE WORLD IN SEVEN DAYS...
It's cute...
ANYWAY, I REALLY AM SORRY.
I JUST HADN'T SEEN ANYTHING ON THE BIG SCREEN IN SO LONG, I GOT OVER-EXCITED...
OH, IT'S FINE. I KNOW HOW YOU FEEL.
LET ME SEE THE PAMPHLET WHEN WE GET HOME, OKAY?
IT LOOKS LIKE THE WEATHER IS GOING TO BE REALLY NICE, SO WHEN WE GET HOME, I CAN HANG THE LAUNDRY...
HALT
...
STOMP
STOMP
STOMP
STOMP
STOMP
HUH? WHAT? WHAT'S WRONG?
OH, RIGHT! YOU HUNG THE LAUNDRY OUT TO DRY BEFORE WE LEFT!
BAM
I WAS DRYING SOME FRESHLY PRINTED SILKSCREEN T-SHIRTS, TOO!
PHWAH
BUT WITH THAT RAIN, THEY'LL BE RUINED...
HUH...?

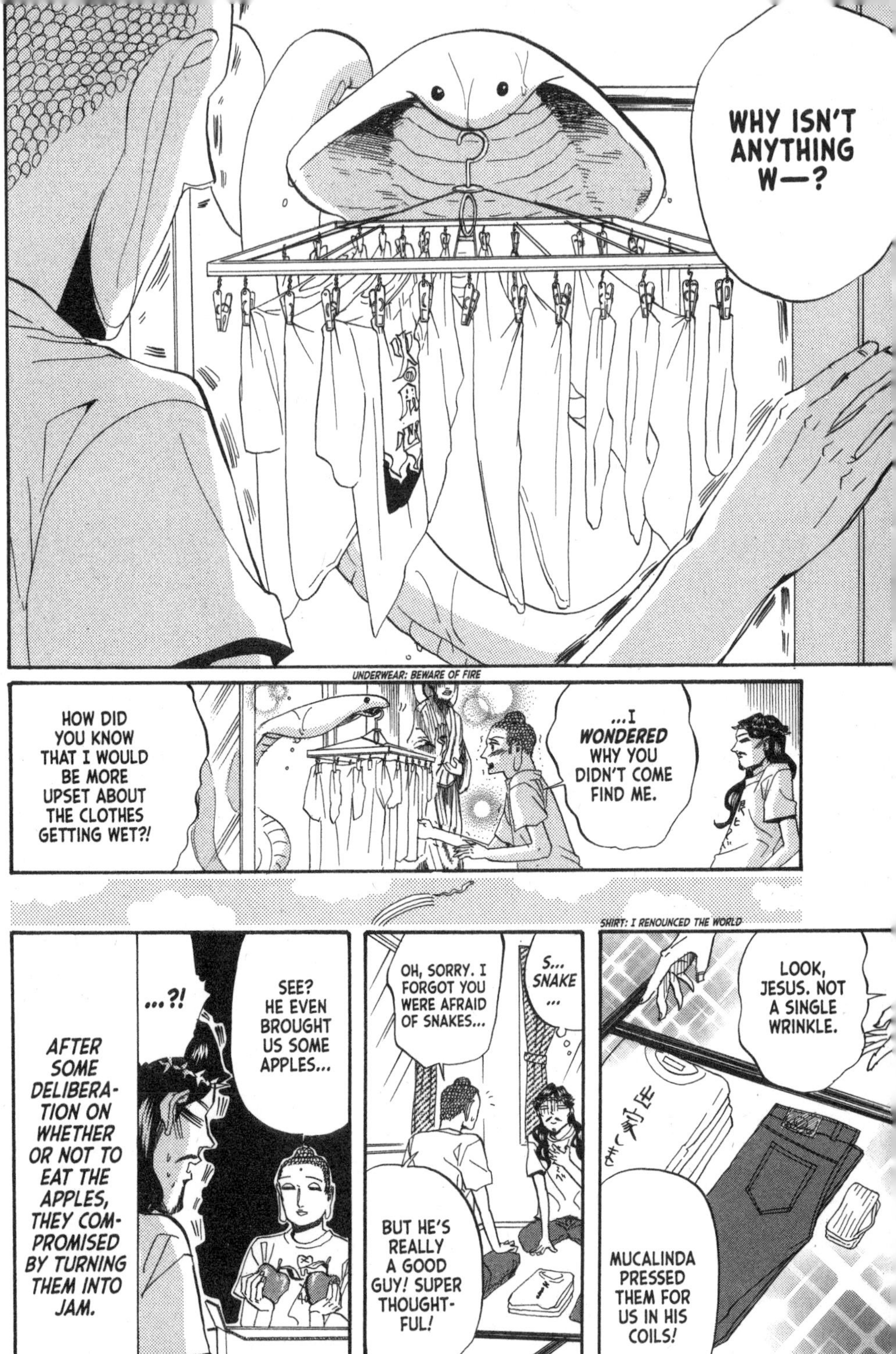
WHY ISN'T ANYTHING W—?
UNDERWEAR: BEWARE OF FIRE
...I WONDERED WHY YOU DIDN'T COME FIND ME.
HOW DID YOU KNOW THAT I WOULD BE MORE UPSET ABOUT THE CLOTHES GETTING WET?!
SHIRT: I RENOUNCED THE WORLD
LOOK, JESUS. NOT A SINGLE WRINKLE.
MUCALINDA PRESSED THEM FOR US IN HIS COILS!
S... SNAKE...
OH, SORRY. I FORGOT YOU WERE AFRAID OF SNAKES...
BUT HE'S REALLY A GOOD GUY! SUPER THOUGHTFUL!
SEE? HE EVEN BROUGHT US SOME APPLES...
...?!
AFTER SOME DELIBERATION ON WHETHER OR NOT TO EAT THE APPLES, THEY COMPROMISED BY TURNING THEM INTO JAM.
APPLES

008 ~Quantum of Cockleshells~
Most Memorable Scenes

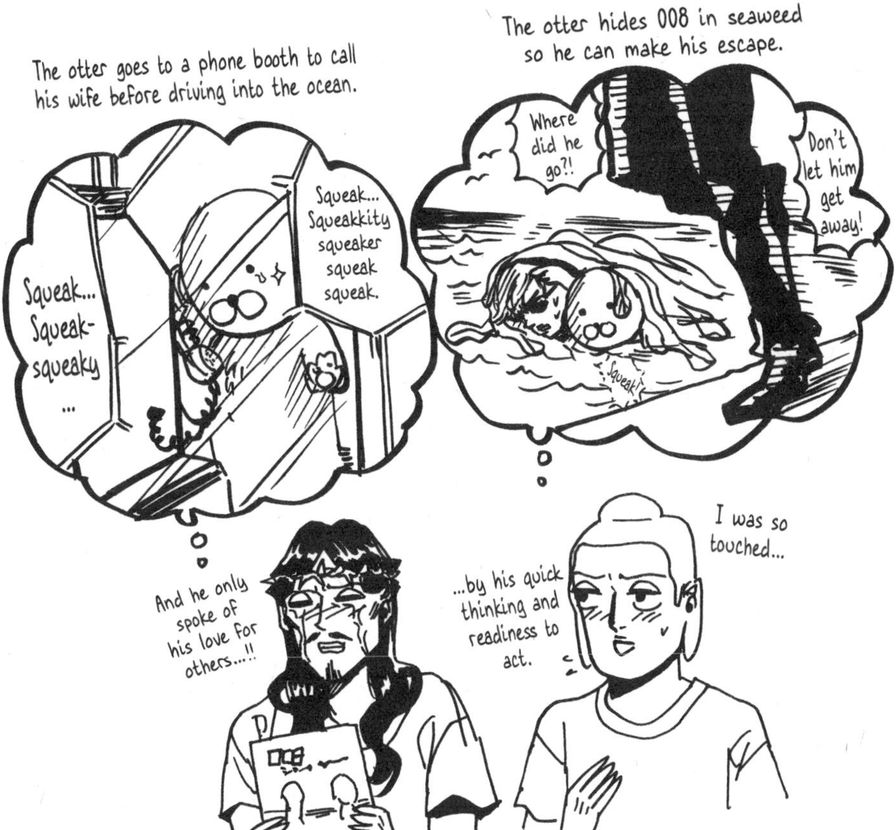

The otter hides 008 in seaweed so he can make his escape.
Where did he go?!
Don't let him get away!
Squeak!
The otter goes to a phone booth to call his wife before driving into the ocean.
Squeak... Squeakkity squeaker squeak squeak.
Squeak... Squeak-squeaky ...
I was so touched...
...by his quick thinking and readiness to act.
And he only spoke of his love for others...!!

CHAPTER 26 TRANSLATION NOTES

40 teeth, page 213
The Buddha's physical appearance is described in part by the list of 32 Characteristics of a Great Man. These include the *urna* on his forehead and the bump on top of his head. Another of these characteristics is that, rather than the 32 teeth most adult humans have, he has 40.

Battle of Wills, page 214
The Japanese word for "battle of wills" is *nekurabe,* literally meaning "root comparison." It happens to sound similar to *konkurabe,* the Japanese pronunciation of "conclave"—the meeting of cardinals to decide the new pope. An especially long conclave to decide who would become pope after the death of Pope Clement IV became a literal battle of wills as the French cardinals and (mostly) Italian cardinals refused to see eye to eye on whom to call to the papacy next. This almost three-year battle of wills has been immortalized in the Japanese pun, "The *konkurabe* is a *nekurabe*," or, "The conclave is a battle of wills."

Cheap movie day, page 215
In Japan, movie tickets generally go for around 1800 to 1900 yen (approximately $18, $19), with discounts for students, seniors, etc. There are also certain days of the week or month when you can get special discounts.

Especially the Old Testament, page 218
While the book of Revelation in the New Testament is generally the go-to book for a description of the end of the world (in fact, the word "apocalypse" literally means "revelation"), there are plenty of prophecies about the last days in the Old Testament, especially in the books of Isaiah, Jeremiah, and Ezekiel.

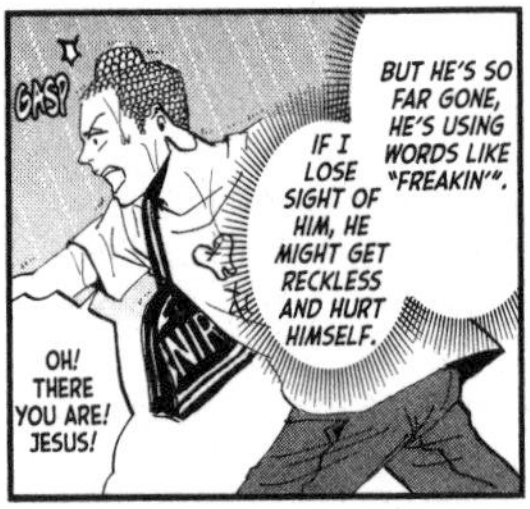
BUT HE'S SO FAR GONE, HE'S USING WORDS LIKE "FREAKIN'".
IF I LOSE SIGHT OF HIM, HE MIGHT GET RECKLESS AND HURT HIMSELF.
GASP
OH! THERE YOU ARE! JESUS!

Using words like freakin', page 225
Originally Buddha says, "He's gotten so wild that he's using *ore* as his first-person pronoun." *Ore* means "I" or "me," and is considered to be among the crudest of Japanese first-person pronouns. Usually Jesus uses the more polite *watashi* to say "I" or "me," but his distress over the loss of the otter has him resorting to the more vulgar pronoun, and speaking more like a member of the Yakuza in general.

I wonder if another saint came down from Heaven, page 226
There are multiple myths and traditions about rainbows forming bridges from Heaven to Earth, the most famous arguably being the Bifrost of Norse mythology, but the concept exists in other cultures as well.

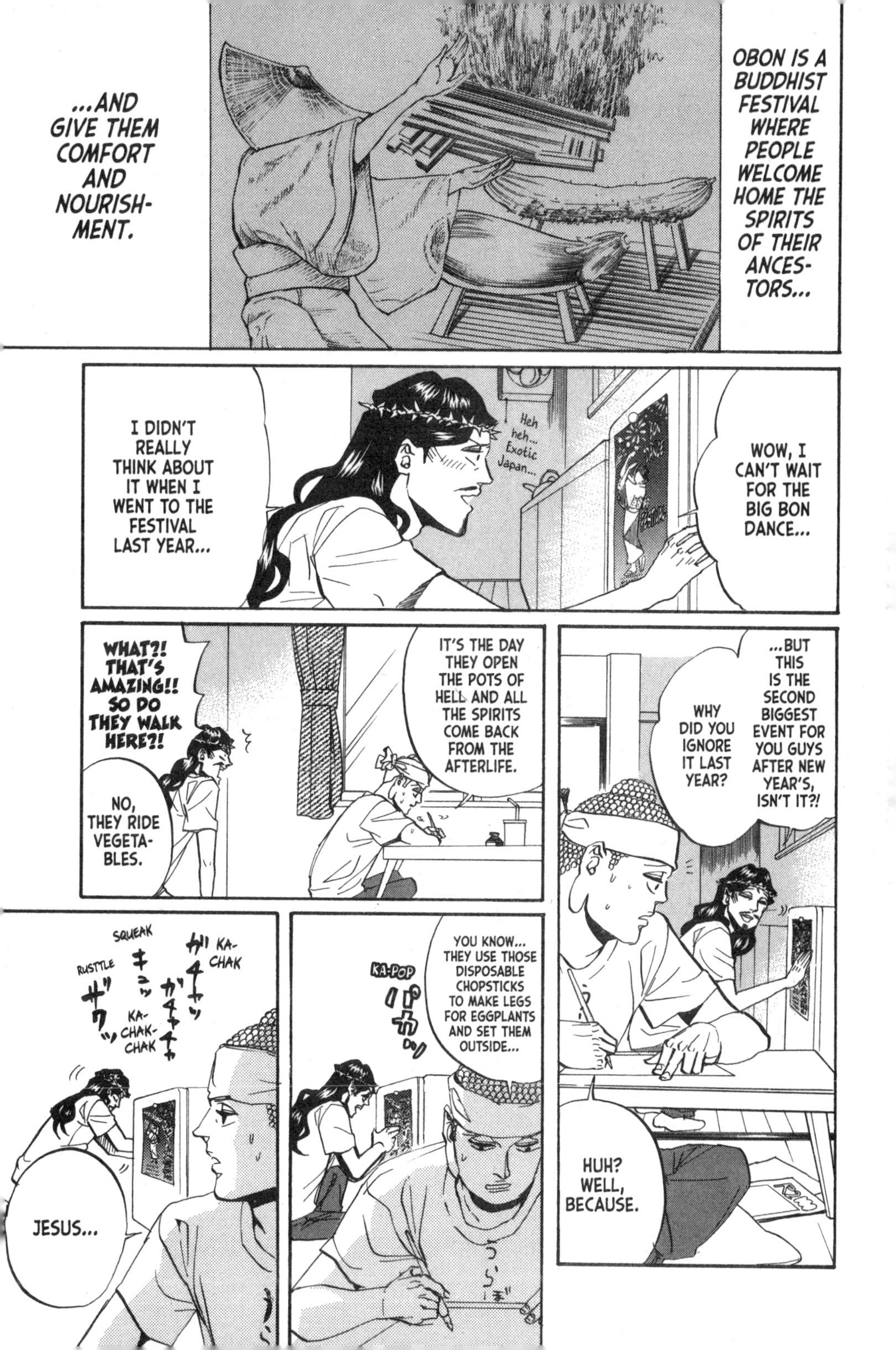
OBON IS A BUDDHIST FESTIVAL WHERE PEOPLE WELCOME HOME THE SPIRITS OF THEIR ANCESTORS...
...AND GIVE THEM COMFORT AND NOURISHMENT.
WOW, I CAN'T WAIT FOR THE BIG BON DANCE...
Heh heh... Exotic Japan...
I DIDN'T REALLY THINK ABOUT IT WHEN I WENT TO THE FESTIVAL LAST YEAR...
...BUT THIS IS THE SECOND BIGGEST EVENT FOR YOU GUYS AFTER NEW YEAR'S, ISN'T IT?!
WHY DID YOU IGNORE IT LAST YEAR?
HUH? WELL, BECAUSE.
IT'S THE DAY THEY OPEN THE POTS OF HELL AND ALL THE SPIRITS COME BACK FROM THE AFTERLIFE.
WHAT?! THAT'S AMAZING!! SO DO THEY WALK HERE?!
NO, THEY RIDE VEGETABLES.
YOU KNOW... THEY USE THOSE DISPOSABLE CHOPSTICKS TO MAKE LEGS FOR EGGPLANTS AND SET THEM OUTSIDE...
KA-POP
KA-CHAK
SQUEAK
RUSTLE
KA-CHAK-CHAK
JESUS...

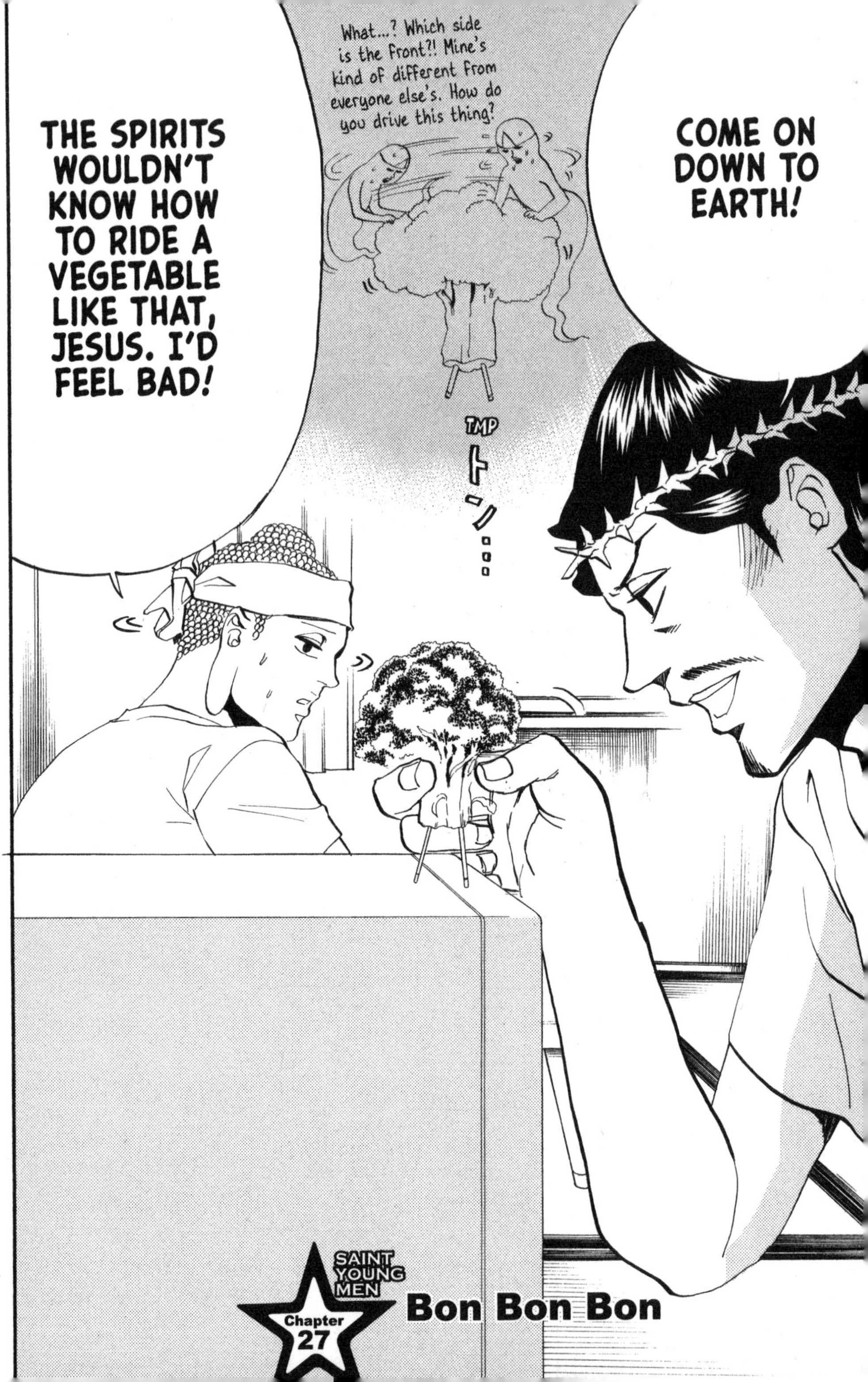
COME ON DOWN TO EARTH!
What...? Which side is the front?! Mine's kind of different from everyone else's. How do you drive this thing?
THE SPIRITS WOULDN'T KNOW HOW TO RIDE A VEGETABLE LIKE THAT, JESUS. I'D FEEL BAD!
TMP
トン…
SAINT YOUNG MEN
Chapter 27
Bon Bon Bon

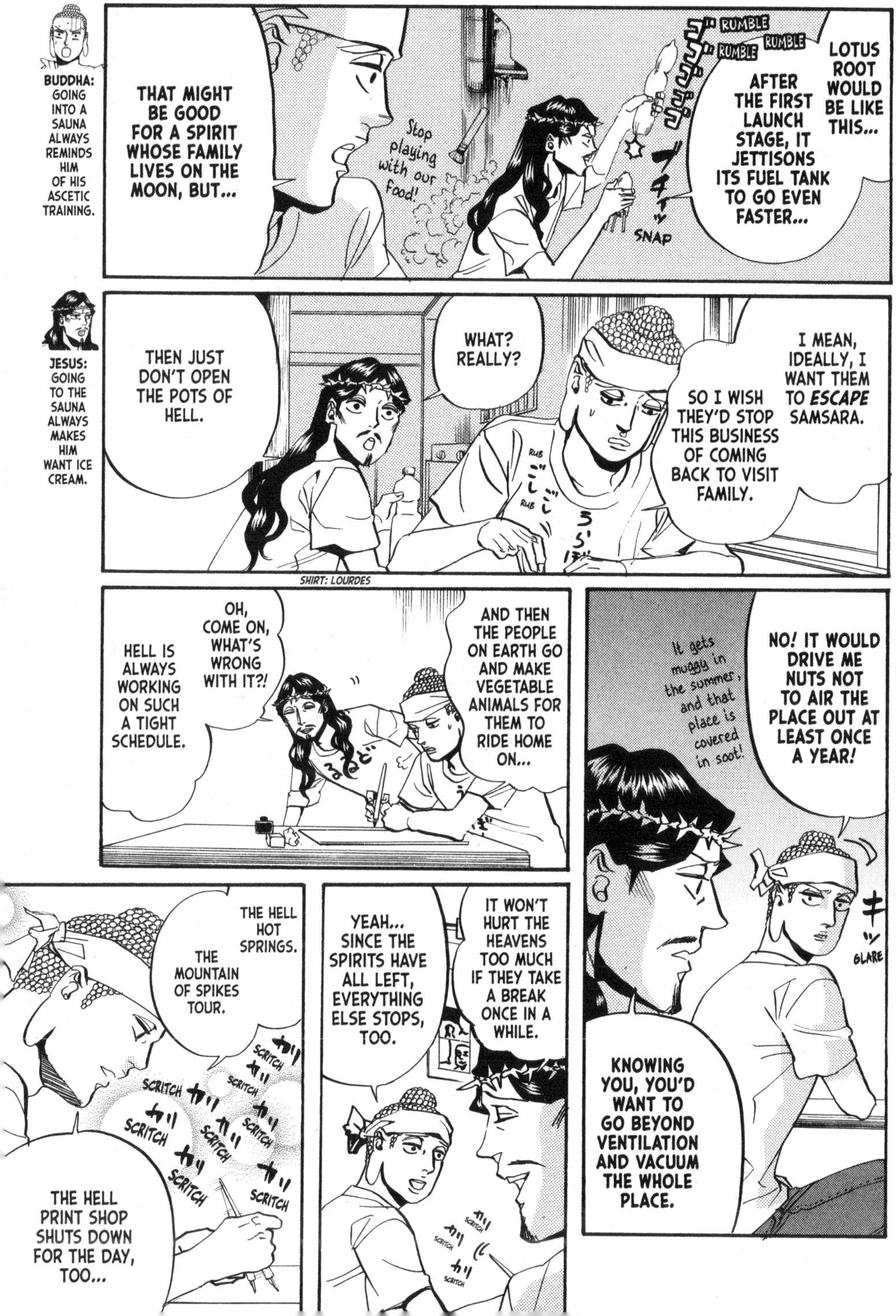
LOTUS ROOT WOULD BE LIKE THIS...
AFTER THE FIRST LAUNCH STAGE, IT JETTISONS ITS FUEL TANK TO GO EVEN FASTER...
RUMBLE RUMBLE RUMBLE
SNAP
Stop playing with our food!
THAT MIGHT BE GOOD FOR A SPIRIT WHOSE FAMILY LIVES ON THE MOON, BUT...
BUDDHA: GOING INTO A SAUNA ALWAYS REMINDS HIM OF HIS ASCETIC TRAINING.
I MEAN, IDEALLY, I WANT THEM TO *ESCAPE* SAMSARA.
SO I WISH THEY'D STOP THIS BUSINESS OF COMING BACK TO VISIT FAMILY.
WHAT? REALLY?
THEN JUST DON'T OPEN THE POTS OF HELL.
RUB RUB
JESUS: GOING TO THE SAUNA ALWAYS MAKES HIM WANT ICE CREAM.
SHIRT: LOURDES
NO! IT WOULD DRIVE ME NUTS NOT TO AIR THE PLACE OUT AT LEAST ONCE A YEAR!
It gets muggy in the summer, and that place is covered in soot!
GLARE
KNOWING YOU, YOU'D WANT TO GO BEYOND VENTILATION AND VACUUM THE WHOLE PLACE.
AND THEN THE PEOPLE ON EARTH GO AND MAKE VEGETABLE ANIMALS FOR THEM TO RIDE HOME ON...
OH, COME ON, WHAT'S WRONG WITH IT?!
HELL IS ALWAYS WORKING ON SUCH A TIGHT SCHEDULE.
IT WON'T HURT THE HEAVENS TOO MUCH IF THEY TAKE A BREAK ONCE IN A WHILE.
YEAH... SINCE THE SPIRITS HAVE ALL LEFT, EVERYTHING ELSE STOPS, TOO.
SCRITCH SCRITCH SCRITCH
THE HELL HOT SPRINGS.
THE MOUNTAIN OF SPIKES TOUR.
SCRITCH SCRITCH SCRITCH SCRITCH SCRITCH SCRITCH SCRITCH
THE HELL PRINT SHOP SHUTS DOWN FOR THE DAY, TOO...

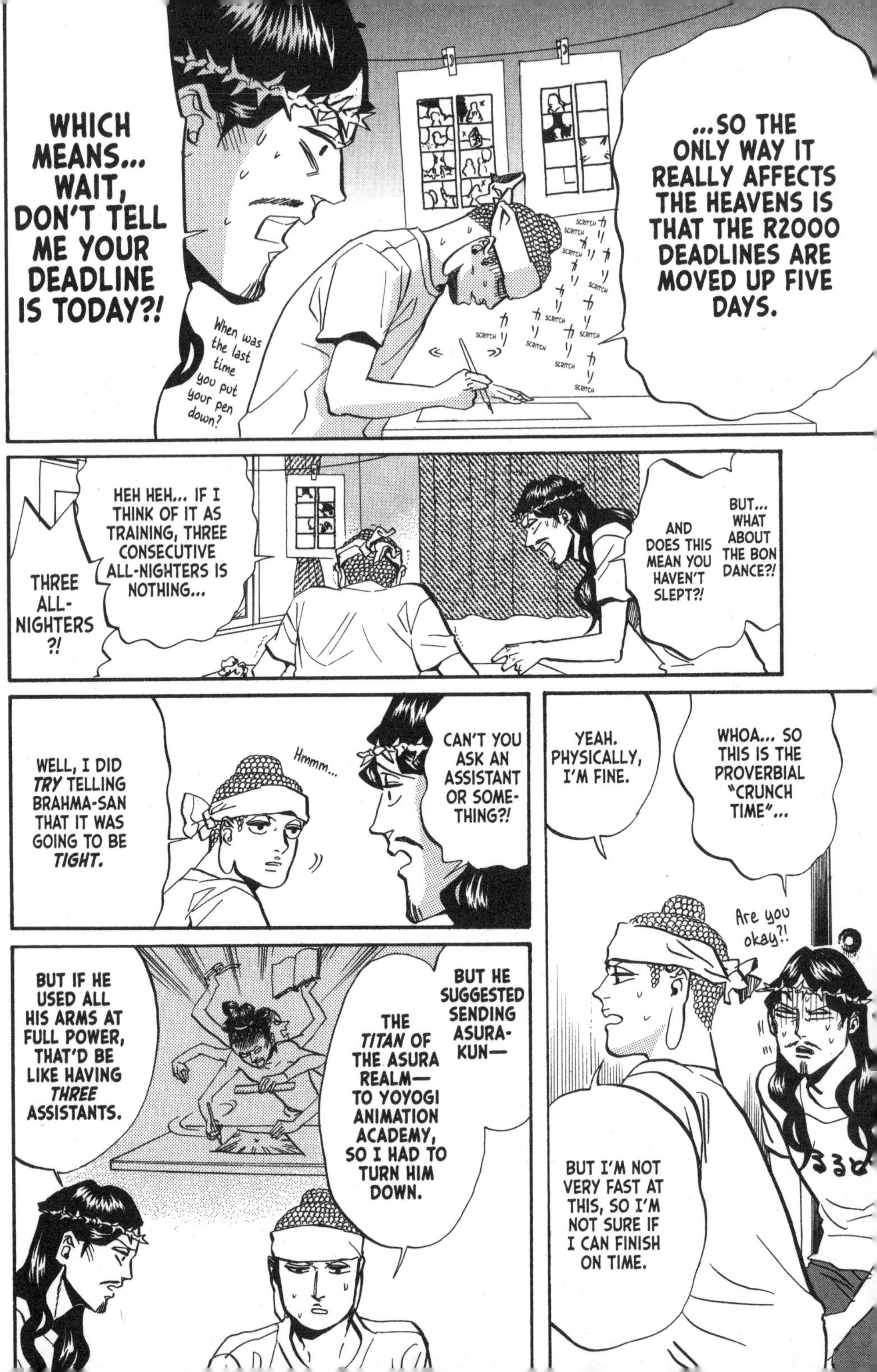
...SO THE ONLY WAY IT REALLY AFFECTS THE HEAVENS IS THAT THE R2000 DEADLINES ARE MOVED UP FIVE DAYS.
SCRITCH
WHICH MEANS... WAIT, DON'T TELL ME YOUR DEADLINE IS TODAY?!
When was the last time you put your pen down?
BUT... WHAT ABOUT THE BON DANCE?!
AND DOES THIS MEAN YOU HAVEN'T SLEPT?!
HEH HEH... IF I THINK OF IT AS TRAINING, THREE CONSECUTIVE ALL-NIGHTERS IS NOTHING...
THREE ALL-NIGHTERS?!
WHOA... SO THIS IS THE PROVERBIAL "CRUNCH TIME"...
YEAH. PHYSICALLY, I'M FINE.
Are you okay?!
BUT I'M NOT VERY FAST AT THIS, SO I'M NOT SURE IF I CAN FINISH ON TIME.
CAN'T YOU ASK AN ASSISTANT OR SOMETHING?!
Hmmm...
WELL, I DID *TRY* TELLING BRAHMA-SAN THAT IT WAS GOING TO BE *TIGHT.*
BUT HE SUGGESTED SENDING ASURA-KUN—
THE *TITAN* OF THE ASURA REALM— TO YOYOGI ANIMATION ACADEMY, SO I HAD TO TURN HIM DOWN.
BUT IF HE USED ALL HIS ARMS AT FULL POWER, THAT'D BE LIKE HAVING *THREE* ASSISTANTS.

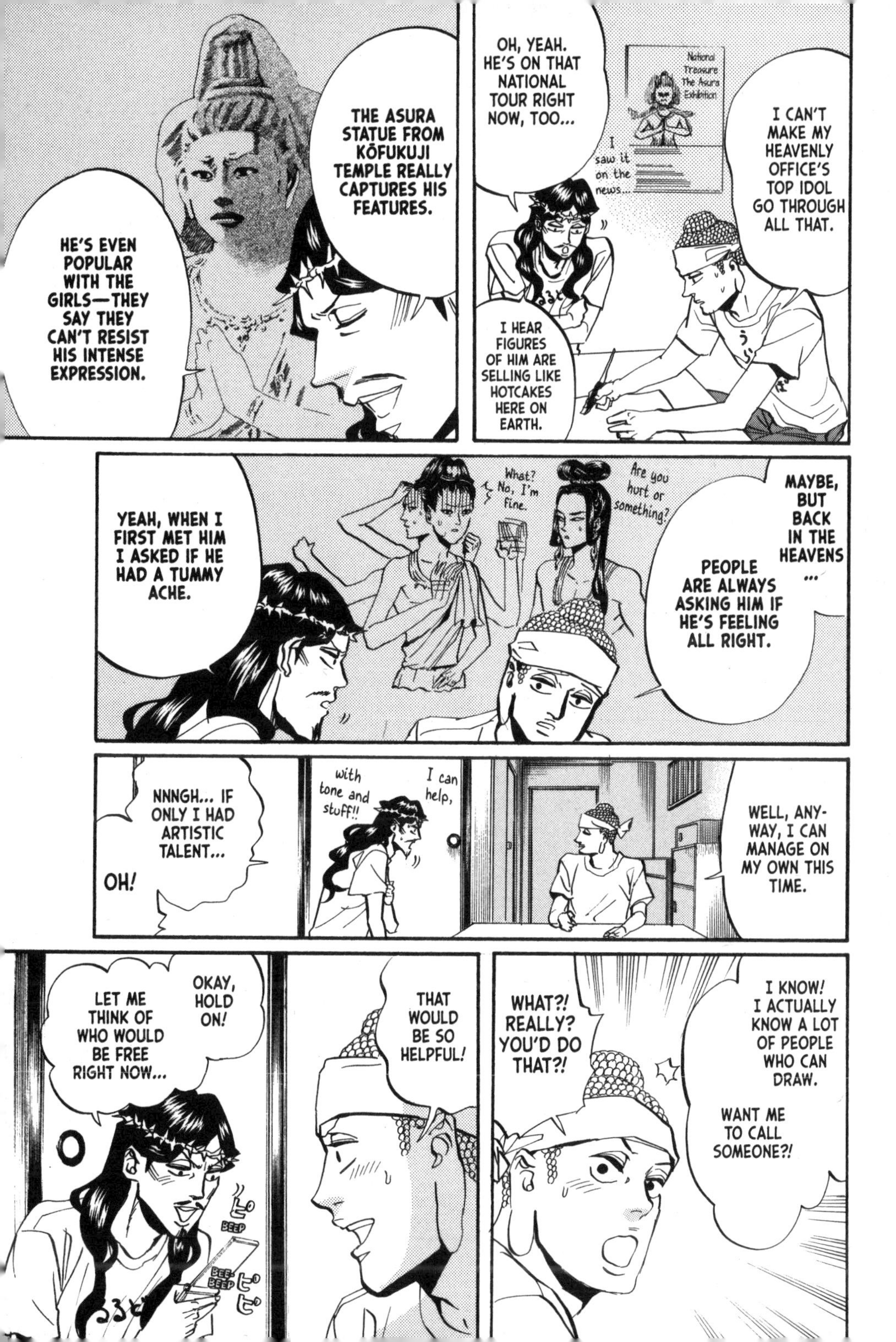
I CAN'T MAKE MY HEAVENLY OFFICE'S TOP IDOL GO THROUGH ALL THAT.
National Treasure The Asura Exhibition
OH, YEAH. HE'S ON THAT NATIONAL TOUR RIGHT NOW, TOO...
I saw it on the news...
I HEAR FIGURES OF HIM ARE SELLING LIKE HOTCAKES HERE ON EARTH.
THE ASURA STATUE FROM KŌFUKUJI TEMPLE REALLY CAPTURES HIS FEATURES.
HE'S EVEN POPULAR WITH THE GIRLS—THEY SAY THEY CAN'T RESIST HIS INTENSE EXPRESSION.
MAYBE, BUT BACK IN THE HEAVENS...
PEOPLE ARE ALWAYS ASKING HIM IF HE'S FEELING ALL RIGHT.
Are you hurt or something?
What? No, I'm fine.
YEAH, WHEN I FIRST MET HIM I ASKED IF HE HAD A TUMMY ACHE.
WELL, ANY-WAY, I CAN MANAGE ON MY OWN THIS TIME.
I can help,
with tone and stuff!!
NNNGH... IF ONLY I HAD ARTISTIC TALENT...
OH!
I KNOW! I ACTUALLY KNOW A LOT OF PEOPLE WHO CAN DRAW.
WANT ME TO CALL SOMEONE?!
WHAT?! REALLY? YOU'D DO THAT?!
THAT WOULD BE SO HELPFUL!
OKAY, HOLD ON!
LET ME THINK OF WHO WOULD BE FREE RIGHT NOW...
ピ BEEP
ピピ BEE-BEEP

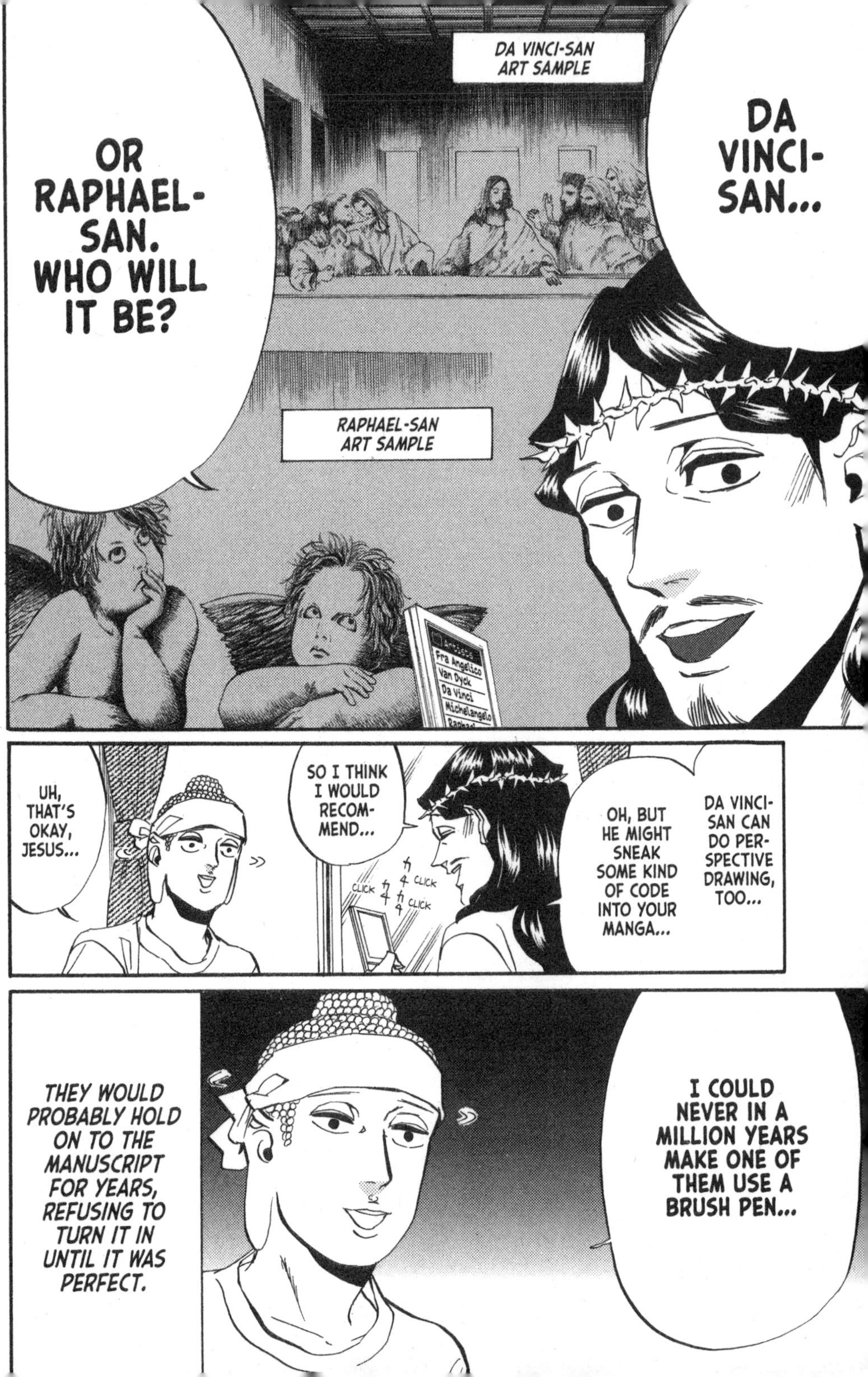
DA VINCI-SAN...
DA VINCI-SAN ART SAMPLE
OR RAPHAEL-SAN. WHO WILL IT BE?
RAPHAEL-SAN ART SAMPLE
Fra Angelico
Van Dyck
Da Vinci
Michelangelo
DA VINCI-SAN CAN DO PERSPECTIVE DRAWING, TOO...
OH, BUT HE MIGHT SNEAK SOME KIND OF CODE INTO YOUR MANGA...
CLICK CLICK CLICK CLICK
SO I THINK I WOULD RECOMMEND...
UH, THAT'S OKAY, JESUS...
I COULD NEVER IN A MILLION YEARS MAKE ONE OF THEM USE A BRUSH PEN...
THEY WOULD PROBABLY HOLD ON TO THE MANUSCRIPT FOR YEARS, REFUSING TO TURN IT IN UNTIL IT WAS PERFECT.

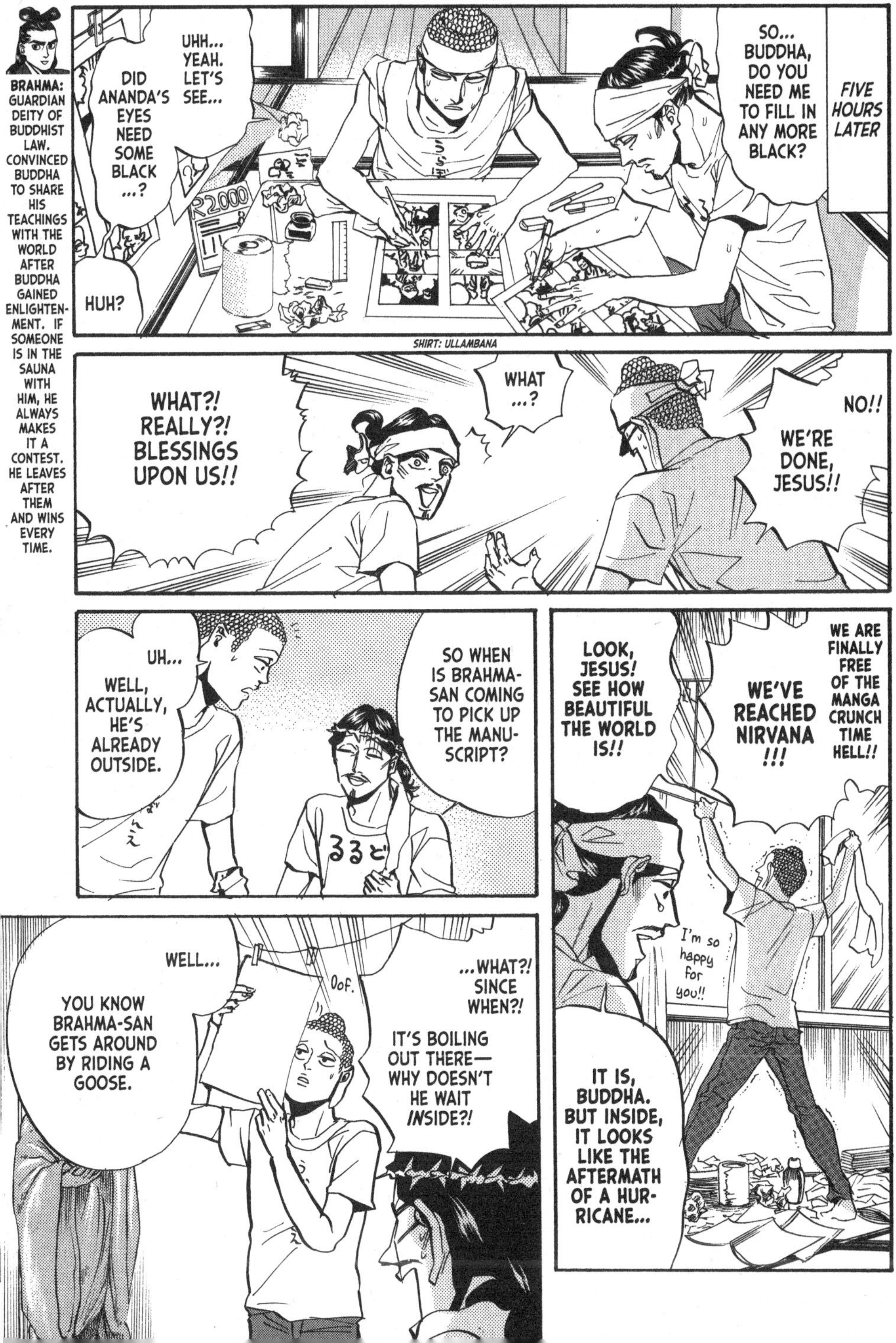

FIVE HOURS LATER
SO... BUDDHA, DO YOU NEED ME TO FILL IN ANY MORE BLACK?
UHH... YEAH. LET'S SEE...
DID ANANDA'S EYES NEED SOME BLACK ...?
HUH?
SHIRT: ULLAMBANA
NO!!
WE'RE DONE, JESUS!!
WHAT ...?
WHAT?! REALLY?! BLESSINGS UPON US!!
WE ARE FINALLY FREE OF THE MANGA CRUNCH TIME HELL!!
WE'VE REACHED NIRVANA !!!
LOOK, JESUS! SEE HOW BEAUTIFUL THE WORLD IS!!
I'm so happy for you!!
IT IS, BUDDHA. BUT INSIDE, IT LOOKS LIKE THE AFTERMATH OF A HURRICANE...
SO WHEN IS BRAHMA-SAN COMING TO PICK UP THE MANUSCRIPT?
るるど
UH...
WELL, ACTUALLY, HE'S ALREADY OUTSIDE.
...WHAT?! SINCE WHEN?!
IT'S BOILING OUT THERE—WHY DOESN'T HE WAIT INSIDE?!
Oof.
WELL...
YOU KNOW BRAHMA-SAN GETS AROUND BY RIDING A GOOSE.
BRAHMA: GUARDIAN DEITY OF BUDDHIST LAW. CONVINCED BUDDHA TO SHARE HIS TEACHINGS WITH THE WORLD AFTER BUDDHA GAINED ENLIGHTENMENT. IF SOMEONE IS IN THE SAUNA WITH HIM, HE ALWAYS MAKES IT A CONTEST. HE LEAVES AFTER THEM AND WINS EVERY TIME.

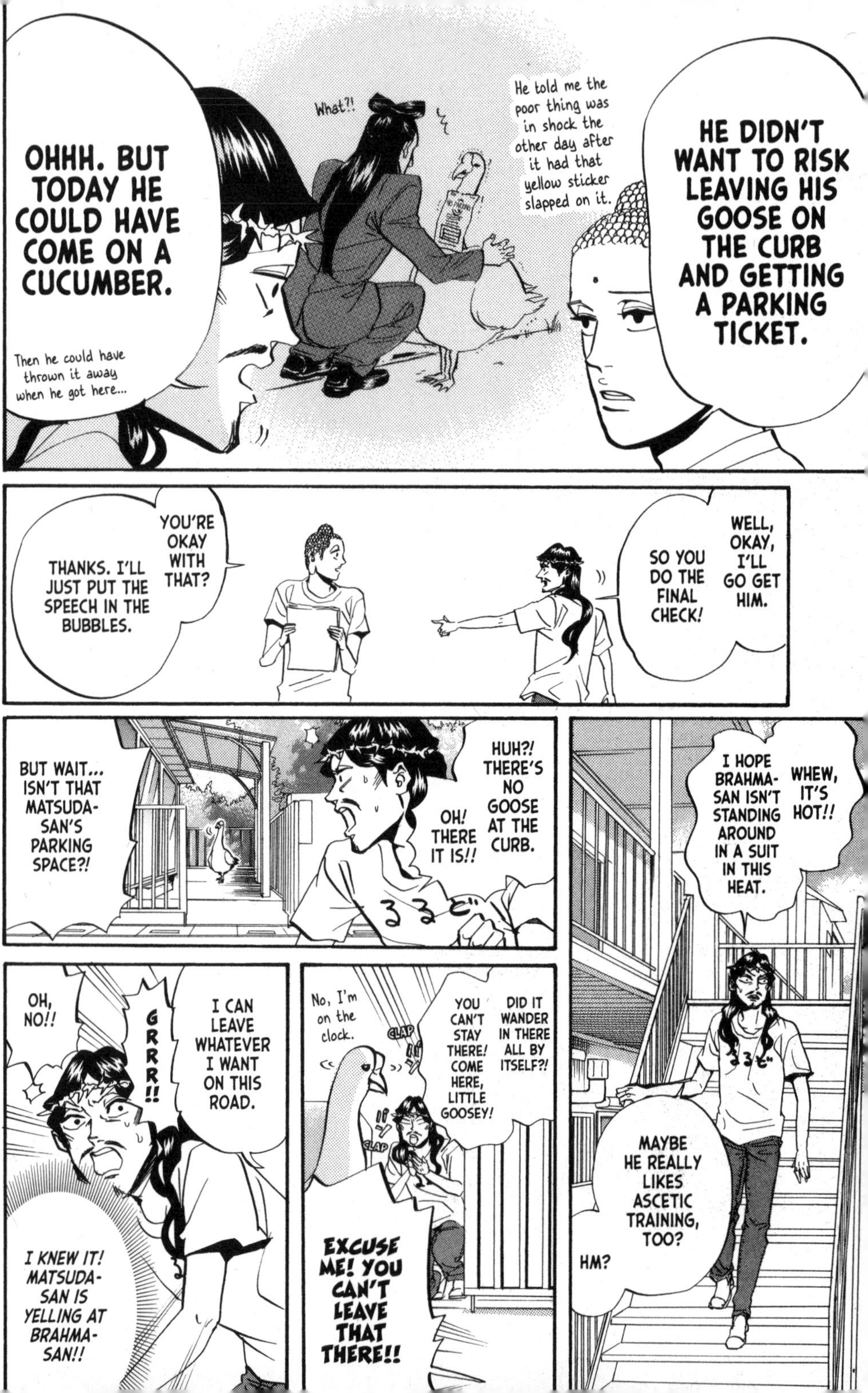
HE DIDN'T WANT TO RISK LEAVING HIS GOOSE ON THE CURB AND GETTING A PARKING TICKET.
He told me the poor thing was in shock the other day after it had that yellow sticker slapped on it.
What?!
OHHH. BUT TODAY HE COULD HAVE COME ON A CUCUMBER.
Then he could have thrown it away when he got here...
WELL, OKAY, I'LL GO GET HIM.
SO YOU DO THE FINAL CHECK!
YOU'RE OKAY WITH THAT?
THANKS. I'LL JUST PUT THE SPEECH IN THE BUBBLES.
WHEW, IT'S HOT!!
I HOPE BRAHMA-SAN ISN'T STANDING AROUND IN A SUIT IN THIS HEAT.
MAYBE HE REALLY LIKES ASCETIC TRAINING, TOO?
HM?
HUH?! THERE'S NO GOOSE AT THE CURB.
OH! THERE IT IS!!
BUT WAIT... ISN'T THAT MATSUDA-SAN'S PARKING SPACE?!
DID IT WANDER IN THERE ALL BY ITSELF?!
YOU CAN'T STAY THERE! COME HERE, LITTLE GOOSEY!
No, I'm on the clock.
CLAP
CLAP
EXCUSE ME! YOU CAN'T LEAVE THAT THERE!!
I CAN LEAVE WHATEVER I WANT ON THIS ROAD.
GRRRR!!
OH, NO!!
I KNEW IT! MATSUDA-SAN IS YELLING AT BRAHMA-SAN!!

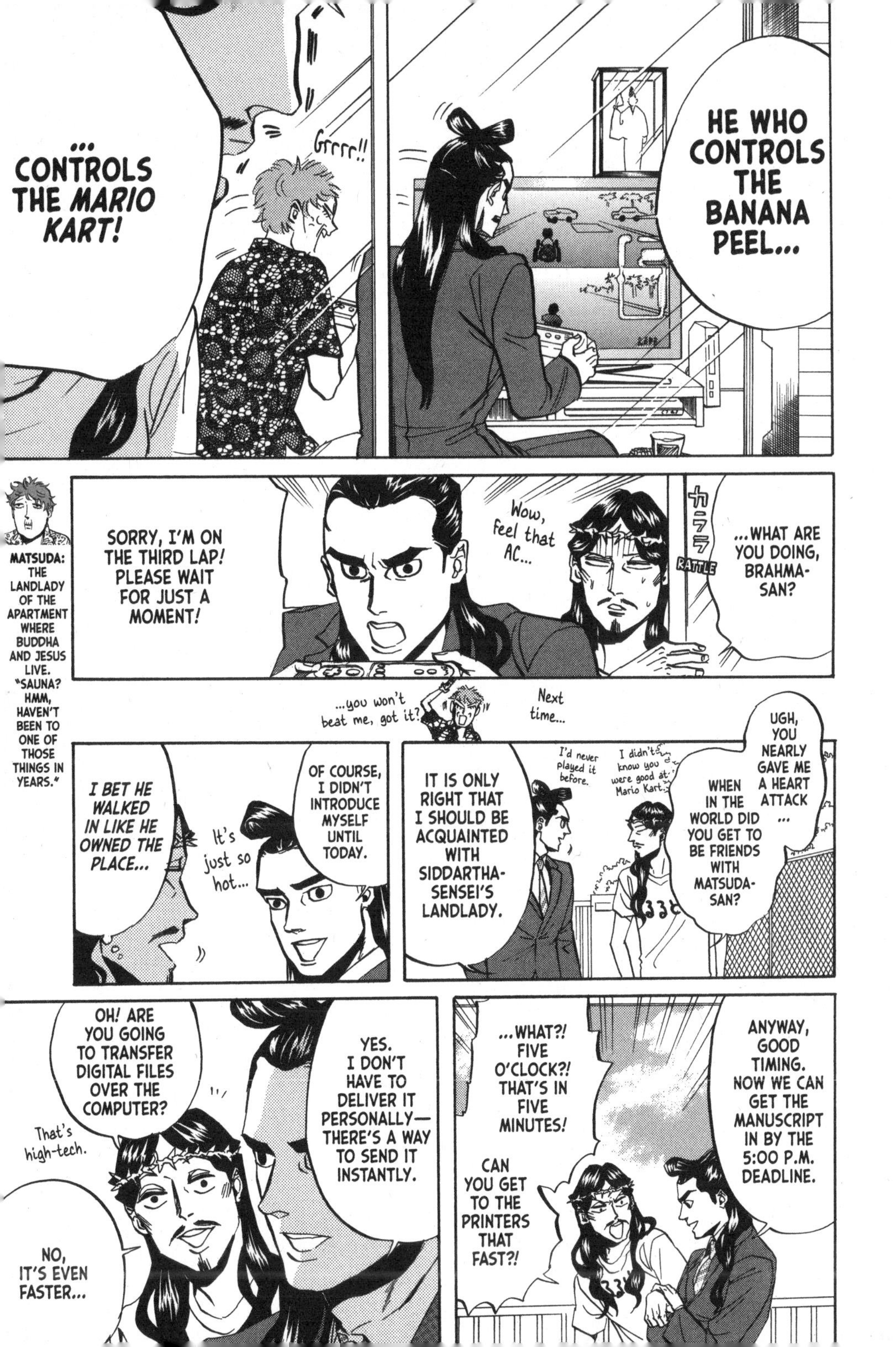
HE WHO CONTROLS THE BANANA PEEL...
Grrrr!!
...CONTROLS THE MARIO KART!
...WHAT ARE YOU DOING, BRAHMA-SAN?
カラ
RATTLE
Wow, feel that AC...
SORRY, I'M ON THE THIRD LAP! PLEASE WAIT FOR JUST A MOMENT!
MATSUDA: THE LANDLADY OF THE APARTMENT WHERE BUDDHA AND JESUS LIVE. "SAUNA? HMM, HAVEN'T BEEN TO ONE OF THOSE THINGS IN YEARS."
Next time...
...you won't beat me, got it?
UGH, YOU NEARLY GAVE ME A HEART ATTACK...
WHEN IN THE WORLD DID YOU GET TO BE FRIENDS WITH MATSUDA-SAN?
I didn't know you were good at Mario Kart.
I'd never played it before.
IT IS ONLY RIGHT THAT I SHOULD BE ACQUAINTED WITH SIDDARTHA-SENSEI'S LANDLADY.
OF COURSE, I DIDN'T INTRODUCE MYSELF UNTIL TODAY.
It's just so hot...
I BET HE WALKED IN LIKE HE OWNED THE PLACE...
ANYWAY, GOOD TIMING. NOW WE CAN GET THE MANUSCRIPT IN BY THE 5:00 P.M. DEADLINE.
...WHAT?! FIVE O'CLOCK?! THAT'S IN FIVE MINUTES!
CAN YOU GET TO THE PRINTERS THAT FAST?!
YES. I DON'T HAVE TO DELIVER IT PERSONALLY—THERE'S A WAY TO SEND IT INSTANTLY.
OH! ARE YOU GOING TO TRANSFER DIGITAL FILES OVER THE COMPUTER?
That's high-tech.
NO, IT'S EVEN FASTER...

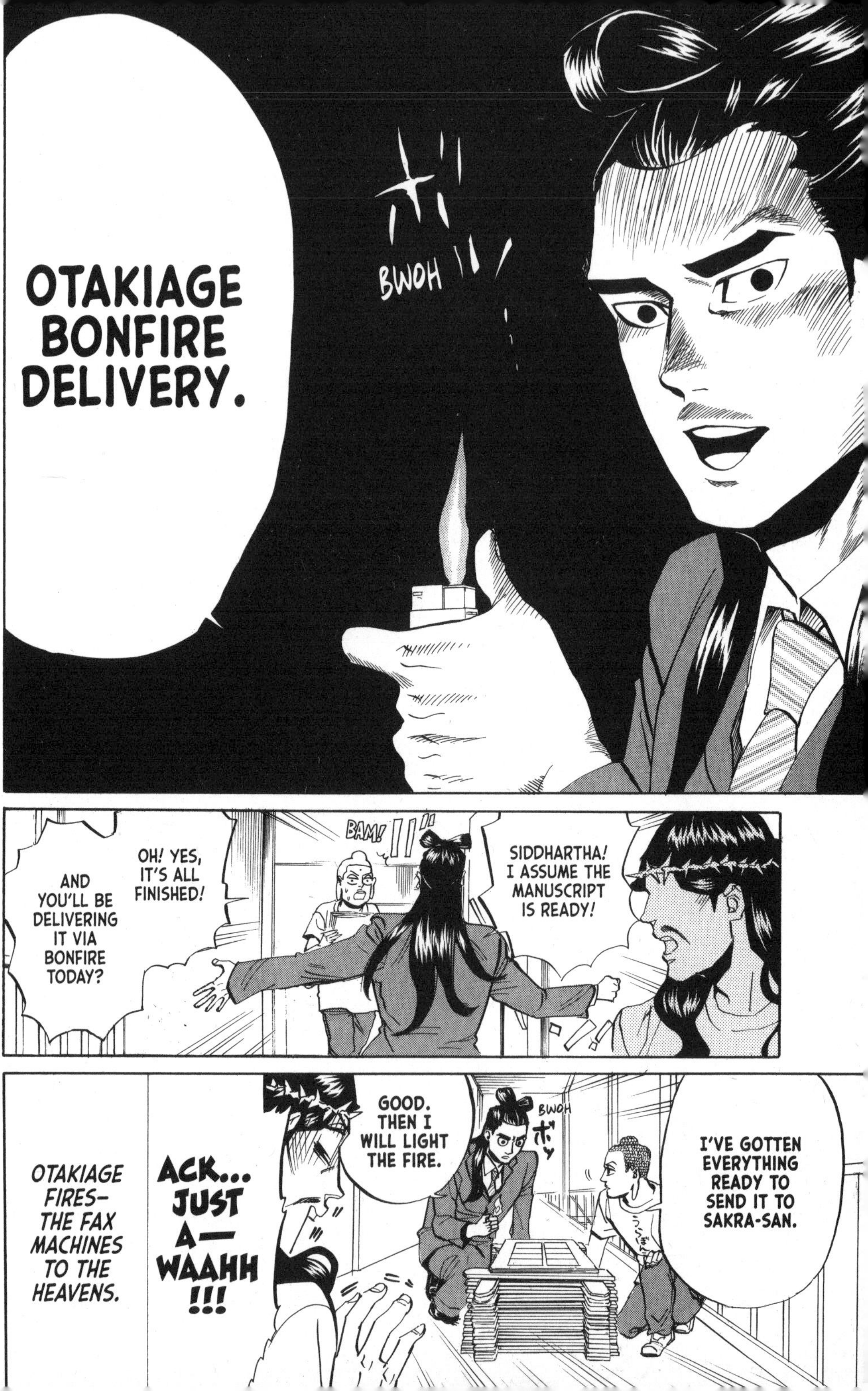
OTAKIAGE BONFIRE DELIVERY.
BWOH
SIDDHARTHA! I ASSUME THE MANUSCRIPT IS READY!
BAM!
OH! YES, IT'S ALL FINISHED!
AND YOU'LL BE DELIVERING IT VIA BONFIRE TODAY?
I'VE GOTTEN EVERYTHING READY TO SEND IT TO SAKRA-SAN.
BWOH
GOOD. THEN I WILL LIGHT THE FIRE.
ACK... JUST A— WAAHH!!!
OTAKIAGE FIRES— THE FAX MACHINES TO THE HEAVENS.

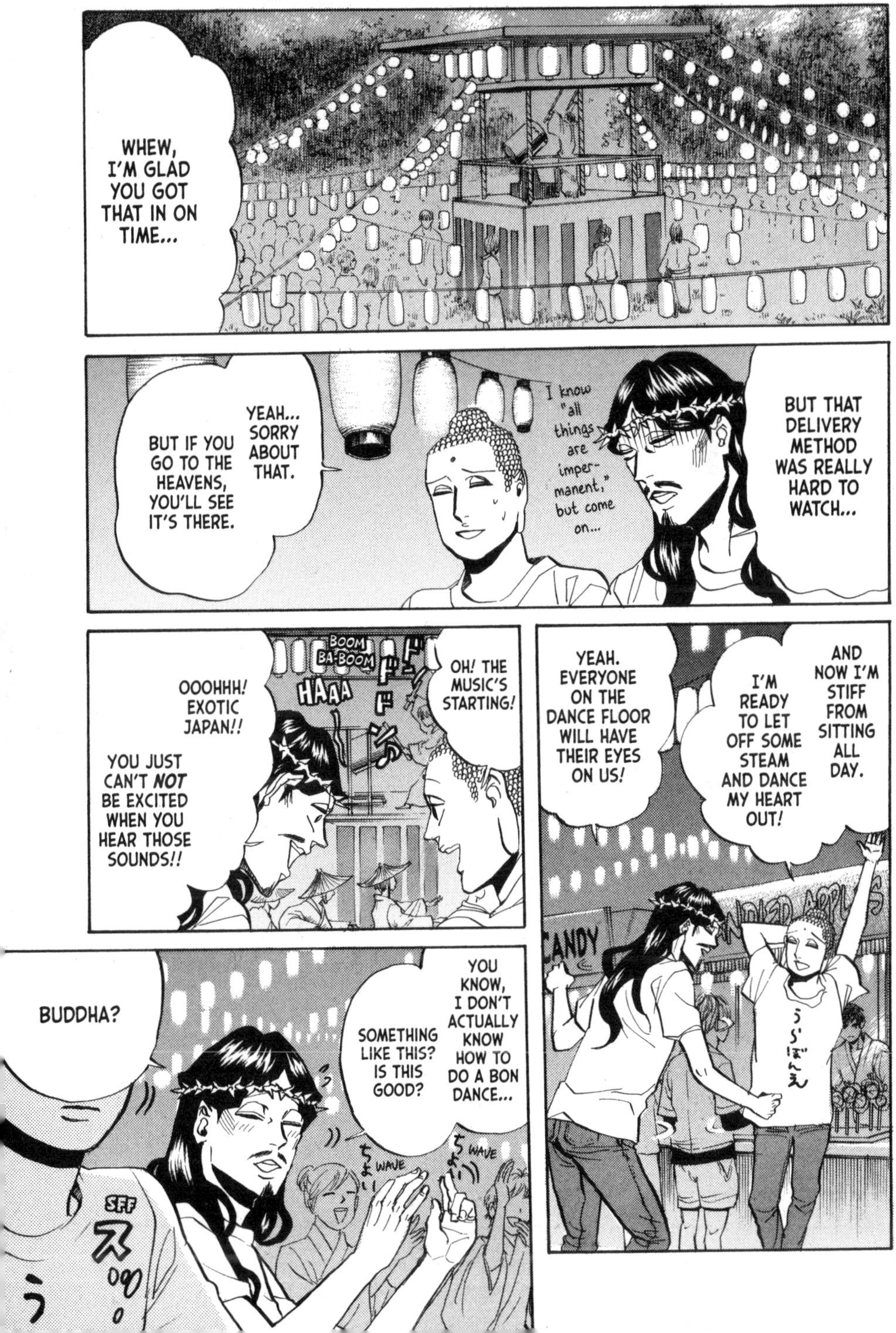
WHEW, I'M GLAD YOU GOT THAT IN ON TIME...
BUT THAT DELIVERY METHOD WAS REALLY HARD TO WATCH...
I know "all things are impermanent," but come on...
YEAH... SORRY ABOUT THAT.
BUT IF YOU GO TO THE HEAVENS, YOU'LL SEE IT'S THERE.
AND NOW I'M STIFF FROM SITTING ALL DAY.
I'M READY TO LET OFF SOME STEAM AND DANCE MY HEART OUT!
YEAH. EVERYONE ON THE DANCE FLOOR WILL HAVE THEIR EYES ON US!
CANDY
うらぼんえ
OH! THE MUSIC'S STARTING!
BOOM BA-BOOM
ドドド
HAAA
OOOHHH! EXOTIC JAPAN!!
YOU JUST CAN'T *NOT* BE EXCITED WHEN YOU HEAR THOSE SOUNDS!!
YOU KNOW, I DON'T ACTUALLY KNOW HOW TO DO A BON DANCE...
SOMETHING LIKE THIS? IS THIS GOOD?
ちょい WAVE
ちょい WAVE
BUDDHA?
SFF
スッ

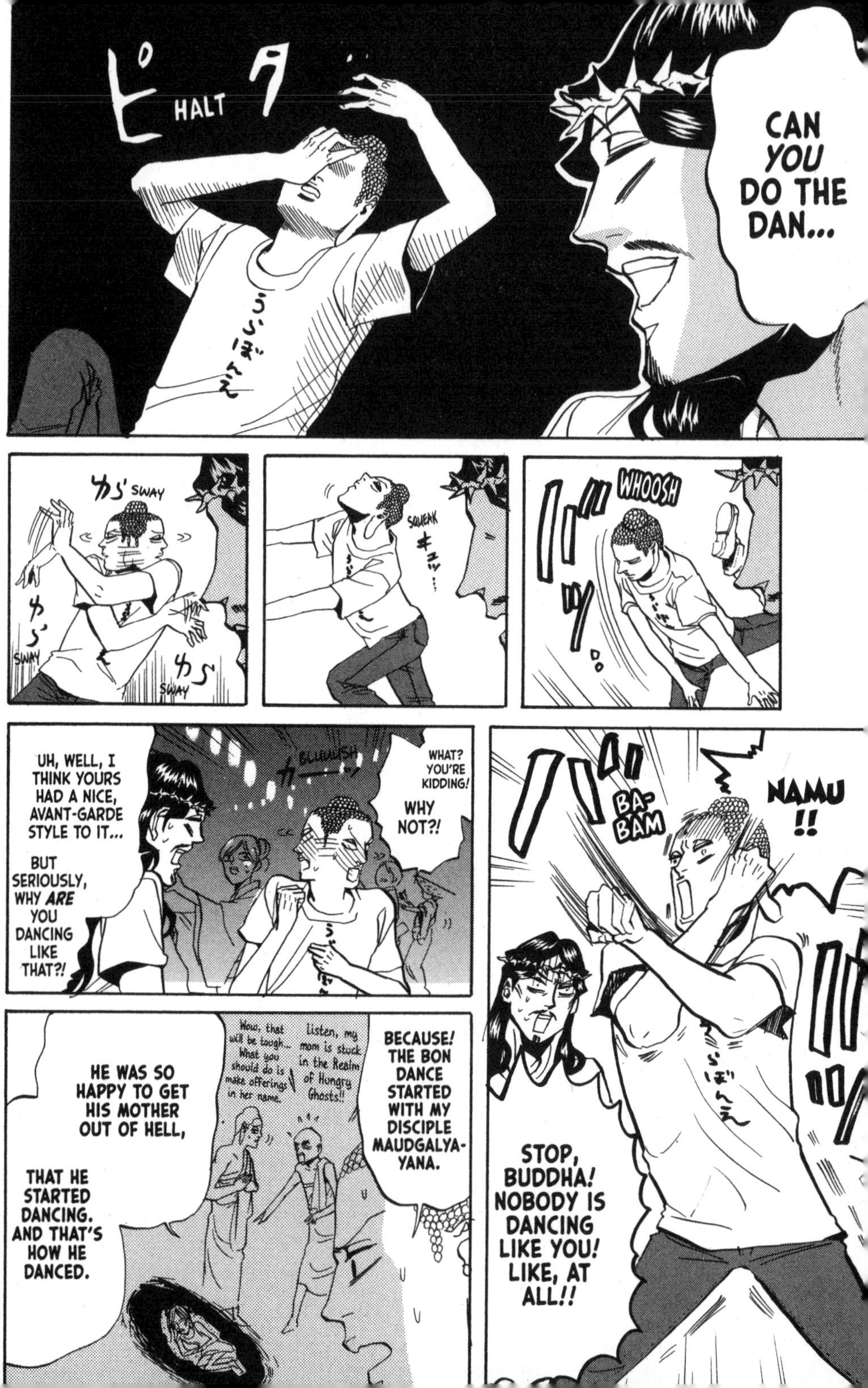
CAN *YOU* DO THE DAN...
ピタ
HALT
うらぼんえ
WHOOSH
キュッ...
SQUEAK
ゆら SWAY
ゆら SWAY
ゆら SWAY
NAMU!!
BA-BAM
STOP, BUDDHA! NOBODY IS DANCING LIKE YOU! LIKE, AT ALL!!
WHAT? YOU'RE KIDDING!
WHY NOT?!
カーッ BLUUUSH
UH, WELL, I THINK YOURS HAD A NICE, AVANT-GARDE STYLE TO IT...
BUT SERIOUSLY, WHY *ARE* YOU DANCING LIKE THAT?!
BECAUSE! THE BON DANCE STARTED WITH MY DISCIPLE MAUDGALYA-YANA.
Listen, my mom is stuck in the Realm of Hungry Ghosts!!
Wow, that will be tough... What you should do is make offerings in her name.
HE WAS SO HAPPY TO GET HIS MOTHER OUT OF HELL,
THAT HE STARTED DANCING. AND THAT'S HOW HE DANCED.

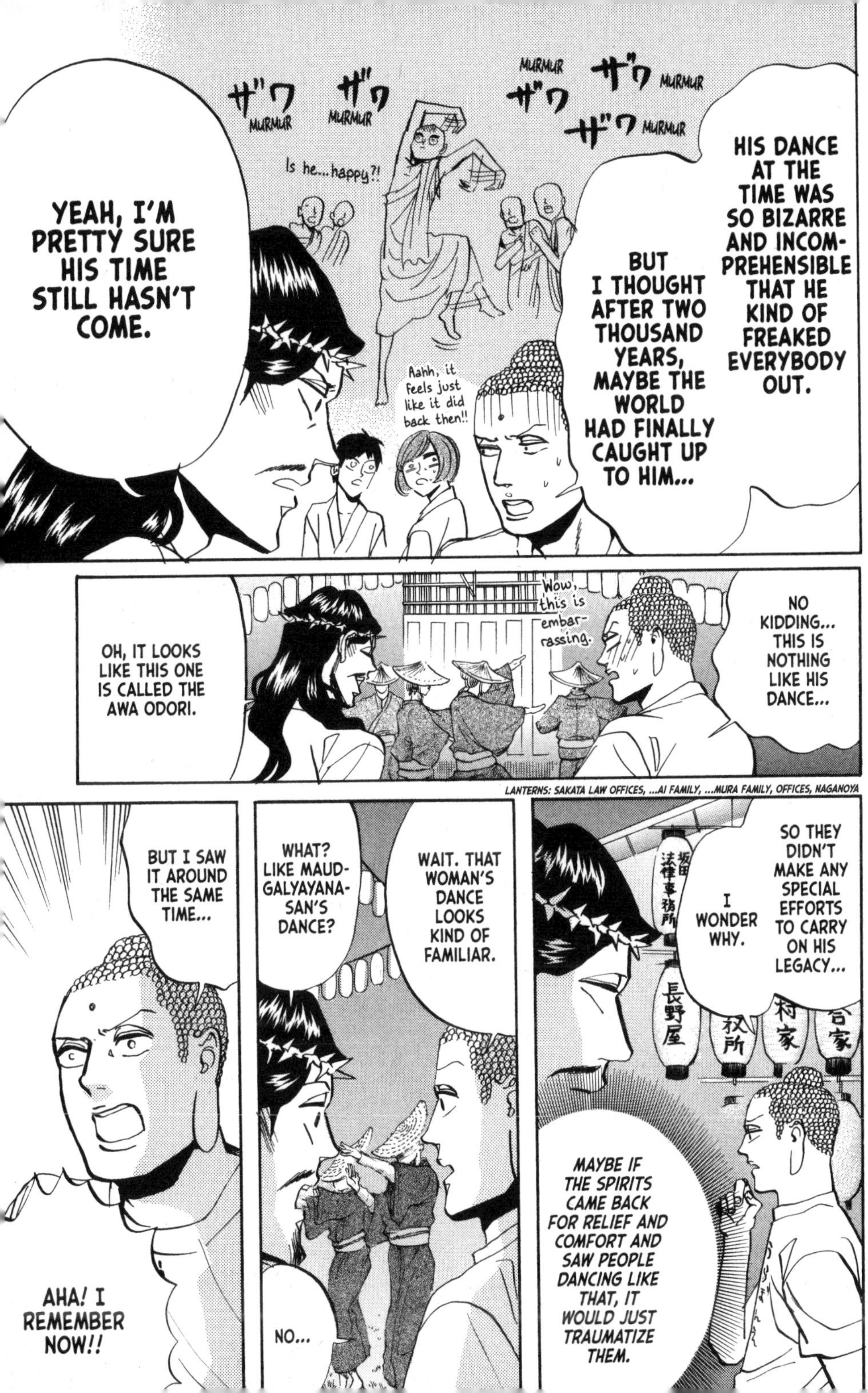
ザワ MURMUR
ザワ MURMUR
ザワ MURMUR
ザワ MURMUR
ザワ MURMUR
ザワ MURMUR
HIS DANCE AT THE TIME WAS SO BIZARRE AND INCOMPREHENSIBLE THAT HE KIND OF FREAKED EVERYBODY OUT.
BUT I THOUGHT AFTER TWO THOUSAND YEARS, MAYBE THE WORLD HAD FINALLY CAUGHT UP TO HIM...
Is he...happy?!
Aahh, it feels just like it did back then!!
YEAH, I'M PRETTY SURE HIS TIME STILL HASN'T COME.
NO KIDDING... THIS IS NOTHING LIKE HIS DANCE...
Wow, this is embarrassing.
OH, IT LOOKS LIKE THIS ONE IS CALLED THE AWA ODORI.
LANTERNS: SAKATA LAW OFFICES, ...AI FAMILY, ...MURA FAMILY, OFFICES, NAGANOYA
坂田法律事務所
長野屋
所
村家
SO THEY DIDN'T MAKE ANY SPECIAL EFFORTS TO CARRY ON HIS LEGACY...
I WONDER WHY.
MAYBE IF THE SPIRITS CAME BACK FOR RELIEF AND COMFORT AND SAW PEOPLE DANCING LIKE THAT, IT WOULD JUST TRAUMATIZE THEM.
WAIT. THAT WOMAN'S DANCE LOOKS KIND OF FAMILIAR.
WHAT? LIKE MAUDGALYAYANA-SAN'S DANCE?
NO...
BUT I SAW IT AROUND THE SAME TIME...
AHA! I REMEMBER NOW!!

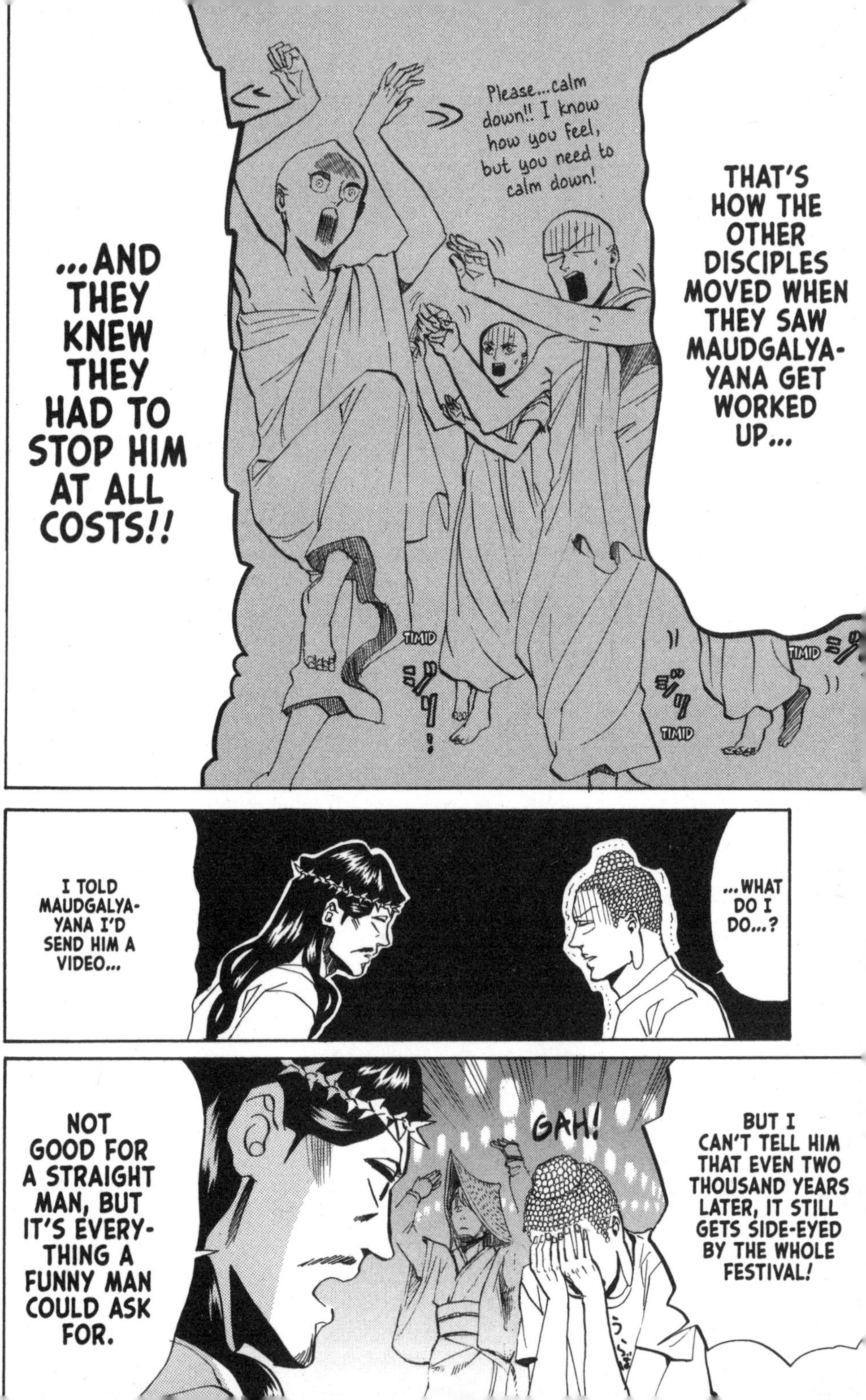
THAT'S HOW THE OTHER DISCIPLES MOVED WHEN THEY SAW MAUDGALYAYANA GET WORKED UP...
Please...calm down!! I know how you feel, but you need to calm down!
...AND THEY KNEW THEY HAD TO STOP HIM AT ALL COSTS!!
TIMID
TIMID
TIMID
...WHAT DO I DO...?
I TOLD MAUDGALYAYANA I'D SEND HIM A VIDEO...
BUT I CAN'T TELL HIM THAT EVEN TWO THOUSAND YEARS LATER, IT STILL GETS SIDE-EYED BY THE WHOLE FESTIVAL!
GAH!
NOT GOOD FOR A STRAIGHT MAN, BUT IT'S EVERYTHING A FUNNY MAN COULD ASK FOR.

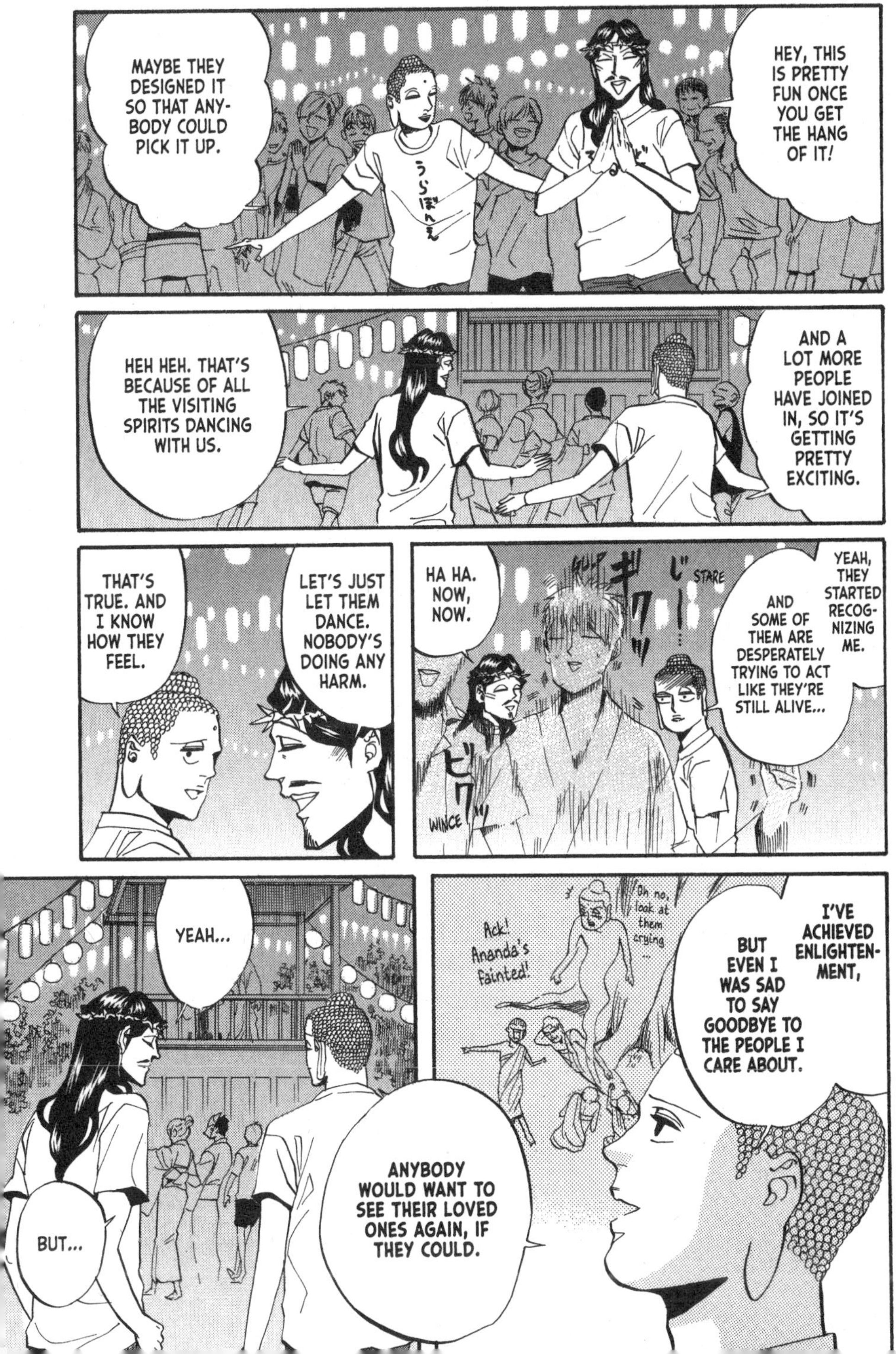
HEY, THIS IS PRETTY FUN ONCE YOU GET THE HANG OF IT!
MAYBE THEY DESIGNED IT SO THAT ANYBODY COULD PICK IT UP.
AND A LOT MORE PEOPLE HAVE JOINED IN, SO IT'S GETTING PRETTY EXCITING.
HEH HEH. THAT'S BECAUSE OF ALL THE VISITING SPIRITS DANCING WITH US.
YEAH, THEY STARTED RECOGNIZING ME.
AND SOME OF THEM ARE DESPERATELY TRYING TO ACT LIKE THEY'RE STILL ALIVE...
STARE
GULP
HA HA. NOW, NOW.
WINCE
LET'S JUST LET THEM DANCE. NOBODY'S DOING ANY HARM.
THAT'S TRUE. AND I KNOW HOW THEY FEEL.
I'VE ACHIEVED ENLIGHTENMENT,
BUT EVEN I WAS SAD TO SAY GOODBYE TO THE PEOPLE I CARE ABOUT.
Oh no, look at them crying...
Ack! Ananda's fainted!
YEAH...
ANYBODY WOULD WANT TO SEE THEIR LOVED ONES AGAIN, IF THEY COULD.
BUT...

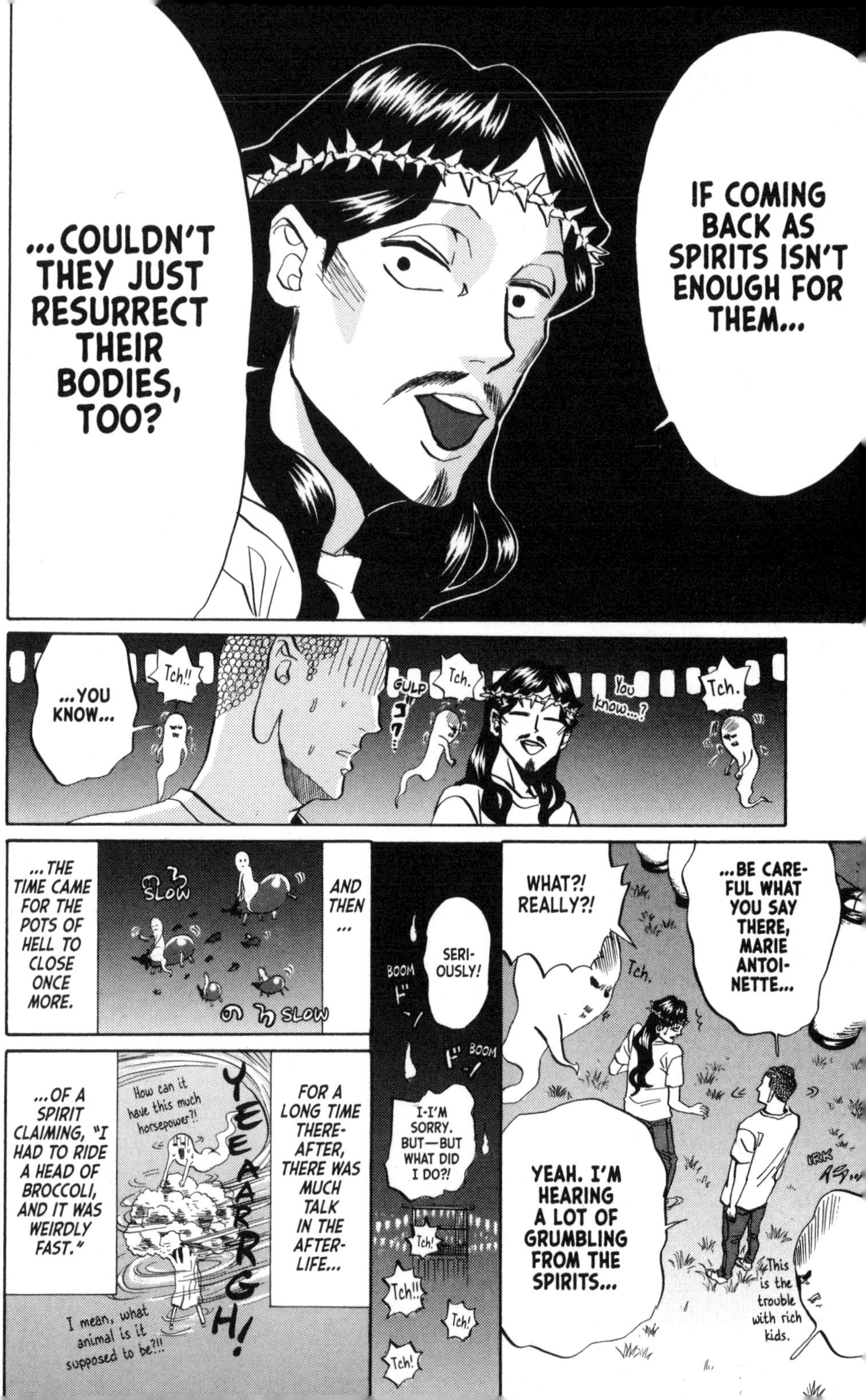
IF COMING BACK AS SPIRITS ISN'T ENOUGH FOR THEM...
...COULDN'T THEY JUST RESURRECT THEIR BODIES, TOO?
Tch.
You know...?
Tch.
GULP
Tch!!
...YOU KNOW...
...BE CAREFUL WHAT YOU SAY THERE, MARIE ANTOINETTE...
WHAT?! REALLY?!
Tch.
IRK
YEAH. I'M HEARING A LOT OF GRUMBLING FROM THE SPIRITS...
This is the trouble with rich kids.
SERIOUSLY!
BOOM
BOOM
I-I'M SORRY. BUT—BUT WHAT DID I DO?!
Tch!
Tch!!
Tch!
Tch!
AND THEN...
...THE TIME CAME FOR THE POTS OF HELL TO CLOSE ONCE MORE.
SLOW
SLOW
FOR A LONG TIME THEREAFTER, THERE WAS MUCH TALK IN THE AFTERLIFE...
YEEAARRGH!
How can it have this much horsepower?!
...OF A SPIRIT CLAIMING, "I HAD TO RIDE A HEAD OF BROCCOLI, AND IT WAS WEIRDLY FAST."
I mean, what animal is it supposed to be?!!

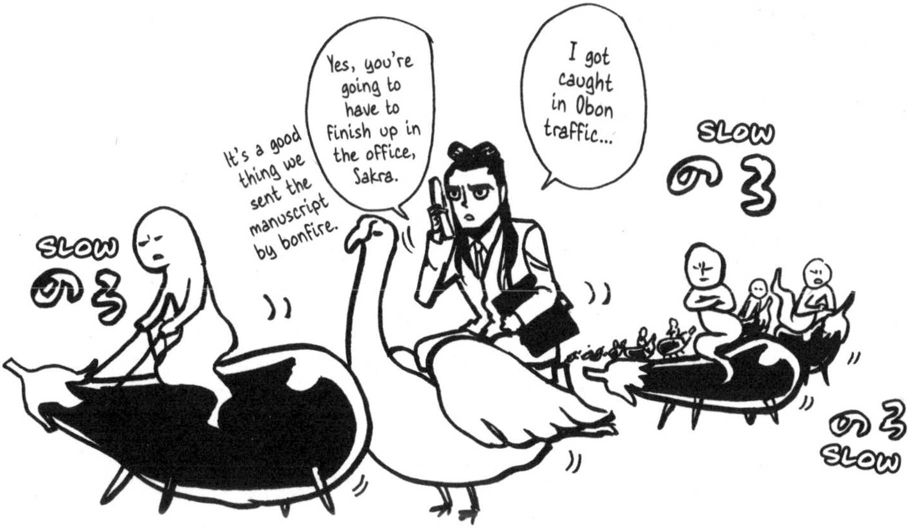

のろ
SLOW
I got caught in Obon traffic...
SLOW
のろ
Yes, you're going to have to finish up in the office, Sakra.
It's a good thing we sent the manuscript by bonfire.
SLOW
のろ

CHAPTER 27 TRANSLATION NOTES

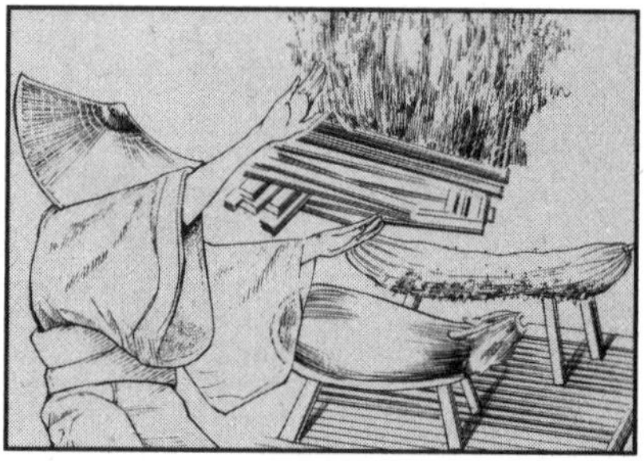

Riding vegetables, page 231
As Buddha describes, this is an Obon custom to help deceased ancestors make their way to and from the afterlife. Giving legs to an eggplant makes a cow, which will give a slow ride back to the afterlife, but cucumbers can also be used, making a horse to bring ancestors home quickly.

Bon Bon Bon, page 232
This title features three different kind of Bons. The first is the Bon of Obon—the aforementioned holiday. The O is added at the beginning to elevate the term and show respect to it, so in that case, Bon and Obon mean the same thing. The second is the Bon of Bonten, which is the Japanese name of Brahma. The last Bon likely refers to the sound of lighting a fire, such as a bonfire, which is not an uncommon feature of Obon festivals.

Lourdes, page 233
A French town at the base of the Pyrenees Mountains. It became a Catholic pilgrimage site after a girl who later became Saint Bernadette saw visions of a woman who identified herself as the Immaculate Conception (a term related to the Virgin Mary) and asked that a chapel be built near the town.

Mountain of Spikes, page 233
One of the most well-known features in the Japanese vision of Hell is the Mountain of Spikes. As the name suggests, it's a mountain made of sharp, pointy spears that sinners are made to walk across.

Asura-kun the Titan going to Yoyogi Animation Academy, page 234

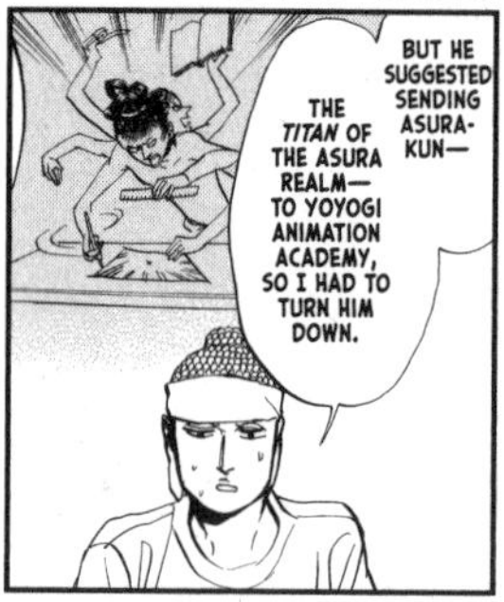
BUT HE SUGGESTED SENDING ASURA-KUN—
THE *TITAN* OF THE ASURA REALM—TO YOYOGI ANIMATION ACADEMY, SO I HAD TO TURN HIM DOWN.

Yoyogi Animation Academy is a school in the Chiyoda Ward of Tokyo that teaches all manner of anime-related trades, including manga artistry. In Japan, when someone is coming up against a tight deadline, it's called a *shuraba,* which translates roughly to "battleground" or, in entertainment contexts, "fight scene." But in this case, it is the word for "crunch time," "hell week," or whatever colorful term a creator may feel like using for the death they feel when all they have time for is work. Literally, it means "place of the asura," where "asura" translates to demigod, titan, or demon, and refers to the creatures that rule over the Asura Realm—one of the six realms in Buddhism, where fighting and death are a constant.

Top Idol Asura, page 235
Around the year 2009, the officials at Kōfukuji Temple in Nara launched a grand endeavor to revive the popularity of their Buddhist statues, particularly of Asura. Their efforts were wildly successful, and when they culminated in an exhibition in which their Asura statue was put on display in Tokyo, people young and old lined up for hours just to see it, and the museum had to extend its opening hours to accommodate them. Meanwhile, 15,000 replicas of the statue sold out in just two weeks. Later, the exhibition was sent to Kyushu, hence the national tour.

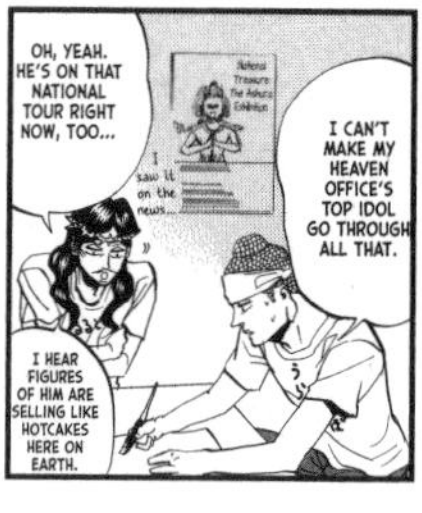
I CAN'T MAKE MY HEAVEN OFFICE'S TOP IDOL GO THROUGH ALL THAT.
OH, YEAH. HE'S ON THAT NATIONAL TOUR RIGHT NOW, TOO...
I saw it on the news...
I HEAR FIGURES OF HIM ARE SELLING LIKE HOTCAKES HERE ON EARTH.

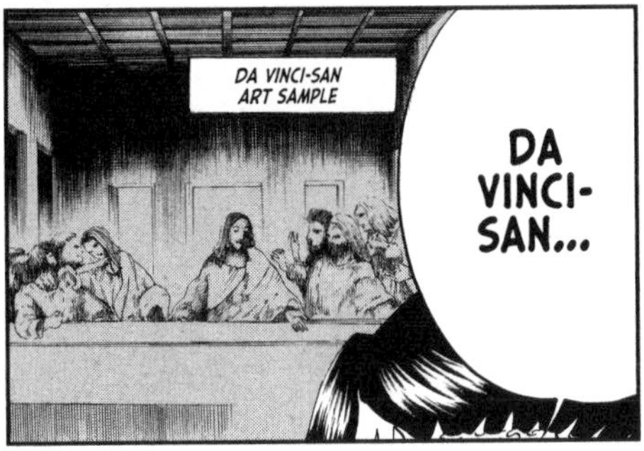
DA VINCI-SAN
ART SAMPLE
DA VINCI-SAN...

Da Vinci and Raphael, page 236

Leonardo da Vinci, more commonly known as Leonardo, is a Renaissance painter, inventor, sculptor, architect, etc. who lived from 1452 to 1519. He is most famous for painting the *Mona Lisa* and *The Last Supper* (pictured here). Raffaello Sanzio da Urbino, more commonly known as Raphael, is another Renaissance painter who lived from 1483 to 1520. His sample artwork shown here is a section of the *Sistine Madonna.*

Ullambana, page 237

This is the Sanskrit word for the Bon Festival.

Riding a goose, page 237

Brahma was adopted into Buddhism from other religions such as Hinduism, in which deities are often depicted with animals known as *vahana,* or "vehicles." The *vahana* that accompanies Brahma is a bird called a *hamsa,* which can refer to a goose or a swan.

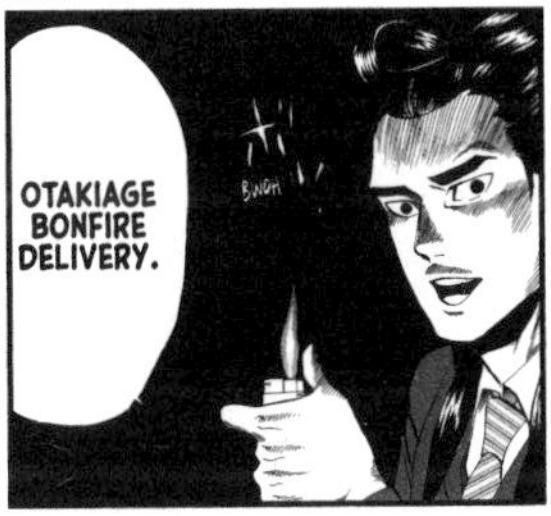
OTAKIAGE BONFIRE DELIVERY.

Otakiage bonfire delivery, page 240

One of the rituals performed on Obon is a ceremonial fire used to released cherished objects from their physical form and return them to the heavens. The objects burned are usually mementos of the deceased or good luck charms purchased or received throughout the previous year.

Sakra-san, page 240

Sakra, or Taishakuten in Japanese, is the ruler of the Devas.

Maudgalyayana rescues his mother, page 242

One of the Buddha's closest disciples was Maudgalyayana. According to a story told in the *Ullambana Sutra* (the origin of the Obon tradition), he used these powers after his parents died to find out what realms they had been reborn into. His father was safely reborn in Heaven, but his mother had been reborn into the Realm of Hungry Ghosts because of her sins. Maudgalyayana tried to feed her, but the food always burst into flames before she could eat any of it. The Buddha's disciple asked his master for help, and the Buddha told him to make offerings to some monks and ask them to pray for his ancestors. They did, and his mother was freed from her hell.

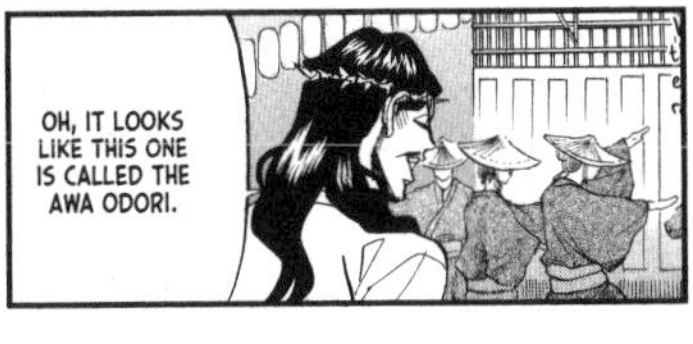
OH, IT LOOKS LIKE THIS ONE IS CALLED THE AWA ODORI.

Awa Odori, page 243

The Bon Odori, or Bon Dance, as it is known today, originated as a folk dance to welcome the spirits of the dead. There are different variations of it in different regions.

SAINT☆YOUNG MEN

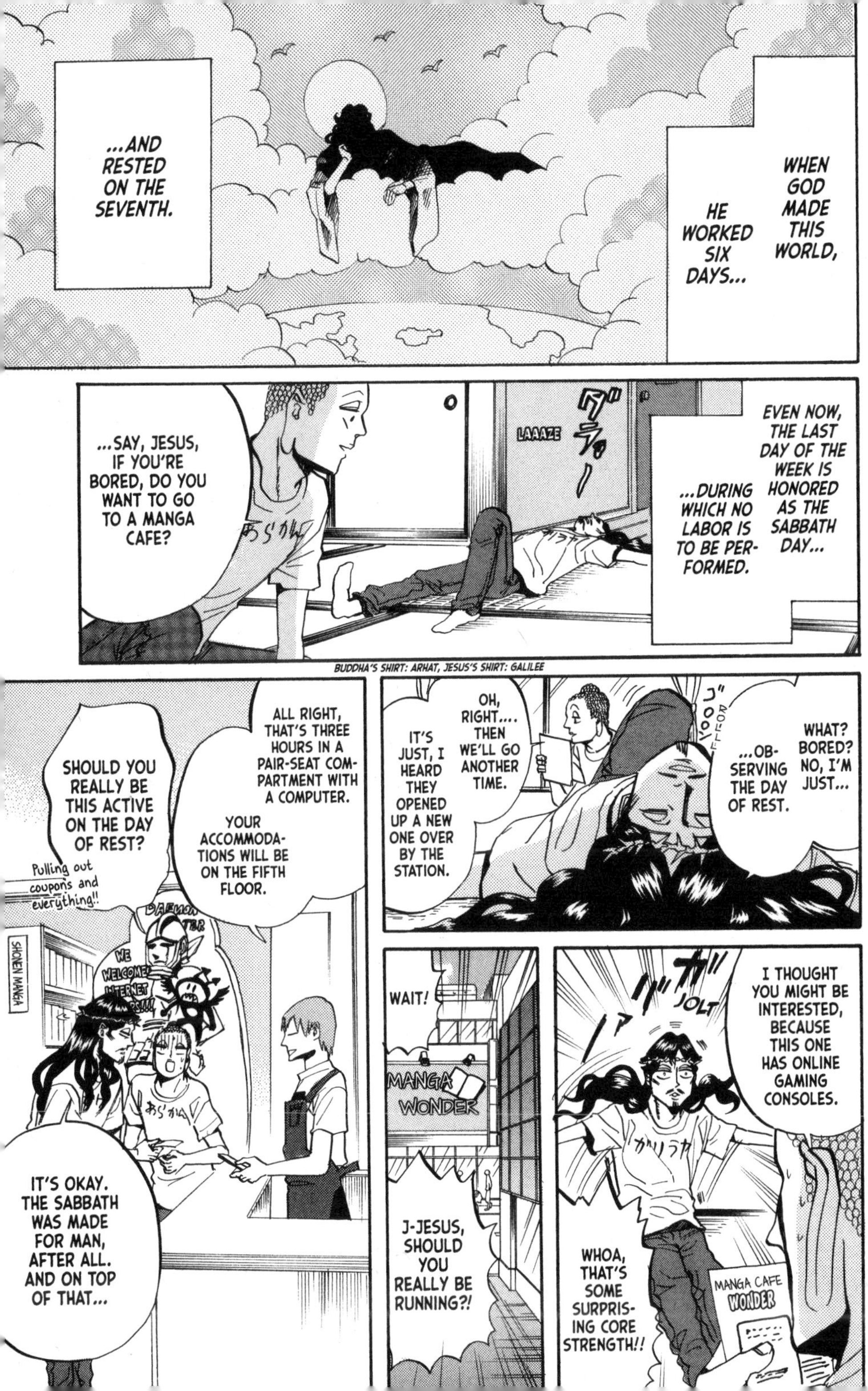
WHEN GOD MADE THIS WORLD,
HE WORKED SIX DAYS...
...AND RESTED ON THE SEVENTH.
EVEN NOW, THE LAST DAY OF THE WEEK IS HONORED AS THE SABBATH DAY...
...DURING WHICH NO LABOR IS TO BE PERFORMED.
LAAAZE
...SAY, JESUS, IF YOU'RE BORED, DO YOU WANT TO GO TO A MANGA CAFE?
BUDDHA'S SHIRT: ARHAT, JESUS'S SHIRT: GALILEE
WHAT? BORED? NO, I'M JUST...
...OB-SERVING THE DAY OF REST.
ROLLL
OH, RIGHT.... THEN WE'LL GO ANOTHER TIME.
IT'S JUST, I HEARD THEY OPENED UP A NEW ONE OVER BY THE STATION.
I THOUGHT YOU MIGHT BE INTERESTED, BECAUSE THIS ONE HAS ONLINE GAMING CONSOLES.
JOLT
WHOA, THAT'S SOME SURPRIS-ING CORE STRENGTH!!
MANGA CAFE WONDER
WAIT!
MANGA WONDER
J-JESUS, SHOULD YOU REALLY BE RUNNING?!
ALL RIGHT, THAT'S THREE HOURS IN A PAIR-SEAT COM-PARTMENT WITH A COMPUTER.
YOUR ACCOMMODA-TIONS WILL BE ON THE FIFTH FLOOR.
SHOULD YOU REALLY BE THIS ACTIVE ON THE DAY OF REST?
Pulling out coupons and everything!!
SHONEN MANGA
IT'S OKAY. THE SABBATH WAS MADE FOR MAN, AFTER ALL. AND ON TOP OF THAT...

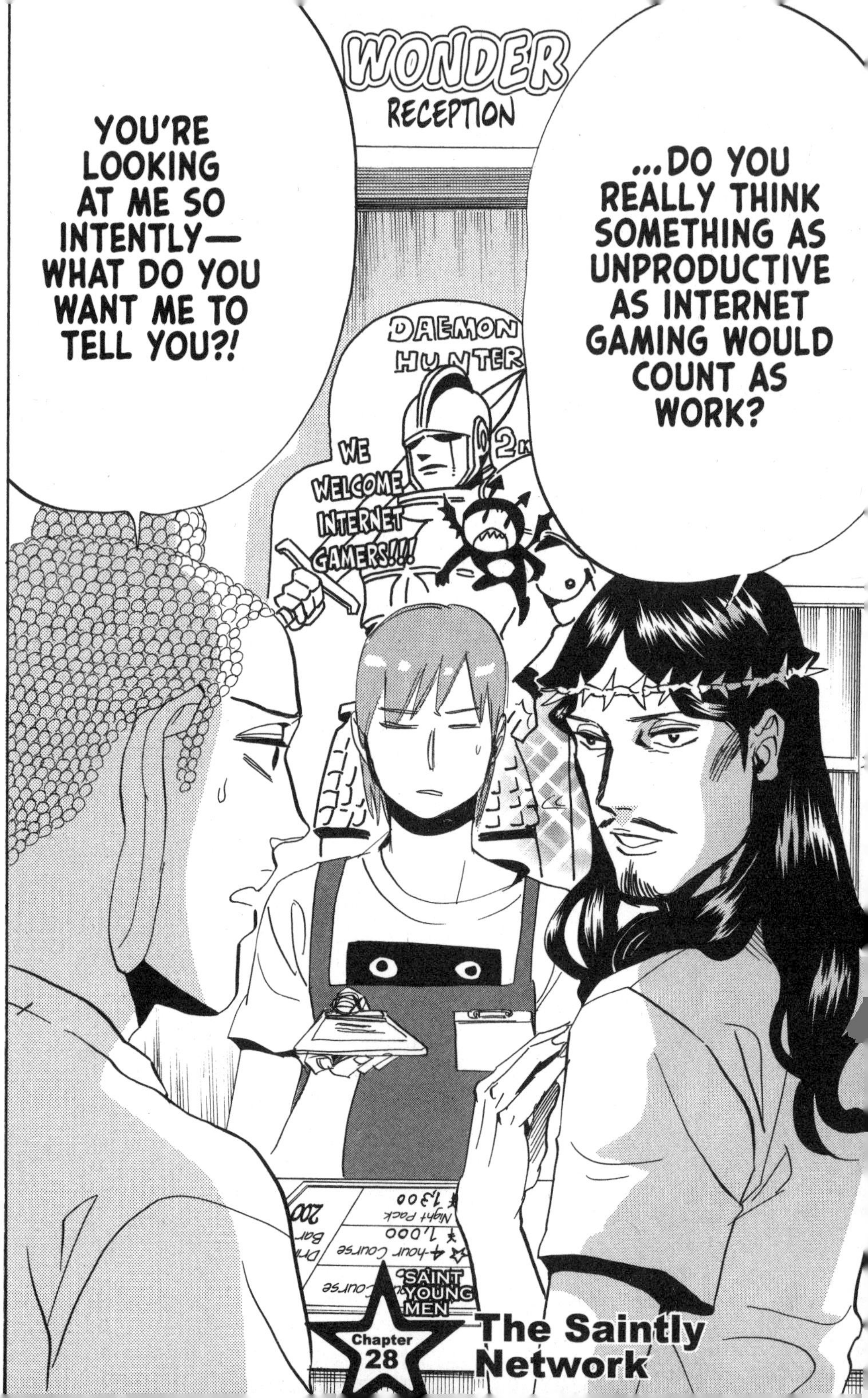
...DO YOU REALLY THINK SOMETHING AS UNPRODUCTIVE AS INTERNET GAMING WOULD COUNT AS WORK?
YOU'RE LOOKING AT ME SO INTENTLY— WHAT DO YOU WANT ME TO TELL YOU?!
WONDER
RECEPTION
DAEMON HUNTER 2
WE WELCOME INTERNET GAMERS!!!
4-hour Course ¥1,000
Night Pack ¥1,300
SAINT YOUNG MEN
Chapter 28
The Saintly Network

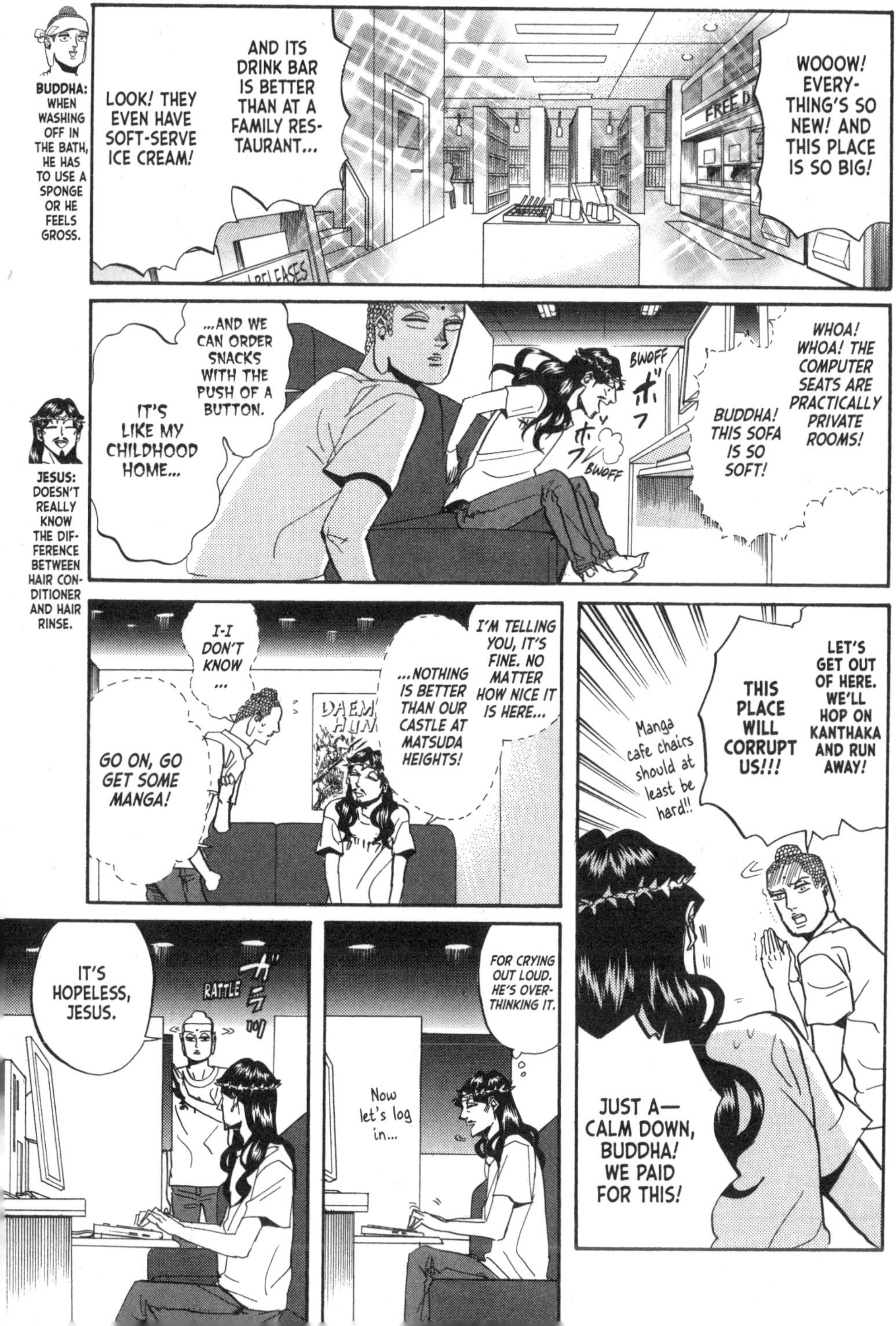
BUDDHA: WHEN WASHING OFF IN THE BATH, HE HAS TO USE A SPONGE OR HE FEELS GROSS.
JESUS: DOESN'T REALLY KNOW THE DIFFERENCE BETWEEN HAIR CONDITIONER AND HAIR RINSE.
WOOOW! EVERYTHING'S SO NEW! AND THIS PLACE IS SO BIG!
AND ITS DRINK BAR IS BETTER THAN AT A FAMILY RESTAURANT...
LOOK! THEY EVEN HAVE SOFT-SERVE ICE CREAM!
WHOA! WHOA! THE COMPUTER SEATS ARE PRACTICALLY PRIVATE ROOMS!
BUDDHA! THIS SOFA IS SO SOFT!
BWOFF
BWOFF
...AND WE CAN ORDER SNACKS WITH THE PUSH OF A BUTTON.
IT'S LIKE MY CHILDHOOD HOME...
LET'S GET OUT OF HERE. WE'LL HOP ON KANTHAKA AND RUN AWAY!
THIS PLACE WILL CORRUPT US!!!
Manga cafe chairs should at least be hard!!
JUST A— CALM DOWN, BUDDHA! WE PAID FOR THIS!
I'M TELLING YOU, IT'S FINE. NO MATTER HOW NICE IT IS HERE...
...NOTHING IS BETTER THAN OUR CASTLE AT MATSUDA HEIGHTS!
I-I DON'T KNOW...
GO ON, GO GET SOME MANGA!
FOR CRYING OUT LOUD. HE'S OVERTHINKING IT.
Now let's log in...
IT'S HOPELESS, JESUS.
RATTLE

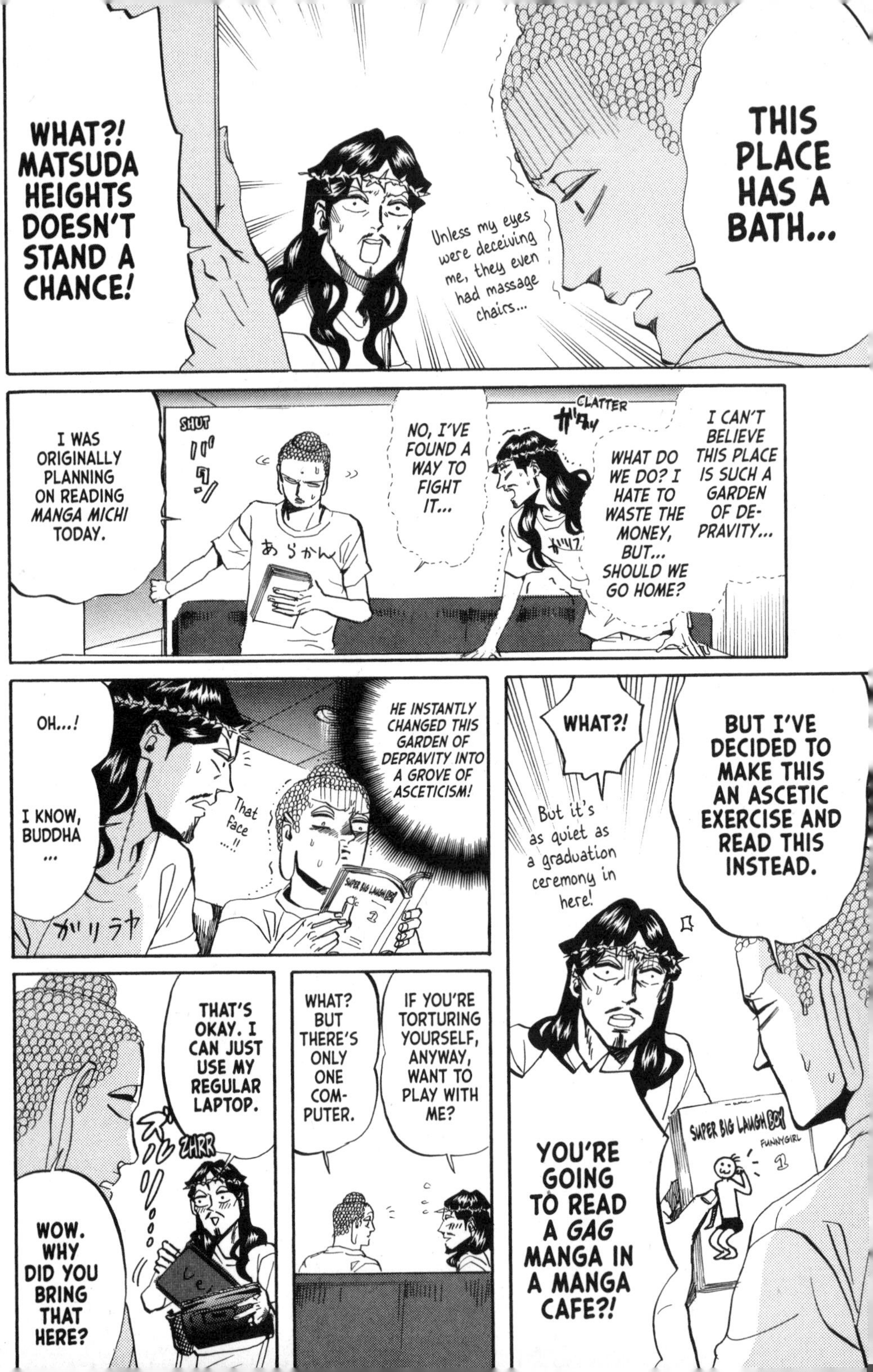
THIS PLACE HAS A BATH...
Unless my eyes were deceiving me, they even had massage chairs...
WHAT?! MATSUDA HEIGHTS DOESN'T STAND A CHANCE!
I CAN'T BELIEVE THIS PLACE IS SUCH A GARDEN OF DE-PRAVITY...
CLATTER
WHAT DO WE DO? I HATE TO WASTE THE MONEY, BUT... SHOULD WE GO HOME?
NO, I'VE FOUND A WAY TO FIGHT IT...
SHUT
I WAS ORIGINALLY PLANNING ON READING *MANGA MICHI* TODAY.
BUT I'VE DECIDED TO MAKE THIS AN ASCETIC EXERCISE AND READ THIS INSTEAD.
WHAT?!
But it's as quiet as a graduation ceremony in here!
SUPER BIG LAUGH BOY
FUNNYGIRL
YOU'RE GOING TO READ A *GAG* MANGA IN A MANGA CAFE?!
HE INSTANTLY CHANGED THIS GARDEN OF DEPRAVITY INTO A GROVE OF ASCETICISM!
That face ...!!
OH...!
I KNOW, BUDDHA ...
SUPER BIG LAUGH BOY
IF YOU'RE TORTURING YOURSELF, ANYWAY, WANT TO PLAY WITH ME?
WHAT? BUT THERE'S ONLY ONE COM-PUTER.
THAT'S OKAY. I CAN JUST USE MY REGULAR LAPTOP.
ZHRR
WOW. WHY DID YOU BRING THAT HERE?

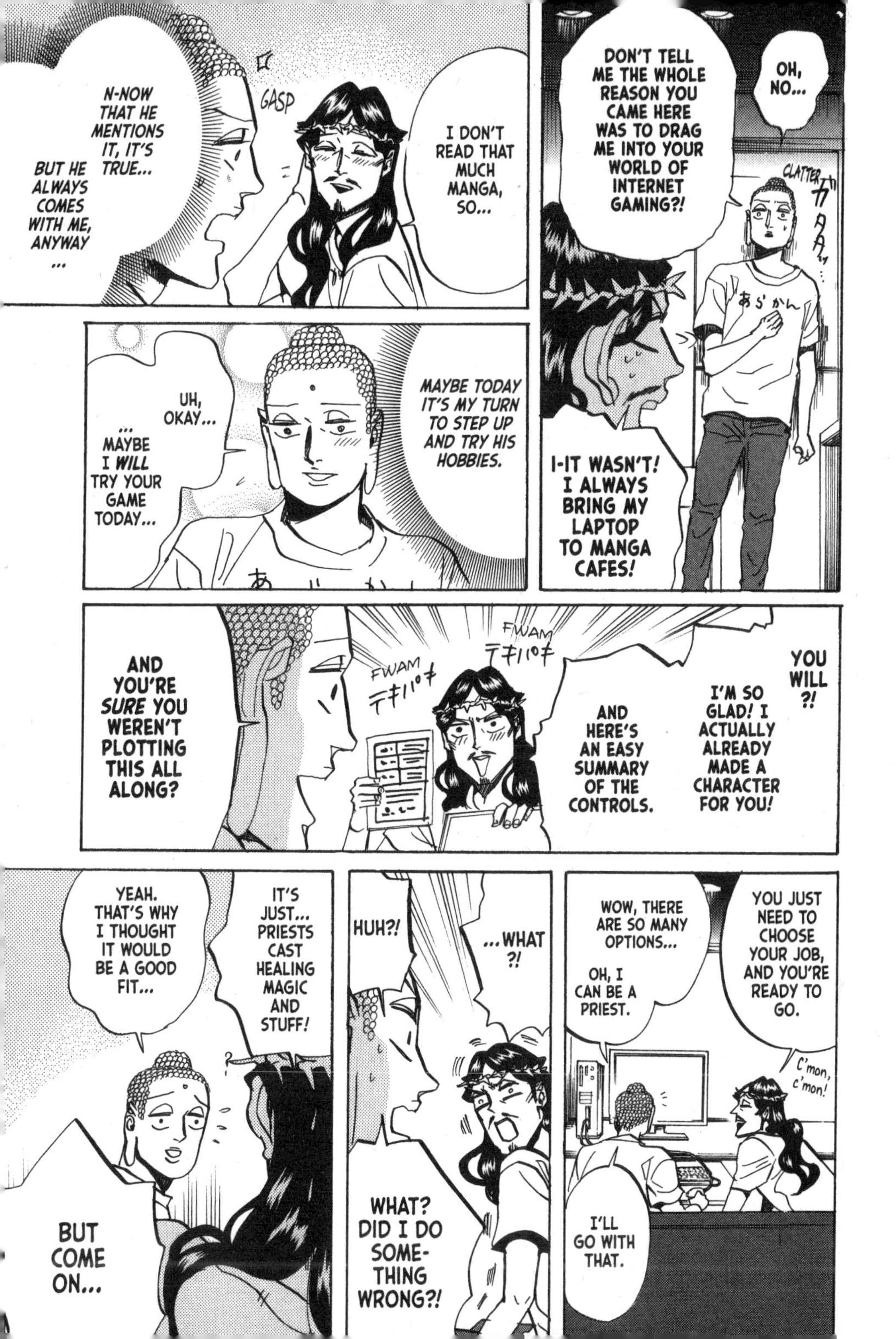
OH, NO...
DON'T TELL ME THE WHOLE REASON YOU CAME HERE WAS TO DRAG ME INTO YOUR WORLD OF INTERNET GAMING?!
CLATTER
I-IT WASN'T! I ALWAYS BRING MY LAPTOP TO MANGA CAFES!
I DON'T READ THAT MUCH MANGA, SO...
GASP
N-NOW THAT HE MENTIONS IT, IT'S TRUE...
BUT HE ALWAYS COMES WITH ME, ANYWAY ...
MAYBE TODAY IT'S MY TURN TO STEP UP AND TRY HIS HOBBIES.
UH, OKAY...
... MAYBE I WILL TRY YOUR GAME TODAY...
YOU WILL ?!
I'M SO GLAD! I ACTUALLY ALREADY MADE A CHARACTER FOR YOU!
AND HERE'S AN EASY SUMMARY OF THE CONTROLS.
FWAM
FWAM
AND YOU'RE SURE YOU WEREN'T PLOTTING THIS ALL ALONG?
YOU JUST NEED TO CHOOSE YOUR JOB, AND YOU'RE READY TO GO.
C'mon, c'mon!
WOW, THERE ARE SO MANY OPTIONS...
OH, I CAN BE A PRIEST.
I'LL GO WITH THAT.
...WHAT ?!
HUH?!
WHAT? DID I DO SOME-THING WRONG?!
IT'S JUST... PRIESTS CAST HEALING MAGIC AND STUFF!
YEAH. THAT'S WHY I THOUGHT IT WOULD BE A GOOD FIT...
BUT COME ON...

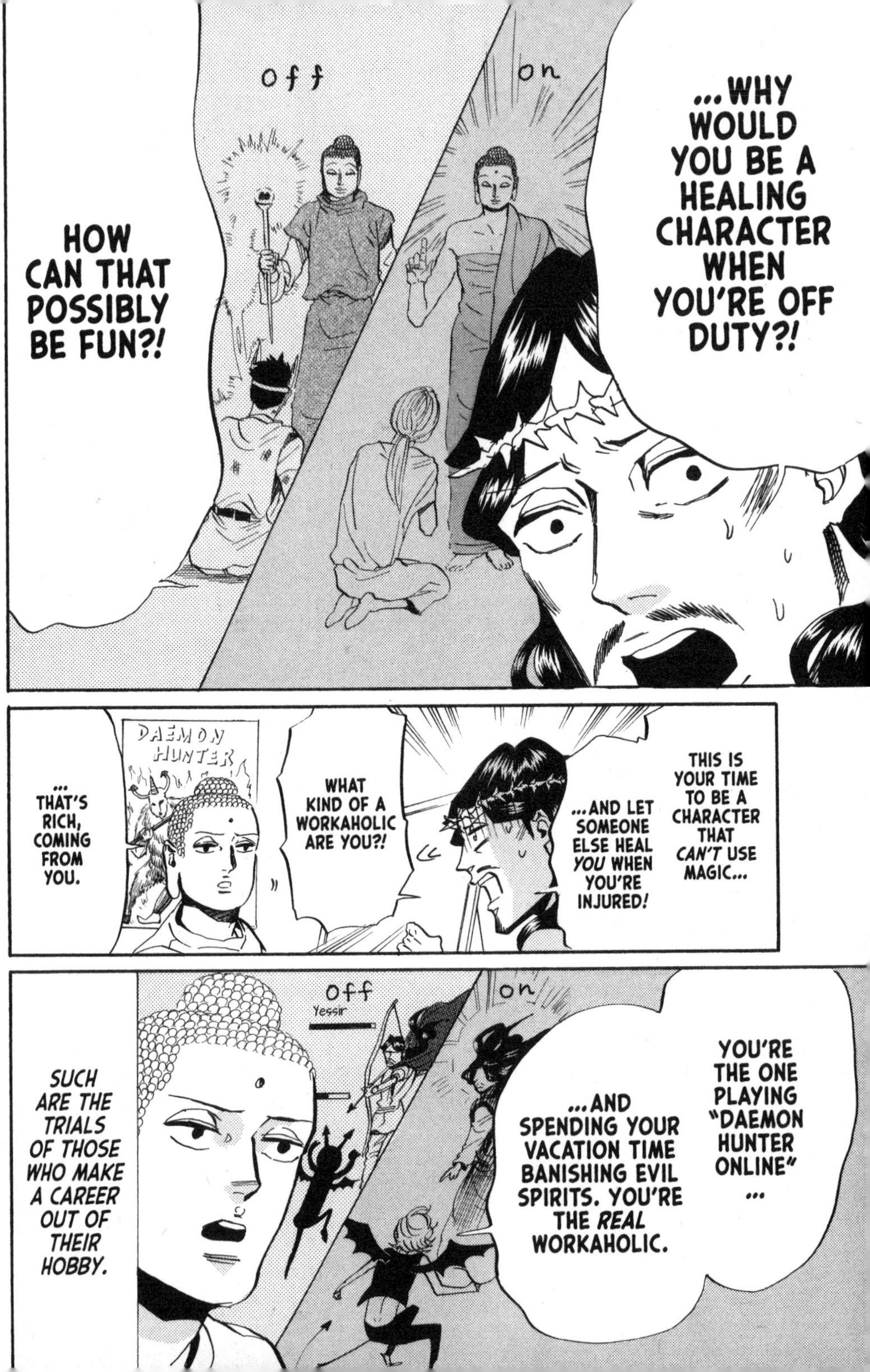
on
off
...WHY WOULD YOU BE A HEALING CHARACTER WHEN YOU'RE OFF DUTY?!
HOW CAN THAT POSSIBLY BE FUN?!
THIS IS YOUR TIME TO BE A CHARACTER THAT *CAN'T* USE MAGIC...
...AND LET SOMEONE ELSE HEAL *YOU* WHEN YOU'RE INJURED!
WHAT KIND OF A WORKAHOLIC ARE YOU?!
DAEMON HUNTER
...THAT'S RICH, COMING FROM YOU.
on
off
Yessir
YOU'RE THE ONE PLAYING "DAEMON HUNTER ONLINE"...
...AND SPENDING YOUR VACATION TIME BANISHING EVIL SPIRITS. YOU'RE THE *REAL* WORKAHOLIC.
SUCH ARE THE TRIALS OF THOSE WHO MAKE A CAREER OUT OF THEIR HOBBY.

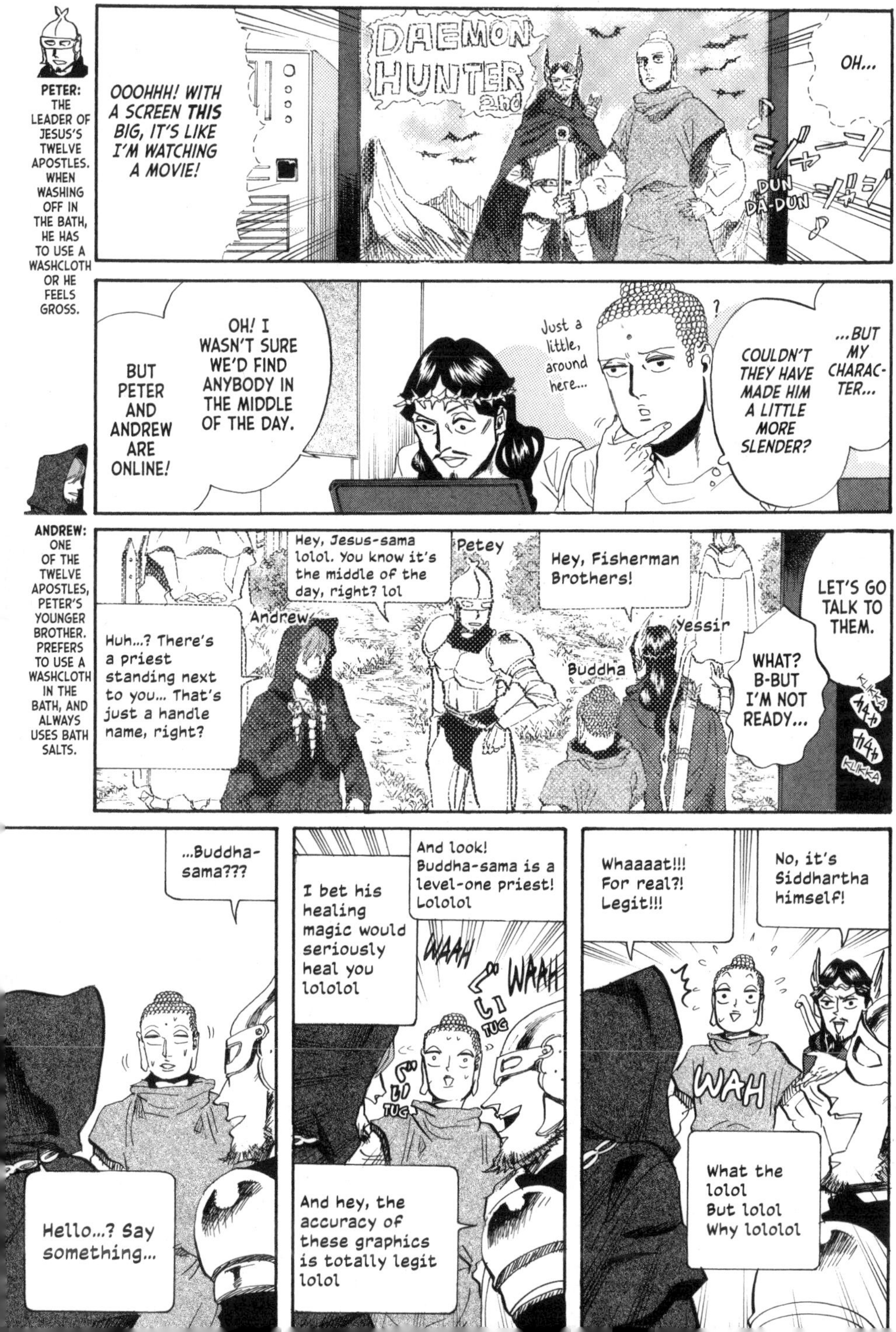
PETER: THE LEADER OF JESUS'S TWELVE APOSTLES. WHEN WASHING OFF IN THE BATH, HE HAS TO USE A WASHCLOTH OR HE FEELS GROSS.
OH...
DUN DA-DUN
DAEMON HUNTER 2nd
OOOHHH! WITH A SCREEN THIS BIG, IT'S LIKE I'M WATCHING A MOVIE!
...BUT MY CHARACTER...
COULDN'T THEY HAVE MADE HIM A LITTLE MORE SLENDER?
?
Just a little, around here...
OH! I WASN'T SURE WE'D FIND ANYBODY IN THE MIDDLE OF THE DAY.
BUT PETER AND ANDREW ARE ONLINE!
ANDREW: ONE OF THE TWELVE APOSTLES, PETER'S YOUNGER BROTHER. PREFERS TO USE A WASHCLOTH IN THE BATH, AND ALWAYS USES BATH SALTS.
LET'S GO TALK TO THEM.
WHAT? B-BUT I'M NOT READY...
KLIKKA
KLIKKA
Hey, Fisherman Brothers!
Yessir
Buddha
Petey
Hey, Jesus-sama lolol. You know it's the middle of the day, right? lol
Andrew
Huh...? There's a priest standing next to you... That's just a handle name, right?
No, it's Siddhartha himself!
Whaaaat!!! For real?! Legit!!!
WAH
What the lolol
But lolol
Why lololol
And look! Buddha-sama is a level-one priest! Lolololol
I bet his healing magic would seriously heal you lolololol
WAAH
WAAH
TUG
TUG
And hey, the accuracy of these graphics is totally legit lolol
...Buddha-sama???
Hello...? Say something...

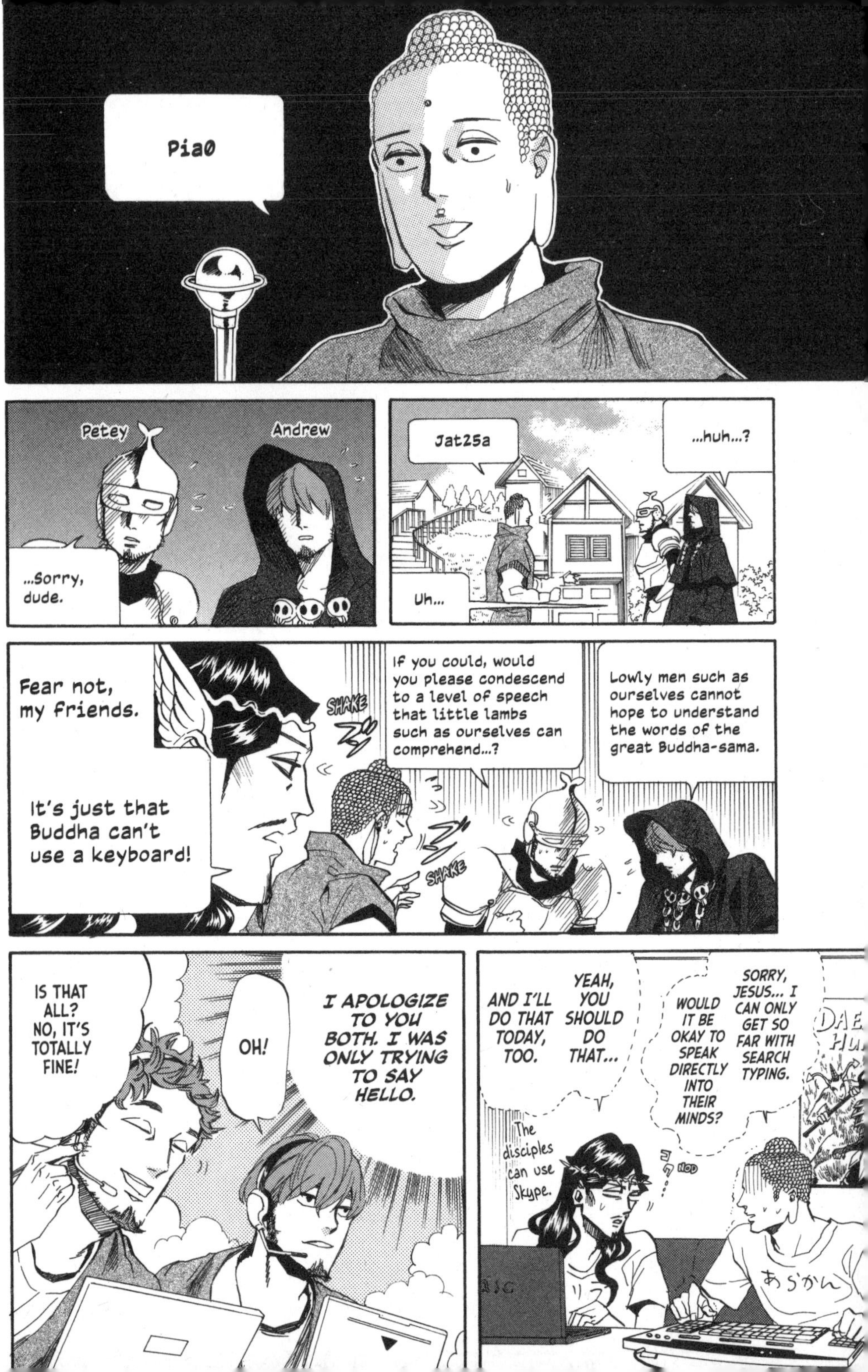
Pia0
...huh...?
Jat25a
Uh...
Andrew
Petey
...Sorry, dude.
Lowly men such as ourselves cannot hope to understand the words of the great Buddha-sama.
If you could, would you please condescend to a level of speech that little lambs such as ourselves can comprehend...?
SHAKE
Fear not, my friends.
It's just that Buddha can't use a keyboard!
SHAKE
SORRY, JESUS... I CAN ONLY GET SO FAR WITH SEARCH TYPING.
WOULD IT BE OKAY TO SPEAK DIRECTLY INTO THEIR MINDS?
YEAH, YOU SHOULD DO THAT...
AND I'LL DO THAT TODAY, TOO.
NOD
The disciples can use Skype.
I APOLOGIZE TO YOU BOTH. I WAS ONLY TRYING TO SAY HELLO.
OH!
IS THAT ALL? NO, IT'S TOTALLY FINE!

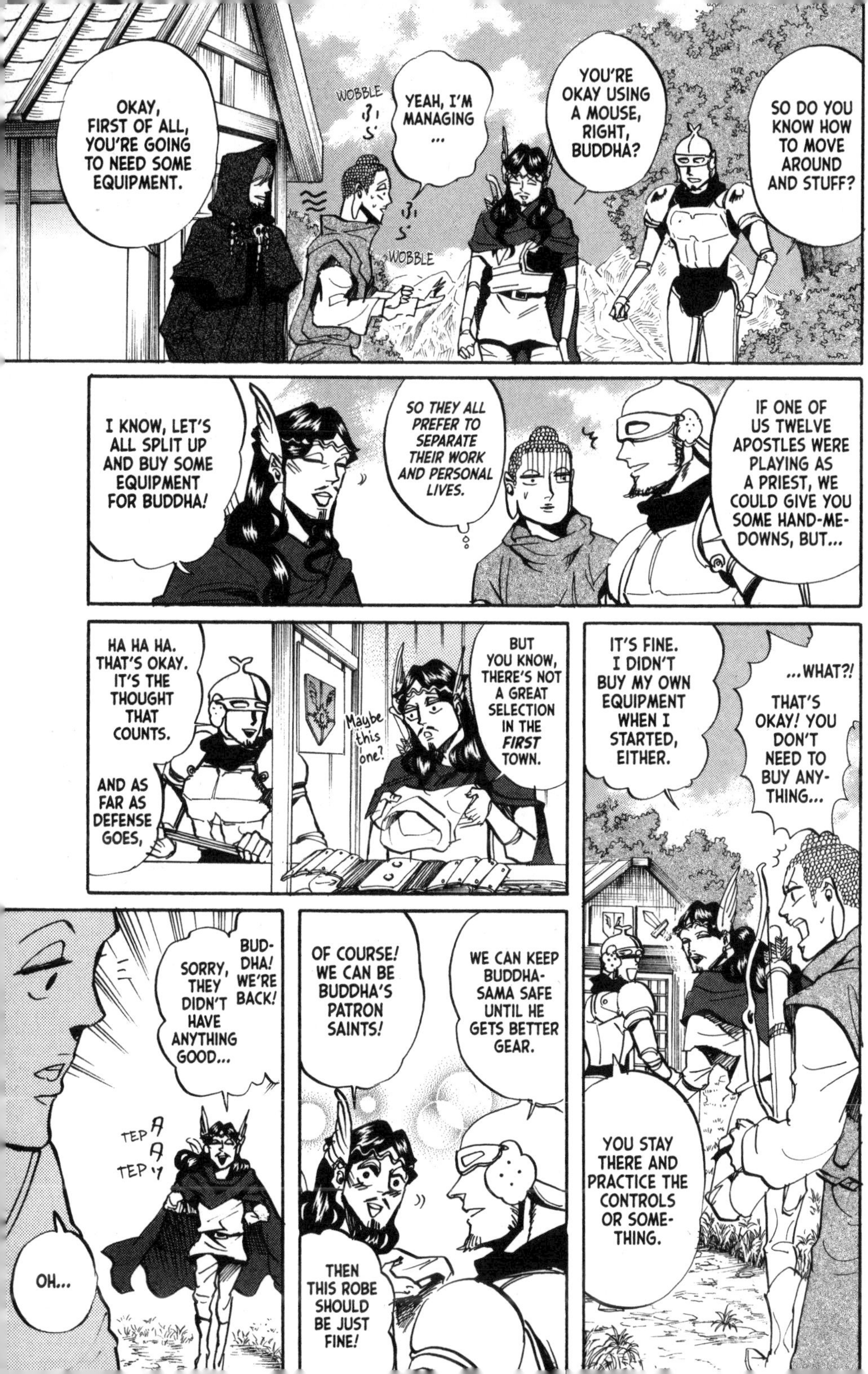
SO DO YOU KNOW HOW TO MOVE AROUND AND STUFF?
YOU'RE OKAY USING A MOUSE, RIGHT, BUDDHA?
YEAH, I'M MANAGING ...
WOBBLE
WOBBLE
OKAY, FIRST OF ALL, YOU'RE GOING TO NEED SOME EQUIPMENT.
IF ONE OF US TWELVE APOSTLES WERE PLAYING AS A PRIEST, WE COULD GIVE YOU SOME HAND-ME-DOWNS, BUT...
SO THEY ALL PREFER TO SEPARATE THEIR WORK AND PERSONAL LIVES.
I KNOW, LET'S ALL SPLIT UP AND BUY SOME EQUIPMENT FOR BUDDHA!
...WHAT?!
THAT'S OKAY! YOU DON'T NEED TO BUY ANYTHING...
IT'S FINE. I DIDN'T BUY MY OWN EQUIPMENT WHEN I STARTED, EITHER.
YOU STAY THERE AND PRACTICE THE CONTROLS OR SOMETHING.
BUT YOU KNOW, THERE'S NOT A GREAT SELECTION IN THE *FIRST* TOWN.
Maybe this one?
HA HA HA. THAT'S OKAY. IT'S THE THOUGHT THAT COUNTS.
AND AS FAR AS DEFENSE GOES,
WE CAN KEEP BUDDHA-SAMA SAFE UNTIL HE GETS BETTER GEAR.
OF COURSE! WE CAN BE BUDDHA'S PATRON SAINTS!
THEN THIS ROBE SHOULD BE JUST FINE!
BUDDHA! WE'RE BACK!
SORRY, THEY DIDN'T HAVE ANYTHING GOOD...
TEP
TEP
OH...

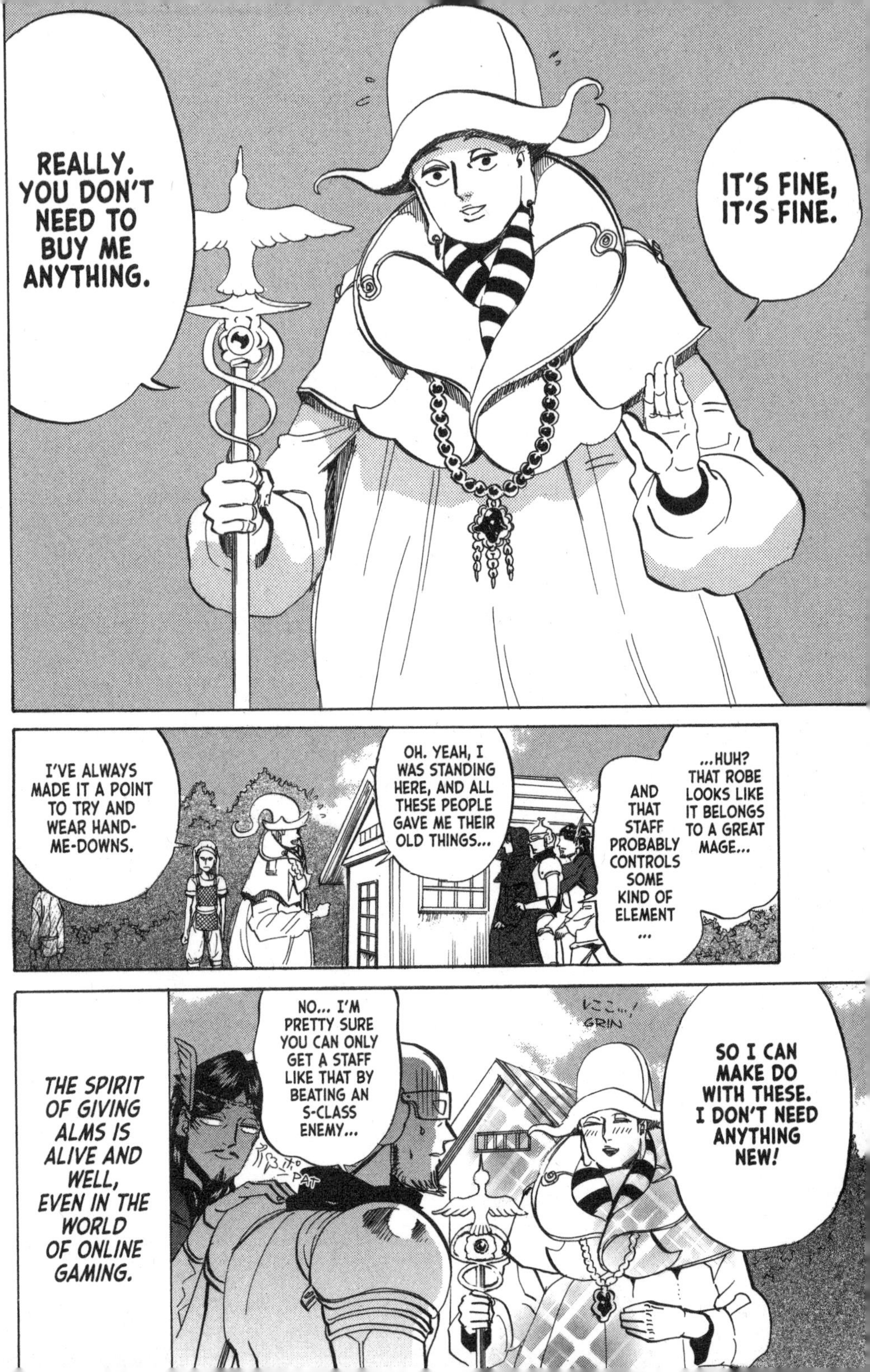
IT'S FINE, IT'S FINE.
REALLY. YOU DON'T NEED TO BUY ME ANYTHING.
...HUH? THAT ROBE LOOKS LIKE IT BELONGS TO A GREAT MAGE...
AND THAT STAFF PROBABLY CONTROLS SOME KIND OF ELEMENT...
OH. YEAH, I WAS STANDING HERE, AND ALL THESE PEOPLE GAVE ME THEIR OLD THINGS...
I'VE ALWAYS MADE IT A POINT TO TRY AND WEAR HAND-ME-DOWNS.
GRIN
SO I CAN MAKE DO WITH THESE. I DON'T NEED ANYTHING NEW!
NO... I'M PRETTY SURE YOU CAN ONLY GET A STAFF LIKE THAT BY BEATING AN S-CLASS ENEMY...
PAT
THE SPIRIT OF GIVING ALMS IS ALIVE AND WELL, EVEN IN THE WORLD OF ONLINE GAMING.

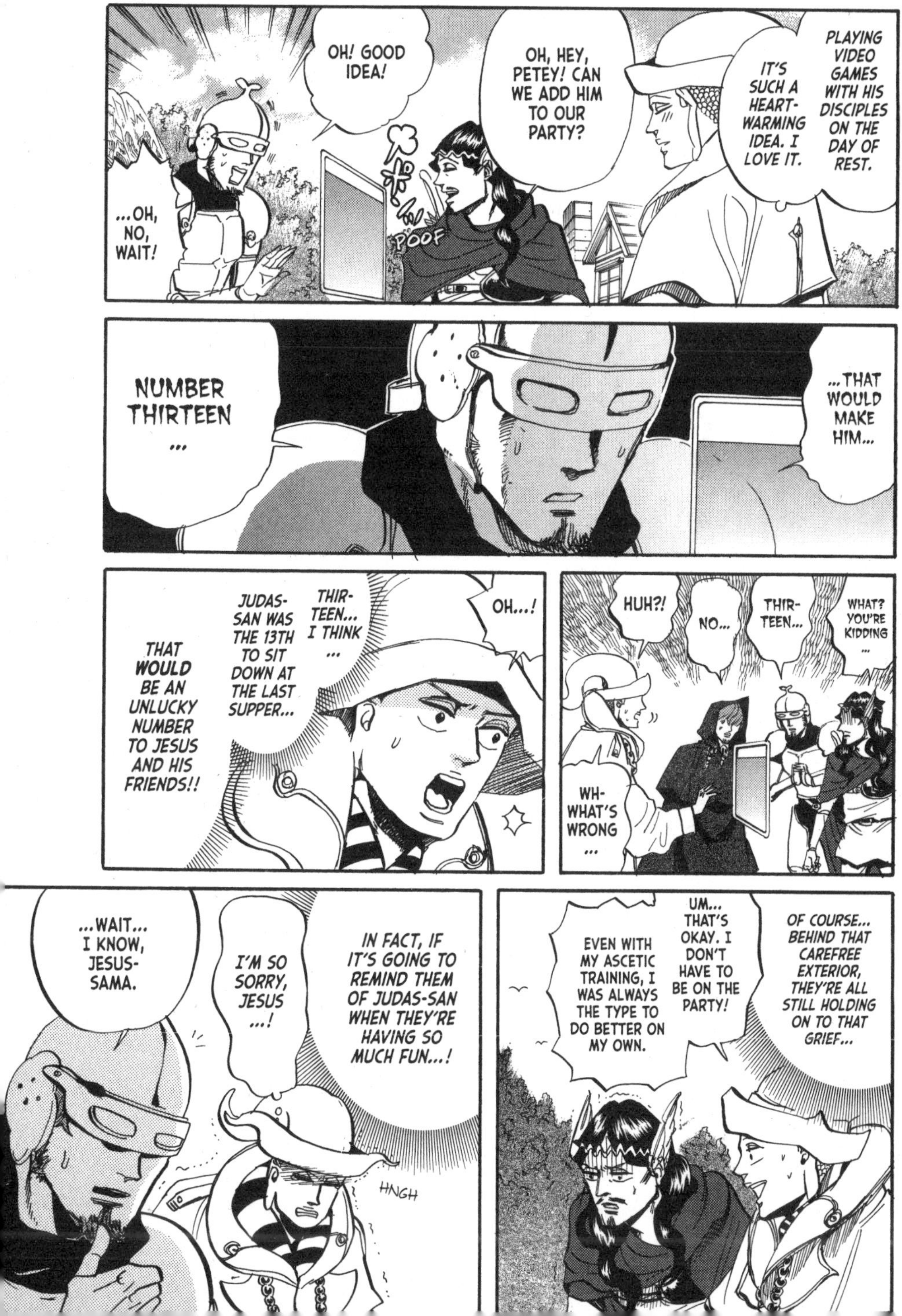
PLAYING VIDEO GAMES WITH HIS DISCIPLES ON THE DAY OF REST.
IT'S SUCH A HEART-WARMING IDEA. I LOVE IT.
OH, HEY, PETEY! CAN WE ADD HIM TO OUR PARTY?
OH! GOOD IDEA!
POOF
...OH, NO, WAIT!
...THAT WOULD MAKE HIM...
NUMBER THIRTEEN ...
WHAT? YOU'RE KIDDING ...
THIR-TEEN...
NO...
HUH?!
WH-WHAT'S WRONG ...
OH...!
THIR-TEEN... I THINK ...
JUDAS-SAN WAS THE 13TH TO SIT DOWN AT THE LAST SUPPER...
THAT *WOULD* BE AN UNLUCKY NUMBER TO JESUS AND HIS FRIENDS!!
OF COURSE... BEHIND THAT CAREFREE EXTERIOR, THEY'RE ALL STILL HOLDING ON TO THAT GRIEF...
UM... THAT'S OKAY. I DON'T HAVE TO BE ON THE PARTY!
EVEN WITH MY ASCETIC TRAINING, I WAS ALWAYS THE TYPE TO DO BETTER ON MY OWN.
IN FACT, IF IT'S GOING TO REMIND THEM OF JUDAS-SAN WHEN THEY'RE HAVING SO MUCH FUN...!
I'M SO SORRY, JESUS ...!
HNGH
...WAIT... I KNOW, JESUS-SAMA.

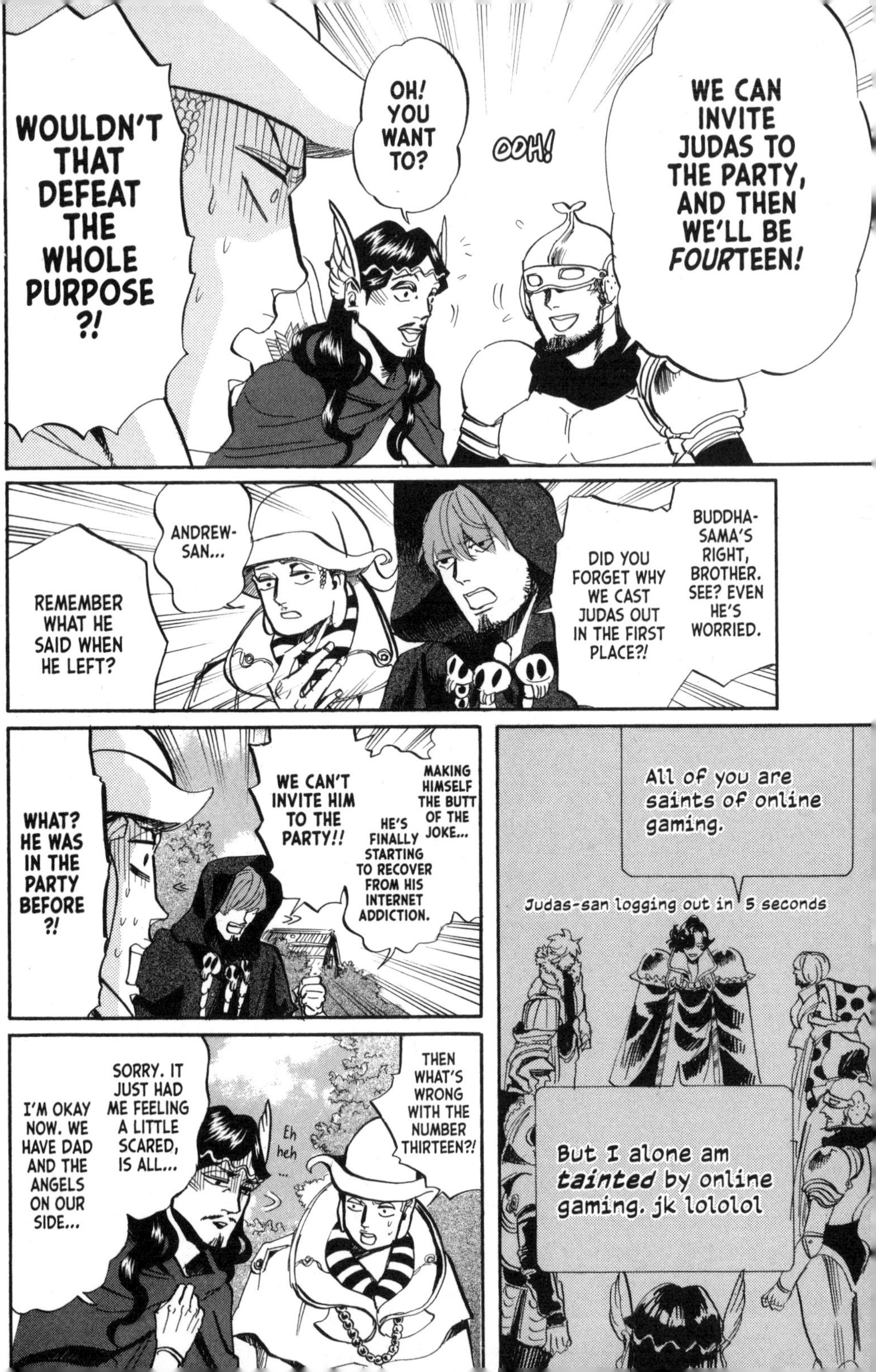
WE CAN INVITE JUDAS TO THE PARTY, AND THEN WE'LL BE *FOUR*TEEN!
OOH!
OH! YOU WANT TO?
WOULDN'T THAT DEFEAT THE WHOLE PURPOSE?!
BUDDHA-SAMA'S RIGHT, BROTHER. SEE? EVEN HE'S WORRIED.
DID YOU FORGET WHY WE CAST JUDAS OUT IN THE FIRST PLACE?!
ANDREW-SAN...
REMEMBER WHAT HE SAID WHEN HE LEFT?
All of you are saints of online gaming.
Judas-san logging out in 5 seconds
But I alone am *tainted* by online gaming. jk lololol
MAKING HIMSELF THE BUTT OF THE JOKE...
WE CAN'T INVITE HIM TO THE PARTY!!
HE'S FINALLY STARTING TO RECOVER FROM HIS INTERNET ADDICTION.
WHAT? HE WAS IN THE PARTY BEFORE?!
THEN WHAT'S WRONG WITH THE NUMBER THIRTEEN?!
Eh heh ...
SORRY. IT JUST HAD ME FEELING A LITTLE SCARED, IS ALL...
I'M OKAY NOW. WE HAVE DAD AND THE ANGELS ON OUR SIDE...

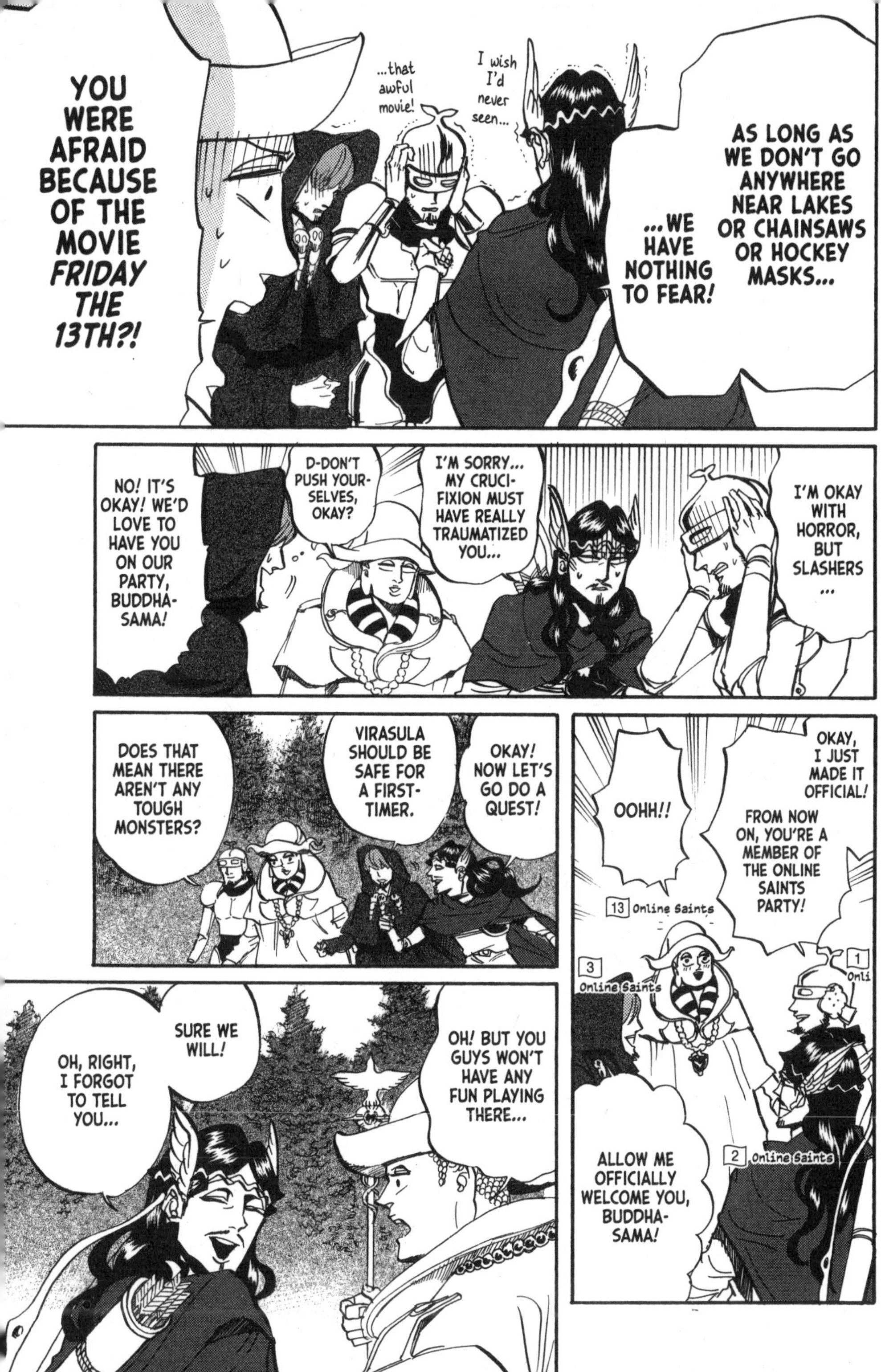
AS LONG AS WE DON'T GO ANYWHERE NEAR LAKES OR CHAINSAWS OR HOCKEY MASKS...
...WE HAVE NOTHING TO FEAR!
I wish I'd never seen...
...that awful movie!
YOU WERE AFRAID BECAUSE OF THE MOVIE *FRIDAY THE 13TH*?!
I'M OKAY WITH HORROR, BUT SLASHERS...
I'M SORRY... MY CRUCIFIXION MUST HAVE REALLY TRAUMATIZED YOU...
D-DON'T PUSH YOURSELVES, OKAY?
NO! IT'S OKAY! WE'D LOVE TO HAVE YOU ON OUR PARTY, BUDDHA-SAMA!
OKAY, I JUST MADE IT OFFICIAL!
FROM NOW ON, YOU'RE A MEMBER OF THE ONLINE SAINTS PARTY!
OOHH!!
13 Online Saints
1 Onli
3 Online Saints
2 Online Saints
ALLOW ME OFFICIALLY WELCOME YOU, BUDDHA-SAMA!
OKAY! NOW LET'S GO DO A QUEST!
VIRASULA SHOULD BE SAFE FOR A FIRST-TIMER.
DOES THAT MEAN THERE AREN'T ANY TOUGH MONSTERS?
OH! BUT YOU GUYS WON'T HAVE ANY FUN PLAYING THERE...
SURE WE WILL!
OH, RIGHT, I FORGOT TO TELL YOU...

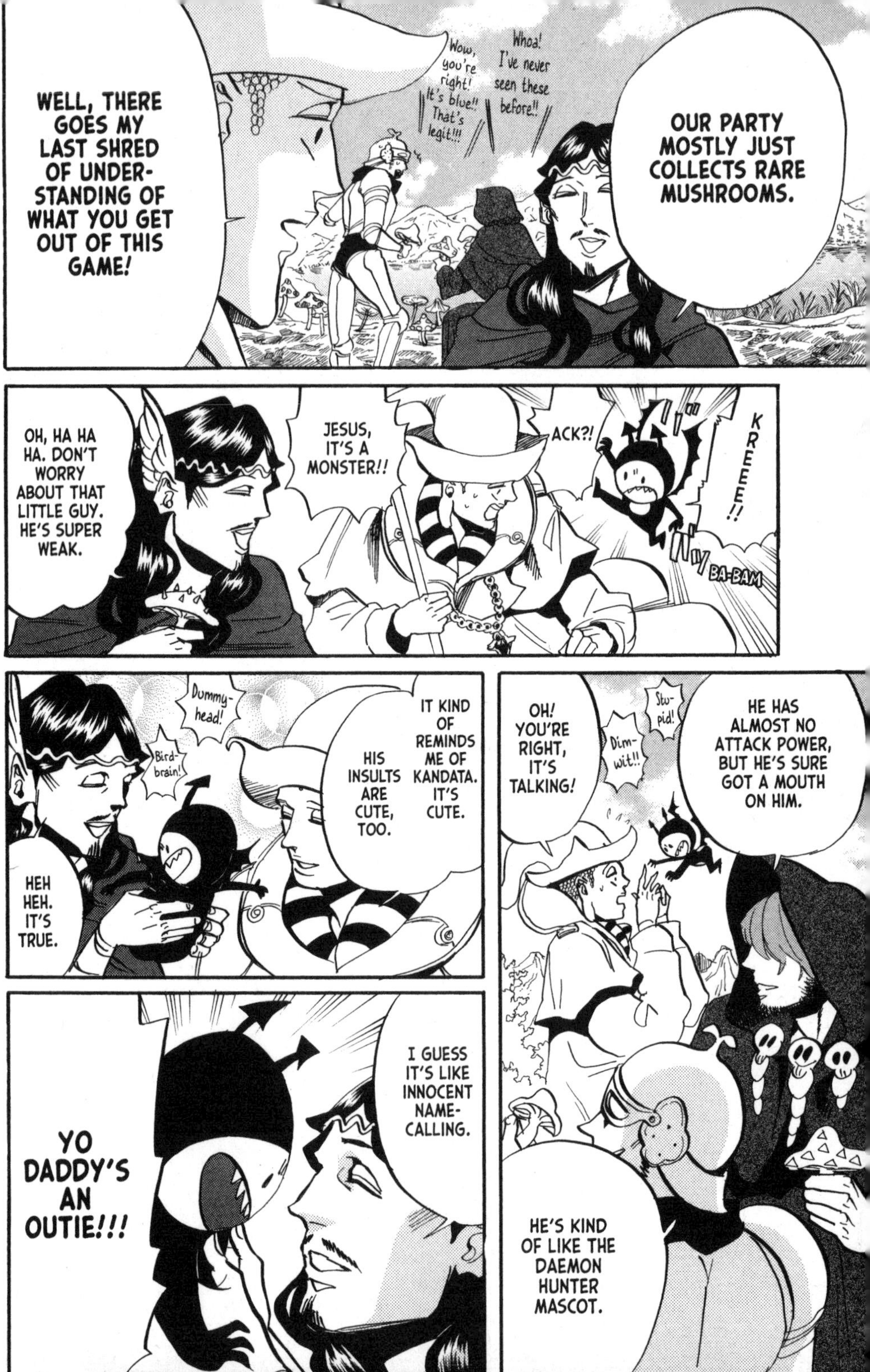
OUR PARTY MOSTLY JUST COLLECTS RARE MUSHROOMS.
Whoa! I've never seen these before!!
Wow, you're right! It's blue!! That's legit!!!
WELL, THERE GOES MY LAST SHRED OF UNDER-STANDING OF WHAT YOU GET OUT OF THIS GAME!
KREEEE!!
BA-BAM
ACK?!
JESUS, IT'S A MONSTER!!
OH, HA HA HA. DON'T WORRY ABOUT THAT LITTLE GUY. HE'S SUPER WEAK.
HE HAS ALMOST NO ATTACK POWER, BUT HE'S SURE GOT A MOUTH ON HIM.
Stu-pid!
Dim-wit!!
OH! YOU'RE RIGHT, IT'S TALKING!
HE'S KIND OF LIKE THE DAEMON HUNTER MASCOT.
IT KIND OF REMINDS ME OF KANDATA. IT'S CUTE.
Dummy-head!
HIS INSULTS ARE CUTE, TOO.
Bird-brain!
HEH HEH. IT'S TRUE.
I GUESS IT'S LIKE INNOCENT NAME-CALLING.
YO DADDY'S AN OUTIE!!!

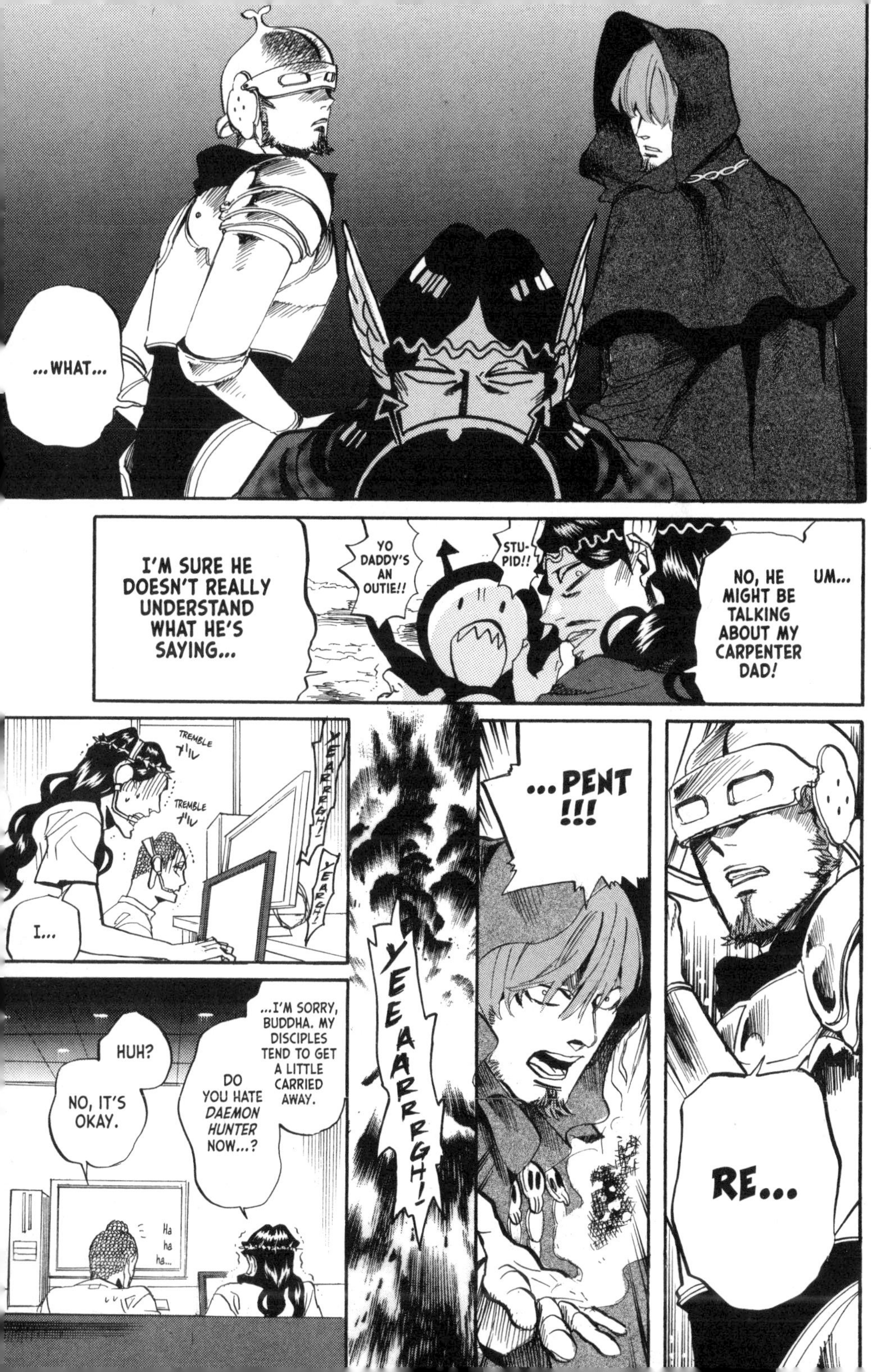
...WHAT...
UM...
NO, HE MIGHT BE TALKING ABOUT MY CARPENTER DAD!
STU-PID!!
YO DADDY'S AN OUTIE!!
I'M SURE HE DOESN'T REALLY UNDERSTAND WHAT HE'S SAYING...
RE...
...PENT !!!
YEEAARRGH!
TREMBLE
TREMBLE
YEARRGH!
YEARGH!
I...
...I'M SORRY, BUDDHA. MY DISCIPLES TEND TO GET A LITTLE CARRIED AWAY.
DO YOU HATE *DAEMON HUNTER* NOW...?
HUH?
NO, IT'S OKAY.
Ha ha ha...

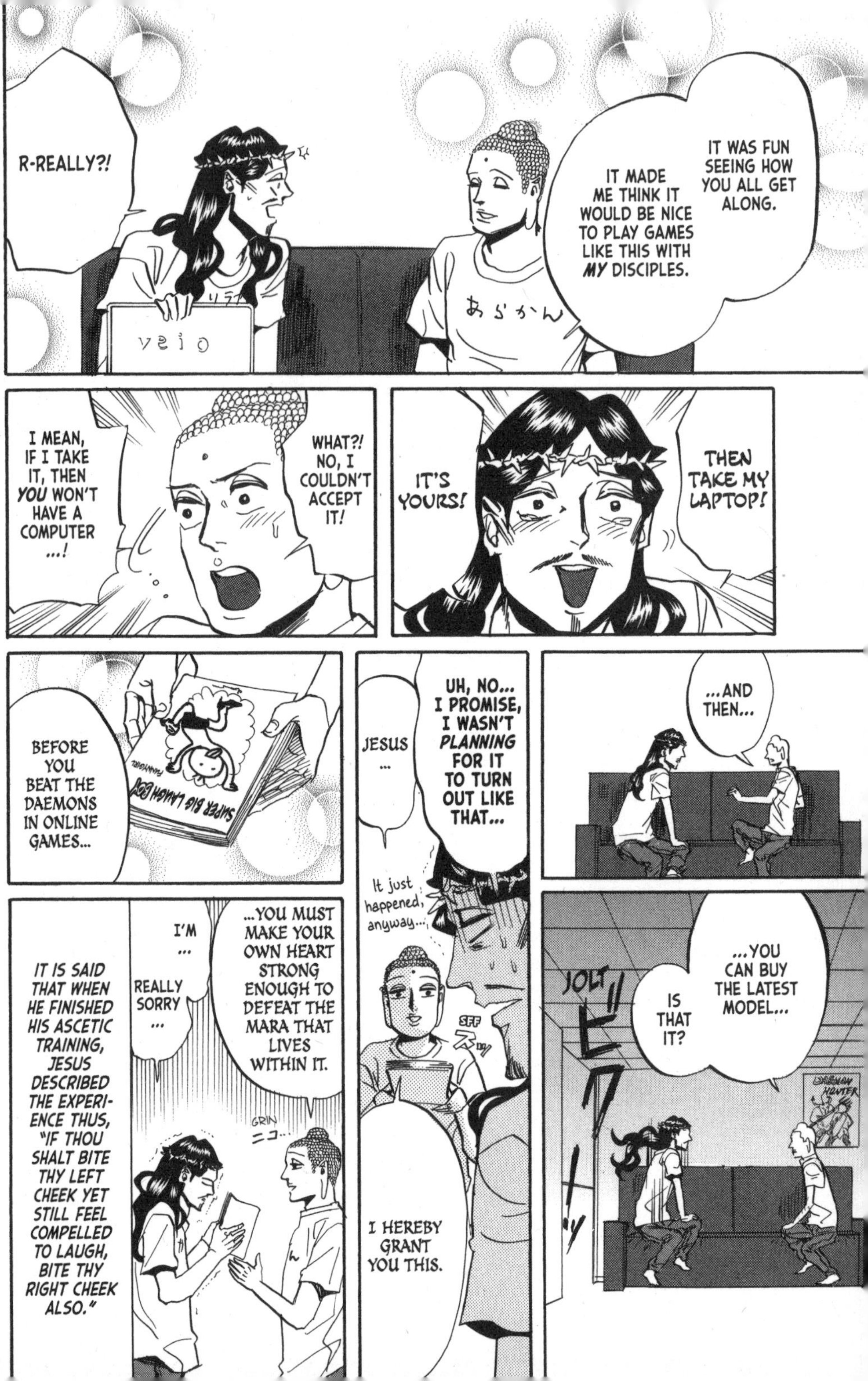
IT WAS FUN SEEING HOW YOU ALL GET ALONG.
IT MADE ME THINK IT WOULD BE NICE TO PLAY GAMES LIKE THIS WITH *MY* DISCIPLES.
R-REALLY?!
THEN TAKE MY LAPTOP!
IT'S YOURS!
WHAT?! NO, I COULDN'T ACCEPT IT!
I MEAN, IF I TAKE IT, THEN *YOU* WON'T HAVE A COMPUTER ...!
...AND THEN...
...YOU CAN BUY THE LATEST MODEL...
IS THAT IT?
JOLT
DAEMON HUNTER
UH, NO... I PROMISE, I WASN'T *PLANNING* FOR IT TO TURN OUT LIKE THAT...
JESUS ...
It just happened, anyway...
SFF
I HEREBY GRANT YOU THIS.
BEFORE YOU BEAT THE DAEMONS IN ONLINE GAMES...
SUPER BIG LAUGH BOX
...YOU MUST MAKE YOUR OWN HEART STRONG ENOUGH TO DEFEAT THE MARA THAT LIVES WITHIN IT.
I'M ... REALLY SORRY ...
GRIN
IT IS SAID THAT WHEN HE FINISHED HIS ASCETIC TRAINING, JESUS DESCRIBED THE EXPERIENCE THUS, "IF THOU SHALT BITE THY LEFT CHEEK YET STILL FEEL COMPELLED TO LAUGH, BITE THY RIGHT CHEEK ALSO."

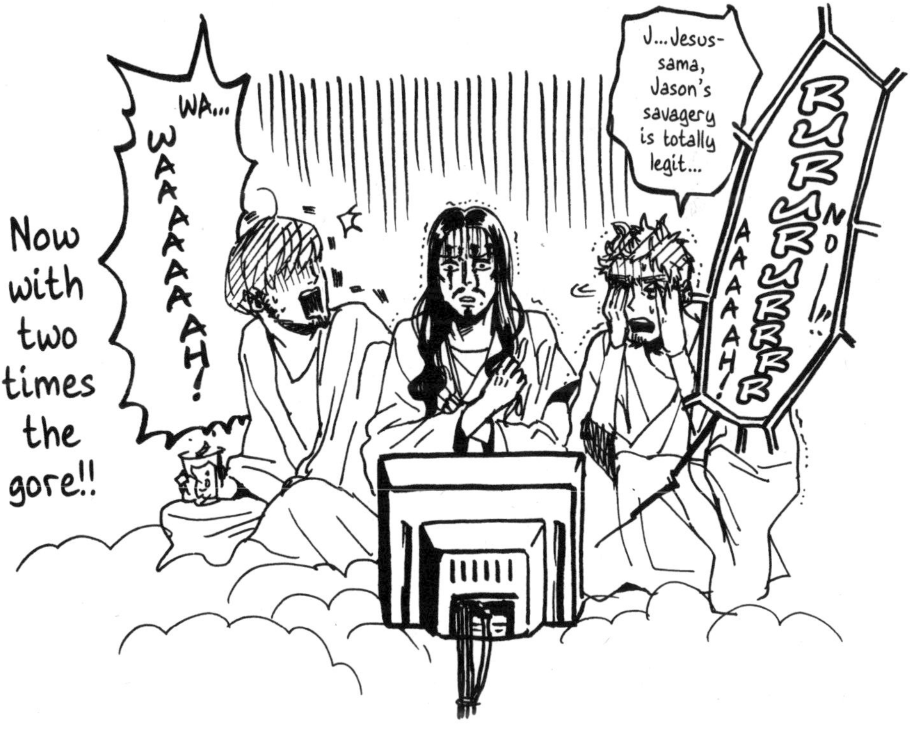
Now with two times the gore!!
J...Jesus-sama, Jason's savagery is totally legit...
RURURURURRRR
NO!!
AAAAAAH!
WA...
WAAAAAAAAH!

CHAPTER 28 TRANSLATION NOTES

Galilee and Arhat, page 251
Galilee is a region in northern Israel where Jesus served most of His ministry. Arhat is a Buddhist term for someone who has gained enlightenment, or has made significant progress on the path to enlightenment.

The Sabbath was made for man, page 251
The Gospel of Mark tells the story of a time when Jesus and his disciples were walking through corn fields (where "corn" is a generic term in the King James Bible used to describe all grain), and his disciples picked the corn and ate it as they went. Because picking food is a form of labor, the Pharisees, who had created several strict and specific rules for proper Sabbath observance, accused these disciples of breaking the Sabbath. One of the things Jesus said in response was, "The Sabbath was made for man, not man for the Sabbath." In other words, the Sabbath was instituted as a way to help people recover from their labors, and so observance of the Day of Rest should not become a chore.

Manga Michi, page 254
Manga Michi, or "Manga Road," is the autobiographical manga of Fujiko Fujio, the manga-making duo famous for creating *Doraemon*.

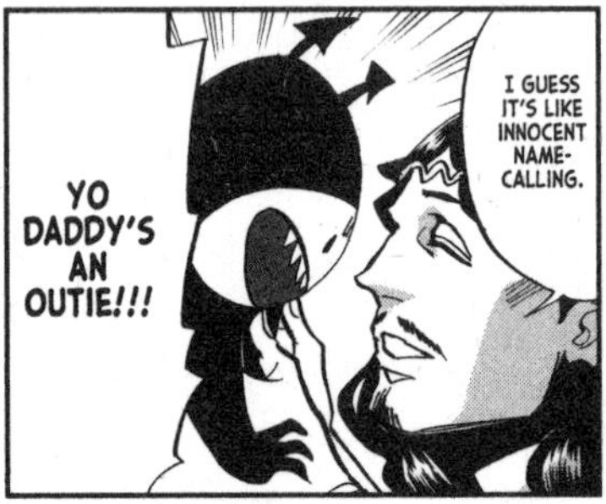
I GUESS IT'S LIKE INNOCENT NAME-CALLING.
YO DADDY'S AN OUTIE!!!

Yo daddy's an outie, page 264
This is a play on the common Japanese children's insult, "Yo mama's an outie!", referring to the shape of said mother's belly button. It carries an implication that the child shouting the insult is insinuating that he or she has seen the addressee's mother in the nude, or would at least have some sort of inside info on what her navel would look like. Some have theorized that the word for "belly button" is also a euphemism for a woman's genitalia, in which case the insult would indicate that the person making the claim thinks the organ in question looks funny (which they would only know if they had seen it). But in modern times, it's a phrase shouted in childish quarrels with no real thought behind it except that it probably sounds funny and insulting at the same time.

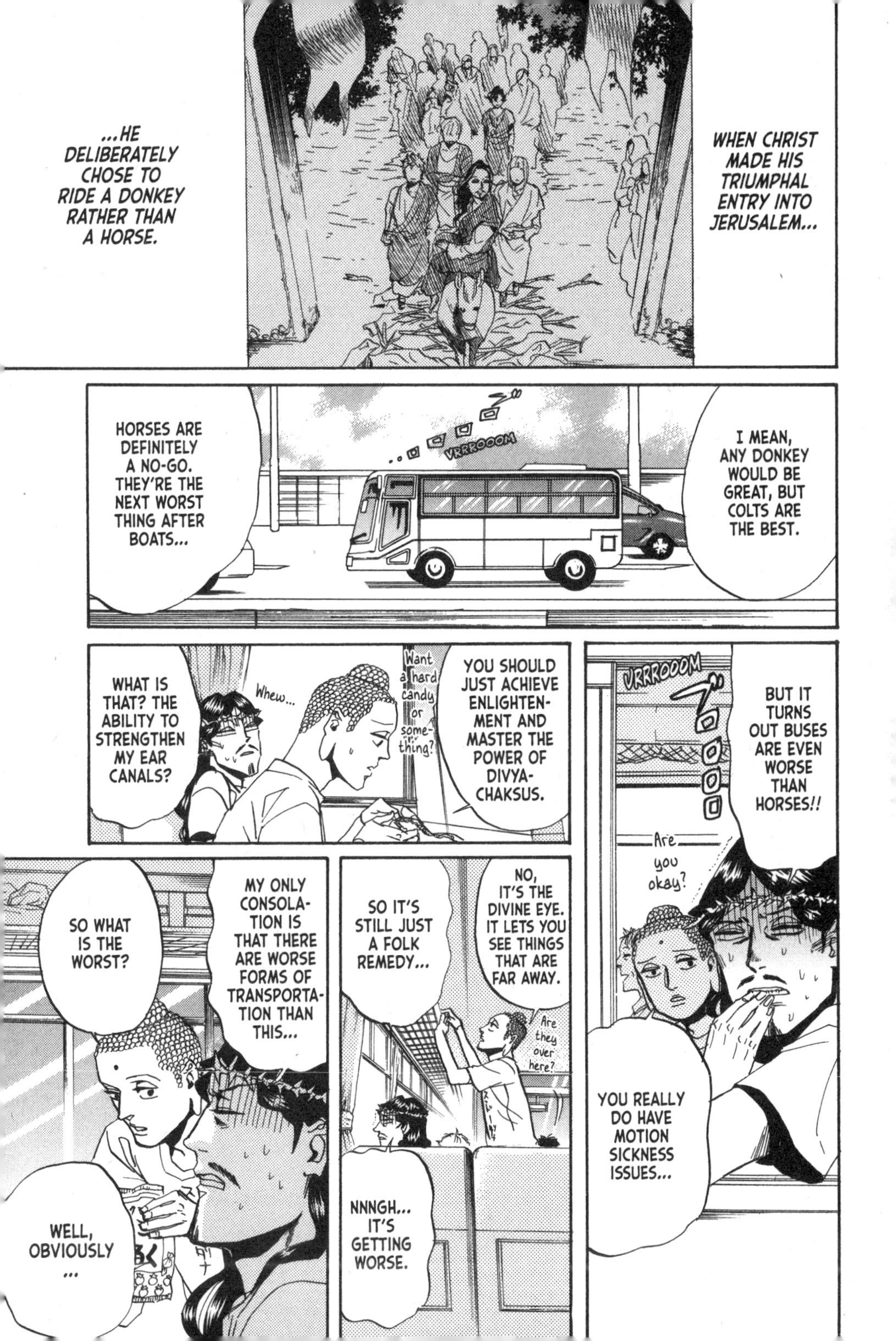
WHEN CHRIST MADE HIS TRIUMPHAL ENTRY INTO JERUSALEM...
...HE DELIBERATELY CHOSE TO RIDE A DONKEY RATHER THAN A HORSE.
I MEAN, ANY DONKEY WOULD BE GREAT, BUT COLTS ARE THE BEST.
VRRROOOM
HORSES ARE DEFINITELY A NO-GO. THEY'RE THE NEXT WORST THING AFTER BOATS...
VRRROOOM
BUT IT TURNS OUT BUSES ARE EVEN WORSE THAN HORSES!!
Are you okay?
YOU REALLY DO HAVE MOTION SICKNESS ISSUES...
YOU SHOULD JUST ACHIEVE ENLIGHTEN-MENT AND MASTER THE POWER OF DIVYA-CHAKSUS.
Want a hard candy or some-thing?
WHAT IS THAT? THE ABILITY TO STRENGTHEN MY EAR CANALS?
Whew...
NO, IT'S THE DIVINE EYE. IT LETS YOU SEE THINGS THAT ARE FAR AWAY.
SO IT'S STILL JUST A FOLK REMEDY...
Are they over here?
NNNGH... IT'S GETTING WORSE.
MY ONLY CONSOLA-TION IS THAT THERE ARE WORSE FORMS OF TRANSPORTA-TION THAN THIS...
SO WHAT IS THE WORST?
WELL, OBVIOUSLY ...

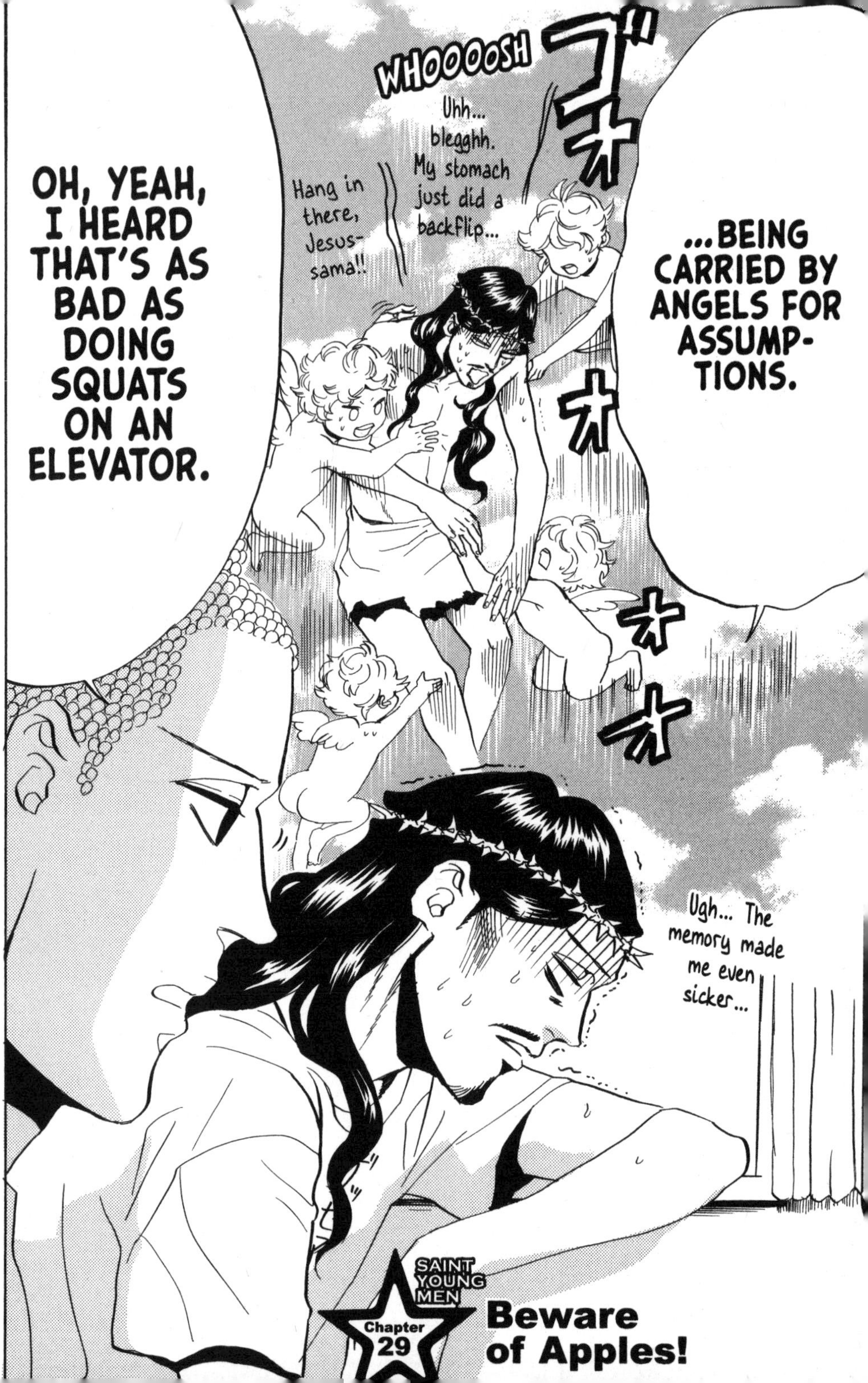
...BEING CARRIED BY ANGELS FOR ASSUMPTIONS.
WHOOOOSH
ゴオオオオ
Uhh... blegghh. My stomach just did a backflip...
Hang in there, Jesus-sama!!
OH, YEAH, I HEARD THAT'S AS BAD AS DOING SQUATS ON AN ELEVATOR.
Ugh... The memory made me even sicker...
SAINT YOUNG MEN
Chapter 29
Beware of Apples!

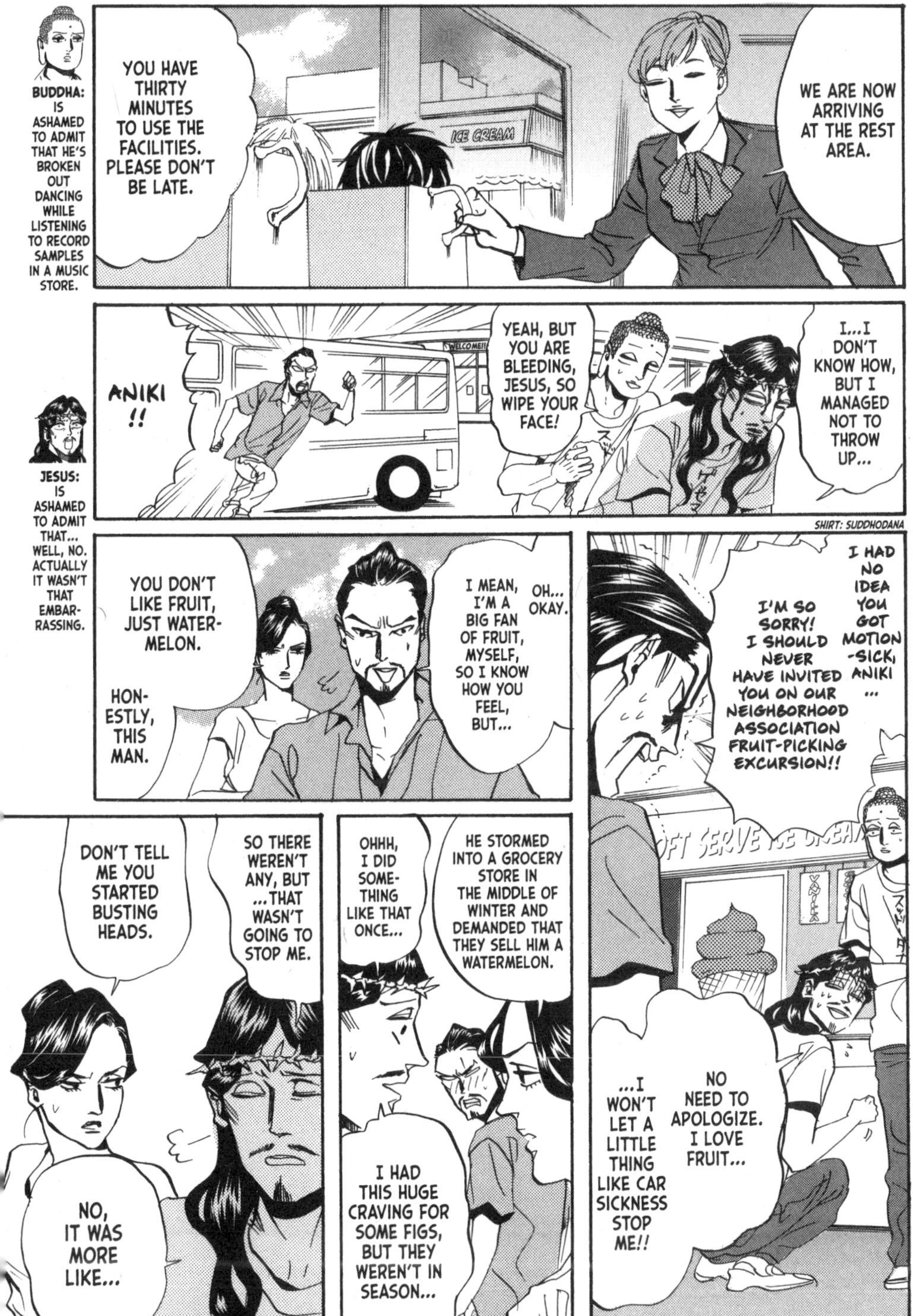
BUDDHA: IS ASHAMED TO ADMIT THAT HE'S BROKEN OUT DANCING WHILE LISTENING TO RECORD SAMPLES IN A MUSIC STORE.
JESUS: IS ASHAMED TO ADMIT THAT... WELL, NO. ACTUALLY IT WASN'T THAT EMBAR-RASSING.
WE ARE NOW ARRIVING AT THE REST AREA.
YOU HAVE THIRTY MINUTES TO USE THE FACILITIES. PLEASE DON'T BE LATE.
ICE CREAM
I...I DON'T KNOW HOW, BUT I MANAGED NOT TO THROW UP...
YEAH, BUT YOU ARE BLEEDING, JESUS, SO WIPE YOUR FACE!
WELCOME!!
ANIKI !!
SHIRT: SUDDHODANA
I HAD NO IDEA YOU GOT MOTION -SICK, ANIKI ...
I'M SO SORRY! I SHOULD NEVER HAVE INVITED YOU ON OUR NEIGHBORHOOD ASSOCIATION FRUIT-PICKING EXCURSION!!
SOFT SERVE ICE CREAM
VANILLA
NO NEED TO APOLOGIZE. I LOVE FRUIT...
...I WON'T LET A LITTLE THING LIKE CAR SICKNESS STOP ME!!
OH... OKAY.
I MEAN, I'M A BIG FAN OF FRUIT, MYSELF, SO I KNOW HOW YOU FEEL, BUT...
YOU DON'T LIKE FRUIT, JUST WATER-MELON.
HON-ESTLY, THIS MAN.
HE STORMED INTO A GROCERY STORE IN THE MIDDLE OF WINTER AND DEMANDED THAT THEY SELL HIM A WATERMELON.
OHHH, I DID SOME-THING LIKE THAT ONCE...
I HAD THIS HUGE CRAVING FOR SOME FIGS, BUT THEY WEREN'T IN SEASON...
SO THERE WEREN'T ANY, BUT ...THAT WASN'T GOING TO STOP ME.
DON'T TELL ME YOU STARTED BUSTING HEADS.
NO, IT WAS MORE LIKE...

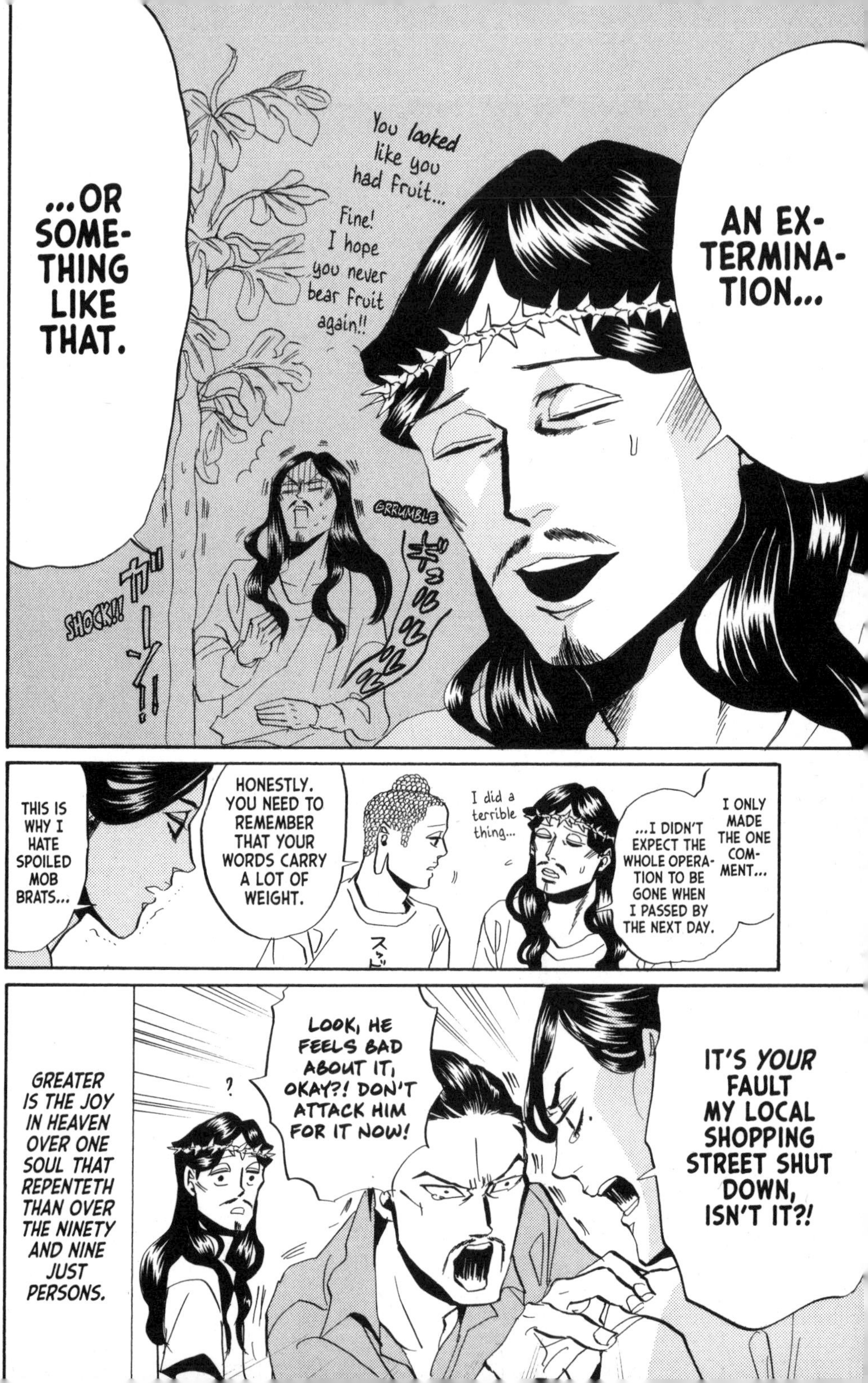
AN EXTERMINATION...
You looked like you had fruit...
Fine! I hope you never bear fruit again!!
GRRUMBLE
SHOCK!!
...OR SOMETHING LIKE THAT.
I ONLY MADE THE ONE COMMENT...
...I DIDN'T EXPECT THE WHOLE OPERATION TO BE GONE WHEN I PASSED BY THE NEXT DAY.
I did a terrible thing...
HONESTLY. YOU NEED TO REMEMBER THAT YOUR WORDS CARRY A LOT OF WEIGHT.
THIS IS WHY I HATE SPOILED MOB BRATS...
IT'S YOUR FAULT MY LOCAL SHOPPING STREET SHUT DOWN, ISN'T IT?!
LOOK, HE FEELS BAD ABOUT IT, OKAY?! DON'T ATTACK HIM FOR IT NOW!
?
GREATER IS THE JOY IN HEAVEN OVER ONE SOUL THAT REPENTETH THAN OVER THE NINETY AND NINE JUST PERSONS.

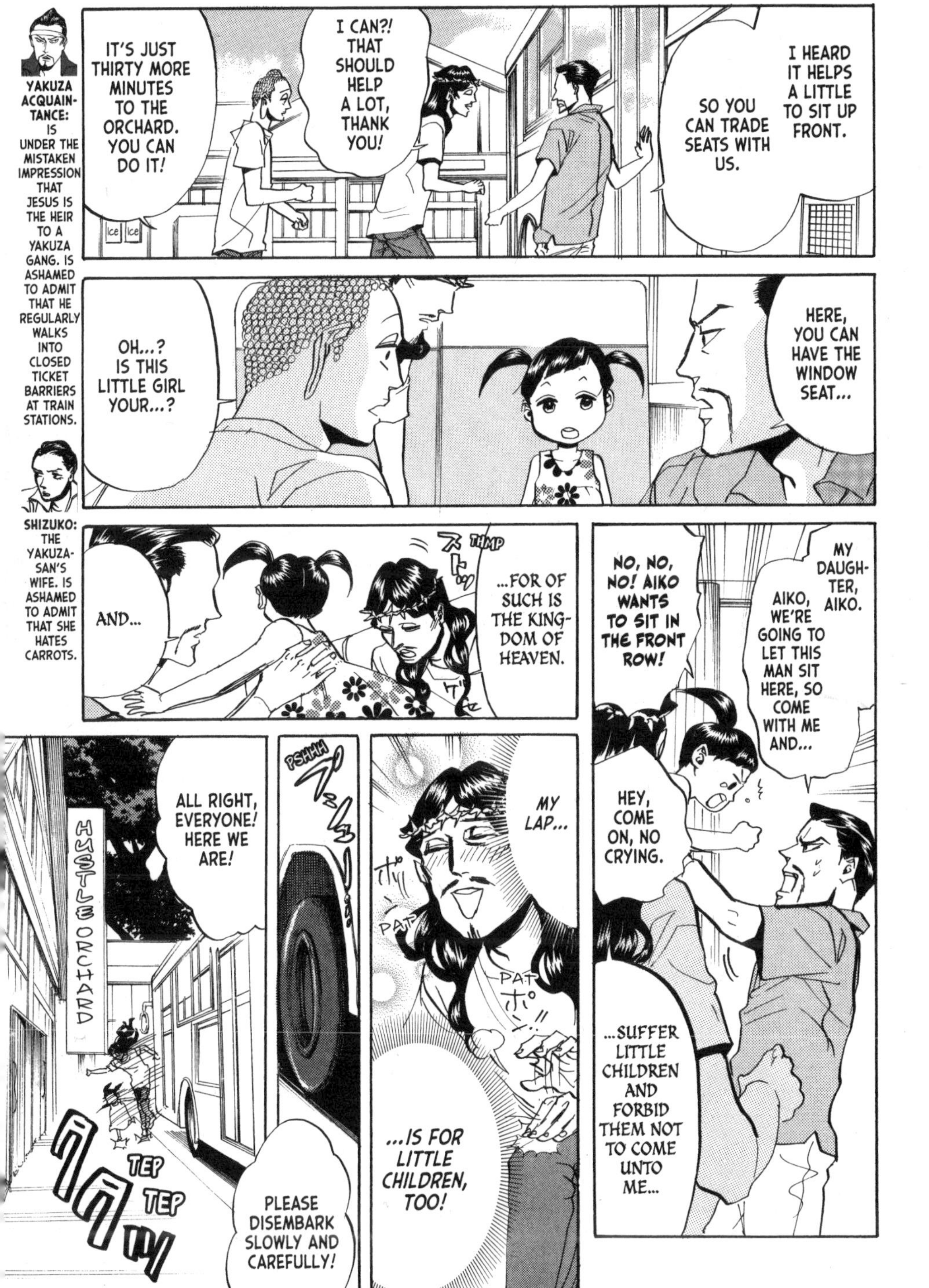
I HEARD IT HELPS A LITTLE TO SIT UP FRONT.
SO YOU CAN TRADE SEATS WITH US.
I CAN?! THAT SHOULD HELP A LOT, THANK YOU!
IT'S JUST THIRTY MORE MINUTES TO THE ORCHARD. YOU CAN DO IT!
Ice Ice
HERE, YOU CAN HAVE THE WINDOW SEAT...
OH...? IS THIS LITTLE GIRL YOUR...?
MY DAUGHTER, AIKO.
AIKO, WE'RE GOING TO LET THIS MAN SIT HERE, SO COME WITH ME AND...
NO, NO, NO! AIKO WANTS TO SIT IN THE FRONT ROW!
HEY, COME ON, NO CRYING.
...SUFFER LITTLE CHILDREN AND FORBID THEM NOT TO COME UNTO ME...
THMP
...FOR OF SUCH IS THE KINGDOM OF HEAVEN.
AND...
MY LAP...
PAT
PAT
...IS FOR LITTLE CHILDREN, TOO!
PSHHH
ALL RIGHT, EVERYONE! HERE WE ARE!
HUSTLE ORCHARD
TEP TEP
PLEASE DISEMBARK SLOWLY AND CAREFULLY!
YAKUZA ACQUAINTANCE: IS UNDER THE MISTAKEN IMPRESSION THAT JESUS IS THE HEIR TO A YAKUZA GANG. IS ASHAMED TO ADMIT THAT HE REGULARLY WALKS INTO CLOSED TICKET BARRIERS AT TRAIN STATIONS.
SHIZUKO: THE YAKUZA-SAN'S WIFE. IS ASHAMED TO ADMIT THAT SHE HATES CARROTS.

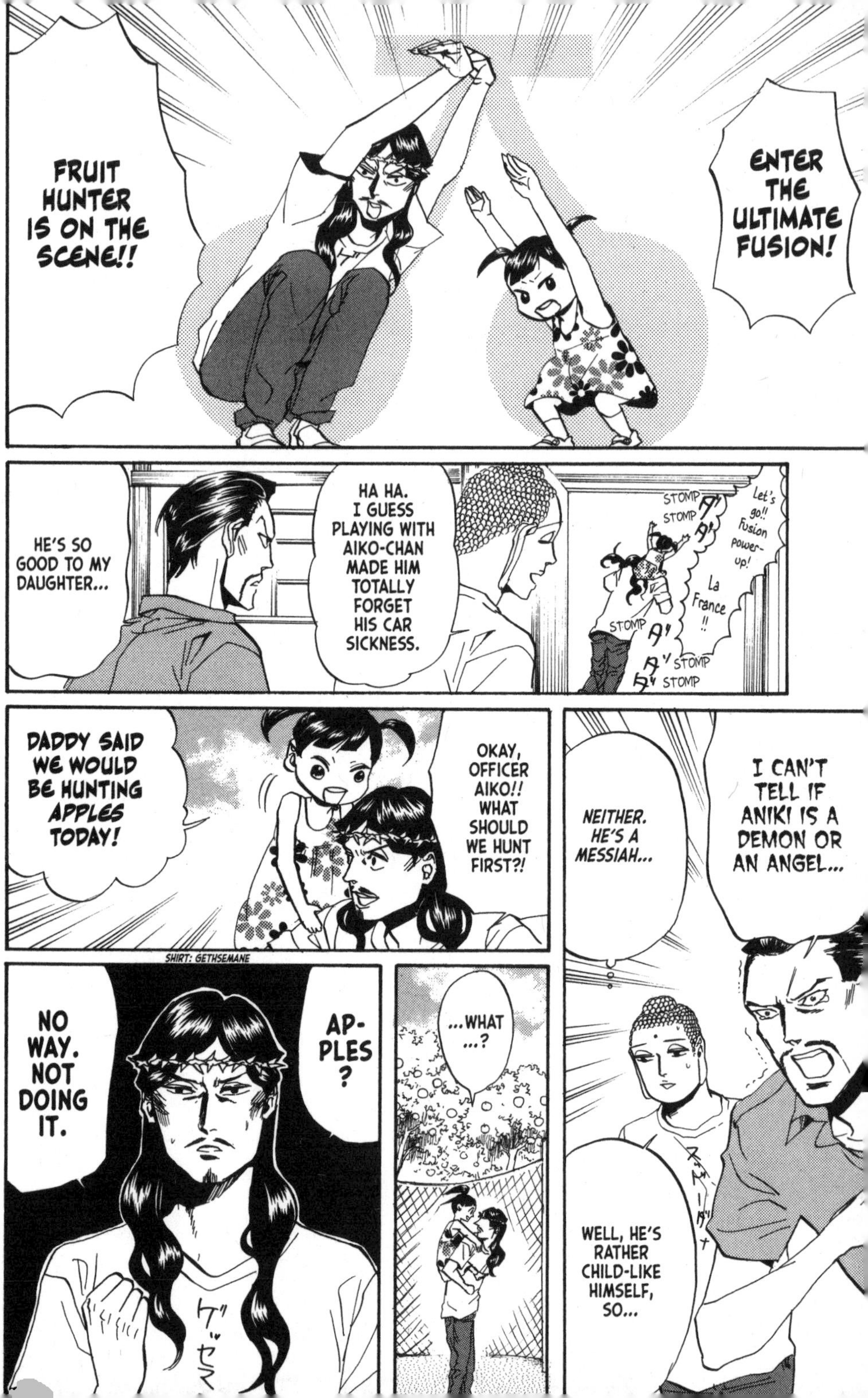
ENTER THE ULTIMATE FUSION!
FRUIT HUNTER IS ON THE SCENE!!
STOMP STOMP
Let's go!! Fusion power-up!
La France !!
STOMP
STOMP STOMP
HA HA. I GUESS PLAYING WITH AIKO-CHAN MADE HIM TOTALLY FORGET HIS CAR SICKNESS.
HE'S SO GOOD TO MY DAUGHTER...
I CAN'T TELL IF ANIKI IS A DEMON OR AN ANGEL...
NEITHER. HE'S A MESSIAH...
WELL, HE'S RATHER CHILD-LIKE HIMSELF, SO...
OKAY, OFFICER AIKO!! WHAT SHOULD WE HUNT FIRST?!
DADDY SAID WE WOULD BE HUNTING APPLES TODAY!
SHIRT: GETHSEMANE
...WHAT ...?
AP-PLES ?
NO WAY. NOT DOING IT.

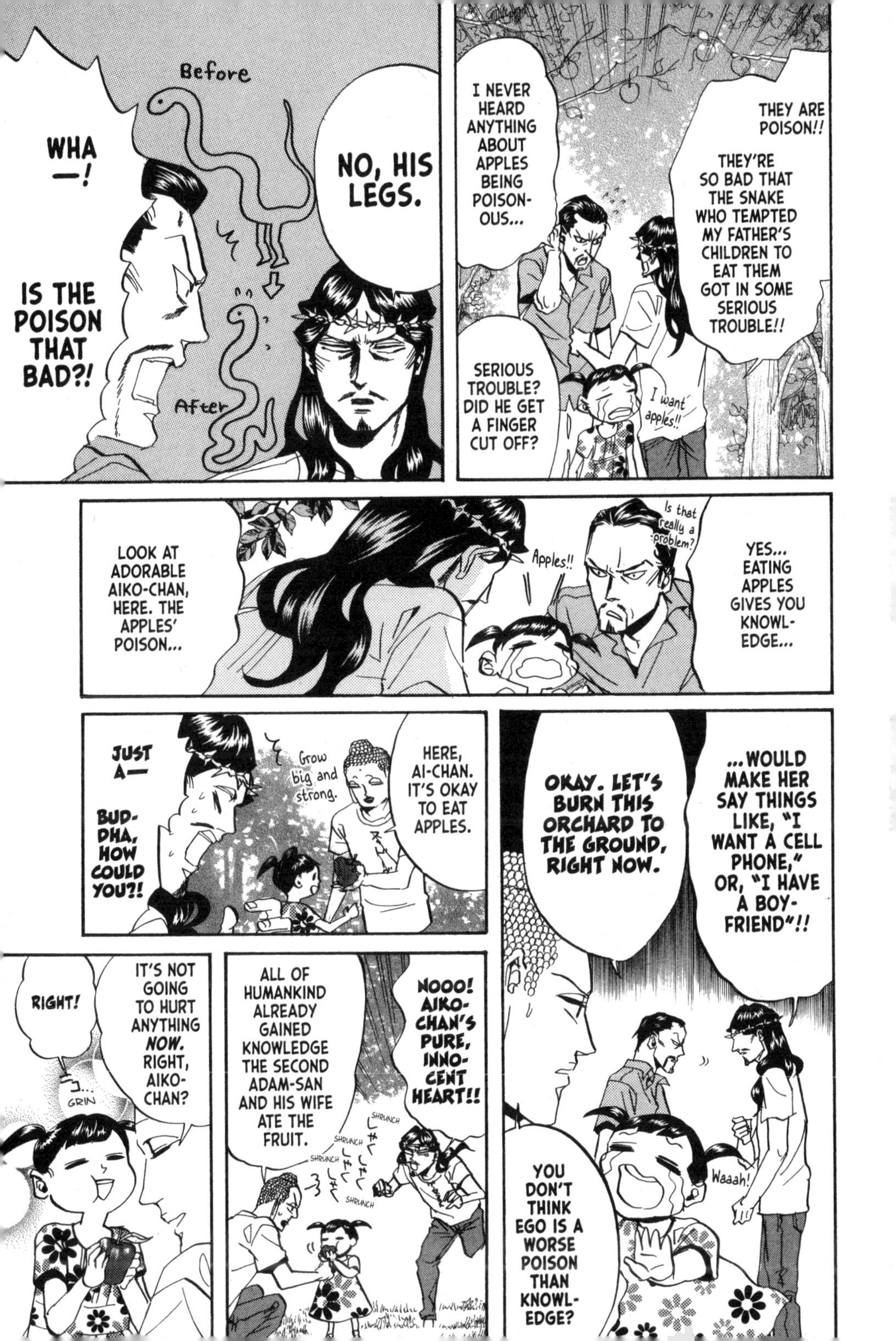
THEY ARE POISON!!
THEY'RE SO BAD THAT THE SNAKE WHO TEMPTED MY FATHER'S CHILDREN TO EAT THEM GOT IN SOME SERIOUS TROUBLE!!
I NEVER HEARD ANYTHING ABOUT APPLES BEING POISON-OUS...
I want apples!!
SERIOUS TROUBLE? DID HE GET A FINGER CUT OFF?
NO, HIS LEGS.
Before
After
WHA—!
IS THE POISON THAT BAD?!
YES... EATING APPLES GIVES YOU KNOWL-EDGE...
Is that really a problem?
Apples!!
LOOK AT ADORABLE AIKO-CHAN, HERE. THE APPLES' POISON...
...WOULD MAKE HER SAY THINGS LIKE, "I WANT A CELL PHONE," OR, "I HAVE A BOY-FRIEND"!!
OKAY. LET'S BURN THIS ORCHARD TO THE GROUND, RIGHT NOW.
Waaah!
YOU DON'T THINK EGO IS A WORSE POISON THAN KNOWL-EDGE?
HERE, AI-CHAN. IT'S OKAY TO EAT APPLES.
Grow big and strong.
JUST A—
BUD-DHA, HOW COULD YOU?!
NOOO! AIKO-CHAN'S PURE, INNO-CENT HEART!!
ALL OF HUMANKIND ALREADY GAINED KNOWLEDGE THE SECOND ADAM-SAN AND HIS WIFE ATE THE FRUIT.
SHRUNCH
SHRUNCH
SHRUNCH
SHRUNCH
IT'S NOT GOING TO HURT ANYTHING NOW. RIGHT, AIKO-CHAN?
RIGHT!
GRIN

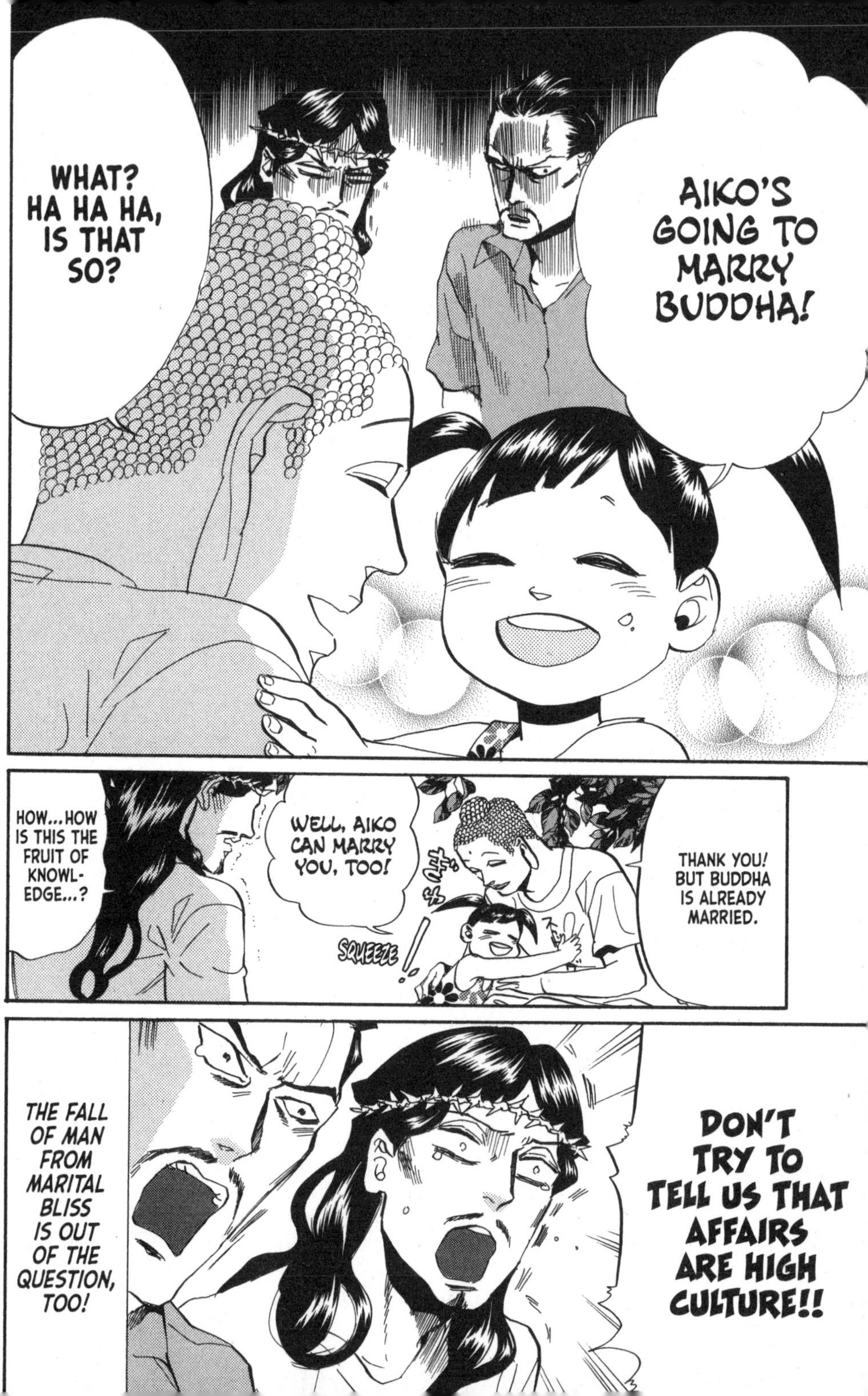
AIKO'S GOING TO MARRY BUDDHA!
WHAT? HA HA HA, IS THAT SO?
THANK YOU! BUT BUDDHA IS ALREADY MARRIED.
WELL, AIKO CAN MARRY YOU, TOO!
SQUEEZE
HOW...HOW IS THIS THE FRUIT OF KNOWL-EDGE...?
DON'T TRY TO TELL US THAT AFFAIRS ARE HIGH CULTURE!!
THE FALL OF MAN FROM MARITAL BLISS IS OUT OF THE QUESTION, TOO!

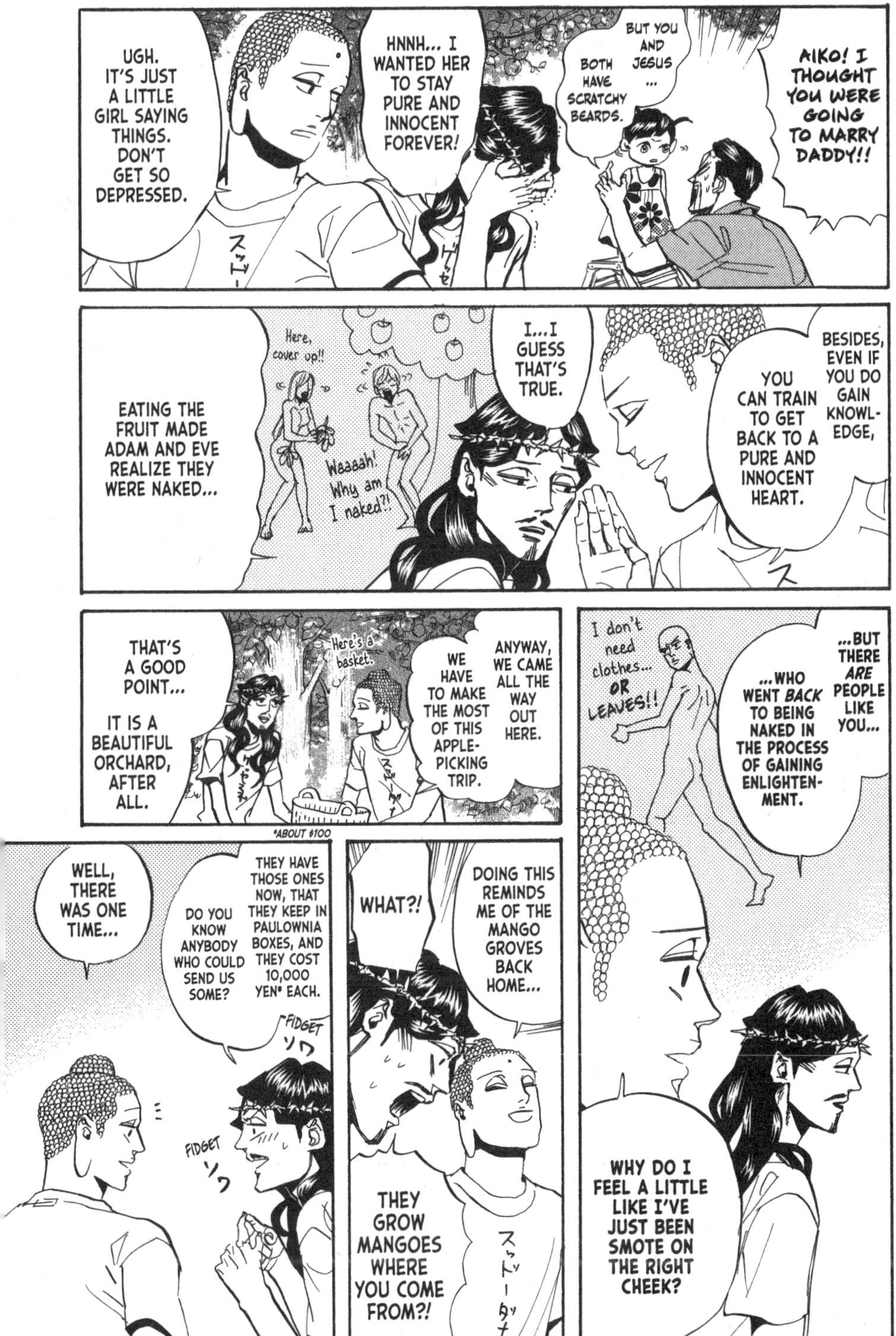
AIKO! I THOUGHT YOU WERE GOING TO MARRY DADDY!!
BUT YOU AND JESUS ... BOTH HAVE SCRATCHY BEARDS.
HNNH... I WANTED HER TO STAY PURE AND INNOCENT FOREVER!
UGH. IT'S JUST A LITTLE GIRL SAYING THINGS. DON'T GET SO DEPRESSED.
BESIDES, EVEN IF YOU DO GAIN KNOWL-EDGE,
YOU CAN TRAIN TO GET BACK TO A PURE AND INNOCENT HEART.
I...I GUESS THAT'S TRUE.
Here, cover up!!
Waaaah! Why am I naked?!
EATING THE FRUIT MADE ADAM AND EVE REALIZE THEY WERE NAKED...
...BUT THERE *ARE* PEOPLE LIKE YOU...
...WHO WENT *BACK* TO BEING NAKED IN THE PROCESS OF GAINING ENLIGHTEN-MENT.
I don't need clothes... OR LEAVES!!
WHY DO I FEEL A LITTLE LIKE I'VE JUST BEEN SMOTE ON THE RIGHT CHEEK?
ANYWAY, WE CAME ALL THE WAY OUT HERE.
WE HAVE TO MAKE THE MOST OF THIS APPLE-PICKING TRIP.
Here's a basket.
THAT'S A GOOD POINT...
IT IS A BEAUTIFUL ORCHARD, AFTER ALL.
DOING THIS REMINDS ME OF THE MANGO GROVES BACK HOME...
WHAT?!
THEY GROW MANGOES WHERE YOU COME FROM?!
THEY HAVE THOSE ONES NOW, THAT THEY KEEP IN PAULOWNIA BOXES, AND THEY COST 10,000 YEN* EACH.
DO YOU KNOW ANYBODY WHO COULD SEND US SOME?
FIDGET ソワ
WELL, THERE WAS ONE TIME...
FIDGET ソワ
*ABOUT $100

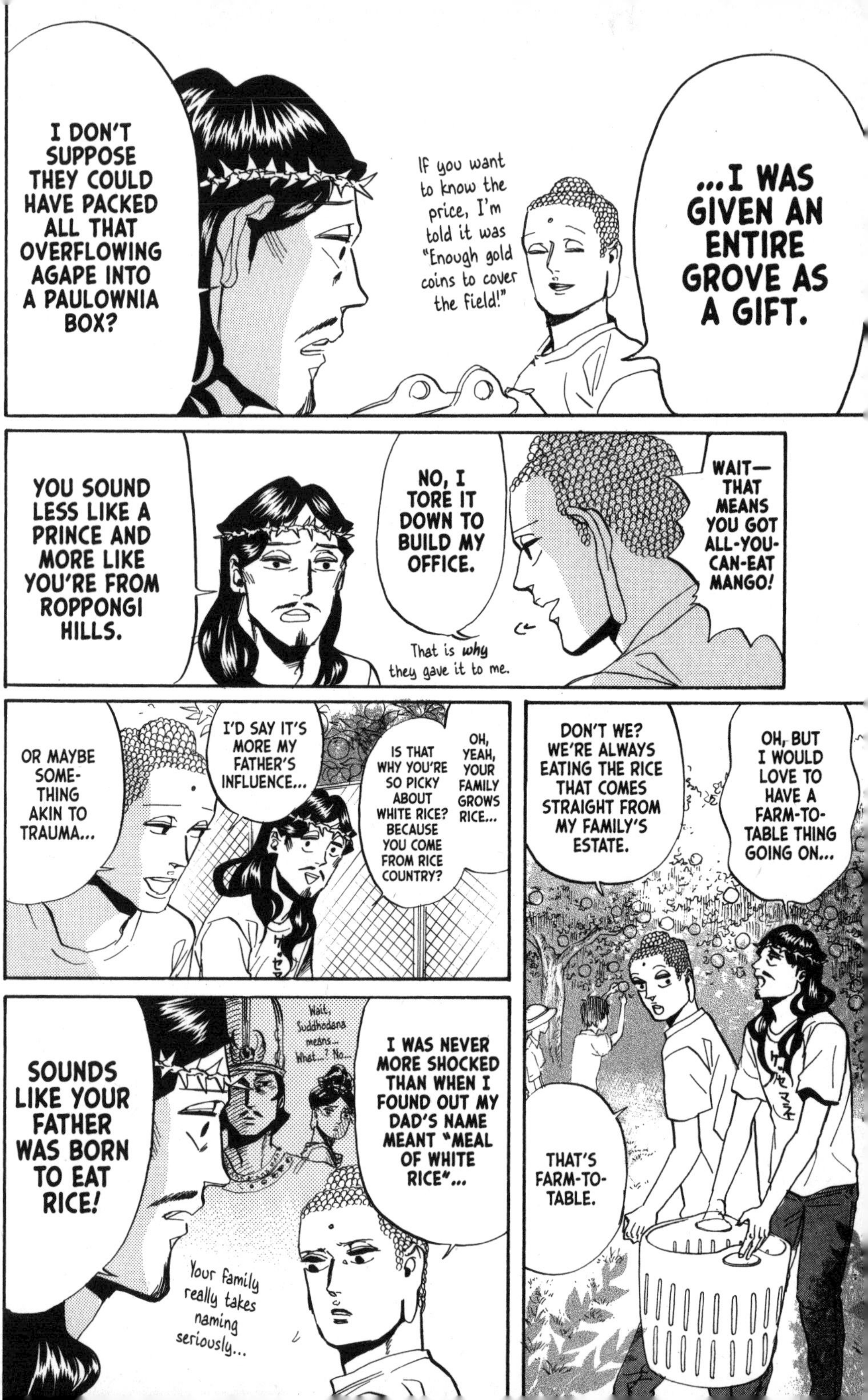
...I WAS GIVEN AN ENTIRE GROVE AS A GIFT.
If you want to know the price, I'm told it was "Enough gold coins to cover the field!"
I DON'T SUPPOSE THEY COULD HAVE PACKED ALL THAT OVERFLOWING AGAPE INTO A PAULOWNIA BOX?
WAIT— THAT MEANS YOU GOT ALL-YOU-CAN-EAT MANGO!
NO, I TORE IT DOWN TO BUILD MY OFFICE.
That is *why* they gave it to me.
YOU SOUND LESS LIKE A PRINCE AND MORE LIKE YOU'RE FROM ROPPONGI HILLS.
OH, BUT I WOULD LOVE TO HAVE A FARM-TO-TABLE THING GOING ON...
DON'T WE? WE'RE ALWAYS EATING THE RICE THAT COMES STRAIGHT FROM MY FAMILY'S ESTATE.
THAT'S FARM-TO-TABLE.
OH, YEAH, YOUR FAMILY GROWS RICE...
IS THAT WHY YOU'RE SO PICKY ABOUT WHITE RICE? BECAUSE YOU COME FROM RICE COUNTRY?
I'D SAY IT'S MORE MY FATHER'S INFLUENCE...
OR MAYBE SOME-THING AKIN TO TRAUMA...
I WAS NEVER MORE SHOCKED THAN WHEN I FOUND OUT MY DAD'S NAME MEANT "MEAL OF WHITE RICE"...
Wait, Suddhodana means... What...? No...
SOUNDS LIKE YOUR FATHER WAS BORN TO EAT RICE!
Your family really takes naming seriously...

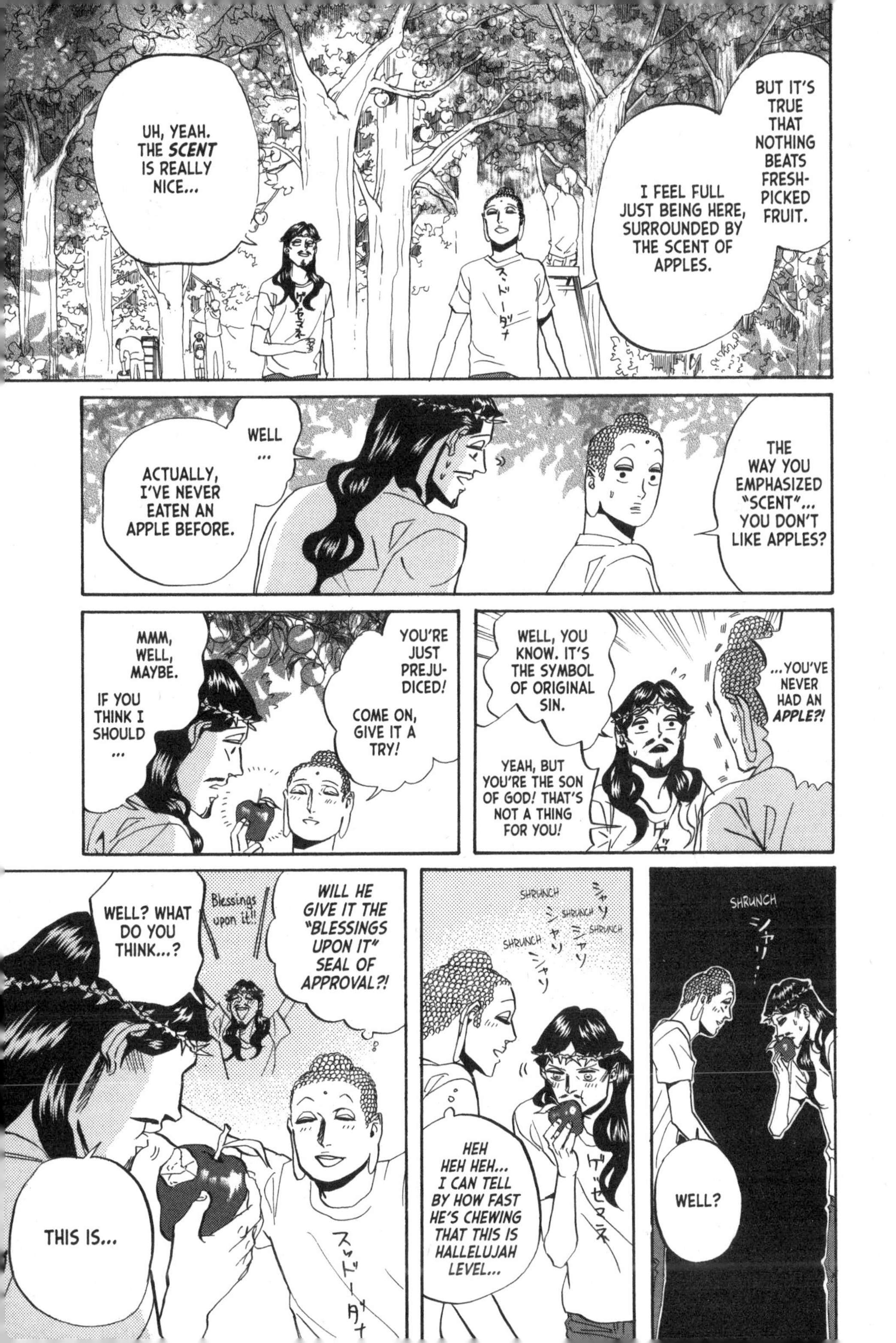
BUT IT'S TRUE THAT NOTHING BEATS FRESH-PICKED FRUIT.
I FEEL FULL JUST BEING HERE, SURROUNDED BY THE SCENT OF APPLES.
UH, YEAH. THE *SCENT* IS REALLY NICE...
THE WAY YOU EMPHASIZED "SCENT"... YOU DON'T LIKE APPLES?
WELL ...
ACTUALLY, I'VE NEVER EATEN AN APPLE BEFORE.
...YOU'VE NEVER HAD AN *APPLE?!*
WELL, YOU KNOW. IT'S THE SYMBOL OF ORIGINAL SIN.
YEAH, BUT YOU'RE THE SON OF GOD! THAT'S NOT A THING FOR YOU!
YOU'RE JUST PREJUDICED!
COME ON, GIVE IT A TRY!
MMM, WELL, MAYBE.
IF YOU THINK I SHOULD ...
SHRUNCH
WELL?
SHRUNCH
SHRUNCH
SHRUNCH
SHRUNCH
HEH HEH HEH... I CAN TELL BY HOW FAST HE'S CHEWING THAT THIS IS HALLELUJAH LEVEL...
WILL HE GIVE IT THE "BLESSINGS UPON IT" SEAL OF APPROVAL?!
Blessings upon it!!
WELL? WHAT DO YOU THINK...?
THIS IS...

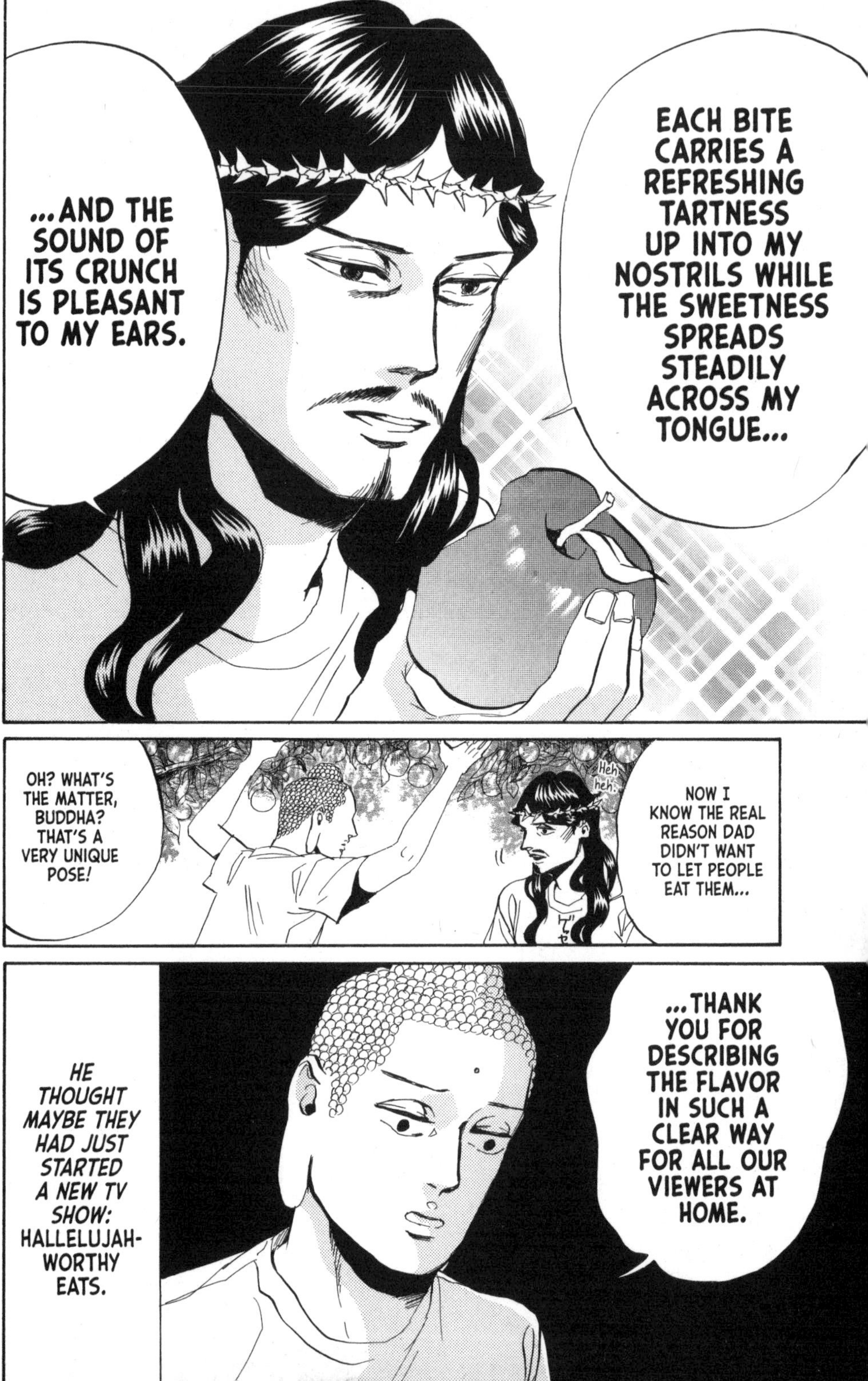
EACH BITE CARRIES A REFRESHING TARTNESS UP INTO MY NOSTRILS WHILE THE SWEETNESS SPREADS STEADILY ACROSS MY TONGUE...
...AND THE SOUND OF ITS CRUNCH IS PLEASANT TO MY EARS.
Heh heh.
NOW I KNOW THE REAL REASON DAD DIDN'T WANT TO LET PEOPLE EAT THEM...
OH? WHAT'S THE MATTER, BUDDHA? THAT'S A VERY UNIQUE POSE!
...THANK YOU FOR DESCRIBING THE FLAVOR IN SUCH A CLEAR WAY FOR ALL OUR VIEWERS AT HOME.
HE THOUGHT MAYBE THEY HAD JUST STARTED A NEW TV SHOW: HALLELUJAH-WORTHY EATS.

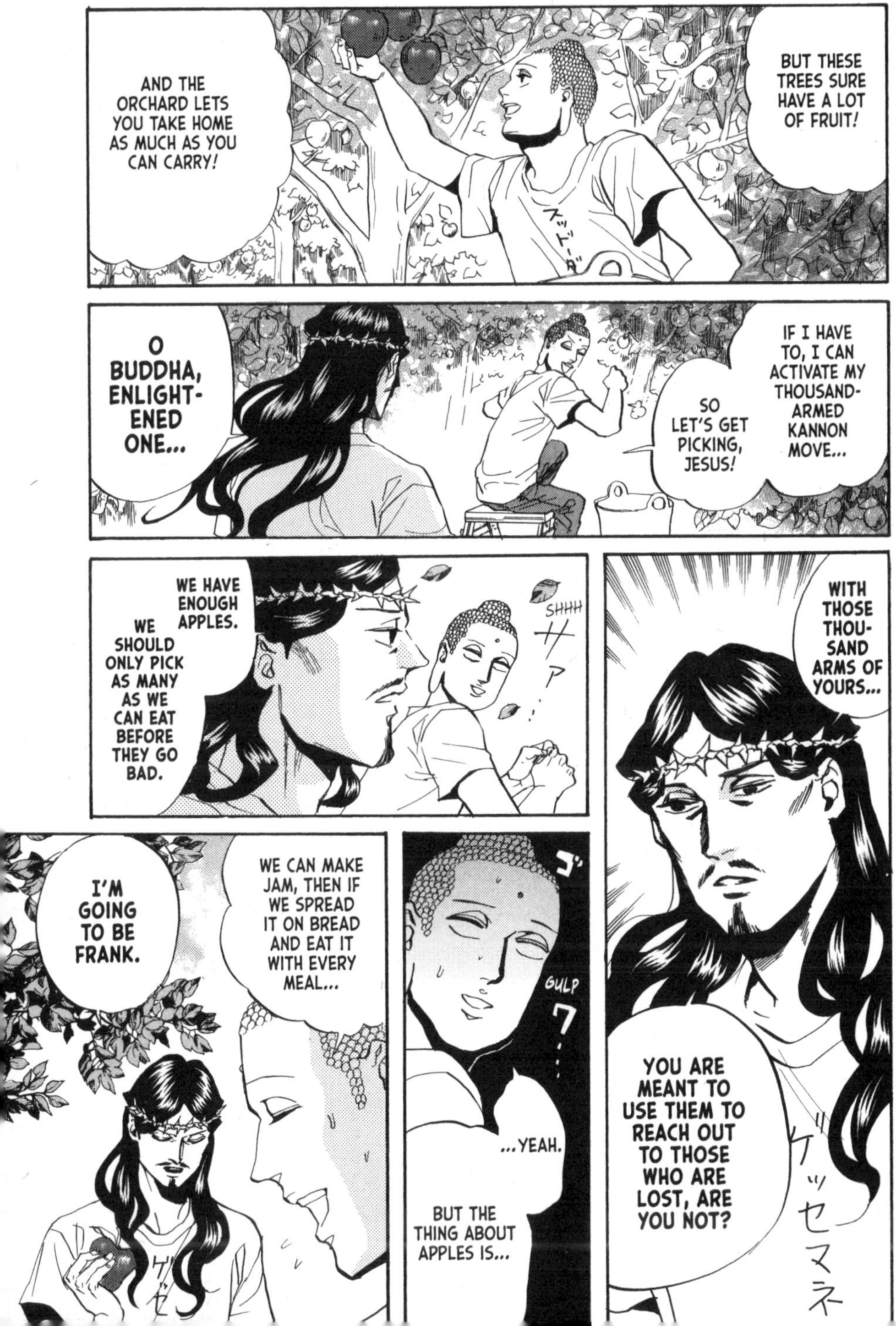
BUT THESE TREES SURE HAVE A LOT OF FRUIT!
AND THE ORCHARD LETS YOU TAKE HOME AS MUCH AS YOU CAN CARRY!
IF I HAVE TO, I CAN ACTIVATE MY THOUSAND-ARMED KANNON MOVE...
SO LET'S GET PICKING, JESUS!
O BUDDHA, ENLIGHTENED ONE...
WITH THOSE THOUSANDS ARMS OF YOURS...
YOU ARE MEANT TO USE THEM TO REACH OUT TO THOSE WHO ARE LOST, ARE YOU NOT?
ゲッセマネ
WE HAVE ENOUGH APPLES.
WE SHOULD ONLY PICK AS MANY AS WE CAN EAT BEFORE THEY GO BAD.
SHHH
サァ
...YEAH.
GULP
ゴク
BUT THE THING ABOUT APPLES IS...
WE CAN MAKE JAM, THEN IF WE SPREAD IT ON BREAD AND EAT IT WITH EVERY MEAL...
I'M GOING TO BE FRANK.

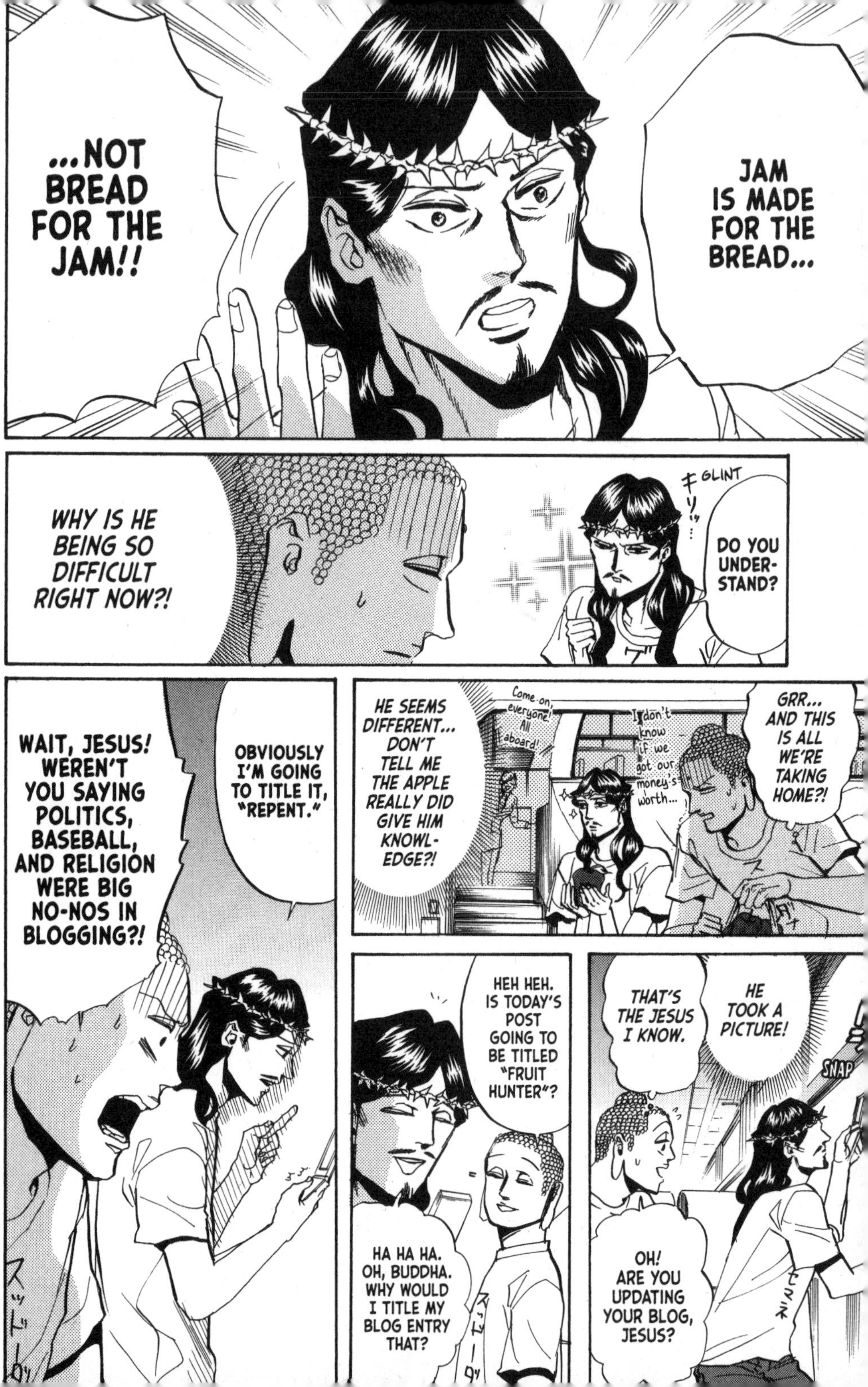
JAM IS MADE FOR THE BREAD...
...NOT BREAD FOR THE JAM!!
GLINT
DO YOU UNDERSTAND?
WHY IS HE BEING SO DIFFICULT RIGHT NOW?!
GRR... AND THIS IS ALL WE'RE TAKING HOME?!
I don't know if we got our money's worth...
Come on, everyone! All aboard!
HE SEEMS DIFFERENT... DON'T TELL ME THE APPLE REALLY DID GIVE HIM KNOWLEDGE?!
HE TOOK A PICTURE!
THAT'S THE JESUS I KNOW.
SNAP
OH! ARE YOU UPDATING YOUR BLOG, JESUS?
HEH HEH. IS TODAY'S POST GOING TO BE TITLED "FRUIT HUNTER"?
HA HA HA. OH, BUDDHA. WHY WOULD I TITLE MY BLOG ENTRY THAT?
OBVIOUSLY I'M GOING TO TITLE IT, "REPENT."
WAIT, JESUS! WEREN'T YOU SAYING POLITICS, BASEBALL, AND RELIGION WERE BIG NO-NOS IN BLOGGING?!

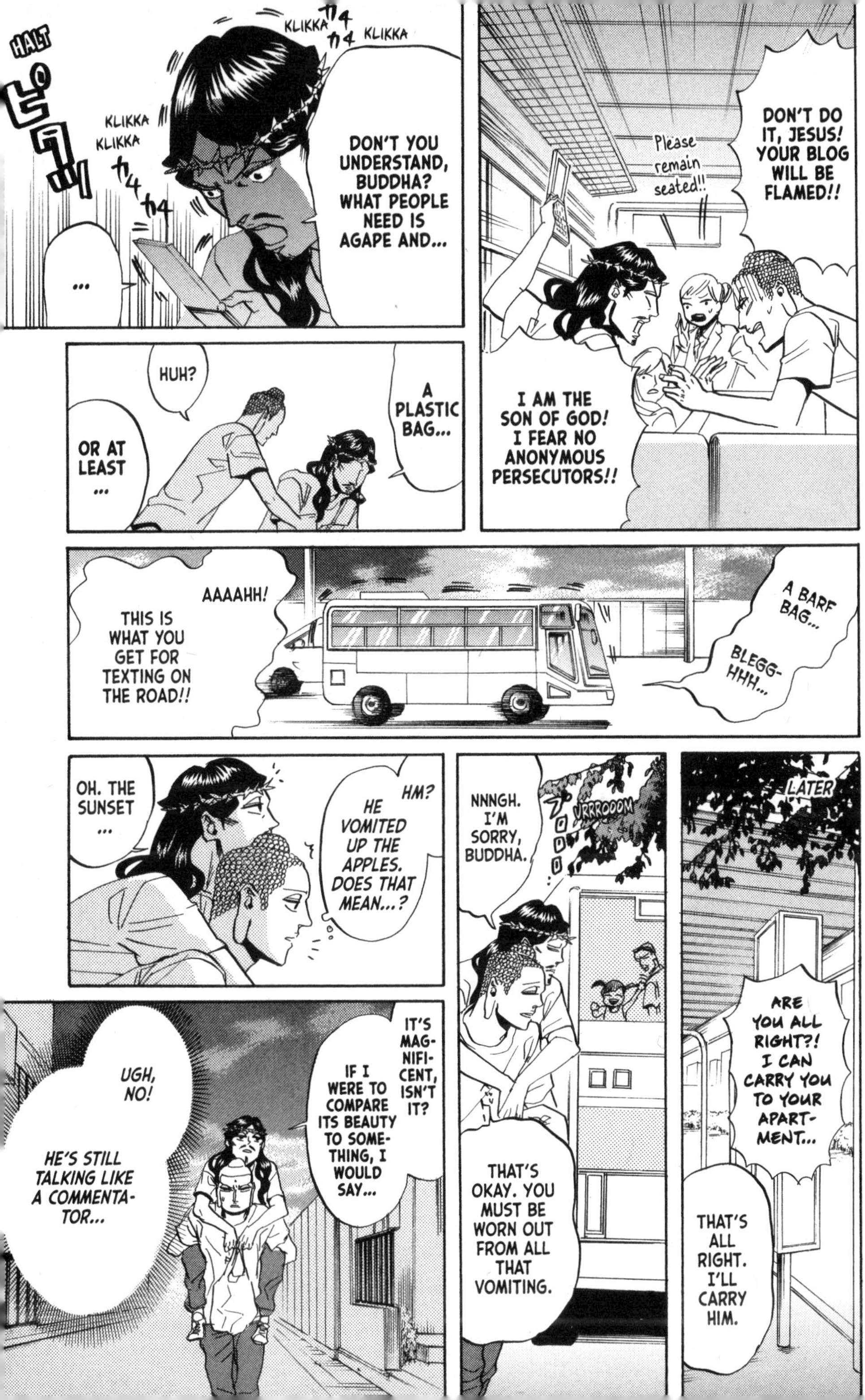
DON'T DO IT, JESUS! YOUR BLOG WILL BE FLAMED!!
Please remain seated!!
I AM THE SON OF GOD! I FEAR NO ANONYMOUS PERSECUTORS!!
KLIKKA KLIKKA
DON'T YOU UNDERSTAND, BUDDHA? WHAT PEOPLE NEED IS AGAPE AND...
HALT
KLIKKA KLIKKA
...
A PLASTIC BAG...
HUH?
OR AT LEAST ...
A BARF BAG...
BLEGGHHH...
AAAAHH!
THIS IS WHAT YOU GET FOR TEXTING ON THE ROAD!!
LATER
ARE YOU ALL RIGHT?! I CAN CARRY YOU TO YOUR APARTMENT...
THAT'S ALL RIGHT. I'LL CARRY HIM.
URRROOOM
NNNGH. I'M SORRY, BUDDHA.
THAT'S OKAY. YOU MUST BE WORN OUT FROM ALL THAT VOMITING.
HM? HE VOMITED UP THE APPLES. DOES THAT MEAN...?
OH. THE SUNSET ...
IT'S MAGNIFICENT, ISN'T IT?
IF I WERE TO COMPARE ITS BEAUTY TO SOMETHING, I WOULD SAY...
UGH, NO!
HE'S STILL TALKING LIKE A COMMENTATOR...

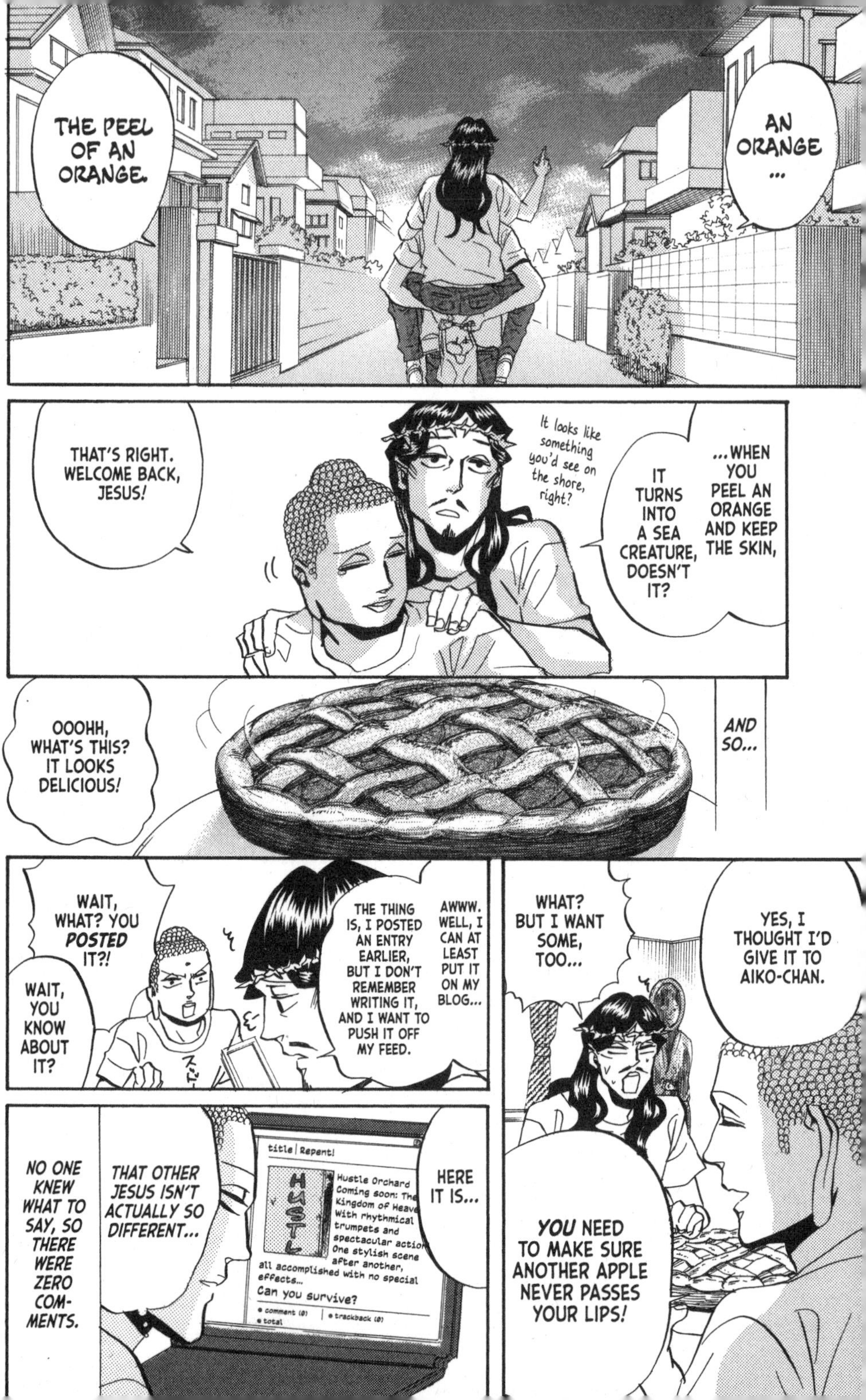
AN ORANGE ...
THE PEEL OF AN ORANGE.
...WHEN YOU PEEL AN ORANGE AND KEEP THE SKIN,
IT TURNS INTO A SEA CREATURE, DOESN'T IT?
It looks like something you'd see on the shore, right?
THAT'S RIGHT. WELCOME BACK, JESUS!
AND SO...
OOOHH, WHAT'S THIS? IT LOOKS DELICIOUS!
YES, I THOUGHT I'D GIVE IT TO AIKO-CHAN.
WHAT? BUT I WANT SOME, TOO...
YOU NEED TO MAKE SURE ANOTHER APPLE NEVER PASSES YOUR LIPS!
AWWW. WELL, I CAN AT LEAST PUT IT ON MY BLOG...
THE THING IS, I POSTED AN ENTRY EARLIER, BUT I DON'T REMEMBER WRITING IT, AND I WANT TO PUSH IT OFF MY FEED.
WAIT, WHAT? YOU *POSTED* IT?!
WAIT, YOU KNOW ABOUT IT?
HERE IT IS...
title | Repent!
HUSTL
Hustle Orchard Coming soon: The Kingdom of Heave With rhythmical trumpets and spectacular actio One stylish scene after another, all accomplished with no special effects...
Can you survive?
comment (0) | trackback (0)
total
THAT OTHER JESUS ISN'T ACTUALLY SO DIFFERENT...
NO ONE KNEW WHAT TO SAY, SO THERE WERE ZERO COMMENTS.

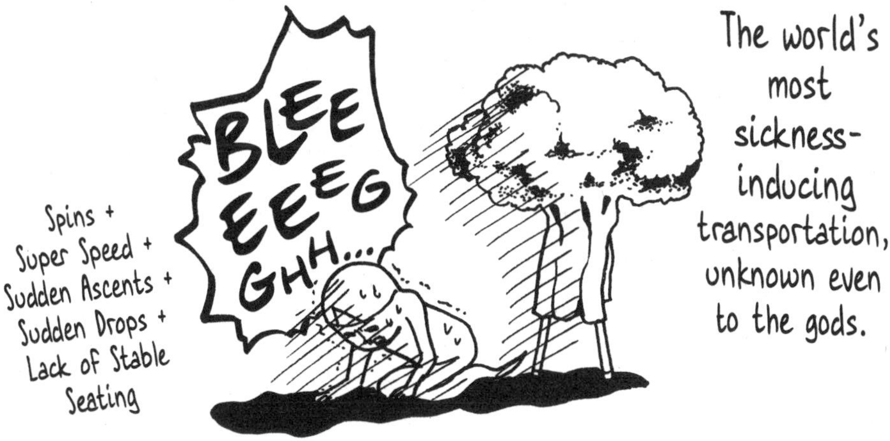
The world's most sickness-inducing transportation, unknown even to the gods.
BLEEEEEEGHH...
Spins + Super Speed + Sudden Ascents + Sudden Drops + Lack of Stable Seating

CHAPTER 29 TRANSLATION NOTES

Deliberately chose to ride a donkey, page 269

Soon before he was crucified, Jesus made his triumphal entry into Jerusalem riding the colt of a donkey, with multitudes of people shouting "Hosanna." There is great significance in his choice of a donkey: first, it was in fulfillment of a prophecy that the Messiah would come riding a donkey. The animal was a token of peace—a king going to war would ride a horse and bring with him all the trappings of war, but a king riding a donkey came in peace. Finally, the donkey is the symbol of Jewish royalty.

Divya-chaksus, page 269

This is one of the *Abhijna*, or six higher knowledges that include extra-sensory perception. Divya-chaksu, or *tengen* in Japanese, means "divine eye," and grants the ability to see all things, including people's past and future lives.

Assumptions, page 270

An assumption, also known as ascension or translation, is when someone is taken bodily into Heaven, as opposed to dying and having only the spirit go to Heaven. After Jesus was resurrected and spent time teaching his apostles, he went back to Heaven in what is known as the Ascension of Jesus Christ.

Suddhodana, page 271

This is the name of Siddhartha Gautama's father.

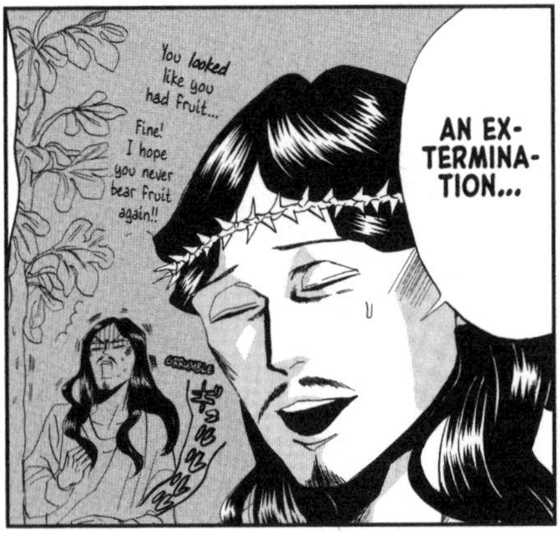

AN EX-TERMINA-TION...
You looked like you had fruit...
Fine! I hope you never bear fruit again!!

Cursing the fig tree, page 272

At one point in his ministry, Jesus came upon a fig tree that was covered in leaves—a sign that the tree also had fruit. When the fig tree proved to be all form and no substance (there was no fruit), he cursed it to an eternity of barrenness for its hypocrisy, and before long the tree withered away and died. This happened in early spring, around the time of Passover, and figs are in season briefly in early summer, then have a longer season that runs from late summer into autumn. However, fruit buds of the fig often appear earlier than the leaves, so any fig tree with leaves is also likely to have mature fruit. In fact, some species of fig are still edible before they are ripe, so it is not unreasonable that a fig tree with leaves on it would have edible fruit even in the spring.

The joy in Heaven, page 272

This is a reference to *The Gospel of Luke*, chapter 15, which tells of the Pharisees criticizing Jesus for associating with sinners.

Suffer the little children, page 273

This is something Jesus said when people brought their children to be blessed by him, and the disciples told them not to bother Jesus. When he saw it, he told them not to forbid the children, because "of such is the Kingdom of Heaven."

Fruit Hunter, page 274

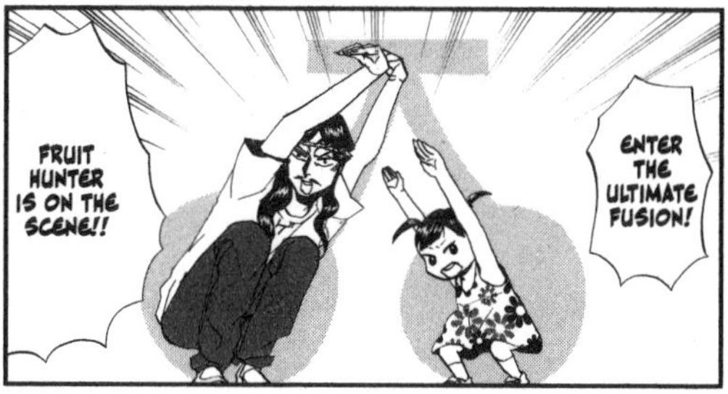
ENTER THE ULTIMATE FUSION!
FRUIT HUNTER IS ON THE SCENE!!

The Japanese word for picking fruit in this sort of situation is *karu,* which in this case would be defined as "to wander the mountains or fields in search of plants, flowers, mushrooms, etc." However, its more common definition is "to chase down and capture birds or beasts," in other words, "to hunt." For this reason, Jesus and Aiko choose "Fruit Hunter" as the cool English name for their ultimate fusion. The Fruit Hunter transforms further into La France, which is the Japanese name for the Claude Blanchet pear. This pear had little success in France, because the climate makes it hard to grow, but in Japan it has thrived and become a bit of a luxury item, nicknamed the Queen of Fruits.

A demon or an angel, page 274

More literally, this Yakuza friend says he can't tell if this terrifying mob heir is an *asura* or a Buddha (where the term "Buddha" is used as a general term for someone who has achieved enlightenment and therefore is very kind and saintly). Buddha replies that Jesus is a messiah, which literally means "anointed one," and more specifically refers to the Messiah—the prophesied Savior.

Gethsemane, page 274

This is the name of the garden where Jesus Christ prayed and suffered for the sins of all humankind. He experienced pain so great that "his sweat was as it were great drops of blood falling down to the ground" (Luke 22:44). The name means "oil press," as it was a place where olives were pressed to make olive oil. As such, there were several olive trees there.

Apples are poison, page 274

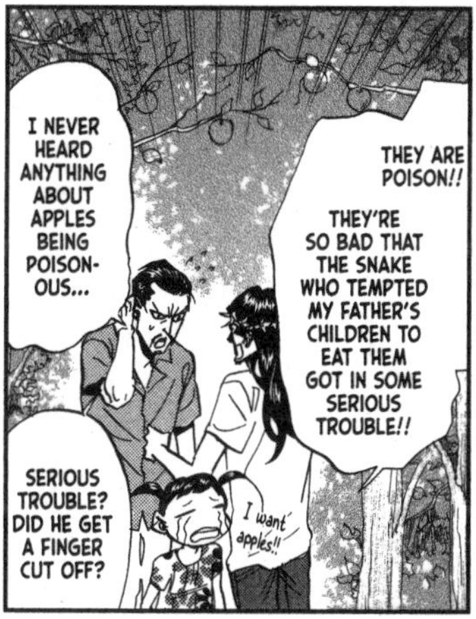
THEY ARE POISON!!
THEY'RE SO BAD THAT THE SNAKE WHO TEMPTED MY FATHER'S CHILDREN TO EAT THEM GOT IN SOME SERIOUS TROUBLE!!
I NEVER HEARD ANYTHING ABOUT APPLES BEING POISON-OUS...
I want apples!!
SERIOUS TROUBLE? DID HE GET A FINGER CUT OFF?

This is a reference to the Biblical tale of the beginning of the human race. Adam and Eve were placed in the Garden of Eden and told they could eat any of the many fruits growing abundantly there—any except for the fruit of the Tree of Knowledge of Good and Evil. The serpent beguiled Eve and convinced her to eat the fruit. She gave some of the fruit to Adam, and sin and death were introduced into the world as a result. God cast Adam and Eve out of the Garden of Eden, and cursed the serpent that it would travel on its belly from that time forward. The Bible never identifies the fruit of the Tree of Knowledge of Good and Evil as any specific fruit extant on the earth today, but the general assumption is that it was an apple. This may have been a play on the Latin word for evil (*malum*) and the Greek word for apple (*melon*), or it may be from the habit of using the word "apple" as an umbrella term for any foreign fruit (a habit that existed as late as the 17th century). Other candidates have been suggested as the real forbidden fruit, including but not limited to figs, pomegranates, grapes, and mushrooms.

It may also be worth noting that while the fruit of the apple is not poisonous, the seeds do contain small amounts of cyanide.

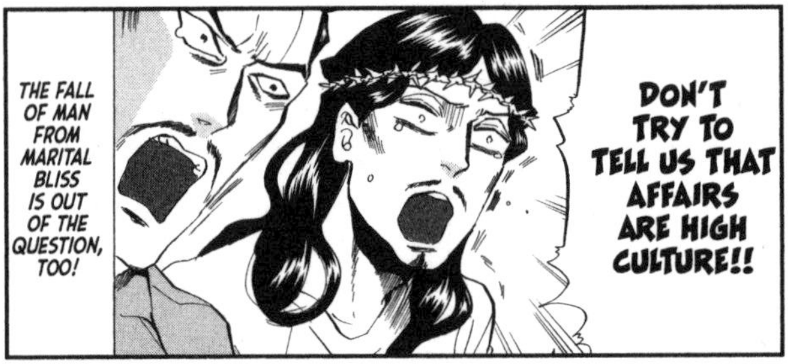
DON'T TRY TO TELL US THAT AFFAIRS ARE HIGH CULTURE!!
THE FALL OF MAN FROM MARITAL BLISS IS OUT OF THE QUESTION, TOO!

Affairs are high culture and the fall of man from marital bliss, page 276
"Affairs are high culture" is a line attributed to the Japanese actor Junichi Ishida, who defended his infamous extramarital activity by saying, "Culture and art often spring from the love affairs we call infidelity." This comment was further sensationalized by the media into simply, "Affairs are high culture." "The fall of man from marital bliss" is an adaptation. This part of the line was originally *shitsurakuen*, which means "lost paradise," as in Milton's *Paradise Lost* (an epic poem about the fall of Adam and Eve), or as in Junichi Watanabe's novel, *A Lost Paradise,* about a former magazine editor, his extramarital affair with a younger woman, and their subsequent double suicide.

Paulownia boxed mango, page 277
Jesus is likely referring to the Egg of the Sun mango that is highly valued in Japan. Although the same variety can be bought in Florida for only a few dollars, in the Miyazaki Prefecture, these mangoes are raised and harvested with a special process that ensures the highest quality. Because they are such prized fruit, they are sold in luxury fruit stores and packaged in paulownia boxes, which are often used for very formal gifts.

Enough gold coins to cover the field, page 278
The land for the Jetavana Temple was purchased by a disciple of the Buddha's, who was challenged by the land's owner to cover the entire plot in gold coins and succeeded in the task, except for one area which the owner donated to the cause. The land was covered in trees (which may or may not have been mango trees), and there is a mango grove on the outskirts of the grounds.

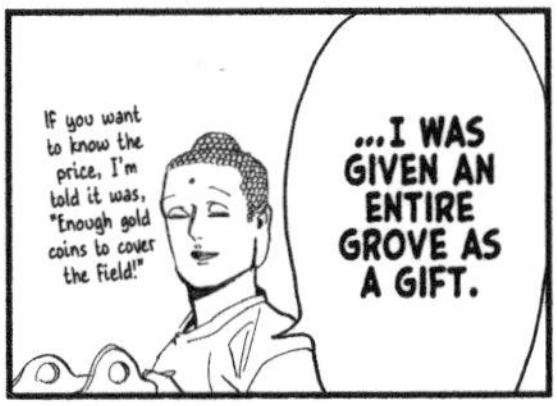
...I WAS GIVEN AN ENTIRE GROVE AS A GIFT.
If you want to know the price, I'm told it was, "Enough gold coins to cover the field!"

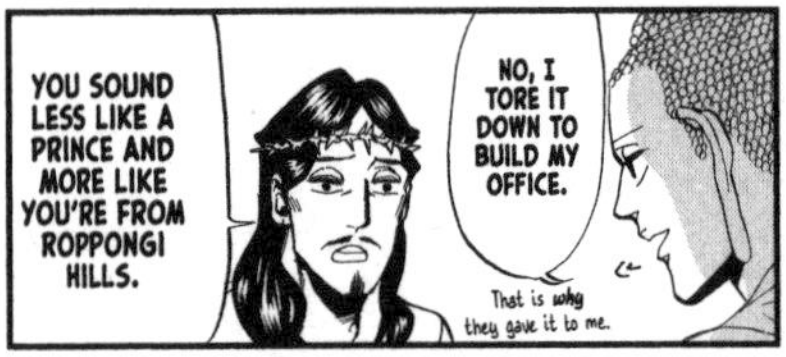
NO, I TORE IT DOWN TO BUILD MY OFFICE.
That is why they gave it to me.
YOU SOUND LESS LIKE A PRINCE AND MORE LIKE YOU'RE FROM ROPPONGI HILLS.

Roppongi Hills, page 278
Roppongi Hills is a mega-complex in the Roppongi district of the Minato Ward of Tokyo. It includes office buildings, apartment complexes, shops, parks, etc. There are many high-profile companies with offices there, whose CEOs also live in the complex.

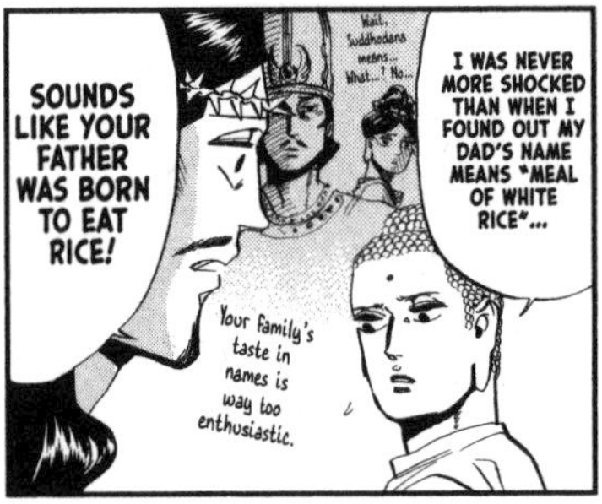
I WAS NEVER MORE SHOCKED THAN WHEN I FOUND OUT MY DAD'S NAME MEANS "MEAL OF WHITE RICE"...
Wait, Suddhodana means... What...? No...
SOUNDS LIKE YOUR FATHER WAS BORN TO EAT RICE!
Your family's taste in names is way too enthusiastic.

Meaning of Suddhodana, page 278
Suddhodana is Sanskrit for "he who grows pure rice." Buddha's interpretation here is likely a derivative of that.

Hallelujah-Worthy Eats, page 279

Buddha suggests that Jesus's commentary on the taste of apples is reminiscent of the Japanese TV show *Kuishinbo! Banzai!* (*Long Live Gourmands!*), a daily five-minute food show in which the host would go all around Japan sampling the local delicacies.

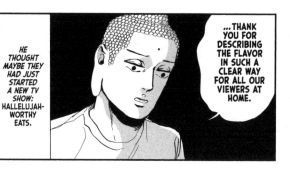

...THANK YOU FOR DESCRIBING THE FLAVOR IN SUCH A CLEAR WAY FOR ALL OUR VIEWERS AT HOME.
HE THOUGHT MAYBE THEY HAD JUST STARTED A NEW TV SHOW: HALLELUJAH-WORTHY EATS.

SAINT☆YOUNG MEN

◄ KAMOME ►
SHIRAHAMA

Witch Hat Atelier

A magical manga adventure for fans of Disney and Studio Ghibli!

Witch Hat Atelier © Kamome Shirahama/Kodansha Ltd.

The magical adventure that took Japan by storm is finally here, from acclaimed DC and Marvel cover artist Kamome Shirahama!

In a world where everyone takes wonders like magic spells and dragons for granted, Coco is a girl with a simple dream: She wants to be a witch. But everybody knows magicians are born, not made, and Coco was not born with a gift for magic. Resigned to her un-magical life, Coco is about to give up on her dream to become a witch...until the day she meets Qifrey, a mysterious, traveling magician. After secretly seeing Qifrey perform magic in a way she's never seen before, Coco soon learns what everybody "knows" might not be the truth, and discovers that her magical dream may not be as far away as it may seem...

THE MAGICAL GIRL CLASSIC THAT BROUGHT A GENERATION OF READERS TO MANGA, NOW BACK IN A DEFINITIVE, HARDCOVER COLLECTOR'S EDITION!

CARDCAPTOR SAKURA
COLLECTOR'S EDITION
C L A M P

Ten-year-old Sakura Kinomoto lives a pretty normal life with her older brother, Tōya, and widowed father, Fujitaka—until the day she discovers a strange book in her father's library, and her life takes a magical turn...

- A deluxe large-format hardcover edition of CLAMP's shojo manga classic
- All-new foil-stamped cover art on each volume
- Comes with exclusive collectible art card

KC
KODANSHA
COMICS

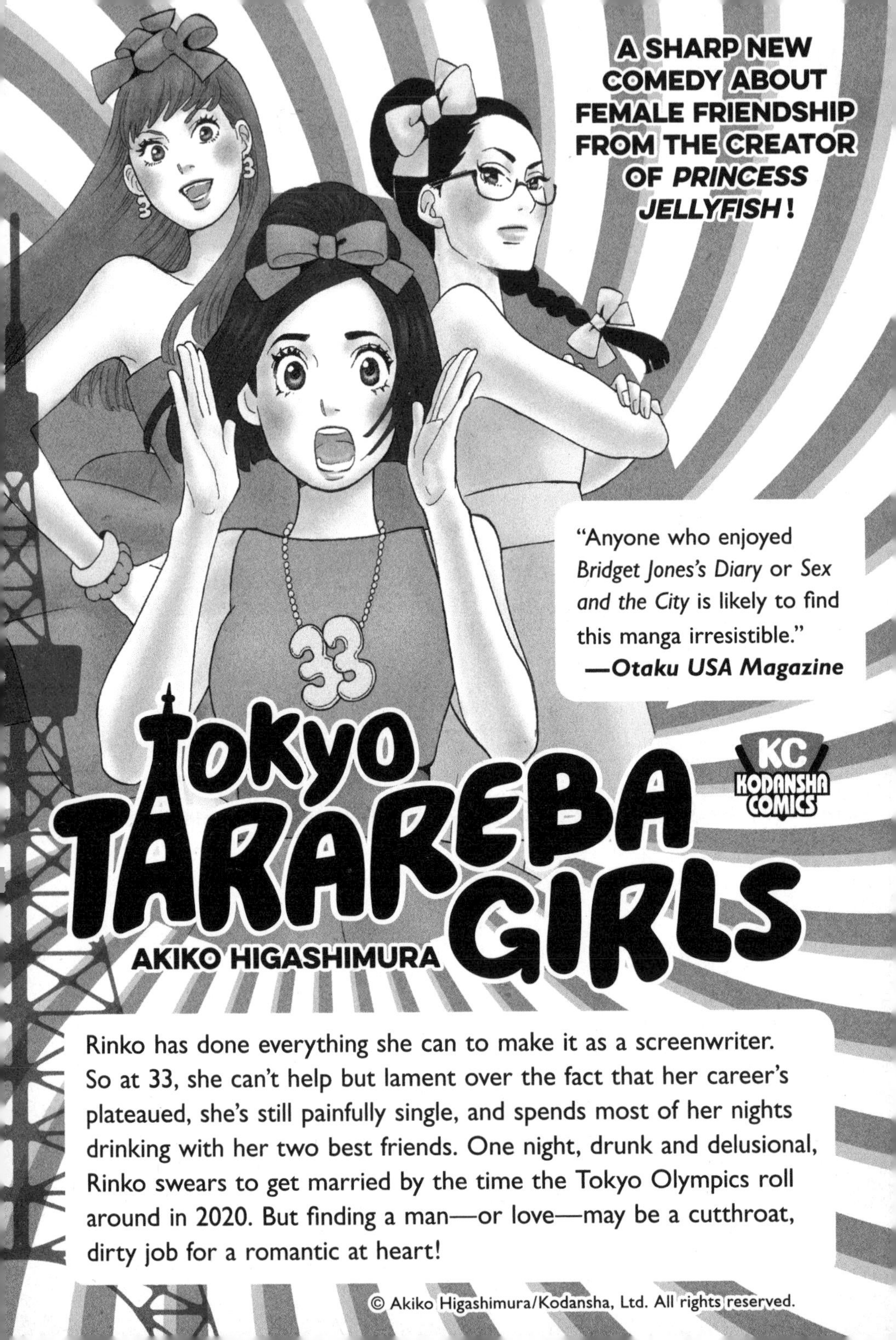
A SHARP NEW COMEDY ABOUT FEMALE FRIENDSHIP FROM THE CREATOR OF *PRINCESS JELLYFISH*!
"Anyone who enjoyed *Bridget Jones's Diary* or *Sex and the City* is likely to find this manga irresistible."
—*Otaku USA Magazine*
TOKYO TARAREBA GIRLS
AKIKO HIGASHIMURA
KC KODANSHA COMICS
Rinko has done everything she can to make it as a screenwriter. So at 33, she can't help but lament over the fact that her career's plateaued, she's still painfully single, and spends most of her nights drinking with her two best friends. One night, drunk and delusional, Rinko swears to get married by the time the Tokyo Olympics roll around in 2020. But finding a man—or love—may be a cutthroat, dirty job for a romantic at heart!
© Akiko Higashimura/Kodansha, Ltd. All rights reserved.

Princess Jellyfish

Akiko Higashimura

ALSO AN ANIME!

"One of the best manga for beginners!"
—*Kotaku*

Tsukimi Kurashita is fascinated with jellyfish. She's loved them from a young age and has carried that love with her to her new life in the big city of Tokyo. There, she resides in Amamizukan, a safe-haven for geek girls where no boys are allowed. One day, Tsukimi crosses paths with a beautiful and fashionable woman, but there's much more to this woman than her trendy clothes...!

Saint Young Men 2 copyright © 2009 Hikaru Nakamura
English translation copyright © 2019 Hikaru Nakamura

All rights reserved.

Published in the United States by Kodansha Comics, an imprint of Kodansha USA Publishing, LLC, New York.

Publication rights for this English edition arranged through Kodansha Ltd., Tokyo.

First published in Japan in 2009 by Kodansha Ltd., Tokyo as *Seinto oniisan*, volumes 3 & 4.

ISBN 978-1-63236-975-8

Original cover design by Hiroshi Niigami (NARTI;S)

Printed in the United States of America.

www.kodanshacomics.com

9 8 7 6 5 4 3 2 1
Translation: Alethea Nibley & Athena Nibley
Lettering: Lys Blakeslee
Editing: Jacob Friedman, Nathaniel Gallant, & Ajani Oloye
Kodansha Comics edition cover design by Phil Balsman

Publisher: Kiichiro Sugawara
Managing editor: Maya Rosewood
Vice president of marketing & publicity: Naho Yamada

Director of publishing services: Ben Applegate
Associate director of operations: Stephen Pakula
Publishing services managing editor: Noelle Webster
Assistant production manager: Emi Lotto, Angela Zurlo